A P Bhardwaj's

UGC/NTA CUET (UG)

English

A P Bhardwaj's

UGC/NTA CUET (UG)

English

First Edition

Published by
OakBridge Publishing Pvt. Ltd.
M 35, 1st Floor, Old DLF, Gurugram, 122001, Haryana, India
Tel.: +91 124 4305970, E-mail: info@oakbridge.in
www.oakbridge.in

ISBN: 978-93-95764-23-0

Printed and bound at Saurabh Printers Pvt. Ltd.

First Edition (First Impression)

DEDICATED

TO

MY PARENTS

LATE SH D S BHARDWAJ

LATE SMT SHUKLA DEVI BHARDWAJ

Their struggling life led me in a way to imbibe the 'Do or Die' spirit to strive and struggle for excellence, inherit positive attitude, progressive thinking, and inculcate the feeling of oneness and goodness for fellow human beings. Writing a book was one of their unfulfilled passions, which I am trying to pursue as a tribute to them and an acknowledgement of their countless blessings in my life.

ACKNOWLEDGEMENTS

Getting an opportunity to write a book like CUET (UG) ENGLISH with a nationally acclaimed Oakbridge Publishing is really a lifetime dream to be translated into reality. Gratitude to the experienced and committed publishing team leaders like Shreesh and Vikesh, who kept motivating, guiding, and supervising the work from time to time. Thanks to marketing and sales master, Naveen Bagga for providing the ground reality of the competition and existing demand of the book in the market.

Such an enormously challenging task cannot be accomplished without the help of near and dear ones. The input of my friend Dr Rajesh Kumar Jaiswal is invaluable.

The inputs and efforts of Priyanka Srivastava are really noteworthy and praiseworthy. A very chosen few can work with me at my pace and momentum without compromising quality and Priyanka is one of them.

My daughter, Anaadi, a student at Vivek High School, Chandigarh (A Brand Name For Quality Education), is very excited for this book as she knows that a number of students from her school are preparing for CUET and this book will be a great help to them.

I wish all the very best to all the CUET aspirants!

Preface to CUET(UG) English

I am extremely glad to present my CUET (UG) English book. CUET (UG) is a common university entrance test for undergraduate courses conducted by NTA (NATIONAL TESTING AGENCY). It is a single window opportunity for admission to central universities.

The English language paper is one of the most important sections of CUET (UG). This is a specific and exclusive book for CUET(UG) English language paper. The CUET English language paper is designed to check proficiency of English including the components such as comprehension passage, vocabulary, grammar, and usage.

This book has been made 6-into-1 book.

Divided into 6 parts and spread over 33 chapters, the book broadly covers:

PART A: VOCABULARY

PART B: GRAMMAR

PART C: ENGLISH USAGE

PART D: COMPREHENSION

PART E: SENTENCE CORRECTION

PART F: MOCK PAPERS AND PREVIOUS YEAR QUESTION PAPERS

Part A Vocabulary building starts with an introductory write up highlighting the importance of vocabulary building and ways to improve it. The opening chapter starts with 2000 basic words with their meanings and usage. The entire part A introduces the students with approximately 10,000 words along with variants of the words like synonyms, antonyms, one word substitution, word clarification, idioms, etc. 1500 MCQs and 500 matching words will further enable students to check their level of retention and usage.

Part B Functional grammar enables the students to revisit and refresh all the basic concepts of grammar, and practice tests would further help to check the level of understanding. The rules governing the use of articles, prepositions, models, conjunctions, etc., further supported with practice tests, will help the students to clear their concepts and solve any question on these topics with ease.

Part C ENGLISH USAGE has been made very intensive and interesting with a variety of PTs and very extensive and equally engaging with approximately 2000 MCQs with answers.

Part D Comprehension introduces the students with the sum and substance of comprehension reading and how to deduce the real substance from the subtle ideas narrated, described, and outlined in any comprehension to find correct answers to the given questions.

Part E Sentence correction chapter has been made as a self-correctional segment to check the 1200 common errors usually made.

Finally, the Part F Mock Papers and Previous Year Question Papers help you assess the preparation and gain confidence before taking the NTA CUET examination.

Having gone through all the 6 parts, spread over 33 chapters supported with 400 plus PTs, 4000 MCQs, 10,000 words with their variants and Mock Papers, the students will be enthused with a renewed confidence. The students will find it a clear, coherent, and comprehensive resource material for CUET (UG) ENGLISH PAPER.

Hope the students will read it, like it, and recommend it!

A P Bhardwaj

Chandigarh

January 2023

CONTENTS

PART B: REFRESH THE CONCEPTS OF GRAMMAR (130 PTs)

PART C: TEST OF USAGE OF ENGLISH LANGUAGE (164 PTs AND APPROX 2000 MCQs)

PART D: COMPREHENSIONS (16 PTs)

PART E: SENTENCE CORRECTION (1200 CE AND 29 PTs)

PART F: MOCK PAPERS AND PREVIOUS YEAR QUESTION PAPERS

PART A:
VOCABULARY BUILDING
(1500 MCQs, 500 MTW and 65 PTs)

IMPORTANCE OF VOCABULARY BUILDING HOW CUET ENGLISH BOOK MEETS THIS REQUIREMENT?

"Words are the body of thought."
–Carlyle

"Good words are worth much, and cost little."
–George Herbert

The test of vocabulary is a very important and crucial segment in the English language papers in almost all the competitive and academic examinations. It can be very scoring if handled carefully and very damaging too if taken casually. It requires a lot of effort, perseverance, and finesse for scoring well in the vocabulary. Vocabulary building is not an easy, and overnight task. Rather, it is a long, tedious, and rigorous process which one has to undergo. Reading, reading, and reading is the only way out. But the first and foremost requirement is to know what to read and from where to read. Exposure to high quality words in good numbers from a good, reliable, and authentic resource material is the first steppingstone towards a good vocabulary building. Hence the VOCABULARY BUILDING SECTION of CUET ENGLISH BOOK will provide a steppingstone towards building a rich, useful, and meaningful vocabulary.

The choice of words is of paramount importance. '***Words***, says Norman Lewis – author of world-renowned book, 'word power made easy,' ***are exciting and mysterious tokens of our thoughts. They are the tools with which ideas are dug up.***' If words are not functional and contextual, the expression will be neither clear nor intelligible. Clarity is the first and foremost prerequisite of good expression and communication.

A good vocabulary enables one to express exactly what one means as clearly and concisely as possible. The economy of words pays off exponentially. One way of ensuring to communicate clearly and to the point is through accurate and effective use of suitable words.

Vocabulary building has been most of the time an Achilles heel for most of the students. They find it no less than *crossing the Rubicon or setting the Thames on fire.* CUET ENGLISH BOOK is an honest attempt in the direction of helping and enabling the CUET ASPIRANTS to overcome this hurdle. Hence the need and necessity of a rich word treasure like VOCABULARY BUILDING SECTION (VBS) which students will find really a concise, compact and comprehensive resource material.

VOCABULARY BUILDING SECTION (VBS) is an outcome of my 20 years class tested teaching skills. The quality of the compiled material is class tested, and trusted by hundreds of students every year. It is a testimony to its authenticity and indispensability. VBS is a highly systematized, step by step graded compilation with 2000 essential words with meanings and usage at the outset, gradually unfolding to its 5,000 variables as synonyms & antonyms and other variants like word substitution, word formation, word clarification etc. All in all, the students would get acquainted with more than 10,000 words in various forms, which are more than sufficient to solve any question related to the vocabulary section. All the chapters are followed by either practice tests or MCQs in profuse numbers so as to enable the students to check their level of understanding of words and enhance the richness of their word bank.

The meanings, usage, examples, and illustrations throughout the book have been given to make the things clear, informative, and interesting. Easy to understand, crystal clear presentation strictly avoiding superficiality and superfluity, and eclectic selection of words are the cornerstones of this book.

The salient features put together will make the tedious task of vocabulary building easy and engaging. Having mastered this book, the students will be enthused with a renewed confidence and develop a special proclivity and knack for vocabulary building. Attempting vocabulary related questions will be a cakewalk after mastering this book.

The depth and breadth of coverage of the book, simplicity of presentation, multiplicity and variety of questions make it a one stop solution for all. The students will find it a clear, compact, coherent, and comprehensive book covering all the essential aspects of vocabulary building, elements of Grammar, test of usage, comprehension, and sentence correction.

A rich vocabulary is an open sesame to the doors of opportunities. It helps not only to score high grades in competitive and academic examinations but also to attain greater heights in specialized fields of activities.

VBS is framed to equip the students with more than sufficient tools of words. Lucidity, accuracy, and laconism are the embellishing ornaments imparting ornamental touches to all the topics covered in the book. The students will develop an uncanny knack of using the right word in the right place at the right time after mastering the VOCABULARY BUILDING SECTION.

Generally, there are two things that are recommended to improve language: more and more activities regarding writing and reading. More writing is an obvious one, since practice makes a man perfect. But writing in a vacuum will not do much good. Reading exposes us to new words, ideas, styles, and better ways of presentation. Reading is the most effective way of developing impressive writing.

'Vocabulary is a matter of word- building as well as word using.'

–David Crystal

Our understanding of what we read & hear is, to a very large degree, determined by our **vocabulary**. 'Words are our most inexhaustible source of magic,' says J K Rowling's character Dumbledore in Harry Potter. Although a great deal of vocabulary is learned unconsciously, some vocabulary should be taught directly and deliberately. Direct instructions help students learn difficult words, such as words that represent complex concepts that are not part of the students' everyday experiences. Direct instructions of vocabulary relevant to a given text leads to better reading comprehension.

'You can't build up a vocabulary if you never meet any new words. And to meet them, you must read. The more you read the better.'

–Rudolf Flesch and Abraham Lass

Here are some of the important ways by which one can improve one's vocabulary.

- Reading is the key to improving one's vocabulary. Read a good English Newspaper daily to improve reading and writing skills
- Go through articles and blogs on different topics. On reading one will come across various new words. Learn these words and look for their meanings.
- Only mugging up the meanings will not help. Try to learn at least 5 to 10 words daily and use them in your day-to-day life. This can help memorize those words more easily.
- When one comes across a new word, find at least 5- 10 synonyms and antonyms for those words, and learn them.
- Practice more and more vocabulary-based questions from previous years papers, it helps to understand the level and variety of words.

- Make a notebook and write all the new words and their variants and keep revising them from time to time.
- Develop the habit of consulting a dictionary as frequently as possible and also explore a thesaurus from time to time. Nowadays a mobile in hands is a gateway to treasures of words.

Words are the bridge between what is said and what is meant.

'Words are important. if you cannot say what you mean, you will never mean what you say. And you should always mean what you say.'

These words are based on a quotation of Bernard Shaw adapted as a dialogue in the film, 'The Last Emperor,' written by Mark Peplos & Bernardo Bertolucci.

This write up will help students understand the importance of vocabulary and highlight the usefulness of my Book CUET English.

A P BHARDWAJ
CHNDIGARH
JANUARY 2023

1 WORDS - MEANINGS AND THEIR USAGE

A		
1.	**abash** *verb* embarrass	*Usage:* Ravi doesn't get abashed even after his open criticism.
2.	**abate** *verb* subside, decrease, lessen	*Usage:* The violence abated when curfew was clamped.
3.	**abbreviate** *verb* shorten	*Usage:* Dr. is an abbreviated form of doctor.
4.	**abdicate** *verb* renounce, give up	*Usage:* Ashoka had abdicated the throne after promulgation of Dhamma.
5.	**abduction** *noun* forcibly taking someone away against their will	*Usage:* The criminals abducted a top doctor of the town for ransom.
6.	**aberrant** *noun* abnormal or deviant	*Usage:* His aberrant behaviour is the outcome of parental pampering.
7.	**abet** *verb* aid, usually in doing something wrong, encourage	*Usage:* Abetting in a crime is an offence in itself.
8.	**abeyance** *noun* suspended action	*Usage:* The session was held in abeyance.
9.	**abhor** *verb* detest, hate	*Usage:* I abhor communalism and communalists.
10.	**abject** *adj.* wretched, lacking pride	*Usage:* The abject poverty of India is still a slap on the face of India's claim of being a welfare state.
11.	**abjure** *verb* renounce upon oath	*Usage:* The top leader abjured his allegiance to his party.
12.	**abolish** *verb* cancel, put an end to	*Usage:* Capital punishment should not be abolished.
13.	**abominable** *adj.* detestable, extremely unpleasant, very bad	*Usage:* The Ruchika molestation case was one of the most abominable cases in which a police officer is involved.
14.	**abortive** *adj.* unsuccessful, fruitless	*Usage:* The terrorists made abortive attempts to kill popular leaders.
15.	**abrade** *verb* wear away by friction, scrape, rub off, erode	*Usage:* If you are not true to your words, then your reputation gets abraded.
16.	**abridge** *verb* condense or shorten	*Usage:* Please abridge this written matter.
17.	**abrogate** *adj.* abolish, cancel or repeal by authority, annul	*Usage:* The government abrogated TADA once the terrorism problem was solved in Punjab.

18.	**abscond** *verb* depart secretly and hide	*Usage:* One who absconds for 90 days from the legal process, is declared a proclaimed offender.
19.	**absolute** *adj.* complete, totally, unlimited, certain	*Usage:* Pakistani President Parvez Musharraf assumed absolute powers once the martial law was imposed.
20.	**absolve** *verb* pardon (an offence)	*Usage:* Charles Sobhraj was absolved by the court.
21.	**abstain** *verb* refrain	*Usage:* One should abstain from excessive drinking and smoking.
22.	**abstract** *adj.* theoretical, not concrete	*Usage:* The discipline of philosophy provides a number of abstract concepts.
23.	**abstruse** *adj.* obscure, profound, difficult to understand	*Usage:* Osho gives the simplest explanations and interpretations of the most abstruse philosophies and philosophers.
24.	**abundant** *adj.* plentiful, possessing riches or resources	*Usage:* The warehouses of Punjab government are abundant with wheat and rice.
25.	**abusive** *adj.* coarsely insulting, physically harmful	*Usage:* The abusive language used by parents leaves very detrimental effects on their children.
26.	**abysmal** *adj.* bottomless	*Usage:* His arrogance is exceeded only by his abysmal ignorance.
27.	**abyss** *noun* enormous chasm, vast bottomless pit	*Usage:* The death of his father created more than an abyss in his life.
28.	**accelerate** *verb* move faster	*Usage:* We must accelerate the pace of our practice if we have to perform well at Olympics.
29.	**accessible** *adj.* easy to approach, obtainable	*Usage:* Jyoti Basu, in spite of being a CM, remained accessible even to the common man.
30.	**acclaim** *verb* great approval	*Usage:* Rang De Basanti was an acclaimed movie.
31.	**acclimate** *verb* adjust to climate	*Usage:* One must be flexible enough to acclimate according to the time and circumstances.
32.	**accolade** *noun* award of merit	*Usage:* Booker prize is the biggest accolade a writer can get in his life.
33.	**accommodate** *verb* oblige or help someone, adjust or bring into harmony, adapt	*Usage:* I always did everything possible to accommodate my elderly relatives.
34.	**accomplice** *noun* partner in crime	*Usage:* Providing a criminal with a lethal weapon makes one an accomplice in the offence.
35.	**accrue** *verb* come about by addition or natural growth or advantage	*Usage:* You must pay the interest that has accrued on your debt as well as the principal sum.
36.	**acknowledge** *verb* recognise, admit	*Usage:* The PM acknowledged the contribution of policemen in managing the pandemic situation.
37.	**acme** *noun* top, pinnacle	*Usage:* Amitabh Bachchan is at the acme of his career.
38.	**acquire** *verb* obtain, get	*Usage:* I acquired everything on my own in my life.
39.	**acquittal** *noun* deliverance from a charge	*Usage:* As the prosecution failed to produce any evidence against the accused, it resulted in his acquittal.

40.	**acrid** *adj.* sharp, bitterly pungent	*Usage:* Kashmir problem is the cause of an acrid relationship between India and Pakistan.
41.	**acrimonious** *adj.* bitter in words or manner	*Usage:* The political opponents condemned each other in acrimonious words over rising fuel prices.
42.	**actuate** *verb* motivate, to put into action or motion	*Usage:* My motivational lecture actuated the students to start preparation with new vigour and vitality.
43.	**acuity** *noun* sharpness, keenness of thought or vision	*Usage:* The inherent acuity of Tatas made them build a business empire.
44.	**acumen** *noun* mental keenness	*Usage:* The business acumen of Dhirubhai Ambani helped him succeed where others had failed.
45.	**acute** *adj.* quickly perceptive, keen, brief and severe	*Usage:* Acute shortage of funds led to closure of projects.
46.	**adage** *noun* wise saying, proverb	*Usage:* 'Honesty is the best policy' is a centuries old adage.
47.	**adamant** *adj.* hard, inflexible	*Usage:* Aadi is very adamant.
48.	**adapt** *verb* alter, modify	*Usage:* One has to learn to adapt oneself according to the requirements of time and circumstances.
49.	**addiction** *noun* compulsive, habitual need	*Usage:* He is addicted to novels.
50.	**addle** *verb* muddle	*Usage:* You must mind your own business and not addle with other's affairs.
51.	**adept** *adj.* expert at, highly skilled	*Usage:* Pradeep is very adept at drafting legal documents.
52.	**adhere** *verb* stick, fasten	*Usage:* Come what may, one should adhere to one's conviction.
53.	**adherent** *noun* supporter, follower	*Usage:* Osho had his adherents all over the world.
54.	**admonish** *verb* warn, reprove	*Usage:* The judge admonished the advocate.
55.	**adorn** *verb* decorate, add beauty, splendour, or distinction to something	*Usage:* Aishwarya was adorned with fine jewellery at the Filmfare festival.
56.	**adroit** *adj.* skilful	*Usage:* Suraj is very adroit in all the typing and composing activities.
57.	**adulation** *noun* flattery, admiration	*Usage:* A number of politicians thrive on adulation.
58.	**adulterate** *verb* make impure by adding inferior or tainted substances	*Usage:* Nowadays many youngsters' impressionistic minds are adulterated with shortcuts to earn money.
59.	**advent** *noun* arrival	*Usage:* With the advent of the Europeans, the Mughal empire began to shrink.
60.	**adversary** *noun* opponent, enemy	*Usage:* The young businessman struggled to defeat his business adversary through innovative strategies.
61.	**adverse** *adj.* unfavourable, hostile	*Usage:* The recession had a highly adverse effect on the economy.

62.	**adversity** *noun* poverty, misfortune	*Usage:* Adversity teaches us lessons of life.
63.	**aesthetic** *adj.* artistic, dealing with or capable of appreciation of the beautiful	*Usage:* Suman has great aesthetic sense.
64.	**affable** *adj.* easily approachable, warm, friendly	*Usage:* Riya's affable attitude makes her adorable among her peer group.
65.	**affected** *adj.* artificial, pretended, assumed in order to impress	*Usage:* His affected mannerisms and pretensions have earned him the reputation of a snob.
66.	**affinity** *noun* kinship, a natural liking or sympathy	*Usage:* She felt an affinity with all who suffered, so much so, that their pains were her pains.
67.	**affliction** *noun* state of distress, cause of suffering	*Usage:* The state should look into the afflictions of Naxals.
68.	**affluence** *noun* abundance, wealth	*Usage:* India is known for affluence of resources.
69.	**affront** *noun* insult	*Usage:* The involvement of Manu Sharma in the Jessica murder case earned affront for the Sharma family.
70.	**aftermath** *noun* consequences, outcome, upshot	*Usage:* Napolean's defeat was the aftermath of the battle of Waterloo.
71.	**agglomeration** *noun* collection, heap	*Usage:* India is an agglomeration of castes, classes, religions, regions and races.
72.	**aggrandise** *verb* increase or intensify	*Usage:* The politicians just focus on aggrandising and maximising their own interests.
73.	**aggregate** *verb* gather, accumulate	*Usage:* With the boom in share market, stakeholders aggregated great wealth in a short period of time.
74.	**aggressor** *noun* attacker	*Usage:* The Aryans are mistakenly understood as aggressors but actually they were immigrants.
75.	**aghast** *adj.* horrified, feeling great horror or dismay	*Usage:* I was aghast at the sudden demise of my friend.
76.	**agility** *noun* nimbleness	*Usage:* The agility of Payal helped her in qualifying all the physical tests in her training very easily.
77.	**agitate** *verb* stir up, disturb	*Usage:* Her fiery remarks agitated the already angry mob.
78.	**agnostic** *noun* one who is sceptical of the existence or 'knowability' of God or any ultimate reality	*Usage:* Buddha was agnostic.
79.	**alacrity** *noun* cheerful, promptness	*Usage:* Ravi is known for alacrity of responses he gives to the audience.
80.	**alienate** *verb* make hostile, separate	*Usage:* The Kashmir issue alienated the local Hindus.
81.	**allay** *verb* calm, pacify	*Usage:* The leader failed to allay the fears of the public.
82.	**allege** *verb* charge	*Usage:* The officer was alleged to have taken a bribe, hence he was suspended.

83.	**allegiance** *noun* loyalty	*Usage:* Mr. Virk's loyalty towards the CM is unwavering.
84.	**alleviate** *verb* relieve, to make less hard to bear, reduce or decrease	*Usage:* The pain killer alleviated my suffering.
85.	**allure** *verb* entice, attract	*Usage:* The kidnappers tried to allure the children with toys.
86.	**aloof** *adj.* apart, reserved	*Usage:* Shy by nature, she remained aloof while the rest conversed.
87.	**altercate** *verb* quarrel, dispute noisily or in a heated manner	*Usage:* They altercated for a long time before coming to blows.
88.	**altruistic** *adj.* unselfishly generous, unselfishly concerned for others	*Usage:* Mother Teresa is known for her altruistic deeds done throughout her life.
89.	**amalgamate** *verb* combine, unite in one body	*Usage:* The elements are amalgamated to make a compound.
90.	**amass** *verb* collect	*Usage:* The minister amassed a huge amount of black money.
91.	**ambience** *noun* environment, atmosphere	*Usage:* She went to the restaurant not for food but for the soul-soothing ambience.
92.	**ambiguous** *adj.* unclear or doubtful in meaning	*Usage:* The ambiguous answers of the speaker baffled the audience.
93.	**amble** *noun* moving at an easy pace	*Usage:* She was ambling at the Shimla Mall.
94.	**ameliorate** *verb* improve, make better	*Usage:* In order to ameliorate the deteriorating situation of the country, we need leaders with wisdom, vision and character.
95.	**amenable** *adj.* readily managed, willing to be led	*Usage:* He was amenable to any suggestions that came from those he looked up to.
96.	**amend** *verb* correct, change, generally for the better	*Usage:* The Parliament can amend the Constitution.
97.	**amenities** *noun* convenient features, courtesies	*Usage:* It is the duty of the local corporation to provide basic amenities.
98.	**amiable** *adj.* agreeable, lovable, warmly, friendly	*Usage:* Surbhi is a very amiable and affable girl.
99.	**amicable** *adj.* polite, friendly, not quarrelsome	*Usage:* We should be amicable and try to find out some solutions to our family problem.
100.	**amiss** *adj.* wrong, faulty	*Usage:* Seeing her frown, he wondered if anything was amiss.
101.	**amoral** *adj.* not moral	*Usage:* Everyone dislikes amoral people.
102.	**amorous** *adj.* moved by sexual love, loving	*Usage:* 'Love them and leave them' was the motto of the amorous don.
103.	**amorphous** *adj.* formless, lacking shape or definition	*Usage:* I have just an amorphous idea of writing a book.
104.	**ample** *adj.* abundant	*Usage:* In order to master any language, one should have ample vocabulary at one's disposal.

105.	**amplify** *verb* broaden or clarify by expanding, intensity, make stronger	*Usage:* The mediator tried to amplify the problem before solving it.
106.	**anarchist** *noun* person who seeks to overturn the established government, advocate of abolishing authority	*Usage:* Osho was an anarchist.
107.	**anarchy** *noun* absence of governing body, state of disorder	*Usage:* After Ashoka's death, the Mauryan Empire witnessed a virtual state of anarchy.
108.	**anecdote** *noun* short account of an amusing or interesting event	*Usage:* Khushwant Singh is known for fabulous anecdotes he writes in his articles.
109.	**anguish** *noun* acute pain, extreme suffering	*Usage:* Visiting the site of the explosion, the officials were surprised to see the anguish of the victims and their families.
110.	**animated** *adj.* lively, spirited	*Usage:* Madhuri's animated expressions are the main USP of her films.
111.	**animosity** *noun* active enmity	*Usage:* For the development of the entire South Asian region, Indo-Pak animosity needs to be ended.
112.	**annals** *noun* records, history	*Usage:* Ashoka's marvels are recorded in the annals of history.
113.	**annex** *verb* attach, take possession of	*Usage:* China wants to annex certain parts of North-Eastern India.
114.	**annihilate** *verb* destroy	*Usage:* The terrorists tried to annihilate the entire population of the Kashmir valley in revenge.
115.	**anonymity** *noun* state of being nameless or anonymous	*Usage:* A senior-most official gave the news on the condition of anonymity.
116.	**anonymous** *adj.* having no name	*Usage:* Some anonymous sayings are very popular since ages.
117.	**antagonism** *noun* hostility, active resistance	*Usage:* We should keep ourselves away from any kind of antagonism.
118.	**antecedents** *noun* preceding events or circumstances, ancestors or early background	*Usage:* The antecedents of the candidates selected for IAS are checked by the police before they join service.
119.	**antipathy** *noun* aversion, dislike	*Usage:* I have strong antipathy for corrupt people.
120.	**antithesis** *noun* contrast, direct opposite of or to	*Usage:* This disaster was the antithesis of all that he had hoped for, but he fought it with all his strength.
121.	**apathy** *noun* lack of caring, indifference	*Usage:* The citizens' apathy is one of the root causes of the sorry state of affairs in the country.
122.	**apex** *noun* tip, summit, climax	*Usage:* The Supreme Court is the apex court in India.
123.	**apogee** *noun* highest point	*Usage:* Amitabh Bachchan is at the apogee of popularity in Bollywood.

124.	**apolitical** *adj.* having an aversion or lack of concern for political affairs	*Usage:* The person to be elected as President of India should be apolitical.
125.	**apostate** *noun* one who abandons his religious faith or political beliefs	*Usage:* Because he switched from one party to another, his former friends shunned him as an apostate.
126.	**appal** *verb* dismay, shock	*Usage:* The human rights activists were appalled by the horrifying conditions in the Naxal affected areas.
127.	**appease** *verb* pacify or soothe, relieve	*Usage:* The government always tried to appease the public with dilatory tactics.
128.	**apposite** *adj.* appropriate, fitting	*Usage:* It was an apposite opportunity for the people to put forward their demand.
129.	**appraise** *verb* estimate value of	*Usage:* We got our house appraised by experts for the right price, before setting out to sell it.
130.	**appreciate** *verb* be thankful for, increase in worth, be thoroughly conscious of	*Usage:* I earnestly appreciate the way you handled the entire situation.
131.	**apprehend** *verb* to suspect	*Usage:* The police always apprehend that the habitual offenders could be the main culprits.
132.	**apprehension** *noun* an anxious feeling of fear	*Usage:* Sometimes our unfounded apprehensions land us in undesirable trouble.
133.	**apprise** *verb* inform or notify	*Usage:* When he was apprised of the dangerous situation, he took certain immediate steps to control it.
134.	**approbation** *noun* approval, sanction or commendation	*Usage:* I need approbation of my boss.
135.	**appropriate** *verb* acquire, take possession of something for one's own use	*Usage:* The government appropriated the private banks for the welfare of the general public.
136.	**arbitrary** *adj.* capricious, randomly chosen, tyrannical	*Usage:* Saddam Hussain's arbitrary rule earned him notoriety.
137.	**arcane** *adj.* secret, mysterious, known only to the initiator	*Usage:* Mystics in ancient India were known to possess certain arcane powers.
138.	**archaic** *adj.* obsolete, no more in use, outdated, outmoded	*Usage:* 'Thee' and 'thou' are archaic words in English language.
139.	**ardent** *adj.* intense, passionate, zealous	*Usage:* My teacher is an ardent follower of Gandhian philosophy.
140.	**arduous** *adj.* hard, strenuous, difficult to do, onerous	*Usage:* Writing a book is really an arduous task.
141.	**aromatic** *adj.* fragrant, having an aroma, sweet smelling	*Usage:* The King's palace had aromatic halls and courtyards,
142.	**arousal** *noun* awakening, provocation (of a response)	*Usage:* A newly published book on the development of our country since independence has aroused a big political debate.
143.	**arrogance** *noun* pride, haughtiness	*Usage:* Everyone dislikes her arrogance.

144.	**articulate** *adj.* effective, distinct	*Usage:* Arun's articulate presentations in the court are without a parallel.
145.	**ascendancy** *noun* controlling influence, domination	*Usage:* India's inherent bickering was really responsible for British ascendancy.
146.	**ascertain** *verb* find out for certain	*Usage:* Police reached the spot to ascertain the situation.
147.	**ascribe** *verb* refer, attribute, assign	*Usage:* Sunita ascribes the credit of her success to her family.
148.	**asinine** *adj.* stupid, silly, obstinate	*Usage:* Your asinine remarks prove your lack of knowledge in this particular area.
149.	**asperity** *noun* sharpness (of temper)	*Usage:* The asperity of his speech led to his expulsion from the party.
150.	**aspire** *verb* seek to attain, long for	*Usage:* One should aspire for realistic career goals based on abilities.
151.	**assail** *verb* assault, attack with arguments, begin working on (a task, problem, etc.) with vigour and determination	*Usage:* The public assailed the speaker for his sarcastic comment about their religious leader.
152.	**assay** *verb* analyse, evaluate	*Usage:* The SSP reached the spot to assay the situation arising out of mob riot.
153.	**assent** *verb* agree, accept	*Usage:* It is my great pleasure to give assent to your proposal.
154.	**assert** *verb* declare or state with confidence, put oneself forward boldly	*Usage:* We must learn to assert for our rights.
155.	**assiduous** *adj.* diligent, done with constant and careful attention, persevering	*Usage:* Construction of the Metro rail is the result of assiduous efforts of a visionary project leader, Mr. Sridharan.
156.	**assimilate** *verb* absorb, cause to become homogeneous	*Usage:* Majority of the students accumulate knowledge but they do not assimilate it.
157.	**assuage** *verb* ease or lessen (pain), satisfy (hunger), soothe (anger)	*Usage:* Have this pain killer, it will assuage your suffering.
158.	**astute** *adj.* wise, shrewd, keen	*Usage:* Narsimha Rao was a very astute politician.
159.	**asunder** *adv.* into parts, apart	*Usage:* The top business families in India stand asunder at times.
160.	**asylum** *noun* place of refuge or shelter, protection	*Usage:* Pakistan has a tendency to give asylum to terrorists operating in India.
161.	**atheistic** *adj.* denying the existence of God	*Usage:* Khushwant Singh claims to have an atheistic attitude.
162.	**atone** *verb* make amends for, pay for	*Usage:* He knew no way in which he could atone for his acts of omission and commission.
163.	**atrocity** *noun* brutal deed	*Usage:* Saddam Hussain was very unpopular for the atrocities he committed on the public.
164.	**attenuate** *verb* make thin, weaken	*Usage:* By withdrawing their forces, the army officer hoped to attenuate the tense situation.

165.	**attest** *verb* testify, bear witness	*Usage:* The judicial magistrate can attest the testimonials.
166.	**attribute** *noun* essential quality	*Usage:* One of his outstanding attributes was his team management skill.
167.	**audacious** *adj.* daring, bold	*Usage:* The new officer took very audacious steps to curb corruption.
168.	**augment** *verb* increase, add to	*Usage:* The induction of the Rafale fighter aircrafts will help augment the power of the Indian Air Force.
169.	**august** *adj.* impressive, majestic	*Usage:* It was really a great pleasure for me to address such an august gathering.
170.	**auspicious** *adj.* favourable	*Usage:* Shivam announced his engagement to Priya on the auspicious occasion of Maha Shivratri.
171.	**austere** *adj.* simple and unornamented	*Usage:* Buddha led an austere life.
172.	**authenticate** *verb* prove genuine	*Usage:* The finger prints of the culprit authenticated his involvement in the crime.
173.	**authoritarian** *adj.* despotic, autocratic, arbitrary, dictatorial	*Usage:* General Musharaf's authoritarian rule in Pakistan came to an end in 2007.
174.	**authoritative** *adj.* having the weight of authority, peremptory and dictatorial	*Usage:* The DGP headed the Punjab police in a very authoritative manner to curb the menace of terrorism.
175.	**autocratic** *adj.* having absolute, unchecked power, dictatorial	*Usage:* Hitler's regime has become a good example of autocratic rule that is talked about all over the world.
176.	**autonomous** *adj.* self-governing	*Usage:* The UPSC is an autonomous body.
177.	**avarice** *noun* greed for wealth	*Usage:* Modern man's avarice has driven him away from a peaceful life.
178.	**averse** *adj.* reluctant, disinclined	*Usage:* The new CM was greatly averse to favouritism and nepotism.
179.	**aversion** *noun* firm dislike	*Usage:* I have great aversion for sycophants.
180.	**avert** *verb* prevent, turn away	*Usage:* In order to avert the incident, the police took strong precautionary measures.
181.	**avid** *adj.* greedy, eager for	*Usage:* He is an avid learner of law.
182.	**avow** *verb* declare openly	*Usage:* Mahatma Gandhi avowed to uproot the British rule from India.
183.	**awe** *noun* solemn wonder	*Usage:* The child was looking at the old man with awe.
184.	**awry** *adv.* distorted, crooked	*Usage:* He gave a very awry version of the entire episode.
	B	
185	**babble** *verb* chatter	*Usage:* I love my daughter babbling with me.
186	**baffle** *verb* frustrate, perplex	*Usage*: The problem of inflation baffled the Finance Minister.
187	**baleful** *adj.* deadly, having malign influence, ominous	*Usage:* The fortune teller made baleful predictions.

188	**balmy** *adj.* mild, fragrant	*Usage:* The balmy breeze of September refreshed us after the sultry days of May and June in Chandigarh.
189	**banal** *adj.* hackneyed, commonplace, trite, lacking originality	*Usage:* Some writers produce very banal articles which make no sense to common people.
190	**bane** *noun* curse	*Usage:* His arrogance proved a bane that obstructed his career.
191	**bask** *verb* luxuriate, take pleasure in warmth	*Usage:* Basking on the beach for hours together is a good refreshment for the body and mind.
192	**bawdy** *adj.* indecent, obscene	*Usage:* He made bawdy remarks about his classmates.
193	**beam** *noun* as verb smile radiantly	*Usage:* As Dinesh got selected for OTA, his face was beaming with confidence.
194	**beatific** *adj.* giving bliss, blissful	*Usage:* The beatific smile on the child's face makes everyone feel relaxed.
195	**beatitude** *noun* blessedness, state of bliss	*Usage:* The Buddha's statue oozes out beatitude.
196	**befuddle** *verb* confuse thoroughly	*Usage:* The abductors of Khushpreet befuddled the police.
197	**beget** *verb* to farther, produce, give rise to	*Usage:* History shows us that violence begets violence.
198	**begrudge** *verb* resent	*Usage:* Both the brothers are begrudged for the last so many years over a property dispute.
199	**beguile** *verb* mislead or delude, pass time	*Usage:* With flattery and big talk of easy money, he beguiled his father into betting his hard-earned money in the share market.
200	**belated** *adj.* delayed	*Usage:* I missed wishing him yesterday, so I will have to wish him a belated happy birthday.
201	**beleaguer** *verb* harass	*Usage:* We should not beleaguer the poor.
202	**belie** *verb* contradict, give a false impression	*Usage:* His coarse and hard-bitten exterior temperament belie his inner beauty.
203	**belittle** *verb* disparage or depreciate, put down	*Usage:* Parents should not belittle their wards for trifling issues because it can have very negative impact on their personality.
204	**bellicose** *adj.* warlike	*Usage:* Hitler's bellicose attitude helped him to be a winner initially.
205	**belligerent** *adj.* quarrelsome	*Usage:* His belligerent wife creates a fuss about very paltry issues and spoils the whole atmosphere at home.
206	**bemoan** *verb* lament, express disapproval of	*Usage:* One should not always keep bemoaning and groaning about one's past.
207	**bemused** *adj.* confused, lost in thought, preoccupied	*Usage:* She was bemused to see the sculptures in the museum.
208	**benediction** *noun* blessing	*Usage:* The appearance of the sun after many rainy days was like a benediction to the farmers.
209	**benefactor** *noun* gift giver, patron	*Usage:* Mughal ruler Akbar was the benefactor of many cultural and religious activities.

210	**beneficial** *adj.* helpful, useful	*Usage:* Her guidance and experience can prove very beneficial to you.
211	**benevolent** *adj.* generous, charitable	*Usage:* Dr. Saxena remained involved in benevolent activities throughout his life.
212	**benign** *adj.* kindly, favourable, not malignant	*Usage:* She is known for her benign attitude towards her employees.
213	**bequeath** *verb* hand down	*Usage:* Civilisation is the cultural legacy which our forefathers bequeathed to us.
214	**berate** *verb* scold strongly	*Usage:* Sometime parents berate their children for no fault.
215	**bereft** *adj.* deprived of, lacking, desolate because of a loss	*Usage:* He was left bereft of his valuables by dacoits.
216	**berserk** *adv.* frenzied, angered	*Usage:* The public of Delhi went berserk after the Damini gang rape case.
217	**beseech** *verb* beg, plead with	*Usage:* You have to beseech with the principal for leave.
218	**beset** *verb* harass or trouble, hem in	*Usage:* India is beset with the problem of acute shortage of onions.
219	**besiege** *verb* surround with armed forces, harass (with requests)	*Usage:* Alauddin Khilji besieged the fort of Chittor.
220	**bestial** *adj.* beastlike, brutal	*Usage:* Any amount of condemnation is less for such bestial acts of attacks on Mumbai.
221	**bestow** *verb* give	*Usage:* Bharat Ratna was bestowed on Pranab Mukherjee, the former President of India, for his service to the nation.
222	**betray** *verb* to deceive	*Usage:* To betray someone is against moral and ethical behavioural norms.
223	**betroth** *verb* become engaged to marry	*Usage:* The announcement that they had become betrothed surprised their friends who had not suspected any romance between them.
224	**biased** *adj.* slanted, prejudiced	*Usage:* The judiciary is not supposed to be biased in favour of anybody, come what may.
225	**bigotry** *noun* stubborn intolerance (as in religion and ideology)	*Usage:* Bigotry is the outcome of ignorance and it breeds intolerance.
226	**bizarre** *adj.* fantastic, violently contrasting	*Usage:* The plot of the film was bizarre but still it received good response.
227	**blandishment** *noun* flattery	*Usage:* Blandishment is wrongly considered nowadays as an important factor for success.
228	**blasphemy** *noun* irreverence, sacrilege, cursing	*Usage:* Calling top religious leaders as anti-national is no less than blasphemy for many.
229	**blatant** *adj.* flagrant violation of law, conspicuously, loudly, offensive	*Usage:* The politicians often make blatant remarks against their opponents.
230	**bleak** *adj.* cold or cheerless, unlikely to be favourable	*Usage:* There are very bleak chances of his survival in this cold weather.

231	**bloated** *adj.* swollen	*Usage:* Excessive drinking made his face look bloated.
232	**blunder** *noun* error, a foolish or stupid mistake	*Usage:* The promise of holding plebiscite in Kashmir was a mountainous blunder.
233	**boisterous** *adj.* violent, rough, noisy	*Usage:* Shashi Tharoor in his book 'Midnight to Millennium' has called Indian democracy as boisterous democracy.
234	**bombardment** *noun* attack with missiles	*Usage:* The enemy army's bombardment demolished the entire town.
235	**bombastic** *adj.* pompous, using inflated language	*Usage:* He writes very bombastic language.
236	**booming** *adj.* resonant, flourishing deep and thriving	*Usage:* The prices of daily necessaries are booming nowadays.
237	**boon** *noun* blessing, benefit	*Usage:* Aman and Honey's association proved a boon for each other.
238	**boorish** *adj.* rude, clumsy, ungentlemanly	*Usage:* Rajesh's wife is very unpopular among the peer group for her boorish behaviour.
239	**boundless** *adj.* unlimited, vast	*Usage:* Tejas had boundless passion for the army.
240	**bountiful** *adj.* abundant, graciously generous	*Usage:* Upasana has a very bountiful nature.
241	**braggart** *noun* snob, foppish, boaster	*Usage:* Some bureaucrats' wards are usually braggart.
242	**brandish** *verb* wave, shake, or exhibit in a menacing, challenging, or exultant way, flourish	*Usage:* The terrorist brandished his gun to intimidate the public.
243	**brazen** *adj.* insolent	*Usage:* Her brazen contempt for authority generated public antipathy against her.
244	**brevity** *noun* conciseness, shortness, terseness	*Usage:* Brevity in professional situations is always appreciated.
245	**brittle** *adj.* easily breakable	*Usage:* The flower pots are made of brittle material.
246	**browbeat** *verb* bully, intimidate	*Usage:* The teacher tried to browbeat the student, but he retaliated.
247	**browse** *verb* graze, skim or glance at casually	*Usage:* I just browsed through the book.
248	**brusque** *adj.* blunt, abrupt	*Usage:* Her brusque reply stunned him.
249	**bucolic** *adj.* rustic	*Usage:* When Ravi came to Chandigarh, he was thoroughly bucolic.
250	**buffoonery** *noun* clowning jesting, evoking fun	*Usage:* Rohan was very notorious in the class for his buffoonery.
251	**bulwark** *noun* defensive wall, fortified rampart or other strong defence, person who defends	*Usage:* The writ of Habeas Corpus is the bulwark of personal freedom.

252	**bumptious** *adj.* self-assertive, disagreeably conceited or arrogant person	*Usage:* The bumptious attitude of Mr. Mahajan has made him an unpopular teacher.
253	**buoyant** *adj.* cheerful and optimistic	*Usage:* Honey had a buoyant mood when he heard the news of him being the topper of PCS Examination.
254	**burlesque** *noun* give an imitation that ridicules	*Usage:* The stage performer's burlesque on corrupt politicians made the audience burst into laughter.
255	**bustle** *verb* move about energetically, teem	*Usage:* Amninder always bustles with vigour and vitality.
256	**buttress** *verb* support, prop up	*Usage:* The defence lawyer came up with several far-fetched arguments to buttress his client's weak case.
C		
257	**cacophonous** *adj.* discordant, inharmonious	*Usage:* In the cacophonous claims and counter claims of politicians, the real issues are ignored.
258	**cajole** *verb* coax, wheedle	*Usage:* Mother tried to cajole her baby by letting her ride her tricycle in the park.
259	**calamity** *noun* disaster, misery	*Usage:* As news of the calamity spread, offers of relief poured in from all sectors into the flood-stricken community.
260	**callous** *adj.* hardened, unfeeling	*Usage:* The king was dethroned by the public for his callous attitude.
261	**camaraderie** *noun* good-fellowship	*Usage:* Our entire peer group enjoys camaraderie with each other.
262	**camouflage** *verb* disguise, conceal	*Usage:* In spite of being one of the most corrupt officials, Mr. Debey tries to camouflage as a very honest and upright person.
263	**candour** *noun* frankness, open honesty	*Usage:* I am highly impressed by her candour both in reel and real life.
264	**canny** *adj.* shrewd, thrifty	*Usage:* Beware of his canny nature.
265	**cantankerous** *adj.* ill humoured, irritable	*Usage:* Jaiswal got irritated with the cantankerous nature of his colleague.
266	**capacious** *adj.* spacious, roomy	*Usage:* In the capacious lobby of the metro station, several travellers lingered on while waiting for their train.
267	**capitulate** *verb* surrender, give up	*Usage:* The enemy was warned to capitulate or face annihilation.
268	**caprice** *noun* whim	*Usage:* You should try your best to come out of your caprice.
269	**capricious** *adj.* unpredictable, fickle	*Usage:* She is a very capricious lady.
270	**caption** *noun* title, chapter heading, text under illustration	*Usage:* The captions that accompany the cartoons are almost as funny as the pictures themselves.
271	**captivate** *verb* delight, charm or enthral	*Usage:* The new movie captivated the imagination of the masses and classes.

272	**cardinal** *adj.* chief, principal	*Usage:* We should focus on the cardinal issues related to the project.
273	**carnage** *noun* destruction of life	*Usage:* The genocide of Jews by Hitler is one of the bloodiest carnages recorded in history.
274	**carnal** *adj.* fleshly, bodily, sensual, sexual	*Usage:* When you are really involved in love with someone then the relationship is not confined to carnal desires.
275	**cascade** *noun* small waterfall	*Usage:* The cascade of his words enamoured the audience.
276	**castigate** *verb* criticise severely, punish	*Usage:* All the politicians should concentrate on developmental issues instead of castigating each other.
277	**cataclysm** *noun* upheaval, deluge, a great flood	*Usage:* India faced the cataclysm of Tsunami in 2004.
278	**catalyst** *noun* agent which brings about a chemical change while itself remaining unaffected and unchanged	*Usage:* He acted as a catalyst between the government and terrorists.
279	**catastrophe** *noun* calamity, disaster	*Usage:* The recent cyclone was a catastrophe that destroyed many coastal towns and cities in and around eastern coast of India.
280	**categorical** *adj.* exceptions, unqualified, absolute	*Usage:* He sent his categorical and unequivocal reply.
281	**cater to** *verb* supply something desired	*Usage:* My Study Package for CLAT and LL.B. Entrance Test caters to the needs of all students preparing for these examinations.
282	**catharsis** *noun* purging or cleansing of any passage of the body	*Usage:* Aristotle maintained that tragedy caused a catharsis by purging the soul of base concepts.
283	**caustic** *adj.* burning, sarcastically biting	*Usage:* The caustic remarks about the leader of a minority community made him unpopular.
284	**cavalcade** *noun* procession, parade	*Usage:* The President was followed by the cavalcade of his bodyguards.
285	**cede** *verb* yield (title, territory) to, surrender formally	*Usage:* India will never cede any part of Kashmir to Pakistan.
286	**celebrated** *adj.* famous, well-known	*Usage:* Salam Rushdie is a celebrated author.
287	**celestial** *adj.* heavenly, divine, of the finest or highest kind, perfect	*Usage:* The beauty of Menaka is celestial.
288	**censorious** *adj.* critical, inclined to find fault, harshly	*Usage:* Some people have very censorious attitude towards others.
289	**censure** *verb* blame, criticise	*Usage:* The councillor was censured for his arrogant behaviour with one of the journalists.
290	**ceremonious** *adj.* marked by formality	*Usage:* The office of Governor is ceremonious.

291	**certitude** *noun* certainty, a feeling of absolute sureness or conviction	*Usage:* Though there was no certitude of his getting the job, Ravish thought that there was no harm in giving it a try.
292	**cessation** *noun* stoppage	*Usage:* Army Generals ordered the cessation of firing.
293	**chaotic** *adj.* completely in disorder	*Usage:* The assassination of Indira Gandhi drove the entire country to a very chaotic state of affairs.
294	**charisma** *noun* divine gift, great popular charm or appeal	*Usage:* Salman has a very exclusive charisma of his personality.
295	**charlatan** *noun* quack, pretender of knowledge	*Usage:* The political charlatans and religious swindlers are basically responsible for the problems of communalism and casteism.
296	**chasm** *noun* rupture, split	*Usage:* The exit of the vice president led to a chasm in the party.
297	**chaste** *adj.* pure, virtuous, sexually abstinent, celibate	*Usage:* Cleopatra is known in history as the most chaste woman.
298	**chasten** *verb* discipline, punish in order to correct or make better	*Usage:* Nature chastens all for good or bad deeds.
299	**chastise** *verb* punish, esp. by beating, scold or condemn sharply	*Usage:* You must chastise her for her rude behaviour.
300	**chauvinist** *noun* blindly devoted, patriot	*Usage:* Subhash Chandra Bose was a great chauvinist.
301	**chequered** *adj.* marked by changes	*Usage:* His resume showed a very chequered record of his academic qualifications.
302	**cherubic** *adj.* angelic, innocent-looking	*Usage:* Tamanna is known for her cherubic beauty.
303	**chicanery** *noun* trickery, deception	*Usage:* Those sneaky lawyers won the case through chicanery.
304	**chide** *verb* scold, reprove mildly	*Usage:* Grandma began to chide Surjeet for his lying.
305	**chimerical** *adj.* fantastically improbable, highly unrealistic, imaginative	*Usage:* His plots are always by and large chimerical, lacking practicability and feasibility.
306	**chivalrous** *adj.* courteous, faithful, brave	*Usage:* Chivalrous behaviour involves noble words and good deeds.
307	**choleric** *adj.* having or showing a quick temper or irascible, bilious	*Usage:* No one likes the new officer because of his choleric nature.
308	**chortle** *verb* chuckle with delight	*Usage:* On hearing that her rival had just been jailed for embezzlement, she chortled with joy.
309	**chronic** *adj.* long established as a disease	*Usage:* Communalism is one of the most chronic ills afflicting the Indian state, society and nation.

310	**churlish** *adj.* boorish, rude, stingy or mean	*Usage:* Dismayed by his churlish manners at the birthday party, the girls vowed never to invite him again.
311	**circumlocution** *noun* indirect or roundabout expression	*Usage:* He was afraid to call a spade a spade and resorted to circumlocutions to avoid direct reference to his subject.
312	**circumscribe** *verb* limit, confine	*Usage:* We should not be circumscribed by our circumstances.
313	**circumspect** *adj.* prudent, cautious	*Usage:* She is very circumspect before signing any contract for a new book.
314	**circumvent** *verb* outwit, baffle	*Usage:* Amartya Sen circumvented Karan Thapar in a TV program 'Devil's Advocate'.
315	**clairvoyant** *adj. noun* having foresight, fortune-teller	*Usage:* It is very difficult to identify a true clairvoyant.
316	**clamour** *noun* noise, uproar, a loud outcry	*Usage:* There had been a great clamour in the parliament about the 3G telecom scam.
317	**clandestine** *adj.* secret, surreptitious, furtive	*Usage:* My friend asked me to join him for a movie in a clandestine manner during college hours.
318	**clasp** *noun* fastening device, firm grip	*Usage:* In a frenzied state of passion, he clasped my hands and jumped from the building to escape the fire.
319	**clemency** *noun* disposition to be lenient, mildness, as of the weather	*Usage:* The President of India has power to grant clemency.
320	**clench** *verb* close tightly, grasp	*Usage:* The mother clenched her child when the bus took an abrupt turn.
321	**coalesce** *verb* combine, fuse	*Usage:* All the parties should coalesce on certain national issues.
322	**coalition** *noun* partnership, union	*Usage:* The UPA coalition formed the government once again in 2010.
323	**coddle** *verb* to treat gently	*Usage:* He was coddling his pet.
324	**coercion** *noun* use of force to get someone to obey	*Usage:* The use of coercion frustrates the validity of the contract.
325	**cogent** *adj.* convincing, forceful, compelling	*Usage:* Pradeep Virk gave such cogent argument before the full bench, that all the judges were dumbfounded.
326	**cogitate** *verb* to think seriously and deeply (about), ponder, meditate, consider	*Usage:* Just cogitate on the course of action you want to pursue in your life and you will find a way forward.
327	**cognizance** *noun* knowledge, official observation of or authority over something	*Usage:* The judge took cognizance of the charge.
328	**cohere** *verb* stick together	*Usage:* In times of emergency, all the members of our family cohered to tackle the situation.
329	**cohesion** *noun* tendency to keep together	*Usage:* With the policy of divide and rule, the Britishers disturbed unity and cohesion of Indians.

330	**collaborate** *verb* work together	*Usage:* The two young writers collaborated in preparing this book.
331	**collage** *noun* work of art put together from fragments	*Usage:* The collage of photos of my daughter Anaadi's first birthday has been appreciated by all.
332	**collate** *verb* examine in order to verify authenticity, arrange in order	*Usage:* The team of editors collated the newly received manuscript to determine saleability of the proposed book.
333	**collateral** *noun* consequent and subsequent	*Usage:* The 1984 anti-Sikh riots were not the collateral outcome of assassination of Indira Gandhi, but a politically instigated massacre.
334	**colloquial** *adj.* pertaining to conversational or common speech	*Usage:* Colloquial language is different from written language.
335	**collusion** *noun* conspiring in a fraudulent scheme	*Usage:* The swindlers were found guilty of collusion.
336	**colossal** *adj.* huge, astonishingly great, extra ordinary	*Usage:* Writing a book is a colossal task.
337	**comely** *adj.* attractive, agreeable	*Usage:* Suman has a very comely outlook.
338	**commemorate** *verb* honour the memory of	*Usage:* Amar Jawan Jyoti commemorates the valiant soldiers who fought in different wars.
339	**commensurate** *adj.* equal in extent	*Usage:* Your reward will be commensurate with your efforts.
340	**commiserate** *verb* feel or express pity or sympathy for	*Usage:* Her friends commiserated at the sudden demise of his father.
341	**commodious** *adj.* spacious and comfortable	*Usage:* The rooms of the hotel were very commodious.
342	**compatible** *adj.* harmonious, in harmony with	*Usage:* Husband and wife have a very compatible nature.
343	**compelling** *adj.* overpowering, irresistible in effect	*Usage:* The prosecutor presented a well-reasoned case, but Pradeep Virk's compelling arguments for leniency won over the jury.
344	**complacency** *noun* self-satisfaction, smugness, contentment	*Usage:* Complacency retards growth.
345	**complaisant** *adj.* trying to please, obliging	*Usage:* The courtiers obeyed the king's orders in a complaisant manner.
346	**complement** *verb* complete, consummate, make perfect	*Usage:* Both Himmat and Simran complement and supplement each other in their nature, look, attitude and vision.
347	**complementary** *adj.* serving to complete something	*Usage:* The publisher gives ten complimentary copies to its authors.
348	**compliance** *noun* readiness to yield, conformity in fulfilling requirements	*Usage:* In compliance with the orders of the government, the Deputy Commissioner made all the arrangements.

349	**compliant** *adj.* yielding	*Usage:* One should not be so compliant that others take you for granted.
350	**complicity** *noun* participation, involvement	*Usage:* The complicity of the police in this kidnapping and murder case has been proved beyond doubt.
351	**compunction** *noun* remorse, a sharp feeling of uneasiness brought on by a sense of guilt	*Usage:* The judge was especially severe in his sentencing because he felt that the criminal had shown no compunction for his heinous crime.
352	**concede** *verb* admit, yield	*Usage:* The Governor conceded our request to inaugurate the function.
353	**conceit** *noun* vanity or self-love, whimsical idea, extravagant metaphor	*Usage:* Self-conceit is a very dangerous perversion of the personality.
354	**conception** *noun* beginning, forming of an idea	*Usage:* Since the conception of an idea, I worked hard to translate it into reality.
355	**concerted** *adj.* mutually agreed on, done together	*Usage:* They made concerted efforts to complete the project.
356	**concession** *noun* an act of yielding	*Usage:* Before they could reach an agreement, both sides had to make certain concessions.
357	**conciliatory** *adj.* reconciling, soothing	*Usage:* They had to find out some conciliatory solution.
358	**concise** *adj.* brief and compact	*Usage:* Precise and concise writing is considered as the best writing exercise.
359	**conclusive** *adj.* decisive	*Usage:* We could not reach any conclusion.
360	**concoct** *verb* prepare by combining, make up in concert	*Usage:* The police concocted the story to implicate Mr. Gupta in false corruption cases.
361	**concomitant** *noun* that which accompanies	*Usage:* Where wealth accumulates, cultural decline is a natural concomitant.
362	**concord** *noun* harmony, agreement between people or things	*Usage:* For success in life, one should have concord between one's capabilities and set goals.
363	**concur** *verb* agree, to occur at the same time, coincide	*Usage:* Did you concur with the decision of the court or did you find it unfair?
364	**concurrent** *adj.* happening at the same time	*Usage:* Non-cooperation movement and Khilafat movement were concurrent movements.
365	**condemn** *verb* censure, sentence, force or limit to particular state	*Usage:* We should condemn corrupt politicians.
366	**condense** *verb* shorten	*Usage:* Please condense this matter in 20 pages.
367	**condole** *verb* express sympathetic sorrow	*Usage:* His friends gathered to condole with him over the death of his father.
368	**condone** *verb* overlook, forgive, give tacit approval, excuse	*Usage:* His lectures were condoned when he produced the death certificate of his father.

369	**conducive** *adj.* making it easy, possible, or likely for something to happen	*Usage:* The atmosphere at his home was very conducive for studies.
370	**confidant** *noun* trusted friend	*Usage:* He had no confidant with whom he could discuss his problems at home.
371	**confine** *verb* shut in, restrict the movement of	*Usage:* Your circumstances should not define you or confine you rather you should define your circumstances.
372	**confirm** *verb* corroborate, verify, support	*Usage:* I have several witnesses who will confirm my account of what happened.
373	**confiscate** *verb* seize, commandeer	*Usage:* The army confiscated all available supplies of uranium.
374	**confluence** *noun* flowing together of two streams, the place where the two rivers join	*Usage:* Prayagraj is situated at the confluence of Ganga and Yamuna.
375	**conformity** *noun* harmony, agreement	*Usage:* In conformity with our rules and regulations, I am calling the general body meeting of our organisation.
376	**confound** *verb* confuse, puzzle	*Usage:* The officer, instead of solving the problem, confounded it.
377	**congenial** *adj.* pleasant, friendly	*Usage:* Life becomes an enjoyable journey with congenial companions by your side.
378	**congenital** *adj.* existing at birth	*Usage:* Some children are born with congenital diseases.
379	**conglomeration** *noun* a huge mixture	*Usage:* India is a conglomeration of castes, classes, religions, regions, races and languages.
380	**conjugal** *adj.* pertaining to marriage	*Usage:* As per law, either of the spouses can approach the court for conjugal rights.
381	**conjure** *verb* imagine	*Usage:* She conjures up very fantastic ideas.
382	**connivance** *noun* involvement	*Usage:* Media exposed the connivance of police with the abductors.
383	**connoisseurs** *noun* a lover of an art	*Usage:* In recent years, she had developed into a connoisseur of fine art.
384	**connotation** *noun* suggested or implied meaning of an expression	*Usage:* Generally, foreigners are unaware of the connotations of the words they use.
385	**consecrate** *verbs* dedicate, sanctify	*Usage:* We shall consecrate our lives to the noble purpose of eradicating illiteracy.
386	**consequential** *adj.* pompous, important, self-important	*Usage:* Convinced of her own importance, Brinda looked around with a consequential air.
387	**consistency** *noun* absence of contradictions, dependability, uniformity, degree of thickness	*Usage:* Consistency is one of the most important constituents in the preparation for Civil Services Examination.
388	**console** *verb* lessen sadness or disappointment, give comfort	*Usage:* I consoled the family members of my friend for their untimely loss in the form of his death.
389	**consonance** *noun* harmony, agreement	*Usage:* Profound writing demands that your thought process should be in consonance with your writing.

390	**conspicuous** *adj.* easily seen, noticeable, striking	*Usage:* The conspicuous absence of the officer raised the sign of suspicion on his capabilities.
391	**conspiracy** *noun* treacherous plot	*Usage:* The offence of conspiracy requires more than one person committing the crime.
392	**constraint** *noun* compulsion, repression of feelings	*Usage:* Time constraint is the biggest challenge to be tackled in competitive examinations.
393	**construe** *verb* explain, interpret	*Usage:* If I construe your remarks correctly, then they convey a very wrong message.
394	**consummate** *adj.* complete or perfect in every way, supreme	*Usage:* You must be a consummate idiot, as I have never seen anyone who makes as many stupid errors as you do.
395	**contaminate** *verb* pollute, to make impure	*Usage:* The regular music nights at the University campus contaminated its conducive atmosphere for studies.
396	**contemporary** *noun* person belonging to the same period	*Usage:* Atal Bihari Vajpayee and Parvez Musharraf were contemporaries.
397	**contempt** *noun* scorn, disdain	*Usage:* Really great people do not show contempt for poor and humble.
398	**contention** *noun* claim, thesis	*Usage:* You must take a stand for your contentions.
399	**contentious** *adj.* quarrelsome, belligerent	*Usage:* Disagreeing violently with the referees, the coach became so contentious that they threw him out of the game.
400	**contiguous** *adj.* adjacent to, touching upon	*Usage:* India and Pakistan are contiguous countries.
401	**continence** *noun* self-restraint, sexual chastity	*Usage:* The popularity of Jainism faded because of overstress on continence.
402	**contingent** *noun* conditions	*Usage:* If you make a contract to be performed contingent upon certain conditions, that contract is known as contingent contract.
403	**contortions** *noun* twisting, distortions	*Usage:* In spite of public prosecutor's contortions in the case to save the accused, the judge did not acquit him.
404	**contraband** *noun,* adj. illegal trade, smuggling	*Usage:* The coast guard tries to prevent traffic in contraband goods.
405	**contrite** *adj.* penitent	*Usage:* The contrite apology tendered by the accused failed to attract any sympathy for him.
406	**contrived** *adj.* forced, artificial, not spontaneous	*Usage:* His contrived behaviour made him unpopular among the entire group.
407	**controvert** *verb* oppose with argument, attempt to refute, contradict	*Usage:* Controverting your statement in a court of law is an offence.
408	**conundrum** *noun* a big problem	*Usage:* Since independence, Kashmir is a big conundrum for both India and Pakistan.
409	**convene** *verb* assemble	*Usage:* The President convened the Governors' meet at Delhi.
410	**conventional** *adj.* ordinary, typical	*Usage:* The conventional style of paper has been changed.

411	**converge** *verb* approach, tend to meet, come together	*Usage:* The doctors from distant places converged in the capital to protest against the proposed reservations.
412	**converse** *noun* opposite	*Usage:* While we agree to his views, the converse is not true.
413	**conversant** *adj.* familiar or acquainted with	*Usage:* The PM is very well conversant with the problems of refugees.
414	**convert** *noun* one who has adopted a different religion or opinion	*Usage:* Religious converts form a tiny minority of the population in our country.
415	**convivial** *adj.* festive, gay, characterised by joviality	*Usage:* Once the news of Abhey's top position in PCS was out, the convivial atmosphere at their home was commendable.
416	**copious** *adj.* plentiful	*Usage:* Rajesh has copious vocabulary of the English language.
417	**coquette** *noun* first	*Usage:* Nobody likes that coquette.
418	**cordial** *adj.* gracious, heartfelt	*Usage:* Our Olympian medal holders were given a cordial welcome.
419	**coronation** *noun* ceremony of crowning a queen or king	*Usage:* The coronation of Shivaji took place at his Ramgarh fort.
420	**corporeal** *adj.* bodily, material	*Usage:* Special laws empower the police to resort to corporeal punishments for the dreaded terrorists.
421	**corpulent** *adj.* very fat, obese	*Usage:* The corpulent man has resolved to reduce his weight.
422	**corroborate** *verb* confirm, support	*Usage:* Until and unless you corroborate your allegation with sufficient evidence, the court cannot do anything.
423	**corrode** *verb* destroy by chemical action	*Usage:* The girders supporting the bridge corroded so gradually that no one suspected any danger until the bridge suddenly collapsed.
424	**cosmic** *adj.* pertaining to the universe, vast	*Usage:* There are certain cosmic laws that regulate the universe.
425	**cosmopolitan** *adj.* sophisticated	*Usage:* He is known for his cosmopolitan outlook and catholicity of vision.
426	**coterie** *noun* group that meets socially, select circle	*Usage:* The leader always had a coterie of his sleuths surrounding him.
427	**countermand** *verb* cancel, revoke	*Usage:* The general countermanded the orders issued in his absence.
428	**covert** *adj.* secret, hidden, implied	*Usage:* He was arrested for all his covert and overt support to the terrorists.
429	**covetous** *adj.* avaricious	*Usage:* The child was covetous by nature and wanted to take away the toys belonging to his classmate.
430	**cow** *verb* terrorize, intimidate: to make someone timid and submissive by filling with fear or awe	*Usage:* Nowadays it is not easy to cow anyone because the public is very aware and informed about laws.

431	**cower** *verb* shrink quivering, as from fear	*Usage:* The frightened child cowered in a corner of the room.
432	**coy** *adj.* shy, modest, coquettish	*Usage:* She is a very coy lady.
433	**cozen** *verb* cheat, hoodwink, swindle	*Usage:* Sometimes even close friends cozen.
434	**crabbed** *adj.* sour, peevish	*Usage:* The crabbed old man was avoided by the children because he scolded them when they made noise.
435	**craftiness** *noun* slyness, trickiness	*Usage:* Advocate Joshi is notorious for his craftiness in the legal fraternity.
436	**crass** *adj.* very unrefined, grossly insensible	*Usage:* She is crass in and out and it is very difficult to refine her.
437	**craven** *adj.* very cowardly, abjectly afraid	*Usage:* His craven refusal to join the protest was criticised by his comrades, who had expected him to be brave enough to stand up for his beliefs.
438	**credence** *noun* credentials	*Usage:* One cannot have any credence in his promises because he has a track record of making false promises.
439	**credibility** *noun* believability, trustworthiness	*Usage:* Nobody can doubt the credibility of Honey.
440	**credulity** *noun* gullibility	*Usage:* Credulity is the major weak point of his personality.
441	**crest** *noun* highest point	*Usage:* She is at the crest of her success.
442	**crestfallen** *adj.* dejected, dispirited	*Usage:* She felt crestfallen when she was humbugged by her lover.
443	**cringe** *verb* shrink back, as if in fear	*Usage:* Indian public at large has developed the habit of cringing and grovelling before the political bosses.
444	**criterion** *noun* standard used in judging	*Usage:* What criterion did you use when you selected this essay as the prize-winner?
445	**crotchety** *adj.* eccentric, whimsical	*Usage:* Although he was infamous to be a crotchety old gentleman, I found his ideas substantially sound and sensible.
446	**crux** *noun* crucial point	*Usage:* This is the crux of the entire problem.
447	**cryptic** *adj.* mysterious, hidden, secret	*Usage:* He gave a very cryptic reply which was not easily understandable.
448	**cull** *verb* pick out, reject	*Usage:* All the Mauryan rulers culled religions of their own choices.
449	**culminate** *verb* attain the highest point, climax	*Usage:* Because of indifferent attitude of the governments, the Naxal problem has culminated into a huge conundrum.
450	**cumbersome** *adj.* heavy, hard to manage	*Usage:* Writing a book is a very tedious, complex and cumbersome job.
451	**cumulative** *adj.* growing by addition	*Usage:* The outburst of the public against the government was a cumulative effect of so many unattended public grievances.
452	**cupidity** *noun* greed, strong desire, esp. for wealth, avarice	*Usage:* The defeated people could not satisfy the cupidity of the conquerors, who demanded excessive tribute.

453	**curmudgeon** *noun* churlish, miserly individual	*Usage:* Mr. Marwaha is a curmudgeon person.
454	**cursory** *adj.* casual, hastily done	*Usage:* I just had a cursory look at the book.
455	**curtail** *verb* shorten, reduce	*Usage:* You cannot curtail this article.
456	**cynical** *adj.* sceptical or distrustful of human motives	*Usage:* She is so cynical that she doesn't trust anyone.
457	**cynosure** *noun* shining star	*Usage:* With her selection in OTA, Suman became the cynosure of the entire clan.
	D	
458	**dauntless** *adj.* bold	*Usage:* Despite the dangerous nature of the undertaking, the dauntless soldier volunteered for the assignment.
459	**dawdle** *verb* loiter, waste time	*Usage:* We have to meet a deadline, so don't dawdle, just get down to work.
460	**deadlock** *noun* standstill, stalemate	*Usage:* Because negotiations had reached a deadlock, some of the delegates had begun to mutter about breaking off the talks.
461	**dearth** *noun* scarcity	*Usage:* There is a dearth of NDA and CDS officers in the Indian army.
462	**debacle** *noun* sudden downfall, complete disaster	*Usage:* We should be mentally strong to face any debacle.
463	**debauch** *verb* corrupt, seduce from virtue	*Usage:* At times the younger generation does not mind being debauched to make easy money.
464	**debilitate** *verb* weaken, enfeeble	*Usage:* Nobody can debilitate the strong ambition of Honey to become an officer.
465	**debonair** *adj.* friendly, aiming to please	*Usage:* The debonair actress draws appreciation from all quarters of the society.
466	**debris** *noun* rubble	*Usage:* The true lessons of history are buried under the debris of history.
467	**debunk** *verb* expose as false, exaggerated, worthless, etc., ridicule	*Usage:* Pointing out that he consistently had voted against strengthening anti-pollution legislation, reporters debunked the candidate's claim that he was a fervent environmentalist.
468	**decadence** *noun* decay	*Usage:* With the British ascendancy, the decadence of the Mughal empire set in.
469	**decimate** *verb* kill, usually one out of ten	*Usage:* We do more to decimate our population in automobile accidents than we do in war.
470	**decipher** *verb* to interpret	*Usage:* The Indus script which is pictographic has not been deciphered as yet.
471	**decorum** *noun* propriety, orderliness and good taste in manners	*Usage:* We have to maintain a decorum in the office, as a team from the Head Office is coming.
472	**decrepitude** *noun* state of collapse caused by illness or old age	*Usage:* I was unprepared for the state of decrepitude in which I had found my old friend, he seemed to have aged twenty years in six months.

473	**decry** *verb* express strong disapproval of, disparage	*Usage:* The fundamentalists decried the woman reservation bill.
474	**deface** *verb* mar, disfigure	*Usage:* The hoardings and banners have defaced the beauty of the city.
475	**defeatist** *adj.* attitude of one who is ready to accept defeat as a natural outcome	*Usage:* If you maintain your defeatist attitude, you will never succeed.
476	**defer** *verb* delay till later, exempt temporarily	*Usage:* The date of the declaration of results may be deferred.
477	**deference** *noun* courteous regard for another's wish	*Usage:* With due deference, he requested the Principal for a fee concession.
478	**defiance** *noun* refusal to yield, resistance	*Usage:* No one could understand the reason of his defiance to marry Neha.
479	**defile** *verb* pollute, profane	*Usage:* The political gangsters, instigated by the opposition, defiled the party office with their scurrilous writings.
480	**deft** *adj.* neat, skilful	*Usage:* Suraj is a deft typist.
481	**defunct** *adj.* dead, no longer in use or existence	*Usage:* We have to rejuvenate the defunct agencies so as to deliver the services properly.
482	**degenerate** *verb* become worse, deteriorate	*Usage:* Nowadays our society is degenerating in the wake of import of western culture.
483	**deify** *verb* turn into a god, idolised	*Usage:* People in India virtually deify Gandhi.
484	**delectable** *adj.* delightful, delicious	*Usage:* We thanked our host for a most delectable meal.
485	**delete** *verb* erase, strike out	*Usage:* If you delete this paragraph, your whole essay will have greater appeal.
486	**deleterious** *adj.* harmful to health or well-being, injurious	*Usage:* If you believe that smoking is deleterious to your health then forgo this habit.
487	**deliberate** *verb* consider, ponder	*Usage:* Offered the new job, she asked for time to deliberate before she told them her decision.
488	**delve** *verb* dig	*Usage:* He delves into details of every topic he reads.
489	**demagogue** *noun* person who appeals to people's prejudice, false leader of people	*Usage:* The spiritual guru was accused of being a demagogue because he made promises that aroused futile hopes in his followers.
490	**demean** *verb* degrade, humiliate	*Usage:* Never try to demean others.
491	**demeanour** *noun* behaviour, bearing	*Usage:* His sober demeanour quietened the noisy revellers.
492	**demise** *noun* death	*Usage:* The sudden demise of his father virtually devastated him.
493	**demolition** *noun* destruction	*Usage:* The municipal body ordered demolition of all illegal structures.
494	**demoniac** *adj.* fiendish	*Usage:* The demoniac designs of politicians are reprehensible.

495	**demystify** *verb* clarify, free from mystery or obscurity	*Usage:* Helpful doctors demystify medical procedures by describing them in common man's language.
496	**denigrate** *verb* defame	*Usage:* All attempts to denigrate his character failed.
497	**denizen** *noun* inhabitant or resident, regular visitor	*Usage:* The denizens of the unauthorised slum area unanimously raised their voice for legalisation of the land.
498	**deplore** *verb* regret, disapprove of	*Usage:* It is very easy to deplore the activities of others.
499	**depose** *verb* dethrone, remove from office	*Usage:* The army attempted to depose the president and set up a military government.
500	**deposition** *noun* removal from office or position of power, testimony under oath	*Usage:* He made his deposition before the magistrate.
501	**depravity** *noun* extreme corruption, wickedness	*Usage:* The depravity of politicians is nowadays questioned by the public at the time of elections.
502	**deprecate** *verb* express disapproval of, protest against, belittle	*Usage:* Mr. Saxena deprecates feminism.
503	**depreciate** *verb* lessen in value	*Usage:* If you neglect this property, it will depreciate.
504	**depredation** *noun* plundering	*Usage:* After the depredations of the Mughal invaders, the once affluent people were left penniless.
505	**deranged** *adj.* insane	*Usage:* He had to be hopitalised because he was mentally deranged.
506	**derelict** *adj.* abandoned, negligent	*Usage:* The derelict child became addicted to smoking and drinking.
507	**deride** *verb* ridicule	*Usage:* We should avoid deriding others.
508	**derogatory** *adj.* expressing a low opinion	*Usage:* The columnist made very derogatory remarks about the present government in his article.
509	**desecrate** *verb* profane, violate the sanctity of	*Usage:* Places of worship should not be desecrated,
510	**despise** *verb* look on with scorn, regard as worthless or distasteful	*Usage:* Mrs. Sharma despised her neighbour's newly bought car.
511	**despoil** *verb* plunder	*Usage:* The bandit chief warned that if the villagers do not yield, they will despoil the entire village.
512	**despondent** *adj.* depressed, gloomy	*Usage:* He is a having a despondent look since he failed in exams.
513	**destitute** *adj.* extremely poor	*Usage:* Because they had no health insurance, the father's costly illness left the family destitute.
514	**desultory** *adj.* aimless, haphazard, digressing at random	*Usage:* He is nowadays leading a very desultory life.
515	**detached** *adj.* emotionally removed, calm and objective, physically unconnected	*Usage:* Buddha has professed the philosophy of leading a detached life.

516	**deterrent** *noun* something that discourages, hindrance	*Usage:* The threat of capital punishment serves as a deterrent to potential killers.
517	**detrimental** *adj.* harmful, damaging	*Usage:* Smoking has very detrimental effects on health.
518	**devious** *adj.* roundabout, erratic, not straightforward	*Usage:* The magician's plan was so devious that it was only with great difficulty we could follow its shifts and dodges.
519	**devise** *verb* think up, invent plan	*Usage:* We have to devise a new strategy to trigger the growth of the company.
520	**devoid** *adj.* lacking, empty	*Usage:* He is devoid of basic civic sense.
521	**dexterous** *adj.* skilful	*Usage:* The magician was so dexterous that we could not follow him as he performed his tricks.
522	**diabolical** *adj.* devilish	*Usage:* Cassius and Brutus hatched a diabolical conspiracy to kill Caesar.
523	**dichotomy** *noun* split, branching into two parts	*Usage:* Vishwas didn't know how to resolve the dichotomy between his ambition to go to college and his childhood longing to run away and join the film industry.
524	**diffidence** *noun* shyness	*Usage:* You must overcome your diffidence if you intend to become a good articulator.
525	**dilapidated** *adj.* ruined because of neglect	*Usage:* The dilapidated historical monument needed far more work than just a new coat of paint.
526	**dilatory** *adj.* delaying	*Usage:* Your dilatory tactics may compel them to cancel the contract.
527	**dilemma** *noun* problem, choice of two unsatisfactory alternatives	*Usage:* In this dilemma, he knew no one to whom he could turn for advice.
528	**dilettante** *noun* aimless follower of the arts, amateur, dabbler	*Usage:* He was not serious in his painting, he was rather a dilettante.
529	**diligence** *noun* steadiness of effort, persistent hard work	*Usage:* Her employers were greatly impressed by her diligence and offered her a partnership in the firm.
530	**dint** *noun* means, effort	*Usage:* By dint of hard work Honey made to the final list of IAS Selections 2010.
531	**dire** *adj.* disastrous, arousing terror or causing extreme distress	*Usage:* You should be prepared to face the dire consequences.
532	**disarray** *noun* a disorderly or untidy state	*Usage:* All the institutions of governance in India are in disarray.
533	**disavowal** *noun* denial, disclaiming	*Usage:* His disavowal of his part in the conspiracy was not believed by the judge.
534	**disburse** *verb* pay-out, spend	*Usage:* When you disburse money on the company's behalf, be sure to get a receipt.
535	**discernible** *adj.* distinguishable, perceivable	*Usage:* The vehicles on the road were not discernible from a distance in the fog.
536	**disclaim** *verb* disown, renounce claim to	*Usage:* If I grant you this privilege, will you disclaim all other rights?

537	**discombobulated** *adj.* confused, discomposed	*Usage:* Ravi Saxena delivered a discombobulated speech which was not at all expected of him.
538	**discomfit** *verb* to frustrate the plans or expectations of, to make uneasy, defeat, disconcert	*Usage:* This strategy to grab the attention of the buyers will certainly discomfit the rival company.
539	**disconcert** *noun* confuse, upset, embarrass	*Usage:* The lawyer was disconcerted by the evidence.
540	**discrepancy** *noun* lack of consistency, difference	*Usage:* The police noticed some discrepancies in his description of the crime and did not believe him.
541	**discrete** *adj.* separate, unconnected	*Usage:* The universe is composed of discrete bodies.
542	**discretion** *noun* prudence, ability to adjust actions to circumstances	*Usage:* It is the discretion of the governor to grant pardon.
543	**discriminating** *adj.* able to see differences, prejudiced	*Usage:* It will be quite discriminating if we do not appreciate the efforts of the young man.
544	**disdain** *verb* view with scorn or contempt	*Usage:* I virtually disdain corrupt people.
545	**dishearten** *verb* discourage, cause to lose courage or hope	*Usage:* The rich should not dishearten the poor.
546	**dishevelled** *adj.* untidy, tousled, rumpled	*Usage:* Our corrupt politicians are responsible for the dishevelled state of affairs.
547	**dismantle** *verb* shatter	*Usage:* At times we are in a very dismantled state of mind.
548	**dismay** *verb* discourage, frighten	*Usage:* Her failure in getting some job immediately to pull her family expenses dismayed her to the very bone.
549	**disparage** *verb* belittle, lower in esteem	*Usage:* Don't disparage the achievement of others.
550	**disparate** *adj.* basically different, unrelated	*Usage:* My brother and I have disparate opinions about marriage.
551	**disparity** *noun* difference, condition of inequality	*Usage:* There is a great disparity in their theory and reality.
552	**dispel** *verb* drive away, cause to vanish	*Usage:* Guru (teacher) is he who dispels darkness.
553	**disperse** *verb* scatter, to dispel	*Usage:* The police fired tear gas into the crowd to disperse the agitators.
554	**disseminate** *verb* distribute, spread, scatter	*Usage:* We have to disseminate knowledge in order to awaken the citizenry and save them from the clutches of terrorist leanings.
555	**dissident** *adj.* dissenting, rebellious	*Usage:* The dissident students and their supporters were arrested by the police.
556	**dissipate** *verb* squander, waste, scatter	*Usage:* He is a fine artist, but I fear he may dissipate his natural ability if he keeps wasting his time playing games.
557	**dissolute** *adj.* loose in morals	Usage: It is indeed shocking to read about the dissolute life led by the ancient Romans.

558	**dissolution** *noun* breaking of a union, decay	*Usage:* The trifling issues led to the dissolution of the empire.
559	**dissuade** *verb* persuade not to do, discourage	*Usage:* The Vice Chancellor failed to dissuade the student leader.
560	**distil** *verb* extract the essence, purify, refine	*Usage:* It is better to distil one's thoughts for the good of humanity instead of going to temples.
561	**distinction** *noun* honour, contrast, discrimination	*Usage:* Suman has the distinction of securing 3rd All India Rank in OTA 2010.
562	**distort** *verb* twist	*Usage:* The lawyers distort all facts.
563	**divergent** *adj.* differing, deviating	*Usage:* All the political parties had divergent views on the reservation issue.
564	**diverse** *adj.* differing in some characteristics, various	*Usage:* The professor suggested diverse ways of approaching the assignment and recommended that we choose one of them.
565	**diversion** *noun* act of turning aside, pastime	*Usage:* After studying for several hours, he needed a diversion from work.
566	**diversity** *noun* variety, dissimilitude	*Usage:* India is a country known for its unity in diversity.
567	**divest** *verb* strip, deprive, or dispose off	*Usage:* He was divested of his power to act and could no longer run the business affairs single-handedly
568	**divulge** *verb* reveal, disclose something confidential	*Usage:* Ravi would never divulge anything that a friend told him in confidence.
569	**docile** *adj.* obedient, easily managed	*Usage:* All the faculty members like him because of his docile nature.
570	**doctrine** *noun* teachings, in general, particular principle (religious, legal, etc.)	*Usage:* The doctrines of Gandhi are taught all over the world.
571	**dogged** *adj.* determined, stubborn	*Usage:* I am sometimes scared of his dogged determination to avenge his father's death.
572	**dogmatic** *adj.* opinionated, arbitrary, doctrinal	*Usage:* We tried to discourage Karan from being so dogmatic, but never could convince him that his opinions might be wrong.
573	**doldrums** *noun* blues, listlessness, slack period	*Usage:* She is always in the doldrums and can never take a strong and concrete decision.
574	**doleful** *adj.* sorrowful, mournful, melancholy	*Usage:* He found the doleful lamentations of the bereaved family emotionally disturbing, so he left the cremation site as quickly as he could.
575	**dolt** *noun* stupid person	*Usage:* Initially I thought I was talking to a mature audience, instead, I found myself addressing a pack of dolts and idiots.
576	**domineer** *verb* rule over tyrannically	*Usage:* Nowadays it is almost impossible to domineer over the public with force or fear.
577	**dormant** *adj.* sleeping, lethargic, latent	*Usage:* Once you are determined to accomplish any gargantuan task, your dormant energies get activated.

578	**dwindle** *verb* shrink, reduce	*Usage:* After Ashoka's death, the Mauryan empire dwindled.
	E	
579	**ebullient** *adj.* showing excitement, overflowing with enthusiasm	*Usage:* His natural ebullience began to return after he recuperated.
580	**eccentric** *adj.* irregular, odd, whimsical, bizarre	*Usage:* He is an eccentric character who likes to wear a beret and dark glasses.
581	**eccentricity** *noun* oddity, idiosyncrasy	*Usage:* His eccentricity has ostracised him from his peer group.
582	**ecclesiastic** *adj.* pertaining to the church	*Usage:* His ambition was to move upwards in the ecclesiastical hierarchy.
583	**eclectic** *adj.* composed of elements drawn from disparate sources	*Usage:* I have got an eclectic collection of paintings, drawings & prints at my place.
584	**eclipse** *verb* darken, extinguish, surpass	*Usage:* The blockbuster of 2010 'Dabangg' has eclipsed all previous revenue records.
585	**ecstasy** *noun* rapture, joy, and overpowering emotion	*Usage:* I am happy but not ecstatic as I had thought of better results.
586	**edify** *verb* instruct, correct morally	*Usage:* In the 18th century art was seen, along with music and poetry, as something edifying.
587	**eerie** *adj.* weird, uncanny, ghostly, spooky, frightful	*Usage:* Old Shimla was known for its eerie surrounding and ghostly alleys.
588	**efface** *verb* rub out, as from a surface, erase, wipe out, obliterate,	*Usage:* The successful hosting of CWG 2010 has effaced India's image as a third world country.
589	**effectual** *adj.* able to produce a desired effect, valid	*Usage:* This is the only effectual way to secure our present and future happiness.
590	**effervescence** *noun* inner excitement or exuberance	*Usage:* He performed the ceremony with great effervescence.
591	**efficacy** *noun* power to produce desired effect	*Usage:* The result will unveil the efficacy of his hard-work.
592	**effrontery** *noun* shameless boldness	*Usage:* His effrontery in front of his teachers caused much embarrassment to his parents.
593	**effusive** *adj.* pouring forth, gushing, unrestrained, unreserved, demonstrative, over demonstrative	*Usage:* Their effusive and unbridled child caused them great embarrassment at the party.
594	**egoism** *noun* excessive interest in one's self, belief that one should be interested in one's self rather than in others	*Usage:* Egoism always acts as a barrier between the enlightened ones and the ordinary ones.
595	**egotistical** *adj.* excessively self-centred, self-important, conceited	*Usage:* His egotistical demeanour has made him infamous among his peers.

596	**egregious** *adj.* notorious, conspicuously bad or shocking	*Usage:* The Islamic countries have seen the most egregious of abuses of human rights in recent times.
597	**egress** *noun* departure, emergence, escape, doorway, passage, way out, exit	*Usage:* The terrorists could not find the egress and were cornered by the security personnel.
598	**ejaculation** *noun* a sudden vehement utterance or exclamation	*Usage:* He was filled with ejaculation of joy and amazement after winning the tournament.
599	**elated** *adj.* overjoyed, in high spirits from	*Usage:* The elated Indian squad was warmly welcomed after winning the World Cup.
600	**elicit** *verb* draw out by discussion	*Usage:* The cabinet tried to elicit the policy to be adopted on climate change.
601	**elixir** *noun* cure-all, something invigorating	*Usage:* The news of getting a job was an elixir for her fear and uncertainty.
602	**eloquence** *noun* vivid, forceful, fluent, graceful, persuasive speech or writing	*Usage:* Winston Churchill was known for eloquence of his speech.
603	**elucidate** *verb* explain, enlighten	*Usage:* The union government appointed a committee to elucidate the dispute.
604	**elusive** *adj.* evasive, baffling, hard to grasp	*Usage:* He couldn't understand her elusive gestures and consequently landed up in a mess.
605	**emaciated** *adj.* thin and wasted	*Usage:* The horrifying scenes of emaciated prisoners being beaten were shown on the TV.
606	**emanate** *verb* to come forth, issue, as from a source, emit	*Usage:* All the major rivers emanate from glaciers.
607	**emancipate** *verb* set free, release from bondage, servitude, or serfdom	*Usage:* The US emancipated many spies of Russia and vice-versa.
608	**embargo** *noun* ban on commerce or other activity	*Usage:* India had to face an embargo after she tested nuclear weapons for the first time.
609	**embark** *verb* commence	*Usage:* The party president has embarked upon his poll campaign for the forthcoming elections.
610	**embellish** *verb* adorn, ornament	*Usage:* Fresh snowfall after a decade has embellished the beauty of Shimla.
611	**embezzlement** *noun* stealing	*Usage:* An IAS couple has been charged for embezzlement of government funds.
612	**embody** *verb* personify, make concrete, incorporate	*Usage:* Jack Kennedy embodied all hopes of 1960s.
613	**embrace** *verb* hug, adopt, or espouse, accept readily, encircle, include	*Usage:* If you want to succeed in life you need to embrace ideas of great people and apply them in your life.
614	**embroil** *verb* throw into confusion, involve in strife, entangle	*Usage:* The counsel made the witness embroil posing with a plethora of questions.

615	**embryonic** *adj.* undeveloped, rudimentary	*Usage:* His skills are embryonic; he is still a rookie.
616	**emend** *verb* correct: corrected by a critic	*Usage:* This book has many errors, it needs to be emended.
617	**eminent** *adj.* high, lofty	*Usage:* The chief guest was a person of eminent stature.
618	**empathy** *noun* ability to identify with another's feelings, ideas, etc.	*Usage:* Politicians need to be very empathetic with the masses to address their problems.
619	**empirical** *adj.* based solely on experiment and observation rather than theory, practical experience without reference to scientific principles.	*Usage:* There is no empirical evidence to support his thesis.
620	**emulate** *verb* to try, often by imitating or copying, to equal or surpass, to imitate	*Usage:* Emulate people of good character and integrity.
621	**enamoured** *adj.* in love	*Usage:* Jahangir was enamoured by the flawless beauty of Kashmir and called it a 'paradise on earth'.
622	**encomium** *noun* high praise, eulogy	*Usage:* Excessive encomium leads to egoism.
623	**encompass** *verb* surround, encircle, contain, include, achieve, contrive	*Usage:* China is trying to encompass India by improving its bilateral ties with our neighbours.
624	**encroachment** *noun* trespassing or gradual intrusion	*Usage:* The municipal corporation razed down the encroachments adjoining the main market.
625	**endorse** *verb* approve, support	*Usage:* All the G-5 countries, except China, have endorsed India's demand for a permanent UNSC seat.
626	**enduring** *adj.* lasting, surviving, durable	*Usage:* The enduring power of this battery can last for a month.
627	**energise** *verb* invigorate	*Usage:* Regular yoga energises my body and soul.
628	**enervate** *verb* weaken	*Usage:* The effect of the storm is likely to enervate in a couple of days.
629	**engage** *verb* attract, hire, pledge oneself, confront	*Usage:* The government engaged a foreign firm for the security of CWG 2010.
630	**engaging** *adj.* charming, attractive	*Usage:* Her engaging looks and eloquence were peerless.
631	**engender** *verb* cause, produce	*Usage:* Confronting the Indian army on the battlefield engendered fear in the enemy.
632	**engross** *verb* occupy fully, express formally or in legal form	*Usage:* The policeman was so much engrossed in his talks that the convict escaped.
633	**enhance** *verb* increase, improve	*Usage:* This supplement will surely enhance your immunity.

634	**enigma** *noun* puzzle, mystery, a perplexing, or baffling matter	*Usage:* The origin of the universe is still an enigma for everyone.
635	**enigmatic** *adj.* obscure, puzzling	*Usage:* The enigmatic vastness of the universe amazes everyone.
636	**ennui** *noun* boredom, weariness and dissatisfaction resulting from inactivity or lack of interest	*Usage:* I was feeling ennui after standing for hours together in a queue to deposit my bill.
637	**enormity** *noun* hugeness	*Usage:* I am amazed at the enormity of this project.
638	**enrapture** *verb* intensely, fill with great pleasure or delight, entrance, enchant, enravish	*Usage:* I was enraptured when I met the star Amartya Sen.
639	**ensemble** *noun* group of (supporting) players, organic unity, costume	*Usage:* I performed with an ensemble of young musicians.
640	**entail** *verb* require, necessitate, involve	*Usage:* Success entails dedication and hard work.
641	**enterprising** *adj.* dynamic initiative	*Usage:* Our company has always embraced enterprising ideas.
642	**enthral** *verb* capture, enslave	*Usage:* The peerless beauty of Katrina enthralled the audience.
643	**entice** *verb* lure, attract, tempt	*Usage:* All governments entice multinationals to invest in their country.
644	**entourage** *noun* group of attendants, retinue	*Usage:* Western celebrities always come with their entourage.
645	**entreat** *verb* plead, ask earnestly	*Usage:* We entreated the landlord to negotiate the rent for the last time.
646	**entrepreneur** *noun* businessman, contractor	*Usage:* India has emerged as a country of IT entrepreneurs.
647	**enumerate** *verb* list, mention one by one	*Usage:* The school principal enumerated his virtues in detail.
648	**enunciate** *verb* speak distinctly, proclaim	*Usage:* He has been enunciated as a hardcore criminal by the court.
649	**ephemeral** *adj.* short-lived, fleeting	*Usage:* Beauty is ephemeral, but knowledge is not.
650	**epicure** *noun* connoisseur of food and drink	*Usage:* Sanjeev Kapoor is one of the finest epicures.
651	**equable** *adj.* tranquil, steady, uniform	*Usage:* His equable remarks settled down the dispute.
652	**equanimity** *noun* calmness of temperament, composure	*Usage:* M.S. Dhoni exhibits equanimity on the field.
653	**equilibrium** *noun* balance	*Usage:* For a smooth economy, equilibrium should be maintained between demand and supply.
654	**equitable** *adj.* fair, impartial	*Usage:* Everyone should be given equitable opportunity to represent himself.

655	**equity** *noun* fairness, justice	*Usage:* Equity in rights leads to an egalitarian society.
656	**equivocal** *adj.* ambiguous, intentionally misleading	*Usage:* Politicians are always ready with their equivocal arguments at press briefs.
657	**equivocate** *verb* mislead, attempt to conceal the truth	*Usage:* The convict tried to equivocate the judge.
658	**erode** *verb* wear away	*Usage:* Every year a lot of agricultural land is eroded in the floods.
659	**erotic** *adj.* pertaining to passionate love	*Usage:* Khajuraho temples are famous for their erotic sculptures.
660	**erratic** *adj.* odd, unpredictable	*Usage:* The monsoons show erratic trends every year.
661	**erroneous** *adj.* mistaken, wrong	*Usage:* The minister apologised for his erroneous remarks.
662	**erudite** *adj.* learned, scholarly	*Usage:* Swami was known for his erudite wits.
663	**escapism** *noun* avoiding reality by diverting oneself with amusements	*Usage:* Escapism is never desirable; one should always face realities.
664	**eschew** *verb* avoid, keep away from (something harmful or disliked), shun, abstain from	*Usage:* Eschewing pessimism is my new year resolution.
665	**esoteric** *adj.* hard to understand, known only to a chosen few	*Usage:* The esoteric mystery of the universe is a puzzle for everyone.
666	**espionage** *noun* spying, in order to maintain its power	*Usage:* A senior Indian diplomat was charged with espionage for the enemy country.
667	**espouse** *verb* adopt, support or advocate	*Usage:* She ran away with him to Mexico and espoused the revolutionary cause.
668	**esteem** *verb* respect, value	*Usage:* I esteem him for his honesty.
669	**estranged** *adj.* separated, alienated	*Usage:* He had estranged relations with his wife.
670	**ethereal** *adj.* light, heavenly, unusually refined	*Usage:* Sameera is an ethereal beauty.
671	**ethnic** *adj.* relating to races	*Usage:* Somalia was marred by an ethnic crisis recently.
672	**ethos** *noun* underlying character of a culture, group, etc.	*Usage:* Real ethos of India lie in its villages.
673	**euphemism** *noun* mild expression in place of an unpleasant one	*Usage:* 'To pass away' is a euphemism for dying.
674	**euphonious** *adj.* pleasing in sound	*Usage:* I like the euphonious vibrations of the guitar.
675	**euphoria** *noun* feeling of great happiness and well-being (sometimes exaggerated)	*Usage:* On the eve of New Year, the atmosphere at the beach was filled with euphoria.

676	**evanescent** *adj.* fleeting, vanishing	*Usage:* The density of fog was evanescent with the rising sun.
677	**evasive** *adj.* not frank, eluding	*Usage:* The people got hold of the thief after he replied evasively.
678	**even-handed** *adj.* impartial, fair	*Usage:* For a healthy democracy, even-handed polls are indispensable.
679	**evince** *verb* to overcome, show plainly	*Usage:* The entire production evinces authenticity and a real respect for the subject matter.
680	**evocative** *adj.* tending to call up (emotions, memories)	*Usage:* Her story is sharply evocative of Indian provincial life.
681	**exacerbate** *verb* worsen, embitter	*Usage:* The Tsunami after an earthquake exacerbated the relief work.
682	**exacting** *adj.* extremely demanding, arduous or onerous	*Usage:* Building the Great Wall of China was an exacting task.
683	**exalt** *verb* raise in rank or dignity, praise	Usage The officer was exalted after he solved a murder mystery in two days.
684	**exasperate** *verb* vex, annoy, irritate	*Usage:* China's indulgence with Pakistan has been exasperating India for a long time.
685	**excerpt** *noun* selected passage (written or musical)	*Usage:* Excerpts from famous literary works are taught at premier schools nowadays.
686	**exclaim** *verb* cry out suddenly as if in surprise	*Usage:* He went back to the lab, Iris exclaimed impatiently.
687	**excoriate** *verb* sold with biting harshness, strip the skin off	*Usage:* He proceeded to excoriate me in front of the nurses.
688	**exculpate** *verb* clear from blame	*Usage:* The judge exculpated the convict.
689	**execrable** *adj.* very bad, due to inferior quality	*Usage:* Chinese electronic goods are execrable as compared to western goods.
690	**exemplary** *adj.* serving as a model, outstanding	*Usage:* The court awarded him exemplary punishment.
691	**exertion** *noun* effort	*Usage:* After a lot of exertion for the last 10 years, Honey finally got selected for the IAS.
692	**exhilarating** *adj.* invigorating and refreshing, cheering	*Usage:* Yoga session for an hour every day is an exhilarating experience.
693	**exhort** *verb* urge earnestly by advice, warning, admonish strongly	*Usage:* The Indian army exhorted the enemy to reduce its activity on the border.
694	**exhume** *verb* dig out of the ground, remove from the grave	*Usage:* The TV channel exhumed the real facts of the case.
695	**exigency** *noun* urgent situation	*Usage:* The action proposed by the PM is an outcome of political exigency.
696	**exodus** *noun* departure, a going out or forth, esp. in a large group	*Usage:* The Kashmir problem led to large scale exodus of Kashmiri Pandits.

697	**exonerate** *verb* acquit, exculpate	*Usage:* He must be exonerated in this case as he has a strong alibi.
698	**exorbitant** *adj.* excessive, going beyond what is reasonable, just, proper, etc.	Usage: The exorbitant prices of onion has baffled the common man.
699	**exorcise** *verb* drive out evil spirits	*Usage:* The swindler cheated on him by promising to exorcise the evil spirit.
700	**exotic** *adj.* not native, strange or different in a way that is striking or fascinating	*Usage:* We are producing many exotic varieties of banana here.
701	**expansive** *adj.* outgoing and sociable, broad and extensive	*Usage:* Tatas have expansive plans to roll out new products in the market.
702	**expatriate** *noun* exile, someone who has withdrawn from his native land	*Usage:* M.F. Hussain has been expatriated because of the life threats he was receiving.
703	**expedient** *adj.* suitable, practical, politic	*Usage:* To socialise, you need to be expedient rather than be idealist.
704	**expedite** *verb* hasten, facilitate	*Usage:* We need to expedite our meeting as we are running out of time.
705	**expeditious** *adj.* fast, speedy, quick	*Usage:* India wants expeditious trial of 26/11 offenders from Pakistan.
706	**expertise** *noun* specialised knowledge, expert skill	*Usage:* He has an expertise in fast bowling.
707	**expiate** *verb* make amends for (a sin)	*Usage:* He paid a visit to a shrine in view of expiating his sins.
708	**explicit** *adj.* totally clear, definite, outspoken	*Usage:* Don't just hint around that you're dissatisfied, be explicit about what's vexing you the most.
709	**exploit** *noun* deed or action, particularly the one which is brave, remarkable and daring	*Usage:* The child was given the President's Award for his exploit of confronting the dacoits.
710	**exploit** *verb* make use of, sometimes unjustly	*Usage:* The upper class in India has always exploited the lower classes.
711	**exposure** *noun* act of laying something open	*Usage:* Lack of exposure is the main hindrance for all round development of the child.
712	**expunge** *verb* cancel, remove	*Usage:* The telecom minister's speech was expunged from the records of the parliamentary proceedings.
713	**expurgate** *verb* clean, remove offensive parts of a book	*Usage:* The critics expurgated the offensive illustrations in the textbook.
714	**extant** *adj.* still in existence	*Usage:* Though its production is dated back to 1774, some copies of this book are still extant.
715	**extent** *noun* degree, magnitude, scope	*Usage:* The minister reviewed the extent of the destruction caused by the quake.
716	**extenuate** *verb* weaken, mitigate	*Usage:* The storm extenuated after rainfall.

717	**extol** *verb* praise, glorify	*Usage:* The police squad was extolled by the minister after solving the case.
718	**extort** *verb* wring from, get money by threats, etc.	*Usage:* The kidnappers extorted money from the victim's parents.
719	**extradition** *noun* surrender of prisoner by one state to another	*Usage:* India could not extradite Headley as we don't have an extradition treaty with USA.
720	**extraneous** *adj.* not essential, superfluous	*Usage:* The case should not be solved on extraneous grounds.
721	**extricate** *verb* free, disentangle	*Usage:* The security personnel at the dock extricated the person caught in the net accidently.
722	**extrinsic** *adj.* external, not essential, extraneous	*Usage:* Nowadays, there are fewer extrinsic pressures to get married.
723	**extrovert** *noun* person interested mostly in external objects and actions	*Usage:* He is an extrovert and likes socialising with people.
724	**exuberance** *noun* overflowing abundance, joyful enthusiasm, flamboyance, lavishness	*Usage:* The outlook of Katrina Kaif oozes out exuberance.
725	**exude** *verb* discharge, give forth	*Usage:* The alpine trees exude some kind of a jelly like syrup.
726	**exult** *verb* rejoice greatly, be jubilant, leap with joy	*Usage:* He was exultant on the successful implementation of the plan.
	F	
727	**fallacious** *adj.* false, misleading	*Usage:* The argument of the opposition party is fallacious.
728	**fallible** *adj.* liable to error, mistaken	*Usage:* Human-beings are fallible.
729	**falter** *verb* hesitate, to lose strength, certainty, etc.	*Usage:* Normal life is at a standstill though the economy is faltering.
730	**fanaticism** *noun* excessive zeal, extreme devotion to a belief or cause	*Usage:* The terrorists were guided by fanaticism.
731	**fancy** *noun* notion, whim, inclination	*Usage:* She didn't suspect that his interest was just a passing fancy.
732	**farce** *noun* mockery	*Usage:* Indian politicians have made Indian democracy a farce.
733	**fastidious** *adj.* difficult to please, squeamish	*Usage:* She is very fastidious about her dress-up.
734	**fatalism** *noun* belief that events are determined by forces beyond one's control	*Usage:* There is a mood of fatalism among the radicals.
735	**faze** *verb* disconcert, dismay	*Usage:* The Indian army was fazed on seeing the enemy's might.

736	**feasible** *adj.* practical, capable of being done, within reason	*Usage:* The demand of the opposition is not feasible.
737	**fecundity** *noun* fertility, fruitfulness	*Usage:* The land of Punjab is known for its fecundity.
738	**feign** *verb* pretend, to make a false show of, to make up (a story, excuse, etc.)	*Usage:* He feigned weakness in the bout but later emerged victorious.
739	**feint** *noun* trick, shift, sham blow	*Usage:* The enemy was befuddled by the Indian army's feint.
740	**felicitous** *adj.* apt, suitably expressed, well chosen	*Usage:* This is a felicitous title for this passage.
741	**felicity** *noun* happiness, appropriateness (of a remark, choice, etc.)	*Usage:* They lived with great felicity after their patch-up.
742	**ferment** *noun* agitation, commotion	*Usage:* Rice-grains are fermented to make beverages.
743	**ferret** *verb* drive or hunt out of hiding	*Usage:* She nonetheless continued to ferret about for possible jobs.
744	**fervent** *adj.* ardent, hot	*Usage:* Some religiously fervent bigots joined the rally.
745	**fervid** *adj.* ardent, hot, glowing, impassioned, fervent	*Usage:* A successful group is always headed by a fervid leader.
746	**fervour** *noun* glowing ardour (zeal emotional warmth), intensity of feeling	*Usage:* The pilgrims moved on with religious fervour.
747	**fester** *verb* rankle, produce irritation or resentment	*Usage:* His condition was festered by successive heart attacks.
748	**festive** *adj.* joyous, celebratory	*Usage:* Indian culture is full of festive occasions.
749	**fetter** *verb* shackle or chain for the feet, anything that holds in check, restraint	*Usage:* The hardcore criminals are fettered while appearing in public.
750	**fiasco** *noun* total failure	*Usage:* Kalmadi was responsible for the CWG fiasco.
751	**fickle** *adj.* changeable, faithless	*Usage:* Fickle minded people are not good decision makers.
752	**fictitious** *adj.* imaginary	*Usage:* She is paranoid and talks about fictitious people.
753	**fidelity** *noun* loyalty	*Usage:* He has a suspicion about his wife's fidelity.
754	**figment** *noun* invention, imaginary thing	*Usage:* It must be a figment of their imagination to travel against time.
755	**figurative** *adj.* not literal, but metaphorical, using a figure of speech	*Usage:* He made some figurative expression at the literary fest and received huge applaud.
756	**finesse** *noun* skill, or ability to handle delicate and difficult situations skilfully and diplomatically	*Usage:* The Taj has finesse in its continental food.

757	**finicky** *adj.* too particular, fussy	*Usage:* The girls are too finicky about their looks.
758	**firebrand** *noun* hothead, troublemaker	*Usage:* Ramu is the only firebrand in the group.
759	**fissure** *noun* crevice, a long, narrow, deep cleft or crack	*Usage:* An underground nuclear test left a huge fissure on the surface.
760	**fitful** *adj.* spasmodic	*Usage:* The electrician made some very fitful attempts to fix the fuse.
761	**flabbergasted** *adj.* astounded, astonished, overcome with surprise	*Usage:* The huge sized asteroids left the scientists flabbergasted
762	**flaccid** *adj.* flabby, weak, feeble	*Usage:* Her skin lost its tone and became flaccid due to old age.
763	**flagrant** *adj.* conspicuously wicked, blatant, outrageous	*Usage:* Her flagrant remarks in front of her teachers annoyed them.
764	**flair** *noun* talent, aptitude	*Usage:* He has a good flair for language.
765	**flamboyant** *adj.* ornate or too showy, florid	*Usage:* Yuvraj is a flamboyant Indian batsman.
766	**flaunt** *verb* display ostentatiously	*Usage:* The son of an MP flaunted the traffic rule, and nobody caught him.
767	**flinch** *verb* hesitate, shrink	*Usage:* The heroine flinched to shoot some bold scenes.
768	**flippant** *adj.* lacking proper seriousness	*Usage:* Flippancy is a barrier between a man and success.
769	**flounder** *verb* struggle and thrash about, proceed clumsily	*Usage:* India's top-bowler floundered while facing the South African batsman.
770	**flourish** *verb* grow well, prosper, decorate with ornaments	*Usage:* The Harappan civilisation flourished on and around the banks of the Indus river.
771	**flout** *verb* reject, mock	*Usage:* He flouted the security ring and headed towards the minister.
772	**fluctuate** *verb* waver, shift	*Usage:* The prices are likely to fluctuate with time.
773	**fluency** *noun* smoothness of speech	*Usage:* Her fluency of language got her extra marks in the interview.
774	**fluster** *verb* confuse, become nervous or befuddled	*Usage:* The sudden arrival of the crowd flustered the security.
775	**flux** *noun* flowing, series of changes	*Usage:* Education remains in a state of flux which will take time to settle down.
776	**foible** *noun* weakness, slight fault	*Usage:* I forgive her for that small foible.
777	**foil** *noun* a person or thing that sets off or enhances another by contrast	*Usage:* The police foiled the terrorists' plot to attack the building.
778	**foment** *verb* stir up, instigate	*Usage:* Enemy country tried to foment the radicals.

779	**foolhardy** *adj.* rash, bold ordering in a foolish way, reckless	*Usage:* This is a foolhardy idea as we have no prior knowledge of this.
780	**forbearance** *noun* patience	*Usage:* His forbearance showed up in his success.
781	**foreshadow** *verb* give an indication beforehand, portend, prefigure	*Usage:* The fate of the parties was foreshowed by exit polls.
782	**foresight** *noun* ability to foresee future happenings, prudence	*Usage:* He must have the foresight to predict the fluctuation in the market.
783	**forestall** *verb* prevent by taking action in advance	*Usage:* The police forestalled any kind of terrorist activity.
784	**forgo** *verb* give up, do without	*Usage:* If you don't come, I will forego.
785	**forlorn** *adj.* sad and lonely, wretched	*Usage:* He is living a dejected and forlorn life.
786	**formidable** *adj.* menacing, threatening	*Usage:* China is a formidable challenge for India.
787	**forsake** *verb* desert, abandon, renounce	*Usage:* He has forsaken his wife.
788	**forswear** *verb* renounce, abandon	*Usage:* The missionaries pressurised the tribal to forswear Hinduism.
789	**forthright** *adj.* outspoken, straightforward, frank	*Usage:* Karan Thapar is known for his forthright and witty remarks.
790	**fortitude** *noun* bravery, courage	*Usage:* He was given President's award for his fortitude.
791	**fortuitous** *adj.* accidental, by chance	*Usage:* We had a fortuitous meeting with her in the market.
792	**foster** *verb* rear, encourage	*Usage:* The government is fostering foreign investment in our country.
793	**fractious** *adj.* unruly, disobedient, irritable	*Usage:* The child showed a fractious and unbridled behaviour.
794	**frail** *adj.* weak, easily broken, shattered, damaged or destroyed, fragile, easily tempted to do wrong, morally weak	*Usage:* The old and frail woman implored her son to provide her basic necessities of life.
795	**frantic** *adj.* marked by frenzy	*Usage:* He made frantic efforts to win the election but lost.
796	**fraternise** *verb* associate in a friendly way	*Usage:* Justin doesn't fraternise widely.
797	**fraudulent** *adj.* cheating, deceitful	*Usage:* He had acquired huge properties by fraudulent means.
798	**fraught** *adj.* filled, charged or loaded (with), emotion, tense, anxious, distressing, etc.	*Usage:* She was fraught with anger when she found her son indulging in mean activities.

799	**fray** *noun* brawl	*Usage:* He need not get involved in this fray.
800	**frenetic** *adj.* frenzied, frantic	*Usage:* It is difficult to sustain the frenetic pace of life in New York.
801	**fret** *verb* to be annoyed or vexed	*Usage:* He must be fretting over his failure.
802	**frivolous** *adj.* lacking in seriousness, self-indulgently carefree, relatively unimportant	*Usage:* These types of frivolous efforts do not ensure success.
803	**frolicsome** *adj.* gay	*Usage:* We had a frolicsome evening.
804	**frugality** *noun* thrift, economy	*Usage:* Frugality and humility are the basis of profundity of personality.
805	**fruition** *noun* bearing of fruit, fulfilment, realisation	*Usage:* His hard work gave him fruition at the end of the year.
806	**frustrate** *verb* thwart, defeat	*Usage:* The wrong application of law frustrates the very purpose of law.
807	**fugitive** *adj.* fleeting or transitory, roving	*Usage:* The war fugitives were freed by the police.
808	**fulcrum** *noun* support on which a lever rests	*Usage:* The Britishers considered Gandhi as the fulcrum of Indian National Movement.
809	**fulsome** *adj.* disgustingly excessive	*Usage:* I was not sure of his fulsome remarks about my performance.
810	**fundamental** *verb* basic, primary, essential	*Usage:* The Constitution provides fundamental rights to all individuals.
811	**furore** *noun* frenzy, great excitement	*Usage:* There has been a great furore over the telecom scam.
812	**furtive** *adj.* stealthy, sneaky	*Usage:* This furtive plot was foiled by the security agency.
813	**fusion** *noun* union, coalition	*Usage:* Fusion music is a big hit these days.
814	**futile** *adj.* useless, hopeless, ineffectual	*Usage:* All the efforts of doctors proved futile.
	G	
815	**galvanise** *verb* stimulate, stir up, revitalise	*Usage:* The speech of the student leader galvanised the students with new vigour and vitality.
816	**gamut** *noun* entire range	*Usage:* The gamut of the 'Dhauladhars' lies proudly in Kangra.
817	**gape** *verb* open widely, stare open-mouthed	*Usage:* When I dictated them the bidding amount, they all stood and gaped.
818	**gargantuan** *adj.* huge, enormous	*Usage:* Writing a book is a gargantuan task.
819	**garner** *verb* gather, store up	*Usage:* They have garnered a buffer stock for any unforeseen event.
820	**garrulous** *adj.* loquacious, wordy, talkative	*Usage:* He being the most garrulous in the group is liked by everyone.

821	**gauche** *adj.* clumsy, coarse and uncouth	*Usage:* Her gauche dress-up embarrassed her as she received many negative comments on it.
822	**gaudy** *adj.* flashy, showy	*Usage:* The traditional and gaudy Indian products are at sale in the fair.
823	**gawk** *verb* stare foolishly, look in open-mouthed awe	*Usage:* When Jot made it to the streets, thousands came to gawk.
824	**generate** *verb* cause, produce, create	*Usage:* The 3-G spectrum generated huge revenues.
825	**generic** *adj.* characteristic of an entire class or species	*Usage:* Mongols have the generic trait of broad chest and height.
826	**genesis** *noun* beginning, origin	*Usage:* The genesis of this species is disputed.
827	**geniality** *noun* cheerfulness, kindliness, sympathy	*Usage:* His geniality made him popular among children.
828	**genteel** *adj.* well-bred, elegant	*Usage:* Her genteel demeanour at the party won her kudos.
829	**gentility** *noun* those of gentle birth, refinement	*Usage:* The clergy showed and boasted of geniality among common men.
830	**gentry** *noun* people of standing, class of people just below nobility	*Usage:* The club had a sea of gentry on the eve of New Year.
831	**ghastly** *adj.* horrible, frightful, very unpleasant	*Usage:* I escaped the ghastly surroundings of his farm house very narrowly.
832	**gibberish** *noun* nonsense, babbling	*Usage:* Nobody paid heed to his gibberish ideas of aliens.
833	**gibe** *verb* mock, jeer or taunt, scoff (at)	*Usage:* To gibe on others, back-fires many a time.
834	**giddy** *adj.* light-hearted, dizzy	*Usage:* His giddy comments were rejoiced by everyone.
835	**gingerly** *adv.* very carefully	*Usage:* The thieves prowled gingerly in the shop.
836	**gist** *noun* essence or main point, as of an article or argument	*Usage:* He grasped the gist of the movie.
837	**glaring** *adj.* highly conspicuous	*Usage:* The glaring problem of poverty, ignorance and unemployment must be tackled as the top-most priority.
838	**glaze** *verb* cover with a thin and shiny surface	*Usage:* The glazed water bodies opened at noon.
839	**glib** *adj.* fluent, facile and slick	*Usage:* To be a media journalist you need to be a sort of glib.
840	**glimmer** *verb* shine erratically, twinkle	*Usage:* Her eyes glimmered in the sunlight.
841	**gloat** *verb* express evil satisfaction, view malevolently	*Usage:* He thinks he has every reason to gloat over his deeds.
842	**gloss over** *verb* explain away	*Usage:* He glossed over every aspect of the policy.
843	**glossy** *adj.* smooth and shining	*Usage:* The glossy new car was the main attraction.
844	**glut** *verb* overstock, fill to excess	*Usage:* The engineering field has been glutted.

845	**glutton** *noun* someone who eats too much	*Usage:* He is a kind of glutton and always likes to eat for free.
846	**gnarled** *adj.* twisted and knotty, roughened, hardened, sinewy	*Usage:* He inherited the gnarled disease from his father.
847	**gory** *adj.* full of, covered with, or like gore bloody, characterised by much bloodshed or slaughter	*Usage:* Hitler did gory genocide of the Jews.
848	**grandeur** *noun* impressiveness, stateliness, majesty	*Usage:* The grandeur of the Buckingham Palace speaks volumes of its majesty.
849	**grandiloquent** *adj.* pompous, bombastic, using high sounding language	*Usage:* He made a grandiloquent speech but failed to impress the audience.
850	**grandiose** *adj.* pretentious, high-flown, ridiculously, exaggerated, impressive	*Usage:* He boasts of his grandiose ancestry among his group but in reality, he belongs to very humble background.
851	**grapple** *verb* wrestle, come to grips with	*Usage:* He was grappling with the problem.
852	**gratify** *verb* to please someone, or to satisfy a wish or need	*Usage:* Nobody can gratify this official's greed for money.
853	**gratuitous** *adj.* given freely, unwarranted, uncalled for	*Usage:* He is the gratuitous guest in the party.
854	**gravity** *noun* seriousness, solemnity or sedateness of manner of character	*Usage:* The leader knew the gravity of the situation and called for a meeting.
855	**gregarious** *adj.* sociable, fond of the company of others	*Usage:* Being gregarious, he is the most popular member of the golf club.
856	**grievance** *noun* cause of complaint	*Usage:* The CM addressed the grievances of the public.
857	**grill** *verb* question severely or relentlessly, torture by applying heat	*Usage:* Kalmadi was grilled in the corruption case.
858	**grisly** *adj.* ghastly, terrifying, horrible	*Usage:* The grisly scenes in the movie horrified everyone.
859	**grouse** *verb* complain, fuss	*Usage:* We have a million s grouses about our rented room.
860	**grotesque** *adj.* strange, unpleasant	*Usage:* The details of the incident were too grotesque for me to sit through its narration.
861	**grovel** *verb* to lie prone or crawl in a prostrate position, esp. abjectly, to behave humbly or abjectly, as before authority, debase oneself in a servile fashion	*Usage:* The drunkards started grovelling on seeing the cops.

862	**grudging** *adj.* unwilling, reluctant, stingy	*Usage:* She had to accept the proposal grudgingly.
863	**gruel** *verb* liquid food made by boiling oatmeal, etc., in milk or water	*Usage:* The doctor has advised her on how to take gruel every morning.
864	**gruelling** *adj.* exhausting	*Usage:* They returned home after a gruelling day of campaigning.
865	**gruesome** *adj.* grisly, horrible	*Usage:* A gruesome murder of a child generated panic in the locality.
866	**gruff** *adj.* surly rough-mannered, brusquely rude	*Usage:* The cops dealt with the trespassers gruffly.
867	**guile** *noun* deceit, duplicity, wiliness, cunning	*Usage:* I love children's innocence and presence of guile.
868	**guileless** *adj.* without deceit, candid, frank	*Usage:* He was exonerated by the court because he was guileless.
869	**guise** *noun* appearance, costume	*Usage:* He guised as a juggler and guiled the cops.
870	**gullible** *adj.* easily deceived, cheated, tricked, credulous	*Usage:* He is gullible to a girl's trickery.
	H	
871	**hackneyed** *adj.* commonplace, trite	*Usage:* Our electronic media is becoming hackneyed as they lack candidness.
872	**haggard** *adj.* wasted away, gaunt	*Usage:* He was weak and a bit haggard.
873	**haggle** *verb* argue about prices	*Usage:* As she haggled for every penny, every vendor allowed her to negotiate for the price.
874	**hallowed** *adj.* blessed, consecrated	*Usage:* The hallowed Dalai Lama paid a visit to the monastery.
875	**hallucination** *noun* delusion	*Usage:* Some of the yogis start taking such medicines which make them to get hallucinations.
876	**halting** *adj.* hesitant, faltering	*Usage:* Every day of strike is halting the daily business.
877	**hamper** *verb* obstruct, hinder, impede, encumber	*Usage:* Economic growth has been hampered by tough competition for the neighbours.
878	**haphazard** *adj.* random, by chance	*Usage:* The court ordered the razing down of a haphazard construction.
879	**harass** *verb* to annoy by repeated attacks	*Usage:* Women employees are harassed sometimes.
880	**harbinger** *noun* forerunner	*Usage:* Sher Shah Suri was the harbinger of administrative reforms in medieval India.
881	**harbour** *verb* provide a refuge for, hide	*Usage:* The terrorists took harbour in Pakistan.
882	**hardy** *adj.* sturdy, robust, able to stand inclement weather	*Usage:* The coastal homes require hardy construction to withstand storms.

883	**harrowing** *adj.* agonising, distressing, traumatic	*Usage:* It was a harrowing experience for him to spend six months in the hospital.
884	**haughtiness** *noun* pride, arrogance	*Usage:* His downfall was caused by his haughtiness.
885	**hazardous** *adj.* dangerous	*Usage:* Mountaineering is a hazardous activity.
886	**hazy** *adj.* slightly obscure	*Usage:* The match couldn't be completed due to haziness.
887	**headlong** *adj.* hasty, rash	*Usage:* His headlong attempt to escape was successful.
888	**heckler** *noun* person who harasses others	*Usage:* Don't associate with Vinay, he is virtually a heckler.
889	**hedonist** *noun* one who believes that pleasure is the sole aim in life	*Usage:* His hedonistic attitude didn't let him succeed in life.
890	**heed** *verb* pay attention to, consider	*Usage:* Pay heed to what is taught in the class.
891	**heinous** *adj.* atrocious, hatefully bad	*Usage:* There should be a death penalty for heinous crimes like rape.
892	**heresy** *noun* opinion contrary to popular belief, opinion contrary to accepted religion	*Usage:* The radicals left him for his heresy views.
893	**heterodox** *adj.* unorthodox, unconventional	*Usage:* Bhagat Singh had heterodox beliefs and ideals about religion and God.
894	**heterogeneous** *adj.* dissimilar, mixed	*Usage:* It was a heterogeneous mixture of colours.
895	**heyday** *noun* time of greatest success, prime	*Usage:* He was known all over the world in his heydays.
896	**hiatus** *noun* gap,	*Usage:* Kashmir problem widened the hiatus between India and Pakistan.
897	**hibernate** *verb* to remain dormant	*Usage:* Cold blooded reptiles hibernate in winter.
898	**hierarchy** *noun* arrangement by rank or standing, authoritarian body divided into ranks	*Usage:* He ranks 4th in order of hierarchy of bureaucracy of Punjab.
899	**hilarity** *noun* boisterous mirth	*Usage:* The whole audience burst out in hilarity.
900	**hindrance** *noun* block, obstacle	*Usage:* It has been a hindrance in the overall development of the world.
901	**hoard** *verb* stockpile, accumulate for future use	*Usage:* The black marketers hoard the necessities of daily life in order to enhance their prices.
902	**hoary** *adj.* white with age	*Usage:* Her hoary looks could tell her age.
903	**hoax** *noun* trick, practical joke	*Usage:* Some brats had caused the hoax of a bomb.
904	**hodgepodge** *noun* jumble, mixture of ill-suited elements	*Usage:* He did a lot of hodgepodges before finally finishing the act.
905	**hone** *verb* sharpen	*Usage:* Before entering the western waters, I wanted to hone my sea-faring skills.

906	**hoodwink** *verb* deceive, delude	*Usage:* It's not an easy job to hoodwink the cops.
907	**hostility** *noun* unfriendliness, hatred	*Usage:* She showed hostility towards the foreigners.
908	**hover** *verb* hang about, wait nearby	*Usage:* The plane kept hovering as it couldn't get a clear landing.
909	**humane** *adj.* marked by kindness or consideration	*Usage:* Her humane efforts towards mankind have bagged her the peace prize.
910	**humdrum** *adj.* dull, monotonous	*Usage:* The intrinsic beauties of life are nowadays lost in the humdrum of life.
911	**humility** *noun* humbleness of spirit	*Usage:* He showed great humility to his guest.
912	**hurtle** *verb* crash, rush	*Usage:* He was hurtled by the quick movement of others.
913	**husband** *verb* use sparingly, conserve, save	*Usage:* You must husband your money for tough times.
914	**hypocritical** *adj.* pretending to be virtuous, deceiving	*Usage:* He is hypocritical and that is why nobody trusts him.
	I	
915	**idiosyncrasy** *noun* particular way of behaving or thinking	*Usage:* Everyone has his own idiosyncrasies which are noticed in their behaviour.
916	**ignominy** *noun* deep disgrace, shame or dishonour	*Usage:* Her behaviour has brought ignominy to his family.
917	**imbibe** *verb* to absorb	*Usage:* I tried to imbibe the ideas of Gandhi.
918	**immaculate** *adj.* spotless, flawless, absolutely clean	*Usage:* Monalisa is an immaculate work.
919	**imminent** *adj.* likely to happen without delay, impending	*Usage:* There appeared an imminent danger.
920	**immune** *adj.* resistant to, free or exempt from, protected against something disagreeable or harmful	*Usage:* He has become immune to criticism.
921	**immutable** *adj.* unchangeable	*Usage:* Now the matter has been decided and it is immutable.
922	**impair** *verb* injure, hurt	*Usage:* She will be given relaxation as she is physically impaired.
923	**impalpable** *adj.* imperceptible, intangible	*Usage:* The arrival of the fighter plane was impalpable for the enemy.
924	**impart** *verb* to transfer or give	*Usage:* The scholars imparted great knowledge at the meet.
925	**impartial** *adj.* not biased, fair	*Usage:* A judge must be impartial.
926	**impassable** *adj.* not able to be travelled or crossed	*Usage:* The mighty Himalayas remained impassable for a long time.
927	**impasse** *noun* predicament, deadlock	*Usage:* The parliament came to an impasse.

928	**impassive** *adj.* without feeling, imperturbable, stoical	*Usage:* The authorities seemed to be impassive to the needs of the mediocre class.
929	**impeach** *verb* charge with crime in office, indict	*Usage:* The President of India can be impeached under Article 61.
930	**impeccable** *adj.* faultless, without defect or error	*Usage:* The impeccable precision of the scientist made the project successful.
931	**impede** *verb* hinder, block, delay	*Usage:* The remoteness of rural areas impedes developmental activities.
932	**impediment** *noun* hindrance, stumbling-block	*Usage:* Stammering is a great impediment to his personality.
933	**impel** *verb* drive or force onward	*Usage:* The fear of scolding from the teacher impelled me to finish my homework.
934	**impenetrable** *adj.* not able to be pierced or entered, beyond understanding	*Usage:* The government network of secret information system is impenetrable.
935	**impending** *adj.* nearing, approaching	*Usage:* The entire administration was busy in making arrangements for the impending visit of Barack Obama.
936	**imperceptible** *adj.* unnoticeable, undetectable	*Usage:* The doctors told him that his disease developed gradually and imperceptibly.
937	**imperious** *adj.* domineering, haughty	*Usage:* The dictator was imperious towards his people.
938	**impermeable** *adj.* impervious, not permitting passage through its substance	*Usage:* The fortification makes the palace impermeable.
939	**impertinent** *adj.* insolent, rude	*Usage:* He made impertinent remarks about the Principal.
940	**imperturbable** *adj.* calm, placid, composed	*Usage:* Dhoni is known as an imperturbable guy on the field.
941	**impervious** *adj.* impenetrable, incapable of being damaged or distressed	*Usage:* Our strong army makes our borders impervious.
942	**impetuous** *adj.* hasty, rash	*Usage:* The meeting resulted in a fiasco.
943	**impetus** *noun* incentive, stimulus, moving force	*Usage:* The new 5-year plan will give impetus to education.
944	**impiety** *noun* irreverence, lack of respect for God	*Usage:* He had an impiety for religious rites, so he decided to have a court marriage.
945	**impinge** *verb* infringe, touch, collide with	*Usage:* Your demand shouldn't impinge upon my interests.
946	**impious** *adj.* lacking reverence for God	*Usage:* His impious demeanour was reprimanded by his elders.
947	**implausible** *adj.* unlikely, unbelievable	*Usage:* It is an implausible argument.
948	**implement** *verb* put into effect, supply with tools	*Usage:* The plan was partly implemented by them.

949	**implicate** *verb* incriminate, show to be involved	*Usage:* Your son seems to be implicated in the notorious robbery.
950	**implication** *noun* something hinted at or suggested	*Usage:* You just imagine the implication of your decision.
951	**implicit** *adj.* understood but not stated	*Usage:* Freedom of press is an implicit right in the Indian Constitution.
952	**implore** *verb* to ask or beg earnestly for, beseech, to ask or beg (a person) to do something, entreat	*Usage:* I implored my teacher to forgive me.
953	**imply** *verb* suggest a meaning not expressed, signify	*Usage:* Your proposed plan should clearly imply the public benefits.
954	**impostor** *noun* someone who assumes a false identity	*Usage:* He is an impostor and has cheated many people.
955	**impotent** *adj.* weak, ineffective	*Usage:* You have to make very frantic efforts because impotent efforts will not bring the desired results.
956	**impoverished** *adj.* poor, deprived	*Usage:* I gave some old clothes to impoverished children.
957	**impregnable** *adj.* invulnerable	*Usage:* The fort of Chittoor was impregnable.
958	**impromptu** *adj.* without previous preparation	*Usage:* He gave an impromptu speech.
959	**impropriety** *noun* improperness, unsuitability	*Usage:* The impropriety of his speech was ridiculed.
960	**improvident** *adj.* thriftless, failing to provide for the future, lacking foresight or thrift	*Usage:* People in cities need to give up their improvident lifestyle to avoid crisis.
961	**imprudent** *adj.* lacking caution, injudicious	*Usage:* He made an imprudent attempt to climb a tree and fell down.
962	**inadvertently** *adv.* unintentionally, mistakenly	*Usage:* He inadvertently took me for someone else.
963	**inalienable** *adj.* not to be taken away, non-transferable	*Usage:* Our Constitution gives us some inalienable rights.
964	**inane** *adj.* silly, senseless	*Usage:* Her inane behaviour made her the laughing stock in class.
965	**incapacitate** *verb* make someone or something disable, make unable or unfit, esp. to make incapable of normal activity	*Usage:* Due to hypothermia his lower limbs were incapacitated.
966	**incarcerate** *verb* imprison, shut up, confine	*Usage:* Bhagat Singh himself got incarcerated so that more people join the freedom struggle.
967	**incarnation** *noun* act of assuming a human body and human nature	*Usage:* Osho is said to be an incarnation of God.

968	**incense** *verb* enrage, infuriate	*Usage:* When Ram jeered at Sham he got incensed and struck a blow on his head.
969	**inception** *noun* start, beginning	*Usage:* Since the inception of the batch, she has been creating problems.
970	**incessant** *adj.* uninterrupted, unceasing	*Usage:* He made incessant efforts till he finally got selected into IAS.
971	**incline** *noun & verb* slope, slant	*Usage:* The US is inclined to Indian side on the issue of climate change.
972	**inclusive** *adj.* tending to include all	*Usage:* We need to have an all-inclusive policy of development.
973	**incoherent** *adj.* unintelligible, muddled, illogical	*Usage:* His thesis was totally incoherent and incomprehensible.
974	**incompatible** *adj.* inharmonious, not going or getting along, well-together, in congruous	*Usage:* That couple has an incompatible nature.
975	**Incongruous** *adj.* not fitting, absurd, conflicting, discordant	*Usage:* Their supply was incongruous with our demand.
976	**inconsequential** *adj.* insignificant, unimportant	*Usage:* I didn't want you to be bothered over such an inconsequential matter.
977	**incontrovertible** *adj.* indisputable, not open to question	*Usage:* His incontrovertible arguments prevailed upon the judge.
978	**incorporeal** *adj.* lacking a material body, insubstantial	*Usage:* Only incorporeal punishment is allowed in our schools.
979	**incorrigible** *adj.* not correctable, that which cannot be corrected, improved, or reformed	*Usage:* I am an incorrigible optimist.
980	**incredulous** *adj.* withholding belief, sceptical	*Usage:* The incredulous nature of Vaishali made her all alone.
981	**incriminate** *verb* accuse	*Usage:* Without any solid evidence it was difficult to incriminate the big fish of the racket.
982	**inculcate** *verb* instil	*Usage:* I want to inculcate in myself the positive outlook and fearlessness of my Guru.
983	**incumbent** *adj.* obligatory, currently holding an	*Usage:* Whenever elections take place, the incumbency factor plays an important role.
984	**incur** *verb* bring upon oneself	*Usage:* They refused to take loan in view of the future losses they might incur.
985	**incursion** *noun* temporary invasion	*Usage:* The BSF Jawans were able to retaliate the incursion successfully.
986	**indefatigable** *adj.* tireless, not yielding to fatigue	*Usage:* The indefatigable labour of Sushil Kumar won laurels for the country.
987	**indelible** *adj.* not able to be erased	*Usage:* That incident left an indelible imprint on my personality.

988	**indeterminate** *adj.* uncertain, not clearly fed, indefinite	*Usage:* They were still indeterminate about their plan.
989	**indicative** *adj.* suggestive, implying	*Usage:* His laborious nature is indicative of good results.
990	**indict** *verb* charge with the commission of a crime	*Usage:* Nobody can be indicted for the same crime more than once.
991	**indifferent** *adj.* unmoved or unconcerned by, mediocre	*Usage:* The citizens' indifferent attitude is equally responsible for the sorry state of affairs.
992	**indigent** *adj.* poor, destitute	*Usage:* His indigent condition is the outcome of his prodigal son.
993	**indignation** *noun* anger at an injustice	*Usage:* The feeling of indignation forced them to revolt against the authorities.
994	**indiscretion** *noun* lack of tactfulness or sound judgment	*Usage:* Some veteran politicians can even take benefit of indiscretion of media persons.
995	**indiscriminate** *adj.* choosing at random, confused	*Usage:* He made indiscriminate misuse of power.
996	**indissoluble** *adj.* permanent	*Usage:* Rajya Sabha is the indissoluble House of the Parliament.
997	**indoctrinate** *verb* instruct in a doctrine or ideology	*Usage:* The mindset of suicide bombers is indoctrinated in a manner that they are ready to sacrifice their life.
998	**indolent** *adj.* lazy	*Usage:* Indolent people should not hope for success.
999	**indomitable** *adj.* unconquerable, unyielding	*Usage:* The indomitable spirit of Napoleon was without a parallel.
1000	**indubitable** *adj.* unable to be doubted, unquestionable	*Usage:* His credentials are indubitable.
1001	**induce** *verb* persuade, bring about	*Usage:* The teacher induced the students to continue the classes.
1002	**indulgent** *adj.* humouring, yielding, lenient	*Usage:* The indulgence of his parents led him astray.
1003	**industrious** *adj.* diligent, hard-working	*Usage:* He seems to be the most industrious boy in the class.
1004	**inebriated** *adj.* habitually intoxicated, drunk	*Usage:* The inebriated security guard was unable to identify his boss.
1005	**ineffable** *adj.* unutterable, cannot be expressed in speech	*Usage:* To top in class gave me an ineffable contentment and joy.
1006	**ineffectual**, *adj.* not effective, weak	*Usage:* The experiment seemed to be ineffectual as many of the objectives were not met.
1007	**inefficacious** *adj.* not effective, unable to produce a desired result	*Usage:* The ISRO test of satellite was inefficacious as compared to their claim.
1008	**inept** *adj.* lacking skill, unsuited, incompetent	*Usage:* The inept tailor made a trouser without pockets.
1009	**inequity** *noun* unfairness, lack of justice	*Usage:* Inequity shown by some judicial officers in recent years has compelled the public to disbelieve in judiciary.

1010	**inert** *adj.* inactive, lacking power to move	*Usage:* Inert gases are filled in lamps.
1011	**inevitable** *adj.* unavoidable	*Usage:* The downfall of everything that goes up is inevitable.
1012	**inexorable** *adj.* relentless, unyielding, implacable	*Usage:* I made inexorable attempts to placate him but couldn't appease him.
1013	**infallible** *adj.* unerring, not liable to fail, go wrong, make a mistake, etc., dependable, reliable	*Usage:* The company claims of an infallible security system.
1014	**infamous** *adj.* notoriously bad	*Usage:* The infamous Jallianwala Bagh massacre took place in 1919.
1015	**infantile** *adj.* childish	*Usage:* He is always mirthful with his infantile acts.
1016	**infer** *verb* deduce, conclude	*Usage:* We can't infer anything from such vague remarks.
1017	**infernal** *adj.* pertaining to hell, devilish	*Usage:* He is a little infernal child always up to some kind of mischief.
1018	**infidel** *noun* unbeliever	*Usage:* Infidels need to be avoided.
1019	**infiltrate** *verb* pass into or through, penetrate (an organisation) sneakily	*Usage:* The attempt of Pakistani rangers to infiltrate our border was foiled by BSF.
1020	**infinitesimal** *adj.* very small	*Usage:* The presence of infinitesimal traces of oxygen have been found on Saturn.
1021	**infirmity** *noun* weakness	*Usage:* Due to his infirmity he didn't stand up against anybody.
1022	**inflated** *adj.* exaggerated, pompous, enlarged (with air or gas)	*Usage:* The inflated price wasn't acceptable to us, so we broke the deal.
1023	**influx** *noun* flowing into, inflow, as of a liquid, gas, etc., a continual coming in of persons or things	*Usage:* A huge influx of foreign students has made American universities a global education hub.
1024	**infuriate** *verb* enrage, make angry	*Usage:* The father was infuriated to know that his daughter rather than studying is busy in developing networking on Facebook.
1025	**ingenious** *adj.* clever, resourceful	*Usage:* Their team has got a bunch of ingenious minds.
1026	**ingenuous** *adj.* naive and trusting, young, unsophisticated	*Usage:* His ingenuous demeanour attracted many free advice givers.
1027	**ingrained** *adj.* deeply established, firmly rooted	*Usage:* These words should be ingrained in your mind.
1028	**inimical** *adj.* unfriendly, hostile, harmful, detrimental	*Usage:* Our country was on inimical terms with Pakistan after 26/11.
1029	**inimitable** *adj.* matchless, not able to be imitated	*Usage:* Shweta is an inimitable beauty.

1030	**iniquitous** *adj.* wicked, immoral, unrighteous	*Usage:* The iniquitous son was responsible for bringing disrepute to the family.
1031	**initiate** *verb* begin, originate, receive into a group	*Usage:* India-Pak has initiated a new round of talks.
1032	**injurious** *adj.* harmful	*Usage:* The doctors have told him to avoid liquor as it is injurious to his liver.
1033	**inkling** *noun* hint, an indirect suggestion, a vague idea or notion	*Usage:* The Indian side never had an inkling of Pakistan intruders.
1034	**innate** *adj.* inborn, existing naturally rather than acquired	*Usage:* He has innate qualities of a team leader.
1035	**innocuous** *adj.* harmless, dull and uninspiring	*Usage:* The politician asserted that her remarks were totally innocuous.
1036	**innovation** *noun* change, introduction of something new	*Usage:* The ISRO and DRDO are responsible for innovation in the defence sector.
1037	**inopportune** *adj.* untimely, poorly chosen	*Usage:* The committee selected an inopportune squad for the world lab.
1038	**inordinate** *adj.* unrestrained, excessive	*Usage:* This employee made inordinate misuse of his position.
1039	**insatiable** *adj.* not easily satisfied, unquenchable, greedy	*Usage:* The officer was very insatiable and ended up taking Rs. 2 lacs as bribe.
1040	**inscrutable** *adj.* impenetrable, not readily understood, mysterious	*Usage:* This fort is virtually inscrutable.
1041	**insensible** *adj.* unconscious, unresponsive	*Usage:* As he is a rookie in this field, he made some insensible remarks on media.
1042	**insidious** *adj.* treacherous, stealth, sly	*Usage:* The insidious member of the group divulged all the secrets.
1043	**insightful** *adj.* discerning, perceptive	*Usage:* His real insightfulness will be tested during war time.
1044	**insipid** *adj.* lacking in flavour, dull	*Usage:* Hari serves us insipid food, so we usually don't prefer visiting him.
1045	**insolence** *noun* impudent disrespect, haughtiness	*Usage:* I will tell about your insolence to your boss, you don't deserve this job.
1046	**insolvent** *adj.* bankrupt, unable to repay one's debts	*Usage:* He declared himself insolvent.
1047	**instigate** *verb* urge, start, provoke	*Usage:* The religious fervour instigated the radicals.
1048	**insurgent** *adj.* rebellious	*Usage:* The Naxal insurgents planted a bomb at the CM's office.
1049	**insurmountable** *adj.* overwhelming, unbeatable, insuperable	*Usage:* The Indian army gained an insurmountable advantage in the Kargil war.

1050	**integral** *adj.* complete	*Usage:* Kashmir is an integral part of India.
1051	**integrate** *verb* make whole, combine, make into one unit	*Usage:* To integrate the nation we need to imbibe a feeling of brotherhood.
1052	**integrity** *noun* uprightness, wholeness	*Usage:* The integrity of our PM is undoubtable.
1053	**intellect** *noun* higher mental powers	*Usage:* Indian intellect is supporting the American IT industry.
1054	**intelligentsia** *noun* the intelligent and educated classes (often used derogatorily)	*Usage:* Much of the intelligentsia migrated to the US in the 70s and 80s.
1055	**intemperate** *adj.* immoderate, excessive, extreme	*Usage:* India took intemperate steps to retaliate the attack.
1056	**interloper** *noun* intruder, unwanted meddler	*Usage:* The guard cornered the interloper in the premises of the parliament.
1057	**intermittent** *adj.* periodic, occurring on and off	*Usage:* The north received intermittent rains yesterday.
1058	**interrogate** *verb* question closely, cross-examine	*Usage:* The NIA went to the US to interrogate Headley.
1059	**intimidate** *verb* frighten	*Usage:* The sudden roaring of the leopard in the zoo intimidated everyone.
1060	**intractable** *adj.* unruly, stubborn, unyielding	*Usage:* The intractable stance of the other party broke off the deal.
1061	**intransigence** *noun* refusal of any compromise, stubbornness	*Usage:* The intransigence shown by the workers left the factory closed for the consecutive day.
1062	**intricate** *adj.* complex, knotty, tangled	*Usage:* You wouldn't be able to understand the intricate language.
1063	**intrinsic** *adj.* essential, inherent, built-in	*Usage:* Fundamental Rights are an intrinsic part of the Constitution of India.
1064	**introspective** *adj.* looking within oneself	*Usage:* The coach advised the team for a self-introspective session.
1065	**introvert** *noun* one who is introspective, inclined to think more about oneself	*Usage:* Introvert people find it difficult to adapt.
1066	**intrude** *verb* trespass, enter as an uninvited person	*Usage:* As he intruded in my premises, I charged him for trespassing.
1067	**intuition** *noun* immediate insight, power of knowing without reasoning	*Usage:* I have an intuition for guessing the right answers in MCQs.
1068	**inundate** *verb* overwhelm, flood, submerge	*Usage:* The flood water inundated all the city homes including the citadel.
1069	**inured** *adj.* accustomed to something difficult, painful, etc, habituated, hardened by any adverse situation	*Usage:* I am inured to such rigors of training.

1070	**invalidate** *verb* weaken, destroy	*Usage:* The court invalidated the orders of the government.
1071	**invasive** *adj*. tending to spread aggressively, intrusive	*Usage:* The invasive weed covered whole of the arable land.
1072	**invigorate** *verb* energise, stimulate	*Usage:* A cup of coffee will surely invigorate him.
1073	**invincible** *adj*. unconquerable	*Usage:* The Indian cricket team at present is invincible.
1074	**invoke** *verb* call upon, ask for	*Usage:* She invoked the jurisdiction of Punjab and Haryana High Court in a case of violation of Fundamental Rights.
1075	**invulnerable** *adj*. incapable of injury	*Usage:* Areas other than coastal areas are invulnerable to tsunamis.
1076	**iota** *noun* very small quantity	*Usage:* An iota of mistake can frustrate the plan from materialising.
1077	**irascible** *adj*. irritable, easily angered	*Usage:* His irascible demeanours make him a poor leader and organiser.
1078	**irate** *adj*. angry, wrathful, incensed	*Usage:* The irate citizenry revolted against the government.
1079	**ire** *noun* anger, wrath	*Usage:* He earned the ire of the boss.
1080	**irksome** *adj*. annoying, tedious	*Usage:* Her idiosyncrasies are irksome.
1081	**ironic** *adj*. resulting in an unexpected and contrary outcome	*Usage:* Her ironic mirth at her failure surprised everyone.
1082	**irony** *noun* hidden sarcasm or satire, use of words that seem to mean the opposite of what they actually convey	*Usage:* It is an irony that those who solve the problems are actually the trouble creators.
1083	**irrational** *adj*. illogical, lacking reason, insane	*Usage:* The demands of the workers are very irrational.
1084	**irreconcilable** *adj*. incompatible, not able to be resolved	*Usage:* The children born to migrated Indian parents are irreconcilable with Indian culture.
1085	**irrefutable** *adj*. indisputable, incontrovertible, undeniable	*Usage:* Vikram was chosen as irrefutable leader of the gang.
1086	**irrelevant** *adj*. not applicable, unrelated	*Usage:* He started giving irrelevant explanations.
1087	**irremediable** *adj*. incurable, not correctable	*Usage:* AIDS is an irremediable disease.
1088	**irreparable** *adj*. not able to be corrected or repaired	*Usage:* The 26/11 attack did irreparable damage to Indo-Pak ties.
1089	**irrepressible** *adj*. unable to be restrained or held back	*Usage:* The irrepressible horses broke the fence and ran amuck.
1090	**irreproachable** *adj*. blameless, impeccable	*Usage:* The PM's integrity is surely irreproachable.

1091	**irresolute** *adj.* uncertain how to act, weak	*Usage:* Their irresolute mindset deprived them of success.
1092	**irreverence** *noun* lack of proper respect	*Usage:* They showed irreverence to their Pakistani counterparts in a cross-border meet.
1093	**irrevocable** *adj.* unalterable, irreversible	*Usage:* The contract is irrevocable.
	J	
1094	**jabber** *verb* chatter rapidly or unintelligibly	*Usage:* The vendor jabbered with maximum intensity.
1095	**jargon** *noun* technical terminology	*Usage:* The academicians are notorious for making use of jargon to impress upon readers.
1096	**jaundiced** *adj.* prejudiced (envious, hostile or resentful), yellowed	*Usage:* She looked at her sister-in-law with jaundiced eyes at the party.
1097	**jeopardise** *verb* endanger, imperil, put at risk	*Usage:* I don't want to jeopardise your safety.
1098	**jettison** *verb* throw overboard, to discard (something) as useless or a burden	*Usage:* The crew started to jettison the unnecessary cargo.
1099	**jingoist** *noun* extremely aggressive and militant patriot, warlike chauvinist	*Usage:* Maoists are the worst form of jingoists.
1100	**jocose** *adj.* given to joking	*Usage:* His jocose remarks made everyone giggle.
1101	**jocular** *adj.* said or done in jest	*Usage:* He was in a less jocular mood than ever.
1102	**jollity** *noun* gaiety, cheerfulness	*Usage:* We enjoyed the singing and jollity of the event.
1103	**jostle** *verb* shove, bump	*Usage:* We spent an hour jostling with the crowds as we did our shopping.
1104	**jovial** *adj.* good-natured, merry	*Usage:* Father Whitaker appeared to be in a jovial mood.
1105	**jubilation** *noun* rejoicing	*Usage:* The team members jumped up in jubilation.
1106	**judicious** *adj.* sound in judgment, wise	*Usage:* This man is known for his judicious approach.
	K	
1107	**kaleidoscope** *noun* something that is made up of a weight of different and frequent changing colours or element	*Usage:* The vivid kaleidoscope of colours is displayed in the plumage of the peacock.
1108	**kernel** *noun* central or vital part, whole seed (as of corn)	*Usage:* I just want to know the kernel of the problem.
1109	**kindle** *verb* start a fire, inspire	*Usage:* The hanging of Bhagat Singh kindled a new spirit among youngsters of 1930.

1110	**kindred** *adj.* related, belonging to the same family	*Usage:* I eagerly wait for the annual get together with my kindred folk.
1111	**knave** *noun* untrustworthy persons, rogue, scoundrel	*Usage:* His knavery has made him notorious among his peer group.
1112	**knotty** *adj.* intricate, difficult, tangled	*Usage:* The new management team faces some knotty problems.
1113	**kudos** *noun* honour, glory, praise	*Usage:* Salman Rushdie enjoys kudos all over the world for his literary genius.
	L	
1114	**laborious** *adj.* demanding much work or care, tedious	*Usage:* Cracking the Civil Services Exam, is a laborious task.
1115	**labyrinth** *noun* a complicated, perplexing arrangement, course of affairs, etc.	*Usage:* The problems of Naxals have assumed labyrinth proportions.
1116	**lackadaisical** *adj.* lacking purpose or zest, half-hearted, languid	*Usage:* India lost the Ramjet Golden Trophy from South Africa due to their lackadaisical efforts.
1117	**lacklustre** *adj.* dull, lacking energy or vitality, boring, unimaginative	*Usage:* He has already been blamed for his party's lacklustre performance during the election campaign.
1118	**laconic** *adj.* brief, terse and to the point in speech or expressions, using a few words	*Usage:* It is difficult to create a laconic piece of writing.
1119	**laggard** *adj.* slow, sluggish	*Usage:* The company has developed a reputation as a technological laggard in the computer arena.
1120	**lament** *verb* grieve, express sorrow	*Usage:* Ken began to lament the death of his only son.
1121	**languid** *adj.* weary, sluggish, listless	*Usage:* Without experienced staff, the company gradually earned the reputation of a languid company.
1122	**languish** *verb* lose animation, or strength	*Usage:* Without experienced staff the company gradually languished.
1123	**languor** *noun* lassitude, depression	*Usage:* She underwent languor after witnessing the horrifying scene of accident.
1124	**latent** *adj.* potential but undeveloped, dormant, hidden	*Usage:* You have to activate your latent potentials to achieve the desired results.
1125	**lavish** *adj.* liberal, wasteful	*Usage:* Mahima gave a lavish party on her 18th birthday.
1126	**lax** *adj.* careless, slack, of a loose texture, not rigid or strict	*Usage:* Lax security at the airport led to the disaster.
1127	**lechery** *noun* lustfulness, impurity, in thought and deed	*Usage:* His lechery has earned him an unfathomable bad reputation.
1128	**legacy** *noun* money or property left to someone by a will, bequest, anything handed down from, or as from, an ancestor, a gift made by a will	*Usage:* You could make a real difference to someone's life by leaving them a generous legacy.

1129	**legend** *noun* explanatory list of symbols on a map	*Usage:* The play was based on an Irish legend.
1130	**leniency** *noun* mildness, permissiveness	*Usage:* The judge rejected pleas for leniency and sentenced him to six months in prison.
1131	**lethal** *adj.* deadly, fatal	*Usage:* Frost and wet are a lethal combination for plants.
1132	**levity** *noun* lack of seriousness, lightness	*Usage:* Arnold disapproved such levity.
1133	**lewd** *adj.* lustful, showing, or intended to excite sexual desire	*Usage:* Playboy depicts a lewd lifestyle.
1134	**liability** *noun* drawback, debts	*Usage:* Kahlon groups depict assets of $138 million and liabilities of $120.5 million.
1135	**licentious** *adj.* amoral, lewd and lascivious, unrestrained	*Usage:* His female colleagues avoid him because of his licentious behaviour.
1136	**Lilliputian** *adj.* extremely small, narrow-minded, petty	*Usage:* A person with a Lilliputian personality can't be a good leader.
1137	**lynchpin** *noun* something that holds or links various parts together	*Usage:* Suman is the lynchpin of our team and crucial to my long-term plan.
1138	**lineage** *noun* descent, ancestry	*Usage:* They can trace their lineage directly back to the 18th century.
1139	**linger** *verb* loiter or dawdle, continue or persist	*Usage:* The scent of her perfume lingered on in the room.
1140	**lionize** *verb* treat as a celebrity	*Usage:* The press began to lionize the new leader as he made his first public appearance.
1141	**liquidate** *verb* to wind up, to eliminate,	*Usage:* Sultan Balban first of all liquidated a group of forty nobles.
1142	**listless** *adj.* lacking in spirit or energy	*Usage:* The tired worker looked around listlessly while working.
1143	**loath** *adj.* reluctant, disinclined	*Usage:* I am loath to go out on such a cold windy night.
1144	**loathe** *verb* detest	*Usage:* She was filled with loathe at his brutality.
1145	**lofty** *adj.* very high, elevated, noble, sublime	*Usage:* Gandhi's lofty ideas have still the same appeal.
1146	**loiter** *verb* hang around, linger	*Usage:* Unemployed young men loiter around in the market.
1147	**longevity** *noun* long life	*Usage:* The main characteristic of the strike has been its longevity.
1148	**loquacious** *adj.* talkative	*Usage:* Ravi is a very loquacious guy.
1149	**lout** *noun* a clumsy, stupid fellow, to treat with contempt, flout	*Usage:* His lout behaviour is criticised by everyone.
1150	**lucid** *adj.* easily understood, clear, intelligible	*Usage:* J.L. Nehru's glimpses of history is a lucid account of the history of mankind.

1151	**lucrative** *adj.* profitable, producing wealth, remunerative	*Usage:* The business didn't turn out to be as lucrative as Ravi hoped it to be.
1152	**ludicrous** *adj.* laughable, trifling	*Usage:* The sight of the grown man wearing a hat was ludicrous.
1153	**lugubrious** *adj.* very sad or mournful	*Usage:* The sight of the death of Ravi's father was lugubrious.
1154	**lull** *noun* moment of calm	*Usage:* There was a lull in the political scenario after the election of the current President.
1155	**luminary** *noun* celebrity, dignitary	*Usage:* The political opinions of such luminaries as Sartre or de Beauvoir are worth emulating.
1156	**lurk** *verb* stealthily lie in waiting, slink, exist unperceived	*Usage:* He thought he saw someone lurking above the chamber during the address.
1157	**luscious** *adj.* pleasing to taste or smell	*Usage:* Katrina Kaif has a luscious outlook which captivates everybody.
1158	**lustrous** *adj.* shining	*Usage:* He has recently bought a lustrous Bugatti Veyron car.
	M	
1159	**machinations** *noun* evil schemes or plots	*Usage:* It is very difficult to unearth the machinations of politicians.
1160	**magnanimous** *adj.* generous, great-hearted	*Usage:* He is very magnanimous and donates to orphanages liberally.
1161	**magnate** *noun* person of prominence or influence	*Usage:* The finance minister addressed the conference of Business Magnates.
1162	**magnitude** *noun* greatness, extent	*Usage:* An operation of this magnitude is going to be difficult.
1163	**maim** *verb* mutilate, injure	*Usage:* After the bomb blasts, there were a number of maimed bodies.
1164	**maladroit** *adj.* clumsy, bungling	*Usage:* Some of his interviews with the press were rather maladroit.
1165	**malady** *noun* illness	*Usage:* He was inflicted at twenty-one with an incurable malady.
1166	**malaise** *noun* uneasiness, vague feeling of ill health	*Usage:* He complained of depression, headache, and malaise.
1167	**malediction** *noun* curse, evil talk about someone, slander	*Usage:* The Indian serials are a major cause of spread of malediction among women.
1168	**malefactor** *noun* evildoer, criminal	*Usage:* Jagat is a well-known criminal lawyer who had saved many a malefactor from going to jail.
1169	**malevolent** *adj.* wishing evil	*Usage:* Her malevolent attitude and ill intentions never let her succeed.
1170	**malfeasance** *noun* wrongdoing or misconduct, esp. by a public official	*Usage:* The court ordered suspension of two I.A.S. officers for their malfeasance.

1171	**malicious** *adj.* hateful, spiteful	*Usage:* He was expelled from the cabinet for his malicious behaviour during conference.
1172	**malign** *verb* speak evil of, bad-mouth, defame	*Usage:* He maligned him dreadfully.
1173	**malignant** *adj.* injurious, tending to cause death, aggressively malevolent	*Usage:* The doctor says that she has developed a malignant tumour.
1174	**malleable** *adj.* impressionable	*Usage:* Harry was malleable with new ideas.
1175	**mammoth** *adj.* gigantic, enormous, huge in size or importance	*Usage:* The Bhakra Dam has mammoth dimensions.
1176	**mandate** *noun* order, charge	*Usage:* The public gave its mandate against the ruling party.
1177	**mandatory** *adj.* obligatory	*Usage:* It is mandatory to undergo probation before getting confirmation.
1178	**manifest** *adj.* evident, visible, obvious	*Usage:* Your inner personality manifests in your conduct.
1179	**manifesto** *noun* declaration statement of policy	*Usage:* The main political parties are currently drawing their election manifesto.
1180	**manipulate** *verb* operate with one's hands, control or play upon (people, forces, etc.) artfully	*Usage:* India was able to manipulate the policy of US over Pakistan.
1181	**maverick** *noun* rebel, nonconformist	*Usage:* A maverick group of scientists confront the existence of God.
1182	**mawkish** *adj.* mushy and gushy, icky-sticky, sentimental, maudlin	*Usage:* Their grim poverty aroused her mawkish sympathy.
1183	**Meagre** *noun* small quantity	*Usage:* This job gives me a meagre salary.
1184	**meander** *verb* wind or turn in its course	*Usage:* Roads meandered round the edges of the fields.
1185	**meddlesome** *adj.* interfering	*Usage:* His meddlesome attitude is not acceptable to other members of the family.
1186	**mediate** *verb* settle a dispute through the services of an outsider	*Usage:* The UN appointed a committee to mediate the Indo-Pak dispute.
1187	**mediocre** *adj.* ordinary, commonplace	*Usage:* There is no need to boast of your result as you had a mediocre performance.
1188	**meditation** *noun* reflection, thought	*Usage:* The man was lost in meditation, walking with slow steps along the shore.
1189	**medley** *noun* mixture	*Usage:* India is a medley of cultures.
1190	**meek** *adj.* quiet and obedient, spiritless	*Usage:* Mr. Banwari never expected his meek daughter would dare defy him.
1191	**melancholy** *adj.* gloomy, morose, blue	*Usage:* He expressed his melancholy in the poetry.

1192	**mellifluous** *adj.* sweetly or smoothly flowing, melodious	*Usage:* We heard the mellifluous singing of choir.
1193	**mendicant** *noun & adj.* beggar, of or characteristic of a beggar	*Usage:* A mendicant pleased me in the market.
1194	**mercurial** *adj.* capricious, changing, fickle, quick as quicksilver to change	*Usage:* His mercurial temperament annoys everybody.
1195	**merger** *noun* combination (of two business corporations)	*Usage:* The rivers merge just north of a vital irrigation system.
1196	**mesmerise** *verb* hypnotise, spellbind	*Usage:* There was something fabulous about DLF flats that mesmerised the customers.
1197	**metamorphosis** *noun* change of form, major transformation	*Usage:* There's been a metamorphosis in his personality and now he is much more extrovert.
1198	**metaphysical** *adj.* very abstract, abstruse, or subtle, often a derogatory	*Usage:* My Guru was more concerned with metaphysical matter than with physical ones.
1199	**methodical** *adj.* systematic	*Usage:* Parveen was methodical in his research, carefully recording his observations and theories.
1200	**meticulous** *adj.* excessively careful, painstaking, scrupulous	*Usage:* Mr. Bhardwaj has meticulously prepared the books for CLAT & LL.B. entrances examinations.
1201	**milieu** *noun* environment, means of expression	*Usage:* They stayed safe and happy, within their own social milieu.
1202	**militant** *adj.* combative, bellicose	*Usage:* Militant mineworkers in the Ukraine have voted for a one-day strike next month.
1203	**mimicry** *noun* imitation	*Usage:* One of his little strengths was his skill at mimicry.
1204	**mincing** *adj.* affectedly dainty	*Usage:* As he was injured, he walked down the steps mincingly.
1205	**minuscule** *adj.* extremely small	*Usage:* The film was shot in 17 days, a minuscule amount of time.
1206	**minute** *adj.* extremely small	*Usage:* Within minutes we realised our mistake.
1207	**minutiae** *noun* petty details	*Usage:* Much of his early work is concerned with the minutiae of rural life.
1208	**mirage** *noun* unreal reflection, optical illusion	*Usage:* It hovered before his eyes like a mirage.
1209	**mire** *verb* entangle, stick in swampy ground	*Usage:* India after independence was mired by poverty, disease and squander.
1210	**mirth** *noun* merriment, laughter	*Usage:* That caused considerable mirth amongst pupils and sports masters alike.
1211	**misapprehension** *noun* error, misunderstanding	*Usage:* Misapprehensions are very dangerous for mutual trust.
1212	**miscellany** *noun* mixture of writings on various subjects	*Usage:* This bowl contains a miscellany of slips.

1213	**mischance** *noun* ill luck	*Usage:* India fails to win the hockey cup by mischance.
1214	**misconception** *noun* mistaken idea	*Usage:* There are many fears and misconceptions about cancer.
1215	**misconstrue** *verb* interpret incorrectly, misjudge	*Usage:* An outsider may misconstrue the understanding level of these friends.
1216	**misdemeanour** *noun* minor crime	*Usage:* Emily knew nothing about her husband's misdemeanours.
1217	**miserly** *adj.* stingy, mean	*Usage:* A person of miserly nature hates to form a friends circle.
1218	**misgivings** *noun* doubts	*Usage:* She had some misgivings about what she was about to do.
1219	**mishap** *noun* an unlucky or unfortunate accident	*Usage:* After a number of mishaps she did manage to get back to Germany.
1220	**misrepresent** *verb* give a false or incorrect impression	*Usage:* He said that the press had misrepresented him as arrogant and bullying.
1221	**mollify** *verb* pacify, appease	*Usage:* The ruling party tried to mollify pressure groups.
1222	**momentous** *adj.* very important	*Usage:* The Planning Commission Deputy Chairman presented a momentous layout of the next 5-year plan.
1223	**momentum** *noun* impetus	*Usage:* After my motivational lecture, the students' preparation got momentum.
1224	**monotony** *noun* sameness leading to boredom	*Usage:* A night in the town may help break the monotony of the week.
1225	**monumental** *adj.* massive	*Usage:* It is a monumental task to get 95 percent marks in CLAT.
1226	**moodiness** *noun* fits of depression or gloom	*Usage:* Due to her recurring moodiness she remained mostly in seclusion.
1227	**morbid** *adj.* given to unwholesome thought, moody, characteristic of disease	*Usage:* He is always up to morbid ideas, maybe he has a morbid mentality.
1228	**morose** *adj.* ill-humoured, sullen, melancholy	*Usage:* One elderly man sat morose at the bar.
1229	**mortify** *verb* humiliate, to cause to feel shame, humiliation	*Usage:* Jane mortified her family by leaving her husband.
1230	**mosaic** *noun* picture made of colourful small inlaid tiles	*Usage:* M.F. Hussain painted a picture depicting the mosaic of Indian culture.
1231	**motley** *adj.* multi-coloured, mixed	*Usage:* People of all hues get absorbed in the motley of Indian culture.
1232	**muddle** *verb* confuse, mix up	*Usage:* Don't muddle into problems of others.
1233	**multifaceted** *adj.* having many aspects, versatile	*Usage:* Pradeep has a multifaceted personality.
1234	**multifarious** *adj.* varied, greatly diversified	*Usage:* The reasons for closure are multifarious.

1235	**mundane** *adj.* worldly, commonplace, ordinary, etc.	*Usage:* He is unwilling to do mundane tasks.
1236	**munificent** *adj.* very generous	*Usage:* Palkhivala was very munificent and donated much of his earnings for philanthropic works.
1237	**murky** *adj.* dark and gloomy, thick with fog, vague	*Usage:* Indian society gives a murky impression to others.
1238	**muse** *verb* ponder	*Usage:* You just muse over your decision of divorce.
1239	**mushroom** *verb* expand or grow rapidly	*Usage:* There has been a mushrooming of four wheelers in Chandigarh over the last decade.
1240	**muster** *verb* gather, assemble	*Usage:* Subhash Chandra Bose mustered support for his movement all over the world.
1241	**musty** *adj.* stale	*Usage:* That terrible musty smell makes everybody uncomfortable to sit.
1242	**mutability** *noun* ability to change in form, fickleness	*Usage:* Mutability is one of the biggest idiosyncrasies of his personality.
1243	**muted** *adj.* silent, muffled, toned down	*Usage:* There is a saga of problems behind muted voices of common man.
1244	**mutinous** *adj.* unruly, rebellious	*Usage:* The situation became mutinous.
1245	**myopic** *adj.* near-sighted, lacking foresight	*Usage:* Politicians of present times have a myopic mindset.
	N	
1246	**nadir** *noun* lowest point	*Usage:* 1945 to 1946 was the nadir in Truman's Presidency.
1247	**narcissist** *noun* conceited person, someone in love with his own image	*Usage:* Normally a narcissist person is not accepted by the public.
1248	**nascent** *adj.* incipient, coming into being	*Usage:* The still nascent science of psychology has not become very popular in India.
1249	**nebulous** *adj.* vague, hazy, cloudy	*Usage:* Children were able to form a nebulous notion of world.
1250	**nefarious** *adj.* very wicked, villainous, iniquitous	*Usage:* He was grilled by the police for nefarious activities.
1251	**negate** *verb* nullify, deny	*Usage:* These weaknesses negated his otherwise progressive attitude toward the staff.
1252	**nemesis** *noun* someone seeking revenge	*Usage:* Nadal proved to be much of a nemesis for Federer in the US open.
1253	**nettle** *verb* annoy, vex	*Usage:* It was the suggestion that he might alter course to win an election that really nettled him.
1254	**nicety** *noun* precision, minute distinction	*Usage:* The niceties and technicalities of law should not obstruct the purpose of justice.
1255	**nip** *verb* stop something's growth or development	*Usage:* We should try to nip the revolt in the bud.

1256	**nonchalance** *noun* indifference, lack of concern, composure	*Usage:* His nonchalance was the cause of spoiling his child.
1257	**noncommittal** *adj.* neutral, unfledged, undecided	*Usage:* The Mayor gave noncommittal answers to questions of the public.
1258	**nondescript** *adj.* indistinctive, ordinary	*Usage:* In spite of being a celebrated author, he bears a nondescript outlook.
1259	**nonentity** *noun* person of no importance, nonexistence	*Usage:* Gandhi felt himself a nonentity and forlorn cry after independence.
1260	**nostalgia** *noun* homesickness, longing for the past	*Usage:* The feelings of nostalgia overpowered him.
1261	**notable** *adj.* conspicuous, important, distinguished	*Usage:* With a few notable exceptions, doctors are a pretty sensible lot.
1262	**notoriety** *noun* disrepute, ill fame	*Usage:* He achieved notoriety as chief counsel to President Nixon in the Watergate break in case.
1263	**novelty** *noun* something new, newness	*Usage:* In the contemporary western world, rapidly changing styles cater to the desires for novelty and individualism.
1264	**novice** *noun* a person new to a particular occupation, activity, etc., beginner	*Usage:* I'm a novice in the film industry.
1265	**noxious** *adj.* harmful	*Usage:* Many household products give off noxious fumes.
1266	**nullify** *verb* to make invalid	*Usage:* He used his vast executive power to nullify decisions by the local government.
	O	
1267	**oaf** *noun* stupid, awkward person	*Usage:* He always dislikes Ravi because he is an oaf.
1268	**obdurate** *adj.* stubborn	*Usage:* He is very unpopular for his obdurate behaviour.
1269	**obfuscate** *verb* confuse, muddle, cause confusion, make needlessly complex	*Usage:* They are just obfuscating the issue.
1270	**obliterate** *verb* destroy completely	*Usage:* The memories of partition cannot be obliterated.
1271	**oblivion** *noun* obscurity, forgetfulness	*Usage:* He has been living life of oblivion for the last 10 years.
1272	**oblivious** *adj.* inattentive or unmindful, wholly absorbed	*Usage:* He was totally oblivious of the careless activities of his son.
1273	**obnoxious** *adj.* offensive	*Usage:* To make promiscuous gestures at a public place is always obnoxious.
1274	**obscure** *adj.* dark, vague, unclear	*Usage:* The origin of this custom is obscure.
1275	**obsequious** *adj.* slavishly attentive, servile, sycophantic	*Usage:* He met the officer in an obsequious manner.

1276	**obsessive** *adj.* related to thinking about something constantly, pre-occupying	*Usage:* William is obsessive about motor racing.
1277	**obsolete** *adj.* no longer useful, outmoded, antiquated	*Usage:* 'Thou and thee' are obsolete words.
1278	**obstinate** *adj.* stubborn, hard to control or treat	*Usage:* He is very obstinate and will not pay any heed to you.
1279	**obstreperous** *adj.* boisterous, noisy	*Usage:* It is impossible to work continuously in this obstreperous industry.
1280	**obtrude** *verb* push (oneself of one's ideas) forward or intrude, butt in, stick out or extrude	*Usage:* He didn't want to obtrude on her privacy.
1281	**obtuse** *adj.* blunt, stupid	*Usage:* It is very difficult to accommodate an obtuse fellow.
1282	**obviate** *verb* make unnecessary, get rid of	*Usage:* The use of a solicitor trained as a mediator would obviate the need for independent legal advice.
1283	**odious** *adj.* hateful, vile	*Usage:* He is certainly the most odious man I have ever met.
1284	**odium** *noun* detestation, hatefulness, disrepute	*Usage:* The corrupt police official has been exposed to public odium and contempt.
1285	**odorous** *adj.* having an odour	*Usage:* The taste is only slightly bitter and little odorous.
1286	**odyssey** *noun* long, eventful journey	*Usage:* Visiting Hon'ble Krishna Iyer was no less than an odyssey for me.
1287	**offensive** *adj.* attacking, insulting, distasteful	*Usage:* His offensive remarks were taken very seriously.
1288	**offhand** *adj.* casual, done without prior thought	*Usage:* His offhand speech bored the audience.
1289	**officious** (*adj.*) meddlesome	*Usage:* I don't like officious interference of the bureaucracy.
1290	**onerous** *adj.* burdensome, taxing	*Usage:* It is an onerous task to bring up the children.
1291	**onset** *noun* beginning, attack	*Usage:* Most of the mountainous passes are closed with the onset of winter.
1292	**onus** *noun* duty, burden, responsibility	*Usage:* The onus is on the shopkeeper to provide goods which come up to the quality of their description.
1293	**opulence** *noun* extreme wealth, luxuriousness, abundance	*Usage:* The opulence of the superstar's new palatial house is the talk of the town in Mumbai.
1294	**orgy** *noun* wild	*Usage:* In an orgy of violence, the mob caused unconscionable destruction.
1295	**orient** *verb* get one's bearings, adjust	*Usage:* You will need the time to orient yourself to your new project.
1296	**orientation** *noun* inclination	*Usage:* Clearing Civil Services Examination demands a special type of orientation and inclination, in addition to labour and knowledge.

1297	**ornate** *adj.* excessively or elaborately decorated	*Usage:* Sculptures of the Ajanta-Ellora Temples are highly ornate.
1298	**orthodox** *adj.* traditional, conservative in belief	*Usage:* Godaras of Haryana are very orthodox people.
1299	**ossify** *verb* change or harden into bone	*Usage:* The opinion of the general public has ossified in a very negative way.
1300	**ostensible** *adj.* apparent, professed, pretended	*Usage:* She always tries to make an ostensible display of learning.
1301	**ostentatious** *adj.* showy, pretentious, trying to attract attention	*Usage:* Her ostentatious way of presenting the things always brings mockery to her.
1302	**ostracise** *verb* exclude from public favour, ban	*Usage:* A rapist should be ostracised from the society.
1303	**oust** *verb* expel out	*Usage:* We wondered if the management would be able to oust Girdhari from the office.
1304	**outlandish** *adj.* bizarre, peculiar, unconventional	*Usage:* He always tries to make his lecture outlandish.
1305	**outmoded** *adj.* no longer stylish, old-fashioned	*Usage:* 'Thou and thee' are outmoded words nowadays.
1306	**outskirts** *noun* fringes	*Usage:* Their residence is situated at the outskirts of Delhi.
1307	**outspoken** *adj.* candid, blunt	*Usage:* Ravi is very outspoken.
1308	**outstrip** *verb* surpass, outdo	*Usage:* It is not easy to outstrip one's immediate boss unless one has made up one's mind to quit or be expelled from one's organisation.
1309	**outwit** *verb* outsmart, trick	*Usage:* By disguising herself as an old woman, Chandini was able to outwit her parents.
	P	
1310	**palpable** *adj.* tangible, easily perceptible, unmistakable	*Usage:* The patient's enlarged spleen was so palpable that even a first-year medical student could feel it.
1311	**paltry** *adj.* insignificant, petty, trifling	*Usage:* One can get the imitation of this diamond neckpiece just by paying a paltry sum to the jeweller.
1312	**panacea** *noun* cure-all, remedy for all diseases	*Usage:* Knowledge is the panacea of all diseases.
1313	**panegyric** *noun* formal praise	*Usage:* The court poets in ancient times used to write panegyric poems in praise of their kings.
1314	**panoramic** *adj.* related to an unobstructed and comprehensive view	*Usage:* On a clear day, from the top of the Qutub Minar you can get a panoramic view of New Delhi.
1315	**paradigm** *noun* model, example	*Usage:* We need a paradigm shift in our judicial system.
1316	**paradox** *noun* something apparently contradictory in nature	*Usage:* Dr. S. Radhakrishnan is called a man of paradoxes.
1317	**paramount** *adj.* foremost in importance, supreme	*Usage:* Discipline is of paramount importance for a successful life.

1318	**paranoia** *noun* mental disorder	*Usage:* Rajesh's wife is a patient of paranoia.
1319	**paraphernalia** *noun* resources	*Usage:* The entire police paraphernalia was busy in making arrangement for the visit of Prime Minister.
1320	**parity** *noun* equality in status or amount, close resemblance	*Usage:* In Presidential election in India, a parity has been struck between the votes of Centre and States.
1321	**parochial** *adj.* narrow in outlook	*Usage:* Politicians sometimes take a very parochial view of certain national issues for the self-aggrandisement.
1322	**parry** *verb* ward off a blow, deflect	*Usage:* The party spokesperson cleverly parried all the enquiries about the arms scandal put up by the reporters in the press conference.
1323	**partial** *adj.* incomplete	*Usage:* The judge cannot afford to take a partial viewpoint to pronounce a sound judgement.
1324	**partiality** *noun* inclination, bias	*Usage:* As a judge, not only must you be unbiased, you must also avoid any evidence of partiality at the time of awarding judgement.
1325	**partisan** *adj.* one-sided, prejudiced, committed to a party	*Usage:* On certain issues of principle, she refused to take a partisan stand, but let her conscience be her guide.
1326	**passive** *adj.* not active, acted upon	*Usage:* Mahatma Gandhi urged his followers to pursue a program of passive resistance as he felt that it was more effective than violence and acts of terrorism.
1327	**pathetic** *adj.* causing sadness, compassion, pity	*Usage:* Arvind Adiga's Booker Prize winner novel 'The White Tiger' virtually depicts the pathetic state of India.
1328	**patronise** *verb* support	*Usage:* ISI of Pakistan patronises all the terrorist absconders of India.
1329	**paucity** *noun* scarcity, dearth, insufficiency	*Usage:* Because of the paucity of funds, all the projects were to be postponed.
1330	**pedagogy** *noun* teaching, art of education	*Usage:* The Oxford University is known for its pedagogy.
1331	**pedant** *noun* a person who makes a vain display of learning	*Usage:* Nobody likes pedants.
1332	**pedantic** *adj.* showing off learning	*Usage:* One should not indulge in pedantic activities.
1333	**peerless** *adj.* having no equal, incomparable	*Usage:* Arundhati is a peerless writer.
1334	**pejorative** *adj.* abusive	*Usage:* The pejorative remarks of politicians triggered the riots.
1335.	**penchant** *noun* strong inclination, liking	*Usage:* I have a penchant for writing.
1336	**penitent** *adj.* repentant	*Usage:* When he realised the enormity of his crime, he became remorseful and penitent.
1337	**pensive** *adj.* thoughtful, contemplative	*Usage:* The pensive lover gazed at the portrait of his beloved and deeply sighed.

1338	**perceptive** *adj.* insightful, aware, wise	*Usage:* One has to develop a very perceptive and critical attitude while preparing for the Civil Services Examination.
1339	**perfidious** *adj.* treacherous, disloyal	*Usage:* The opposition party leaders described the new reservation bill as a perfidious attack on the Education System of the country.
1340	**perforate** *verb* pierce, put a hole through	*Usage:* Before you can open the cough syrup bottle, you must first perforate the plastic safety seal that covers the cap.
1341	**perfunctory** *adj.* superficial, not thorough, lacking interest, care, or enthusiasm	*Usage:* The editor's perfunctory inspection of the book overlooked many errors.
1342	**peripheral** *adj.* marginal, outer	*Usage:* They lived, not in central Mumbai, but in one of those peripheral suburbs that spring up on the outskirts of a great city.
1343	**periphery** *noun* edge, especially of a round surface	*Usage:* He sensed that there was something just beyond the periphery of his vision.
1344	**perjury** *noun* false testimony while under oath	*Usage:* Perjury is a very serious offence under the Indian Penal Code
1345	**permeable** *adj.* penetrable, porous, allowing liquids or gas to pass through	*Usage:* If your jogging clothes weren't made out of permeable fabric, you'd drown in your own perspiration.
1346	**permeate** *verb* pass through, spread	*Usage:* The foul smell of stale beer permeated the air.
1347	**pernicious** *adj.* very destructive	*Usage:* His pernicious remarks infuriated the public.
1348	**perpetrate** *verb* commit an offense	*Usage:* Only an insane person could perpetrate such a horrible crime.
1349	**perpetual** *adj.* everlasting	*Usage:* Hon'ble Justice Krishna Iyer is a perpetual source of inspiration for the entire legal fraternity.
1350	**perpetuate** *verb* make something last	*Usage:* The judgments of Hon'ble Justice Krishna Iyer perpetuate in the entire legal system as a perennial source of knowledge.
1351	**perspicacious** *adj.* having insight, penetrating, astute	*Usage:* Pradeep Virk is known for his perspicacious and polemical arguments.
1352	**pertinacious** *adj.* stubborn, persistent	*Usage:* He is bound to succeed because his pertinacious nature will not permit him to quit.
1353	**pertinent** *adj.* to the point, relevant	*Usage:* Virginia Woolf's words on women's rights are as pertinent today as they were when she wrote them nearly a century ago.
1354	**perturb** *verb* disturb greatly	*Usage:* The demolition of the Babri Masjid perturb the Hindu-Muslim relationships.
1355	**peruse** *verb* to read through something.	*Usage:* He opened the newspaper and began to peruse the vacancy ads.
1356	**philanthropist** *noun* lover of mankind, doer of good	*Usage:* Mother Teresa was a great philanthropist.

1357	**philistine** *noun* narrow-minded person, uncultured and exclusively interested in material gain	*Usage:* We need more men of culture and enlightenment, we have too many philistines among us.
1358	**pillage** *verb* plunder	*Usage:* The enemy pillaged the quiet village and left it in ruins.
1359	**pinnacle** *noun* peak, the highest point, culmination, acme	*Usage:* Amitabh Bachchan is at the pinnacle of his career.
1360	**pious** *adj.* devout, religious	*Usage:* Her mother is a very pious lady.
1361	**piquant** *adj.* pleasantly sharp or biting, stimulating to the taste	*Usage:* The piquant sauce added to our enjoyment of the meal.
1362	**pique** *verb* provoke or arouse, annoy	*Usage:* 'I know something you don't know', said Anita, trying to pique Lata's interest.
1363	**pitfall** *noun* hidden danger, concealed trap	*Usage:* Her parents warned young Pragya against the many pitfalls that lay in wait for her in the big city.
1364	**pithy** *adj.* concise, meaningful, substantial	*Usage:* One has to put a lot of labour to develop pithy and profound language.
1365	**pivotal** *adj.* crucial, key, vital	*Usage:* The new 'smart weapons' technology played a pivotal role in the quick resolution of the war with Iraq.
1366	**placate** *verb* pacify, conciliate	*Usage:* All the efforts of India to placate Pakistan on the Kashmir issue failed.
1367	**placid** *adj.* peaceful, calm	*Usage:* After his vacation in this placid section, he felt soothed and rested.
1368	**plagiarism** *noun* theft of another's ideas or writings passed off as original	*Usage:* Plagiarism is an offence punishable under law.
1369	**plasticity** *noun* ability to be moulded	*Usage:* The Indus valley people are known to have no plasticity of mind.
1370	**platitude** *noun* trite remark	*Usage:* The platitude of the speaker irritated the Vice Chancellor.
1371	**plausible** *adj.* having a show of truth but open to doubt, specious	*Usage:* 'I don't see your excuse to be plausible so I can't grant you leave', said the dissatisfied employer.
1372	**plenitude** *noun* abundance, completeness	*Usage:* Looking in the pantry, we admired the plenitude of fruits and pickles he had preserved during the summer.
1373	**plethora** *noun* excess, overabundance	*Usage:* We have a plethora of laws but still we are not able to punish the real culprits because of loopholes in the law.
1374	**pliable** *adj.* flexible, yielding, adaptable	*Usage:* She has a very pliable nature.
1375	**plight** *noun* state (especially a bad state or condition)	*Usage:* The movie Slumdog Millionaire has depicted the real plight of India.

1376	**poignancy** *noun* quality of being deeply moving, keenness of emotion	*Usage:* Watching the tearful reunion of the long-separated mother and child, the social worker was touched by the poignancy of the scene.
1377	**polarise** *verb* split into opposite extremes or camps	*Usage:* On the Mandir-Masjid issue, all the parties polarised.
1378	**polemical** *adj.* aggressive in verbal attack, disputatious	*Usage:* Pradeep is known for his polemical arguments.
1379	**politic** *adj.* expedient, prudent, well advised	*Usage:* It will not be politic to raise this issue at this time.
1380	**pomposity** *noun* self-important behaviour, acting like a stuffed shirt	*Usage:* The pomposity of his behaviour has earned him the title of a snob.
1381	**ponderous** *adj.* weighty, unwieldy	*Usage:* His humour lacked the light thought, his jokes were always ponderous.
1382	**pore** *verb* study industriously, ponder	*Usage:* Determined to be a lawyer, Mahima spent hours poring over law books.
1383	**portend** *verb* foretell, presage	*Usage:* The astrologers had portended that Buddha will leave the world and become a recluse.
1384	**portent** *noun* sign, omen, forewarning	*Usage:* He regarded the black cloud as a portent of evil.
1385	**posthumous** *adj.* after death	*Usage:* Her son was awarded posthumously.
1386	**potent** *adj.* powerful, persuasive, greatly influential	*Usage:* Writing is a potent weapon.
1387	**potential** *adj.* expressing possibility, latent	*Usage:* He has all the potential to become an IAS officer.
1388	**pragmatic** *adj. & noun* practical	*Usage:* His ideas are always very pragmatic and practical.
1389	**prate** *verb* speak foolishly, boastfully	*Usage:* Let us not prate about our good qualities, rather, let our virtues speak for themselves.
1390	**prattle** *verb* to speak in a childish way, babble	*Usage:* Baby Pinky prattled on and on about the cats and her Barbie doll.
1391	**precarious** *adj.* uncertain, risky	*Usage:* Investment in the share market is always very precarious.
1392	**precept** *noun* practical rule, guiding conduct	*Usage:* The precepts of Christianity are very simple and profound.
1393	**precinct** *noun* periphery	*Usage:* The terrorist was killed in the precincts of the holy place.
1394	**precise** *adj.* accurately stated	*Usage:* Try to be precise and concise while writing answers if you want it to fetch handsome marks.
1395	**precocious** *adj.* advanced in development	*Usage:* Mahima is a very precocious girl.
1396	**precursor** *noun* forerunner	*Usage:* Rishabhanatha was the precursor of Jainism.

1397	**predator** *noun* creature that seizes and devours another animal, person who robs or exploits others	*Usage:* Politicians are the vilest form of predators.
1398	**predecessor** *noun* former occupant of a post	*Usage:* Sher Shah Suri was the predecessor of Akbar.
1399	**predicament** *noun* tricky or dangerous situation, dilemma	*Usage:* It was a big predicament to solve the issue.
1400	**predilection** *noun* preference	*Usage:* I have a predilection for multinational publishers.
1401	**preeminent** *adj.* outstanding, superior	*Usage:* The ex-cabinet minister travelled to the US because he wanted the preeminent surgeon in the field to perform the operation.
1402	**pre-empt** *verb* to acquire (public land) by pre-emption, to seize before anyone else can, excluding others, appropriate beforehand	*Usage:* Hoping to pre-empt any attempts by the opposition to make educational reform a hot political issue, the candidate set out her own plan to revitalise the public schools.
1403	**premeditate** *verb* plan in advance	*Usage:* Before plunging into preparation for Civil Services, you should premeditate about your priorities and capabilities.
1404	**premise** *noun* assumption, postulate	*Usage:* The division of the society into haves and have nots is the basic premise of Marxism.
1405	**premonition** *noun* forewarning	*Usage:* We ignored these premonitions of disaster because they appeared to be based on childish fears.
1406	**preposterous** *adj.* absurd, ridiculous	*Usage:* We all were amused at her preposterous performance.
1407	**prerogative** *noun* privilege, unquestionable right	*Usage:* It is the prerogative of the President to grant pardon under Article 72.
1408	**presumptuous** *adj.* overconfident	*Usage:* His presumptuous attitude was the reason of his failure.
1409	**pretentious** *adj.* ostentatious, pompous	*Usage:* His pretentious display of learning failed to attract the attention of the audience.
1410	**pretext** *noun* excuse	*Usage:* She always tries to remain absent in the classes on one pretext or the other.
1411	**prevail** *verb* induce, triumph over	*Usage:* Corruption is prevailing all over the country.
1412	**prevalent** *adj.* widespread, generally accepted	*Usage:* Corruption, bribery and nepotism is prevalent in every sector, public or private, in India.
1413	**prevaricate** *verb* to turn aside from, or evade the truth, equivocate, to lie	*Usage:* She was prevaricating between yes and no for the matrimonial proposal she had got.
1414	**prey** *noun* victim	*Usage:* The public is prey to false and staggering promises of politicians.
1415	**prim** *adj.* very precise and formal, exceedingly proper	*Usage:* The new leader has a knack for delivering prim speeches.

1416	**primordial** *adj.* existing at the beginning (of time), rudimentary	*Usage:* The tribes of Madhya Pradesh are perhaps one of our primordial ancestors.
1417	**pristine** *adj.* characteristic of earlier times, primitive, unspoiled	*Usage:* The pristine glory of Ashokan times is recorded in the annals of history.
1418	**privation** *noun* hardship, want	*Usage:* In his young days, he had his first-hand experience of hunger and privation.
1419	**probe** *verb* to investigate	*Usage:* The CBI is probing the Aarushi murder case.
1420	**proclivity** *noun* inclination	*Usage:* She has a strange proclivity for cleanliness, rather I would say she is a cleanliness freak.
1421	**procrastinate** *verb* postpone, delay or put off	*Usage:* 'Procrastination robs you of opportunity', says Napoleon Hill.
1422	**prod** *verb* poke, stir up, urge	*Usage:* If you prod him hard enough, he'll eventually reveal all the secrets.
1423	**prodigal** *adj.* wasteful, spendthrift	*Usage:* His prodigal son would squander away all his ancestral properties.
1424	**prodigious** *adj.* marvellous, enormous	*Usage:* Suman Godara is a prodigious daughter of her parents.
1425	**prodigy** *noun* marvel, highly gifted child	*Usage:* Suman is a prodigy.
1426	**profane** *verb* violate, desecrate, treat unworthily	*Usage:* We should not profane the religious faith of any person.
1427	**profligate** *adj.* dissipated, wasteful, wildly immoral	*Usage:* His profligate behaviour has established him as a lecher.
1428	**profound** *adj.* deep, not superficial, complete	*Usage:* Pithy and profound language cannot be mastered easily.
1429	**profusion** *noun* overabundance, lavish expenditure, excess	*Usage:* There is a profusion of castes, classes, languages, regions and races in India.
1430	**progenitor** *noun* ancestor	*Usage:* Aryans are the progenitors of Indian civilisation.
1431	**progeny** *noun* children, offspring	*Usage:* Maya was proud of her progeny in general but regarded Suman as the most promising of all her children.
1432	**prognosis** *noun* prediction	*Usage:* If the doctor's prognosis is correct, the patient will not survive.
1433	**proliferation** *noun* rapid growth, spread, multiplication	*Usage:* The proliferation of the violence by the state generates counter violence.
1434	**prolific** *adj.* fertile	*Usage:* Paulo Coelho is a prolific writer.
1435	**prolixity** *noun* tedious wordiness, verbosity	*Usage:* Prolixity of his writing make him an unpopular writer with general readers at large.
1436	**prominent** *adj.* conspicuous, notable, sticking out	*Usage:* Siddhartha is one of the most prominent novels of Herman Hess.
1437	**promiscuous** *adj.* looseness of sexuality	*Usage:* All the tele serials broadcast nowadays legitimise promiscuous relationships.

1438	**prompt** *verb* cause, provoke	*Usage:* What prompted you to take this decision?
1439	**propagate** *verb* multiply, spread	*Usage:* Since bacteria propagate more quickly in unsanitary environments, it is important to keep hospital rooms clean.
1440	**propensity** *noun* natural inclination	*Usage:* Convinced of his own talent, Ravi has an unfortunate propensity to belittle the talents of others.
1441	**prophetic** *adj.* foretelling the future	*Usage:* I have no magical prophetic powers, when I predict what will happen, I base my predictions on my intuitions.
1442	**propitiate** *verb* to cause to become favourably inclined, win or regain the good will of, appease	*Usage:* The tribal devotees offered sacrifices to propitiate the deity.
1443	**Propitious** *adj.* favourable, fortunate, advantageous	*Usage:* Mr. Bhagat consulted his horoscope to see whether Tuesday would be a propitious day to start his new business.
1444	**proponent** *noun* supporter	*Usage:* He is one of the leading proponents of capital punishment.
1445	**propound** *verb* put forth for analysis	*Usage:* In your discussion, you have propounded several questions, let us consider each one separately.
1446	**propriety** *noun* fitness, correct conduct	*Usage:* You have to take care of the propriety required while talking to your teacher.
1447	**propulsive** *adj.* driving forward	*Usage:* India has a great propulsive power to become a superpower.
1448	**proscribe** *verb* ostracise, banish, outlaw, denounce or forbid	*Usage:* Criminals should be proscribed to enter politics.
1449	**proselytise** *verb* convert to a religion or belief	*Usage:* Proselytising the people of other faiths should be strongly discouraged.
1450	**prosperity** *noun* good fortune, financial physical well-being	*Usage:* I wish you peace, progress and prosperity on the eve of New Year.
1451	**prostrate** *verb* stretch out full on ground	*Usage:* Sultan Balban made all the courtiers to prostrate before him .
1452	**protean** *adj.* easily or continually changing, versatile, able to take on any shape or role	*Usage:* The protean talents of Amitabh Bachchan are amazing.
1453	**protege** *noun* person receiving protection and support from a patron	*Usage:* V.S. Naipaul is a protégé of the British government nowadays.
1454	**protocol** *noun* diplomatic etiquette	*Usage:* We must run this state dinner according to protocol if we are to avoid offending any of our guests.
1455	**prototype** *noun* original work used as a model by others	*Usage:* The crude typewriter on display in this museum is the prototype of the elaborate machines in use today.
1456	**protract** *verb* prolong, lengthen in duration	*Usage:* Protracting the issue is one of the most notorious dilatory tactics.

1457	**provocative** *adj.* arousing anger or interest, annoying	*Usage:* The demagogue made a provocative speech in order to generate violence.
1458	**provoke** *verb* stir to anger, cause retaliation	*Usage:* The involvement of the wife with husband's friend provoked him to such an extent that he killed both of them when caught red-handed in an obnoxious manner.
1459	**prowess** *noun* extraordinary ability, military bravery	*Usage:* He always boasts of his athletic prowess.
1460	**proximity** *noun* nearness	*Usage:* Blind people sometimes develop a compensatory ability to sense the proximity of objects around them.
1461	**proxy** *noun* authorised agent	*Usage:* Pakistan is waging a proxy war against India in the name of Kashmir problem.
1462	**prudent** *adj.* cautious, careful	*Usage:* He is a very prudent fellow.
1463	**prune** *verb* cut away, trim	*Usage:* With the help of her editor, she was able to prune her overlong manuscript into a publishable form.
1464	**prurient** *adj.* having or causing lustful thoughts or sexual behaviour	*Usage:* The prurient remarks made by the teacher in an indirect way on a girl student landed him in trouble.
1465	**puerile** *adj.* childish	*Usage:* His puerile habits sometimes become very repulsive.
1466	**pugnacity** *noun* combativeness, disposition to fight	*Usage:* At times I am offended by the false show of his pugnacity.
1467	**pulchritude** *noun* beauty, comeliness	*Usage:* The pulchritude of Usha is without a parallel in Bollywood.
1468	**pulverise** *verb* crush or grind into dust	*Usage:* The politicians are pulverising and vulgarising our rich composite culture.
1469	**pungent** *adj.* stinging	*Usage:* The pungent remarks of the leader led to his expulsion from the party.
1470	**punitive** *adj.* punishing, inflicting	*Usage:* He asked for punitive measures against the offender.
1471	**pusillanimous** *adj.* cowardly, faint-hearted	*Usage:* He is too pusillanimous to stand up to his opponents.
	Q	
1472	**quack** *noun* charlatan, impostor	*Usage:* Do not be misled by the exorbitant claims of this quack, he cannot cure you.
1473	**quagmire** *noun* complex or dangerous	*Usage:* Our judicial system is in quagmire. It needs radical judicial reforms so as to revive the faith of public in the judiciary.
1474	**quaint** *adj.* odd, old-fashioned, picturesque	*Usage:* Her quaint clothes and old-fashioned language marked her as an eccentric.
1475	**quandary** *noun* dilemma	*Usage:* Mumbai attacks left the Indian government in a quandary.
1476	**quell** *verb* extinguish, put down, quieten	*Usage:* In order to quell the mob, the police made use of tear gas.

1477	**quench** *verb* assuage or satisfy	*Usage:* It is very difficult to quench the insatiable thirst of a corrupt officer.
1478	**quietude** *noun* tranquillity	*Usage:* He was impressed by the air of quietude and peace that pervaded the valley.
1479	**quirk** *noun* starting twist, caprice	*Usage:* By a quirk of fate he virtually minted money in a short span of time.
1480	**quiver** *verb* to shake slightly, often because of strong emotion, tremble, shake	*Usage:* Her bottom lips quivered and tears started rolling down her eyes.
1481	**quixotic** *adj.* idealistic but impractical	*Usage:* Constantly coming up with quixotic unworkable schemes to save the world he has his heart in the right place, but his head somewhere in the clouds.
	R	
1482	**ramification** *noun* branching out, sub division	*Usage:* We must examine all the ramifications of this problem.
1483	**rampant** *adj.* growing in profusion, unrestrained	*Usage:* The rampant corruption in the country is one of the most glaring ills to be cured at the earliest.
1484	**ramshackle** *adj.* loose and rickety, likely to fall to pieces, falling apart	*Usage:* The ramshackle aspiration cannot produce the desired results.
1485	**rancid** *adj.* having the odour of stale fat	*Usage:* You should not nurture rancid thoughts.
1486	**rancour** *noun* bitterness, hatred	*Usage:* Thirty years after the war, she could not let go of the past but was still consumed with rancour against her foe.
1487	**random** *adj.* without definite purpose, plan, or arm, haphazard	*Usage:* We made a random survey and came to know about the sorry state of affairs prevailing in our education system.
1488	**rankle** *verb* irritate, fester	*Usage:* The memory of having been jailed rankled him for years.
1489	**rant** *verb* rave, talk excitedly, scold, make a grandiloquent speech	*Usage:* When he heard that I'd sold the family car, dad began to rant at me like a complete madman.
1490	**rapacious** *adj.* excessively greedy, predatory	*Usage:* The Indian bureaucracy has turned out to be very rapacious and instead of being servants of the public they are behaving like masters.
1491	**rapport** *noun* emotional closeness, harmony	*Usage:* For healthy teaching, a good rapport between the teacher and students is of utmost importance.
1492	**ratify** *verb* approve formally, confirm, verify	*Usage:* Party leaders doubted that they had enough votes in both Houses of the Parliament to ratify the constitutional amendment.
1493	**rationale** *noun* fundamental reason or justification, grounds for an action	*Usage:* He couldn't adduce any rationale in support of his theory.
1494	**rationalise** *verb* give a plausible reason	*Usage:* We have to rationalise the problem before offering any final solution.

1495	**raucous** *adj.* harsh and shrill, disorderly and boisterous	*Usage:* The raucous crowd of New Year's Eve revellers got progressively noisier as midnight drew nearer.
1496	**rave** *noun* overwhelmingly favourable review	*Usage:* His latest book received rave reviews in the homeland as well as abroad.
1497	**ravenous** *adj.* extremely hungry	*Usage:* He gave a ravenous glance at the girl which offended her.
1498	**raze** *verb* to completely destroy a city, building, etc.	*Usage:* The American air-force's attacks on Iraq razed all their buildings to the ground.
1499	**realm** *noun* kingdom, field or sphere	*Usage:* In the animal realm, the lion is the king of beasts.
1500	**rebuff** *verb* snub, beat back	*Usage:* She rebuffed his invitation so smoothly that he did not realise he had been snubbed.
1501	**rebuke** *verb* scold harshly, criticise severely	*Usage:* The boss rebuked the steno.
1502	**rebuttal** *noun* refutation, response with contrary evidence	*Usage:* In his rebuttal, the defence lawyer rebutted all the allegations of the public prosecutor.
1503	**recalcitrant** *adj.* obstinately stubborn, determined to resist authority, unruly	*Usage:* Her recalcitrant attitude at the office earned her blatant criticism.
1504	**recapitulate** *verb* summarise	*Usage:* Let us recapitulate what has been said in the meeting before proceeding to implement it.
1505	**receptive** *adj.* quick or willing to receive ideas, suggestions, etc.	*Usage:* One should always be receptive to others' opinions, but one should always take action according to one's own will.
1506	**recession** *noun* withdrawal, retreat, time of low economic activity	*Usage:* The world witnessed economic recession in 2009.
1507	**reciprocal** *adj.* mutual, exchangeable, interacting	*Usage:* The two nations signed a reciprocal trade agreement.
1508	**reciprocate** *verb* repay in kind	*Usage:* We are supposed to reciprocate others' feelings in the same mode and manner, tone and tanner.
1509	**recrimination** *noun* counter charges	*Usage:* Our politicians always indulge in recriminations instead of focusing on development.
1510	**rectify** *verb* set right, correct	*Usage:* You have to rectify your course of action if you want to succeed.
1511	**rectitude** *noun* uprightness, moral virtue, correctness of judgment	*Usage:* The DGP was virtually venerated by his subordinates for his unparalleled rectitude.
1512	**recuperate** *verb* recover, get back (said of losses, health etc.)	*Usage:* We had just not recuperated from the trauma of partition that we had to face Pakistan attack in 1948.
1513	**recurrent** *adj.* occurring again and again	*Usage:* Dad's recurrent asthma attacks disturbed us, so we consulted a physician.

1514	**redress** *noun* remedy, compensation	*Usage:* The government is supposed to provide a redress for the problem of poverty, unemployment and ignorance.
1515	**redundant** *adj.* superfluous, repetitious, excessively wordy	*Usage:* Both the superficial as well as redundant writings are not considered as good writings.
1516	**refrain** *verb* abstain from, resist	*Usage:* We should refrain from smoking and drinking.
1517	**refurbish** *verb* renovate	*Usage:* Mr. Gupta was busy in refurbishing his house.
1518	**refute** *verb* disprove, to prove (a person or an argument) to be wrong, confute	*Usage:* One cannot refute the authenticity of the prophetic words of Buddha that 'all composite things decay'.
1519	**regale** *verb* entertain by providing a splendid feast	*Usage:* He regaled us with a grand feast after his return from Oxford.
1520	**rehabilitate** *verb* restore to proper condition	*Usage:* Rehabilitating the refugees of partition was one of the biggest problems before the Indian government.
1521	**reiterate** *verb* repeat	*Usage:* He reiterated the warning to make sure everyone understood it.
1522	**rejuvenate** *verb* make feel or seem young again, bring back to youthful strength, appearance, etc.	*Usage:* We need to rejuvenate our judicial system.
1523	**relegate** *verb* banish to an inferior position, delegate, assign	*Usage:* The advent of the Rococo culture has relegated our traditional values to the background.
1524	**relent** *verb* give in	*Usage:* Her father relented her love marriage.
1525	**relevant** *adj.* pertinent, referring to the case in hand	*Usage:* We should jot down the most relevant points as a ready reckoner for the revision.
1526	**replete** *adj.* filled to the brim or to the point of being stuffed, abundantly supplied	*Usage:* Indian history is replete with stories of Chivalry and Valour.
1527	**replica** *noun* a reproduction or copy of original	*Usage:* His son is his exact replica.
1528	**repository** *noun* storehouse	*Usage:* Libraries are repositories of the world's best thoughts.
1529	**reprehensible** *adj.* deserving blame	*Usage:* Shocked by the viciousness of the bombing, politicians of every party uniformly condemned the terrorists' reprehensible deed.
1530	**repress** *verb* restrain, crush, oppress	*Usage:* Anne's parents tried to curb her impetuosity without repressing her boundless high spirits.
1531	**reprieve** *noun* temporary stay	*Usage:* During the twenty-four-hour reprieve, the lawyers sought to make the stay of execution permanent.
1532	**reprimand** *verb* reprove severely, rebuke	*Usage:* His boss gave him a severe reprimand for being negligent in his work.
1533	**reproach** *verb* express disapproval or disappointment	*Usage:* His mother reproached him for not eating all his dinner.

1534	**reprobate** *noun* person hardened in sin, devoid of a sense of decency, person of bad character and habits	*Usage:* I cannot understand why he has so many admirers if he is such a reprobate.
1535	**repudiate** *verb* disown, disavow, to refuse to accept something or someone as true, good or reasonable	*Usage:* He repudiated the allegations that he had tried to deceive his clients.
1536	**repugnant** *adj.* loathsome, hateful	*Usage:* I find flattery as one of the most repugnant activities.
1537	**repulsion** *noun* distaste, act of driving back, hating bloodshed	*Usage:* I have a repulsion for backbiting and leg-pulling.
1538	**reputed** *adj.* generally accounted or supposed to be such	*Usage:* Suraj Chopra is reputed for his typing skills.
1539	**requisite** *noun* necessary requirement	*Usage:* You should have requisite qualifications to apply for this post.
1540	**requite** *verb* repay, revenge	*Usage:* The thankless fellow requited his benefactors by betraying them.
1541	**rescind** *verb* to revoke, repeal or cancel (a law, order, etc.)	*Usage:* TADA was rescinded once the Punjab problem was solved.
1542	**resentment** *noun* indignation, bitterness, displeasure	*Usage:* He showed his resentment at his father's choice.
1543	**resilient** *adj.* elastic	*Usage:* Indian democracy is very resilient.
1544	**resolve** *noun* determination, firmness of purpose	*Usage:* We have to take a resolve to solve the basic problems of infrastructure.
1545	**resolve** *verb* decide, settle, solve	*Usage:* The people of India resolved to constitute India into a sovereign, socialist, secular and democrat republic.
1546	**resonant** *adj.* echoing, resounding, deep and full in sound	*Usage:* The deep, resonant voice of the actor, Amitabh Bachchan makes him particularly effective when he appears on screen.
1547	**respite** *noun* interval of relief, time for rest, delay in punishment	*Usage:* After working nonstop on this nerve-racking project for three straight months, I need a respite.
1548	**resplendent** *adj.* dazzling, glorious, brilliant	*Usage:* We saw the bride at the centre of the hall, resplendent in a red sequined bridal costume.
1549	**restitution** *noun* reparation, indemnification	*Usage:* Mr. Jaiswal filed a writ for restitution of conjugal rights.
1550	**restive** *adj.* restlessly impatient	*Usage:* He is restive to become an IAS officer.
1551	**restraint** *noun* moderation or self-control, controlling force, restriction	*Usage:* The security forces exercised great restraint by not responding to the hostile attacks of the demonstrators.
1552	**resurge** *verb* rise again, flow to and from	*Usage:* The wave of nationalism was resurging during 1930s when Bhagat Singh and others were hanged.

1553	**retain** *verb* hold or keep in possession, employ	*Usage:* I have to retain the same accommodation.
1554	**retaliation** *noun* repayment (usually for bad treatment)	*Usage:* In retaliation, India also bombarded the terrorist camps in POK.
1555	**reticence** *noun* reserved, uncommunicativeness, inclination to silence	*Usage:* Her reticence is one of her biggest assets because nobody is able to form any opinion about her.
1556	**retinue** *noun* following, attendants	*Usage:* The President travels with a large retinue of aides and bodyguards.
1557	**retort** *noun* quick sharp reply	*Usage:* Even when it was advisable for her to keep her mouth shut, she was always ready with a quick retort.
1558	**retract** *verb* withdraw, take back	*Usage:* When questioned on TV, the minister retracted his allegations.
1559	**retrench** *verb* cut down, economise	*Usage:* The company had to retrench because of failing orders.
1560	**retribution** *noun* vengeance, compensation, punishment for offenses	*Usage:* They fled because they feared retribution for the genocide.
1561	**retrieve** *verb* recover, find and bring in	*Usage:* Computers are used to store and retrieve information efficiently.
1562	**retrograde** *verb* go backwards, degenerate	*Usage:* Instead of advancing, our civilisation seems to have retrograded in ethics and culture.
1563	**retrospective.** *adj.* looking back on the past	*Usage:* One should make regular, repeated, and retrospective introspection.
1564	**revelry** *noun* boisterous merrymaking	*Usage:* New Year's Eve is a night of revelry.
1565	**reverent** *adj.* respectful, worshipful	*Usage:* Hon'ble Justice P.N. Bhagwati enjoys a very reverent reputation among the legal fraternity.
1566	**reverie** *noun* daydream, musing	*Usage:* He was awakened from his reverie by the teacher's question.
1567	**revert** *verb* relapse, backslide, turn back to	*Usage:* I shall revert to you once I finish my groundwork.
1568	**revile** *verb* vilify	*Usage:* It is a very useless activity to revile others so as to hide your own weakness.
1569	**revoke** *verb* cancel, retract	*Usage:* The ordinance was revoked.
1570	**revulsion** *noun* sudden violent change of feeling, reaction	*Usage:* Many people in this country who admired dictatorships underwent revulsion when they realised what Hitler and Mussolini were trying to do.
1571	**rhetoric** *noun* art of effective communication, insincere language	*Usage:* All writers, by necessity, must be skilled in rhetoric.
1572	**ribald** *adj.* wanton, profane	*Usage:* He sang a song in such a ribald manner that it offended many of the more prudish listeners.
1573	**rife** *adj.* abundant, current	*Usage:* The atmosphere in the country was rife with communal feelings.

1574	**rig** *verb* fix or manipulate	*Usage:* Rigging in elections in India is very common.
1575	**rigor** *noun* extreme hardship or difficulty	*Usage:* Everybody has to undergo the rigors of life.
1576	**rigorous** *adj.* severe, harsh, demanding, exact, disliked by his superiors	*Usage:* They had to undergo a rigorous training program before they finally joined the army.
1577	**robust** *adj.* vigorous, strong	*Usage:* After training at OTA Chennai, he had a very robust physique.
1578	**rousing** *adj.* lively, stirring	*Usage:* She delivered a rousing speech full of anger and passion.
1579	**rout** *verb* stampede, drive out	*Usage:* The reinforcements were able to rout the enemy.
1580	**rubble** *noun* broken fragments	*Usage:* Ten years after World War II, some of the rubble left by enemy bombings can still be seen.
1581	**rudimentary** *adj.* elementary	*Usage:* You are supposed to have rudimentary knowledge of all the topics like History, Geography, Science and others for the Civil Services Examinations.
1582	**ruffian** *noun* bully, scoundrel	*Usage:* The ruffians threw stones at the police.
1583	**ruminate** *verb* ponder	*Usage:* We have to ruminate over the consequences of our action.
1584	**rustic** *adj.* pertaining to country people, uncouth	*Usage:* He looked out of place in the party with his rustic attire.
1585	**ruthless** *adj.* pitiless, cruel	*Usage:* Some people believe that to succeed in this world one has to be ruthless.
	S	
1586	**sacrilege** *noun* treating something holy or important without respect	*Usage:* In Sikhism it is sacrilege to enter a Gurudwara bare-headed.
1587	**sacrilegious** *adj.* desecrating, profane	*Usage:* Some radicals assassinated him as they considered his remarks sacrilegious.
1588	**sacrosanct** *adj.* most sacred, inviolable	*Usage:* Muslims consider 'Koran' as their most sacrosanct book.
1589	**saga** *noun* Scandinavian myth, any legend	*Usage:* He wrote a 6000-page saga about 18th century slavery.
1590	**sagacious** *adj.* perceptive, shrewd, having insight	*Usage:* Judges are known for their sagacious spontaneity.
1591	**salacious** *adj.* lascivious, lustful	*Usage:* Rani Mukherjee played the role of a salacious reporter in the movie 'No One Killed Jessica'.
1592	**salient** *adj.* prominent	*Usage:* Auto-gear is the most salient feature of this bike.
1593	**salubrious** *adj.* promoting health or welfare, healthful, wholesome, salutary	*Usage:* The doctor advised him to take a salubrious diet and roam in fresh air.
1594	**salutary** *adj.* tending to improve, beneficial, wholesome	*Usage:* His early failures had a salutary effect on his performance.

1595	**salvage** *verb* rescue from loss	*Usage:* The team's first task was to decide what equipment could be salvaged.
1596	**sanctimonious** *adj.* displaying ostentatious or hypocritical devoutness	*Usage:* His sanctimonious behaviour apprised every one of his truthfulness.
1597	**sanction** *verb* approve, ratify	*Usage:* The project is required to be sanctioned by the Defence Ministry before starting the work.
1598	**sanguine** *adj.* cheerful, hopeful	*Usage:* The scientists were quite sanguine about the launch but to their utter disbelief it failed.
1599	**sap** *verb* to weaken, diminish, undermine	*Usage:* Working out constantly for four hours sapped him of all his energy.
1600	**sarcasm** *noun* scornful remarks, stinging rebuke	*Usage:* The politician of the opposition party ridiculed with sarcasm the proposal of our party.
1601	**sardonic** *adj.* disdainful, sarcastic, cynical	*Usage:* The author took a sardonic note of the events.
1602	**satiate** *verb* satisfy fully	*Usage:* It was very difficult to satiate the bench of highly qualified judges.
1603	**satire** *noun* form of literature in which irony, sarcasm, and ridicule are employed to attack vice and folly	*Usage:* This piece of writing is a satire on Indian democracy.
1604	**satirical** *adj.* mocking	*Usage:* Gauri's satirical poems are often very humorous.
1605	**saunter** *verb* stroll slowly	*Usage:* As we were free for an hour, we took a saunter in the Bougainvillea Garden.
1606	**savant** *noun* eminent scholar, a learned person	*Usage:* Mr. Sudhir Sharma is a well-known savant of Punjab University.
1607	**savour** *verb* enjoy, have a distinctive flavour smell, or quality	*Usage:* He likes to savour other's defeat more than his success.
1608	**savoury** *adj.* tasty, pleasing, attractive, or agreeable	*Usage:* There is something savoury in the air of Shimla.
1609	**scanty** *adj.* meagre, insufficient	*Usage:* Our doctors in rural areas do well with scanty resources.
1610	**scapegoat** *noun* someone who bears the blame for others	*Usage:* The party has some junior leaders who are made scapegoats every time.
1611	**schism** *noun* a division or split in an organised group or society, any of the sects, parties, etc., formed by such a split	*Usage:* The bone of contention led to a schism in the party.
1612	**scintillate** *verb* sparkle, flash	*Usage:* My nephew gave a scintillating performance for his age.
1613	**scoff** *verb* mock, ridicule	*Usage:* He scoffed at his adversaries until he had to face them in the battlefield.

1614	**scourge** *noun* lash, whip, severe punishment	*Usage:* The offenders will scourge for the breach of contract.
1615	**scruple** *verb* fret about, hesitate, for ethical reasons	*Usage:* He is man with no moral scruples.
1616	**scrupulous** *adj.* conscientious, extremely thorough	*Usage:* He held the notes scrupulously and performed well in exams.
1617	**scrutinise** *verb* examine closely and critically	*Usage:* The committee scrutinised all the documents in depth.
1618	**scuffle** *noun* struggle, a short and sudden fight	*Usage:* Rather than scuffling with these ruffians, it's better to call the police.
1619	**scurrilous** *adj.* obscene, indecent	*Usage:* The scurrilous scenes in the movies attracted many viewers.
1620	**scuttle** *verb* to hinder, to impede	*Usage:* The flow of water was scuttled by a temporary bridge of stones.
1621	**seamy** *adj.* sordid, unwholesome	*Usage:* He is always attracted to the seamy side of things.
1622	**seasoned** *adj.* experienced	*Usage:* Mr. Mishra is the most seasoned doctor at PGI.
1623	**secession** *noun* withdrawal	*Usage:* The security forces were forced to make a secession.
1624	**seclusion** *noun* isolation, solitude	*Usage:* The hermit led a life of seclusion.
1625	**sectarian** *adj.* relating to a religious faction or sub group, narrow-minded, limited	*Usage:* During the pre-independence era, sectarian ideas were mainly promoted.
1626	**secular** *adj.* worldly, not pertaining to church matters, temporal	*Usage:* These secular matters are to be addressed by their religious group.
1627	**sedate** *adj.* composed, grave	*Usage:* Dhoni is known for his sedate demeanour.
1628	**sedentary** *adj.* requiring sitting	*Usage:* Meditation is a sedentary task.
1629	**seditious** *adj.* resistant to authority	*Usage:* Binayak Sen is arrested for his anti-national and seditious activities.
1630	**sedulous** *adj.* diligent, hardworking	*Usage:* To complete the construction of 400 flats in 24 hours was very sedulous job on the part of the workers.
1631	**seemly** *adj.* proper, appropriate	*Usage:* Param and Jot obviously look like a seemly couple as they have many things in common.
1632	**seep** *verb* ooze, trickle	*Usage:* The water seeping through the tank made the floor wet and slippery.
1633	**seethe** *verb* be disturbed, boil, smoulder	*Usage:* She seethed with anger as if I had committed a blunder.
1634	**sensual** *adj.* devoted to the pleasures of the senses, carnal, voluptuous	*Usage:* His sensuality has made him inefficient in his work and has affected his performance graph.

1635	**sententious** *adj.* terse, concise, aphoristic	*Usage:* We couldn't introduce ourselves as the meeting was quite sententious.
1636	**sentinel** *noun* sentry, lookout	*Usage:* While the robbers did their business, two of them were acting as sentinel.
1637	**sequester** *verb* isolate, retire from public life, segregate, seclude	*Usage:* The much-hyped baba has now become a sequester.
1638	**serenity** *noun* calmness, placidity	*Usage:* We admired the serenity of the quiet village.
1639	**serpentine** *adj.* winding, twisting	*Usage:* His serpentine moves on the road flabbergasted the patrolling team.
1640	**servile** *adj.* slavish, cringing	*Usage:* Being servile, Ram was preferred by his boss over his other colleagues.
1641	**servitude** *noun* slavery, compulsory labour	*Usage:* Many women organisations are mooting in support of egalitarian society with no woman subjected to servitude.
1642	**sever** *verb* cut, separate	*Usage:* Due to hypothermia, her finger had to be severed.
1643	**severity** *noun* harshness, intensity, sternness, austerity	*Usage:* The convict pleaded for reduction in severity of the punishment.
1644	**shackle** *verb* chain, fetter	*Usage:* India became free in 1947 breaking the shackles of imperialism.
1645	**sham** *verb* pretend	*Usage:* The child shammed anger to force his parents buy him the toy.
1646	**shambles** *noun* wreck, mess	*Usage:* After an earthquake jolted the city, the transport system was in shambles.
1647	**simper** *verb* smirk, smile affectedly	*Usage:* Caught simpering in the classroom, the professor made him stand outside.
1648	**simplistic** *adj.* oversimplified	*Usage:* Her simplistic attitude led everyone to overpower her.
1649	**simulate** *verb* feign, pretend	*Usage:* He simulated to be naïve but soon overpowered his adversary.
1650	**sinecure** *noun* well-paid position with little responsibility	*Usage:* Though he is the head of HR department, his job seems to be a sinecure to me.
1651	**sinewy** *adj.* tough, strong and firm	*Usage:* The bank has now got a sinewy locker to avoid any kind of infiltration.
1652	**singular** *adj.* unique, extraordinary, odd	*Usage:* Param has a singular taste for desi music.
1653	**sinister** *adj.* evil, threatening harm or misfortune, portentous, disastrous	*Usage:* M.A. Jinnah had come up with a sinister idea of the partition of India.
1654	**sinuous** *adj.* winding, bending in and out, not morally honest	*Usage:* The IT department raided the dubious IAS officer for his sinuous dealings.
1655	**sceptic** *noun* doubter	*Usage:* Khushwant Singh is much of a sceptic in religious affairs.

1656	**skirmish** *noun* minor fight or encounter or conflict	*Usage:* I insisted on resolving the issue but the skirmish with Veerappan gang seemed inevitable.
1657	**sluggard** *noun* lazy person	*Usage:* His friends are very interested in gym, sports and athletics but he on the contrary is much of a sluggard.
1658	**sluggish** *adj.* slow, lazy, lethargic	*Usage:* The government foreign policy is responsible for the sluggish recovery of our economy.
1659	**slur** *verb* speak indistinctly	*Usage:* She slurs while speaking
1660	**slur** *noun* insult to one's character or reputation, slander	*Usage:* Mrs. Kahlon sued the newspaper which had reportedly slurred her image.
1661	**smelt** *verb* melt or blend ores, changing their chemical composition	*Usage:* Pure iron is procured from iron ore by smelting.
1662	**smirk** *noun* conceited smile, smile in an annoyingly complacent way	*Usage:* The teacher said 'you both are always smirking in the class. What's the matter with you guys'?
1663	**smoulder** *verb* burn without flame,	*Usage:* The Indo-Pak border dispute is still smouldering despite efforts since 1947.
1664	**sobriety** *noun* temperance or moderation, seriousness	*Usage:* Sobriety is the key to a profound personality.
1665	**sojourn** *noun* temporary stay, live somewhere temporarily, as on a visit, stay for a while	*Usage:* My sojourn in New York lasted for two days only.
1666	**solace** *noun* something that eases or relieves, comfort in trouble	*Usage:* The negative test report after a successful operation gave him a quantum of solace.
1667	**solicit** *verb* request earnestly, seek	*Usage:* India solicited USSR's help to set up its first IIT.
1668	**solicitous** *adj.* worried, concerned	*Usage:* India is solicitous of Pakistan's proliferation of its nuclear arsenal.
1669	**solitude** *noun* state of being alone, seclusion	*Usage:* The reaper worked the whole day at the farm in solitude.
1670	**sophisticated** *adj.* worldly-wise and urbane, complex	*Usage:* Much of his sophistication was of no use as the audience had judged his lack of knowledge.
1671	**sophistry** *noun* seemingly plausible but fallacious reasoning	*Usage:* His sophistry couldn't satisfy the jury.
1672	**sordid** *adj.* filthy, base, vile, squalid, depressingly wretched	*Usage:* The sordid surroundings of Dharavi (Mumbai) has gained it infamy across the globe.
1673	**sparse** *adj.* not thick, thinly scattered, scanty	*Usage:* Natural resources are sparsely available in northern India.
1674	**spartan** *adj.* avoiding luxury and comfort, sternly disciplined	*Usage:* The disciples took oath to lead a spartan and austere life.
1675	**spasmodic** *adj.* fitful, periodic,	*Usage:* The spasmodic rains ruined our plan to go for trekking.

1676	**spat** *noun* squabble, minor dispute	*Usage:* His repetitive checking at the airport led to a spat with the security personnel.
1677	**spate** *noun* sudden strong outburst, unusually large outpouring, as of words, a sudden, heavy rain	*Usage:* The rich countries have come under increasing pressure amid a *spate* of weather disasters.
1678	**spatial** *adj.* relating to space	*Usage:* None of his spatial theories was accepted by the space agency.
1679	**specious** *adj.* seemingly reasonable but incorrect, misleading (often intentionally)	*Usage:* The specious information provided by the witness was taking the case far from being solved.
1680	**spendthrift** *noun* someone who wastes money, squanderer, prodigal	*Usage:* The hip-hop generation of present India is much of a spendthrift.
1681	**spontaneity** *noun* naturalness	*Usage:* The spontaneity in her acting won her kudos from the audience.
1682	**sporadic** *adj.* occurring irregularly	*Usage:* The sporadic rains confirmed that there would be no match.
1683	**spry** *adj.* vigorously active, nimble, brisk, etc., esp. though elderly	*Usage:* The brook moves down the hills spraying and sizzling.
1684	**spurious** *adj.* false, counterfeit, forged, illogical	*Usage:* The bank officials hinted some foreign hands in the spreading of spurious currency in India.
1685	**spurn** *verb* reject, scorn	*Usage:* She spurned Param's proposal to marry him due to his financial instability.
1686	**squabble** *noun* minor quarrel, bickering	*Usage:* The dealers are always squabbling on prices in the fish market.
1687	**squalor** *noun* filth, degradation, dirty, neglected state	*Usage:* The alleys of Dharavi were full of squalor.
1688	**squander** *verb* waste, to spend wastefully	*Usage:* Being from a humble background, Param could never think of being a squanderer.
1689	**stagnant** *adj.* motionless state	*Usage:* The mosquitoes are usually found on stagnant water bodies.
1690	**staid** *adj.* sober, sedate	*Usage:* Her behaviour in the party put a question mark on her staid attitude.
1691	**stalemate** *noun* deadlock	*Usage:* The parliament was caught in a stalemate over the JPC issue.
1692	**stalwart** *adj.* strong, brawny, steadfast	*Usage:* Nehru and Patel were two stalwarts of India after independence.
1693	**stamina** *noun* strength, staying power	*Usage:* Saina walked on a treadmill for two hours every day to increase her stamina.

1694	**steadfast** *adj.* loyal, unswerving, straight, unbending	*Usage:* Nehru was a steadfast follower of Gandhi.
1695	**stealth** *noun* slyness, sneakiness, secretiveness	*Usage:* Every developed nation is trying to develop stealth technology in aircrafts.
1696	**steep** *verb* soak, saturate	*Usage:* You need to steep the wound in antiseptic water.
1697	**stifle** *verb* suppress, extinguish, inhibit	*Usage:* You should not stifle the feelings of children.
1698	**stigma** *noun* token of disgrace, brand	*Usage:* Abject poverty is a great stigma on India's image of a welfare state.
1699	**stigmatise** *verb* brand, mark as wicked or disgraceful	*Usage:* One mistaken deed of Manu Sharma stigmatised his whole life.
1700	**stilted** *adj.* bombastic, inflate	*Usage:* The stilted speech of the leader was very popular among the masses.
1701	**stint** *noun* a fixed period of time that you spend doing something	*Usage:* He did a brief stint in the army after leaving school.
1702	**stint** *verb* be thrifty, set limits	*Usage:* Don't stint yourself, take another slice of cake.
1703	**stipend** *noun* a regular or fixed payment for services	*Usage:* The meagre stipend I used to get here couldn't sustain my family of eight members.
1704	**stipulate** *verb* make express conditions, specify	*Usage:* You need to finish the project in the stipulated time in order to get your pay cheque.
1705	**stratagem** *noun* deceptive scheme	*Usage:* His stratagems are known to me and he can no longer deceive us.
1706	**stratify** *verb* divide into classes, be arranged into strata	*Usage:* The Indian society is stratified from mythological age.
1707	**stratum** *noun* layer of earth's surfaces, layer of society	*Usage:* The Indian priestly class – the Brahmans have set a hierarchy of rules for every stratum of society.
1708	**strew** *verb* spread randomly, sprinkle, scatter	*Usage:* The doctor advised to strew some powder on the wound and then drape it.
1709	**striated** *adj.* marked with parallel bands, grooved	*Usage:* The nuclear test left striated marks in the desert of Pokhran.
1710	**stricture** *noun* restriction, adverse criticism	*Usage:* The court passed a stricture against the government.
1711	**strident** *adj.* loud and harsh, insistent	*Usage:* Nobody came out of his house despite strident appeals from the authorities.
1712	**stringent** *adj.* binding, rigid	*Usage:* Khap panchayats are known for their stringent rules.
1713	**stultify** *verb* cause to appear or become stupid or inconsistent, frustrate or hinder, to render worthless, useless or futile	*Usage:* His intelligence was stultified as he had to live in the prison for four years with hardcore criminals.
1714	**stupefy** *verb* make numb, stun, amaze	*Usage:* I was stupefied to see the 165-storey high Burj-Khalifa.

1715	**suavity** *noun* urbanity, polished	*Usage:* The Mumbaikars boast of their suavity compared to their rural counterparts.
1716	**subdued** *adj.* less intense, quieter	*Usage:* Subdued music was being played in the background, as I was enjoying my candlelight dinner.
1717	**subjective** *adj.* unreal, fanciful, resulting from a mental construct	*Usage:* His thinking was not at par with other thinkers at the meet, but it was merely subjective.
1718	**subjugate** *verb* conquer, bring under control	*Usage:* The Mughal ruler Akbar was able to subjugate most of India under one umbrella.
1719	**subsequent** *adj.* following, later	*Usage:* The subsequent offers from many firms led him to auction his vintage car.
1720	**subservient** *adj.* behaving like a slave, servile, obsequious	*Usage:* Indians during the British Raj were meant to be subservient to their white bosses.
1721	**subside** *verb* settle down, descend, grow quiet	*Usage:* The storm will subside in a week's time.
1722	**subsidiary** *adj.* subordinate, secondary	*Usage:* The GM group has Chevrolet as one of its subsidiaries.
1723	**subsidy** *noun* direct financial aid by government, etc.	*Usage:* The Punjab government provides huge subsidies to Kinnow growers.
1724	**subsistence** *noun* existence, means of support, livelihood	*Usage:* Every youth today wants to earn much more than a subsistence salary for a happy and secured future.
1725	**substantial** *adj.* ample, solid, in essentials	*Usage:* I need a substantial amount of money for my studies.
1726	**substantiate** *verb* establish by evidence, verify, support	*Usage:* The US is ready to substantiate India's bid for a permanent UNSC seat.
1727	**substantive** *adj.* essential, pertaining to the substance	*Usage:* Long term planning is substantive for India's all-round development.
1728	**subterfuge** *noun* pretence, evasion	*Usage:* Most people can see right through this subterfuge.
1729	**subtlety** *noun* perceptiveness, ingenuity, delicacy	*Usage:* Her subtlety at the conference appraised every one of her ingenuity.
1730	**subversive** *adj.* tending to overthrow, destructive	*Usage:* The subversive public wanted to have a new government.
1731	**succinct** *adj.* brief, terse, compact	*Usage:* I had a succinct media briefing that couldn't answer many questions.
1732	**succour** *noun* aid, assistance, comfort or help given, especially to someone who is suffering or is in need	*Usage:* The USSR provided succour to India during the Chinese offensive in 1962.
1733	**succulent** *adj.* juicy, full of richness	*Usage:* He procured succulent fruits from the market for breakfast.
1734	**succumb** *verb* yield, give in, die	*Usage:* The victim succumbed to injuries on his way to the hospital.
1735	**sully** *verb* tarnish, soil	*Usage:* Her image has been sullied by the media.

1736	**sultry** *adj.* sweltering	*Usage:* The atmosphere between the two parties was quite sultry during the negotiations.
1737	**summit** *noun* utmost height or pinnacle, highest point (of a mountain, etc.)	*Usage:* The summit of his sporting career met with many controversies.
1738	**sumptuous** *adj.* lavish, rich	*Usage:* The sumptuous surrounding of the Connaught Place attracts everyone.
1739	**supercilious** *adj.* arrogant, condescending,	*Usage:* Her supercilious attitude forced me to exclude her from my friend's list.
1740	**superficial** *adj.* trivial, shallow	*Usage:* He escaped the accident unhurt barring some superficial injuries.
1741	**superfluous** *adj.* unnecessary, excessive, overabundant	*Usage:* The government must cut short its expenses on superfluous foreign visits of its ministers.
1742	**supersede** *verb* place over something else	*Usage:* The Chinese economy is expected to supersede US by 2030.
1743	**superimpose** *verb* cause to be set aside, replace, make obsolete	*Usage:* The company tried to superimpose its adversary with similar plans to reduce customer base.
1744	**supple** *adj.* flexible, pliable	*Usage:* We need to have a new and supple foreign policy to meet the growing energy needs.
1745	**suppress** *verb* stifle, overwhelm, subdue, inhibit	*Usage:* Don't suppress your feelings.
1746	**surly** *adj.* rude, cross	*Usage:* Her surliness is a cause of concern for her parents as it is increasing day by day.
1747	**surmise** *verb* guess	*Usage:* I surmised most of the MCQs but only 1/4th was correct.
1748	**surmount** *verb* overcome	*Usage:* The superior technology of the Chinese army surmounted the Indian troops in the 1962 war.
1749	**surpass** *verb* exceed	*Usage:* India will surpass China as the most populous country by 2050.
1750	**surreptitious** *adj.* secret, furtive, sneaky, hidden	*Usage:* The surreptitious nuclear tests by India led to US imposing sanctions on India.
1751	**susceptible** *adj.* impressionable, easily influenced, having little resistance, as to a disease, receptive to	*Usage:* The US considered India susceptible on climate change issue but India took a different note of the matter.
1752	**sustain** *verb* experience, support, nourish	*Usage:* Many emerging entrepreneurs in America weren't able to sustain the might of recession.
1753	**sustenance** *noun* means of support, food, nourishment	*Usage:* The tribals depended on the ill-fated government supplier for their sustenance.
1754	**swagger** *verb* behave arrogantly or pompously, strut or walk proudly	*Usage:* The fashion of swaggering in an open jeep with loud music is prevalent in Punjab University.

T		
1755	**taciturn** *adj.* habitually silent, talking little	*Usage:* In matters related to police and law, one needs to be taciturn in the absence of a lawyer.
1756	**talisman** *noun* charm to bring good luck and avert misfortune	*Usage:* Gandhi provided a talisman to the entire humanity.
1757	**tangible** *adj.* able to be touched, real, palpable	*Usage:* There should be some tangible evidence, remarked Justice Sanghvi.
1758	**tantalise** *verb* tease, torture with disappointment	*Usage:* The politicians tantalise the imagination of the public with their staggering promises.
1759	**tantamount** *adj.* equivalent in effect or value	*Usage:* Providing shelter to any ISI agent tantamounts to sedition.
1760	**tantrum** *noun* fit of petulance, caprice	*Usage:* To my disbelief I saw Jot throwing a tantrum as I had considered her to be a mature girl.
1761	**tawdry** *adj.* cheap and gaudy	*Usage:* The rural fair was packed with tawdry items.
1762	**tedious** *adj.* boring, tiring	*Usage:* The job of a watchman seems to be very tedious and tiring.
1763	**temerity** *noun* boldness, rashness	*Usage:* Some actresses show a brazen temerity.
1764	**temper** *verb* moderate, tone down or restrain, toughen (steel)	*Usage:* The Pakistani bowlers reportedly tampered with the ball.
1765	**temperament** *noun* characteristic frame of mind, disposition, emotional excess	*Usage:* Miss Sekhon seems to be of a haughty temperament though she pretends to be calm and composed.
1766	**temperate** *adj.* restrained, self-controlled, moderate in respect to temperature	*Usage:* Try to be temperate in your eating this holiday season, if you control your appetite, you won't gain too much weight.
1767	**tempestuous** *adj.* stormy, impassioned, violent	*Usage:* The winter session of the parliament is expected to be very tempestuous.
1768	**tempo** *noun* speed of music, rate of activity	*Usage:* The unforeseen event broke the tempo of the group and delayed the project.
1769	**temporise** *verb* avoid committing oneself, gain time, to suit one's actions to the time, occasion or circumstances	*Usage:* 'Don't temporise the things, I want to implement it with effect from now onwards', said the Minister.
1770	**tenacious** *adj.* holding fast, that retains well, retentive, persistent, stubborn	*Usage:* Her tenacious hug didn't let me go as I was getting late.
1771	**tenacity** *noun* firmness, persistence	*Usage:* The tenacity of the farmer made it possible to fix his appointment with the Minister.
1772	**tendentious** *adj.* having an aim, biased, designed to further a cause	*Usage:* The media with paid news has now become tendentious.
1773	**tender** *verb* offer, extend	*Usage:* The company floated an open tender for the project.

1774	**tenet** *noun* doctrine, dogma	*Usage:* The tenets of Gandhi are followed all over the world.
1775	**tentative** *adj.* hesitant, not fully worked out or developed, experimental, not definite or positive	*Usage:* The tentative dates of CSAT 2022 may be out by next week.
1776	**tenuous** *adj.* thin, rare, slim	*Usage:* The cultural and historical links between many provinces were seen to be very tenuous.
1777	**terrestrial** *adj.* earthly (as opposed to celestial), pertaining to the land	*Usage:* Our institute is purely dedicated towards research of terrestrial life forms.
1778	**terse** *adj.* concise, abrupt, pithy	*Usage:* The agents had a terse conversation and they parted in a jiffy.
1779	**testy** *adj.* irritable, short-tempered	*Usage:* The city life is taking much out of me and hence making me testy.
1780	**tether** *verb* tie with a rope, limit one's abilities, resources, etc.	*Usage:* It's not good to tether your child's creativity by imposing your will.
1781	**thrive** *verb* prosper, flourish	*Usage:* The Harappans thrived on the bank of the Indus.
1782	**throes** *noun* violent, anguish	*Usage:* We were in the throes of battle when the reinforcements arrived.
1783	**throng** *noun* crowd, any great number of things massed or considered together, multitude	*Usage:* Many pilgrims throng the shrine of Amarnath boosting the tourism related industry.
1784	**thwart** *verb* baffle, frustrate	*Usage:* The police thwarted the futile attempts of the culprits.
1785	**timidity** *noun* lack of self-confidence or courage	*Usage:* Despite his timidity, Yusuf Pathan presents himself well in the media briefings.
1786	**timorous** *adj.* fearful, demonstration of fear	*Usage:* The timorous palace of the deceased king is a haunting place.
1787	**titanic** *adj.* of or like the Titans, gigantic, of great size, strength or power	*Usage:* Osho was a titanic genius.
1788	**titter** *noun* laugh in a half-suppressed way, giggle, nervous laugh	*Usage:* The students don't even dare to titter at the time of their practical.
1789	**titular** *adj.* nominal holding of title without obligations	*Usage:* The POI is the titular head of the state.
1790	**torrid** *adj.* passionate, hot or scorching	*Usage:* Britishers made Shimla their summer capital to avoid the torrid Indian plains.
1791	**tortuous** *adj.* full of twists and turns, winding, full of curves, not straight forward, devious, deceitful or tricky	*Usage:* These long and tortuous negotiations are aimed at ending the conflict.

1792	**totter** *verb* move unsteadily, sway, as if about to fall	*Usage:* He tottered to the fridge, got a beer and skimped at the table.
1793	**touchstone** *noun* criterion	*Usage:* Job security has become the touchstone of a prosperous career.
1794	**touchy** *adj.* easily offended, over-sensitive, irascible, very risky	*Usage:* The movie was very touchy and I couldn't overcome my emotions for the next two days.
1795	**tout** *verb* publicise, praise excessively	*Usage:* His gimmickry attracted everyone's attention as he was touting his product.
1796	**traduce** *verb* expose to slander, say untrue or malicious things about someone, vilify	*Usage:* That political party has been traduced in the press as a xenophobic party.
1797	**trajectory** *noun* path taken by a projectile	*Usage:* The fielder judged the trajectory of the ball rightly and caught hold of it.
1798	**tranquillity** *noun* calmness, peace, serenity	*Usage:* The sculpture of Buddha exudes great tranquillity.
1799	**transcendent** *adj.* surpassing, exceeding ordinary limits, superior	*Usage:* They advocated the idea of a transcendent God who stood apart from mankind.
1800	**transgression** *noun* violation of a law, sin	*Usage:* It seemed to me that he had transgressed the boundaries of good taste.
1801	**transient** *adj.* momentary, temporary, staying for a short time	*Usage:* Life is transient and ephemeral, but nobody understands it.
1802	**transition** *noun* going from one state of action to another	*Usage:* The transition to a multiparty democracy is proving to be difficult.
1803	**transitory** *adj.* impermanent, fleeting	*Usage:* Most of the teenage romances are transitory.
1804	**Transmute** *verb* change, convert to something different	*Usage:* Scientists transmuted matter into pure energy and exploded the first atomic bomb.
1805	**transparent** *adj.* easily detected, permitting light to pass through freely	*Usage:* The finance minister emphasised for open and transparent government business.
1806	**traumatic** *adj.* pertaining to an injury caused by violence	*Usage:* I suffered a nervous breakdown. It was a traumatic experience.
1807	**traverse** *verb* go through or across, go back and forth over or along, oppose, thwart, to survey, inspect or examine carefully	*Usage:* I traversed the narrow pedestrian bridge.
1808	**travesty** *noun* comical parody, treatment aimed at making something appear ridiculous	*Usage:* Her research suggests that Smith's reputation is the travesty of what he really stood for.
1809	**trepidation** *noun* fear, nervousness, apprehension	*Usage:* It was with some trepidation that I viewed the prospect of cycling across the desert.

1810	**trespass** *verb* unlawfully enter the boundaries of someone else's property	*Usage:* You can be prosecuted for trespass.
1811	**tribute** *noun* tax levied by a ruler, mark of respect	*Usage:* He paid tribute to the organising committee.
1812	**trifling** *adj.* trivial, unimportant	*Usage:* The law does not take notice of trifles.
1813	**trigger** *verb* set off, initiate, fire or activate by pulling or pressing a trigger	*Usage:* A man pointed a gun at them and pulled the trigger.
1814	**trite** *adj.* hackneyed: commonplace	*Usage:* The movie is teeming with obvious and trite ideas.
1815	**trivial** *adj.* unimportant, trifling	*Usage:* The director tried to wave aside these issues as trivial details that could be settled later.
1816	**truculence** *noun* aggressiveness, ferocity	*Usage:* Your secretary said you'd be wanting a cleaner, she announced with her usual truculence.
1817	**truism** *noun* self-evident truth	*Usage:* It is truism that nothing succeeds like success.
1818	**truncate** *verb* cut the top off	*Usage:* The review body truncated the annual report.
1819	**tryst** *noun* an appointment to meet at a specified time and place	*Usage:* Nehru's 'tryst with destiny' speech has become immortal.
1820	**tumult** *noun* commotion, riot, noise	*Usage:* A tumult of feelings agitated her over the sudden demise of her father.
1821	**turbulence** *noun* state of violent agitation	*Usage:* The 1960s and early 1970s were a time of change and turbulence.
1822	**turgid** *adj.* not flowing easily, swollen, distended	*Usage:* He used to make extremely dull, turgid, and boring speeches.
1823	**turmoil** *noun* great commotion and confusion	*Usage:* Her married life is in turmoil because of her husband's extramarital relations.
1824	**turpitude** *noun* depravity, baseness, vileness	*Usage:* His turpitude led to declare him as persona-non-grata in our country.
1825	**tutelage** *noun* guardianship, training, the condition of being under a guardian or tutor	*Usage:* Kanwar is under the tutelage of Bhardwaj at Chandigarh to prepare for CLAT 2022.
	U	
1826	**unassailable** *adj.* not subject to question, not open to attack	*Usage:* With ordinary talent and extraordinary perseverance, nothing is unassailable.
1827	**unassuming** *adj.* modest	*Usage:* Mr. Karan was known for his unassuming lifestyle.
1828	**unbridled** *adj.* violent, uncontrollable	*Usage:* The alchemy by Tarun Tejpal is a tale of lust and unbridled passion.
1829	**uncanny** *adj.* strange, mysterious	*Usage:* The hero, Danny, bears an uncanny resemblance to Kirk Douglas.

1830	**unconscionable** *adj.* unscrupulous, excessive	*Usage:* It's unconscionable for the government to do anything for a man who admits to smuggling 135 tons of cocaine into the country.
1831	**uncouth** *adj.* outlandish, clumsy, boorish	*Usage:* Many consider that idea as uncouth and it doesn't have public support.
1832	**undermine** *verb* weaken, sap	*Usage:* Never undermine your enemy.
1833	**unearth** *verb* dig up	*Usage:* The investigating agencies unearthed the plot of terrorists.
1834	**unequivocal** *adj.* plain, obvious, unmistakable	*Usage:* He gave him a reply in unequivocal terms.
1835	**unerringly** *adj.* infallibly	*Usage:* It was wonderful to watch her fingers moving deftly and unerringly.
1836	**unfathomable** *adj.* incomprehensible, impenetrable	*Usage:* Indian sages had unfathomable knowledge of life and its myths.
1837	**unfetter** *verb* liberate, free from chains	*Usage:* Unfettered by the bounds of reality, my imagination flourished.
1838	**ungainly** *adj.* awkward, clumsy, unwieldy	*Usage:* The dog, an ungainly mongrel pup, was loping about the road.
1839	**unimpeachable** *adj.* blameless and exemplary	*Usage:* He said all five were men of unimpeachable character.
1840	**unintimidating** *adj.* unfrightening	*Usage:* The burglars entered the shop intimidatingly despite an active security system.
1841	**unmitigated** *adj.* unrelieved or immoderate, absolute, out-and-out	*Usage:* The unmitigated drone attacks lead to sabotage of larger parts of Pak.
1842	**unpalatable** *adj.* distasteful, disagreeable	*Usage:* It is an unpalatable fact that rape makes a good news story.
1843	**unprecedented** *adj.* unparalleled	*Usage:* Such a move is rare, but not unprecedented.
1844	**unravel** *verb* disentangle, solve	*Usage:* The UPA government began to unravel the banking scandal.
1845	**unrequited** *adj.* not reciprocated	*Usage:* His unrequited love for a married woman resulted in his divorce.
1846	**unruly** *adj.* disobedient, lawless	*Usage:* 'Unruly behaviour is not acceptable in the house', the Speaker announced.
1847	**unscathed** *adj.* unharmed	*Usage:* The officer in the encounter was unscathed.
1848	**untenable** *adj.* indefensible, not to be maintained	*Usage:* This argument is untenable from an intellectual, moral and practical stand point.
1849	**unwieldy** *adj.* awkward, cumbersome, unmanageable	*Usage:* They came panting up to his door with their unwieldy baggage.
1850	**unwitting** *adj.* unintentional, not knowing	*Usage:* We in India are unwitting victims of the system.

1851	**upbraid** *verb* severely scold, reprimand	*Usage:* His wife set about upbraiding him for neglecting the children.
1852	**uproarious** *adj.* marked by commotion, extremely funny, very noisy	*Usage:* He had spent several uproarious evenings at the embassy club.
1853	**upshot** *noun* the conclusion, result or outcome	*Usage:* The upshot is that we have lots of good but not very skilled employees.
1854	**usurp** *verb* seize another's power or rank	*Usage:* The mafia was accused of usurping the land of the tribals.
1855	**utopia** *noun* ideal place, state, or society	*Usage:* The agitations of the peasants were guided by utopian ideas of their leaders.
	V	
1856	**vacillate** *verb* waver, fluctuate	*Usage:* She vacillates between two marriage proposals.
1857	**vagabond** *noun* wanderer, tramp	*Usage:* The vagabond was ignored by all.
1858	**vagrant** *noun* a homeless wanderer	*Usage:* The vagrant was offered a night's stay and some supper at my home.
1859	**valid** *adj.* logically convincing, should legally be acceptable	*Usage:* He put forward many valid arguments in support of his client.
1860	**validate** *verb* confirm, ratify	*Usage:* Your identity needs to be validated by the police.
1861	**valour** *noun* bravery	*Usage:* The President gave away the medals to the army for their valour in battle.
1862	**vanguard** *noun* forerunners, advance forces	*Usage:* The IT industry is the vanguard of the corporate sector.
1863	**vantage** *noun* position giving an advantage	*Usage:* The Kangra fort stands at a vantage point.
1864	**vapid** *adj.* dull and unimaginative, insipid and flavourless	*Usage:* His ideas being vapid didn't arise much interest.
1865	**variegated** *adj.* many coloured/having varieties in character or form	*Usage:* The trees here have unique variegated flowers.
1866	**vehement** *adj.* forceful, intensely emotional, with marked vigour	*Usage:* She suddenly becomes very vehement and agitated, jumping around and shouting.
1867	**venal** *adj.* capable of being bribed or corrupted	*Usage:* The Indian administration is full of venal bureaucrats.
1868	**vendetta** *noun* feud	*Usage:* The Vice President said that the cartoonist has a personal vendetta against him.
1869	**venerable** *adj.* deserving high respect	*Usage:* A venerable old man with grey hair stood silently before the agitating youngsters.

1870	**venerate** *verb* look upon with feelings of deep respect, regard as venerable, revere	*Usage:* My father virtually venerated Abraham Lincoln.
1871	**venial** *adj.* forgivable, trivial, excusable	*Usage:* It is one of his venial quicks which I usually ignore.
1872	**venom** *noun* poison, hatred, malignancy, spite	*Usage:* The venom had got mixed with his blood after a snakebite.
1873	**vent** *verb* express, utter, to allow to escape	*Usage:* She telephoned her best friend to vent her frustration.
1874	**venturesome** *adj.* a person who is willing to take risks, or an action or behaviour that is risky	*Usage:* The venturesome young man is determined to succeed come what may.
1875	**veracity** *noun* truthfulness, in accordance with truth, accuracy of statement	*Usage:* We have total confidence in the veracity of our research.
1876	**verbalise** *verb* put into words	*Usage:* His inability to verbalise his feeling proved him wrong.
1877	**verbatim** *adv.* word for word, in exactly the same words	*Usage:* The President's speeches are regularly reproduced verbatim in the state-run newspaper.
1878	**verbiage** *noun* pompous array of words	*Usage:* His verbiage was not very impressive in view of the jury.
1879	**verbose** *adj.* someone who speaks much or high-flown language	*Usage:* Nobody appreciates verbose writing.
1880	**verge** *noun* border, edge	*Usage:* The country was on the verge of becoming bankrupt.
1881	**verity** *noun* quality of being true, lasting truth of principle	*Usage:* Some verities of human nature cannot be falsified.
1882	**versatile** *adj.* having many talents, capable of working in many fields	*Usage:* Ramjot Kaur is a versatile girl as she is an expert in many fields.
1883	**vertex** *noun* summit, the highest point, apex	*Usage:* The vertex of Himalayas known as Mt. Everest is very tough to conquer.
1884	**verve** *noun* enthusiasm, liveliness	*Usage:* He composes music with great verve.
1885	**vex** *verb* annoy, distress	*Usage:* It vexed me to think of others gossiping behind my back.
1886	**viable** *adj.* practical or workable, capable of maintaining life	*Usage:* The government is not having much viable options and it can lead to a stalemate.
1887	**vicarious** *adj.* acting as a substitute, done by a deputy, endured, suffered, or performed by one person in place of another	*Usage:* The master has vicarious liability for his servant.

1888	**vicissitude** *noun* ups and downs	*Usage:* Whatever the vicissitudes of her past life, Gill now seems to have come through.
1889	**vie** *verb* contend, complete	*Usage:* In hospitals, business plans vie with patients for doctor's attention.
1890	**vigilance** *noun* watchfulness	*Usage:* Protestors are holding a twenty-four-hour vigilance outside the socialist party headquarters.
1891	**vigour** *noun* active strength	*Usage:* His body lacks the bounce and vigour of a normal two-year-old.
1892	**vilify** *verb* slander	*Usage:* He was vilified, hounded, and forced into exile by the FBI.
1893	**vindicate** *verb* clear from blame, exonerate, justify or support	*Usage:* The director said he has been vindicated by the expert's report.
1894	**vindictive** *adj.* out for revenge, malicious	*Usage:* He was made a victim of the official's vindictive attitude.
1895	**virile** *adj.* manly, having manly strength or vigour, capable of copulation	*Usage:* He wanted his sons to become strong, virile, and athletic like him.
1896	**virtual** *adj.* in essence, for practical purposes	*Usage:* Argentina came to a virtual standstill while the game was being played.
1897	**virtue** *noun* goodness, moral excellence, good quality	*Usage:* She could have established her own innocence and virtue easily enough.
1898	**virtuoso** *noun* highly skilled artist, a savant or dilettante	*Usage:* He was gaining a reputation as a remarkable virtuoso.
1899	**virulent** *adj.* extremely poisonous, hostile, venomous, rancorous	*Usage:* Now he faces virulent attack from Italian media.
1900	**vital** *adj.* vibrant and lively, living, breathing	*Usage:* The port is vital to supply relief to millions of drought victims.
1901	**vitriolic** *adj.* corrosive, sarcastic	*Usage:* Acids have a vitriolic effect on most of the metals.
1902	**vituperative** *adj.* abusive, scolding	*Usage:* He is often the victim of vituperative remarks concerning his wealth.
1903	**vivacious** *adj.* animated, lively	*Usage:* They gave a vivacious performance.
1904	**vociferous** *adj.* clamorous, noisy	*Usage:* He was vociferous opponent of reservation.
1905	**vogue** *noun* popular fashion	*Usage:* In the 21st century, mobile phones are a vogue.
1906	**volatile** *adj.* changeable, explosive, evaporating rapidly	*Usage:* The international oil markets have been highly volatile since the early 1970s.
1907	**volition** *noun* act of making a conscious choice	*Usage:* Everything we do and everything we think is a product of our volition.
1908	**voluptuous** *adj.* gratifying the senses	*Usage:* Katrina Kaif has a very voluptuous figure.
1909	**voracious** *adj.* insatiable	*Usage:* Joseph Smith was a voracious reader.

1910	**vortex** *noun* whirlwind, whirlpool, centre of turbulence, predicament into which one is inexorably plunged	*Usage:* The polar vortex is a system of wintertime winds.
1911	**vulnerable** *adj.* susceptible to wounds	*Usage:* The most vulnerable areas of the district should be provided with immediate relief.
	W	
1912	**waffle** *verb* speak equivocally about an issue	*Usage:* The child started waffling and demanding sweets.
1913	**waggish** *adj.* mischievous, humorous tricky	*Usage:* Ajay is a waggish chap and pretends to be very sincere.
1914	**waive** *verb* give up temporarily, yield	*Usage:* The government, waived all the outstanding loans of the peasants.
1915	**wary** *adj.* very cautious	*Usage:* People didn't teach their children to be wary of strangers.
1916	**wax** *verb* increase in strength, intensity, volume, etc., grown	*Usage:* Portugal and Spain possessed vast empires that waxed and waned with passage of time.
1917	**whet** *verb* sharpen, stimulate	*Usage:* A really good catalogue can also whet customers' appetite for merchandise.
1918	**whimsical** *adj.* capricious, fanciful	*Usage:* Patrick French termed Gandhi as whimsical and unpredictable.
1919	**wilful** *adj.* intentional, headstrong	*Usage:* His wilful decisions are not acceptable to me.
1920	**wily** *adj.* cunning, artful, crafty, sly	*Usage:* His appointment as Prime Minister owed much to the wily manoeuvring by party leaders.
1921	**windfall** *noun* unexpected lucky event	*Usage:* My name in the list of winners of lucky draw was like a windfall.
1922	**winnow** *verb* sift, separate good parts from bad	*Usage:* Administration officials have winnowed the list of candidates to three.
1923	**winsome** *adj.* agreeable, gracious, engaging	*Usage:* She gives him her best winsome smile.
1924	**wispy** *adj.* thin, slight, barely discernible	*Usage:* Her wispy arms couldn't hold much weight.
1925	**wistful** *adj.* vaguely longing, sadly thoughtful	*Usage:* I can't help feeling slightly wistful about the perks I'm giving up.
1926	**withdrawn** *adj.* introverted, remote	*Usage:* Jinnah after his marriage had become withdrawn and moody.
1927	**wither** *verb* shrivel, decay	*Usage:* After Ashoka's death, the Mauryan Empire withered away.
1928	**withhold** *verb* refuse to give, hold back	*Usage:* The President withheld the bill of reservation passed by the parliament.
1929	**withstand** *verb* stand up against successfully, resists	*Usage:* Armoured vehicles are designed to withstand chemical attack.

1930	**witless** *adj.* foolish, idiotic	*Usage:* Please don't repeat such witless questions and make us disturbed.
1931	**witticism** *noun* witty saying, wisecrack	*Usage:* His speech was full of witticism.
1932	**wizardry** *noun* sorcery, magic	*Usage:* A piece of technical wizardry mesmerised all.
1933	**woe** *noun* deep, inconsolable grief, affliction, suffering, pale and wan with grief	*Usage:* He listened to my tale of woe.
1934	**worldly** *adj.* engrossed in matters of this earth	*Usage:* I am not much bothered about the worldly affairs.
1935	**wrath** *noun* anger, fury	*Usage:* He incurred the wrath of the authorities for speaking out against the government's injustice.
1936	**wrench** *verb* pull, strain, twist	*Usage:* Two men wrenched the suitcase from his hand.
1937	**writhe** *verb* twist in coils, contort in pain	*Usage:* The shark was writhing around wildly trying to get free.
1938	**wry** *adj.* twisted, with a humorous twist	*Usage:* There is a wry sense of humour in his literary works.
	Y	
1939	**yield** *noun* amount produced, crop, income on investment	*Usage:* Will she yield to growing pressure and take voluntary retirement?
1940	**yield** *verb* give in, surrender	*Usage:* The high yields available on the dividend shares made them attractive to private investors.
1941	**yore** *noun* time past	*Usage:* The images provoked a strong surge of nostalgia for the days of yore.
	Z	
1942	**zany** *adj.* crazy, comic	*Usage:* She is a zany fellow.
1943	**zeal** *noun* eager enthusiasm	*Usage:* Mr. Lopez approached his task with a religious zeal.
1944	**zealot** (*noun*) fanatic, person who shows excessive zeal	*Usage:* One cannot be a religious zealot and tolerant at the same time.
1945	**zenith** (*noun*) point directly overhead in the sky, summit	*Usage:* His career is now at its zenith.

2 CHECK YOUR WORD POWER - PRACTICE TESTS

48 PRACTICE TESTS

Directions: Match the words from the left column with those in the right column and check your answers against the answer key provided at the end.

PRACTICE TEST – 1				PRACTICE TEST – 2			
1.	Disparage	a.	Flatter lavishly	1.	Parity	a.	Belittlement
2.	Equivocate	b.	Work against	2.	Disparity	b.	Act of being deliberately vague or indirectly deceptive
3.	Titillate	c.	Prohibit	3.	Disparagement	c.	Quality of being open to misinterpretation
4.	Adulate	d.	Forgive	4.	Peer	d.	Statement or word with two meanings, one of them rigid
5.	Proscribe	e.	Appease	5.	Equivocation	e.	Inequality
6.	Obviate	f.	Vague and misleading reply	6.	Ambiguity	f.	Equality
7.	Militate	g.	Slander	7.	Double entendre	g.	One's equal
8.	Malign	h.	Belittle	8.	Unequivocal	h.	Completely different
9.	Condone	i.	Make unnecessary	9.	Par	i.	Definitely positive or negative
10.	Placate	j.	Tickle; stimulate pleasurably	10.	Disparate	j.	Equal

PRACTICE TEST – 3				PRACTICE TEST – 4			
1.	Equity	a.	Time when night and day are of equal length	1.	Titillation	a.	Prohibition
2.	Inequity	b.	Balance of mind; composure	2.	Adulation	b.	Hatefulness; harmfulness, illness
3.	Iniquity	c.	Short-lived	3.	Proscription	c.	Clumsiness
4.	Equinox	d.	Torturous	4.	Militancy	d.	Quality of wishing evil, ill-will

5.	Nostalgia	e.	Sinfulness; wickedness	5.	Malignity	e.	Fact or act of making unnecessary or of doing away with
6.	Equanimity	f.	Unfairness, injustice	6.	Malediction	f.	Worship; excessive flattery
7.	Equilibrium	g.	Noisy, clamorous	7.	Maladroitness	g.	A wrongdoer
8.	Ephemeral	h.	Home sickness	8.	Obviation	h.	Pleasurable stimulation; tickling
9.	Vociferous	i.	Fairness, justice	9.	Malevolence	i.	A curse
10.	Excruciating	j.	Balance	10.	Malefactor	j.	Aggressiveness

PRACTICE TEST – 5				***PRACTICE TEST – 6***			
1.	Benign	a.	Free will	1.	Taciturn	a.	Chattering meaninglessly
2.	Benedictory	b.	Domineering, giving orders in a manner permitting no refusal	2.	Laconic	b.	Wordy
3.	Volition	c.	Not to be soothed or pacified; unyielding to pity or entreaty	3.	Inarticulate	c.	Trite, hackneyed, unoriginal
4.	Bona fide	d.	Tending to pacify or to change hostility to friendliness	4.	Garrulous	d.	Fluent and rapid
5.	Dictatorial	e.	Kindly, good-natured, not cancerous	5.	Banal	e.	Noisy, loud
6.	Placatory	f.	Faithfulness	6.	Verbose	f.	Spluttering unintelligibly
7.	Implacable	g.	Self-satisfied, smug	7.	Voluble	g.	Talkative
8.	Placid	h.	Of the nature of, or relating to, blessings	8.	Cogent	h.	Brilliantly compelling, persuasive
9.	Complacent	i.	In good faith, sincere, valid	9.	Vociferous	i.	Unwilling to engage in conversation
10.	Fidelity	j.	Calm, unruffled, undisturbed	10.	Loquacious	j.	brief

PRACTICE TEST – 7				***PRACTICE TEST – 8***			
1.	Taciturnity	a.	Fond of talking a lot	1.	Laconicity	a.	Floweriness, pompousness, or elegance in speech
2.	Tacitness	b.	Talking, or a speech, 'to oneself'	2.	Eloquence	b.	Incessant chatter with little meaning

PRACTICE TEST – 7				*PRACTICE TEST – 8*			
3.	Circumlocution	c.	Art of throwing one's voice	3.	Magniloquence	c.	Important or influential persons
4.	Loquacity	d.	Reticence	4.	Verbosity	d.	A gradual unfolding or development, a 'rolling out'
5.	Soliloquy	e.	Informal expression used in everyday conversation	5.	Volubility	e.	'a rolling round', radical change, political upheaval
6.	Ventriloquism	f.	State of being understood though not actually expressed	6.	Garrulity	f.	Great economy in speech
7.	Colloquialism	g.	Method of talking indirectly or in a roundabout way	7.	Magnate	g.	Fluency, ease, and/ or rapidity of speech
8.	Loquacious	h.	Talkativeness	8.	Revolution	h.	Great, artistic, or emotional expressiveness
9.	Reticence	i.	A person speaking to himself	9.	Evolution	i.	Wordiness
10.	Soliloquist	j.	Unwillingness to talk	10.	Cogency	j.	Persuasiveness through logic, keen-mindedness in reasoning

PRACTICE TEST – 9				*PRACTICE TEST – 10*			
1.	Vigorous	a.	Unable to fall asleep	1.	Notorious	a.	Beyond correction
2.	Dormant	b.	Pertaining to sleepwalking	2.	Consummate	b.	Continuing over a long period of time, recurring
3.	Somniferous	c.	Drowsy	3.	Incorrigible	c.	Diseased
4.	Insomnious	d.	Support, backing	4.	Inveterate	d.	From long-standing habit
5.	Somnolent	e.	Walk aimlessly	5.	Congenital	e.	Smooth
6.	Somnambulist	f.	Skilled	6.	Chronic	f.	Without conscience or scruples
7.	Endorsement	g.	Introduction	7.	Pathological	g.	Outstandingly bad or vicious
8.	Amble	h.	Energetic	8.	Unconscionable	h.	Unpopular

9.	Preamble	i.	Sleep-inducing	9.	Glib	i.	By birth
10.	Adroit	j.	Lying latent	10.	Egregious	j.	Finished, perfect, artistic

PRACTICE TEST – 11				*PRACTICE TEST – 12*			
1.	Notoriety	a.	State of artistic height	1.	Chronicity	a.	Out of place
2.	Consummate	b.	Beginning, origin	2.	Anachronism	b.	Timepiece, device that measures time very accurately
3.	Consummacy	c.	Science of heredity	3.	Incongruous	c.	Condition of continual or repeating the same time
4.	Incorrigibility	d.	Bring to completion	4.	Chronology	d.	Act of occurring, or of causing to occur, at the same time
5.	Genetics	e.	Study of ancestry	5.	Chronometer	e.	Calendar of events in order of occurrence
6.	Genealogy	f.	Referring to characteristics passed on to offspring by parents	6.	Apathy	f.	Something, or someone, out of time
7.	Genital	g.	Referring to the reproductive or sexual organs	7.	Synchronisation	g.	Lack of feeling
8.	Genesis	h.	Infamy	8.	Pathology	h.	To share or understand another's feelings
9.	Hereditary	i.	Particle that transmits hereditary characteristics	9.	Sympathise	i.	Communication from a distance
10.	Gene	j.	State of being beyond reform or correction	10.	Telepathy	j.	Disease, study of disease

PRACTICE TEST – 13				*PRACTICE TEST – 14*			
1.	Unconscionability	a.	Knowing nothing	1.	Habitual criminal	a.	Veteran
2.	Omniscience	b.	Outstanding badness	2.	Inducing sleep	b.	Introvert
3.	Prescience	c.	Religious group, a massing together	3.	Confined to himself	c.	Somnambulist
4.	Nescient	d.	Total, mass, whole	4.	Scientist of inheritance	d.	Pathologist

PRACTICE TEST – 13				*PRACTICE TEST – 14*			
5.	Glibness	e.	Exclusion from the herd, a setting apart	5.	Skilled old hand	e.	Soporific
6.	Egregiousness	f.	Infinite knowledge	6.	Studies family trees	f.	Recidivist
7.	Gregarious	g.	Friendly, fond of mixing with people	7.	Studies the cause of diseases	g.	Genealogist
8.	Congregation	h.	Lack of conscience	8.	Rides a horse	h.	Vocalist
9.	Segregation	i.	Suspiciously smooth fluency	9.	Sings a song	i.	Equestrian
10.	Aggregate	j.	Foreknowledge	10.	Walks in his sleep	j.	Geneticist

PRACTICE TEST – 15				*PRACTICE TEST – 16*			
1.	Catholic	a.	Equivocal	1.	Martinet	a.	Amateur
2.	Listless, lifeless	b.	Garrulous	2.	Sycophancy	b.	Patriotism
3.	Incapable of reform	c.	Consummate	3.	Dilettante	c.	Godlessness
4.	Saying two things at once	d.	Beneficent	4.	Impostor	d.	Single-mindedness
5.	Mindlessly talkative	e.	Apathetic	5.	Chauvinist	e.	Anti-tradition
6.	Noisy, clamorous	f.	Universal	6.	Monomaniac	f.	Lascivious
7.	Generous, forgiving	g.	Vociferous	7.	Iconoclast	g.	Grading
8.	Economical of speech	h.	Magnanimous	8.	Atheist	h.	Discipline
9.	Having the highest skill	i.	Incorrigible	9.	Lecher	i.	Charlatan
10.	Doing good	j.	Laconic	10.	Hierarchy	j.	Flattery

PRACTICE TEST – 17				*PRACTICE TEST – 18*			
1.	Stridency	a.	Fastly changing	1.	Dipsomania	a.	Women's society
2.	Patricide	b.	One's school or college	2.	Acrophobia	b.	Excessively fond of one's wife
3.	Matriarch	c.	The same in sound but not in spelling or meaning	3.	Uxorial	c.	Delusions of grandeur
4.	Chimerical	d.	Similar in meaning	4.	Kleptomania	d.	Insignia of rank or office
5.	Alma mater	e.	Force	5.	Incendiarism	e.	Characteristic of a wife
6.	Diaphanous	f.	Killing of one's father	6.	Megalomania	f.	Compulsive stealing

PRACTICE TEST – 17				PRACTICE TEST – 18			
7.	Synonyms	g.	Murder	7.	Uxorious	g.	Fear of enclosed spaces
8.	Antonyms	h.	Filmy, gauzy	8.	Regalia	h.	Alcoholism
9.	Homicide	i.	Mother-ruler	9.	Claustrophobia	i.	Fear of heights
10.	Homophones	j.	Opposite in meaning	10.	Sorority	j.	Maliciously starting fires

PRACTICE TEST – 19				PRACTICE TEST – 20			
1.	Hypotension	a.	Excessive fault-finding	1.	Convivial	a.	Frank
2.	Iconoclasm	b.	View that God is unknowable	2.	Indefatigable	b.	Unflinching
3.	Pantheism	c.	Study of religion	3.	Ingenuous	c.	Generous
4.	Hypochondria	d.	Belief that God is in nature	4.	Perspicacious	d.	Capable in many directions
5.	Agnosticism	e.	Ascertainment by examination or testing	5.	Magnanimous	e.	Tireless
6.	Hypercritical	f.	Morbid anxiety about health	6.	Versatile	f.	Fearless
7.	Diagnosis	g.	Denial of existence of God	7.	Stoical	g.	Keen-minded
8.	Theology	h.	A foretelling of future developments	8.	Intrepid	h.	Witty
9.	Prognosis	i.	Abnormality of low blood pressure	9.	Scintillating	i.	Friendly
10.	Atheism	j.	Contempt for tradition	10.	Urbane	j.	Polished, sophisticated

PRACTICE TEST – 21				PRACTICE TEST – 22			
1.	Conviviality	a.	Release of the egg	1.	Ingenious	a.	Easily tricked
2.	Vivacious	b.	One who lives lavishly	2.	Credulous	b.	Religious belief
3.	Devitalise	c.	Strong, sharp	3.	Gullible	c.	Inexperienced, unworldly
4.	Ovulation	d.	Egg-shaped	4.	Incredible	d.	Document proving identity
5.	Vitality	e.	Effervescence, joy of living	5.	Creed	e.	Unbelievable
6.	Joie de vivre	f.	Take life from	6.	Credentials	f.	Shrewdness, cleverness

PRACTICE TEST – 21				PRACTICE TEST – 22			
7.	Ennui	g.	High-spirited	7.	Ingenuity	g.	Clever, inventive, shrewd
8.	Bon vivant	h.	Boredom	8.	Naive	h.	Willing to believe
9.	Vivid	i.	Love of good company	9.		i.	
10.	Ovoid	j.	Strength, vigour	10.		j.	

PRACTICE TEST – 23				PRACTICE TEST – 24			
1.	Perspicacious	a.	Extremely careful, exact, or proper in procedure	1.	Magnanimity	a.	Calmness, composure
2.	Acumen	b.	Clear, easy to understand	2.	Urbanity	b.	Ability either to do many different things well, or to function successfully in many areas
3.	Specious	c.	A forward look	3.	Unanimity	c.	Fearlessness, great courage
4.	Punctilious	d.	Looking inside	4.	Equanimity	d.	Unemotionality, bearing of pain, etc. without complaint
5.	Pungent	e.	Keen-minded	5.	Animus	e.	Big-heartedness, generosity
6.	Perspicuous	f.	Sharp, spicy, piercing	6.	Versatility	f.	Sparkling with wit, cleverness
7.	Retrospect	g.	Wary, cautious, 'looking around'	7.	Stoicism	g.	Fear and trembling, alarm
8.	Prospect	h.	Sharpness of mind or thinking	8.	Intrepidity	h.	Complete agreement, all being of one mind
9.	Introspective	i.	A backward look	9.	Trepidation	i.	Sophistication, courtesy, etc.
10.	Circumspect	j.	Plausible but actually false	10.	Scintillation	j.	Hostility, hatred

PRACTICE TEST – 25				PRACTICE TEST – 26			
1.	A masterly musician	a.	Iconoclast	1.	Love of parties	a.	Creed
2.	Sneers at tradition	b.	Dilettante	2.	City sophistication	b.	Animus
3.	Fears being shut in	c.	Theologian	3.	Religious belief	c.	Urbanity
4.	Fatherly ruler	d.	Pyromaniac	4.	Sharp thinking	d.	Patriotism
5.	A dabbler	e.	Virtuoso	5.	Hostility	e.	Patronymic
6.	Studies religion	f.	Claustrophobe	6.	Marriage	f.	Credo

7.	A beginner	g.	Tyro	7.	Named after the father	g.	Conviviality
8.	Has imaginary ailments	h.	Monotheist	8.	Pride in one's country	h.	Diagnosis
9.	Compulsively starts fires	i.	Hypochondriac	9.	Personal code of ethics	i.	Matrimony
10.	Believes in one God	j.	Patriarch	10.	Identifying a disease	j.	Acuity

PRACTICE TEST – 27				*PRACTICE TEST – 28*			
1.	Egoist	a.	Turns thoughts inwards	1.	Ego	a.	One who is excessively fixated on his own desires, needs, etc.
2.	Egotist	b.	Hates foreigners	2.	Egocentric	b.	To change
3.	Altruist	c.	Talks about accomplishments	3.	Altruism	c.	Argument
4.	Introvert	d.	Hates people	4.	Alter ego	d.	One's concept of oneself
5.	Extrovert	e.	Does not pursue pleasures of the flesh	5.	To alternate	e.	To take one, skip one, etc.
6.	Ambivert	f.	Is interested in the welfare of others	6.	Egomaniacal	f.	Philosophy of putting another's welfare above one's own
7.	Misanthrope	g.	Believes in self-advancement	7.	To alter	g.	One who talks about himself
8.	Misogynist	h.	Turns thoughts both inwards and outwards	8.	Altercation	h.	A choice
9.	Xenophobe	i.	Hates women	9.	Alternative	i.	Morbidly obsessed with oneself
10.	Ascetic	j.	Turns thoughts outwards	10.	Egotist	j.	One's other self

PRACTICE TEST – 29				*PRACTICE TEST – 30*			
1.	Anthropology	a.	System of only one marriage	1.	Obsequious	a.	Snobbish
2.	Gynaecology	b.	Ability to use either hand	2.	Querulous	b.	Harmless
3.	Monogamy	c.	Clumsiness in social situations	3.	Supercilious	c.	Gaunt
4.	Xenophobia	d.	Study of humanity	4.	Obstreperous	d.	Short of funds
5.	Gaucherie	e.	Study of women's ailments	5.	Impecunious	e.	Ingratiatingly polite
6.	Introvert	f.	Devotion to a lonely and austere life	6.	Chivalrous	f.	Sorrowful

7.	Asceticism	g.	Skill, cleverness	7.	Innocuous	g.	Addicted to drink
8.	Philanthropy	h.	A person whose thoughts turn inwards	8.	Bibulous	h.	Courteous to women
9.	Adroitness	i.	Love of mankind	9.	Cadaverous	i.	Complaining
10.	Ambidexterity	j.	Hatred of foreigners	10.	Dolorous	j.	Unmanageable

PRACTICE TEST – 31				*PRACTICE TEST – 32*			
1.	Obsequies	a.	Proper order	1.	Penury	a.	Always honest
2.	Sequence	b.	Corpse	2.	Vicarious	b.	Talkative
3.	Pecuniary	c.	Procession of mounted riders	3.	Fluent	c.	Homesickness
4.	Noxious	d.	Pertaining to money	4.	Euphemism	d.	Meat-eating
5.	Doleful	e.	Funeral rites	5.	Veracious	e.	Circumlocution
6.	Cavalcade	f.	Exaggeratedly sorrowful	6.	Bovine	f.	Harsh noise
7.	Equine	g.	Horselike	7.	Nostalgia	g.	Poverty
8.	Cadaver	h.	Spiritual or artistic decline	8.	Cacophony	h.	Secret
9.	Decadence	i.	Poisonous, harmful	9.	Carnivorous	i.	Placid, stolid, cow-like
10.	Condolence	j.	Expression of sympathy	10.	Clandestine	j.	Experienced by watching or reading about somebody else doing something

PRACTICE TEST – 33				*PRACTICE TEST – 34*			
1.	Fluent	a.	Mental well-being	1.	Canine	a.	Found everywhere
2.	Destitute	b.	Smooth-talking	2.	Feline	b.	Greedy, devouring
3.	Opulent	c.	Truthful	3.	Voracious	c.	All-powerful
4.	Vicarious	d.	Hackneyed phrase	4.	Omnipotent	d.	Stealthy, clandestine
5.	Euphonic	e.	Ostentatiously wealthy	5.	Omniscient	e.	All-knowing
6.	Veracious	f.	Likeness to the truth	6.	Surreptitious	f.	Cat-like
7.	Euphoria	g.	Pleasant-sounding	7.	Nostalgic	g.	Harsh-sounding
8.	Eulogise	h.	In want	8.	Cacophonous	h.	Eating everything
9.	Verisimilitude	i.	Second-hand	9.	Omnivorous	i.	Dog-like
10.	Cliché	j.	Praise	10.	Ubiquitous	j.	Homesick

PRACTICE TEST – 35				PRACTICE TEST – 36			
1.	Vicarious	a.	Excessively polite or servile	1.	Condolence	a.	Outgoing personality
2.	Cavalier	b.	Gaunt, corpse-like	2.	Decadent	b.	Harsh sound
3.	Egocentric	c.	Noisy, boisterous	3.	Altruistic	c.	Having many wives
4.	Obsequious	d.	Wealthy	4.	Extrovert	d.	A return to life in a new form
5.	Querulous	e.	High-handed	5.	Surreptitious	e.	Eating everything
6.	Obstreperous	f.	Sad	6.	Cacophony	f.	Expression of sympathy
7.	Innocuous	g.	Nagging, complaining	7.	Reincarnation	g.	Cowlike, phlegmatic, stolid
8.	Cadaverous	h.	Harmless	8.	Omnivorous	h.	Morally deteriorating
9.	Dolorous	i.	Second-hand	9.	Polygamous	i.	Unselfish
10.	Opulent	j.	Self-centred	10.	Bovine	j.	Stealthy, secret

PRACTICE TEST – 37				PRACTICE TEST – 38			
1.	Mental or emotional disturbances	a.	Gynaecologist	1.	Gynaecology	a.	Rhinoceros
2.	Nervous system	b.	Obstetrician	2.	Obstetrics	b.	Stuffing of skins of animals
3.	Skin	c.	Paediatrician	3.	Paediatrics	c.	Speciality dealing with delivering babies
4.	Infants	d.	Dermatologist	4.	Pedagogue	d.	Stirring up discontent among the masses
5.	Female reproductive organs	e.	Ophthalmologist	5.	Demagoguery	e.	One who measures eyesight
6.	Eyes	f.	Orthopaedist	6.	Dermatology	f.	Speciality in dealing with the female reproductive system
7.	Heart	g.	Cardiologist	7.	Taxidermy	g.	Speciality in dealing with the treatment of children
8.	Blood	h.	Neurologist	8.	Pachyderm	h.	Treatment of skin diseases
9.	Pregnancy, childbirth	i.	Haematologist	9.	Ophthalmologist	i.	Eye doctor
10.	Skeletal system	j.	Psychiatrist	10.	Optometrist	j.	Teacher

PRACTICE TEST – 39				PRACTICE TEST – 40			
1.	Orthopaedics	a.	Record of heart beats	1.	Chiropodist	a.	Designer of buildings and interiors
2.	Orthodontics	b.	Speciality dealing with medical problems of the elderly	2.	Architect	b.	Risk calculator
3.	Neuralgia	c.	Treatment of personality disorders	3.	Actuary	c.	Manipulator of bones
4.	Neuritis	d.	Nerve pain	4.	Radiographer	d.	Drug dispenser
5.	Geriatrics	e.	Treatment of bone problems	5.	Psychologist	e.	Exercise healer
6.	Cardiogram	f.	Inflammation of the nerves	6.	Pharmacist	f.	Assessor of buildings
7.	Cardiograph	g.	Mental unbalance	7.	Surveyor	g.	Financial expert
8.	Neurosis	h.	Emotional disturbance	8.	Osteopath	h.	X-ray expert
9.	Psychosis	i.	Straightening of teeth	9.	Physiotherapist	i.	One who studies human behaviour
10.	Psychiatry	j.	Instrument for recording heartbeats	10.	Economist	j.	Foot healer

PRACTICE TEST – 41				PRACTICE TEST – 42			
1.	Psychology	a.	Mental or emotional disturbance	1.	Podium	a.	Drugs workshop
2.	Psyche	b.	Psychological treatment based on Freudian techniques	2.	Osteopathy	b.	Ballet design
3.	Psychic	c.	General term for non-technical psychological treatment	3.	Pharmacy	c.	Chart of heart function
4.	Psychopathy	d.	Originating in the mind or emotions	4.	Chiropody	d.	Egg-laying water mammal
5.	Psychosomatic	e.	Medical treatment of mental symptoms, e.g. with drugs	5.	Platypus	e.	Treatment of feet
6.	Psychoanalysis	f.	One's inner or mental life, or self-image	6.	Pharmacology	f.	Exercises in water
7.	Psychogenic	g.	Study of the human mind and behaviour	7.	Cardiograph	g.	Speaker's platform

8.	Psychotherapy	h.	Describing the interaction of mind and body	8.	Choreography	h.	Person who makes up drugs
9.	Psychopath	i.	Pertaining to the mind, extrasensory	9.	Hydrotherapy	i.	The science of drug action
10.	Psychiatry	j.	Person lacking in social conscience or inner censor	10.	Apothecary	j.	Treatment by manipulation of bones

PRACTICE TEST – 43				*PRACTICE TEST – 44*			
1.	Purveyor	a.	Fireworks	1.	Physics	a.	The science of the plant kingdom
2.	Barometer	b.	Accurate timepiece	2.	Archaeology	b.	The science of humanity's past
3.	Pyrotechnics	c.	Person who calculates risks	3.	Astronomy	c.	The science of stars and planets
4.	Visionary	d.	Political agitator	4.	Mathematics	d.	The science of all living creatures
5.	Econometrics	e.	An idealist	5.	Botany	e.	The science of insects
6.	Ecology	f.	Someone who sells provisions	6.	Entomology	f.	The science of the basis of material world
7.	Supervisor	g.	Pressure gauge	7.	Geology	g.	The science of the atmosphere and weather
8.	Actuary	h.	Foreman	8.	Biology	h.	The science of number, shape, space
9.	Chronometer	i.	Study of financial statistics	9.	Meteorology	i.	The science of the animal kingdom
10.	Activist	j.	Study of plants and animals in their environment	10.	Zoology	j.	The science of the Earth

PRACTICE TEST – 45				*PRACTICE TEST – 46*			
1.	Astronaut	a.	Studies volcanoes	1.	Zodiac	a.	The study of fungi
2.	Cartographer	b.	Foretells happenings by the stars	2.	Palaeography	b.	The study of word origins
3.	Seismologist	c.	'Sailor of the universe'	3.	Mycology	c.	The science of very small creatures
4.	Arithmetician	d.	Manipulates numbers	4.	Biotechnology	d.	The study of the body's workings
5.	Astrophysicist	e.	Studies the universe	5.	Appendectomy	e.	The science of fossils
6.	Volcanologist	f.	Foretells the weather	6.	Microbiology	f.	Removal of the appendix

PRACTICE TEST – 45				*PRACTICE TEST – 46*			
7.	Cosmologist	g.	Studies earthquakes	7.	Physiology	g.	The study of living things in their environment
8.	Meteorologist	h.	Studies the nature of the stars	8.	Palaeontology	h.	An astrological diagram
9.	Cosmonaut	i.	Draws maps	9.	Ecology	i.	The use of bacteria in industry
10.	Astrologer	j.	'Sailor of the stars'	10.	Etymology	j.	The study of old handwriting

PRACTICE TEST – 47				*PRACTICE TEST – 48*			
1.	Studies volcanoes	a.	Actuary	1.	Delivers babies	a.	Paediatrician
2.	Draws maps	b.	Astrologer	2.	Treats women's ailments	b.	Cardiologist
3.	Calculates risks	c.	Entomologist	3.	Treats infants and children	c.	Psychiatrist
4.	Studies drug action	d.	Cartographer	4.	Treats skin diseases	d.	Chiropodist
5.	Designs buildings	e.	Cosmologist	5.	Treats skeletal problems	e.	Dermatologist
6.	Studies the universe	f.	Pharmacologist	6.	Is a heart specialist	f.	Haematologist
7.	Studies word origins	g.	Etymologist	7.	Treats mental or emotional disturbances	g.	Obstetrician
8.	Works with X-rays	h.	Volcanologist	8.	Treats disorders of the nervous system	h.	Neurologist
9.	Uses a zodiac	i.	Architect	9.	Treats minor ailments of the feet	i.	Orthopaedist
10.	Studies insects	j.	Radiographer	10.	Treats disorders of the blood	j.	Gynaecologist

ANSWERS – CHECK YOUR WORD POWER – PRACTICE TESTS

PRACTICE TEST – 1			PRACTICE TEST – 2		
1.	h	belittle	1.	f	Equality
2.	f	vague and misleading reply or act	2.	e	Inequality
3.	j	Tickle, stimulate pleasurably	3.	a	Belittlement
4.	a	Flatter lavishly	4.	g	One's equal
5.	c	Prohibit	5.	b	Act of being deliberately vague or indirectly deceptive
6.	i	Make unnecessary	6.	c	Quality of being open to misinterpretation
7.	b	Work against	7.	d	Statement or word with two meanings, one of them rigid
8.	g	Slander	8.	i	Definitely positive or negative, clearly
9.	d	Forgive	9.	j	Equal
10.	e	Appease	10.	h	Completely different

PRACTICE TEST – 3			PRACTICE TEST – 4		
1.	i	Fairness, justice	1.	h	Pleasurable stimulation, tickling
2.	f	Unfairness, injustice	2.	f	Excessive flattery
3.	e	Sinfulness, wickedness	3.	a	Prohibition
4.	a	Time when night and day are of equal length	4.	j	Aggressiveness
5.	h	Home sickness	5.	b	Hatefulness, harmfulness
6.	b	Balance of mind, composure	6.	i	A curse
7.	j	Balance	7.	c	Clumsiness
8.	c	Short lived	8.	e	Fact or act of making unnecessary or of doing away with
9.	g	Noisy, clamorous	9.	d	Quality of wishing evil, ill-will
10.	d	Torturous	10.	g	A wrongdoer

PRACTICE TEST – 5			PRACTICE TEST – 6		
1.	e	Kindly, good-natured, not cancerous	1.	i	Reserved
2.	h	Of the nature of, or relating to, blessings	2.	j	Brief
3.	a	Free will	3.	f	Spluttering unintelligibly
4.	i	In good faith, sincere, valid	4.	a	Chattering meaninglessly
5.	b	Domineering, giving orders in a manner permitting no refusal	5.	c	Trite, hackneyed, unoriginal
6.	d	Tending to pacify or to change hostility to friendliness	6.	b	Wordy

7.	c Not to be soothed or pacified, unyielding to pity or entreaty	7.	d Fluent and rapid
8.	j Calm, unruffled, undisturbed	8.	h Brilliantly compelling, persuasive
9.	g Self-satisfied, smug	9.	e Noisy, loud
10.	f Faithfulness	10.	g Talkative

PRACTICE TEST – 7		*PRACTICE TEST – 8*	
1.	d Reticence	1.	f Great economy of words
2.	f State of being understood though not actually expressed	2.	h Great, artistic, or emotional expressiveness
3.	g Method of talking indirectly or in a roundabout way	3.	a Floweriness, pompousness, or elegance in speech
4.	h Talkativeness	4.	i Wordiness
5.	b Talking, or a speech, 'to oneself'	5.	g Fluency, ease, and/ or rapidity of speech
6.	c Art of throwing one's voice	6.	b Incessant chatter with little meaning
7.	e Informal expression used in everyday conversation	7.	c Important or influential person
8.	a Fond of talking a lot	8.	e 'a rolling round', radical change, political upheaval
9.	j Unwillingness to talk	9.	d A gradual unfolding or development, a 'rolling out'
10.	i A person speaking to himself	10.	j Persuasiveness through logic, keen-mindedness in reasoning

PRACTICE TEST – 9		*PRACTICE TEST – 10*	
1.	h Energetic	1.	h Unpopular
2.	j Lying latent	2.	j Finished, perfect, artistic
3.	i Sleep-inducing	3.	a Beyond correction
4.	a Unable to fall asleep	4.	d From long-standing habit
5.	c Drowsy	5.	i By birth
6.	b Pertaining to sleepwalking	6.	b Continuing over a long period of time, recurring
7.	d Support, backing	7.	c Diseased
8.	e Walk aimlessly	8.	f Without conscience or scruples
9.	g Introduction	9.	e Smooth
10.	f Skilled	10.	g Outstandingly bad or vicious

PRACTICE TEST – 11		PRACTICE TEST – 12	
1.	h Infamy	1.	c Condition of continual or repeating the same time
2.	d Bring to completion	2.	f Something, or someone, out of time
3.	a State of artistic height	3.	a Out of place
4.	j State of being beyond reform or correction	4.	e Calendar of events in order of occurrence
5.	c Science of heredity	5.	b Timepiece, device that measures time very accurately
6.	e Study of ancestry	6.	g Lack of feeling
7.	g Referring to the reproductive or sexual organs	7.	d Act of occurring, or of causing to occur, at the same time
8.	b Beginning, origin	8.	j Disease, study of disease
9.	f Referring to characteristics passed on to offspring by parents	9.	h To share or understand another's feelings
10.	i Particle that transmits hereditary characteristics	10.	i Communication from a distance

PRACTICE TEST – 13		PRACTICE TEST – 14	
1.	h Lack of conscience	1.	f Recidivist
2.	f Infinite knowledge	2.	e Soporific
3.	j Foreknowledge	3.	b Introvert
4.	a Knowing nothing	4.	j Geneticist
5.	i Suspiciously smooth fluency	5.	a Veteran
6.	b Outstanding badness	6.	g Genealogist
7.	g Friendly, fond of mixing with people	7.	d Pathologist
8.	c Religious group, a massing together	8.	i Equestrian
9.	e Exclusion from the herd, a setting apart	9.	h Vocalist
10.	d Total, mass, whole	10.	c Somnambulist

PRACTICE TEST – 15		PRACTICE TEST – 16	
1.	f Universal	1.	h Discipline
2.	e Apathetic	2.	j Flattery
3.	i Incorrigible	3.	a Amateur
4.	a Equivocal	4.	i Charlatan
5.	b Garrulous	5.	b Patriotism
6.	g Vociferous	6.	d Single-mindedness
7.	h Magnanimous	7.	e Anti-tradition

8.	j Laconic	8.	c Godlessness
9.	c Consummate	9.	f Lascivious
10.	d Beneficent	10.	g Grading

PRACTICE TEST – 17		*PRACTICE TEST – 18*	
1.	e Force	1.	h Alcoholism
2.	f Killing of one's father	2.	i Fear of heights
3.	i Mother-ruler	3.	e Characteristic of a wife
4.	a Fastly changing	4.	f Compulsive stealing
5.	b One's school or college	5.	j Maliciously starting fires
6.	h Filmy, gauzy	6.	c Delusions of grandeur
7.	d Similar in meaning	7.	b Excessively fond of one's wife
8.	j Opposite in meaning	8.	d Insignia of rank or office
9.	g Murder	9.	g Fear of enclosed spaces
10.	c The same in sound but not in spelling or meaning	10.	a Women's society

PRACTICE TEST – 19		*PRACTICE TEST – 20*	
1.	i Abnormality of low blood pressure	1.	i Friendly
2.	j Contempt for tradition	2.	e Tireless
3.	d Belief that God is in nature	3.	a Frank
4.	f Morbid anxiety about health	4.	g Keen-minded
5.	b View that God is unknowable	5.	c Generous
6.	a Excessive fault-finding	6.	d Capable in many directions
7.	e Ascertainment by examination or testing	7.	b Unflinching
8.	c Study of religion	8.	f Fearless
9.	h A foretelling of future developments	9.	h Witty
10.	g Denial of existence of God	10.	j Polished, sophisticated

PRACTICE TEST – 21		*PRACTICE TEST – 22*	
1.	i Love of good company	1.	g Clever, inventive, shrewd
2.	g High-spirited	2.	h Willing to believe
3.	f Take life from	3.	a Easily tricked
4.	a Release of the egg	4.	e Unbelievable
5.	j Strength, vigour	5.	b Religious belief
6.	e Effervescence, joy of living	6.	d Document proving identity
7.	h Boredom	7.	f Shrewdness, cleverness
8.	b One who lives lavishly	8.	c Inexperienced, unworldly

9.	c Strong, sharp	9.	
10.	d Egg-shaped	10.	

PRACTICE TEST – 23		PRACTICE TEST – 24	
1.	e Keen-minded	1.	e Big-heartedness, generosity
2.	h Sharpness of mind or thinking	2.	i Sophistication, courtesy, etc.
3.	j Plausible but actually false	3.	h Complete agreement, all being of one mind
4.	a Extremely careful, exact, or proper in procedure	4.	a Calmness, composure
5.	f Sharp, spicy, piercing	5.	j Hostility, hatred
6.	b Clear, easy to understand	6.	b Ability either to do many different things well, or to function successfully in many areas
7.	i A backward look	7.	d Unemotionality, bearing of pain, etc., without complaint
8.	c A forward look	8.	c Fearlessness, great courage
9.	d Looking inside	9.	g Fear and trembling, alarm
10.	g Wary, cautious, 'looking around'	10.	f Sparkling with wit, cleverness

PRACTICE TEST – 25		PRACTICE TEST – 26	
1.	e Virtuoso	1.	g Conviviality
2.	a Iconoclast	2.	c Urbanity
3.	f Claustrophobe	3.	a Creed
4.	j Patriarch	4.	j Acuity
5.	b Dilettante	5.	b Animus
6.	c Theologian	6.	i Matrimony
7.	g Tyro	7.	e Patronymic
8.	i Hypochondriac	8.	d Patriotism
9.	d Pyromaniac	9.	f Credo
10.	h Monotheist	10.	h Diagnosis

PRACTICE TEST – 27		PRACTICE TEST – 28	
1.	g Believes in self-advancement	1.	d One's concept of oneself
2.	c Talks about accomplishments	2.	a One who is excessively fixated on his own desires, needs, etc.
3.	f Is interested in the welfare of others	3.	f Philosophy of putting another's welfare above one's own
4.	a Turns thoughts inwards	4.	j One's other self
5.	j Turns thoughts outwards	5.	e To take one, skip one, etc.

6.	h Turns thoughts both inwards and outwards	6.	i Morbidly obsessed with oneself
7.	d Hates people	7.	b To change
8.	i Hates women	8.	c Argument
9.	b Hates foreigners	9.	h A choice
10.	e Does not pursue pleasures of the flesh	10.	g One who talks about himself

PRACTICE TEST – 29		*PRACTICE TEST – 30*	
1.	d Study of humanity	1.	e Ingratiatingly polite
2.	e Study of women's ailments	2.	i Complaining
3.	a System of only one marriage	3.	a Snobbish
4.	j Hatred of foreigners	4.	j Unmanageable
5.	c Clumsiness in social situations	5.	d Short of funds
6.	h A person whose thoughts turn inwards	6.	h Courteous to women
7.	f Devotion to a lonely and austere life	7.	b Harmless
8.	i Love of mankind	8.	g Addicted to drink
9.	g Skill, cleverness	9.	c Gaunt
10.	b Ability to use either hand	10.	f Sorrowful

PRACTICE TEST – 31		*PRACTICE TEST – 32*	
1.	e Funeral rites	1.	g Poverty
2.	a Proper order	2.	j Experienced by watching or reading about somebody else doing something
3.	d- Pertaining to money	3.	b Talkative
4.	i Poisonous, harmful	4.	e Circumlocution
5.	f Exaggeratedly sorrowful	5.	A Always honest
6.	c Procession of mounted riders	6.	i Placid, stolid, cow-like
7.	g Horselike	7.	c Homesickness
8.	b Corpse	8.	f Harsh noise
9.	h Spiritual or artistic decline	9.	d Meat-eating
10.	j Expression of sympathy	10.	h Secret

PRACTICE TEST – 33		*PRACTICE TEST – 34*	
1.	b Smooth-talking	1.	i Dog-like
2.	h In want	2.	f Cat-like
3.	e Ostentatiously wealthy	3.	b Greedy, devouring
4.	i Second-hand	4.	c All-powerful
5.	g Pleasant-sounding	5.	e All-knowing
6.	c Truthful	6.	d Stealthy, clandestine

7.	a Mental well-being	7.	j Homesick
8.	j Praise	8.	g Harsh-sounding
9.	f Likeness to the truth	9.	h Eating everything
10.	d Hackneyed phrase	10.	a Found everywhere

PRACTICE TEST – 35		*PRACTICE TEST – 36*	
1.	i Second-hand	1.	f Expression of sympathy
2.	e High-handed	2.	h Morally deteriorating
3.	j Self-centred	3.	i Unselfish
4.	a Excessively polite or servile	4.	a Outgoing personality
5.	g Nagging, complaining	5.	j Stealthy, secret
6.	c Noisy, boisterous	6.	b Harsh sound
7.	h Harmless	7.	d A return to life in a new form
8.	b Gaunt, corpse-like	8.	e Eating everything
9.	f Sad	9.	c Having many wives
10.	d Wealthy	10.	g Cowlike, phlegmatic, stolid

PRACTICE TEST – 37		*PRACTICE TEST – 38*	
1.	j Psychiatrist	1.	f Speciality dealing with the female reproductive system
2.	h Neurologist	2.	c Speciality dealing with delivering babies
3.	d Dermatologist	3.	g Speciality dealing with the treatment of children
4.	c Paediatrician	4.	j Teacher
5.	a Gynaecologist	5.	d Stirring up discontent among the masses
6.	e Ophthalmologist	6.	h Treatment of skin diseases
7.	g Cardiologist	7.	b Stuffing of skins of animals
8.	i Haematologist	8.	a Rhinoceros
9.	b Obstetrician	9.	i Eye doctor
10.	f Orthopaedist	10.	e One who measures eyesight

PRACTICE TEST – 39		*PRACTICE TEST – 40*	
1.	e Treatment of bone problems	1.	j Foot healer
2.	i Straightening of teeth	2.	a Designer of buildings and interiors
3.	d Nerve pain	3.	b Risk calculator
4.	f Inflammation of the nerves	4.	h X-ray expert
5.	b Speciality dealing with medical problems of the elderly	5.	i One who studies human behaviour
6.	a Record of heart beats	6.	d Drug dispenser
7.	j Instrument for recording heartbeats	7.	f Assessor of buildings

8.	h Emotional disturbance	8.	c Manipulator of bones
9.	g Mental unbalance	9.	e Exercise healer
10.	c Treatment of personality disorders	10.	g Financial expert

PRACTICE TEST – 41		*PRACTICE TEST – 42*	
1.	g Study of the human mind and behaviour	1.	g Speaker's platform
2.	f One's inner or mental life, or self-image	2.	j Treatment by manipulation of bones
3.	i Pertaining to the mind, extrasensory	3.	a Drugs workshop
4.	a Mental or emotional disturbance	4.	e Treatment of feet
5.	h Describing the interaction of mind and body	5.	d Egg-laying water mammal
6.	b Psychological treatment based on Freudian techniques	6.	i The science of drug action
7.	d Originating in the mind or emotions	7.	c Chart of heart function
8.	c General term for non-technical psychological treatment	8.	b Ballet design
9.	j Person lacking in social conscience or inner censor	9.	f Exercises in water
10.	e Medical treatment of mental symptoms, e.g. with drugs	10.	h Person who makes up drugs

PRACTICE TEST – 43		*PRACTICE TEST – 44*	
1.	f Someone who sells provisions	1.	f The science of the basis of material world
2.	g Pressure gauge	2.	b The science of humanity's past
3.	a Fireworks	3.	c The science of stars and planets
4.	e An idealist	4.	h The science of number, shape, space
5.	i Study of financial statistics	5.	a The science of the plant kingdom
6.	j Study of plants and animals in their environment	6.	e The science of insects
7.	h Foreman	7.	j The science of the Earth
8.	c Person who calculates risks	8.	d The science of all living creatures
9.	b Accurate timepiece	9.	g The science of the atmosphere and weather
10.	d Political agitator	10.	i The science of the animal kingdom

PRACTICE TEST – 45		*PRACTICE TEST – 46*	
1.	j 'Sailor of the stars'	1.	h An astrological diagram
2.	i Draws maps	2.	j The study of old handwriting
3.	g Studies earthquakes	3.	a The study of fungi
4.	d Manipulates numbers	4.	i The use of bacteria in industry
5.	h Studies the nature of the stars	5.	f Removal of the appendix

6.	a Studies volcanoes	6.	c The science of very small creatures
7.	e Studies the universe	7.	d The study of the body's workings
8.	f Foretells the weather	8.	e The science of fossils
9.	c 'Sailor of the universe'	9.	g The study of living things in their environment
10.	b Foretells happenings by the stars	10.	b The study of word origins

PRACTICE TEST – 47		PRACTICE TEST – 48	
1.	h Volcanologist	1.	g Obstetrician
2.	d Cartographer	2.	j Gynaecologist
3.	a Actuary	3.	a Paediatrician
4.	f Pharmacologist	4.	e Dermatologist
5.	i Architect	5.	i Orthopaedist
6.	e Cosmologist	6.	b Cardiologist
7.	g Etymologist	7.	c Psychiatrist
8.	j Radiographer	8.	h Neurologist
9.	b Astrologer	9.	d Chiropodist
10.	c Entomologist	10.	f Haematologist

3 SYNONYMS AND ANTONYMS

Synonym is a word with the same meaning or nearly the same meaning in the same language. It has often different implications and associations.

The meanings of synonymous words are not exactly the same. Take for example, *smell* and *stink*; *steal* and *rob*. A *smell* can be good or bad but a *stink* is always a bad or foul smell; as –

How sweet is the *smell* of the roses!

I can't stand the *stink* of burning rubber.

One *steals* things but *robs* people (of things); as – He has *stolen* my watch.

He has *robbed* me of all my belongings.

The English language abounds in synonymous words, delicately differentiated to make possible the expression of all shades of human thought.

Here is a list of synonyms with antonyms of some of the head-words:

A		
1	**Abandon**	leave, forsake, resign, relinquish (***Ant.*** retain)
2	**Abase**	humiliate, humble, disgrace (***Ant.*** exalt, honour, uplift)
3	**Abash**	confound, confuse, shame (***Ant.*** encourage)
4	**Abate**	subside, lessen, diminish, decline, reduce (***Ant.*** raise, rise, increase)
5	**Abbreviate**	shorten, condense, reduce (***Ant.*** expand, lengthen)
6	**Abet**	assist, encourage, help (***Ant.*** hinder, discourage)
7	**Abhor**	detest, hate, loathe (***Ant.*** like, approve)
8	**Abject**	mean, degraded, servile (***Ant.*** proud, independent)
9	**Abjure**	repudiate, disclaim, disavow (***Ant.*** claim, accept)
10	**Aboriginal**	indigenous, native (***Ant.*** immigrant)
11	**Abortive**	fruitless, futile, unsuccessful (***Ant.*** effective, successful)
12	**Abscond**	bolt, decamp, run off (***Ant.*** stay)
13	**Abstruse**	obscure, hidden, deep, profound (***Ant.*** open, simple)
14	**Accelerate**	hasten, quicken, expedite (***Ant.*** retard)
15	**Acclivity**	incline, ascent (***Ant.*** declivity)
16	**Accoutrement(s), Accoutrement**	dress, outfit, equipment
17	**Accredited**	authorised, entrusted (***Ant.*** unauthorised)
18	**Acerbity**	acrimony, bitterness, harshness (***Ant.*** sweetness, mildness)
19	**Actuate**	impel, instigate (***Ant.*** stop, arrest)

20	**Addicted**	devoted, accustomed to (***Ant.*** free)
21	**Adjacent**	near, contiguous, close to (***Ant.*** distant)
22	**Adjourn**	defer, delay, postpone (***Ant.*** advance)
23	**Admonish**	chide, rebuke, warn (***Ant.*** praise, commend)
24	**Adroit**	clever, skilful, expert (***Ant.*** unskilled)
25	**Adversity**	misfortune, hardship, calamity (***Ant.*** prosperity)
26	**Affable**	polite, courteous, civil, accessible (***Ant.*** impolite, uncivil)
27	**Affliction**	trouble, distress, grief, sorrow (***Ant.*** comfort, ease)
28	**Affluence**	opulence, wealth, riches (***Ant.*** poverty)
29	**Affright**	alarm, confound, terrify, intimidate (***Ant.*** encourage)
30	**Aggravate**	intensify, heighten (***Ant.*** lighten)
31	**Alacrity**	alertness, readiness, promptitude, activity (***Ant.*** inactivity)
32	**Alienate**	transfer, estrange (***Ant.*** reconcile)
33	**Allay**	soothe, calm, alleviate, assuage (***Ant.*** excite)
34	**Allure**	attract, entice, ensnare (***Ant.*** repel)
35	**Altercation**	wrangle, quarrel, dispute (***Ant.*** agreement)
36	**Ambiguous**	doubtful, uncertain, equivocal (***Ant.*** obvious, clear)
37	**Ameliorate**	improve, amend, make better (***Ant.*** worsen)
38	**Amenable**	responsive, responsible, accountable (***Ant.*** surly)
39	**Amiable**	charming, lovable, winning (***Ant.*** unlovable)
40	**Amicable**	friendly, sociable, cordial (***Ant.*** unfriendly)
41	**Anguish**	agony, pain, suffering (***Ant.*** ease, comfort)
42	**Annex**	add, join, append (***Ant.*** detach)
43	**Annihilate**	destroy, ruin, annul (***Ant.*** preserve)
44	**Annul**	abrogate, cancel, quash, rescind (***Ant.*** ratify, confirm)
45	**Appease**	pacify, quiet, assuage, soothe (***Ant.*** provoke)
46	**Appraise**	estimate, price
47	**Apprise**	acquaint, inform, notify
48	**Approbation**	authority, praise, approval, sanction (***Ant.*** disapproval)
49	**Arduous**	laborious, difficult, trying (***Ant.*** easy)
50	**Arrogant**	haughty, imperious, overbearing (***Ant.*** humble)
51	**Aspiration**	longing, ambition, yearning (***Ant.*** apathy)
52	**Assail**	assault, attack, invade (***Ant.*** defend)
53	**Astute**	crafty, cunning, sharp (***Ant.*** stupid)
54	**Atrocious**	heinous, monstrous, flagrant (***Ant.*** decent)
55	**Attire**	dress, garment, apparel (***Ant.*** nakedness)
56	**Audacious**	impudent, bold, daring (***Ant.*** timid)
57	**Augment**	extend, enlarge, increase (***Ant.*** lessen)

58	**August**	dignified, stately, imposing, majestic (***Ant.*** humble, lowly)
59	**Auspicious**	fortunate, lucky, propitious (***Ant.*** inauspicious)
60	**Austere**	severe, rigorous, stern (***Ant.*** mild)
61	**Authentic**	trustworthy, true, genuine (***Ant.*** spurious)
		B
62	**Baleful**	hurtful, injurious, noxious (***Ant.*** harmless)
63	**Barbarous**	savage, wild, rude (***Ant.*** civilised)
64	**Beguile**	cheat, deceive, amuse, divert
65	**Behest**	order, command, charge
66	**Benevolent**	charitable, benign (***Ant.*** malevolent)
67	**Beseech**	beg, pray, entreat (***Ant.*** command, give)
68	**Bitter**	sharp, severe, acrid, harsh (***Ant.*** sweet)
69	**Bland**	gentle, mild, courteous (***Ant.*** discourteous)
70	**Blasphemy**	impiety, profanity (***Ant.*** reverence)
71	**Bleak**	cold, chilly, bare (***Ant.*** sunny, warm, lush)
72	**Bliss**	rapture, felicity, delight (***Ant.*** unhappiness)
73	**Blithe**	happy, merry, joyous (***Ant.*** sad, sorrowful)
74	**Boisterous**	clamorous, noisy, rowdy (***Ant.*** quiet)
75	**Bondage**	servitude, subjection (***Ant.*** liberty)
76	**Boorish**	rude, rustic, uncivilised (***Ant.*** civilised)
77	**Brawl**	altercation, fight, squabble (***Ant.*** harmony)
78	**Brittle**	fragile, breakable (***Ant.*** Unbreakable, durable, flexible)
79	**Broach**	utter, tap, open (***Ant.*** close, stop)
80	**Burlesque**	farcical, comical (***Ant.*** serious)
		C
81	**Cabal**	faction, clique, coterie, party, plot (***Ant.*** disband)
82	**Cadaverous**	pale, ghastly, pallid, wan (***Ant.*** flushed, lively)
83	**Cajole**	coax, entice, flatter (***Ant.*** repel)
84	**Calumny**	slander, aspersion (***Ant.*** praise)
85	**Candid**	just, frank, fair (***Ant.*** unfair)
86	**Caprice**	whim, freak, vagary (***Ant.*** steadfastness)
87	**Cardinal**	primary, principal, main, chief (***Ant.*** nonessential, additional)
88	**Caress**	pet, fondle, cuddle, kiss (***Ant.*** repel)
89	**Carnal**	sensuous, fleshy, lascivious (***Ant.*** spiritual)
90	**Castigate**	punish, chastise (***Ant.*** praise)
91	**Catholic**	tolerant, whole, universal (***Ant.*** limited, exclusive)
92	**Cavil**	censure, criticise, carp (***Ant.*** approve)
93	**Chagrin**	mortification, disappointment, dissatisfaction (***Ant.*** satisfaction)

94	**Chary**	wary, cautious, careful (***Ant.*** reckless)
95	**Childish**	juvenile, puerile, silly, weak (***Ant.*** grave, sensible)
96	**Chivalrous**	heroic, brave, gallant (***Ant.*** cowardly)
97	**Choleric**	angry, irascible, hasty (***Ant.*** calm)
98	**Churlish**	uncivil, sullen, rude (***Ant.*** civil)
99	**Circumspect**	prudent, careful, cautious (***Ant.*** incautious)
100	**Circumvent**	outwit, overreach, ensnare (***Ant.*** aid, assist)
101	**Clandestine**	sly, underhand, secret (***Ant.*** open)
102	**Coalesce**	join, blend, mingle (***Ant.*** divide, separate)
103	**Coalition**	alliance, combination, league (***Ant.*** split)
104	**Colossal**	huge, enormous, gigantic (***Ant.*** puny)
105	**Comely**	fair, good-looking, pretty (***Ant.*** ugly)
106	**Communion**	fellowship, intercourse, agreement (***Ant.*** disagreement, disunity)
107	**Compatible**	suitable, consistent, consonant (***Ant.*** incompatible)
108	**Compunction**	remorse, regret (***Ant.*** recklessness)
109	**Concord**	accord, agreement, harmony (***Ant.*** discord)
110	**Confound**	confuse, perplex, embarrass (***Ant.*** enlighten)
111	**Congruous**	fit, consistent, appropriate (***Ant.*** discordant, unfit)
112	**Conjecture**	guess, surmise, hypothesis (***Ant.*** certainty)
113	**Connive**	overlook, conspire, intrigue (***Ant.*** oppose)
114	**Conscientious**	exact, scrupulous, honourable (***Ant.*** unscrupulous)
115	**Consecrate**	sanctify, hallow, devote (***Ant.*** desecrate)
116	**Conspicuous**	manifest, remarkable, noticeable (***Ant.*** obscure, unknown)
117	**Consummate**	perfect, complete, finished (***Ant.*** imperfect)
118	**Contaminate**	pollute, infect, defile, taint (***Ant.*** purify)
119	**Contemptuous**	disdainful, scornful, haughty (***Ant.*** laudatory)
120	**Contentious**	quarrelsome, litigious, captious (***Ant.*** peaceful)
121	**Contravene**	oppose, interfere, contradict (***Ant.*** assist)
122	**Convivial**	merry, joyous, festive, hilarious (***Ant.*** unsocial)
123	**Corporeal**	physical, bodily (***Ant.*** spiritual)
124	**Corpulent**	fleshy, fat, portly (***Ant.*** thin)
125	**Corroborate**	confirm, establish, strengthen (***Ant.*** disprove)
126	**Counterfeit**	false, forged (***Ant.*** genuine)
127	**Covert**	secret, hidden, clandestine, disguised (***Ant.*** overt)
128	**Coy**	bashful, shy, modest, reserved (***Ant.*** pert, saucy)
129	**Crafty**	cunning, wily, artful (***Ant.*** ingenuous)
130	**Credulous**	simple, gullible (***Ant.*** sceptical)
131	**Culpable**	faulty, blameworthy, guilty (***Ant.*** innocent)
132	**Cursory**	superficial, transient, rapid (***Ant.*** thorough)

D		
133	**Dainty**	palatable, delicious, delicate, nice (***Ant.*** unpalatable)
134	**Dearth**	want, scarcity, lack (***Ant.*** plenty)
135	**Debase**	humiliate, degrade (***Ant.*** exalt)
136	**Debility**	weakness, infirmity (***Ant.*** invigoration)
137	**Decay**	decompose, putrefy, rot, spoil (Ant. grow, develop)
138	**Deception**	guile, deceit, cunning, delusion (***Ant.*** sincerity, honesty)
139	**Decorum**	decency, propriety (***Ant.*** impropriety)
140	**Decree**	edict, ordinance, law, mandate (***Ant.*** lawlessness, request)
141	**Defer**	postpone, suspend, adjourn (***Ant.*** advance, continue)
142	**Deference**	reverence, honour, respect (***Ant.*** disrespect)
143	**Defile**	corrupt, stain, spoil, contaminate (***Ant.*** purify)
144	**Delectable**	pleasant, delightful (***Ant.*** displeasing)
145	**Delicious**	dainty, exquisite, luscious, savoury (***Ant.*** unpalatable)
146	**Demeanour**	conduct, behaviour, bearing (***Ant.*** boorishness)
147	**Demolish**	destroy, raze, ruin (***Ant.*** build)
148	**Desecrate**	pollute, profane (***Ant.*** consecrate)
149	**Design**	outline, sketch, plan, purpose, intention (***Ant.*** disorganise, neglect)
150	**Designate**	nominate, appoint, name (***Ant.*** reject)
151	**Desolate**	lonely, deserted, ruined (***Ant.*** populous)
152	**Despicable**	mean, worthless, contemptible (***Ant.*** commendable)
153	**Despot**	oppressor, tyrant, autocrat (***Ant.*** democrat)
154	**Destitute**	poor, indigent, needy (***Ant.*** well-off)
155	**Desultory**	casual, rambling (***Ant.*** steady)
156	**Deviate**	digress, wander, diverge (***Ant.*** be direct)
157	**Diffident**	hesitating, doubtful, bashful (***Ant.*** confident)
158	**Diligence**	industry, perseverance, care (***Ant.*** idleness)
159	**Discern**	behold, observe, perceive, judge (***Ant.*** confuse)
160	**Discursive**	erratic, rambling (***Ant.*** coherent)
161	**Disparage**	discredit, undervalue, decry, belittle (***Ant.*** applaud)
162	**Docile**	pliant, amenable, submissive (***Ant.*** stubborn, inflexible)
163	**Dubious**	doubtful, uncertain (***Ant.*** certain)
E		
164	**Eager**	earnest, keen, enthusiastic (***Ant.*** apathetic)
165	**Ecstasy**	rapture, trance, transport (***Ant.*** consciousness, despair)
166	**Effete**	exhausted, barren, effeminate (***Ant.*** vigorous)
167	**Egotism**	vanity, conceit, self-esteem (***Ant.*** modesty)
168	**Elegant**	refined, graceful (***Ant.*** inelegant)
169	**Elucidate**	explain, interpret, illuminate (***Ant.*** obfuscate)

170	**Embellish**	adorn, beautify, grace (***Ant.*** spoil)
171	**Emolument**	pay, remuneration, gain, reward (***Ant.*** penalty, loss)
172	**Encomium**	praise, eulogy (***Ant.*** censure)
173	**Encroach**	trespass, intrude, invade (***Ant.*** keep off, retreat)
174	**Enervated**	debilitated, enfeebled, unnerved (***Ant.*** invigorated, strengthened)
175	**Enlighten**	edify, illuminate, instruct (***Ant.*** darken)
176	**Equanimity**	coolness, calmness, composure (***Ant.*** agitation, discomposure)
177	**Equivocate**	evade, shuffle, prevaricate (***Ant.*** admit, confess)
178	**Eradicate**	extirpate, root out (***Ant.*** spare)
179	**Eruption**	explosion, outburst, outbreak (***Ant.*** calmness, implosion)
180	**Ethereal**	airy, rare, celestial (***Ant.*** earthly)
181	**Evanescent**	transitory, fleeting, vanishing (***Ant.*** permanent)
182	**Exacerbate**	vex, embitter, exasperate (***Ant.*** soothe)
183	**Excerpt**	extract, quotation (***Ant.*** whole)
184	**Excruciate**	torment, torture, agonise (***Ant.*** alleviate)
185	**Exculpate**	acquit, pardon, absolve (***Ant.*** accuse)
186	**Expatriate**	exile, banish, expel (***Ant.*** repatriate)
187	**Exquisite**	delicate, refined, perfect (***Ant.*** unrefined)
188	**Extenuate**	reduce, lessen, qualify (***Ant.*** intensify)
189	**Extravagant**	lavish, wild, excessive (***Ant.*** economical)
190	**Exult**	rejoice, delight (***Ant.*** grieve)
		F
191	**Fabricate**	forge, invent, coin, produce
192	**Fabulous**	fictitious, marvellous, mythical (***Ant.*** true)
193	**Facetious**	funny, humorous, merry, jesting (***Ant.*** dull, serious)
194	**Faction**	clique, discord, cabal (***Ant.*** individual, harmony)
195	**Fallible**	uncertain, erring (***Ant.*** infallible)
196	**Fastidious**	dainty, meticulous, over-nice (***Ant.*** uncritical, easy)
197	**Fatigue**	tiredness, exhaustion, weariness (***Ant.*** liveliness, strength)
198	**Fatuous**	silly, imbecile, idiotic, weak (***Ant.*** sensible)
199	**Fervour**	warmth, ardour (***Ant.*** coolness)
200	**Filibuster**	pirate, buccaneer, freebooter (***Ant.*** police, law)
201	**Flaccid**	weak, loose, soft (***Ant.*** firm)
202	**Flavour**	relish, taste, savour (***Ant.*** dislike, bland)
203	**Fleece**	rob, clip, despoil (***Ant.*** guard, protect)
204	**Flexible**	pliable, yielding (***Ant.*** inflexible)
205	**Flinch**	wince, recoil (***Ant.*** face, confront)
206	**Flippant**	saucy, irreverent, pert (***Ant.*** reverent, humble)
207	**Flock**	pack, herd, group, brood, litter, set (***Ant.*** individual)

208	**Florid**	ornate, flowery (***Ant.*** plain)
209	**Fluctuate**	vacillate, waver, hesitate, vary (***Ant.*** stick)
210	**Foray**	raid, inroad, incursion, invasion (***Ant.*** release, retreat)
211	**Fortitude**	courage, strength, grit (***Ant.*** cowardice)
212	**Frigid**	unfeeling, cool, chilling (***Ant.*** warm)
213	**Frugal**	economical, thrifty (***Ant.*** extravagant)
214	**Furbish**	burnish, brighten, polish (***Ant.*** damage, ruin)
		G
215	**Garrulous**	chattering, loquacious, talkative (***Ant.*** silent)
216	**Gaunt**	lean, emaciated, thin (***Ant.*** corpulent)
217	**Glut**	surfeit, satiate, cloy, gorge (***Ant.*** lack, abstain)
218	**Grotesque**	odd, bizarre, whimsical (***Ant.*** ordinary, standard)
		H
219	**Hackneyed**	stale, trite, common (***Ant.*** novel)
220	**Hallucination**	illusion, delusion (***Ant.*** real)
221	**Hapless**	unfortunate, unlucky (***Ant.*** lucky)
222	**Headstrong**	stubborn, obstinate, strong-willed (***Ant.*** docile)
223	**Hirsute**	hairy, bearded, shaggy (***Ant.*** smooth)
224	**Homogeneous**	akin, uniform, similar (***Ant.*** heterogeneous)
225	**Hubbub**	uproar, tumult, din (***Ant.*** calm, peace)
		I
226	**Ignominious**	shameful, humiliating, disgraceful (***Ant.*** honourable)
227	**Imbecile**	silly, idiotic, feeble, feeble-minded (***Ant.*** sane)
228	**Immaculate**	faultless, spotless, unblemished (***Ant.*** blemished)
229	**Immunity**	exception, freedom, protection (***Ant.*** defenselessness)
230	**Imperious**	arrogant, authoritative, dictatorial (***Ant.*** servile)
231	**Imposter**	rogue, cheat, knave, charlatan (***Ant.*** square shooter)
232	**Incisive**	trenchant, sharp, biting (***Ant.*** mild)
233	**Indefatigable**	untiring, unwearied, assiduous (***Ant.*** weary)
234	**Indite**	frame, write, dictate, compose (***Ant.*** destroy)
235	**Industrious**	laborious, active, hard-working (***Ant.*** indolent)
236	**Inexorable**	relentless, unyielding (***Ant.*** lenient)
237	**Infernal**	hellish, fiendish, diabolical (***Ant.*** heavenly, godlike)
238	**Infringe**	transgress, violate, break, encroach (***Ant.*** comply, observance)
239	**Ingenuous**	sincere, frank, candid (***Ant.*** disingenuous)
240	**Iniquitous**	unjust, vicious, wicked (***Ant.*** fair)
241	**Irascible**	irritable, touchy (***Ant.*** good-natured)
242	**Itinerant**	roving, wandering, nomadic (***Ant.*** settled, permanent)

	J	
243	**Jaundiced**	biased, prejudiced (***Ant.*** unbiased)
244	**Jocose**	humorous, playful (***Ant.*** grave)
	K	
245	**Knack**	art, feat, dexterity (***Ant.*** clumsiness)
	L	
246	**Labyrinthine**	intricate, mazy, confused (***Ant.*** straightforward)
247	**Laconic**	terse, brief, short (***Ant.*** verbose)
248	**Laggard**	sluggish, tardy, loitering (***Ant.*** prompt, energetic)
249	**Languid**	listless, weak, faint (***Ant.*** vigorous)
250	**Lascivious**	lewd, wanton (***Ant.*** chaste)
251	**Lethal**	deadly, fatal, mortal (***Ant.*** harmless)
252	**Lucrative**	paying, profitable (***Ant.*** unprofitable)
253	**Lucre**	gain, profit (***Ant.*** loss)
254	**Ludicrous**	ridiculous, absurd, comic (***Ant.*** grave)
255	**Lugubrious**	sad, doleful, mournful (***Ant.*** gay, cheerful)
256	**Lurid**	gruesome, dismal, murky (***Ant.*** bright)
	M	
257	**Magnanimous**	generous, unselfish, forgiving (***Ant.*** ungenerous, selfish)
258	**Magniloquent**	inflated, bombastic (***Ant.*** humble, quiet)
259	**Mandate**	command, edict, authorisation (***Ant.*** request)
260	**Maudlin**	emotional, sentimental (***Ant.*** pragmatic, unemotional)
261	**Maxim**	proverb, adage, precept (***Ant***. ambiguity)
262	**Meddlesome**	officious, interfering, intrusive (***Ant.*** non-interfering)
263	**Mendacious**	false, untruthful, lying (***Ant.*** veracious)
264	**Mercenary**	avaricious, mean, venal (***Ant.*** generous, incorrupt)
265	**Meticulous**	precise, scrupulous (***Ant.*** sloppy)
266	**Mollify**	soften, pacify, assuage, appease (***Ant.*** aggravate, depress)
267	**Mundane**	worldly, earthly (***Ant.*** heavenly)
	N	
268	**Nebulous**	confused, hazy, cloudy (***Ant.*** clear)
269	**Niggardly**	stingy, miserly (***Ant.*** generous)
270	**Noxious**	harmful, poisonous, dangerous (***Ant.*** harmless)
	O	
271	**Obdurate**	stubborn, unyielding, obstinate (***Ant.*** yielding, submissive)
272	**Obviate**	counteract, prevent, preclude (***Ant.*** help)
273	**Offal**	garbage, refuse (***Ant***. assets)
274	**Opulent**	wealthy, rich, affluent (***Ant.*** poor)
275	**Ostentation**	pomp, parade, display, boasting (***Ant.*** modesty)

	P	
276	**Paltry**	little, mean, despicable, beggarly (***Ant.*** large, worthy)
277	**Pallid**	pale, colourless (***Ant.*** colourful)
278	**Pandemonium**	uproar, racket (***Ant.*** harmony, order)
279	**Paramount**	supreme, eminent (***Ant.*** trivial)
280	**Pellucid**	clear, limpid, transparent (***Ant.*** obscure, unclear)
281	**Picturesque**	vivid, graphic, picture- like (***Ant.*** unsightly)
282	**Pillage**	plunder, loot, rob (***Ant.*** protect, safeguard)
283	**Poltroon**	coward, dastard (***Ant.*** hero)
284	**Ponderous**	heavy, weighty, bulky (***Ant.*** light)
285	**Precipitate**	hurry, hasten, expedite (***Ant.*** halt, slow)
286	**Preclude**	stop, hinder, prevent (***Ant.*** help)
287	**Predicament**	plight, dilemma, state (***Ant.*** blessing, boon)
288	**Predilection**	prejudice, fondness, preference (***Ant.*** dislike, indifference)
289	**Preposterous**	unbelievable, nonsensical (***Ant.*** reasonable)
290	**Prevaricate**	shuffle, equivocate, lie (***Ant.*** be honest, confront)
291	**Proclivity**	aptitude, leaning, disposition, bias (***Ant.*** disinclination)
292	**Progeny**	offspring, descendant (***Ant.*** antecedents)
293	**Propitious**	pleasing, favourable (***Ant.*** antagonistic)
294	**Puerile**	trivial, childish, silly (***Ant.*** sensible)
295	**Punctilious**	precise, careful, scrupulous (***Ant.*** careless)
	Q	
296	**Quell**	crush, stop, put down (***Ant.*** promote)
297	**Quiescent**	inactive, latent, resting (***Ant.*** dynamic)
298	**Quixotic**	imaginary, impractical (***Ant.*** realistic)
	R	
299	**Rancour**	hatred, malice, spite (***Ant.*** affection)
300	**Rapacious**	greedy, covetous, avaricious (***Ant.*** generous)
301	**Raucous**	harsh, hoarse, loud (***Ant.*** quiet)
302	**Realm**	state, kingdom, sphere (***Ant.*** no-man's-land)
303	**Recapitulate**	repeat, summarise, enumerate (***Ant.*** expand, lengthen)
304	**Recompense**	reward, compensation (***Ant.*** penalty)
305	**Rectitude**	integrity, honesty, virtue (***Ant.*** immorality, dishonesty)
306	**Redundant**	excessive, superfluous, exuberant (***Ant.*** concise)
307	**Refulgent**	shining, glittering, splendid (***Ant.*** dull, dark)
308	**Replete**	stuffed, full (***Ant.*** starved, empty)
309	**Replica**	copy, reproduction (***Ant.*** original)
310	**Reprimand**	rebuke, censure, blame (***Ant.*** praise, reward)
311	**Repudiate**	reject, disown, renounce (***Ant.*** adopt)

312	**Repugnant**	hostile, distasteful (***Ant.*** pleasing)
313	**Resplendent**	bright, shining, glittering (***Ant.*** dull, dark)
314	**Rife**	common, widespread, prevalent, abundant (***Ant.*** insufficient)
315	**Rubicund**	reddish, ruddy, florid (***Ant.*** plain, unornate)
316	**Rueful**	sorrowful, unhappy (***Ant.*** cheerful)
		S
317	**Saucy**	rude, impudent, impertinent (***Ant.*** polite)
318	**Savoury**	nice, tasty, palatable (***Ant.*** flavourless, bland, unappetising)
319	**Scurrilous**	abusive, vulgar (***Ant.*** refined)
320	**Sedulous**	busy, industrious, diligent (***Ant.*** inactive)
321	**Servitude**	slavery, bondage (***Ant.*** freedom)
322	**Simulate**	imitate, pretend, resemble (***Ant.*** real)
323	**Slovenly**	untidy, disorderly (***Ant.*** tidy)
324	**Sombre**	dark, gloom, dismal, dull (***Ant.*** hopeful, happy)
325	**Somnolent**	drowsy, sleepy (***Ant.*** alert)
326	**Sorcery**	witchcraft, magic, necromancy (***Ant.*** *reality, mundane)*
327	**Spurious**	counterfeit, fake, illegitimate (***Ant.*** genuine)
328	**Squalid**	filthy, dirty (***Ant.*** clean)
329	**Stolid**	impassive, unemotional (***Ant.*** sensitive)
330	**Stratagem**	trick, ruse, artifice (***Ant.*** honesty, reality)
331	**Subjugate**	overthrow, conquer, subdue (***Ant.*** encourage, liberate, release)
332	**Succinct**	terse, concise (***Ant.*** wordy)
333	**Surmise**	conjecture, guess (***Ant.*** fact, certainty)
334	**Swarthy**	black, dark, dusky (***Ant.*** fair, pale)
335	**Sycophant**	flatterer, hanger-on, parasite (***Ant.*** independent, proud)
		T
336	**Taciturn**	silent, uncommunicative, reserved (***Ant.*** garrulous)
337	**Tangible**	solid, real, material (***Ant.*** unreal)
338	**Tarnish**	stain, taint, blemish (***Ant.*** purify, improve)
339	**Temerity**	recklessness, rashness, audacity (***Ant.*** caution)
340	**Thrifty**	prudent, economical, saving (***Ant.*** spendthrift)
341	**Thwart**	defeat, frustrate, oppose (***Ant.*** further)
342	**Torpor**	sluggishness, inertness, dullness (***Ant.*** vivacity)
343	**Torrid**	scorching, hot, passionate (***Ant.*** cool)
344	**Tortuous**	winding, circuitous (***Ant.*** straight)
345	**Tranquil**	calm, serene, quiet (***Ant.*** noisy)
346	**Transgress**	violate, exceed, trespass (***Ant.*** behave, obey)

347	**Transient**	fleeting, brief (***Ant.*** permanent)
348	**Tremulous**	trembling, shivering, quaking ***(Ant.*** calm, steady)
349	**Truculent**	savage, ferocious, belligerent ***(Ant.*** tame, mild)
350	**Tumid**	turgid, distended, swollen (***Ant.*** flaccid)
	U	
351	**Umbrage**	displeasure, offence, resentment ***(Ant.*** delight, glee)
352	**Unkempt**	neglected, untidy (***Ant.*** neat)
353	**Urbane**	suave, refined (***Ant.*** uncouth)
	V	
354	**Verdant**	green, unripe, growing ***(Ant.*** declining, dying)
355	**Vestige**	trace, sign, remnant ***(Ant.*** information, lot)
356	**Victuals**	food, bread, meat, provisions (***Ant.*** deprivation, starvation)
357	**Vivacious**	lively, gay, merry (***Ant.*** depressed)
358	**Voluble**	garrulous, glib, loquacious (***Ant.*** curt)
	W	
359	**Wanton**	reckless, unruly (***Ant.*** restrained)
360	**Wastrel**	profligate, vagabond ***(Ant.*** settled, inhabiting)
361	**Whet**	stimulate, sharpen ***(Ant.*** blunt, dull)
362	**Wistful**	yearning, pensive, thoughtful ***(Ant.*** cheerful, joyful)
363	**Wonted**	usual, customary, accustomed (***Ant.*** unwanted)

4 SYNONYMS - PRACTICE TESTS (MCQs)

500 MCQs

DIRECTIONS: *Given below the words are in alphabetic order. Every word is followed by four options. You have to find out the option which is nearest in meaning to the given word. NOTA means None of the Above given answers.*

A

1. Absolute
(a) reasonable (b) narrow
(c) limitless (d) reliable

2. abandon
(a) neglect (b) condense
(c) discontinue (d) abscond

3. Affable
(a) helpful (b) neutral
(c) friendly (d) cheerful

4. Abash
(a) acuity (b) confuse
(c) blush (d) condemn

5. Accomplice
(a) friend (b) abettor
(c) criminal (d) thief

6. Allegiance
(a) disaffection (b) satisfactory
(c) loyalty (d) enmity

7. Amicable
(a) poisonous (b) friendly
(c) satisfying (d) heartening

8. Apogee
(a) middle (b) bottom
(c) climax (d) beginning

9. **Adversity**
(a) failure (b) helplessness
(c) crisis (d) misfortune

10. Acumen
(a) beauty (b) appearance
(c) insight (d) skill

11. Abstain
(a) influence (b) refrain
(c) retain (d) retard

12. Abase
(a) low (b) peaceful
(c) humble (d) cruel

13. Abet
(a) force (b) discourage
(c) assist (d) neglect

14. Abridge
(a) desire (b) condense
(c) graceful (d) disconnect

15. Admonish
(a) appeal (b) support
(c) warn (d) praise

16. Accolade
(a) applause (b) award
(c) affection (d) arrival

17. Antique
(a) old (b) rare
(c) modern (d) unique

18. Ascend
(a) leap (b) mount
(c) deviate (d) grow

19. Adept
(a) professional (b) proficient
(c) sufficient (d) intelligent

20. Admonition
(a) award (b) amazement
(c) pardon (d) warning

21. Applaud
(a) pray (b) flatter
(c) request (d) praise

22. Appraisal
(a) investigation (b) estimation
(c) praise (d) approval

23. Anxiety
(a) worry (b) comfort
(c) faith (d) reassurance

24. Accord
(a) agreement (b) disagreement
(c) dispute (d) disparity

25. Aromatic
(a) stinking (b) sentimental
(c) fragrant (d) crippled

26. Ambit
(a) eviction (b) scope
(c) restriction (d) barrier

27. Adjourn
(a) postpone (b) avoid
(c) complain (d) suppress

28. Accentuated
(a) mitigated (b) projected
(c) exhibited (d) sharpened

29. Acute
(a) rice (b) accidental
(c) severe (d) curious

30. Abscond
(a) flee (b) manage
(c) avoid (d) turn

31. Albeit
(a) although (b) further more
(c) because (d) not only

32. Amalgamate
(a) try (b) collect
(c) mix (d) hate

33. Assay
(a) attack (b) accept
(c) case (d) evaluate

34. Acrid
(a) unripe (b) pungent
(c) bitter (d) dirty

35. Adage
(a) order (b) request
(c) proverb (d) mystery

36. Abominable
(a) odd (b) weird
(c) fine (d) awful

37. Abstemious
(a) moderate (b) proud
(c) excessive (d) rustic

38. Abomination
(a) revulsion (b) disgust
(c) criticism (d) attack

39. Alacrity
(a) eagerly (b) suspicion
(c) unhesitatingly (d) unwillingly

40. Augur
(a) heal (b) hurt
(c) signify (d) reform

41. Assuage
(a) rub (b) prohibit
(c) ease (d) enlarge

42. Addle
(a) soar (b) strike
(c) stop (d) confuse

43. Animosity
(a) vanity (b) hostility
(c) indifference (d) treason

44. Abrupt
(a) pure (b) alert
(c) sudden (d) quick

45. Abstruse
(a) abstract (b) profound
(c) perfect (d) ignorant

46. Altercation
(a) drastic change (b) angry dispute
(c) noisy dialogue (d) loud explosion

47. Anomaly
(a) abnormality (b) ignorance
(c) accident (d) rarity

48. Aphorism
(a) wise saying (b) digression
(c) casual remark (d) repetition

49. Abrade
(a) twist (b) wear off
(c) attach (d) scold

50. Abstruse
(a) missing (b) sprawling
(c) obscure (d) stupid

51. Abnegation
(a) association (b) renunciation
(c) affirmation (d) indignation

B

52. Barbarian
(a) ruffian (b) impolite
(c) partiality (d) distortion

53. Biased
(a) careful (b) partial
(c) expert (d) unskilled

54. Brutal
(a) humane (b) adamant
(c) ruthless (d) criminal

55. Boisterous
(a) boiling (b) hot
(c) noisy (d) dangerous

56. Berserk
(a) clever (b) morose
(c) cheerful (d) wild

57. Benefactor
(a) guardian (b) saint
(c) do-gooder (d) friend

58. Baffle
(a) puzzle (b) tease
(c) hoodwink (d) trick

59. Belligerent
(a) pacifist (b) generous
(c) aggressive (d) reasonable

60. Bifurcated
(a) reduced (b) stabbed
(c) ploughed (d) segregated

61. Bewail
(a) tear apart (b) envy
(c) lament (d) accuse

62. Balmy
(a) soothing (b) fruitful
(c) modest (d) tempestuous

63. Blithe
(a) other worldly (b) giddy
(c) graceful (d) joyous

64. Befuddled
(a) wounded (b) crowded
(c) enlightened (d) confused

65. Besiege
(a) acquire (b) attack
(c) seize (d) surround

66. Bandit
(a) convict (b) robber
(c) thief (d) cut-throat

67. Bankrupt
(a) insolvent (b) debtor
(c) creditor (d) solvent

68. Bane
(a) accuse (b) curse
(c) reject (d) abolish

69. Barter
(a) return (b) exchange
(c) borrow (d) buy

70. Bucolic
(a) angry (b) revengeful
(c) rustic (d) imaginative

71. Bizarre
(a) joyful (b) colourful
(c) grotesque (d) hearty

72. Brutal
(a) humane (b) adamant
(c) ruthless (d) criminal

73. Burlesque
(a) irritate (b) insult
(c) annoy (d) mock

74. Bumptious
(a) ill-tempered
(b) colliding
(c) brashly self-assertive
(d) illiterate

75. Baleful
(a) overflowing (b) pernicious
(c) unethical (d) NOTA

76. Bemused
(a) enchanted (b) entertained
(c) lost in thought (d) ridiculous

C

77. Connoisseur
(a) delinquent (b) interpreter
(c) expert judge (d) ignorant

78. Callous
(a) large (b) hardened
(c) thick (d) dangerous

79. Colossal
(a) dangerous (b) gigantic
(c) fatal (d) honourable

80. Conciseness
(a) correctness (b) frankness
(c) brevity (d) refines

81. Candid
(a) sweet (b) pleasing
(c) frank (d) dishonest

82. Cowardice
(a) timidity (b) gallantry
(c) criminal (d) humanity

83. Compendium
(a) glossary (b) reference
(c) index (d) summary

84. Concise
(a) small (b) strong
(c) solid (d) brief

85. Coterie
(a) institution (b) group
(c) mob (d) family

86. Corroborate
(a) verify (b) refute
(c) disprove (d) disapprove

87. Chimerical
(a) imaginary (b) uncertain
(c) short-lived (d) erratic

88. Conundrum
(a) discussion (b) explanation
(c) solution (d) imbroglio

89. Castigate
(a) delegate (b) evaluate
(c) reprimand (d) enforce

90. Concealed
(a) disclosed (b) opened
(c) camouflaged (d) released

91. Caveat
(a) dispute (b) challenge
(c) advice (d) warning

92. Condemn
(a) blame (b) underrate
(c) hate (d) avoid

93. Congregation
(a) combination (b) meeting
(c) assembly (d) collection

94. Colossus
(a) huge (b) towering
(c) lofty (d) tall

95. Cantankerous
(a) rash (b) disrespectful
(c) noisy (d) quarrelsome

96. Consequence
(a) manner (b) result
(c) cause (d) order

97. Clairvoyance
(a) foretelling (b) recklessness
(c) astrology (d) none of these

98. Culpable
(a) correct (b) guilty
(c) right (d) innocent

99. Chivalry
(a) bravery (b) cowardice
(c) joviality (d) gleefulness

100. Crass
(a) spiritless (b) wicked
(c) insensitive (d) rustic

101. Catapult
(a) restrain (b) control
(c) contain (d) shoot

102. Console
(a) solace (b) sympathise
(c) pacify (d) courage

103. Convivial
(a) aloof (b) shy
(c) jovial (d) lively

104. Construe
(a) meaning (b) interpret
(c) narration (d) confuse

105. Callous
(a) hard (b) cruel
(c) big (d) mighty

106. Censure
(a) condemn (b) blame
(c) pin point (d) charge

107. Careen
(a) secure (b) sway
(c) decay (d) fondle

108. Cherubic
(a) mischievous (b) expensive
(c) rustic (d) angelic

109. Consternation
(a) group of stars
(b) humble service
(c) large display
(d) great amazement/ terror

110. Cumbersome
(a) taxing (b) sorrowful
(c) unwieldy (d) laborious

111. Complicity
(a) deceit
(b) variety
(c) connivance
(d) relief from debt

112. Categorically
(a) purposefully (b) introductorily
(c) unequivocally (d) relatively

113. Confabulate
(a) embroider on (b) private chat
(c) muddle (d) put an end to

D

114. Deride
(a) mock (b) confuse
(c) shout (d) snarl

115. Deify
(a) challenge (b) face
(c) worship (d) flatter

116. Delusion
(a) actuality (b) illusion
(c) clarity (d) emulating

117. Decry
(a) deviate (b) despoil
(c) demure (d) disparage

118. Doleful
(a) bright (b) mournful
(c) colourful (d) jovial

119. Delegate
(a) officer (b) participant
(c) member (d) representative

120. Deplete
(a) exhaust (b) vanish
(c) finish (d) destroy

121. Docile
(a) gentle (b) vague
(c) stubborn (d) stupid

122. Denounce
(a) support (b) sustain
(c) maintain (d) condemn

123. Disrupt
(a) join (b) disturb
(c) refuse (d) deny

124. Dodge
(a) avoid (b) thwart
(c) frustrate (d) confuse

125. Domain
(a) area (b) main
(c) marketing (d) fielding

126. Dynamic
(a) active (b) robust
(c) forceful (d) vigorous

127. Delirious
(a) happy (b) content
(c) amused (d) deranged

128. Dilettante
(a) expert (b) adventure
(c) specialist (d) amateur

129. Delectable
(a) desirable (b) attractive
(c) delicate (d) delightful

130. Dominion
(a) recreation (b) separation
(c) issue (d) realm

131. Desultory
(a) regular (b) obedient
(c) abandoned (d) punctual

132. Drowsy
(a) soothing (b) energetic
(c) exhausted (d) sleepy

133. Disparage
(a) discourage (b) compare
(c) separate (d) belittle

134. Diligent
(a) modest (b) spare
(c) intelligent (d) industrious

135. Deference
(a) obligation (b) respect
(c) postponement (d) pride

136. Dilemma
(a) hard (b) severe
(c) difficult choice (d) scarcity

137. Derisive
(a) mocking (b) copied
(c) limited (d) borrowed

138. Derogatory
(a) questionable (b) inquisitive
(c) humble (d) depreciating

139. Diurnal
(a) news account (b) solar
(c) daily (d) everlasting

140. Dolorous
(a) sorrowful (b) financial
(c) sacred (d) parsimonious

141. Debauch
(a) corrupt (b) open a bottle
(c) branch off (d) cheapen

142. Debilitate
(a) attack
(b) weaken
(c) become accustomed
(d) overwhelm

143. Decadent
(a) aristocratic
(b) subtle
(c) occurring every ten years
(d) deteriorating

144. Demise
(a) false statement (b) death
(c) message (d) stage set

145. Depredation
(a) disapproval
(b) decrease in value
(c) warding off
(d) plundering

146. Denigrate
(a) deny (b) defame
(c) ridicule (d) irritate

E

147. Ephemeral
(a) short-living (b) mythical
(c) unreal (d) artificial

148. Extempore
(a) praise worth (b) impromptu
(c) extraordinary (d) essential

149. Ecstatic
(a) animated (b) enraptured
(c) bewildered (d) fitful

150. Equivocal
(a) ambiguous (b) quarrelsome
(c) reasonable (d) feasible

151. Estrange
(a) endanger (b) alienate
(c) miscalculate (d) puzzling

152. Excruciate
(a) torture (b) extract
(c) imprison (d) refine

153. Enthusiastic
(a) angry (b) excited
(c) noisy (d) violent

154. Echelon
(a) rank (b) opponent
(c) follower (d) identity

155. Exude
(a) ooze (b) wither
(c) overflow (d) evaporate

156. Enigmatic
(a) pithy (b) puzzling
(c) complicated (d) illusive

157. Erotic
(a) attractive (b) beautiful
(c) sensuous (d) sexual

158. Exceedingly
(a) politely (b) extremely
(c) freely (d) outwardly

159. Effete
(a) affected (b) injured
(c) feeble (d) sick

160. Enigma
(a) puzzle (b) elusive
(c) praise (d) clear

161. Extravaganza
(a) profligacy
(b) spectacular show
(c) over reaching
(d) falsification

162. Enthuse
(a) pester (b) provoke
(c) excite (d) annoy

163. Ebullient
(a) exorbitant (b) exuberant
(c) obscure (d) still

164. Edify
(a) consume (b) satisfy
(c) instruct (d) amuse

165. Entice
(a) cheat (b) lure
(c) flight (d) love

166. Emancipate
(a) set free (b) exist
(c) correct morally (d) restrain

167. Elan
(a) flair (b) spiritual
(c) inspiration (d) boredom

168. Empirical
(a) spiritual (b) practical
(c) theoretical (d) royal

169. Erudite
(a) scholar (b) strong
(c) courteous (d) precious

170. Encumbrance
(a) disturbance (b) liability
(c) distraction (d) hindrance

171. Enthral
(a) annoy (b) glorify
(c) charm (d) persuade

172. Explicit
(a) clear (b) exciting
(c) precise (d) refined

173. Epoch
(a) turning point (b) time point
(c) neutral (d) ancient

174. Equivocal
(a) thought (b) uncertain
(c) hard (d) mistrust

175. Enigma
(a) riddle (b) dilemma
(c) fiddle (d) NOTA

176. Eradicate
(a) remove (b) evaporate
(c) eliminate (d) complete

177. Enervate
(a) calm down (b) weaken
(c) pep up (d) lure on

178. Exorcise
(a) expel an evil spirit (b) impress
(c) train thoroughly (d) torture

179. Escheat
(a) confiscate
(b) swindle
(c) avoid
(d) chew thoroughly

180. Exordium
(a) beginning of a speech
(b) plea
(c) essence
(d) final appeal

181. Empirical
(a) relating to a market
(b) based upon experience
(c) ruling despotically
(d) expansionist

F

182. Fraternise
(a) associate (b) organise
(c) expel (d) cheat

183. Forsake
(a) forgive (b) punish
(c) abandon (d) benefit

184. Fatigue
(a) tension (b) drowsiness
(c) tiredness (d) sweating

185. Forlorn
(a) uncared (b) funny
(c) fearful (d) fortunate

186. Fickle
(a) nervous (b) changeable
(c) poor (d) constant

187. Fiddle
(a) frown (b) discard
(c) examine (d) trifle

188. Foreigner
(a) alien (b) native
(c) local (d) national

189. Feign
(a) hesitate (b) pretend
(c) deserve (d) attend

190. Fragment
(a) scrap (b) crumble
(c) dissection (d) cut

191. Foment
(a) pacify (b) incite
(c) rectify (d) restrict

192. Foster
(a) encourage (b) fabricate
(c) foment (d) nurture

193. Filthy
(a) healthy (b) ugly
(c) dirty (d) angry

194. Flak
(a) adventure (b) advice
(c) criticism (d) praise

195. Forthright
(a) straight forward (b) open
(c) frank (d) typical

196. Fiasco
(a) failure (b) hope
(c) strength (d) success

197. Flippancy
(a) levity (b) dexterity
(c) easiness (d) clumsiness

198. Fecundity
(a) validity (b) poverty
(c) fertility (d) depth

G

199. Gratify
(a) pacify (b) indulge
(c) frank (d) appreciate

200. Genesis
(a) relevant (b) beginning
(c) style (d) movement

201. Gist
(a) contribution (b) substance
(c) prestige (d) accessory

202. Glorious
(a) delightful (b) painful
(c) cowardly (d) humiliating

203. Gainsay
(a) advantage (b) proposal
(c) contradict (d) suggestion

204. Gregarious
(a) pugnacious (b) turbulent
(c) sociable (d) morbid

205. Glib
(a) tough (b) smooth
(c) rough (d) rouge

206. Grandiloquent
(a) generous (b) domineering
(c) pompous (d) genuine

H

207. Haggle
(a) bargain (b) reject
(c) postpone (d) accept

208. Hinder
(a) obstruct (b) challenge
(c) damage (d) ruin

209. Humbug
(a) desire (b) craving
(c) illusion (d) deceit

210. Handsome
(a) polite (b) noble
(c) gentle (d) good looking

211. Hassle
(a) greed (b) jealousy
(c) gossip (d) wrangle

212. Hoodlum
(a) devotee (b) criminal
(c) pioneer (d) scholar

213. Hanker
(a) renounce (b) denounce
(c) desire (d) run after

214. Hood-wink
(a) collide (b) deceive
(c) prefer (d) stab

215. Helm
(a) corner (b) handle
(c) head (d) edge

216. Hegemony
(a) domination (b) materialism
(c) subordination (d) booty

217. Hiatus
(a) contempt (b) narrow
(c) tight (d) gap

218. Hallowed
(a) holy (b) reverend
(c) sacred (d) respected

219. Harass
(a) grieve (b) injure
(c) excite (d) annoy

220. Harbinger
(a) pilot (b) forerunner
(c) steward (d) messenger

221. Heterogeneous
(a) similar parts
(b) unlike elements
(c) smooth surfaces
(d) complex problems

222. Hybrid
(a) of mixed origin (b) spirited
(c) well-mannered (d) poor

223. Histrionic
(a) theatrical (b) informed
(c) famous (d) microscopic

I

224. Icon
(a) monument (b) memorial
(c) painting (d) statue

225. Indict
(a) accuse (b) condemn
(c) allege (d) reprimand

226. Imposter
(a) imposer (b) lazy
(c) cheat (d) painful

227. Innate
(a) unique (b) important
(c) inborn (d) essential

228. Indigence
(a) poverty (b) prosperity
(c) suffering (d) scarcity

229. Incite
(a) discourage (b) encourage
(c) internal (d) crime

230. Impertinent
(a) impudent (b) sceptical
(c) thoughtless (d) irritable

231. Impediment
(a) passage (b) obstruction
(c) fateful (d) destruction

232. Indomitable
(a) inactive (b) authoritative
(c) rebellious (d) unconquerable

233. Indolence
(a) leniency (b) relaxation
(c) laziness (d) stagnation

234. Innocent
(a) guilty (b) clean
(c) deadly (d) sinful

235. Ingenuous
(a) active (b) skilful
(c) smart (d) none of these

236. Insidious
(a) slow (b) pessimistic
(c) treacherous (d) patriotic

237. Improvident
(a) thriftiness (b) incautious
(c) unhappy (d) shabby

238. Incensed
(a) inspired (b) encouraged
(c) incited (d) affected

239. Inconsistent
(a) unrestrained (b) restless
(c) inconstant (d) uncertain

240. Infirm
(a) dull (b) sickly
(c) slim (d) unyielding

241. Inexplicable
(a) unconnected (b) chaotic
(c) unaccountable (d) confusing

242. Irk
(a) bore (b) insult
(c) urge (d) irritate

243. Industrious
(a) intelligent (b) hard-working
(c) clever (d) reserved

244. Insolvent
(a) penniless (b) bankrupt
(c) broke (d) poor

245. Ironic
(a) sarcastic (b) inflexible
(c) bitter (d) good natured

246. Impeccable
(a) fussy (b) precise
(c) having integrity (d) faultless

247. Intimidate
(a) hint (b) harass
(c) bluff (d) frighten

248. Insipid
(a) flat (b) lucid
(c) wily (d) witty

249. Imminent
(a) impending (b) inherent
(c) urgent (d) soon

250. Internecine
(a) deadly (b) foolhardy
(c) stealthy (d) international

251. Imbroglio
(a) difficulty (b) impossibility
(c) confrontation (d) stalemate

252. Impasse
(a) confrontation (b) stalemate
(c) difficulty (d) impossibility

253. Immaculate
(a) shining (b) dirty
(c) clean (d) spotless

254. Interim
(a) temporary (b) internal
(c) interval (d) timely

255. Imprecation
(a) oath (b) blessing
(c) bliss (d) abuse

256. Inordinate
(a) subordinate (b) inanimate
(c) excessive (d) extraordinary

257. Inevitable
(a) fixed (b) unavoidable
(c) expected (d) probable

258. Insidious
(a) slow (b) treacherous
(c) pessimistic (d) unfortunate

259. Iota
(a) little (b) scintilla
(c) uncountable (d) dole

260. Intrinsic
(a) shy (b) inherent
(c) talkative (d) aloof

261. Intrepid
(a) hopeless (b) fearless
(c) bold (d) strong

262. Insolent
(a) arrogant (b) lethargic
(c) rude (d) helpful

263. Infrequent
(a) never (b) usual
(c) rare (d) sometimes

264. Infernal
(a) hateful (b) exciting
(c) devilish (d) damaging

265. Indict
(a) accuse (b) condemn
(c) allege (d) reprimand

266. Idiosyncrasy
(a) personality
(b) lack of intelligence
(c) absolute rule
(d) characteristic

267. Impinge
(a) paint (b) constrict
(c) steal (d) encroach

268. Incisive
(a) penetrating (b) short
(c) compendious (d) assured

269. Insinuate
(a) spy upon (b) suggest slyly
(c) set free (d) indicate

270. Immutable
(a) debatable (b) unalterable
(c) impractical (d) not susceptible

271. Inscrutable
(a) mad (b) malicious
(c) misleading (d) unfathomable

272. Imponderable
(a) incapable (b) very small
(c) unthinkable (d) tremendous

273. Ineffable
(a) speechless (b) feminine
(c) rude (d) indescribable

274. Inuendo
(a) investigation (b) insinuation
(c) injustice (d) hinting

275. Immanent
(a) inherent (b) decisive
(c) impending (d) prominent

J

276. Juvenile
(a) hidden (b) young
(c) humorous (d) tedious

277. Jovial
(a) smart (b) funny
(c) triumphant (d) merry

278. Jeer
(a) clean (b) deride
(c) pulsate (d) hear

279. Jocular
(a) merry (b) jolting
(c) craving (d) imperial

280. Jubilant
(a) disturbed (b) scared
(c) gloomy (d) exultant

281. Jingoistic
(a) dashing (b) victorious
(c) compromise (d) patriotic

282. Jocose
(a) trite (b) playful
(c) useless (d) illusory

K

283. Knavery
(a) stupidity (b) heroism
(c) cowardice (d) dishonesty

284. Kindle
(a) set on fire (b) light
(c) conserve (d) preserve

285. Knack
(a) own (b) skill
(c) job (d) quality

286. Kowtow
(a) blockhead (b) illuminate
(c) practise (d) flatter

L

287. Lethal
(a) deadly (b) sluggish
(c) uncivilised (d) smooth

288. Ludicrous
(a) simple (b) dismal
(c) clear (d) absurd

289. Loquacious
(a) quiet (b) talkative
(c) secretive (d) sad

290. Levitate
(a) evaporate (b) fall
(c) rise (d) subsidise

291. Lurid
(a) sensational (b) old
(c) showy (d) pale

292. Latent
(a) hard (b) concealed
(c) visible (d) display

293. Lenient
(a) cruel (b) rough
(c) kind (d) harsh

294. Lethargy
(a) dynamism (b) laziness
(c) cool headed (d) lavish

295. Loquacious
(a) verbose (b) taciturn
(c) rational (d) alluring

296. Loath
(a) tired (b) unwilling
(c) sickly (d) latest

297. Licentious
(a) gay (b) immoral
(c) generous (d) hungry

298. Lamentable
(a) remorseful (b) deplorable
(c) scornful (d) contemptible

299. Lugubrious
(a) sleek (b) consolatory
(c) mournful (d) deceitful

300. Lascivious
(a) fragrant (b) foul
(c) naughty (d) lustful

301. Languish
(a) destroy (b) decay
(c) lack vigour (d) imprisonment

302. Livid
(a) discoloured (b) sensational
(c) bilious (d) smarting

303. Libidinous
(a) lustful (b) disagreeable
(c) discoloured (d) headstrong

M

304. Moribund
(a) stagnant (b) superfluous
(c) dying (d) gloomy

305. Massacre
(a) murder (b) assassinate
(c) stab (d) slaughter

306. Mollify
(a) chastise (b) testify
(c) rebuke (d) appease

307. Morose
(a) cam (b) disappointed
(c) gloomy (d) diseased

308. Machination
(a) labour saving (b) evil plot
(c) factory work (d) engine part

309. Malaise
(a) stagnation (b) spite
(c) curse (d) sickness

310. Mystical
(a) imaginary (b) vague
(c) prophetic (d) spiritually

311. Muffle
(a) soften (b) soften
(c) wrap (d) hasten

312. Masticate
(a) swallow (b) organise
(c) meander (d) reduce

313. Macabre
(a) innocent (b) tarried
(c) gruesome (d) pleasing

314. Marvellous
(a) pleasing (b) wonderful
(c) charming (d) attractive

315. Morbid
(a) angry (b) diseased
(c) irritated (d) dying

316. Mellifluous
(a) sweet (b) stale
(c) tasteful (d) stupid

317. Malign
(a) depreciate (b) deviate
(c) perforate (d) assign

318. Moot
(a) unexpected (b) obsequious
(c) controversial (d) invisible

319. Moronic
(a) imbecile (b) invective
(c) abusive (d) sharp

320. Magnanimous
(a) kind (b) generous
(c) loyal (d) loving

321. Myopic
(a) astigmatic (b) short-sighted
(c) cross-eyed (d) blind

322. Magnifying
(a) enlarging (b) discriminating
(c) reducing (d) denying

323. Modish
(a) adorned (b) sentimental
(c) stylish (d) vacillating

324. Maverick
(a) novice (b) reformer
(c) wonderful (d) unorthodox

325. Malady
(a) ill will (b) ill luck
(c) ill feeling (d) illness

326. Mundane
(a) luxurious (b) worldly
(c) spiritual (d) global

327. Magniloquent
(a) tactful (b) amusing
(c) humorous (d) boastful

328. Mutation
(a) variation (b) display
(c) severance (d) silence

329. Mordant
(a) festering (b) sarcastic
(c) depressed (d) mild

330. Monotonous
(a) uniform (b) equal
(c) same (d) dull

331. Maim
(a) copy (b) imitate
(c) disfigure (d) severe

332. Manifesto
(a) cargo list
(b) secret treaty
(c) revolutionary plot
(d) public declaration

333. Motley
(a) of various colours
(b) undistinguished
(c) dirty
(d) abundant

334. Mayhem
(a) depth (b) measurement
(c) havoc (d) murder

335. Meticulous
(a) lying (b) painstaking
(c) irascible (d) tawdry

336. Mollification
(a) magnification (b) pacification
(c) amplification (d) NOTA

337. Malleable
(a) permeable (b) pliant
(c) stringy (d) puncture proof

338. Miasma
(a) stench (b) aroma
(c) sweetness (d) NOTA

339. Mordant
(a) trenchant (b) festering
(c) sweet (d) fragrant

N

340. Nepotism
(a) favouritism (b) carelessness
(c) inefficiency (d) corruption

341. Nostalgic
(a) soothing (b) homesick
(c) diseased (d) indolent

342. Naive
(a) natural (b) novice
(c) credulous (d) primitives

343. Niggard
(a) cunning (b) miser
(c) shrewd (d) clever

O

344. Obfuscate
(a) push (b) compete
(c) confuse (d) remove

345. Onerous
(a) awesome (b) dutiful
(c) difficult (d) burdensome

346. Omnipotent
(a) all knowing (b) all powerful
(c) everlasting (d) all merciful

347. Ostensibly
(a) actually (b) conspicuously
(c) apparently (d) quietly

348. Ostentation
(a) protruding (b) wealthy
(c) decorative (d) showy

349. Ostracise
(a) fearful (b) fortunate
(c) uncared (d) cut off

350. Ostensible
(a) apparent (b) elaborate
(c) traditional (d) showy

351. Optimistic
(a) optician (b) favourable
(c) wishful (d) hopeful

352. Obdurate
(a) adamant (b) helpful
(c) simple (d) flexible

353. Ostentatious
(a) showy (b) noisy
(c) wealthy (d) talkative

354. Ogle
(a) look (b) stare
(c) peep (d) see

355. Overtures
(a) glimpses (b) promises
(c) rewards (d) offers

356. Overweening
(a) crushing (b) arrogant
(c) pampering (d) massive

P

357. Placid
(a) calm (b) dull
(c) enjoyable (d) clear

358. Prolific
(a) fertile (b) destroy
(c) modest (d) pretty

359. Placate
(a) appease (b) amuse
(c) pity (d) embroil

360. Prohibit
(a) banish (b) punish
(c) forbid (d) exhibit

361. Penchant
(a) disability (b) dislike
(c) like (d) eagerness

362. Pertinacious
(a) determined (b) delicate
(c) defensive (d) humble

363. Pilferage
(a) steal (b) snatch
(c) destroy (d) damage

364. Prudent
(a) skilled (b) experienced
(c) cautious (d) wise

365. Parochial
(a) gloomy
(b) reluctant
(c) troublesome
(d) narrow-minded

366. Prevaricate
(a) anticipate (b) lie
(c) delay (d) authenticate

367. Penitence
(a) retribution (b) submission
(c) confinement (d) repentance

368. Profound
(a) fathomless (b) scanty
(c) scary (d) shallow

369. Prerogative
(a) command (b) privilege
(c) request (d) desire

370. Paramour
(a) rival (b) lover
(c) companion (d) friend

371. Precarious
(a) critical (b) cautious
(c) perilous (d) brittle

372. Paramount
(a) urgent (b) supreme
(c) valuable (d) prestigious

373. Perilous
(a) tempting (b) obsolete
(c) dangerous (d) concrete

374. Preposterous
(a) formal (b) judicious
(c) ridiculous (d) ceremonious

375. Pristine
(a) traditional (b) expensive
(c) original (d) meritorious

376. Prowess
(a) eagerness (b) keenness
(c) understanding (d) bravery

377. Prattle
(a) chatter (b) construct
(c) meditate (d) loiter

378. Proliferate
(a) generate (b) proclaim
(c) support (d) assist

379. Pettifogging
(a) stable (b) unimportant
(c) strong (d) lenient

380. Paradigm
(a) theme (b) example
(c) proof (d) paragon

381. Prune
(a) lend (b) reduce
(c) expand (d) prolong

382. Promulgate
(a) proclaim (b) inform
(c) promote (d) enforce

383. Paparazzo
(a) actor (b) director
(c) dancer (d) photographer

384. Proscribe
(a) banish (b) prohibit
(c) allow (d) accept

385. Palpable
(a) subtle (b) persuasive
(c) excited (d) obvious

386. Parsimonious
(a) stingy (b) hypocritical
(c) stiff (d) miserly

387. Pragmatic
(a) perplexing (b) ideal
(c) practical (d) experienced

388. Perfidy
(a) confidence (b) treachery
(c) obstinacy (d) insolence

389. Peruse
(a) exhaust (b) change
(c) analyse (d) condense

390. Platitudinous
(a) banal (b) level
(c) boastful (d) oratorical

391. Pertinacious
(a) stubbornly (b) related
(c) bold (d) unabashed

392. Polemic
(a) eloquent (b) awkward
(c) scathing (d) disparaging

393. Predatory
(a) plundering (b) anticipating
(c) powerful (d) carnivorous

394. Predilection
(a) forecast (b) preference
(c) remembrance (d) gratification

395. Pre-empt
(a) vacate (b) substitute
(c) prevent (d) place a bet

396. Protagonist
(a) opponent (b) proponent
(c) rebel (d) wrestler

397. Paucity
(a) costliness (b) short rest
(c) scantiness (d) misuse

398. Prodigality
(a) lavishness (b) stimulus
(c) sinfulness (d) negligence

Q

399. Quack
(a) pyromaniac (b) charlatan
(c) dilemma (d) victim

400. Quell
(a) kill (b) destroy
(c) overwhelm (d) overthrow

401. Quibble
(a) discuss (b) deliberate
(c) argue (d) haggle

402. Quizzical
(a) puzzling (b) queer
(c) ill-tempered (d) antiquated

403. Quagmire
(a) large clam (b) bog
(c) underbrush (d) gradual rise

R

404. Ribald
(a) refined (b) indifferent
(c) vulgar (d) attractive

405. Reiterate
(a) reassess (b) rewrite
(c) repeat (d) stutter

406. Replenish
(a) refill (b) supply
(c) provide (d) restore

407. Reverberate
(a) resonate (b) accelerate
(c) revitalise (d) gibberish

408. Reticence
(a) generosity (b) frankness
(c) sincerity (d) taciturnity

409. Robust
(a) wear (b) useless
(c) forceful (d) stupid

410. Reluctant
(a) inclined (b) ready
(c) hesitating (d) willing

411. Reckless
(a) courageous (b) daring
(c) bold (d) rash

412. Repercussion
(a) remuneration (b) consequence
(c) reaction (d) recollection

413. Retrograde
(a) pushback (b) backward
(c) go back (d) draw

414. Reverberations
(a) repetition (b) reverse
(c) echo (d) imitate

415. Resilient
(a) rigid (b) flexible
(c) convenient (d) hard

416. Rakish
(a) illegitimate (b) illegal
(c) immoral (d) heinous

417. Retribution
(a) contempt (b) revenge
(c) punishment (d) discount

418. Replica
(a) mythical creature
(b) answer
(c) duplicate
(d) public building

419. Recluse
(a) miser (b) aged person
(c) woman-hater (d) hermit

420. Recrudescence
(a) rawness
(b) revival
(c) refinement
(d) lack of manners

S

421. Savvy
(a) deformed (b) understanding
(c) dissatisfied (d) NOTA

422. Serene
(a) calm (b) meek
(c) solemn (d) delicate

423. Sanguine
(a) hopeful (b) modest
(c) clever (d) proud

424. Stamina
(a) endurance (b) intensity
(c) eagerness (d) energy

425. Stubborn
(a) willing (b) pliable
(c) easy (d) obstinate

426. Stalemate
(a) deadly (b) dead-end
(c) diffusion (d) dead-drunk

427. Slander
(a) circular (b) spherical
(c) fragile (d) defame

428. Stringent
(a) causing to shrink (b) strict
(c) stringy (d) tense

429. Shrewd
(a) naive (b) clever
(c) raw (d) youthful

430. Serenity
(a) agitation (b) protest
(c) stir (d) calmness

431. Sustain
(a) support (b) review
(c) believe (d) survive

432. Succour
(a) search (b) flow
(c) raise (d) support

433. Severe
(a) rigid (b) aggressive
(c) offensive (d) acute

434. Stridency
(a) flippancy (b) stress
(c) consistency (d) harshness

435. Simon-pure
(a) false (b) genuine
(c) holy (d) artificial

436. Surreptitious
(a) mysterious (b) abstract
(c) secretive (d) secret

437. Scintillating
(a) touching (b) warming
(c) guttering (d) smouldering

438. Sycophant
(a) flatterer (b) follower
(c) admirer (d) suppliant

439. Salacity
(a) depression (b) recession
(c) bliss (d) indecency

440. Surreal
(a) unreal (b) reality
(c) bizarre (d) precise

441. Stringent
(a) tough (b) principled
(c) strict (d) harmful

442. Sultry
(a) foul (b) bad
(c) hot (d) oppressive

443. Spasmodic
(a) intestinal (b) internal
(c) intermittent (d) gradual

444. Solicit
(a) request (b) beseech
(c) demand (d) expectation

445. Stalemate
(a) deadlock (b) stoppage
(c) blockade (d) postpone

446. Sagacity
(a) morality (b) knowledge
(c) wisdom (d) sanctity

447. Salacious
(a) briny (b) purchasable
(c) obscene (d) flavoured

448. Savant
(a) cleansing agent
(b) learned person
(c) young student
(d) French courtier

449. Sanguinary
(a) hopeful (b) unlimited
(c) unnecessary (d) bloody

450. Salubrious
(a) flavoured (b) healthy
(c) lewd (d) pathetic

T

451. Terrific
(a) tragic (b) terrible
(c) big (d) excellent

452. Tête-à-tête
(a) delightful (b) penetrating
(c) piercing (d) conversation

453. Triumph
(a) gain (b) victory
(c) excitement (d) joy

454. Tedious
(a) lengthy (b) tiresome
(c) saint (d) widower

455. Temperate
(a) cool (b) moderate
(c) favourable (d) dangerous

456. Twain
(a) discarded (b) worthless
(c) couple (d) strong

457. Trivial
(a) economical (b) uneconomical
(c) frivolous (d) commonplace

458. Testify
(a) witness (b) describe
(c) recognise (d) appreciate

459. Tentative
(a) final (b) provisional
(c) current (d) unreliable

460. Tenacious
(a) bold (b) poisonous
(c) uncomfortable (d) piercing

461. Taciturnity
(a) silence (b) violence
(c) insolence (d) prudence

462. Truncate
(a) cut off (b) end swiftly
(c) act cruelly (d) cancel

463. Tutelage
(a) rejection (b) perfection
(c) protection (d) dejection

464. Teeter
(a) hesitate (b) descend
(c) pretend (d) toddle

465. Tranquil
(a) sedate (b) calm
(c) quite (d) dull

466. Tycoon
(a) leader (b) ruler
(c) prophet (d) magnate

467. Tantamount
(a) equivalent (b) gigantic
(c) superior (d) far-removed

468. Talisman
(a) charm/formula (b) juror
(c) informer (d) lecturer

469. Transcend
(a) move (b) degrade
(c) surpass (d) delay

470. Tonsure
(a) baldness (b) furry
(c) hairy (d) NOTA

471. Transmogrify
(a) transmute (b) haunt
(c) pierce (d) terrify

472. Traumatic
(a) dreamy (b) magic
(c) emphatic (d) turbulent

U

473. Undaunted
(a) careless (b) unafraid
(c) worthless (d) prudent

474. Unanimously
(a) friendly (b) forcefully
(c) unquestionably (d) democratically

475. Ulterior
(a) revealed (b) undisclosed
(c) extreme (d) decisive

476. Upbraid
(a) plait (b) reproach
(c) elevate (d) foster

477. Unconscionable
(a) unmindful (b) excessive
(c) unmanageable (d) distasteful

V

478. Venality
(a) hope (b) sacrifice
(c) respect (d) corruption

479. Votary
(a) devotee (b) conscious
(c) religious (d) amiable

480. Virginity
(a) decency (b) maidenhood
(c) beauty (d) attractiveness

481. Venture
(a) entrust (b) risk
(c) travel (d) adventure

482. Venerate
(a) defame (b) abuse
(c) respect (d) accuse

483. Vendetta

(a) revenge (b) proposal
(c) compromise (d) feud

484. Vituperate

(a) encourage (b) pretend
(c) appraise (d) vilify

485. Vilify

(a) deceive (b) desert
(c) deprive (d) defame

486. Vindicate

(a) approve (b) justify
(c) express (d) exonerate

487. Virile

(a) childish (b) womanly
(c) manly (d) brave

488. Voracious

(a) voluptuous (b) victorious
(c) hungry (d) wild

W

489. Wary

(a) cautious (b) accurate
(c) quick (d) practical

490. Waive

(a) restrict (b) relax
(c) permit (d) admit

491. Wry

(a) sad (b) twisted
(c) smiling (d) undeserved

492. Worthless

(a) cheap (b) valuable
(c) invalid (d) variable

493. Wither

(a) dry up (b) shrivel
(c) destroy (d) die

494. Whim

(a) thought (b) dream
(c) fit (d) fantasy

495. Wallow

(a) fantasy (b) suffer
(c) luxuriate (d) comfort

496. Wrath

(a) jealousy (b) hatred
(c) anger (d) violence

Z

497. Zenith

(a) sharp (b) bright
(c) bravery (d) climax

498. Zany

(a) thief (b) magician
(c) clown (d) pet

499. Zeal

(a) ardour (b) apathy
(c) indifference (d) NOTA

500. Zealot

(a) fanatic (b) moderate
(c) liberal (d) feminist

ANSWERS – SYNONYMS PRACTICE TESTS (MCQS)

1	(c)	38	(a)	75	(b)	112	(c)	149	(b)	186	(b)	223	(a)
2	(c)	39	(a)	76	(c)	113	(b)	150	(a)	187	(d)	224	(d)
3	(c)	40	(a)	77	(c)	114	(a)	151	(b)	188	(a)	225	(a)
4	(b)	41	(c)	78	(b)	115	(c)	152	(a)	189	(b)	226	(c)
5	(b)	42	(d)	79	(b)	116	(b)	153	(b)	190	(a)	227	(c)
6	(c)	43	(b)	80	(c)	117	(d)	154	(a)	191	(b)	228	(a)
7	(b)	44	(c)	81	(c)	118	(b)	155	(a)	192	(d)	229	(b)
8	(c)	45	(a)	82	(a)	119	(b)	156	(b)	193	(b)	230	(a)
9	(d)	46	(c)	83	(d)	120	(a)	157	(d)	194	(c)	231	(b)
10	(d)	47	(a)	84	(d)	121	(a)	158	(b)	195	(a)	232	(d)
11	(b)	48	(a)	85	(b)	122	(d)	159	(c)	196	(a)	233	(c)
12	(c)	49	(b)	86	(a)	123	(b)	160	(a)	197	(a)	234	(b)
13	(c)	50	(c)	87	(a)	124	(b)	161	(b)	198	(c)	235	(b)
14	(b)	51	(b)	88	(d)	125	(a)	162	(c)	199	(a)	236	(d)
15	(c)	52	(a)	89	(c)	126	(d)	163	(b)	200	(b)	237	(a)
16	(a)	53	(b)	90	(c)	127	(d)	164	(c)	201	(b)	238	(c)
17	(a)	54	(c)	91	(d)	128	(d)	165	(b)	202	(a)	239	(c)
18	(b)	55	(c)	92	(a)	129	(d)	166	(a)	203	(c)	240	(b)
19	(b)	56	(d)	93	(c)	130	(d)	167	(a)	204	(c)	241	(c)
20	(d)	57	(c)	94	(a)	131	(c)	168	(b)	205	(b)	242	(d)
21	(d)	58	(a)	95	(d)	132	(b)	169	(a)	206	(c)	243	(b)
22	(b)	59	(c)	96	(b)	133	(d)	170	(b)	207	(a)	244	(b)
23	(a)	60	(d)	97	(a)	134	(d)	171	(c)	208	(a)	245	(a)
24	(a)	61	(c)	98	(b)	135	(b)	172	(a)	209	(d)	246	(d)
25	(c)	62	(a)	99	(a)	136	(c)	173	(b)	210	(d)	247	(d)
26	(b)	63	(d)	100	(d)	137	(a)	174	(b)	211	(d)	248	(c)
27	(a)	64	(d)	101	(d)	138	(d)	175	(a)	212	(b)	249	(a)
28	(d)	65	(c)	102	(b)	139	(c)	176	(c)	213	(d)	250	(a)
29	(c)	66	(b)	103	(c)	140	(a)	177	(b)	214	(b)	251	(a)
30	(a)	67	(a)	104	(b)	141	(a)	178	(a)	215	(c)	252	(b)
31	(a)	68	(b)	105	(a)	142	(b)	179	(a)	216	(a)	253	(d)
32	(c)	69	(b)	106	(a)	143	(d)	180	(a)	217	(d)	254	(a)
33	(a)	70	(c)	107	(d)	144	(b)	181	(b)	218	(a)	255	(d)
34	(b)	71	(c)	108	(d)	145	(d)	182	(a)	219	(d)	256	(c)
35	(c)	72	(c)	109	(d)	146	(c)	183	(c)	220	(b)	257	(b)
36	(d)	73	(d)	110	(a)	147	(a)	184	(c)	221	(b)	258	(b)
37	(a)	74	(c)	111	(c)	148	(b)	185	(a)	222	(a)	259	(b)

260	(b)	299	(c)	338	(a)	377	(a)	416	(c)	455	(b)	494	(d)
261	(c)	300	(d)	339	(a)	378	(a)	417	(b)	456	(c)	495	(d)
262	(b)	301	(d)	340	(a)	379	(b)	418	(c)	457	(c)	496	(c)
263	(c)	302	(b)	341	(b)	380	(b)	419	(d)	458	(a)	497	(d)
264	(c)	303	(a)	342	(b)	381	(b)	420	(b)	459	(b)	498	(c)
265	(a)	304	(d)	343	(b)	382	(a)	421	(b)	460	(a)	499	(a)
266	(d)	305	(a)	344	(c)	383	(d)	422	(a)	461	(a)	500	(a)
267	(d)	306	(d)	345	(d)	384	(b)	423	(a)	462	(a)		
268	(a)	307	(c)	346	(b)	385	(b)	424	(a)	463	(c)		
269	(d)	308	(b)	347	(c)	386	(d)	425	(d)	464	(d)		
270	(b)	309	(d)	348	(d)	387	(c)	426	(b)	465	(b)		
271	(d)	310	(d)	349	(d)	388	(b)	427	(d)	466	(d)		
272	(c)	311	(b)	350	(d)	389	(c)	428	(b)	467	(a)		
273	(d)	312	(a)	351	(d)	390	(a)	429	(b)	468	(a)		
274	(b)	313	(c)	352	(a)	391	(a)	430	(d)	469	(c)		
275	(a)	314	(b)	353	(a)	392	(c)	431	(d)	470	(a)		
276	(b)	315	(b)	354	(b)	393	(a)	432	(d)	471	(a)		
277	(d)	316	(a)	355	(d)	394	(b)	433	(d)	472	(d)		
278	(b)	317	(a)	356	(b)	395	(c)	434	(d)	473	(b)		
279	(a)	318	(c)	357	(a)	396	(b)	435	(c)	474	(d)		
280	(d)	319	(a)	358	(a)	397	(c)	436	(a)	475	(b)		
281	(d)	320	(b)	359	(a)	398	(a)	437	(d)	476	(b)		
282	(b)	321	(b)	360	(c)	399	(b)	438	(a)	477	(a)		
283	(d)	322	(a)	361	(c)	400	(b)	439	(d)	478	(d)		
284	(a)	323	(c)	362	(a)	401	(c)	440	(a)	479	(a)		
285	(b)	324	(d)	363	(a)	402	(a)	441	(c)	480	(b)		
286	(d)	325	(d)	364	(d)	403	(b)	442	(c)	481	(d)		
287	(a)	326	(b)	365	(d)	404	(c)	443	(c)	482	(c)		
288	(d)	327	(d)	366	(c)	405	(c)	444	(a)	483	(d)		
289	(b)	328	(a)	367	(d)	406	(a)	445	(a)	484	(d)		
290	(c)	329	(c)	368	(a)	407	(a)	446	(c)	485	(d)		
291	(a)	330	(a)	369	(b)	408	(d)	447	(c)	486	(b)		
292	(b)	331	(c)	370	(b)	409	(c)	448	(b)	487	(a)		
293	(c)	332	(d)	371	(a)	410	(c)	449	(a)	488	(c)		
294	(b)	333	(a)	372	(b)	411	(d)	450	(b)	489	(a)		
295	(a)	334	(c)	373	(c)	412	(b)	451	(b)	490	(b)		
296	(c)	335	(b)	374	(c)	413	(c)	452	(d)	491	(b)		
297	(b)	336	(b)	375	(c)	414	(c)	453	(b)	492	(a)		
298	(a)	337	(a)	376	(d)	415	(b)	454	(b)	493	(a)		

5 ANTONYMS - PRACTICE TESTS (MCQs)

352 MCQs

DIRECTIONS: *Given below are words in alphabetical order. Every word is followed by four options. You have to find out the word which is exactly opposite in meaning to the given word. NOTA means None of the Above given answers.*

A

1. **Autonomy**
(a) freedom (b) dependence
(c) authority (d) independence
2. **Abhorrence**
(a) aversion (b) liking
(c) appreciation (d) fear
3. **Audacious**
(a) timid (b) vulgar
(c) low (d) unpractised
4. **Absolute**
(a) scarce (b) limited
(c) faulty (d) efficient
5. **Acute**
(a) sharp (b) critical
(c) dull (d) sensitive
6. **Antipathy**
(a) obedience (b) admiration
(c) agreement (d) fondness
7. **Apposite**
(a) inappropriate (b) intemperate
(c) inconsistent (d) irregular
8. **Amplify**
(a) mummify (b) shock
(c) curtail (d) embalm
9. **Acumen**
(a) intelligence (b) imbecility
(c) potentiality (d) unfamiliarity
10. **Adversity**
(a) enmity (b) severity
(c) prosperity (d) calamity
11. **Auspicious**
(a) spicy (b) unfavourable
(c) clever (d) cunning
12. **Adherent**
(a) rival (b) alien
(c) detractor (d) enemy
13. **Amicable**
(a) friendly (b) shy
(c) hostile (d) crazy
14. **Applaud**
(a) request (b) criticise
(c) pray (d) flatter
15. **Abundant**
(a) long (b) heavy
(c) scarce (d) excessive
16. **Adroit**
(a) deterred (b) skilful
(c) foolish (d) unskilled
17. **Appease**
(a) sympathise (b) irritate
(c) peaceful (d) apart
18. **Absurd**
(a) awkward (b) unreasonable
(c) reasonable (d) worthless
19. **Ancient**
(a) latent (b) raw
(c) recent (d) historical
20. **Acquittal**
(a) warrant (b) condemnation
(c) conviction (d) castigation
21. **Affluent**
(a) talkative (b) poor
(c) prosperous (d) close
22. **Agony**
(a) pleasure (b) bliss
(c) ecstasy (d) fear

23. Aberration
(a) typical behaviour
(b) correct manners
(c) straight aim
(d) full truthfulness

24. Ameliorate
(a) increase (b) deteriorate
(c) clasp (d) dissemble

25. Artificial
(a) solid (b) truthful
(c) authentic (d) natural

26. Abominate
(a) praise (b) attract
(c) like (d) adorn

27. Adamant
(a) reluctant (b) yielding
(c) burly (d) unwanted

28. Abusive
(a) wretched (b) decent
(c) complimentary (d) respectful

29. Averse
(a) willing (b) unwilling
(c) refusal (d) rejection

30. Agile
(a) underfit (b) lazy
(c) clumsy (d) lethargic

31. Arduous
(a) ordinary (b) easy
(c) expected (d) NOTA

32. Abridge
(a) expand (b) increase
(c) lengthen (d) continue

B

33. Bliss
(a) anguish (b) sorrow
(c) agony (d) suffering

34. Blatant
(a) noisy (b) quiet
(c) barren (d) slow

35. Boost
(a) hinder (b) obstruct
(c) discourage (d) rebuke

36. Base
(a) roof (b) height
(c) top (d) climax

37. Bridge
(a) divide (b) bind
(c) release (d) open

38. Beautiful
(a) ugly (b) dark
(c) rough (d) dirty

39. Bashful
(a) daring (b) boastful
(c) upright (d) confident

40. Beseech
(a) bully (b) solicit
(c) demand (d) dismiss

41. Boorish
(a) handsome (b) happy
(c) quite (d) genteel

42. Benign
(a) gracious (b) sinister
(c) novel (d) humane

43. Blemish
(a) preserve (b) purify
(c) defect (d) tarnish

44. Bizarre
(a) soft (b) usual
(c) gentle (d) same

45. Brazen
(a) respectful (b) innocent
(c) delicious (d) helpful

46. Benevolence
(a) contempt (b) malevolence
(c) hatred (d) derision

47. Balmy
(a) hard (b) genuine
(c) mild (d) fragrant

48. Brutality
(a) criminal (b) humanity
(c) adamant (d) without fear

49. Boisterous
(a) calm (b) comfortable
(c) good (d) happy

50. Blithe
(a) soft (b) aloof
(c) cheerless (d) gloomy

51. Brief
(a) short (b) abridged
(c) concise (d) detailed

52. Baffle
(a) elaborate (b) clarify
(c) explain (d) in order

C

53. Condense
(a) lengthen (b) expand
(c) distribute (d) interpret

54. Comply
(a) accept (b) agree
(c) disagree (d) consent

55. Commodious
(a) limited (b) expensive
(c) numerous (d) leisurely

56. Cajole
(a) dissuade (b) detract
(c) disclose (d) confide

57. Carnal
(a) sensuous (b) spiritual
(c) visionary (d) imaginary

58. Conspicuous
(a) indifferent (b) harmless
(c) insignificant (d) unknown

59. Criticise
(a) judge (b) appreciate
(c) flatter (d) analyse

60. Catholic
(a) rough (b) orthodox
(c) open (d) NOTA

61. Chide
(a) praise (b) fear
(c) criticise (d) flatter

62. Crass
(a) gross (b) refined
(c) coarse (d) dense

63. Culpable
(a) irresponsible (b) careless
(c) blameless (d) defendable

64. Covert
(a) clandestine (b) overt
(c) virtuous (d) wide

65. Considerate
(a) harsh (b) infuriated
(c) opposed (d) indifferent

66. Coarse
(a) beautiful (b) soft
(c) fine (d) attractive

67. Callous
(a) confident (b) sentimental
(c) sensitive (d) capable

68. Concealment
(a) identification (b) broadness
(c) evidence (d) indication

69. Consistency
(a) stability (b) harmony
(c) defective (d) inconsistency

70. Capacious
(a) changeable (b) foolish
(c) caring (d) limited

71. Culminate
(a) frustrate (b) fail
(c) abort (d) defeat

72. Chaos
(a) symmetric (b) inexperienced
(c) disturb (d) mould

73. Clandestine
(a) above ground (b) public
(c) outside (d) burnt out

74. Cognisance
(a) idiom (b) ignorance
(c) abeyance (d) anecdote

75. Clumsy
(a) mercy (b) dull
(c) bright (d) dexterous

76. Cohesion
(a) disintegration (b) anomaly
(c) disunity (d) internal

77. Cosy
(a) honestly (b) cold
(c) treacherous (d) falsehood

78. Circumscribed
(a) unrestricted (b) unconfined
(c) open (d) free

79. Crafty
(a) simple (b) artless
(c) ingenious (d) improper

80. Confiscate
(a) release (b) allow
(c) use (d) confer

81. Competent
(a) intelligent (b) diligent
(c) inefficient (d) deficit

B

82. Dissent
(a) agreement (b) dispute
(c) disunity (d) controversy

83. Dissuade
(a) incite (b) persuade
(c) advise (d) instigate

84. Delete
(a) impound (b) insert
(c) inspire (d) injure

85. Despondency
(a) humility (b) cheerlessness
(c) cheerfulness (d) NOTA

86. Degenerate
(a) create (b) progress
(c) restore (d) reproduce

87. Deliberate
(a) premeditated (b) sparking
(c) methodical (d) impulsive

88. Debauchee
(a) moralist (b) thinker
(c) schemer (d) dreamer

89. Dreary
(a) plenty (b) monotonous
(c) unhappy (d) cheerful

90. Depraved
(a) great (b) enhanced
(c) moral (d) prosperous

91. Dauntless
(a) courageous (b) thoughtful
(c) weak (d) NOTA

92. Deplete
(a) refund (b) replenish
(c) fulfil (d) recover

93. Deviate
(a) follow (b) locate
(c) break (d) concentrate

94. Deficit
(a) superfluous (b) surplus
(c) explicit (d) implicit

95. Debilitating
(a) strengthening (b) enfeebling
(c) occupying (d) inhabiting

96. Dainty
(a) splendid (b) aggressive
(c) vigorous (d) towering

97. Disdain
(a) depreciate (b) admiration
(c) penitence (d) contempt

98. Debacle
(a) regain (b) solution
(c) rise (d) movement

99. Doleful
(a) poor (b) happy
(c) rich (d) steady

100. Diabolic
(a) patient (b) generous
(c) kind (d) simple

101. Discrepancy
(a) variance (b) inappropriate
(c) consistency (d) inconsistency

102. Denounce
(a) defend (b) gather
(c) fight (d) rally

103. Debonair
(a) worried (b) pensive
(c) grim (d) serious

104. Disperse
(a) collect (b) considerate
(c) clever (d) cunning

105. Dissipate
(a) sustain (b) conserve
(c) preserve (d) maintain

106. Dormant
(a) active (b) modern
(c) permanent (d) transient

107. Defection
(a) resignation (b) invitation
(c) joining (d) co–operation

108. Dusky
(a) visible (b) fair
(c) obscure (d) shadowy

109. Dither
(a) cry (b) refer
(c) decide (d) defer

110. Derogatory
(a) immediate (b) praising
(c) opinionated (d) roguish

111. Disastrous
(a) constructive (b) demolishing
(c) positive (d) none

112. Deleterious
(a) impulsive (b) salubrious
(c) pathetic (d) inclusive

113. Disdain
(a) depreciate (b) admiration
(c) penitence (d) contempt

114. Diverge
(a) repulse (b) converge
(c) resurge (d) constrict

115. Disperse
(a) collect (b) assemble
(c) hoard (d) save

116. Defiance
(a) dismay (b) suspicion
(c) obedience (d) anxiety

117. Discrete
(a) loud (b) combined
(c) loose (d) circle

118. Diminish
(a) decrease (b) increase
(c) lower (d) rise

119. Desecrate
(a) manage (b) build
(c) consecrate (d) concentrate

E

120. Endow
(a) borrow (b) steal
(c) snatch (d) extort

121. Exhibit
(a) conceal (b) prevent
(c) withdraw (d) concede

122. Enough
(a) inadequate (b) scarce
(c) deficit (d) less

123. Erudite
(a) professional (b) immature
(c) unimaginative (d) ignorant

124. Escalate
(a) lessen (b) subside
(c) reduce (d) fashionable

125. Evacuate
(a) admit (b) emerge
(c) abandon (d) invade

126. Eclipse
(a) shine (b) enlarge
(c) goggle (d) gleam

127. Embrace
(a) suspect (b) harm
(c) reject (d) hurt

128. Exonerate
(a) compel (b) accuse
(c) imprison (d) boldness

129. Extension
(a) condensation (b) subtraction
(c) deletion (d) weakening

130. Execrable
(a) importable (b) acceptable
(c) desirable (d) irritable

131. Euphonious
(a) strident (b) lethargic
(c) literary (d) musical

132. Exterior
(a) internal (b) inner
(c) interior (d) inward

133. Exodus
(a) restoration (b) return
(c) home–coming (d) influx

134. Edification
(a) lamentation (b) annotation
(c) corruption (d) segregation

135. Exasperate
(a) belittle (b) annoy
(c) please (d) tarnish

136. Exotic
(a) poor (b) inexpensive
(c) ugly (d) conventional

137. Explicit
(a) inspiring (b) plain
(c) invigorating (d) implied

138. Exalt
(a) depreciate (b) ennoble
(c) glorify (d) simplify

139. Encourage
(a) warn (b) discourage
(c) dampen (d) disapprove

140. Erratic
(a) reliable (b) right
(c) punctual (d) free

141. Engulfed
(a) encircled (b) groped
(c) disfigured (d) detached

142. Epilogue
(a) conversation (b) dialogue
(c) dramatic (d) prologue

143. Execrate
(a) care (b) praise
(c) love (d) bless

144. Extravagant
(a) miserly
(b) uneconomical
(c) mean
(d) narrow-minded

145. Equanimity
(a) excitement (b) duplicity
(c) dubiousness (d) resentment

146. Extirpate
(a) preserve (b) inseminate
(c) ingratiate (d) enter

147. Exaggerate
(a) minimise (b) maximise
(c) cessation (d) difficult

148. Eloquent
(a) inarticulate (b) clear
(c) lucid (d) coherent

149. Enervate
(a) debilitate (b) fortify
(c) introduce (d) conclude

150. Eschew
(a) traduce (b) invite
(c) use (d) emanate

151. Effulgence
(a) murky (b) harshness
(c) mercenary (d) quiet

152. Ensemble
(a) complement (b) cacophony
(c) coordination (d) solo

153. Ethereal
(a) heavenly (b) earthly
(c) lifelike (d) affectionate

F

154. Fecund
(a) barren (b) solid
(c) unploughed (d) hard

155. Facsimile
(a) reproduction (b) sincere
(c) original (d) engineered

156. Frailty
(a) emaciation (b) strength
(c) health (d) boldness

157. Furtive
(a) straight (b) obvious
(c) unambiguous (d) open

158. Frantic
(a) calm (b) hopeful
(c) active (d) bitter

159. Fickle
(a) diseased (b) fast
(c) constant (d) quick

160. Frugal
(a) gaudy (b) generous
(c) extravagant (d) charitable

161. Fraction
(a) ignition (b) acceleration
(c) mummification (d) NOTA

162. Factitious
(a) bogus (d) fake
(c) spurious (d) genuine

163. Forbidden
(a) allowed (b) prohibited
(c) agreed (d) forsaken

164. Frail
(a) vigorous (b) sturdy
(c) hardy (d) strong

165. Forbid
(a) provoke (b) appreciate
(c) celebrate (d) permit

166. Fluctuate
(a) strong (b) sturdy
(c) slow (d) steady

167. Furious
(a) mild (b) restrained
(c) ticklish (d) disjointed

168. Fallacious
(a) true (b) faulty
(c) wrong (d) dirty

169. Forlorn
(a) elated (b) gloomy
(c) joyless (d) credible

170. Frugality
(a) showy (b) exhibition
(c) extravagance (d) visage

171. Fierce
(a) wild (b) docile
(c) calm (d) timid

172. Fabricate
(a) damage (b) destroy
(c) disintegrate (d) implicate

173. Filthy
(a) stainless (b) shining
(c) sterilised (d) clean

G

174. Gorgeous
(a) desperate (b) plain
(c) fashionable (d) sumptuous

175. Glut
(a) dearth (b) limit
(c) drain (d) supply

176. Gruesome
(a) pleasant (b) rude
(c) fresh (d) clear

177. Gigantic
(a) huge (b) small
(c) dangerous (d) fantastic

178. Glamour
(a) silence (b) incubate
(c) murmur (d) whisper

179. Gusto
(a) sadness (b) distaste
(c) discolour (d) gloom

180. Gratitude
(a) wretched (b) ingratitude
(c) unfaithfulness (d) wickedness

H

181. Hoard
(a) deposit (b) supply
(c) satisfy (d) accumulate

182. Humble
(a) dominant (b) proud
(c) despotic (d) pompous

183. Hide
(a) search (b) show
(c) shine (d) NOTA

184. Haughty
(a) pitiable (b) scared
(c) humble (d) cowardly

185. Hawk
(a) peaceful (b) pigeon
(c) fighter (d) dove

186. Homely
(a) rough (b) outgoing
(c) smooth (d) beautiful

187. Hostile
(a) friendly (b) sudden
(c) costly (d) unfair

188. Homogeneous
(a) heterogeneous (b) consciousness
(c) variegated (d) loquacious

189. Hesitant
(a) proud (b) confident
(c) shy (d) reluctant
(e) tacit

190. Hapless
(a) lucky (b) kind
(c) helpful (d) futile

191. Hamper
(a) open (b) release
(c) hold (d) hasten

I

192. Insipid
(a) nervous (b) pungent
(c) saucy (d) sour

193. Infallible
(a) dubious (b) mistaking
(c) erring (d) unreliable

194. Impeccable
(a) good (b) sound
(c) faulty (d) candid

195. Impervious
(a) penetrable (b) hidden
(c) tolerable (d) gentle

196. Impropriety
(a) decorum (b) purity
(c) ideal (d) conformity

197. Intrude
(a) withhold (b) withdraw
(c) accept (d) surrender

198. Indulge
(a) avoid (b) abstain
(c) forego (d) neglect

199. Impound
(a) generate (b) strengthen
(c) stimulate (d) release

200. Ignore
(a) support (b) favour
(c) redress (d) accept

201. Innocent
(a) sinful (b) guilty
(c) deadly (d) corruption

202. Illegible
(a) clear (b) imitable
(c) clean (d) readable

203. Inimical
(a) related (b) friendly
(c) neutral (d) cheerful

204. Immediate
(a) delayed (b) gradual
(c) leisurely (d) slow

205. Illustrious
(a) uneducated (b) uncivilised
(c) unintelligent (d) unknown

206. Innocence
(a) crime (b) mischief
(c) guilt (d) sin

207. Intransigent
(a) ever–ready (b) faithful
(c) flexible (d) obedient

208. Insolent
(a) sullen (b) rich
(c) determined (d) affable

209. Illusory
(a) nimble (b) realistic
(c) powerful (d) underrated

210. Inadequate
(a) glossy (b) rapid
(c) aspiring (d) sufficient

211. Intrude
(a) to tear away (b) keep away
(c) force (d) compelled

212. Implicate
(a) involve (b) exonerate
(c) corrupt (d) accuse

213. Implode
(a) extract (b) explode
(c) burst (d) erupt

214. Impede
(a) demote (b) promote
(c) eclipse (d) NOTA

215. Illicit
(a) lawful (b) delusive
(c) legitimate (d) NOTA

216. Inclement
(a) pleasant (b) bad
(c) beautiful (d) NOTA

217. Impudent
(a) discourteous (b) courteous
(c) kind (d) helpful

218. Inveterate
(a) stupid (b) uneducated
(c) ignorant (d) inexperienced

219. Indolent
(a) desirable (b) adequate
(c) energetic (d) consistent

J

220. Judicious
(a) unequal (b) unlawful
(c) impure (d) indiscreet

221. Jeer
(a) mourn (b) praise
(c) mock (d) sneer

222. Jettison
(a) rejoice (b) surrender
(c) accept (d) defend

223. Jittery
(a) relax (b) tense
(c) bold (d) shaky

224. Jocose
(a) dull (b) humorous
(c) playful (d) diseased

225. Justify
(a) accuse (b) infuriate
(c) absolve (d) vindicate

226. Jubilant
(a) scared (b) disturbed
(c) gloomy (d) quiet

227. Juxtapositions
(a) unity (b) opposition
(c) separation (d) difference

K

228. Knowledge
(a) ignorance (b) illiteracy
(c) foolishness (d) backwardness

229. Knack
(a) dullness (b) rested
(c) talent (d) dexterity

230. Keen
(a) dull (b) progue
(c) ardent (d) shrewd

231. Kindle
(a) ignite (b) encourage
(c) ignore (d) merciless

L

232. Luscious
(a) dry (b) sour
(c) ugly (d) stale

233. Laconic
(a) prolix (b) profligate
(c) prolific (d) bucolic

234. Languid
(a) smart (b) energetic
(c) fast (d) ferocious

235. Lethal
(a) safe (b) playful
(c) virulent (d) forgiving

236. Lofty
(a) assessed (b) debased
(c) general (d) intrusive

237. Livid
(a) faded (b) shining
(c) discoloured (d) polished

M

238. Magnify
(a) induce (b) diminish
(c) destroy (d) shrink

239. Malicious
(a) boastful (b) indifferent
(c) kind (d) generous

240. Meticulous
(a) slovenly (b) meretricious
(c) shaggy (d) mutual

241. Mundane
(a) extraordinary (b) superb
(c) heavenly (d) excellent

242. Musty
(a) fresh (b) expensive
(c) clean (d) fine

243. Marvellous
(a) pleasing (b) charming
(c) attractive (d) shabby

244. Mendacious
(a) broken (b) efficacious
(c) truthful (d) destructive

245. Morbid
(a) healthy (b) clever
(c) upright (d) sickly

246. Magnanimous
(a) selfish (b) naïve
(c) generous (d) small

247. Mammoth
(a) dull (b) weak
(c) tiny (d) bright

248. Mawkish
(a) sentimental (b) intelligent
(c) certain (d) carefree

N

249. Naive
(a) cunning (b) wealthy
(c) sophisticated (d) complicated

250. Nadir
(a) progress (b) liberty
(c) zenith (d) modernity

O

251. Obsolete
(a) conductive (b) rare
(c) useless (d) recent

252. Obstinate
(a) agreeing
(b) accepting
(c) yielding
(d) accommodating

253. Overweening
(a) humble (b) sedate
(c) miserly (d) clever

254. Onerous
(a) rough (b) burdensome
(c) easy (d) tough

255. Obfuscate
(a) simplify (b) explain
(c) describe (d) clarify

256. Ostentatious
(a) awkward (b) bankrupt
(c) ignorant (d) unpretentious

257. Outmoded
(a) polished (b) practicable
(c) stylish (d) fashionable

P

258. Precarious
(a) dangerous (b) safe
(c) cautious (d) easy

259. Profane
(a) arrogant (b) benign
(c) respectful (d) pious

260. Paucity
(a) surplus (b) scarcity
(c) presence (d) richness
(e) want

261. Pretentious
(a) deranged (b) small
(c) depressing (d) humble

262. Parsimonious
(a) generous (b) frugal
(c) crude (d) stingy

263. Prim
(a) rash (b) extravagant
(c) foul (d) shameful

264. Pertinent
(a) indifferent (b) detached
(c) determined (d) irrelevant

265. Prevent
(a) excite (b) support
(c) invite (d) incite

266. Predilection
(a) denial (b) concealment
(c) aversion (d) attraction

267. Persistent
(a) wavering (b) obstinate
(c) enduring (d) steady

268. Provocation
(a) destruction (b) peace
(c) pacification (d) vocation

269. Pompous
(a) feeble (b) normal
(c) humble (d) mild

270. Persuasive
(a) demoralising (b) false
(c) discouraging (d) unconvincing

271. Paltry
(a) strong (b) worthy
(c) mean (d) bitter

272. Putrid
(a) fresh (b) fragrant
(c) sweet (d) agreeable

273. Passionate
(a) calm (b) arrogant
(c) sure (d) fervent

274. Preposterous
(a) complaisant (b) conceited
(c) apologetic (d) credible

275. Pungent
(a) clear (b) turbid
(c) sharp (d) harmless

276. Piquant
(a) spicy (b) tasty
(c) pungent (d) insipid

277. Partisan
(a) supporter (b) follower
(c) devotee (d) unbiased

278. Perpetual
(a) just (b) discontinue
(c) momentary (d) ordinary

R

279. Recede
(a) rush (b) advance
(c) approach forward (d) none of these

280. Retrieve
(a) respond (b) dismiss
(c) foil (d) abandon

281. Ruthless
(a) mindful (b) compassionate
(c) majestic (d) merciful

282. Respite
(a) tension (b) exertion
(c) regularity (d) delay

283. Reject
(a) agree (b) accept
(c) embrace (d) adopt

284. Robust
(a) thin (b) emaciated
(c) light (d) strong

285. Relinquish
(a) withdraw (b) attack
(c) assume (d) conquer

286. Requisite
(a) dispensable (b) random
(c) inappropriate (d) chaotic

287. Reluctant
(a) inclined (b) worried
(c) willing (d) ready

288. Remorseful
(a) grateful (b) unrepentant
(c) wretched (d) arrogant

289. Repugnant
(a) inoffensive (b) loving
(c) caring (d) pleasing

290. Ramshackle
(a) study (b) ruinous
(c) dilapidated (d) NOTA

291. Ruthless
(a) mindful (b) compassionate
(c) majestic (d) merciful

S

292. Superficial
(a) artificial (b) deep
(c) shallow (d) real

293. Seldom
(a) rarely (b) daily
(c) often (d) never

294. Smooth
(a) ugly (b) awkward
(c) hard (d) rough

295. Synthetic
(a) cosmetic (b) plastic
(c) affable (d) natural

296. Shallow
(a) high (b) hidden
(c) deep (d) hallow

297. Sordid
(a) miserly (b) generous
(c) hopeful (d) open

298. Shrewd
(a) turbid (b) naive
(c) muffled (d) mundane

299. Sluggish
(a) quick (b) sharp
(c) alert (d) vigilant

300. Strenuous
(a) unfaltering (b) irresolute
(c) unwavering (d) lazy

301. Setback
(a) bonus (b) misfortune
(c) shock (d) upset

302. Scold
(a) enamour (b) rebuke
(c) criticise (d) praise

303. Segregation
(a) appreciation (b) alteration
(c) integration (d) NOTA

304. Succumb
(a) curb (b) resist
(c) injure (d) shoot

305. Significant
(a) distinct (b) extreme
(c) alive (d) unimportant

306. Subjugate
(a) enrich (b) liberate
(c) enslave (d) free

307. Sanctity
(a) sacred (b) sophistic
(c) unlawfulness (d) eagerness

308. Serene
(a) jovial (b) moving
(c) agitated (d) nervous

309. Sagacious
(a) casual (b) cunning
(c) foolish (d) false

310. Strident
(a) stable (b) pleasant
(c) musical (d) melodious

T

311. Tragedy
(a) humorous (b) comedy
(c) romance (d) calamity

312. Transparent
(a) coloured (b) childlike
(c) opaque (d) imminent

313. Terrible
(a) horrible (b) awesome
(c) delightful (d) hideous

314. Tragic
(a) funny (b) comic
(c) light (d) humorous

315. Terse
(a) concise (b) detailed
(c) expressive (d) descriptive

316. Timid
(a) fearful (b) tasteless
(c) bold (d) busy

317. Tranquil
(a) peaceful (b) disturbed
(c) painful (d) punishing

318. Timidity
(a) gallantry (b) fearing
(c) weakness (d) guilty

319. Taciturn
(a) dubious (b) garrulous
(c) strategic (d) pleasant

U

320. Unsullied
(a) untrained (b) trained
(c) spotless (d) NOTA

V

321. Validate
(a) legalise (b) spurious
(c) authenticate (d) disprove

322. Violent
(a) tame (b) humble
(c) gentle (d) harmless

323. Virtue
(a) vice (b) fraud
(c) wickedness (d) crime

324. Vulgar
(a) refined (b) cheerful
(c) jolly (d) relevant

325. Vanquish
(a) surrender (b) debase
(c) destroy (d) ruin

326. Voluntary
(a) ordered (b) alternative
(c) compulsory (d) essential

327. Vigour
(a) failure (b) negligence
(c) frailty (d) healthy

328. Virtuous
(a) scandalous (b) vicious
(c) wicked (d) corrupt

329. Virulent
(a) harmless (b) malignant
(c) hostile (d) vicious

330. Vanity
(a) modesty (b) kindness
(c) compassion (d) moderation

331. Vivacious
(a) quarrelsome (b) sober
(c) notorious (d) sluggish

332. Vital
(a) peripheral (b) dead
(c) outer (d) unimportant

333. Vilify
(a) flattery (b) pray
(c) admonish (d) worship

334. Vindictive
(a) praise (b) forgiving
(c) useless (d) piercing

335. Vociferous
(a) laudable (b) quiet
(c) dangerous (d) powerful

336. Vague
(a) foggy (b) cloudy
(c) clear (d) rare

337. Vomit
(a) swallow (b) ingest
(c) deplore (d) endure

338. Vie
(a) guard (b) maintain
(c) discover (d) yield

339. Validate
(a) legalise (b) avoid
(c) disprove (d) disallow

340. Verbose
(a) compact (b) brief
(c) concise (d) NOTA

341. Voluminous
(a) long (b) sleek
(c) belittle (d) loud

342. Valuable
(a) inferior (b) invaluable
(c) lowly (d) worthless

W

343. Wrath
(a) angry (b) peace
(c) delight (d) choler

344. Wane
(a) swell (b) prosper
(c) wax (d) widen

345. Wonder
(a) expectation (b) surprise
(c) possibility (d) probability

346. Wicked
(a) sober (b) helpful
(c) conscientious (d) faithful

347. Within
(a) without (b) past
(c) over (d) beyond

348. Woeful
(a) smiling (b) cheerful
(c) demanding (d) lively

349. Wreck
(a) work (b) build
(c) restore (d) relieve

Z

350. Zany
(a) cautious (b) calculating
(c) cunning (d) sane

351. Zest
(a) restive (b) callous
(c) indifference (d) distaste

352. Zeal
(a) lithe (b) apathy
(c) verbatim (d) NOTA

ANSWERS - ANTONYMS PRACTICE TESTS (MCQs)													
1	(b)	36	(c)	71	(a)	106	(a)	141	(d)	176	(a)	211	(b)
2	(b)	37	(a)	72	(a)	107	(c)	142	(d)	177	(b)	212	(b)
3	(a)	38	(a)	73	(b)	108	(b)	143	(b)	178	(a)	213	(b)
4	(b)	39	(c)	74	(b)	109	(c)	144	(a)	179	(d)	214	(b)
5	(c)	40	(a)	75	(c)	110	(b)	145	(c)	180	(b)	215	(a)
6	(b)	41	(d)	76	(a)	111	(a)	146	(a)	181	(b)	216	(a)
7	(a)	42	(b)	77	(b)	112	(b)	147	(a)	182	(b)	217	(b)
8	(c)	43	(b)	78	(a)	113	(b)	148	(a)	183	(a)	218	(b)
9	(b)	44	(b)	79	(b)	114	(b)	149	(a)	184	(c)	219	(c)
10	(c)	45	(a)	80	(a)	115	(b)	150	(b)	185	(a)	220	(d)
11	(b)	46	(b)	81	(c)	116	(c)	151	(a)	186	(b)	221	(b)
12	(c)	47	(a)	82	(a)	117	(c)	152	(d)	187	(a)	222	(b)
13	(c)	48	(b)	83	(b)	118	(b)	153	(b)	188	(a)	223	(a)
14	(b)	49	(a)	84	(b)	119	(c)	154	(a)	189	(b)	224	(a)
15	(c)	50	(d)	85	(c)	120	(c)	155	(b)	190	(a)	225	(a)
16	(d)	51	(d)	86	(b)	121	(a)	156	(b)	191	(b)	226	(c)
17	(b)	52	(b)	87	(d)	122	(a)	157	(d)	192	(c)	227	(c)
18	(c)	53	(b)	88	(a)	123	(d)	158	(a)	193	(c)	228	(a)
19	(c)	54	(c)	89	(d)	124	(b)	159	(c)	194	(c)	229	(a)
20	(c)	55	(a)	90	(c)	125	(d)	160	(c)	195	(a)	230	(a)
21	(b)	56	(b)	91	(a)	126	(b)	161	(d)	196	(a)	231	(c)
22	(b)	57	(b)	92	(b)	127	(c)	162	(d)	197	(d)	232	(d)
23	(b)	58	(d)	93	(d)	128	(b)	163	(a)	198	(b)	233	(c)
24	(b)	59	(b)	94	(b)	129	(a)	164	(d)	199	(d)	234	(b)
25	(d)	60	(b)	95	(a)	130	(b)	165	(d)	200	(a)	235	(a)
26	(c)	61	(a)	96	(c)	131	(b)	166	(d)	201	(b)	236	(b)
27	(b)	62	(b)	97	(b)	132	(c)	167	(a)	202	(d)	237	(a)
28	(d)	63	(c)	98	(b)	133	(c)	168	(a)	203	(b)	238	(b)
29	(a)	64	(b)	99	(b)	134	(a)	169	(a)	204	(a)	239	(a)
30	(b)	65	(d)	100	(c)	135	(c)	170	(c)	205	(d)	240	(a)
31	(b)	66	(b)	101	(c)	136	(d)	171	(c)	206	(c)	241	(c)
32	(a)	67	(c)	102	(a)	137	(d)	172	(b)	207	(b)	242	(a)
33	(c)	68	(a)	103	(d)	138	(a)	173	(d)	208	(d)	243	(d)
34	(b)	69	(d)	104	(a)	139	(b)	174	(b)	209	(b)	244	(c)
35	(c)	70	(c)	105	(b)	140	(c)	175	(b)	210	(d)	245	(a)
246	(a)	262	(b)	278	(b)	294	(d)	310	(d)	326	(c)	342	(b)

247	(c)	263	(b)	279	(b)	295	(d)	311	(b)	327	(c)	343	(c)
248	(a)	264	(d)	280	(a)	296	(c)	312	(c)	328	(b)	344	(c)
249	(c)	265	(b)	281	(b)	297	(b)	313	(c)	329	(a)	345	(d)
250	(c)	266	(c)	282	(d)	298	(b)	314	(b)	330	(a)	346	(d)
251	(d)	267	(a)	283	(b)	299	(c)	315	(b)	331	(d)	347	(a)
252	(c)	268	(c)	284	(a)	300	(d)	316	(c)	332	(d)	348	(b)
253	(a)	269	(c)	285	(d)	301	(a)	317	(b)	333	(d)	349	(b)
254	(c)	270	(d)	286	(c)	302	(d)	318	(a)	334	(b)	350	(d)
255	(a)	271	(b)	287	(c)	303	(c)	319	(b)	335	(b)	351	(c)
256	(d)	272	(a)	288	(b)	304	(b)	320	(b)	336	(c)	352	(b)
257	(d)	273	(a)	289	(d)	305	(d)	321	(d)	337	(a)		
258	(b)	274	(a)	290	(a)	306	(b)	322	(c)	338	(d)		
259	(d)	275	(a)	291	(b)	307	(c)	323	(a)	339	(c)		
260	(a)	276	(d)	292	(b)	308	(c)	324	(a)	340	(b)		
261	(d)	277	(c)	293	(c)	309	(c)	325	(a)	341	(b)		

6 IDIOMS AND PHRASES

A – Z, ALPHABETICALLY ARRANGED WITH MEANING AND USAGE

INTRODUCTION

Idioms appear in every language, and English has thousands of them. They are often confusing because the meaning of the whole group of words taken together has little, often nothing, to do with the meanings of the words taken one by one.

For instance, to 'let the cat out of the bag' means to reveal a secret. Today the phrase has nothing to do with a cat or a bag, but hundreds of years ago it actually did.

In order to understand a language, you must know what the idioms in that language mean. If you try to figure out the meaning of an idiom literally, word by word, you will get befuddled. You have to know its 'intended' meaning.

Idioms come from all different sources, from the Bible to horse racing, from ancient fables to modern slang. Sometimes famous authors and storytellers such as Homer, Aesop, Geoffrey Chaucer, or William Shakespeare made them up to add spark to their writings. The authors were popular, so the expression they created became popular. Often, however, we don't know the name of the first author or speaker who used a particular expression.

In all the competitive examinations, test of knowledge of idioms is one of the essential ingredients of the English language section. So, in order to help the students to learn the most relevant idioms, this chapter has been compiled to apprise the students with 525 idioms.

These idioms have been culled and finalised after a thorough and eclectic search. The students would find them highly useful for their competitive exams, and in their day-to-day usage for making their writing skills ornamental and consequently impressive & rewarding. The idioms asked in various previous examinations have been examined before finalising these 525 most relevant idioms. These would really serve the purpose of the students.

	A	
1	**Ace up your sleeve**	***Meaning:*** a surprise or secret advantage; especially something tricky that is kept hidden until needed I do not know how Anaadi is going to get her mom to buy her a cycle, but I'm sure she has an ***ace up her sleeve.***
2	**Achilles' heel**	***Meaning:*** one's weakness; fault; flaw; or vulnerable spot in one's otherwise strong character I am good in Math and Science, but English is my ***Achilles' heel.***
3	**Add fuel to the fire**	***Meaning:*** to make a bad situation worse; to do or say something that causes more trouble, makes someone angrier I was already angry with you, and when you forgot to pick me up, that really ***added fuel to the fire.***

4	**Air your dirty laundry in public**	***Meaning:*** to talk about your private disagreements or embarrassing matters in public, usually while quarrelling My neighbours fight a lot and ***air their dirty laundry in public.***
5	**Albatross around your neck**	***Meaning:*** a very difficult burden that you cannot get rid of or a reminder of something you did that was wrong Everywhere I go, my mother compels me to take my nagging sister along. She is an ***albatross around my neck.***
6	**All ears**	***Meaning:*** eager to listen; sharply attentive; curious Good students give ***all ears*** to their teachers in the class.
7	**All that glitters is not gold**	***Meaning:*** something that seems attractive and valuable at first might turn out to be worthless Normally the goods bought online turn out to be ***all that glitters is not gold.***
8	**Ants in your pants**	***Meaning:*** extreme restlessness; over activity You never sit still. You must have ***ants in your pants.***
9	**Apple of your eye**	***Meaning:*** a person or thing that is greatly loved, treasured, and adored Anaadi is the ***apple of my eye.***
10	**As the crow flies**	***Meaning:*** by the shortest and most direct route; measured in a straight, direct line between two places We live at a stone's through from my daughter Anaadi's school ***as the crow flies.***
11	**Asleep at the switch**	***Meaning:*** not attending to one's job or failing to react quickly; not being alert Ravi lost his job because he was ***asleep at the switch.***
12	**At the drop of a hat**	***Meaning:*** right away; at once; without delay; willing at any moment The children are all ready to switch on their TVs ***at the drop of a hat.***
13	**At the end of your rope**	***Meaning:*** at the limit of your ability, endurance, or patience to do something I have tried everything, but nothing has worked. I am at ***the end of my rope.***
14	**Axe to grind**	***Meaning:*** something to gain for yourself for a selfish reason; flattery or trickery used to get a favour from another person Nowadays relationships are nothing but opportunities where everyone has one's ***axe to grind.***
	B	
15	**Babe in the woods**	***Meaning:*** a person who is inexperienced; naive, trusting person Sameer thinks so much of himself as a very shrewd person, but he is actually a ***babe in the woods***.
16	**Back to square one**	***Meaning:*** return to the beginning because of a failure to arrive at the desired result N.K. Sharma's plans are always making castles in the air, that is why he is always ***back to square one.***

17	**Backseat driver**	***Meaning:*** a bossy person who tells another person what to do; a person who gives unwanted advice and directions In Indian folk jokes, the wife is referred to as the ***backseat driver.***
18	**Bark is worse than your bite**	***Meaning:*** the way a person sounds is much more frightening than the way she or he acts; the threat is often worse than the action taken The new director yells a lot, but her ***bark is worse than her bite.***
19	**Bark up the wrong tree**	***Meaning:*** to direct your attention or efforts towards the wrong person or thing; to have the wrong idea about something Avni's father wants to make her an IAS Officer, but he was ***barking up the wrong tree*** because she wanted to be a doctor.
20	**Batten down the hatches**	***Meaning:*** to get ready for trouble; prepare for any emergency In the present time of Covid-19 pandemic, everyone ***battens down the hatches.***
21	**Beat a dead horse**	***Meaning:*** to pursue a useless goal; to continue fighting a battle that has been lost; to keep arguing a point that has already been decided. He tried to convince his sister, but he was ***beating a dead horse.***
22	**Beat around the bush**	***Meaning:*** to avoid answering a question; to approach something carefully or in a roundabout way The politicians normally do not come to the point, they keep ***beating around the bush.***
23	**Beat the band**	***Meaning:*** with much noise; excitement, or commotion; very much, very fast; outdoing all others At his selection in IAS 2020, his entire family was ***beating the band.***
24	**Beat your swords into ploughshare**	***Meaning:*** to stop fighting and turn your attention toward peaceful activities It is advisable for Pakistan to shun the path of terrorism and ***beat its swords into ploughshare.***
25	**Beauty is in the eye of the beholder**	***Meaning:*** there is no standard for beauty, so what one person likes or sees in someone or something is not necessarily what others see; different people have different opinions Only a beautiful mind can appreciate others' beauty because ***beauty is in the eye of the beholder.***
26	**Bed of roses**	***Meaning:*** a wonderful, pleasant situation or position; an easy, comfortable life The position of a leader is not a ***bed of roses*** but a responsibility towards the public.
27	**Bee in your bonnet**	***Meaning:*** a crazy idea; an obsession with an idea Mr. Saxena always weaves fanciful and chimerical ideas; he always has a ***bee in his bonnet.***
28	**Beggars cannot be choosers**	***Meaning:*** needy people have to take whatever they can get and cannot be concerned about the quality if they cannot afford to buy it for themselves One with limited resources should not raise eyebrows at whatever they are offered because ***beggars cannot be choosers.***

29	**Bells and whistles**	***Meaning:*** impressive accessories, especially flashy, high-technology features, and frills, which may sometimes be more decorative than necessary Our teacher says we are getting a new computer with all the latest ***bells and whistles:*** CD-burner, stereo speakers, colour printer, and full multimedia.
30	**Below the belt**	***Meaning:*** cruel, unfair, hurtful; against the rules of sportsmanship Normally incompetent players resort to clumsy ways of hitting ***below the belt.***
31	**Better half**	***Meaning:*** either partner in marriage I am not making a decision until I check with my ***better half.***
32	**Better safe than sorry**	***Meaning:*** be careful; avoid risks and possible injury that you will regret. The mother told her daughter to put on her seat belt, even for a short drive. ***'Better safe than sorry',*** she said.
33	**Between a rock and a hard place**	***Meaning:*** being in a very tight spot and faced with a difficult decision For a soldier, looking after the family& fighting for the country is always like a choice between ***a rock and a hard place.***
34	**Between the devil and the deep blue sea**	***Meaning:*** between two great dangers and not knowing what to do; in a very difficult position Leaving my present assignment of teaching and joining a new assignment was like choosing between the ***devil and the deep blue sea.***
35	**Beware of Greeks bearing gifts**	***Meaning:*** be suspicious of presents from certain people who are just looking for something from you; be on guard against treachery in the disguise of a gift Nowadays presenting gifts on festivals have become opportunities of seeking undue favours. ***Beware of Greeks bearing gifts.***
36	**A bird in the hand is worth two in the bush**	***Meaning:*** what you already have is better than what you might or might not get in the future; a guarantee is worth more than a promise Take this job now because you do not know if you will get another one. Remember that a ***bird in the hand is worth two in the bush.***
37	**Birds of a feather flock together**	***Meaning:*** people who have things in common, such as interests and ideas, usually hang out together; people who are alike often become friends Everyone at that table plays soccer, I guess that ***birds of a feather flock together.***
38	**Bread and butter**	***Meaning:*** basic necessities of life Earning his daily ***bread and butter*** is the main focus of a common man's life.
39	**By and by**	***Meaning:*** after a time ***By and by***, you will come to know everything.
40	**Bite off more than you can chew**	***Meaning:*** to take on a task that is more than you can accomplish; or too ambitious by taking on more jobs or responsibilities than you can deal with at one time You cannot accomplish so many tasks at the same time, don't ***bite off more than you can chew.***

41	**Bite the bullet**	***Meaning:*** prepare for an unpleasant experience; brace yourself to endure with courage something painful but necessary The principal wants to see you in her office. Get ready to ***bite the bullet.***
42	**Bite the dust**	***Meaning:*** to die; to fall in defeat; to fail to succeed The Indian Army compelled the Pakistan Army to ***bite the dust*** in the battle of 1971.
43	**Bite the hand that feeds you**	***Meaning:*** to turn against someone who helps you; to do harm to someone who does good things for you He is a chronic wrong doer; he always ***bites the hand that feeds him.***
44	**Bite your tongue**	***Meaning:*** take back or be ashamed of what you have said. For his wrong doings, he had to ***bite his tongue.***
45	**Black sheep of the family**	***Meaning:*** the most unsuccessful, least admirable member of a family or similar group; a disgraced person Subash is the ***black sheep of the family,*** always causes trouble.
46	**Bleeding heart**	***Meaning:*** an extremely soft-hearted person who feels compassion or pity towards all people Bhagat Puran Singh had a ***bleeding heart*** for the poor, needy, and helpless people.
47	**Blessing in disguise**	***Meaning:*** something that at first seems bad but turns out to be good. Online coaching proves to be a ***blessing in disguise*** in the wake of Covid-19.
48	**Blind as a bat**	***Meaning:*** totally blind When the heavy fog rolled in, she was as ***blind as a bat*** because she could not see an inch in front of her.
49	**Blind leading the blind**	***Meaning:*** the uninformed attempting to inform others When an ill-informed person teaches the ignorant, it is just like ***blind leading the blind.***
50	**Blood is thicker than water**	***Meaning:*** one can expect more kindness from a family member than from a stranger ***Blood is thicker than water,*** that is why family is the first and last choice for everyone.
51	**Blow your own horn**	***Meaning:*** to praise yourself; to call attention to your own merits (intelligence, skills, success, or abilities); to brag about yourself Incapable and incompetent people keep ***blowing their own horn.***
52	**Blue blood**	***Meaning:*** of high or noble birth; an aristocrat; from the upper class of society The ***blue-blooded*** people do not prefer to mix up with commoners.
53	**Bolt from the blue**	***Meaning:*** something sudden, unexpected, and shocking His father's untimely demise came as a ***bolt from the blue***.
54	**Born with a silver spoon in your mouth**	***Meaning:*** born to wealth, comfort, and privilege Jawahar Lal Nehru was ***born with a silver spoon in his mouth.***
55	**Born yesterday**	***Meaning:*** inexperienced and easily fooled; not alert to trickery Ramesh is naive; just seems to have ***born yesterday.***

56	**Bottom line**	***Meaning:*** the most crucial fact; the net result The ***bottom line*** stuck up between the farmers and the government of India is the repeal of three farming laws or amendments to be incorporated.
57	**Break a leg**	***Meaning:*** good luck; do a great job in the show Avni ***broke a leg*** and stole the show at the annual function of the school.
58	**Break the ice**	***Meaning:*** to start a conversation Kapil was very shy when he met Savita. He did not know how to ***break the ice.***
59	**Breath of fresh air**	***Meaning:*** someone or something new, stimulating, invigorating, and refreshing The Hindi movie Manto was like a ***breath of fresh air*** for movie lovers.
60	**Bright-eyed and bushy-tailed**	***Meaning:*** healthy, fit, bright, and lively After her morning walk, she always looks ***bright-eyed and bushy tailed.***
61	**Bring down the house**	***Meaning:*** to get an audience to clap enthusiastically or laugh loudly Kapil Sharma show's artists' stellar performance ***brings down the house.***
62	**Bring home the bacon**	***Meaning:*** to support a family by working; to earn a living He is struggling hard to ***bring home the bacon*** for his old parents.
63	**Bug off**	***Meaning:*** to leave someone alone; go away; stop annoying someone Sita earnestly requested her sister to ***bug off*** for a moment.
64	**Bug someone**	***Meaning:*** to irritate, annoy, and bother someone a lot I wish you would just stop ***bugging me*** and leave me in peace!
65	**Bull in a china shop**	***Meaning:*** a clumsy person who deals too roughly with a delicate situation; a tactless person who says or does something that angers people or upsets their plans Inviting a wrestler as a jury member at a dance show is just like a ***bull in a china shop.***
66	**Burn the candle at both ends**	***Meaning:*** to overwork yourself mentally or physically and until you're exhausted He is ***burning the candle at both ends*** to qualify for IAS in his first attempt.
67	**Burn the midnight oil**	***Meaning:*** to stay up very late at night studying or working One has to ***burn the midnight oil,*** to qualify for IIT Examination.
68	**Burn your bridges behind you**	***Meaning:*** to make a decision you cannot change; to commit yourself to a course of action If you drop out of school now, you will be ***burning your bridges behind you.***
69	**Bury the hatchet**	***Meaning:*** to settle an argument; end a war; make peace; become friends after being enemies Stop fighting and ***bury the hatchet.***
70	**Bury your head in the sand**	***Meaning:*** to ignore danger by pretending you do not see it; to hide from obvious signs of danger You are ***burying your head in the sand*** if you think that smoking isn't bad for your health.

71	**Busy as a beaver**	***Meaning:*** working very hard; extremely industrious Avni is as ***busy as a beaver,*** to navigate through tough times of Covid-19 pandemic.
72	**Butter someone up**	***Meaning:*** to flatter someone; to try to get a favour by praising someone Maybe if you ***butter up*** the math teacher, she will raise your final grade.
73	**Butterflies in the stomach**	***Meaning:*** a fluttery feeling in the stomach, usually caused by nervousness During my first public speech to an august gathering, there were ***butterflies in the stomach.***
74	**Button your lip**	***Meaning:*** to stop talking; be quiet The teacher asked all students to ***button their lips.***
75	**Buy a pig in a poke**	***Meaning:*** to buy something without seeing or examining it Without bare knowledge of a computer, buying a second-hand computer will be like ***buying a pig in a poke.***
76	**By hook or by crook**	***Meaning:*** by any means possible (legal or not) He is crazy to win the match ***by hook or by crook.***
77	**By the book**	***Meaning:*** exactly according to the rules; precisely as instructed The law-abiding citizens prefer to go ***by the book.***
78	**By the skin of your teeth**	***Meaning:*** just barely; by the narrowest of margins He needed only 400 marks to qualify for NEET Examination, but by securing 399 marks he lost it ***by the skin of his teeth.***
	C	
79	**Call it a day**	***Meaning:*** to stop work for the day; to bring a project to an end for the time being You have been working on that history report since breakfast. Why don't you ***call it a day?***
80	**Call the shots**	***Meaning:*** to make the decision; to be in charge; to give orders He is a henpecked husband, and his wife ***calls the shots.***
81	**Call you on the carpet**	***Meaning:*** to call a person before an authority for a scolding The principal ***called*** the erring teacher ***on the carpet*** to make her realise what wrong she had done.
82	**Call your bluff**	***Meaning:*** to demand that someone prove a claim; to challenge, someone to carry out a threat The Taxila House was bragging of winning the final trophy, but Nalanda ***called their bluff.***
83	**Calm before the storm**	***Meaning:*** a period of unusual peace before a disturbance or crisis; an unnatural or false calm before a storm The meeting may be peaceful now, but this is only the ***calm before the storm.***
84	**Cannot fight city hall**	***Meaning:*** an ordinary person cannot win a struggle against an administrative system A commoner who has to slog to make both ends meet ***cannot fight the city hall.***

85	**Cannot get blood from a stone**	***Meaning:*** you cannot ask for or do the impossible Do not expect any favours from the Sharma family because you ***can't get blood from a stone.***
86	**Cannot hold a candle to**	***Meaning:*** to be second-rate in a certain skill; to be greatly inferior; to be not good as someone else When it comes to the question of topping the class, Avni ***cannot hold a candle to*** anyone else.
87	**Cannot see the forest for the trees**	***Meaning:*** to overlook the overall situation because of a focus on small details My teacher catches all my grammar mistakes, but he misses my brilliant writing. He ***cannot see the forest for the trees.***
88	**Carry coals to Newcastle**	***Meaning:*** to bring something to a place where it is already plentiful Taking flowers to the florist's daughter is like ***carrying coals to Newcastle.***
89	**Carry the ball**	***Meaning:*** to be in charge or be responsible; to make sure that a job gets done right Mrs. Sharma heads her company; she will ***carry the ball*** during annual function.
90	**Carry the weight of the world on your shoulders**	***Meaning:*** to be burdened by all the problems in the world Some people unnecessarily ***carry the weight of the world on their shoulders*** instead of focusing on their own lives.
91	**Carved in stone**	***Meaning:*** permanent and unalterable The teacher's rule about no cell phones in class is ***carved in stone.*** Do not even think about making a call here.
92	**Cast pearls before swine**	***Meaning:*** to waste something good or valuable on someone who won't appreciate or understand it Your investment in your pastime friends is just like ***casting pearls before swine.***
93	**Cast the first stone**	***Meaning:*** to be the first to attack, blame, or criticise someone Do not criticise. You have done it yourself, so you shouldn't ***cast the first stone.***
94	**Cat got your tongue**	***Meaning:*** is there a reason that you are not speaking? Why don't you answer me? Has the ***cat got your tongue?***
95	**Cat that swallowed the canary**	***Meaning:*** very self-satisfied Once after the final selection of Ravi in the defence services, he seemed like the ***cat that swallowed the canary.***
96	**Catch more flies with honey than with vinegar**	***Meaning:*** more can be accomplished by being pleasant than by being disagreeable Ask her nicely. Remember, you can ***catch more flies with honey than with vinegar.***
97	**Catch someone red-handed**	***Meaning:*** to catch someone in the act of doing something wrong Kasab was ***caught red-handed*** on the spot during the attack on Taj Mumbai in 2011.
98	**Catch you later**	***Meaning:*** good-bye; I'll see or speak to you at another time Leaving for home, Suresh asked Rajesh to ***catch him later.***

99	**Champing at the bit**	***Meaning:*** to be impatient to start; to be ready and enthusiastic to do something Anaadi was ***champing at the bit*** to play with her friends after announcement of her school results.
100	**Chew someone out**	***Meaning:*** to scold severely or roughly; to bawl someone out Leena's mother-in-law ***chewed her out*** publicly in the colony.
101	**Chew the fat**	***Meaning:*** to have a friendly, informal talk; to chat in a relaxed way The old friends ***chewed the fat*** till midnight.
102	**Chew up the scenery**	***Meaning:*** to overact; to exaggerate your emotions Veena is a great artist expert at ***chewing the scenery*** before others.
103	**Chew your cud**	***Meaning:*** to think deeply to oneself; to turn a matter over and over in your mind Some people have the habit of ***chewing the cud.***
104	**Chicken feed**	***Meaning:*** a very small or insignificant amount of money During Covid-19, there was heavy salary cuts in the private sector and the employees were paid only ***chicken feed.***
105	**Chickens come home to roost**	***Meaning:*** bad words or actions come back to haunt a person; evil acts will return to plague the doer You better be careful what you say when you're happy. ***Chickens come home to roost.***
106	**Chill out**	***Meaning:*** relax, calm down After almost two years torture of Corona, people ***chilled out*** in the New Year 2023.
107	**Chip off the old block**	***Meaning:*** a child who resembles a parent in behaviour, looks, or abilities My wife is the exact replica of her mother. She is really a ***chip off the old block.***
108	**Chip on your shoulder**	***Meaning:*** to be quarrelsome, aggressive, or crude; to be ready to fight Avoid him today because he has a real ***chip on his shoulders.***
109	**Chips are down**	***Meaning:*** the situation is urgent and has to be dealt with now Girls, the ***chips are down.*** If we do not win this game, we are out of the playoffs.
110	**Clam up**	***Meaning:*** to refuse to talk; to become silent When the teacher asked who had broken the windowpanes, all students ***clammed up.***
111	**Clean as a whistle**	***Meaning:*** completely free from dirt; perfectly neat The science lab is as ***clean as a whistle.***
112	**Clean bill of health**	***Meaning:*** declaration of satisfaction, healthy condition, or proven innocence The gas station that inspected Dad's old car gave it a ***clean bill of health.***
113	**Clear as a bell**	***Meaning:*** easily and clearly understood with no confusion whatsoever The principal's message was ***clear as a bell*** to all the late comers.

114	**Clear the decks**	***Meaning:*** to get all of the minor details out of the way in order to focus on a major project Before we can build our model for the science fair, we have to ***clear the decks*** of other homework.
115	**Climb the walls**	***Meaning:*** to be frustrated or anxious during a challenging situation; to be unable to endure The assembly was so dull that all the kids were ***climbing the walls.***
116	**Clip your wings**	***Meaning:*** to end a person's privileges; to take away someone's power or freedom to do something It is said that Raja's favours are not permanent, he can ***clip anyone's wings*** anytime.
117	**Cloak-and-dagger**	***Meaning:*** concerning or involving spies, secret agents, intrigue, and mystery; involving plotting and scheming ***Cloak-and-dagger*** stories were the most favourite area of Sunita.
118	**Close shave**	***Meaning:*** a very narrow escape from danger During the head-on-collision Raju had a ***close shave*** with the grace of God.
119	**Cold feet**	***Meaning:*** a fear of doing something; a loss of nerve or confidence Waiting for the first result, she had ***cold feet.***
120	**Cold shoulder**	***Meaning:*** unfriendly treatment of a person by ignoring him or her Though William met his old friend with warmth, his friend gave him the ***cold shoulder.***
121	**Cold turkey**	***Meaning:*** the sudden stopping of any habit (smoking or drugs) I stopped ***cold turkey*** on my smoking habit.
122	**Come apart at the seams**	***Meaning:*** to become so upset that all self-control is gone If anyone tries to check the family antecedents of Parvesh, he ***comes apart at the seams.***
123	**Come out of your shell**	***Meaning:*** to stop being so shy; to become more friendly In the present times, one cannot excel being introvert, one has to ***come out of his shell.***
124	**Come up smelling like a rose**	***Meaning:*** to get out of a possibly embarrassing or disgraceful situation without hurting your reputation, and maybe even improving it Even though my sister forgot to do her chores last week, she still ***came up smelling like a rose.***
125	**Cook your goose**	***Meaning:*** to wreck someone's plans; to ruin someone's project; to spoil someone's happiness Milkha Singh's opponents tried to ***cook his goose*** but could not succeed.
126	**Cooking with gas**	***Meaning:*** performing with skill, energy, enthusiasm, and excellence Yesterday, he did not score a single point. But in tonight's game, he was really ***cooking with gas.***
127	**Cool as a cucumber**	***Meaning:*** very calm, not nervous, or emotional Ravish Kumar was as ***cool as a cucumber*** when he got the Magsaysay Award from the President of the Philippines.

128	**Cool your heels**	***Meaning:*** to be kept waiting for a long time, usually by someone in power or authority The officer made the delegates to ***cool their heels*** before meeting them.
129	**Cost an arm and a leg**	***Meaning:*** very expensive; high-priced, though possibly not worth the cost Though it may ***cost an arm and a leg*** for a commoner to go abroad, but nowadays it is a status symbol.
130	**Couch potato**	***Meaning:*** a person who spends a lot of time watching television He will not come out to play because he is a ***couch potato.***
131	**Cream of the crop**	***Meaning:*** the best person or thing of all; the top choice; the best part Among all the chefs at hotel Taj Mumbai, Mr. Saxena is ***cream of the crop.***
132	**Crocodile tears**	***Meaning:*** fake tears; false grief I begged and cried to go to the party, but Dad said I was shedding ***crocodile tears.***
133	**Cross the bridge when you come to it**	***Meaning:*** don't predict problems until they actually happen; don't worry about future events now; don't deal with a difficulty until you have to The optimists ***cross the bridge when they come to it*** and the pessimist keeps moaning and groaning.
134	**Cry over spilled milk**	***Meaning:*** to cry or complain about an event that has already taken place and can't be changed It is no use to ***cry over spilled milk.***
135	**Cry wolf**	***Meaning:*** to give a false alarm of danger; to warn of a peril that you know is not real Don't worry if my little brother starts screaming that there's a ghost in his room. He always ***cries wolf.***
136	**Cut off your nose to spite your face**	***Meaning:*** to injure yourself out of anger toward another; to make a situation worse for yourself when angry with someone Out of anger some people ***cut off their nose to spite their face.***
137	**Cut the mustard**	***Meaning:*** to be able to handle a job or fulfil the requirements He was forty and many people thought he was too old to ***cut the mustard,*** but he handled it skilfully.
138	**Cut to the quick**	***Meaning:*** to hurt someone's feelings very deeply; to be extremely unkind or nasty The teacher was ***cut to the quick*** when the parents unnecessarily complained against him.
139	**Cut your eyeteeth on something**	***Meaning:*** to acquire wisdom; to gain valuable experience, often at a young age The life's ups and downs enables ***everyone to cut one's eyeteeth on something.***
140	**Cutting edge**	***Meaning:*** the forefront, the most advanced or important position, usually in science and technology Nipun always had a ***cutting edge*** over others in the pre-board examination.

D		
141	**Dark-horse candidate**	***Meaning:*** a contestant about whom little is known and who wins unexpectedly Everyone was surprised when Tejasvi Yadav came out victorious with his party as the single largest party in Bihar elections because he was a ***dark horse candidate***.
142	**Dead as a doornail**	***Meaning:*** totally dead or hopeless; without a chance of success Congress party in the present times seems ***dead as a doornail,*** but it needs to be reorganised to rejuvenate.
143	**Dead duck**	***Meaning:*** a person who is ruined When Ravi lost all the money in the share market, he was a ***dead duck.***
144	**Diamond in the rough**	***Meaning:*** someone or something that doesn't look so good now, but that has great merit and the potential to be beautiful Nowadays, the simple and innocent people are mistakenly considered as ***diamond in the rough.***
145	**Do or die**	***Meaning:*** to succeed or fail completely Gandhiji gave the slogan of ***'Do or Die'*** during the Quit India Movement.
146	**Dog days of summer**	***Meaning:*** the hottest and most humid days of summer Sales of air conditioners are usually highest during the ***dog days of summer.***
147	**Dog-eat-dog world**	***Meaning:*** a way of life marked by fierce competition in which people compete ruthlessly for survival or success In the era of fierce and cutthroat competition, the present-day world is no less than ***dog-eat-dog world.***
148	**Dog's life**	***Meaning:*** a bleak, terrible existence without much happiness or freedom Covid-19 has totally rendered poor people's life worse than a ***dog's life.***
149	**Do not count your chickens before they hatch**	***Meaning:*** do not count on profits before you earn them or have them in hand It is advisable that one should ***not count one's chickens before they hatch.***
150	**Do not look a gift horse in the mouth**	***Meaning:*** don't complain if a gift is not perfect; take what you've been given without criticism or emphasis on its worth When Mona complained about her present, her dad told her ***not to look a gift horse in the mouth.***
151	**Do not take any wooden nickels**	***Meaning:*** do not let anyone cheat you or take advantage of you One should learn the ways of society with passage of time so as ***not to take any wooden nickels.***
152	**Dose of one's own medicine**	***Meaning:*** the same or a similar bad thing done back to the person who did it first Indians believe in the theory of karma, according to which one gets a ***dose of one's own medicine,*** if he puts others in trouble.
153	**Dot your i's and cross your t's**	***Meaning:*** to take great care over details Before taking a final decision of starting a new project ***dot your i's and cross your t's.***

154	**Down in the dumps**	***Meaning:*** sad and depressed When Geeta could not figure in the final merit list of IAS, she was ***down in the dumps.***
155	**Down the drain**	***Meaning:*** lost forever; wasted During Covid-19 pandemic, the businesses of a number of people went ***down the drain.***
156	**Down the hatch**	***Meaning:*** swallow a drink in one gulp Grandma handed me a glass of smelly medicine and said, ***'Down the hatch'.***
157	**Down-to-earth**	***Meaning:*** practical; sensible; realistic Even though Lokesh's parents are millionaires, they do not act snobbishly, they are really quite ***down-to-earth.***
158	**Down-to-the-wire**	***Meaning:*** running out of time; at the very last minute I cannot talk to you now. I am ***down-to-the-wire*** on this research report.
159	**Draw the line at**	***Meaning:*** to set a specific limit, especially about behaviour My parents give me a lot of freedom, but they ***draw the line at*** letting me stay out late on school nights.
160	**Dressed to the nines**	***Meaning:*** wearing fashionable clothing; dressed to attract attention Indians are normally ***dressed to the nines*** at weddings.
161	**Drive a hard bargain**	***Meaning:*** to buy or sell at a good price Real Estate property dealers are smart enough to ***drive a hard bargain.***
162	**Drive you crazy**	***Meaning:*** to make someone uncontrolled I can't help stopping myself when I see any book of Paulo Coelho, it literally ***drives me crazy.***
163	**Drop in the bucket**	***Meaning:*** a very small, insignificant amount Because of Covid-19, a majority of the people are left with a ***drop in their buckets.***
164	**Drop you like a hot potato**	***Meaning:*** to get rid of something or somebody as quickly as possible The father advised his son to ***drop his*** bad friend ***like a hot potato.***
165	**Dull as dishwater**	***Meaning:*** not inspiring; uninteresting Programs on that channel are as ***dull as dishwater.***
166	**Dyed-in-the-wool**	***Meaning:*** complete, permanent, stubborn A number of people are ***dyed-in-the-wool*** BPJ voters, who do not wavier or falter.
		E
167	**Early bird catches the worm**	***Meaning:*** a person who gets up early and starts a project ahead of others has the best chance of accomplishing his or her goal Jaskaran slept overnight in front of the stadium in order to get tickets. The ***early bird catches the worm.***
168	**Easy as pie**	***Meaning:*** not difficult; requiring practically no effort Nowadays scoring more than 90% in boards is as ***easy as pie.***

169	**Easy as rolling off a log**	***Meaning:*** very, very easy; requiring little or no effort Anaadi made me realise that running online classes is as ***easy as rolling off a log.***
170	**Easy come, easy go**	***Meaning:*** something that is easily obtained, as money, can be lost or parted with just as easily It is commonly said that ill gotten money goes like ***easy come, easy go.***
171	**Eat crow**	***Meaning:*** to be forced to do something very disagreeable; to acknowledge a mistake or defeat I made Arun admit that he was wrong, and now he has to ***eat crow.***
172	**Eat humble pie**	***Meaning:*** to be apologetic or suffer humiliation; to act humble or admit guilt When he finds out how wrong he has been, he will ***eat humble pie.***
173	**Eat out of your hand**	***Meaning:*** to be very cooperative or submissive Abhimanyu ***eats out of your hand*** once you assign him a job.
174	**Eat you out of house and home**	***Meaning:*** to be so expensive to feed and keep that the person paying cannot afford it Mandy grew four inches, he is ***eating his*** parents ***out of house and home.***
175	**Eat your hat**	***Meaning:*** a statement made when you are positive that something will happen Mr. Sharma was always boastful of his children, but he had to ***eat his hat*** when they finally failed in all the exams.
176	**Eat your heart out**	***Meaning:*** to feel extremely unhappy about a hopeless situation; to make yourself sick with grief and worry After Serena lost the plane tickets, she ***ate her heart out*** over the mistake.
177	**Eat your words**	***Meaning:*** to have to take back what you said; to admit humbly that you were wrong Mr. Kaushal had predicted that Chandan can never be selected in IAS, but when selected, he had to ***eat his words.***
178	**Egg on your face**	***Meaning:*** to be very embarrassed or humiliated for something foolish that you did or said The farmers laws passed by government may be ***egg on the government's face.***
179	**Elbow grease**	***Meaning:*** hard, energetic manual labour Put a little ***elbow grease*** into the hat job. Polish that car until it shines!
180	**Eleventh hour**	***Meaning:*** at the latest possible time, just before the absolute deadline Prof. Jaiswal is habitual to complete everything at the ***eleventh hour.***
181	**Every cloud has a silver lining**	***Meaning:*** there is something good in every bad situation When the night is deep, dead & dark, it means dawn is about to break as ***every cloud has a silver lining.***
182	**Every Tom, Dick, and Harry**	***Meaning:*** every person possible, especially very ordinary people One cannot satisfy ***every Tom, Dick and Harry,*** rather one should focus on one's own life.

183	**Eye for an eye and a tooth for a tooth**	***Meaning:*** revenge or punishment exactly like the original crime or offense In ancient times, the philosophy of ***eye for an eye and a tooth for a tooth*** was the most acceptable philosophy.
184	**Eyes in the back of your head**	***Meaning:*** ability to sense what is happening outside of one's field of vision; ability to know what happens when one's back is turned My teacher always knows when we are passing notes. He must have ***eyes in the back of his head.***
		F
185	**Face the music**	***Meaning:*** to endure the consequence of one's actions I was caught cheating and now I have to ***face the music.***
186	**Fair-weather friend**	***Meaning:*** a person who is a faithful friend only when everything is going well but who deserts you in times of difficulty One must beware of one's ***fair-weather friends.***
187	**Fat cat**	***Meaning:*** a wealthy person; a rich benefactor The ***fat cats*** must contribute towards funds for victims of earthquake.
188	**Feast or famine**	***Meaning:*** great success or total failure; either too much or too little of something Covid-19 made businesses ***feast or famine*** because grocery and the pharmaceutical sector flourished manifold, whereas many others lost.
189	**Feather in your cap**	***Meaning:*** a great achievement or special honour The new book of Bhardwaj is a ***feather in his cap.***
190	**Feather your nest**	***Meaning:*** to be more interested in taking care of yourself The bureaucracy in India is more interested in ***feathering its own nest.***
191	**Feel your oats**	***Meaning:*** to be in high spirits, energetic; to act in a proud way The whole class was celebrating the farewell party and all the classmates were ***feeling their oats.***
192	**Feet of clay**	***Meaning:*** a hidden fault of character; a weak point If one is able to fix his ***feet of clay,*** one can rectify it.
193	**Fiddle while Rome burns**	***Meaning:*** do nothing or busy yourself with unimportant matters instead of acting in an urgent situation The government ***fiddled while Rome burned,*** doing nothing to control the Covid-19 pandemic.
194	**Field day**	***Meaning:*** to have unlimited opportunities; to have it all your own way Anaadi had a ***field day*** on her birthday to get all the toys of her choice.
195	**Fifth wheel**	***Meaning:*** extra person The office of the Comptroller and Auditor-General is known as the ***fifth wheel*** of the coach.
196	**Fight tooth and nail**	***Meaning:*** to fight fiercely, furiously, and ferociously Alauddin Khilji had to ***fight tooth and nail*** to win over Padmavati of Chittor.
197	**Fill the bill**	***Meaning:*** to be very competent, effective Rajesh as the accountant in office ***fills the bill.***

198	Finger in every pie	***Meaning:*** to have a part in something; to be involved in many matters, businesses, or activities Mrs. Lokhande has her ***finger in every pie*** when it comes to music, dance, and theatre.
199	Fish out of water	***Meaning:*** a person who is out of his or her usual place Getting into the police force, Deepak was feeling like a ***fish out of water.***
200	Fit as a fiddle	***Meaning:*** in good health; in fine shape Mr. Bhushan is nearly ninety, but he is still ***fit as a fiddle.***
201	Fit like a glove	***Meaning:*** to fit a person or thing perfectly; to be exactly right These new curtains match your bedspread perfectly. They ***fit*** your bedroom ***like a glove.***
202	Fix your wagon	***Meaning:*** to get even with or punish someone; to thwart or frustrate another or cause his or her failure in something Mr. Singh was found to derelict his duty and now his superiors would ***fix his wagon.***
203	Flash in the pan	***Meaning:*** a temporary success which yields no long-term results Thought initially the team of Punjab exhibited a great performance, but it was just a ***flash in the pan.***
204	Flotsam and jetsam	***Meaning:*** a collection of mostly worthless and useless objects; rubbish and refuse I am cleaning out my room of all ***flotsam and jetsam.***
205	Fly-by-night	***Meaning:*** selling for quick profit, then disappearing; a swindler or unreliable person The store from where I bought that defective computer was a ***fly-by-night*** operation.
206	Fly by the seat of your pants	***Meaning:*** to do something by instinct and feel without any earlier experience or instruction Though I took a chance to write a book on Legal Aptitude when I had no earlier experience, but I ***flew by the seat of my pants.***
207	Fly in the ointment	***Meaning:*** a small annoyance that spoils an otherwise pleasant situation The food, the music, and the decorations were prefect, but her camera broke. That was the ***fly in the ointment.***
208	Fly off the handle	***Meaning:*** to lose your temper; to become furiously angry When he saw the report card of his son, he ***flew off the handle.***
209	Fly the coop	***Meaning:*** to escape; to leave suddenly and secretly I tried to chain my dog. When I was looking for the chain, he ***flew the coop.***
210	Foam at the mouth	***Meaning:*** to be uncontrollably furious, like a mad dog When the father found the son sleeping just before the exam, he was ***foaming at the mouth.***
211	Follow your nose	***Meaning:*** to go straight ahead in the same direction When he asked me the way to the cafeteria, I told him to ***follow his nose.***

212	**Food for thought**	***Meaning:*** an interesting idea worth thinking about carefully The column 'Inner Voice', in Hindustan Times daily literally provides ***food for thought.***
213	**Footloose and fancy-free**	***Meaning:*** not attached to anyone; not involved with anyone romantically; free Nowadays people are losing sensitivity and sensibility and they are just ***footloose and fancy-free.***
214	**For the birds**	***Meaning:*** worthless; useless; stupid That movie was ***for the birds.*** I am sorry I wasted my money on it.
215	**Forty winks**	***Meaning:*** a short nap I just need ***forty winks*** and I will be able to work all night.
216	**Four corners of the earth**	***Meaning:*** from all over the planet; all parts of a place The death of soccer Venezuelan legend Maradona was mourned by all from the ***four corners of the earth.***
217	**From soup to nuts**	***Meaning:*** the whole things from beginning to end I want to listen to your life history ***from soup to nuts.***
218	**From the word go**	***Meaning:*** from the very beginning Her mother did not like her boyfriend ***from the word go.***
219	**Full of beans**	***Meaning:*** lively, happy and energetic, high-spirited After final exams, some of us were exhausted and others were ***full of beans.***
220	**Full of hot air**	***Meaning:*** being foolish and talking nonsense; pompous; vain I do not believe a word he says. He is ***full of hot air.***
221	**Full steam ahead**	***Meaning:*** proceed with all possible speed and power The captain of the team shouted, ***'Full steam ahead!'*** to get his tired players out onto the field.
	G	
222	**Get a handle on something**	***Meaning:*** to start to overcome a difficult problem or situation Nipun had a lot of trouble with geometry, but I think he is ***getting a handle on it.***
223	**Get a kick out of something**	***Meaning:*** to enjoy doing something; to get a thrill out of something My grandmother really ***gets a kick out of*** playing these video games with me.
224	**Get away with murder**	***Meaning:*** to do something bad, wrong, or illegal and not get caught or punished Most of the accused, most of the time think that they will ***get away with murder.***
225	**Get in on the ground floor**	***Meaning:*** to be a part of some big or important project or business at its start Shukla Ji ***got in on the ground floor*** with the Aadhaar Card project of Govt. of India.

226	**Get into the swing of things**	***Meaning:*** to become accustomed to routine activities Once the Covid-19 pandemic will be over, people will ***get into the swing of things.***
227	**Get off the hook**	***Meaning:*** to free yourself or someone from a distasteful obligation; to get out of trouble; to evade a punishment Though he carried all the responsibilities of the family after his father's death, now he wants to ***get off the hook.***
228	**Get out of my face**	***Meaning:*** stop standing in front of me in a provocative manner, arguing with me You would better ***get out of my face*** right now or you will be sorry!
229	**Get real**	***Meaning:*** face reality; stop fantasising Mr. Digvijay must ***get real*** to the feel of divorce proceedings, instead of flying in the air.
230	**Get something off your chest**	***Meaning:*** to make known something that is bothersome, but kept secret for a time Something is bothering me, and I want to ***get it off my chest.*** Please do not smoke here.
231	**Get the green light**	***Meaning:*** get permission to go ahead with a project Mrs. Nischint Kaur hoped to ***get the green light*** from the principal to redesign her science lab.
232	**Get the lead out of your feet**	***Meaning:*** to get busy; to move or work more quickly The captain encourages the team to ***get the lead out of its feet.***
233	**Get the sack**	***Meaning:*** to be fired A number of employees in the private sector ***got the sack*** because of Covid-19.
234	**Get this show on the road**	***Meaning:*** get going; move forward; get the work started; do it Every morning, Dad shouts, 'Let us ***get this show on the road.*** You do not want to be late for school'.
235	**Get to the bottom of something**	***Meaning:*** to find out the real cause of something The police left no stone unturned to ***get to the bottom of*** *the* crime.
236	**Get under your skin**	***Meaning:*** to bother or upset someone It really ***gets under my skin*** when my parents clean up my room.
237	**Get-up-and-go**	***Meaning:*** energy and motivation; pep; enthusiasm; ambition Since grandmother joined that health club, she has had a lot more ***get-up-and-go.***
238	**Get up on the wrong side of the bed**	***Meaning:*** to awake in a bad temper or mood, feeling cross or grouchy It is advisable to start the day afresh and not ***get up on the wrong side of the bed.***
239	**Get your feet wet**	***Meaning:*** to have a first experience in something; to begin to do something for the first time Mansi had never been in a play, but she took a small part just to ***get her feet wet.***

240	**Get your goat**	***Meaning:*** to annoy very badly; to make a person angry It really ***got his goat*** when he cooked for three hours and no one ate the meal.
241	**Gift of gab**	***Meaning:*** skill in talking, especially in an interesting and colourful way A good politician makes best time of his ***gift of the gab.***
242	**Gild the lily**	***Meaning:*** to spoil something that is already beautiful by adding something extra Anamika really doesn't need all that makeup. That is like ***gilding the lily.***
243	**Give me five**	***Meaning:*** to slap a person's hand as a hearty greeting or a sign of solid agreement My little cousin always yells, ***'Give me five!'***
244	**Give someone the shift off your back**	***Meaning:*** to be extremely generous Mr. Rajesh would ***give you the shift off his back*** if you needed it.
245	**Give someone the third degree**	***Meaning:*** use mental or physical pressure to get information or a confession from someone The teacher ***gave the third degree*** to every student to find out who had glued his briefcase shut.
246	**Give up the ghost**	***Meaning:*** to die; to stop running His computer ***gave up the ghost*** when he was taking online classes.
247	**Give your eyeteeth for something**	***Meaning:*** to want something very badly I'd ***give my eyeteeth*** to own a book like the ones by Abdul Kalam.
248	**Go against the grain**	***Meaning:*** to say or to do something in an unconventional way that annoys people He really ***goes against her grain*** when he says that a woman cannot be president.
249	**Go along for the ride**	***Meaning:*** to watch but not take part in an activity; to keep someone company Aman swore that she did not trash any laws. She just ***went along for the ride.***
250	**Go bananas**	***Meaning:*** to be or go crazy Your brother has ***gone bananas*** for Hindi movies.
251	**Go fly a kite**	***Meaning:*** go away; leave; stop bothering me When he asked for her help, she told him to ***go fly a kite.***
252	**Go for broke**	***Meaning:*** to risk everything on one big goal or effort; to try as hard as possible Instead of applying for separate law entrance, he ***went for broke*** and applied only for CLAT.
253	**Go over like a lead balloon**	***Meaning:*** to fail miserably I wanted to go to Antarctica for a vacation, but my idea ***went over like a lead balloon.***

254	**Go over with a fine-tooth comb**	***Meaning:*** to search with great care or attention She went ***over the lawn with a fine-tooth comb,*** but she could not find her contact lens.
255	**Go to bat for someone**	***Meaning:*** to help someone out; to defend someone Ravi ***went to bat for his friend*** Chander when he defended him in front of the investigating agencies.
256	**Go to the dogs**	***Meaning:*** to decline in looks or health; to be ruined or destroyed; to ruin oneself Because of his addiction to drugs, the star of yesteryears has ***gone to the dogs.***
257	**Gone to pot**	***Meaning:*** become ruined; to get worse and worse This was once a beautiful park, but now it has all ***gone to pot.***
258	**Goody two-shoes**	***Meaning:*** a person who thinks he or she is perfect and tries to be Mona is such a ***goody two-shoes*** that everyone hates her for her vain display.
259	**Grease someone's palm**	***Meaning:*** to bribe someone In government offices, one has to ***grease the concerned officer's palm*** to get things done on time.
260	**Greek to me**	***Meaning:*** too difficult to understand; unknown Taking online classes was literally ***Greek to me.***
261	**Green thumb**	***Meaning:*** having a special talent for making flowers and green plants grow well My uncle has a ***green thumb.*** You should see his roses.
262	**Green with envy**	***Meaning:*** extremely jealous Mrs. Sharma goes ***green with envy*** at anyone's success.
263	**Grit your teeth**	***Meaning:*** to not show one's feelings; to put up with difficulty; to bear pain In the present times of selfishness, one has to ***grit one's teeth*** to avoid unnecessary mockery.
		H
264	**Handle with kid gloves**	***Meaning:*** to treat gently and carefully ***Handle*** the little one's problems ***with kid gloves.***
265	**Hand-to-mouth existence**	***Meaning:*** to spend your salary as fast as it's earned without saving any for the future He lives a ***hand-to-mouth existence*** doing odd jobs around the town.
266	**Handwriting on the wall**	***Meaning:*** a sign that something bad is going to happen; a warning of danger The Covid-19 damages are clearly like the ***handwriting on the wall.***
267	**Hanging by a thread**	***Meaning:*** to be in a dangerous or unsafe position The jobs of many in the private sector are ***hanging by a thread*** in the wake of Covid-19.
268	**Hat in hand**	***Meaning:*** to beg or plead for a favour or a pardon ***Hat in hand,*** I went to the judge pleading for mercy.

269	**Have a bone to pick with you**	***Meaning:*** to have an argument or unpleasant matter to settle with someone My new boss said she ***had a bone to pick with me*** and called me into her office.
270	**Have a screw loose**	***Meaning:*** to behave or look in a strange or foolish manner; to be odd and not ordinary The substitute English teacher must ***have a screw loose.***
271	**Have your cake and eat it too**	***Meaning:*** to spend or use something but still have it You can either go to a movie or get a pizza, but you cannot ***have your cake and eat it too.***
272	**Have your heart in your mouth**	***Meaning:*** to be extremely frightened about something My ***heart was in my mouth*** when I reached the top of the roller coaster.
273	**Head and shoulders above someone**	***Meaning:*** far superior; much better than She is ***head and shoulders above*** all her classmates in English language.
274	**Head honcho**	***Meaning:*** the person in charge; the chief, boss, leader Do what the ***head honcho*** tells you if you want to keep your job.
275	**Head in the clouds**	***Meaning:*** absentminded; daydreaming; lost in thought My report card said that I should pay more attention in class and avoid keeping my ***head in the clouds.***
276	**Head over heels in love**	***Meaning:*** completely and helplessly in love He fell ***head over heels in love*** with the Science teacher.
277	**Hear a pin drop**	***Meaning:*** so silent you can hear very soft things happening; without sound; noiseless At the break of dawn, you can ***hear a pin drop,*** including the ticking of a clock.
278	**Heart of gold**	***Meaning:*** an extremely kind, generous, humane, and forgiving nature Upasna has a ***heart of gold,*** and everyone loves her for it.
279	**Heart's in the right place**	***Meaning:*** to be well-meaning and kind-hearted; to have good intentions even though mistakes occur Atul messes up sometimes, but his ***heart's in the right place.***
280	**High horse**	***Meaning:*** acting superior and arrogant as if you were better than other people Neetu always runs his ***high horse*** without being aware of his ground reality.
281	**Highway robbery**	***Meaning:*** an extremely high price or charge for something Shopping at malls is no less than a ***highway robbery.***
282	**Hit below the belt**	***Meaning:*** to use unfair tactics or be unsportsmanlike He ***hit below the belt*** to top in the exam.
283	**Hit the jackpot**	***Meaning:*** to be very lucky; to achieve amazing success Today I ***hit the jackpot;*** I got the highest grade in the spelling test.
284	**Hit the nail right on the head**	***Meaning:*** to be exactly correct about a description or come to the right conclusion She really ***hit the nail right on the head***, when she instantly identified the accused in an identification parade.

285	**Hit the road**	***Meaning:*** to begin a journey, to leave The car rallyists ***hit the road*** early in the morning.
286	**Hit the roof**	***Meaning:*** to lose your temper suddenly; to become violently angry On seeing the report card, Arnav's father ***hit the roof.***
287	**Hit the spot**	***Meaning:*** to fully satisfy and refresh, especially with food or drink After a long hike through the desert, a cold drink ***hit the spot.***
288	**Hitch your wagon to a star**	***Meaning:*** to aim high; to try to reach the highest level; to follow a great ambition Dr. APJ Abdul Kalam always advised youngsters to ***hitch their wagon to a star.***
289	**Hold the fort**	***Meaning:*** to temporarily be responsible for watching over a place Our teacher was late, so the teacher next door ***held the fort*** in until he showed up.
290	**Hold your horses**	***Meaning:*** slow down; wait a minute; be patient ***Hold your horses,*** why are you walking so fast?
291	**Horse of a different colour**	***Meaning:*** a different matter altogether Making arrangements for the English class was a ***horse of a different colour*** than that of a hobby class.
292	**Hot under the collar**	***Meaning:*** very angry; upset Better say good night. My father is starting to get ***hot under the collar.***
		I
293	**If the shoe fits, wear it**	***Meaning:*** if a remark applies to you, you should admit that it is true Some students never clean up after art class. I am not mentioning names, but ***if the shoe fits, wear it.***
294	**Ignorance is bliss**	***Meaning:*** it is better not to know the bad news sometimes, especially if you're happy Sometimes it causes losses to be wise and, in that situation, ***ignorance is bliss.***
295	**In a nutshell**	***Meaning:*** in very few words; briefly; clearly and to the point ***In a nutshell,*** tell me what the show was about.
296	**In hot water**	***Meaning:*** in serious trouble or in an embarrassing situation with someone of authority The officer was ***in hot water*** for disobeying the orders of the court.
297	**In one ear and out the other**	***Meaning:*** not listening to what is being said, not attentive In case of the majority of children, the parents' advice goes ***in one ear and out the other.***
298	**In the bag**	***Meaning:*** absolutely certain to be won, gotten, or achieved; sure, definite Our soccer team had the championship ***in the bag*** when the other team's best player fell sick.
299	**In the catbird seat**	***Meaning:*** in a position of advance or superiority The students with a good family background are always ***in the catbird seat.***

300	**In the driver's seat**	***Meaning:*** in control; in the position of authority Mrs. Saxena is always ***in the driver's seat*** as Mr. Sharma is a henpecked husband.
301	**In the lap of luxury**	***Meaning:*** surrounded by luxuries; having the most lavish things that money can buy Pradeep lives ***in the lap of luxury*** in his mansion in Sector 2, Chandigarh.
302	**In the limelight**	***Meaning:*** at the centre of attention Kangana Ranaut was ***in the limelight*** after the death of Sushant Singh Rajput.
303	**In the nick of time**	***Meaning:*** just at the exact time; at the precise moment Though he seemed to be late, he reached just ***in the nick of time*** before the program started.
304	**In the pink**	***Meaning:*** in excellent health physically and emotionally I was pleased to see that Mr. Singh was ***in the pink*** of health.
305	**In the same boat**	***Meaning:*** in the same bad situation; sharing the same problem or difficulty In the present times of lockdown, most people are sailing ***in the same boat.***
	J	
306	**Jack-of-all-trades**	***Meaning:*** a person who can do different kinds of jobs It is advised to be the master of a few rather than be a ***jack-of-all-trades.***
307	**Jet set**	***Meaning:*** the wealthy, fashionable, and famous people who travel frequently The ***jet set*** section of the society do not mix with the riff-raff and bob-tail.
308	**Johnny-come-lately**	***Meaning:*** someone who is new to a place or group; an inexperienced person The older teachers in the math department call the new teacher a ***Johnny-come-lately.***
309	**Jump down your throat**	***Meaning:*** to talk or scream at someone in a sudden, angry way The father ***jumped down his throat*** at the children making noise.
310	**Jump off the deep end**	***Meaning:*** to act emotionally without carefully thinking about the end result Inter-caste marriage in India even today is no less than ***jumping off the deep end.***
311	**Jump on the bandwagon**	***Meaning:*** to become part of the newest activity because many other people are Last year nobody liked my idea of a school carnival. Now everyone wants to ***jump on the bandwagon.***
312	**Jump the gun**	***Meaning:*** to act prematurely or hastily I could not wait to give my mother her Mother's Day gift, so I ***jumped the gun*** and gave it to her a week early.
313	**Just deserts**	***Meaning:*** the punishment a person deserves; receive what one deserves The rape accused need to be given the ***just deserts.*** Those who caused great torment to others rarely get their just deserts.

K		
314	**Keep a stiff upper lip**	***Meaning:*** to be brave and not show emotion in a time of trouble Even while undergoing the worst and toughest times of her life, she ***keeps a stiff upper lip.***
315	**Keep a straight face**	***Meaning:*** to keep from laughing It is very difficult to ***keep a straight face*** after watching the clownish behaviour of Mrs. Poonam.
316	**Keep body and soul together**	***Meaning:*** to keep alive; to have just enough to survive He got a job that paid so little, he was barely able to ***keep body and soul together.***
317	**Keep something under your hat**	***Meaning:*** to keep something secret The Chandigarhians are so introvert that they ***keep everything under their hats.***
318	**Keep the wolf from the door**	***Meaning:*** to keep away from suffering, poverty or starvation He got two extra jobs just to ***keep the wolf from the door.***
319	**Keep your ear to the ground**	***Meaning:*** know what is going on; pay attention and be well informed Mr. Mittal always ***keeps his ear to the ground*** and knows who is who and what is what.
320	**Keep your fingers crossed**	***Meaning:*** to wish for good luck and success for someone or something Before the final results, all the candidates were ***keeping their fingers crossed.***
321	**Keep your head above water**	***Meaning:*** to earn enough to stay out of debt and avoid financial ruin Business is in doldrums because of Covid-19, and Dad is barely ***keeping his head above water.***
322	**Kick up your heels**	***Meaning:*** to celebrate and have a wonderful time After the good results, the successful candidates kept ***kicking up their heels*** the whole night.
323	**Kill the goose that lays the golden eggs**	***Meaning:*** to spoil or destroy something good out of stupidity, greed, or impatience Sometimes people out of sheer greed ***kill the goose that lays the golden eggs.***
324	**Kill two birds with one stone**	***Meaning:*** to do two things by one action; to get two results with just one effort Anaadi prepared her English language with twin purpose of school examination as well as English Olympiad thereby ***killing two birds with one stone.***
325	**Knock your socks off**	***Meaning:*** thrill, amaze, delight, overwhelm, startle, excite, shock At an Indian Idol music talent hunt show, Kamakshi ***knocked the jury's socks off.***
L		
326	**Lame duck**	***Meaning:*** an elected official in the last days of his or her time on the job After defeat in the US 2020 Presidential Elections, Donald Trump was a ***lame duck*** for the remainder of his term.

327	**Laugh out of the other side of your mouth**	***Meaning:*** to be made to feel sorrow, to cry at a change in luck after experiencing some happiness Once the news gets out that Donald Trump bought votes to win the election, he'll be ***laughing out of the other side of his mouth.***
328	**Lay an egg**	***Meaning:*** to give an embarrassing performance She really ***laid an egg*** at the talent show with her clumsy performance.
329	**Lay your cards on the table**	***Meaning:*** to reveal all the facts openly and honestly; to reveal one's purpose and plans The mayor ***laid his cards on the table*** about the beautification project.
330	**Lead you by the nose**	***Meaning:*** to dominate or control someone Everyone knows that Mr. Sharma is a henpecked husband, his wife ***leads him by the nose.***
331	**Leave no stone unturned**	***Meaning:*** to make all possible efforts to carry out a task She vowed that she would ***leave no stone unturned*** in finding out who let the air out of her car's tyres.
332	**Leave someone holding the bag**	***Meaning:*** to force someone to take blame when it should be shared When the teacher demanded to know who wrote the joke on the blackboard, Arnav was ***left holding the bag.***
333	**Left out in the cold**	***Meaning:*** to not tell someone something; to exclude someone from a place or activity Ravi told everyone else about the party, but he ***left me out in the cold.***
334	**Lend an ear**	***Meaning:*** to listen and pay attention to Good students always ***lend their ears*** to their teachers.
335	**Let sleeping dogs lie**	***Meaning:*** to not make someone angry by stirring up trouble Do not remind the director that you missed two rehearsals. Better to ***let sleeping dogs lie.***
336	**Let the cat out of the bag**	***Meaning:*** to give away a secret Ravi's younger brother ***let the cat out of the bag*** by telling about the surprise party.
337	**Life in the fast lane**	***Meaning:*** a fast, busy way of life In the present age of fast foods, the youngsters are leading their ***lives in the fast lane.***
338	**Light at the end of the tunnel**	***Meaning:*** a long-searched-for answer, goal, or success After 10 years of long legal battle, the victim finally saw the ***light at the end of the tunnel.***
339	**Like a bump on a log**	***Meaning:*** inactive and not responding Do not just sit there ***like a bump on a log.*** Help the people in distress because of Covid-19.
340	**Like it or lump it**	***Meaning:*** whether you like it or not; certain to happen Covid-19 is a grim reality. We ***like it or lump it*** but we need to take precautions.
341	**Like pulling teeth**	***Meaning:*** something very hard to do Asking Sameer to follow a disciplined routine is ***like pulling teeth.***

342	**Like two peas in a pod**	***Meaning:*** identical; alike in looks and behaviour Anaadi and Upasna are ***like two peas in a pod.***
343	**Lock, stock, and barrel**	***Meaning:*** the whole of something; all the parts of a thing; everything The company was sold – ***lock, stock, and barrel.***
344	**Long in the tooth**	***Meaning:*** old; aged; elderly Mr. & Mrs. Dhawan are a quite ***long in the tooth.***
345	**Look down your nose at someone**	***Meaning:*** to think of and treat people as if they were lower in quality or ability The newly rich class ***look down their nose at poor people.***
346	**Loose cannon**	***Meaning:*** a person who is unpredictable and sometimes out of control He got fired because he was a ***loose cannon*** and caused everybody a lot of trouble.
347	**Lose your shirt**	***Meaning:*** to lose everything; especially money Mr. Mahajan ***lost his shirt*** in the share market.
348	**Lower the boom**	***Meaning:*** to scold or punish strictly; to make someone follow the rules Sometimes the parents unnecessarily ***lower the boom*** on their children.
		M
349	**Mad as a hatter**	***Meaning:*** completely crazy, strange, eccentric Chaudhary is as ***mad as a hatter,*** but he is my first friend.
350	**Mad as a wet hen**	***Meaning:*** very upset; extremely angry; ready to fight When Avni realised that her brother had eaten all the cookies, she was as ***mad as a wet hen.***
351	**Make a mountain out of a molehill**	***Meaning:*** to turn a small, unimportant issue into a big, important one; to exaggerate Some people are in the habit of ***making a mountain out of a molehill.***
352	**Make ends meet**	***Meaning:*** to earn just enough to live within one's income With a 50 percent salary cut because of Covid-19, the salaried class find it difficult to ***make ends meet.***
353	**Make hay while the sun shines**	***Meaning:*** to make the best of a limited opportunity For some people Covid-19 proved to be a blessing in disguise, they ***made hay while the sun shined.***
354	**Make heads or tails out of something**	***Meaning:*** to understand how something works; to figure something out We are not able to ***make heads or tails out of the instructions*** for assembling the new weather-forecasting machine.
355	**Make no bones about something**	***Meaning:*** to speak directly, plainly, honestly, and without hesitation or doubt The substitute teacher ***made no bones about the colourful hats*** worn in the class.
356	**Make your mouth water**	***Meaning:*** to look so attractive and desirable that it makes you want to have it very much; to want to eat or drink something that looks or smells delicious The egg parathas ***made my mouth water.***

357	**March to the beat of a different drummer**	***Meaning:*** be an individual; do your own thing; don't do what everybody else does; be original and creative Arnav never imitates others, he ***marched to the beat of a different drummer.***
358	**Mess with someone**	***Meaning:*** to annoy, argue with, hassle, or otherwise anger and irritate a person Do not even think of ***messing with the new teacher.*** She is tough.
359	**Midas touch**	***Meaning:*** to make a lot of money at whatever you do Dhirubhai Ambani is said to have a ***Midas touch.***
360	**Mince words**	***Meaning:*** not to come right to the point; to be less than 100% honest Please don't ***mince words.*** Tell me exactly what you think of me.
361	**Mind over matter**	***Meaning:*** the power of your mind is stronger than the body ***Mind over matter*** is a centuries old established philosophy.
362	**Mind your Ps and Qs**	***Meaning:*** to be extremely exact; be careful not to say or do anything wrong Please try to ***mind your Ps and Qs*** when the Prime Minister visits the school.
363	**Money burns a hole in your pocket**	***Meaning:*** cannot stop yourself from spending whatever money you have He is a pathological spendthrift who can't save a single penny, ***money burns a hole in his pocket.***
364	**Monkey business**	***Meaning:*** silliness or fooling around; dishonest or illegal activities; idiotic pranks No more ***monkey business!*** Settle down.
365	**More than meets the eye**	***Meaning:*** there are hidden facts that can't be seen or understood right away The police could easily make out that there was ***more than what met the eye.***
		N
366	**Needle in a haystack**	***Meaning:*** something hard or impossible to find; anything hopeless (in a search) Without any clue about the offence or offender, the police felt like they were looking for a ***needle in a haystack.***
367	**Nickel-and-dime**	***Meaning:*** unimportant, small-time, trivial, petty He said he worked for a big corporation, but in reality, it was only a ***nickel-and-dime*** company.
368	**Nitty-gritty**	***Meaning:*** the specific heart of the matter; the practical details; the fundamental core of something A judge must look into the ***nitty-gritty*** of every case; let's get down to the ***nitty-gritty*** of finding a job
369	**Nose out of joint**	***Meaning:*** angry, jealous, or annoyed at someone When Mannat could not win in Olympiad, her ***nose was out of joint*** for a week.

370	**Not your cup of tea**	***Meaning:*** not what one likes or prefers; not suitable; not to your taste He advised me to join an MNC and I told him that it was ***not my cup of tea.***
371	**Nothing new under the sun**	***Meaning:*** everything is just a little different but pretty much the same as an earlier invention This expensive pasta is really just macaroni. There's ***nothing new under the sun.***
372	**Nothing to sneeze at**	***Meaning:*** not small or unimportant; something to be taken seriously He won the silver medal, not the gold, but that is still ***nothing to sneeze at.***
373	**Nothing ventured, nothing gained**	***Meaning:*** if you don't try to do something, you'll never accomplish it Keep trying because if you stop trying, ***nothing ventured, nothing gained.***
	O	
374	**Off your rocker**	***Meaning:*** crazy; silly; foolish; not thinking correctly The Head of the company is ***off his rocker,*** nobody likes his ways.
375	**Old hat**	***Meaning:*** out-of-date; not new; too familiar; uninteresting Let us try a new place for our next vacation. Shimla is so ***old hat.***
376	**On cloud nine**	***Meaning:*** blissfully happy; joyous Anaadi was ***on cloud nine*** when she won the scholar's badge.
377	**On pins and needles**	***Meaning:*** waiting anxiously for something; extremely nervous I was ***on pins and needles*** until I got the phone call that the plane had landed safely.
378	**On tenterhooks**	***Meaning:*** uncertain, anxious, very tense; in painful suspense about how something will turn out The police was ***on tenterhooks*** to nab the offender.
379	**On the ball**	***Meaning:*** alert; effective; skilful; knowledgeable Those who are selected for the hot seat in the KBC program, always prefer their friends ***on the ball*** to be consulted.
380	**On the horns of a dilemma**	***Meaning:*** having to choose between two unavoidable options Having selected for P.O. in bank and Inspector in Police, he was ***on the horns of a dilemma,*** as to which to join and which to leave.
381	**On the hot seat**	***Meaning:*** in a difficult or uncomfortable position When Akshay was found absent from duty, he was really ***on the hot seat.***
382	**On the rocks**	***Meaning:*** financially ruined or wrecked; near disaster; finished I need a loan because of my dog-walking business is ***on the rocks.***
383	**On the ropes**	***Meaning:*** almost failing; on the verge of collapse; nearly ruined Because of Covid-19 pandemic, a number of businessmen are ***on the ropes.***
384	**On the spur of the moment**	***Meaning:*** suddenly; acting without thinking about it first, impulsively He took a decision ***on the spur of the moment*** to take the accident victims to the hospitals.

385	**On the tip of your tongue**	***Meaning:*** temporarily forgotten but at the point where one can almost say it The name of the song was ***on the tip of her tongue,*** but she could not remember it fast enough to win the contest.
386	**On the warpath**	***Meaning:*** in a very angry mood; infuriated Mr. Sharma is ***on the warpath*** because his car broke down again.
387	**On top of the world**	***Meaning:*** feeling extremely happy When my first book got published, I was ***on top of the world.***
388	**Once in a blue moon**	***Meaning:*** almost never; very seldom; hardly ever The teacher is tough, but ***once in a blue moon*** she does not give us homework.
389	**One good turn deserves another**	***Meaning:*** one good deed should be paid back with another One must always recognise others' contributions. ***One good turn deserves another.***
390	**Open a can of worms**	***Meaning:*** to cause trouble; to set unpleasant events in motion If you mention my report card to my mother, you will ***open a can of worms.***
391	**Other side of the coin**	***Meaning:*** opposite side or point of view He conducts himself in public decently but in his private life, you can see the ***other side of the coin.***
392	**Out of sight, out of mind**	***Meaning:*** if you do not see something for a long time, you'll eventually stop thinking about it It is the prevalent practice that when you go away from someone it means ***out of sight, out of mind.***
393	**Out of the frying pan and into the fire**	***Meaning:*** from a bad situation into one that is worse The thief escaped from the dog and ran into a policeman thereby being ***out of the frying pan and into the fire.***
		P
394	**Penny-wise and pound-foolish**	***Meaning:*** careful in small matters but carless about important things; saving small amounts of money while wasting large amounts Mrs. Sharma makes a cut on her health expenses but wastes too much money on unnecessary things. It is like being ***penny-wise and pound-foolish.***
395	**People who live in glass houses should not throw stones**	***Meaning:*** you should not criticise others if you are just as bad as they are He complained about her driving, but he has already had two accidents. ***People who live in glass houses should not throw stones***
396	**Piece of cake**	***Meaning:*** an especially easy and pleasant task Writing an essay on any topic is just a ***piece of cake*** for Rajesh.
397	**Play cat and mouse**	***Meaning:*** to tease or fool someone She ***plays cat and mouse*** with her little brother, pretending to hand him a lollipop, then taking it away when he reaches for it.

398	**Play fast and loose**	***Meaning:*** to do whatever pleases you without caring about what will happen to others Promising help and dodging at a critical moment is not good. You should not ***play fast and loose*** with your friends.
399	**Play second fiddle**	***Meaning:*** to be a follower; to be in an inferior position The employees habitual of flattery always ***play second fiddle*** to the bosses.
400	**Play with fire**	***Meaning:*** to take an unnecessary and dangerous risk; to court danger Openly intimidating your neighbour in front of all was no less than ***playing with fire.***
401	**Point of no return**	***Meaning:*** the position or time after which it is impossible to go back, change your mind, or do something different We cannot cancel the show now. We have reserved the theatre and sold tickets. We have reached the ***point of no return.***
402	**Poor as a church mouse**	***Meaning:*** very poor; poverty-stricken The Sharmas used to be wealthy, but after the stock market crash, they are as ***poor as a church mouse.***
403	**Pour oil on troubled waters**	***Meaning:*** to calm an angry quarrel My brothers were having a terrible fight in the car, but my mother ***poured oil on troubled waters*** by saying they were both right.
404	**Power behind the throne**	***Meaning:*** the actual, but unrecognised, person in charge The Gandhi family runs the Congress Party, though Sonia Gandhi is not the President, she is the real ***power behind the throne.***
405	**Pull a rabbit out of a hat**	***Meaning:*** to produce something that is needed as if by magic; to unexpectedly find a solution to a problem We were very hungry, and suddenly Mr. Jindal took some cookies out of his pocket. It was like ***pulling a rabbit out of a hat.***
406	**Pull no punches**	***Meaning:*** to hit as hard as possible; to attack with full force; to be perfectly honest; to not hold back Tell me what you thought of my acting. Do not ***pull any punches.***
407	**Pull out all the stops**	***Meaning:*** to do everything possible to succeed; to do something as enthusiastically as you can He ***pulled out all the stops*** to persuade his parents for love marriage.
408	**Pull strings**	***Meaning:*** to exert behind-the-scenes influence; to secretly control others from a distance as if they were puppets The Party President ***pulls strings*** of all party workers after election defeat.
409	**Pull the wool over your eyes.**	***Meaning:*** to fool, deceive, or trick someone He was ***pulling the wool over the eyes*** of his parents and instead of focusing on studies he was just watching movies.
410	**Pull your leg**	***Meaning:*** to tease or fool someone; to jokingly try to lie to somebody Oh, do not get so annoyed at them for teasing you. They are just ***pulling your leg.***
411	**Pull yourself together**	***Meaning:*** to regain control over one's emotions and become calm after being very upset Calm down, ***pull yourself together,*** and plan a new trip.

412	**Put all your eggs into one basket**	***Meaning:*** to risk everything you have at once on a single idea or plan; to commit all your resources at one time One should apply for different jobs instead of trying only for Civil Services just like ***putting all your eggs into one basket.***
413	**Put the cart before the horse**	***Meaning:*** do things in backward or reverse order If you pull your shoes on before your socks, you were ***putting the cart before the horse.***
414	**Put your best foot forward**	***Meaning:*** to make the best attempt possible; to do your best to make the greatest impression you can When you go in for your interview, try to ***put your best foot forward.***
		Q
415	**Quiet as a mouse**	***Meaning:*** silent or still; making very little noise; saying nothing; hushed, subdued ***Quiet as a mouse,*** she slipped back into her dormitory after hours.
		R
416	**Rain on your parade**	***Meaning:*** to spoil someone's day, performance, special occasion, celebration, plans Heavy rains spoiled the marriage celebrations and it ***rained on his parade.***
417	**Raining cats and dogs**	***Meaning:*** to rain very heavily; to pour It is ***raining cats and dogs,*** and our picnic is ruined.
418	**Rat race**	***Meaning:*** a fierce, unending, stressful competition in business or society All Indian youngsters, without evaluating their potentials run a ***rat race*** for Civil Services preparations.
419	**Rats abandoning a sinking ship**	***Meaning:*** disloyal people who desert a failing enterprise before it is too late Like ***rats abandoning a sinking ship,*** they switched to the other candidate when theirs began to lose.
420	**Read between the lines**	***Meaning:*** to discern the true, hidden meaning or fact in any document or action The spiritual mystic show always advised to ***read between the lines.***
421	**Red-carpet treatment**	***Meaning:*** great respect and hospitality given to someone important; special treatment The Booker Prize winner is given ***red-carpet treatment.***
422	**Red-letter day**	***Meaning:*** a day remembered as especially happy and significant 15 August, 1947 is a ***red-letter day*** in the Indian history.
423	**Red tape**	***Meaning:*** excessive formality and time-consuming, rigid adherence to rules and regulations ***Red-tapism*** is the most serious malady afflicting Indian bureaucracy.
424	**Ring a bell**	***Meaning:*** to sound familiar; to call something to mind; to stir a vague memory I do not remember her face, but her name ***rings a bell.***

425	**Roll with the punches**	***Meaning:*** to adjust to a difficult situation Try not to be too discouraged with your new job. Just ***roll with the punches*** a while.
426	**Rolling stone gathers no moss**	***Meaning:*** a person who is always on the move or who changes jobs often will not be able to save or keep much He has changed 5 jobs in 2 years which goes against his credentials as a ***rolling stone gathers no moss.***
427	**Rome was not built in a day**	***Meaning:*** a difficult or important goal or task cannot be achieved quickly or all at once Writing a book for IAS Examination is not an overnight job as ***Rome was not built in a day.***
428	**Rotten apple spoils the barrel**	***Meaning:*** one bad person or thing may spoil an entire group A tiny group of kids starts fights in our school, and people think that one ***rotten apple spoils the barrel.***
429	**Round peg in a square hole**	***Meaning:*** a person whose abilities, character, or personality are not suited to his or her position Though Sunita opted for Science on her parent's insistence it is as she is a ***round peg in a square hole.***
430	**Rub the wrong way**	***Meaning:*** to annoy and irritate someone; to handle someone insensitively Repeated reminders to the bosses for promotion proved to be ***rubbing the wrong way.***
431	**Rule with an iron hand**	***Meaning:*** to be strict, stern, a harsh ruler Sardar Patel could unify the princely Indian states because he ***ruled with an iron hand.***
432	**Run off at the mouth**	***Meaning:*** to talk too much; to talk nonstop Ravi keeps ***running off at the mouth*** about the University Faculty.
		S
433	**Salt of the earth**	***Meaning:*** a person or group considered to be the finest, most admirable, and noble Martyrs like Bhagat Singh and Subhash Chander Bose are considered the ***salt of the earth.***
434	**Same old song and dance**	***Meaning:*** dull, nonsense that has been said many times before; a lie or excuse that's been told before Mr. Saxena keeps blowing the same trumpet like the ***same old song and dance.***
435	**Save for a rainy day**	***Meaning:*** to save for a time of need; to put something away for the future It is advisable to make savings so as to ***save some money for a rainy day.***
436	**Scarce as hen's teeth**	***Meaning:*** very, very rare or totally non-existent During the holidays, seats on any flight were as ***scarce as hen's teeth.***
437	**School of hard knocks**	***Meaning:*** challenging experiences that can teach you a lot Mrs. Suri never went to college, but she learned how to be successful in the ***school of hard knocks.***

438	Scratch the surface	***Meaning:*** to just begin to deal with a problem; to deal with only a very small part of a subject Scientists have only ***scratched the surface*** in finding the vaccine for Covid-19.
439	See eye to eye	***Meaning:*** to agree fully; to have the same opinion My parents and I do not always ***see eye to eye*** about my allowance.
440	Sell like hotcakes	***Meaning:*** to sell quickly, effortlessly, and in quantity My book LA/ LR is ***selling like hotcakes*** for the last 10 years.
441	Set your teeth on edge	***Meaning:*** to cause annoyance or discomfort to someone When I watch any Indian media channel except NDTV, it ***sets my teeth on edge.***
442	Settle an old score	***Meaning:*** to get back at; to get revenge for past wrongs The ruling parties in power always try to ***settle an old score*** with opponents.
443	Shape up or ship out	***Meaning:*** to correct your behaviour, improve your performance Neetu has been asked to be regular and punctual to ***shape up or ship out.***
444	Shoe is on the other foot	***Meaning:*** the situation is now the opposite of what it once was; places are reversed Once you drove right by me in the rain and did not stop. Now the ***shoe is on the other foot,*** I would be driving, and you would be walking.
445	Shoot from the hip	***Meaning:*** to speak or act without first thinking about the consequences Mr. Singh is known for his impulsive behaviour, he just ***shoots from the hip*** and lands himself into trouble.
446	Shot in the arm	***Meaning:*** something that lifts your spirits, energy, and confidence Mr. Sharma was feeling pretty low in the hospital, but your letter really gave him a ***shot in the arm.***
447	Show must go on	***Meaning:*** the proceedings must continue regardless of any catastrophe or difficulty; nothing can stop what has been planned The bride had planned a wedding outdoors, and even when it rained, she insisted that the ***show must go on.***
448	Show your true colours	***Meaning:*** to reveal what you are really like Fair weather friends ***show their true colours*** in bad times.
449	Sight for sore eyes	***Meaning:*** a most welcome, unexpected sight; a pleasant surprise After prolonged illness, when the reports of gradual recovery came, Mr. Sharma saw a ***sight for sore eyes.***
450	Sink or swim	***Meaning:*** to fall or succeed by one's own efforts without anyone's help or interference Once I had taken the risk to run the institute, it was a ***sink or swim*** situation.
451	Sitting pretty	***Meaning:*** to be in a lucky, superior, or advantageous position The Indian hockey team had scored four goals in the first half, so it was ***sitting pretty.***

452	**Six of one and a half dozen of the other**	***Meaning:*** one and the same thing; nothing to choose between; equal I do not care if we eat veg or non-veg food. To me, it is ***six of one and a half dozen of the other.***
453	**Skeleton in your closet**	***Meaning:*** a shameful and shocking secret that people try to keep hidden Everyone has bright and dark facets of life, but people prefer to keep the dark as a ***skeleton in the closet.***
454	**Sky is the limit**	***Meaning:*** there is no limit to what you can spend or how far you can go or what you can achieve In the field of journalism, ***sky is the limit.***
455	**Slow on the draw**	***Meaning:*** slow to understand or figure something out; slow to respond or react; not alert; not a deep thinker Some of Albert Einstein's teachers thought he was a little ***slow on the draw.***
456	**Smell a rat**	***Meaning:*** to be suspicious; to feel that something is wrong Although everything looked right, the investigator ***smelled a rat.***
457	**Smell like a rose**	***Meaning:*** to look good in a bad situation; to avoid a damaged reputation when involved with corruption; to appear pure and innocent Though the officer was caught red-handed while taking bribe, he came ***smelling like a rose.***
458	**Snake in the grass**	***Meaning:*** an unfaithful, untrustworthy, underhanded, and deceitful person; a traitor Beware of opportunists, they are like a ***snake in the grass.***
459	**Snug as a bug in a rug**	***Meaning:*** cosy and comfortable; safe and secure Grandma tucked her in, as ***snug as a bug in a rug,*** shut off the lights, and tiptoed out of the room.
460	**Sow your wild oats**	***Meaning:*** to behave wildly and foolishly, especially when young Can you believe that our quiet, dignified grandfather ***sowed his wild oats*** when he was just out of college?
461	**Spare the rod and spoil the child**	***Meaning:*** to physically punish children when they misbehave so they will learn to behave properly in the future ***'Spare the rod and spoil the child',*** practice is quite imperative to make the children behave properly.
462	**Spick-and-span**	***Meaning:*** extremely clean, tidy, neat Mr. Balwant Chaudhary always had ***spick-and-span*** surroundings and lived life in the same style.
463	**Spill the beans**	***Meaning:*** to give away a secret to someone who is not supposed to know it He was afraid that his wife would ***spill the beans.***
464	**Spitting image**	***Meaning:*** a perfect resemblance; an exact likeness He must be Aarav's father. He is the ***spitting image*** of Aarav.
465	**Stick-in-the-mud**	***Meaning:*** a person with old-fashioned ideas who avoids anything new, ignores progress, and fights change Mr. Wilson is still stuck up in old duddy fuddy ideas. He is just a ***stick-in-the-mud.***

466	**Stick to your guns**	***Meaning:*** to stand firm and hold to one's position in the face of opposition; to stand up for your rights no matter what trouble you get into In the sharp opposition of new farmers' laws, the entire farmers' community ***stuck to its guns.***
467	**Stick your neck out**	***Meaning:*** to take a bold or dangerous risk; to expose yourself to criticism You should not have to be the only one to complain. Why should you ***stick your neck out?***
468	**Still waters run deep**	***Meaning:*** somebody can be more knowledgeable or emotional than he or she first appears to be; a silent person may be intelligent Arnav was a quiet student, but he was very brilliant. ***Still waters run deep.***
469	**Stir up a hornet's nest**	***Meaning:*** to make many people furious; to cause trouble The new farmers laws have ***stirred up a hornet's nest*** all over India.
470	**Straight from the horse's mouth**	***Meaning:*** directly from the person or place that is the most reliable source or the best authority I got it ***straight from the horse's mouth*** that there is going to be a surgical strike against Pakistan.
471	**Straight from the shoulder**	***Meaning:*** frankly, honestly This is ***straight from the shoulder:*** I do not want to share a room with you because you smoke.
472	**Strike a happy medium**	***Meaning:*** to find a compromise to a problem; to find a sensible solution midway between two opposite desires In order to pacify the agitating farmers, the government has to ***strike a happy medium.***
473	**Strike while the iron is hot**	***Meaning:*** to act at the most favourable time or moment to get the best results; to take advantage of favourable conditions One must have patience to think for the best opportunity and must ***strike while the iron is hot.***
474	**Stuffed shirt**	***Meaning:*** a self-important person who shows a lot of phony dignity The chairman of the board is such a ***stuffed shirt.***
475	**Swallow hook, line, and sinker**	***Meaning:*** to believe a story completely without questioning it; to be very gullible I told him a ghost story, and he ***swallowed it hook, line, and sinker.***
476	**Swan song**	***Meaning:*** the final, farewell performance of an actor or singer; one's last words or actions The Hindi movie Chichore was the ***swan song*** of Sushant Singh Rajput.
477	**Sweep under the rug**	***Meaning:*** to hide or ignore unpleasant matters Her parents found out about her failing grades, even though she tried to ***sweep them under the rug.***
478	**Sweep you off your feet**	***Meaning:*** to make a favourable impression; to effect with strong emotion or enthusiasm; to overcome someone with feelings of love or happiness so strong that he or she can't resist you Being the topper of IAS 2020, Kanchan Singla ***swept everyone off their feet.***

		T
479	**Take off your hat to someone**	***Meaning:*** to admire or praise someone for a notable accomplishment Even with her arm in a sling, she cooked a marvellous meal. I have to ***take my hat off to her.***
480	**Take someone under your wing**	***Meaning:*** to help, guide, or protect someone Looking at his deteriorating results, the father ***took his son under his wing*** for final the Boards Examination.
481	**Take the bitter with the sweet**	***Meaning:*** to accept the bad things that happen along with the good Life in sum total of good and bad happenings, it is better to learn to ***take the bitter with the sweet.***
482	**Take the bull by the horns**	***Meaning:*** to act bravely in a troublesome situation The Covid-19 pandemic is a grim reality, but everyone has to ***take the bull by its horns.***
483	**Take with a grain of salt**	***Meaning:*** to not believe completely; to be doubtful Happy Singh tends to exaggerate. ***Take*** what he says ***with a grain of salt.***
484	**Talk through your hat**	***Meaning:*** to talk nonsense Do not let what Micky said upset you. He is just ***talking through his hat.***
485	**Throw caution to the wind**	***Meaning:*** to take a huge risk; to act recklessly and hastily Many people are ***throwing cautions to the wind*** without wearing a mask and not maintaining social distance in spite of Covid-19 prevalence.
486	**Throw cold water on something**	***Meaning:*** to say or do something discouraging; to dampen one's enthusiasm for something Rekha's father refused her to take part in the dance competition and ***threw cold water on her plans.***
487	**Throw your hat into the ring**	***Meaning:*** to announce one's candidacy for election to office; to issue a challenge Dayal Partap ***threw his hat into the ring*** today. He is running for the post of President of the High Court Bar Association
488	**Tickle your funny bone**	***Meaning:*** to make you laugh; to amuse somebody The Kapil Sharma show literally ***tickles everyone's funny bone.***
489	**Tighten your belt**	***Meaning:*** to live on less money; to make sacrifices and lower one's standard of living Everyone is constrained to ***tighten their belt*** because of shrinking sources of income in the Covid-19 times.
490	**Till the cows come home**	***Meaning:*** for a long, long time I'll stand here ***till the cows come home*** unless you pay me back the money, I lent you.
491	**Tip of the iceberg**	***Meaning:*** just a small part of a larger problem or a worse situation In Chemistry, learning the symbols for the elements is just the ***tip of the iceberg.***
492	**Toe the line**	***Meaning:*** do what you are supposed to do; obey all rules and orders All the employees were supposed to ***toe the line*** and follow all the regulations of the company or they were out of a job.

493	**Too many cooks spoil the broth**	***Meaning:*** a project is set back rather than helped by too many organisers; the more people who work on one project, the worse it will turn out The decorations look terrible because the committee could not agree on anything. ***Too many cooks spoil the broth.***
494	**Top banana**	***Meaning:*** the leading comedian in a variety show; a boss Kapil Sharma has been a ***top banana*** in Indian comedian shows.
495	**Tough nut to crack**	***Meaning:*** something very complicated to understand or to do; an extremely tough or thorny problem to solve Mr. Sharma never seeks the help of anyone and never opens up his heart; he is a ***tough nut to crack.***
496	**True-blue**	***Meaning:*** very loyal, dependable, and faithful Ahmed Patel, who expired recently, was a ***true-blue*** supporter of the Congress.
497	**Turn over a new leaf**	***Meaning:*** to correct one's behaviour or attitude; to begin anew; to make a fresh start If you have not been feeling fit, maybe it is time to ***turn over a new leaf*** and start exercising.
498	**Turn the tables**	***Meaning:*** to reverse the situation; to make the opposite happen Our school football team ***turned the tables*** at the last moment and won the match.
		U
499	**Under the table**	***Meaning:*** in secret, dishonestly; not out in the open Bribe ***under the table*** is a norm in India – nobody minds.
500	**Up a creek without a paddle**	***Meaning:*** in deep trouble and unable to do anything about it; in serious trouble Ravi lost his notes just one day before the exams, he is ***up a creek without a paddle.***
501	**Up against the wall**	***Meaning:*** in big trouble; in a difficult or desperate situation The Covid-19 pandemic has left a large number of employees ***up against the wall.***
502	**Upper crust**	***Meaning:*** high society; social or financial elite; important people The poor student fell hopelessly in love with a girl from the ***upper crust.***
503	**Upset the applecart**	***Meaning:*** to spoil or interfere with a plan; to obstruct progress; to mess everything up by surprise or accident The elder sister ***upset the applecart*** when she came to know about her younger sister's trip to Agra.
		W
504	**Walking on air**	***Meaning:*** to be exuberantly happy, excited, and joyful When she found out that she was having a baby, she left the doctor's clinic ***walking on air.***
505	**Walk on eggs**	***Meaning:*** to be very cautious; to proceed warily Ashima was ***walking on eggs*** when she tried to return the necklace she had borrowed without asking.

506	**Wash your hands of something**	***Meaning:*** to withdraw from something; to end one's association or responsibility for something; to disavow, disclaim, or disown I am tired of arguing with my lab partners, so I am ***washing my hands of the science project.***
507	**Water over the dam**	***Meaning:*** something that is past and cannot be changed Lost your ring last week? It's ***water over the dam now.***
508	**Wear your heart on your sleeve**	***Meaning:*** to show one's emotions and feelings openly A person with a weak personality ***wears his heart on his sleeves.***
509	**Wet behind the ears**	***Meaning:*** young, inexperienced, and immature The big companies prefer experienced people but they don't engage those who are ***wet behind the ears.***
510	**Wet blanket**	***Meaning:*** a person who spoils other people's fun by being depressing, dull, sour, nagging, or humourless I never prefer to invite Mr. Singh in any gathering because he is a ***wet blanket.***
511	**What's good for the goose is good for the gander**	***Meaning:*** a rule or method of treatment that applies to one person or group must also apply to others, especially your mate If the girls' team cannot travel to the championship, neither should the boys' team. ***What's good for the goose is good for the gander.***
512	**Wheel and deal**	***Meaning:*** to skilfully and aggressively make big plans with important business, usually to earn a lot of money Sasha's uncle is an international businessman who ***wheels and deals*** all over the world.
513	**When the cat's away, the mice will play**	***Meaning:*** when the person in charge is absent, people will usually do as they please and take advantage of the freedom It is a joke here in India about husband-wife relationship that in the absence of wife, the husband is free as ***when the cat is away, the mice will play.***
514	**Where there's smoke, there's fire**	***Meaning:*** there is always a basis for a rumour, no matter how untrue it appears There cannot be ***smoke without fire*** meaning that rumours also have a background.
515	**Which way the wind blows**	***Meaning:*** the direction in which something is going or may go; how matters stand Before privatising the electricity, the Chandigarh Corporation Mayor just wanted to know ***which way the wind blows.***
516	**White elephant**	***Meaning:*** any possession that is useless, unwanted, or costs a lot of money to keep He is good for nothing just like a ***white elephant*** and an unnecessary burden on the family.
517	**Wild-goose chase**	***Meaning:*** a useless or hopeless search, especially because something does not exist or cannot be found It is a ***wild-goose chase*** trying to discover from whom you got infected with Covid-19.

518	**With flying colours**	***Meaning:*** with ease and great success; in triumph As expected, Nippun passed his tests ***with flying colours.***
519	**Without batting an eyelash**	***Meaning:*** without showing emotion or interest; impassive Ranbir Kapoor accepted the award ***without batting an eyelash.***
520	**Wolf in sheep's clothing**	***Meaning:*** somebody who appears to be harmless but is really dangerous The new landlord acts friendly, but he might be a ***wolf in sheep's clothing.***
521	**Word of mouth**	***Meaning:*** by one person telling another; by speaking, rather than writing The movie got bad reviews, but it became popular by ***word by mouth.***
522	**Worth your salt**	***Meaning:*** deserving the pay or reward that you get In order to get a raise, you have to prove that you are ***worth your salt.***
523	**Wrong side of the tracks**	***Meaning:*** from a less socially desirable part of town; the poor, unfashionable Mukesh's father was upset when he started dating a girl from the ***wrong side of the tracks.***
	Y	
524	**You can lead a horse to water but you can't make him drink**	***Meaning:*** you can encourage, but not force, someone to do something You can guide someone to do something worthwhile but cannot make it happen as ***you can lead a horse to water but you can't make him drink.***
525	**You can't teach an old dog new tricks**	***Meaning:*** people who find it difficult or impossible to change their ways or adjust to new ideas The old generations find it difficult to develop a taste for junk food. ***You cannot teach an old dog new tricks.***

7 IDIOMS AND PHRASES - PRACTICE TESTS (MCQs)

327 MCQs

CATEGORY – ONE

DIRECTIONS: Every idiom/ phrase provided in bold & italics is followed by four options. You have to find out the exact option from the given options. NOTA means None of the Above given answers.

Q 1. ***All agog***

(a) restless (b) everybody
(c) almighty (d) all ready

Q 2. ***A snake in the grass***

(a) unreliable person
(b) secret or hidden enemy
(c) unforeseen happening
(d) unrecognisable danger

Q 3. ***A tall order***

(a) a big problem
(b) a task difficult to perform
(c) a big demand
(d) untenable claim

Q 4 ***All and sundry***

(a) all of a sudden
(b) greater share
(c) everyone without distinction
(d) completion of work

Q 5 ***A storm in a teacup***

(a) a danger signal
(b) a great noise
(c) much excitement over something trivial
(d) unexpected event

Q 6 ***Adam's ale***

(a) water (b) grace
(c) wine (d) pleasure

Q 7 ***A jaundiced eye***

(a) angry
(b) jealousy
(c) prejudice
(d) a generous view

Q 8 ***A bull in a china shop***

(a) a person who becomes too excited where no excitement is warranted
(b) a person who is very ugly but loves the beautiful things of life
(c) a person who is rough and clumsy where skill and care are required
(d) a person who takes a sadistic delight in harming innocent people

Q 9 ***At one's beck and call***

(a) to be in an advantageous position
(b) enjoying oneself without caring for others
(c) to be always at one's service
(d) to be under one's subjugation

Q 10 ***By fair means or foul***

(a) in any way, honest or dishonest
(b) without difficulty
(c) having been instigated
(d) without using common sense

Q 11 ***By the rule of thumb***

(a) by cheating and deception
(b) by the use of force
(c) by practical experience which is rather rough
(d) by the use of trickery

Q 12 ***Castles in the air***

(a) perfect plans
(b) visionary projects
(c) fanciful schemes
(d) romantic designs

Q 13 ***Don't stick your neck out***

(a) move
(b) invite trouble unnecessarily
(c) interfere
(d) look outside

Q 14 ***Do not add fuel to the fire***

(a) aggravate trouble
(b) create problem
(c) calm down
(d) harass

Q 15 ***Hush money***

(a) easy money
(b) money overdue
(c) bribe paid to secure silence
(d) money earned by wrong means

Q 16 ***In a jiffy***

(a) in a hurry (b) in a moment
(c) in a funny mood (d) immediately

Q 17 ***Leave one to sink or swim***

(a) to put one in difficulty
(b) to be in a dilemma
(c) not to help one
(d) to leave to one's fate

Q 18 ***Pin–money***

(a) money paid for compensation
(b) bribery
(c) allowance made to a lady for her expenses
(d) alimony

Q 19 ***Spick and span***

(a) a ready–made thing
(b) neat and clean
(c) garrulous
(d) outspoken

Q 20 ***Seema is a little hard of hearing***

(a) deaf (b) inaudible
(c) insensitive (d) disinterested

Q 21 ***To turn over a new leaf***

(a) to change the old habits and adopt new ones
(b) to cover up one's faults by wearing new masks
(c) to change completely one's course of action
(d) to shift attention to new problems after having studied the old ones thoroughly

Q 22 ***To frame a person***

(a) to make one appear guilty
(b) a narrow escape
(c) to befool someone
(d) to praise someone

Q 23 ***To cross swords***

(a) to defend (b) to fight
(c) to rob (d) to kill

Q 24 ***To give up the ghost***

(a) to become rational
(b) to suffer
(c) to fight evil forces
(d) to die

Q 25 ***Hobson's choice***

(a) feeling of strength
(b) feeling of insecurity
(c) excellent choice
(d) accepts or leave the offer

Q 26 ***To be at loggerheads***

(a) to face stiff opposition
(b) to have a tough encounter
(c) to tax one's mind and body
(d) to be at enmity or strife

Q 27 ***To talk through one's hat***

(a) to talk wisdom
(b) to speak fluently
(c) to speak at random
(d) to talk nonsense

Q 28 ***To snap one's fingers***

(a) to accept immediately
(b) to be anxious
(c) to become contemptuous of
(d) to speak abruptly

Q 29 ***To lose one's head***

(a) to become nervous
(b) to become confused and over excited
(c) to lose balance
(d) to go mad

Q 30 ***To smell a rat***

(a) to misunderstand
(b) to suspect a trick or deceit
(c) to see a hidden meaning
(d) none of these

Q 31 ***To hit below the belt***

(a) to harm physically
(b) to work confidentially
(c) to hit the correct mark
(d) to harm unfairly

Q 32 ***To get cold feet***

(a) to fall sick
(b) to run for life
(c) to become discourteous
(d) to be afraid

Q 33 ***To take a leap in the dark***
(a) to do a task secretly
(b) to run for life
(c) to do a hazardous thing without any idea of the result
(d) to be afraid

Q 34 ***To be at daggers drawn***
(a) to threaten one
(b) to be frightened
(c) to be bitter enemy
(d) to be ready to face danger

Q 35 ***To turn up one's nose at a thing***
(a) to treat it with contemptuous dislike or disgust
(b) to show eagerness to have something
(c) to start to grapple with it
(d) to show indifference

Q 36 ***To save one's face***
(a) to oppose
(b) to hide oneself
(c) to say plainly
(d) to evade disgrace

Q 37 ***To throw dust in one's eyes***
(a) to harm someone
(b) to show false things
(c) to deceive
(d) to make blind

Q 38 ***To be rolling in money***
(a) borrowing money liberally
(b) wasting a lot of money
(c) spending more than his income
(d) very rich

Q 39 ***To get into hot waters***
(a) to get into trouble
(b) to be impatient
(c) to be in a confused state of mind
(d) to suffer a huge financial loss

Q 40 ***To read between the lines***
(a) to suspect
(b) to concentrate
(c) to grasp the hidden meaning
(d) to read carefully

Q 41 ***To be lost in the cloud***
(a) to be concealed from view
(b) to be perplexed
(c) to find oneself in a very uncomfortable position
(d) to meet with one's death

Q 42 ***To turn the tables***
(a) to change completely the position of disadvantage
(b) to create chaos
(c) to change the sorry scheme
(d) to oppose

Q 43 ***To keep the ball rolling***
(a) to work constantly
(b) to make the best use of
(c) to earn more and more
(d) to keep the conversation going

Q 44 ***To play fast and loose***
(a) to be winning sometimes and losing at other times
(b) to play with someone's feelings
(c) to play tricks
(d) to beguile others

Q 45 ***To give currency***
(a) to misinterpret
(b) to bestow importance
(c) to originate
(d) to make publicly known

Q 46 ***To lose face***
(a) to be helpless
(b) to look angry
(c) to look vacant
(d) to be humiliated

Q 47 ***To bite one's lips***
(a) to have double
(b) to be angry
(c) to laugh at others
(d) to feel sorry

Q 48 ***To blow hot and cold***
(a) to be untrustworthy
(b) changing weather
(c) to be rich and poor frequently
(d) to be inconsistent

Q 49 ***To set the people by ears***
(a) to insult and disgrace the people
(b) to box the people
(c) to excite people to a quarrel
(d) to punish heavily

Q 50 ***To hit the jackpot***
(a) to inherit money
(b) to gamble
(c) to become bankrupt
(d) to make money unexpectedly

Q 51 ***To fight to the bitter end***
(a) to die fighting
(b) to drink little
(c) to carry on a contest regardless of consequences
(d) to fight to the last point of enemy position

Q 52 ***To give a false colouring***

(a) to be dishonest
(b) to misrepresent
(c) to conceal the facts
(d) to submit a false report

Q 53 ***To see eye to eye with***

(a) to stare fixedly (b) to agree
(c) to take revenge (d) to be angry

Q 54 ***To be in two minds***

(a) to work on somebody else's advice
(b) to be dominated by someone else
(c) to be in a critical state
(d) to be uncertain

Q 55 ***To show the white feather***

(a) to show arrogance
(b) to show signs of cowardice
(c) to become polite
(d) to seek peace

Q 56 ***To take the wind out of another's sails***

(a) to defeat the motives of another
(b) to manoeuvre to mislead another on the high seas
(c) to anticipate another and to gain advantage over him
(d) to cause harm to another

Q 57 ***To carry the coal to Newcastle***

(a) to do unnecessary things
(b) to work hard
(c) to do menial jobs
(d) to finish a job

Q 58 ***To turn the cover***

(a) to pass the crises
(b) to take a new way of life
(c) to hide the reality
(d) to work hard

Q 59 ***The pros and cons***

(a) good and evil
(b) for and against a thing
(c) former and latter
(d) foul and fair

Q 60 ***To hit the nail on the head***

(a) to guess right
(b) to hit the target
(c) to settle an old score
(d) to catch someone napping

Q 61 ***To run amuck***

(a) to feel exhausted
(b) to run a race
(c) to run to somebody's help
(d) to run about in frenzy

Q 62 ***To be at one's finger's end***

(a) to be highly perplexed
(b) to be completely conversant with
(c) to count things
(d) to be hopeless

Q 63 ***To be as old as the hills***

(a) to be wise and learned
(b) not being worth the age
(c) to be very ancient
(d) to be old but foolish

Q 64 ***To show one's teeth***

(a) to adopt a threatening attitude
(b) to ridicule
(c) to be humble
(d) to face difficulties

Q 65 ***To pour oil on troubled water***

(a) to instigate
(b) to foment trouble
(c) to calm a quarrel with soothing words
(d) to add to the trouble

Q 66 ***To play on a fiddle***

(a) to be busy over trifles
(b) to play upon a musical instrument
(c) to be busy over an important matter
(d) to play an important role

Q 67 ***To mind one's P's and Q's***

(a) to be careful of one's accounts
(b) to be cautious
(c) to be careful of one's personality
(d) to be careful about one's language

Q 68 ***To break the ice***

(a) to end the hostility
(b) to start a conversation
(c) to end the partnership
(d) to start quarrelling

Q 69 ***To pull one's socks up***

(a) to depart (b) to prepare
(c) to get ready (d) to try–hard

Q 70 ***To rule the roost***

(a) to advance in harmony
(b) to preserve oneself from harm
(c) to move forward on the same path
(d) to domineer over others with whom one is associated

Q 71 ***To keep somebody at bay***

(a) to make someone a close friend
(b) to keep at distance
(c) to keep someone in bad condition
(d) to face the challenge

Q 72 ***To cock a snook at somebody***
(a) to make a rude gesture
(b) to ridicule someone
(c) to help somebody secretly
(d) to deceive somebody

Q 73 ***Ad hoc***
(a) for the special purpose
(b) arranged systematically
(c) arranged in order
(d) none of these

Q 74 ***Raining cats and dogs***
(a) heavily (b) drizzling
(c) scattered (d) thinly

Q 75 ***To look down one's nose***
(a) to show anger
(b) to retaliate
(c) to insult in the presence of others
(d) to regard with contempt

Q 76 ***Sought after***
(a) highly paid
(b) pursued by
(c) in great demand
(d) with great talent

Q 77 ***To set the Thames on fire***
(a) do a heroic deed
(b) do something to suit one's own purpose
(c) to turn someone alive
(d) destroy with fire

Q 78 ***Wet blanket***
(a) good companion
(b) warm and friendly
(c) who kills joy
(d) helpful

Q 79 ***To bury the hatchet***
(a) to obtain money
(b) to make friends
(c) to keep a secret
(d) to make peace

Q 80 ***To win laurels***
(a) to be victorious in a game
(b) to memorise
(c) to be disappointed
(d) to earn great prestige/ honour

Q 81 ***To put two and two together***
(a) to mix several things
(b) to make an arithmetical calculation
(c) to keep people in pairs
(d) to deduce from given facts

Q 82 ***To beat about the bush***
(a) to cut down trees
(b) to plant more trees
(c) to hurt someone
(d) not to come to the point

Q 83 ***Watch his step***
(a) behave with caution
(b) observe the threshold
(c) walk carefully
(d) watch his friends

Q 84 ***A bird's eye view***
(a) a beautiful view
(b) a narrow view
(c) an overview
(d) an ugly view

Q 85 ***To be in hot water***
(a) to be in trouble
(b) to bath in hot water
(c) to jump into a pool
(d) to commit suicide

Q 86 ***To keep in abeyance***
(a) in a state of permanence
(b) in a state of emergency
(c) in a state of suspension
(d) in a state of revision

Q 87 ***To be in a fix***
(a) in pain
(b) in distress
(c) depressed
(d) in a difficult situation

Q 88 ***To grease the palm***
(a) to rub oil on the hand
(b) to lubricate the machine parts
(c) to bribe
(d) to cut the tree

Q 89 ***Sit on the fence***
(a) to be in a tricky situation
(b) to be relaxed and comfortable
(c) avoid making a decision or choice
(d) to be defeated and dejected

Q 90 ***A sacred cow***
(a) a person never to be criticised
(b) a saintly person
(c) a helpful person
(d) a very religious person

Q 91 ***At one's wit's end***
(a) to be very witty
(b) to confuse others
(c) to be completely confused
(d) to minimise expenses

Q 92 ***Have a finger in every pie***
(a) to be greedy
(b) to be meddlesome
(c) to be efficient
(d) to be quarrelsome

Q 93 ***The jury is out***
(a) no decision has been reached
(b) a jury member is absent
(c) the entire jury decided to stay out of the proceedings
(d) the jury has taken a break between hearings

Q 94 ***Took to her heels***
(a) bent down
(b) ran off
(c) kicked off her shoes
(d) rubbed her heels

Q 95 ***Plain sailing***
(a) was very easy
(b) was complicated
(c) was competitive
(d) was uncomfortable

Q 96 ***A bolt from the blue***
(a) struck by thunder
(b) a piece of bad luck
(c) a flash of lighting
(d) a complete surprise

Q 97 ***Gift of the gab***
(a) lucky
(b) a big surprise
(c) an honest person
(d) persuasive way of speaking

Q 98 ***A wild goose chases***
(a) run after a bird
(b) a fruitful search
(c) long pursuit
(d) a fruitless pursuit

Q 99 ***A close-fisted person***
(a) a powerful person
(b) a miser
(c) a close friend
(d) a cowardly person

Q 100 ***To feather one's nest***
(a) to harbour ill feelings
(b) to build one's house
(c) to enrich oneself when opportunity occurs
(d) to get something in abundance

Q 101 ***A close shave***
(a) a narrow escape from danger
(b) stubble
(c) very short hair
(d) hairless skin

Q 102 ***To keep up one's appearances***
(a) to make public appearances now and then
(b) to maintain one's look and appearance
(c) to keep up an outward show of prosperity
(d) to make it appear that one is not concerned

Q 103 ***To call a spade a spade***
(a) to be biased
(b) to be impartial
(c) to be frank
(d) to be a hypocrite

Q 104 ***A shot in the dark***
(a) be very violent
(b) an attempt to guess something
(c) to love to go out on adventures
(d) be able to work very quickly

Q 105 ***In a nut shell***
(a) writing (b) briefly
(c) angrily (d) casually

Q 106 ***From the bottom of my heart***
(a) totally (b) wholly
(c) sincerely (d) casually

Q 107 ***A hard nut to crack***
(a) a foolish search
(b) a difficult problem
(c) an easy question
(d) an expensive thing

Q 108 ***To cut one short***
(a) to insult one
(b) to criticise one
(c) to interrupt one
(d) to love one

Q 109 ***To fight tooth and nail***
(a) to fight heroically
(b) to fight like a brute
(c) to make every possible effort to win
(d) to fight a losing battle

Q 110 ***To make castles in the air***
(a) to day-dream
(b) to be boastful
(c) to be conceited
(d) to be too ambitious

Q 111 ***Turn the tide***
(a) save
(b) reverse a situation
(c) touch
(d) spare

Q 112 ***Let the cat out of the bag***
(a) to leak out the secrets
(b) to release the cat
(c) to help the cat
(d) to kill the cat

Q 113 ***To make both ends meet***
(a) to unite
(b) to reconcile
(c) to mix
(d) to live within one's means

Q 114 ***To bell the cat***
(a) to run after the cat
(b) to avoid an encounter
(c) to run away in fear
(d) to lead and face danger

Q 115 ***Cock and bull stories***
(a) stories of birds and animals
(b) unbelievable stories
(c) stories dealing with fight
(d) stories of adventure

Q 116 ***Turn down***
(a) accept (b) reject
(c) twist (d) weave

Q 117 ***Stem the tide***
(a) save (b) stop
(c) touch (d) spare

Q 118 ***To read between the lines***
(a) to read loudly
(b) to understand the hidden meaning of the word
(c) to do some important work
(d) to escape from reality

Q 119 ***Feathering one's nest***
(a) enriching oneself at the expense of the public
(b) buying insurance in time
(c) taking adequate precaution against danger
(d) making a new home

Q 120 ***Throw cold water***
(a) encourage (b) discourage
(c) attack (d) drench

Q 121 ***Under a cloud***
(a) sheltered from the sun
(b) under suspicion
(c) out in the open
(d) get wet

Q 122 ***Get the sack***
(a) look for a sack (b) find a sack
(c) get a call back (d) be dismissed

Q 123 ***Die hard***
(a) unwilling to change
(b) ready to change
(c) egoist
(d) arrogant

Q 124 ***At the eleventh hour***
(a) at eleven o' clock
(b) at the wrong time
(c) at the last possible moment
(d) at the initial moment

Q 125 ***To catch a tartar***
(a) to deal with a person who is more than one's match
(b) to catch a dangerous person
(c) to trap a wanted criminal with great difficulty
(d) to meet with disaster

Q 126 ***Kith and kin***
(a) relatives (b) neighbours
(c) villagers (d) friends

Q 127 ***To explore every avenue***
(a) to search all streets
(b) to scout the wilderness
(c) to find adventure
(d) to try every opportunity

Q 128 ***To shed crocodile tears***
(a) to weep profusely
(b) to pretend grief
(c) to grieve seriously
(d) to mock at something

Q 129 ***A red-letter day***
(a) a dangerous day in one's life
(b) a sorrowful day in one's life
(c) an important or joyful occasion in one's life
(d) both a dangerous and a sorrowful day in one's life

Q 130 ***Hand in glove***
(a) very difficult (b) open enemy
(c) very intimate (d) very rude

Q 131 ***To break the ice***
(a) to shatter peace
(b) to cause harm
(c) to break free
(d) to initiate something

Q 132 ***In apple pie order***
(a) last in the sequence
(b) by government order
(c) everything in its place
(d) neatly demolished

Q 133 ***By leaps and bounds***
(a) in calculated ways
(b) rapidly and speedily
(c) as proposed
(d) very slowly

Q 134 ***Wet behind the ears***
(a) skilful
(b) young and rich with experience
(c) young and without much experience
(d) hearing impaired

Q 135 ***Carry out***
(a) bring
(b) continue
(c) complete something
(d) to take in

Q 136 ***To cut the Gordian knot***
(a) to perform a difficult task
(b) to cut a piece of cloth
(c) to perform an easy task
(d) to do a job perfunctorily

Q 137 ***Out of sorts***
(a) not rich (b) out of reach
(c) out of sight (d) not well

Q 138 ***A golden mean***
(a) comfortable and easy work
(b) middle course between two extremes
(c) a sudden sad event
(d) a subject of contention

Q 139 ***A Herculean task***
(a) an easy puzzle
(b) a good contest
(c) a difficult thing
(d) a hurried job

Q 140 ***All at sea***
(a) very proud (b) overjoyed
(c) in great loss (d) excited

Q 141 ***To cry wolf***
(a) to listen eagerly
(b) to give false alarm
(c) to turn pale
(d) to keep off starvation

Q 142 ***To be above board***
(a) to have a good height
(b) to be honest in any business deal
(c) to have no doubts
(d) to try to be beautiful

Q 143 ***The pros and cons***
(a) arguments in favour and against
(b) the summary
(c) the merits
(d) the demerits

Q 144 ***Ins and outs***
(a) both sides
(b) complete details
(c) inside information
(d) full history

Q 145 ***Between the devil and the deep sea***
(a) to be in a dilemma
(b) to be in a temper
(c) to choose correctly
(d) to live dangerously

Q 146 ***To take to heels***
(a) to run away (b) to jump out
(c) to hurry (d) to take out

Q 147 ***At sixes and sevens***
(a) in disorder
(b) at a certain point
(c) very few
(d) altogether thirteen

Q 148 ***To feel like a fish out of water***
(a) disgusted (b) knowingly
(c) disappointed (d) homeless

Q 149 ***To take to one's heels***
(a) to measure up to one's standard
(b) to shake in one's shoes
(c) to run away
(d) to run slowly

Q 150 ***To call it a day***
(a) to concluded proceedings
(b) to initiate proceedings
(c) to work through the day
(d) to call somebody

Q 151 ***To face the music***
(a) to enjoy a musical recital
(b) to bear the consequences
(c) to live in a pleasant atmosphere
(d) to have a difficult time

Q 152 ***To strain every nerve***
(a) to make utmost efforts
(b) to feel weak and tired
(c) to be diligent workers
(d) to be methodical in work

Q 153 ***With open arms***
(a) with free arms (b) with warmth
(c) with restraint (d) with gratitude

Q 154 ***At the eleventh hour***
(a) too late
(b) too early
(c) immediately
(d) at the last moment

Q 155 ***To throw dust in one's eyes***
(a) to deceive
(b) to show false things
(c) to make blind
(d) to harm someone

Q 156 ***To have an axe to grind***
(a) a private end to serve

(b) to fail to arouse interest
(c) to have no result
(d) to work for both sides

Q 157 ***To drive home***

(a) to find one's root
(b) to return to place of rest
(c) back to original position
(d) to emphasise

Q 158 ***A storm in a tea cup***

(a) useless work
(b) stampede
(c) rare achievement
(d) much ado about nothing

Q 159 ***A white elephant***

(a) a very huge item
(b) a costly and useless possession
(c) a very expensive investment
(d) a useful material

Q 160 ***On the cards***

(a) impossible (b) shocking
(c) evident (d) due

Q 161 ***By hook or by crook***

(a) by compromising or other responsibilities
(b) by impressing the interviewer
(c) by any means, right or wrong
(d) by becoming a specialist in the field

Q 162 ***To give the cold shoulder***

(a) to run shoulder
(b) to give unfriendly response
(c) to take notice of
(d) to give a cold shower

Q 163 ***Bad blood***

(a) war
(b) ill feeling
(c) threatening attitude
(d) in an infected state of being

CATEGORY – TWO

DIRECTIONS: Every idiom/ phrase provided in bold, italics & underlined is followed by four options. You have to find out the exact option from the given options.

Q 1 **At a party, he is always in *high spirits.***

(a) drunk (b) talkative
(c) uncontrollable (d) cheerful

Q 2 **A movement for the world *unity is in the offing.***

(a) at the end (b) about to start
(c) one decline (d) in the air

Q 3 **At Christmas, even the elderly fathers *paint the town red.***

(a) have a lovely time
(b) indulge in rioting
(c) paint the houses red
(d) spill red wine

Q 4 **Akshay can *turn his hand* to anything.**

(a) take advantage of
(b) refuse to do
(c) find fault with
(d) adapt himself to

Q 5 **As our army attacked, the enemy retreated *pell–mell.***

(a) in a disorderly manner
(b) hurriedly
(c) without the least thought
(d) in a heap

Q 6 **A henpecked husband *plays second fiddle to his wife.***

(a) humours
(b) pleases
(c) plays a subordinate role to
(d) fondles with

Q 7 **All his schemes to murder the king *ended up in smoke.***

(a) were discarded
(b) fructified gradually
(c) were partially carried out
(d) came to nothing

Q 8 **At the *eleventh hour,* Mridul arrived and saved him from the crisis.**

(a) at the last minute
(b) one hour before twelve
(c) when in trouble
(d) right at the end

Q 9 **Being an introvert, he will only *eat his heart out.***

(a) suffer silently (b) eat too much
(c) keep brooding (d) invite trouble

Q 10 **By putting on the mimic act, Deepak *stole some of the thunder of Peter's speech.***

(a) filched something
(b) made unimpressive
(c) detracted the listeners from
(d) made a lot of noise

Q 11 **By doing these errands he is merely trying to *curry favour* with his boss.**

(a) gain favour
(b) earn goodwill
(c) gain influence
(d) expect promotion

Q 12 Chandu used very ugly words against his kind uncle; he *threw down the gauntlet* before him.
(a) he showed his readiness to leave the place
(b) he abused and insulted him
(c) he put several conditions for negotiation
(d) he behaved as if he was a very great and important person

Q 13 Caesar was *done to death* by the conspirators.
(a) eliminated (b) murdered
(c) removed (d) attacked

Q 14 Dowry is a *burning question* of the day
(a) an irrelevant problem
(b) a relevant problem
(c) a widely debated issue
(d) a dying issue

Q 15 Discipline is *on the wane* in schools and colleges these days
(a) spreading (b) increasing
(c) spiraling (d) declining

Q 16 Don't *thrust your nose* into my affairs
(a) advise me about
(b) be in opposition to
(c) meddle officiously in
(d) deal with

Q 17 Dishonesty is *at a premium* in almost all spheres of public life.
(a) encouraged
(b) prevalent
(c) valued highly
(d) practiced openly

Q 18 Do you know why I avoid this man? He has *a bee in his bonnet.*
(a) is over confident
(b) is crazy
(c) self-possessed or self-obsessed
(d) is ambitious

Q 19 Eloquent lamentations regarding the fate of the flora and fauna are certain to be rendered a *cry in the wilderness*
(a) a cry with a laughter
(b) a cry in vain
(c) a laughter having no end
(d) an unpleasant situation

Q 20 His voice gets *on my nerves.*
(a) makes me sad
(b) irritates me
(c) makes me ill
(d) pierces my eardrums

Q 21 He works by *fits and starts*
(a) irregularly (b) consistently
(c) enthusiastically (d) in high spirits

Q 22 He *threw cold water* over the project that the secretary had prepared
(a) discouraged (b) encouraged
(c) rejected (d) cleared

Q 23 He is a plain, simple and sincere man He will always *call a spade a spade.*
(a) be outspoken in language
(b) say something to be taken seriously
(c) avoid controversial situations
(d) find meaning or purpose in your action

Q 24 He is *at loggerheads* with his assistants about the management of the concern.
(a) undecided
(b) differing strongly
(c) in agreement
(d) in confusion

Q 25 He is in the habit of *fishing in troubled waters.*
(a) aggravating the situation
(b) putting others in trouble
(c) taking advantage of troubled conditions for personal profit
(d) indulging in evil conspiracies

Q 26 Harassed by repeated acts of injustice, he decided to *put his foot down.*
(a) accept the proposal unconditionally
(b) withdraw
(c) not to yield
(d) resign

Q 27 His father advised him to be *fair and square* in his dealings lest he should fall into trouble.
(a) careful (b) considerate
(c) polite (d) upright

Q 28 He has made his *mark in politics.*
(a) distinguish himself
(b) attained notoriety
(c) ruined his wealth
(d) acquired wealth

Q 29 He *rides the high horse* because of his high connections.
(a) talks flatteringly (b) is famous
(c) is prosperous (d) puts on airs

Q 30 He is a person *after my own heart*
(a) a happy–go–lucky fellow
(b) an object of mockery
(c) exactly to one's own liking
(d) an emotional man

Q 31 He felt *ill at ease* after receiving the letter from his son.

(a) embarrassed (b) disturbed
(c) sick (d) relieved

Q 32 His hard–earned money has *gone down the drain.*

(a) has been collected
(b) has been wasted
(c) has been looted
(d) has been spent

Q 33 His best jokes *fell flat.*

(a) became completely unnerved
(b) were not paid attention to
(c) faced total failure
(d) had no effect

Q 34 Having sold off his factory, Mr. Roy is now a gentleman *at large.*

(a) respected by everybody
(b) living comfortably
(c) held in high esteem
(d) has no serious occupation

Q 35 He always says that he will help. But when it *comes to the crunch*, he does nothing.

(a) confused situation
(b) decisive moment
(c) troublesome moment
(d) difficult time

Q 36 He will win this election *hands down.*

(a) win with narrow margin
(b) win easily
(c) scrape through
(d) win with a big margin

Q 37 He has been working *on and off* for several years on this research project.

(a) rarely (b) at intervals
(c) painstakingly (d) continuously

Q 38 He was a king who ruled his subjects with *a high hand*

(a) democratically (b) oppressively
(c) sympathetically (d) conveniently

Q 39 He got hold of the wrong *end of the stick*

(a) fixed wrong priorities
(b) committed a blunder
(c) felt uneasy
(d) misjudged a situation

Q 40 He was *cool as a cucumber*

(a) dead
(b) nervous
(c) calm and composed
(d) fainted

Q 41 He *took to heart* the death of his wife as he was very much attached to her.

(a) was deeply affected by
(b) was shocked by
(c) was condoled
(d) was ruined by

Q 42 He always *cuts both ends.*

(a) behaves dishonestly
(b) works for both sides
(c) creates discord among friends
(d) argues in support of both sides of the issue

Q 43 He is temporarily in charge of the company and is trying to *feather his nest.*

(a) act for his own future benefits
(b) raise the image of the company
(c) practice his own brand of management philosophy
(d) bring order and discipline in the company

Q 44 He left his friend *in lurch.*

(a) left temporarily
(b) left forever
(c) left when he needed help
(d) left to his fate

Q 45 He has accomplished *a Herculean task.*

(a) impossible job
(b) allotted work
(c) incomplete work
(d) work requiring great effort

Q 46 His phenomenal success shows that he has got *the Midas touch.*

(a) super human qualities
(b) fabulous wealth
(c) ability to succeed in all projects
(d) tremendous acquaintances and resources

Q 47 He is on the *wrong side of fifty.*

(a) a sinner
(b) not yet fifty
(c) old and haggard
(d) over fifty years old

Q 48 He was undecided He let the *grass grow under his feet.*

(a) stayed out
(b) moved away
(c) sat unmoving
(d) loitered around

Q 49 He cannot make *both ends meet.*

(a) earn enough
(b) manage the business

(c) control affairs
(d) work hard

Q 50 He *made light* of his father's advice

(a) rejected
(b) followed readily
(c) disregarded
(d) treated lightly

Q 51 He believes in the policy of *making hay while the sun shines*

(a) helping those who help him
(b) giving bribes to get his work done
(c) seeking advice from one and all
(d) making the best use of a favourable situation

Q 52 He gave his erring son *a piece of his mind.*

(a) encouraged him (b) advised him
(c) suggested anew (d) scolded him

Q 53 His boss was always *breathing down his neck.*

(a) shouting loudly at him
(b) abusing and ill–treating him
(c) giving him strenuous work
(d) watching all his actions closely

Q 54 His *oily tongue* has won him promotion.

(a) word power
(b) fluency in speech
(c) soft speech
(d) flattery

Q 55 He had to *eat a humble pie* owing to his misdeeds

(a) be humiliated
(b) feel downtrodden
(c) accept abuses
(d) apologise humbly

Q 56 He managed to secure the job through *back stairs influence.*

(a) strong recommendation
(b) sheer merit
(c) underhand means
(d) hard effort

Q 57 He is really *worth his salt.*

(a) of value (b) loyal
(c) untrustworthy (d) affectionate

Q 58 He *blew out all the candles at one go.*

(a) simultaneously (b) suddenly
(c) at one attempt (d) at once

Q 59 He finds no difficulty in *keeping the wolf away* from the door.

(a) keeping off starvation
(b) guarding against wild animals
(c) guarding himself against enemies
(d) keeping aloof from disputed matters

Q 60 He knows which side his *bread is buttered.*

(a) knows how to flatter
(b) knows the art of cooking
(c) knows where his advantage lies
(d) knows how to accomplish a task

Q 61 His promotion is *on the cards.*

(a) certain (b) due
(c) probable (d) evident

Q 62 He resigned the post of his *own accord.*

(a) voluntarily and willingly
(b) according to his judgement
(c) according to his convenience
(d) which he liked

Q 63 He *faced the music* for reaching home late.

(a) faced reprimand
(b) faced punishment
(c) faced pleasure
(d) faced entertainment

Q 64 He has too many *irons in the fire.*

(a) is very selfish and greedy
(b) wants to grab everything
(c) is engaged in too many enterprises simultaneously
(d) pokes his nose in every affair

Q 65 He is disliked because of his habit of *making a mountain of a mole hill.*

(a) taking undue advantage of a favourable opportunity
(b) giving great importance to trifles
(c) boasting
(d) exaggerating

Q 66 His *prodigal son* was a constant source of trouble to him.

(a) extravagant
(b) given into bad habits
(c) step-son
(d) poor and miserly

Q 67 He was *carried off his feet* when he was declared to have won the prize.

(a) was dizzy
(b) became delirious
(c) was wild with excitement
(d) danced on his toes

Q 68 He has *turned the tables* on his enemy.

(a) hit
(b) behaved hospitably towards
(c) changed possible defeat into victory
(d) created obstacle for

Q 69 I won't mind even if he *goes to dogs.*
(a) is insulted (b) goes mad
(c) becomes brutal (d) is ruined

Q 70 In parliament, every member can have the *floor with the permission* of the speaker.
(a) speak against his own party
(b) leave the house
(c) make a speech
(d) raise an issue

Q 71 I did not mind what he was saying, he was only *talking through his hat*.
(a) talking ignorantly
(b) talking insultingly
(c) talking nonsense
(d) talking irresponsibly

Q 72. If you pass this difficult examination. It will be a *feather in your cap.*
(a) you will get a scholarship for higher studies
(b) you will get a very good job
(c) it will be one more achievement
(d) your parents will be very happy

Q 73 In the Armed Forces, it is considered a great privilege *to die in harness.*
(a) die with honour
(b) die on a horse back
(c) die while still working
(d) die in the battle field

Q 74 If you *rub him the wrong way*, he is bound to react.
(a) annoy (b) abuse
(c) flatter (d) encourage

Q 75 I am afraid the two brothers are at *cross purposes.*
(a) are working against each other
(b) quarrel with each other
(c) are misunderstanding each other
(d) dislike each other

Q 76 It will be wise on your part to *let bygones be bygones.*
(a) recollect the past
(b) resist the past
(c) revive the past
(d) ignore the past

Q 77 I am afraid he is *burning the candle* at both ends.
(a) working hard
(b) putting in sustained effort
(c) overtaxing his energies
(d) working at night also

Q 78 In the organised society of today, an individual or nation cannot *plough a lonely furrow.*
(a) survive in isolation
(b) remain unaffected
(c) remain non–aligned
(d) do without the help of others

Q 79 It has been *raining cats and dogs.*
(a) endlessly (b) incessantly
(c) continuously (d) heavily

Q 80 It requires unparalleled courage to set the *Thames on fire* .
(a) do something extraordinary or brilliant
(b) do a heroic deed
(c) wreak evil on something
(d) destroy with fire

Q 81 It is Rashmi who *wears the trousers* in their house.
(a) is dominant
(b) dresses glamorously
(c) makes all the decisions
(d) earns a living

Q 82 In modern democratic societies *lynch law* seems to have become a common feature in almost all the spheres of life.
(a) law of the underworld
(b) law of the parliament
(c) law of the Constitution
(d) law of the mob

Q 83 It is difficult for me to believe you, so please put down everything in *black and white.*
(a) sequentially, as it happened
(b) in detail
(c) what you saw
(d) in written form

Q 84 If we give them this concession it will be the *thin end of the wedge.*
(a) the beginning of further concessions
(b) a compromise on principles
(c) inadequate for their needs
(d) the least we could do for them

Q 85 It was such a strange affair that I could not make *head or tail* of it.
(a) remember it (b) face it
(c) believe it (d) understand it

Q 86 I saw him make a *wry face*
(a) abuse
(b) feel sick
(c) show disappointment
(d) cry with pain

Q 87 I have been betrayed by my own *flesh and blood.*
(a) children (b) relatives
(c) acquaintances (d) friends

Q 88 It has been the first time in this office that a clerk *wiped the nose of the boss.*
(a) cheated
(b) abused
(c) complained against
(d) slapped

Q 89 In life, we have to take the *rough with the smooth.*
(a) accept unpleasant as well as pleasant things
(b) make unpleasant things better
(c) use pleasant words to make things smooth
(d) be tough in order to be successful

Q 90 It was discovered that the young man was over *head and ears* in love with her.
(a) completely (b) secretly
(c) sufficiently (d) openly

Q 91 It is *high time* that India did something about the population problem.
(a) appropriate time
(b) auspicious moment
(c) already late
(d) desired occasion

Q 92 *I berated* my assistant soundly for his slackness.
(a) dismissed
(b) suspended
(c) criticised
(d) censured strongly

Q 93 If you give Ashish all your money, you are likely to *burn your fingers.*
(a) suffer (b) be happy
(c) be helpful (d) be unhappy

Q 94 I did not know that he was *pulling my leg* all the time.
(a) defaming me
(b) befooling me
(c) complimenting me
(d) degrading me

Q 95 Kunika was *cocksure* that she was able to do the job as desired.
(a) least worried
(b) doubtful
(c) perfectly confident
(d) not able to imagine

Q 96 Kishan is a *chicken–hearted* fellow.
(a) hold (b) weak
(c) cowardly (d) kind hearted

Q 97 Let us admit that we could not *heap coals of fire* on his head.
(a) put him to shame
(b) agitate him
(c) make him feel sorry
(d) incite him to a fight

Q 98 Lord Clive *won his laurels* in the Battle of Plassey.
(a) overpowered his enemies
(b) fought bravely
(c) defeated his enemies
(d) acquired distinction

Q 99 Mrs. Khanna has been in the *blues for the last* several weeks.
(a) depressed (b) unwell
(c) lonely (d) penniless

Q 100 Manoj always *keeps himself to himself.*
(a) is unsociable
(b) is selfish
(c) is too busy
(d) does not take sides

Q 101 My father strained *every nerve to enable* me to get settled in life.
(a) tried all tricks
(b) worked very hard
(c) bribed several persons
(d) spent a huge amount

Q 102 My aunt was *in a flutter* last night.
(a) in a jovial mood
(b) frightened
(c) in a state of nervous excitement
(d) very angry

Q 103 None of this *hanky-panky*; please talk straight.
(a) diversification (b) indifference
(c) obsession (d) jugglery

Q 104 Our school is within a *stone's throw* of the railway station.
(a) within a definite circumference
(b) within a certain radius
(c) very far off
(d) at a short distance

Q 105 One should be prepared to get a *bolt from the blue* in life, but should not get unnerved by them.
(a) unexpected loss
(b) sad experience
(c) depreciation
(d) sudden shock

Q 106 One should not indulge *in tall talks*
(a) ideal talk (b) flattering
(c) irrelevant talk (d) boasting

Q 107 Please do not indulge in *double dealing.*
(a) two standards
(b) dealing improperly
(c) two jobs
(d) deception

Q 108 Rahul fought *tooth and nail* to save his company.
(a) with strength and fury
(b) with weapons
(c) as best as he could
(d) using unfair means

Q 109 Rajeev achieved success by resorting to a *hole and corner* method.
(a) underhand (b) obscure
(c) clever (d) usual

Q 110 Rajesh and Vikas have remained friends through *thick and thin.*
(a) through days of struggle
(b) in spite of all difficulties
(c) through happy days
(d) always

Q 111 Sumit had to look *high and low* before he could find his scooter key
(a) always (b) nowhere
(c) somewhere (d) everywhere

Q 112 She rejected his proposal of marriage *point–blank.*
(a) pointedly (b) directly
(c) briefly (d) abruptly

Q 113 Some people have a habit of wearing their *heart on their sleeve.*
(a) wasting their time on unnecessary details
(b) avoiding being friendly with others
(c) saying something which is not to be taken
(d) exposing their innermost feelings to others

Q 114 She was received by her friends with *open arms.*
(a) warmly (b) casually
(c) coldly (d) indifferently

Q 115 Some of us are really in a *catch–22* situation
(a) hopeful (b) absurd
(c) depressive (d) dangerous

Q 116 She exhibited remarkable *sangfroid* during the crisis.
(a) composure (b) temper
(c) anger (d) irritation

Q 117 Some people now wonder whether we just *pay lip service* or genuinely subscribe to democracy.
(a) remain indifferent
(b) pay oral tribute
(c) show only outward respect
(d) attach no value

Q 118 There was opposition to the new policy by the *rank and file* of the government.
(a) the majority
(b) the ordinary members
(c) the cabinet members
(d) the official machinery

Q 119 The parliamentary inquiry into the Bofors deal has not *brought to light* any startling facts.
(a) probed (b) proved
(c) highlighted (d) disclosed

Q 120 To all *intents and purposes,* he is a good man
(a) above all
(b) practically
(c) to censure someone in strong terms
(d) in practice

Q 121 I am ambitious too and never want to *rest on my laurels.*
(a) be satisfied (b) be good
(c) be dissatisfied (d) be complacent

Q 122 The casting vote of the chairman *clinched the issue*
(a) finished (b) closed
(c) started (d) decided

Q 123 The aroma from the kitchen makes my *mouth water*
(a) stimulates my appetite
(b) makes me sick
(c) makes me giddy
(d) makes me vomit

Q 124 This place affords *a bird's eye view* of the green valley below.
(a) narrow view (b) beautiful view
(c) ugly view (d) general view

Q 125 The doctor says the patient has *turned the corner.*
(a) died
(b) completely recovered
(c) become worse
(d) passed the crisis

Q 126 The robbery was committed *in the wee hours* of the day.
(a) in the evening
(b) at noontime
(c) after midnight
(d) at dawn

Q 127 The popularity of the yester years superstar is *on the wane.*
(a) growing less
(b) at rock – bottom
(c) at its peak
(d) growing more

Q 128 The young heir to his father's huge estate made *ducks and drakes* of his patrimony.
(a) invested wisely
(b) squandered lavishly
(c) made best use of
(d) took stock of

Q 129 There is no *love lost* between the two neighbours.
(a) cool indifference
(b) close friendship
(c) intense dislike
(d) a love–hate relationship

Q 130 The company has been handed over to new masters *lock, stock and barrel.*
(a) completely (b) financially
(c) administratively (d) partially

Q 131 The sailor found himself between *the devil and the deep sea.*
(a) confronting two opportunities
(b) lost in the deep ocean
(c) facing two challenges
(d) facing two equally bad alternatives

Q 132 The sight of the accident *made my flesh creep.*
(a) confused me (b) worried me
(c) drew my attention (d) frightened me

Q 133 The sworn enemies have decided to *bury the hatchet.*
(a) to make peace
(b) to help each other
(c) to become partners
(d) to avoid each other

Q 134 The politician was able to sway the mob with his *gift of the gab.*
(a) abundance of promises
(b) fluency of speech
(c) political foresight
(d) flattering words

Q 135 The detective left *no stone unturned* to trace the culprit.
(a) took no pains
(b) did very irrelevant things
(c) resorted to illegitimate practices
(d) used all available means

Q 136 They sold their house because it was a real *white elephant.*
(a) a useless one
(b) an expensive one
(c) a rare find
(d) a big one

Q 137 The captors of the kidnapped kept his family *on tenterhooks.*
(a) on constant move
(b) in excited wait
(c) in anxious suspense
(d) in seething anger

Q 138 There is no *hard and fast* rule regarding this subject.
(a) rule that cannot be broken or modified
(b) rule that is difficult
(c) rule that can be broken or modified
(d) rule that is fast–changing

Q 139 The question of abolition of private property is still a *moot point.*
(a) not clear (b) unknown
(c) uncertain (d) undecided

Q 140 Your words can't *throw cold water* on my plans to start a business.
(a) to discourage
(b) to make someone calm
(c) to listen
(d) to get a loss

Q 141 An athlete must be *as fit as a fiddle* to remain competitive.
(a) very weak
(b) free from illness
(c) ready to compete
(d) strong and healthy

Q 142 He took *a leap in the dark* with his latest investment in stocks.
(a) an adventure
(b) jump from a high place
(c) a daring step whose consequences are unpredictable
(d) a thoughtless action

Q 143 There is a lot of work to do, so *roll up your sleeves* and get busy.
(a) speed up
(b) to prepare oneself for work

(c) in corporate
(d) decrease

Q 144 I'll bet you *dollar to doughnuts* she won't accept his marriage proposal.
(a) most probably
(b) almost certainly
(c) not at all
(d) considerably

Q 145 You may become successful in your business someday. *Every dog has his day.*
(a) sooner or later, everyone has his share of good fortune
(b) will get a contract of worth in future
(c) will be successful in establishing business
(d) sooner or later one will get the result of hard work

Q 146 The politician was in the *eye of a storm* because of the accounting scandal.
(a) to trap wanted criminal with great difficulty
(b) to catch a dangerous person
(c) the center of a problem
(d) to meet with disaster

Q 147 A good student has *an eagle eye* for his errors.
(a) an ignoring way
(b) an eye for detail
(c) slow and ignorant to discover
(d) quick to discover

Q 148 Finding a violin in my attic I started *flogging the dead horse.*
(a) to weep for something lost
(b) to enjoy even if something lost
(c) to revive interest in old matters
(d) to forget old matters

Q 149 Look at that painting. It is really *a feast for the eyes.*
(a) reality
(b) very beautiful thing or person
(c) a dream
(d) something ugly

Q 150 Seeing the invasion, the army *grid up the lions.*
(a) to get ready to protect
(b) to prepare for hard work
(c) to get ready for attack
(d) none of above

Q 151 If you *grease the palm,* your work will be done easily.
(a) to break a promise
(b) to break trust
(c) to help
(d) to bribe

Q 152 One should *give a wide berth* to evil persons.
(a) to welcome (b) to applaud
(c) to motivate (d) to avoid

Q 153 The robber disappeared from the bank *in the blink of an eye.*
(a) very easily (b) in an instant
(c) with closed eyes (d) open eyes

Q 154 My mother always keeps my room *spick and span.*
(a) in order (b) disorder
(c) all qualities (d) no quality

Q 155 She was unemployed and homeless, but somehow managed to *keep body and soul together.*
(a) stay fit and fine
(b) remain outstanding in work
(c) managed to be competitive
(d) manage to survive

Q 156 A *lion's share* is always desired in the business.
(a) a non-uniform distribution
(b) a disproportionate distribution
(c) small part in a distribution
(d) large part in a distribution

Q 157 Major newspapers predict a *landslide victory* for the BJP
(a) by an overwhelming majority
(b) not a considerable victory
(c) a victory with difficulty
(d) an unexpected victory

Q 158 These days students try to *mince matters* from their parents.
(a) make use of opportunity
(b) hide the truth of and pretend
(c) to be calm when matters gets worse
(d) to make matters worse

Q 159 Communal riots are something to *set people by ears.*
(a) to incite people
(b) to listen carefully
(c) to give a long speech
(d) to abuse

Q 160 His condescending attitude *made my blood boil.*

(a) made me angry (b) insulted me
(c) abused me (d) ignored me

Q 161 I would move *heaven and Earth* to get into politics.

(a) struggle
(b) do one's utmost
(c) fight with others
(d) destroy everything

Q 162 By changing her job to an unknown company, she *jumped from the frying pan into the fire.*

(a) to enter in a comfortable situation
(b) from bad situation to worse
(c) in a dangerous situation
(d) difficult to please

Q 163 Employers don't like employees who *play truant.*

(a) to be happy
(b) to be away from home
(c) to be absent from duty without permission
(d) to be sad

Q 164 There is no use *paying lip service* when you don't do it from the heart.

(a) false appreciation
(b) pretend to regard
(c) true relation
(d) false commitment

ANSWERS – IDIOMS AND PHRASES PRACTICE TESTS (MCQS) CATEGORY – ONE

1	(a)	30	(b)	59	(a)	88	(c)	117	(b)	146	(a)
2	(a)	31	(d)	60	(a)	89	(c)	118	(b)	147	(a)
3	(d)	32	(d)	61	(d)	90	(a)	119	(a)	148	(c)
4	(c)	33	(c)	62	(b)	91	(c)	120	(b)	149	(c)
5	(c)	34	(c)	63	(c)	92	(b)	121	(b)	150	(a)
6	(a)	35	(a)	64	(b)	93	(a)	122	(d)	151	(b)
7	(c)	36	(d)	65	(b)	94	(b)	123	(a)	152	(a)
8	(c)	37	(c)	66	(a)	95	(a)	124	(c)	153	(b)
9	(c)	38	(d)	67	(d)	96	(d)	125	(a)	154	(d)
10	(a)	39	(a)	68	(b)	97	(d)	126	(a)	155	(a)
11	(b)	40	(c)	69	(c)	98	(d)	127	(d)	156	(a)
12	(c)	41	(c)	70	(d)	99	(b)	128	(b)	157	(d)
13	(c)	42	(a)	71	(b)	100	(c)	129	(c)	158	(d)
14	(a)	43	(d)	72	(b)	101	(a)	130	(c)	159	(b)
15	(c)	44	(d)	73	(a)	102	(c)	131	(d)	160	(d)
16	(a)	45	(d)	74	(a)	103	(c)	132	(c)	161	(c)
17	(d)	46	(d)	75	(d)	104	(b)	133	(b)	162	(b)
18	(d)	47	(d)	76	(c)	105	(b)	134	(c)	163	(b)
19	(b)	48	(d)	77	(a)	106	(c)	135	(c)		
20	(a)	49	(a)	78	(c)	107	(b)	136	(a)		
21	(c)	50	(d)	79	(d)	108	(c)	137	(d)		
22	(a)	51	(d)	80	(d)	109	(a)	138	(b)		
23	(b)	52	(b)	81	(d)	110	(a)	139	(c)		
24	(b)	53	(c)	82	(d)	111	(b)	140	(c)		
25	(d)	54	(d)	83	(c)	112	(a)	141	(b)		
26	(a)	55	(b)	84	(c)	113	(d)	142	(b)		
27	(d)	56	(c)	85	(a)	114	(d)	143	(a)		
28	(b)	57	(a)	86	(c)	115	(b)	144	(b)		
29	(c)	58	(b)	87	(d)	116	(b)	145	(a)		

ANSWERS – IDIOMS AND PHRASES (MCQs) CATEGORY – TWO											
1	(d)	31	(b)	61	(b)	91	(a)	121	(a)	151	(d)
2	(b)	32	(b)	62	(a)	92	(d)	122	(d)	152	(d)
3	(a)	33	(b)	63	(a)	93	(a)	123	(a)	153	(b)
4	(d)	34	(d)	64	(c)	94	(a)	124	(d)	154	(a)
5	(a)	35	(c)	65	(b)	95	(c)	125	(b)	155	(d)
6	(c)	36	(b)	66	(a)	96	(b)	126	(c)	156	(d)
7	(d)	37	(a)	67	(c)	97	(c)	127	(a)	157	(a)
8	(a)	38	(b)	68	(c)	98	(d)	128	(b)	158	(b)
9	(a)	39	(d)	69	(d)	99	(a)	129	(a)	159	(a)
10	(c)	40	(c)	70	(d)	100	(a)	130	(a)	160	(a)
11	(a)	41	(a)	71	(c)	101	(b)	131	(d)	161	(b)
12	(d)	42	(a)	72	(c)	102	(c)	132	(d)	162	(b)
13	(d)	43	(a)	73	(d)	103	(d)	133	(a)	163	(c)
14	(c)	44	(c)	74	(a)	104	(d)	134	(b)	164	(b)
15	(d)	45	(d)	75	(a)	105	(d)	135	(d)		
16	(c)	46	(c)	76	(d)	106	(d)	136	(b)		
17	(b)	47	(d)	77	(c)	107	(d)	137	(a)		
18	(c)	48	(c)	78	(a)	108	(c)	138	(a)		
19	(d)	49	(a)	79	(d)	109	(a)	139	(d)		
20	(b)	50	(d)	80	(a)	110	(b)	140	(a)		
21	(a)	51	(d)	81	(c)	111	(d)	141	(d)		
22	(c)	52	(b)	82	(d)	112	(b)	142	(c)		
23	(a)	53	(b)	83	(d)	113	(d)	143	(b)		
24	(b)	54	(d)	84	(d)	114	(a)	144	(b)		
25	(c)	55	(a)	85	(d)	115	(d)	145	(a)		
26	(d)	56	(c)	86	(c)	116	(b)	146	(c)		
27	(d)	57	(b)	87	(b)	117	(b)	147	(d)		
28	(a)	58	(d)	88	(c)	118	(b)	148	(c)		
29	(d)	59	(c)	89	(a)	119	(d)	149	(b)		
30	(c)	60	(c)	90	(a)	120	(b)	150	(c)		

8 ONE WORD SUBSTITUTION

One-word substitution is important when it comes to writing and speaking precisely, concisely, and clearly. Rather than using verbose sentences, precise words are always understood more easily. In English language, there are many groups of words which can best be described with the help of one single word. Presented in this chapter is a collection of such one-word substitutes along with their respective groups.

WORDS PERTAINING TO THE GOVERNMENT		
1	Government of the people, for the people, and by the people	**Democracy**
2	Government by a sovereign with uncontrolled authority	**Autocracy, Despotism**
3	Government by the nobility	**Aristocracy**
4	Government by departments of state	**Bureaucracy**
5	Government by a few	**Oligarchy**
6	Government by the wealthy	**Plutocracy**
7	Government by priests or ecclesiastics	**Hierarchy, Hagiarchy, Hagiocracy**
8	Government by divine guidance	**Theocracy**
9	Government of the church by Bishops	**Episcopacy**
10	Government by a military class	**Stratocracy**
11	Government by the worst citizens	**Kakistocracy**
12	The right of self-government	**Autonomy**
13	The science of government	**Politics**
14	A radical change in government	**Revolution**
15	To decide a political question by the direct vote of the whole electorate	**Referendum**
16	The period between two reigns	**Interregnum**
17	One who governs a kingdom during infancy, absence, or disability of the sovereign	**Regent**
18	The wife or husband of a king or queen	**Consort**
19	An official numbering of the population	**Census**
20	Facts and figures	**Statistics**

WORDS BY WHICH PEOPLE WITH CERTAIN CHARACTERISTICS ARE KNOWN		
21	One who looks on the bright side of things	**Optimist**
22	One who looks on the dark side of things	**Pessimist**
23	One who devotes his service or wealth for the love of mankind	**Philanthropist**
24	A hater of mankind	**Misanthrope, Misanthropist**
25	One who becomes the favourite of a distinguished personage and serves him as a slave	**Minion**
26	One who sneers at the aims and beliefs of his fellow men	**Cynic**
27	One who walks in his sleep	**Somnambulist**
28	One who talks in his sleep	**Somniloquist**
29	One who has the art of speaking in such a way that the sound seems to come from another person	**Ventriloquist**
30	One who delights to speak about himself or thinks only of his own welfare	**Egotist**
31	One who devotes his life to the welfare and interests of other people	**Altruist**
32	One who runs away from justice or the law	**Fugitive**
33	One who takes refuge in a foreign country	**Refugee, Alien**
34	One who is banished from his home or his country	**Exile**
35	One who maliciously sets	**Incendiary**
36	One who has an irresistible tendency to steal	**Kleptomaniac**
37	One who steals books	**Biblioklept**
38	One who breaks images or church ornaments	**Iconoclast**
39	One who dies for a noble cause	**Martyr**
40	One who retires from society to live a solitary life	**Recluse, Hermit**
41	One who offers his service of his own free will	**Volunteer**
42	One who is compelled by law to serve as a soldier	**Conscript**
43	A soldier or a sailor newly enlisted	**Recruit**
44	One new to anything	**Novice, Tyro, Neophyte**
45	A lover of animals	**Zoophilist**
46	One who engages in any pursuit for the love of it, and not for gain	**Amateur**
47	One who feeds on fruits	**Fruitarian**
48	One who eats no animal flesh	**Vegetarian**
49	One who feeds on human flesh	**Cannibal**
50	One who journeys from place to place	**Itinerant**
51	One who journeys on foot	**Pedestrian**
52	One who journeys to a holy place	**Pilgrim**

53	One who goes from place-to-place begging alms	**Mendicant, Beggar**
54	A leader of the people who can sway his followers by his oratory	**Demagogue**
55	One whose reasoning is clever yet false	**Sophist**
56	One who makes a display of his learning	**Pedant**
57	One who has special skill in judging art, music, tastes, etc.	**Connoisseur**
58	An expert at story-telling	**Raconteur**
59	One who listens to the conversation of others	**Eavesdropper**
60	One who loves his country and serves it devotedly	**Patriot**
61	One who foretells events	**Prophet**
62	One devoted to the pleasures of eating and drinking	**Epicure**
63	One given to luxurious living	**Sybarite**
64	One given to sensual pleasures and bodily enjoyment	**Voluptuary**
65	One who pretends to be what he is not	**Hypocrite, Impostor**
66	One who pretends to know a great deal about everything	**Mountebank, Charlatan, Quack**
67	One who imitates the voice, gestures, etc., of another	**Mimic**
68	One who can enable people speaking different languages to understand each other	**Interpreter**
69	One versed in many languages	**Linguist**
70	One who can use both hands	**Ambidexter**
71	One who entertains another	**Host, Hostess**
72	One who accompanies a young lady to public places	**Chaperon**
73	One under the protection of another	**Protege, Ward**
74	One who searches for minerals or mining sites	**Prospector**
75	A messenger sent in great haste	**Courier**
76	One who steers a boat	**Coxswain**
77	An acrobat who bends his body into various shapes	**Contortionist**
78	A hater of marriage	**Misogamist**
79	A hater of women	**Misogynist**
80	A person in a low state of health, or over-anxious about his health	**Valetudinarian**
81	One who worries a candidate for election by interruption and awkward questions	**Heckler**
82	One who tries to get votes for an election candidate	**Canvasser**
83	An authority on pronunciation	**Orthoepist**
84	An unthankful person	**Ingrate**
85	One sent out on a mission	**Emissary**
86	A person who collects things belonging to ancient times	**Antiquary**
87	One who collects coins	**Numismatist**

88	One who has been before another in office or employment	**Predecessor**
89	One who takes over after another in office or employment	**Successor**
90	One who kills political figures	**Assassin**
91	A partner in crime	**Accomplice**
92	One who works along with another	**Coadjutor**
93	One living at the same time as another	**Contemporary**
94	One who is opposed to intellectual progress	**Obscurant**
95	One who eats all kinds of food	**Pantophagist**
96	One who has an irresistible desire for alcoholic drinks	**Dipsomaniac, Alcoholic**
97	One who abstains from alcoholic drinks	**Teetotaller**
98	A woman with light coloured hair	**Blonde**
99	A woman with dark hair	**Brunette**
100	A person who dresses up women's hair	**Hairdresser, Coiffeur**
101	A noisy, abusive, scolding woman	**Termagant**
102	A young lady who is making her first appearance at a public dance or being presented at Court	**Debutante**
103	One who hides away on a ship to obtain a free passage	**Stowaway**
104	One who shoots with bows and arrows	**Archer**
105	One who fishes with a rod	**Angler**
	WORDS PERTAINING TO PROFESSION OR TRADE	
106	One who attends to the diseases of the eye	**Oculist**
107	One who tests eyesight and sells spectacles	**Optician**
108	One who attends to sick people and prescribes medicines	**Physician**
109	One who treats diseases by performing operations	**Surgeon**
110	One who attends to the teeth	**Dentist**
111	A physician who assists women at child-birth	**Obstetrician, Accoucheur**
112	One who cuts precious stones	**Lapidary, Lapidist**
113	One who writes for the newspapers	**Reporter, Correspondent**
114	One who sets type for books, newspapers, etc.	**Compositor**
115	One who plans and draws the design of buildings and superintends their erection	**Architect**
116	One who draws plans	**Draughtsman**
117	One who deals in flowers	**Florist**
118	One who deals in fruits	**Fruiterer**
119	One who deals in cattle	**Drover**
120	One who deals in clothes and other fabrics	**Draper**
121	A professional rider in horse races	**Jockey**
122	One who studies rocks and soils	**Geologist**

123	One who studies the past through objects left behind	**Archaeologist**
124	One who studies the stars	**Astronomer**
125	One who foretells things by the stars	**Astrologer**
126	One who flies an aeroplane	**Pilot**
127	One who converts raw hide into leather	**Tanner**
128	One who cleans the street	**Scavenger**
129	One who lends money at exorbitant interest	**Usurer**
130	One who draws maps	**Cartographer**
131	One who collects postage stamps	**Philatelist**
132	One who performs tricks by sleight of hand	**Conjuror, Prestidigitator, Juggler**
133	One who performs daring gymnastic feats	**Acrobat**
134	One who travels from place to place selling miscellaneous articles	**Pedlar, Chapman, Hawker**
135	One who watches over students taking an examination	**Invigilator**
136	The person in charge of a library	**Librarian**
137	The head of a town council or corporation	**Mayor**
138	One who writes shorthand	**Stenographer**
139	One who writes poetry	**Poet**
140	One who writes novels	**Novelist**
141	One who writes books	**Author**
142	One who compiles a dictionary	**Lexicographer**
143	One who studies the evolution of mankind	**Anthropologist**
144	One who studies the working of the human mind	**Psychologist**
WORDS PERTAINING TO PLACES		
145	A place where birds are kept	**Aviary**
146	A place where fishes are kept	**Aquarium**
147	A house or shelter for a dog	**Kennel**
148	A house or shelter for a horse	**Stable**
149	A house or shelter for a cow	**Pen, Byre**
150	The home of a lion	**Den**
151	A residence for monks or priests	**Monastery**
152	A residence for nuns	**Convent**
153	A place where milk is converted into butter and cheese	**Dairy**
154	A place where bread and cakes are made	**Bakery**
155	A place where animals are slaughtered for the market	**Abattoir**
156	A factory for manufacturing beer	**Brewery**
157	A place where spirituous liquors are produced	**Distillery**

158	A place where clothes are washed and ironed	**Laundry**
159	A place for housing cars	**Garage**
160	A place for housing aeroplanes	**Hangar**
161	A place where travellers may obtain lodging and refreshment	**Hotel, Inn**
162	A place where people may obtain food and refreshment	**Restaurant**
163	A house for the residence of students	**Hostel**
164	A place where books are kept	**Library**
165	A place where government records are kept	**Archives**
166	A place where any manufacture is carried on	**Factory**
167	A place where scientific experiments are conducted	**Laboratory**
168	A place where athletic exercises are performed	**Gymnasium**
169	A place where treasures of art, curiosities, etc., are preserved or exhibited	**Museum**
170	A building for the lodging and accommodation of soldiers	**Barracks**
171	A place where soldiers are quartered	**Cantonment**
172	A place where money is coined	**Mint**
173	A place where astronomical observations are taken	**Observatory**
174	A place where fruit trees are grown	**Orchard**
175	A place where orphans are housed	**Orphanage**
176	An institution for the reformation of young offenders	**Reformatory**
177	A square courtyard bounded by buildings	**Quadrangle**
178	A Muslim place of worship	**Mosque**
179	A place where water is collected and stored	**Reservoir**
180	A place frequented for reasons of pleasure or health	**Resort**
181	A place with gambling tables, etc.	**Casino**
182	The sleeping-rooms in a college or public institution	**Dormitory**
183	A refreshment hall in monasteries and convents	**Refectory**
184	A school for infants and young children	**Kindergarten**
	WORDS DENOTING NUMBERS	
185	A number of sheep	**Flock**
186	A number of fish taken in a net	**Catch, Haul**
187	A number of horses, ponies, etc., driven together	**Drove**
188	A number of cattle or swine feeding or driving together	**Herd**
189	A collection of wild animals	**Menagerie, Zoo**
190	A number of people at church	**Congregation**
191	A number of people listening to a concert or lecture	**Audience**
192	A number of people looking on at a football match, etc.	**Spectators**

193	A number of people collected together in the street	**Crowd**
194	A number of people gathered together for some common purpose	**Gathering, Assembly, Society**
195	A group of people who get together to work for some cause or common interest	**Coterie**
196	A number of disorderly people	**Mob, Rabble, Canaille**
197	A number of savages	**Horde**
198	A number of singers in a church	**Choice**
199	A number of artistes, dancers or acrobats	**Troupe**
200	A number of actors	**Company**
201	A number of servants	**Staff**
202	A number of soldiers	**Army, Troop, Battalion, Regiment**
203	A number of jurymen engaged on a case	**Jury, Panel**
204	A number (more than two) of judges or bishops	**Bench**
205	A number of directors of a company	**Board**
206	A collection of poems	**Anthology**
207	A collection of books	**Library**
208	A number of pictures, curiosities, etc.	**Collection**
209	A number of ships	**Fleet**
WORDS PERTAINING TO MARRIAGE		
210	One who has only one wife or husband at a time	**Monogamist**
211	One who marries a second wife or husband while the legal spouse is alive	**Bigamist**
212	Man, who has more than one wife at a time	**Polygynist**
213	Woman who has more than one husband at a time	**Polyandrist**
214	A hater of marriage	**Misogamist**
215	One vowed to a single or unmarried life	**Celibate**
216	Legal dissolution of the marriage of husband and wife	**Divorce**
217	Payment of money allowed to a wife on legal separation from her husband	**Alimony**
218	A man whose wife is dead	**Widower**
219	A woman whose husband is dead	**Widow**
220	The property which a new wife brings to her husband	**Dowry**
221	One engaged to be married	**Fiancé, Fiancée**
222	Engaged to be married	**Betrothed, Affianced**
223	A bride's outfit	**Trousseau**
224	Proclamation of intended marriage	**Banns**
225	To run away with a lover in order to get married secretly	**Elope**

WORDS PERTAINING TO SCIENCE AND ARTS		
226	An institution for education in the arts and sciences	**Polytechnic**
227	The study of all heavenly bodies and the earth in relation to them	**Astronomy**
228	The art of tilling the soil	**Agriculture**
229	The art of cultivating and managing gardens	**Horticulture**
230	The science of land management	**Agronomics**
231	The science of family descent	**Genealogy**
232	The study of ancient buildings and prehistoric remains	**Archaeology**
233	The study of ancient writings	**Palaeography**
234	The art of beautiful handwriting	**Calligraphy**
235	The art of making maps and charts	**Cartography**
236	The art of metal-working	**Metallurgy**
237	The study of coins	**Numismatics**
238	The science of numbers	**Mathematics**
239	The science of measuring	**Mensuration**
240	The art of measuring land	**Surveying**
241	The science of triangles	**Trigonometry**
242	The art of preserving skins	**Taxidermy**
243	The art of making fireworks	**Pyrotechnics**
244	The science of colours	**Chromatics**
245	The art of elegant speech or writing	**Rhetoric**
246	The art of effective speaking or oral reading	**Elocution**
247	The art of telling the future by the study of the stars	**Astrology**
248	The study of mankind	**Anthropology**
249	The science which deals with the varieties of the human race	**Ethnology**
250	The science of the structure of the human body	**Anatomy**
251	The science which deals with the way in which the human body works	**Physiology**
252	The scientific study of industrial arts	**Technology**
253	The study of the human mind	**Psychology**
254	The study of the human face	**Physiognomy**
255	The study of physical life or living matter	**Biology**
256	The study of plants	**Botany**
257	The natural history of animals	**Zoology**
258	The study of rocks and soils	**Geology**
259	The study of birds	**Ornithology**
260	The study of eggs	**Oology**

261	The study of mountains	**Orology**
262	The study of languages	**Philology**
263	The study of the origin and history of words	**Etymology**
264	The study of stars	**Astronomy**
265	The study of lakes or of pond life	**Limnology**
	WORDS PERTAINING TO THE FIELD OF MEDICINE	
266	A disease affecting many persons at the same place and time	**Epidemic**
267	A disease widely epidemic	**Pandemic**
268	A disease confined to a particular district or place	**Endemic**
269	A disease affecting widely scattered groups of people	**Sporadic**
270	A substance which destroys or weakens germs	**Antiseptic**
271	A substance used by dentists to deaden the gum and nerve	**Cocaine**
272	A substance used in surgery to produce unconsciousness	**Chloroform**
273	Any medicine which produces insensibility	**Anaesthetic**
274	A medicine which alleviates pain	**Anodyne**
275	The mark or scar left after a wound is healed	**Cicatrice, Cicatrix**
276	A powder or paste (usually sweet-smelling) used for cleaning the teeth	**Toothpaste, Dentifrice**
277	A medicine to counteract poison	**Antidote**
278	An instrument used by physicians for listening to the action of the heart and lungs	**Stethoscope**
279	Free or exempt from infection	**Immune**
280	To place apart to prevent from infecting others	**Isolate**
281	A medicine for producing sleep	**Narcotic, Opiate**
282	A medicine to cause vomiting	**Emetic**
283	Confinement to one place to avoid spread of infection	**Quarantine**
284	To cut off a part of a person's body which is infected	**Amputate**
285	A cure for all diseases	**Panacea**
286	One who is recovering from illness	**Convalescent**
287	Gradual recovery from illness	**Convalescence**
288	A vehicle for conveying sick or injured people to the hospital	**Ambulance**
289	Want or poorness of blood	**Anaemia**
290	Affecting the lungs	**Pulmonary**
291	A substance to keep down evil smells	**Deodorant**
292	To be able to tell the nature of a disease by its symptoms	**Diagnose**
293	A forecast of the result of a disease or illness	**Prognosis**
294	To disinfect by smoke	**Fumigate**
295	The science of diseases of the human body	**Pathology**

296	The mosquito which transmits filariasis	**Culex**
297	The mosquito which transmits malaria	**Anopheles**
298	The mosquito which transmits yellow fever	**Stegomyia**
	WORDS PERTAINING TO DEATH	
299	Fainting or death due to being deprived of air	**Asphyxia**
300	The dead body of a human being	**Corpse**
301	The dead body of an animal	**Carcass**
302	A place where dead bodies are temporarily placed	**Mortuary**
303	Disposal of a dead body by burning	**Cremation**
304	To preserve a dead body from putrefaction	**Embalm**
305	A pile of wood on which a dead body is burned	**Pyre**
306	An examination of a dead body	**Post-mortem, Autopsy**
307	Occurring after death	**Posthumous**
308	An inscription on a tomb	**Epitaph**
309	An account in the newspaper of the funeral of one deceased	**Obituary**
310	To die, without leaving a will	**Intestate**
311	The property left to someone by a will	**Legacy**
312	The act of killing oneself	**Suicide**
313	The act of killing a human being	**Homicide**
314	Murder of a new-born child	**Infanticide**
315	Murder of a brother	**Fratricide**
316	Murder of a sister	**Sororicide**
317	Murder of a mother	**Matricide**
318	Murder of a father	**Patricide**
319	Murder of a parent	**Parricide**
320	Murder of a king	**Regicide**
321	Rising from the dead	**Resurrection**
322	Killed by an electric current	**Electrocuted**
	WORDS PERTAINING TO FIELD OF NATURE	
323	At home equally on land or in water	**Amphibious**
324	Living or going in flocks or herds	**Gregarious**
325	The dormant condition in which plants and animals pass the winter	**Hibernation**
326	(Trees) which lose their leaves annually	**Deciduous**
327	A cud-chewing animal, e.g., the cow	**Ruminant**
328	A gnawing animal, e.g., the rat	**Rodent**
329	A four-footed animal	**Quadruped**

330	Animals which carry their young in a pouch, e.g., kangaroo	**Marsupials**
331	Soil composed largely of decayed vegetable matter	**Humus**
332	Soil washed down and carried away by rivers	**Alluvium**
333	A preparation for killing insects	**Insecticide**
334	A plant or animal growing on another	**Parasite**
335	Lasting for a single year or season	**Annual**
336	Lasting for two years	**Biennial**
337	Living for many years	**Perennial**
338	That part of the seed which develops into a plant	**Embryo, germ**
339	The part of the embryo which forms the root	**Radicle**
340	The part of the embryo which forms the stem	**Plumule**
341	The process by which the young plant begins to grow	**Germination**
342	The process by which plants give off excess water through their leaves	**Transpiration**
343	The process by which plants manufacture food	**Assimilation**
344	The process by means of which plants and animals breathe	**Respiration**
345	The process by which plants take up mineral salts in solution through their roots	**Absorption**
346	Tiny openings on the under-surface of leaves through which the plant breathes	**Stomata**
347	The green colouring matter in the leaves of plants	**Chlorophyll**
348	The process by which pollen dust is transferred from the stamen to the pistil	**Pollination**
349	The entrance of the pollen grains into the ovules in the ovary	**Fertilisation**
350	An instrument for making holes in the soil for seeds or seedlings	**Dibble**
351	One who studies plant and animal life	**Naturalist**
352	The parts of an animal killed for food which are rejected or considered waste	**Offal**
353	Rock from which metal is extracted	**Ore**
354	The track of a wild animal	**Spoor**
355	The meat of deer	**Venison**
356	The flesh of sheep	**Mutton**
357	A cluster of flowers on a branch	**Inflorescence**
358	The seed-leaves of the embryo	**Cotyledon**
359	Plants with one seed-leaf, e.g., corn	**Monocotyledon**
360	Plants with two seed leaves, e.g., lime	**Dicotyledons**
361	A thick underground stem	**Rhizome**
362	Animals with backbone	**Vertebrates**
363	Animals without backbone	**Invertebrates**

364	The inside of a nut	**Kernel**
365	The central or innermost part of a fruit	**Core**
366	The animals of a certain region	**Fauna**
367	The plants and vegetation of a certain region	**Flora**
368	The last stage through which an insect passes before it becomes a perfect insect	**Chrysalis**
369	Absence of rain for a long time	**Drought**
370	To supply land with water by artificial means	**Irrigate**
371	The feelers of an insect	**Antennae**
372	The dead skin cast off by a snake	**Slough**
	ONE WORD SUBSTITUTES AND THEIR OPPOSITES	
373	Writing that is easy to read	**Legible**
374	Writing that is difficult to decipher	**Illegible**
375	Able to read	**Literate**
376	Unable to read	**Illiterate**
377	Fit for food	**Edible**
378	Unfit for human consumption	**Inedible**
379	Fit to be chosen or selected	**Eligible**
380	Not having the qualities of being chosen	**Ineligible**
381	Loud enough to be heard	**Audible**
382	Not distinct enough to be heard	**Inaudible**
383	Born of married parents	**Legitimate**
384	Born of unmarried parents	**Illegitimate**
	WITH THESE MAY BE GROUPED THE FOLLOWING	
385	To move from one country to another	**Migrate**
386	One who leaves his country to settle in another	**Emigrant**
387	One who comes into a foreign country to settle there	**Immigrant**
388	To send back a person to his own country	**Repatriate**
389	To banish from one's country	**Expatriate**
390	Love of one's country	**Patriotism**
391	Goods brought into a country	**Imports**
392	Goods carried out of a country	**Exports**
393	A list or table of duties payable on exports or imports	**Tariff**
394	A list of goods despatched with quantity and price to the purchaser	**Invoice**
395	One to whom goods are dispatched	**Consignee**

ONE WORD SUBSTITUTES AND THEIR NEGATIVES		
396	That which cannot be pierced or penetrated	**Impenetrable**
397	That which cannot be taken by assault	**Impregnable**
398	That which cannot be passed	**Impassable**
399	That which cannot be conquered	**Invincible**
400	That which cannot be wounded or injured	**Invulnerable**
401	That which cannot be lessened	**Irreducible**
402	That which cannot be repaired or remedied	**Irreparable**
403	That which cannot be made good in case of loss	**Irreplaceable**
404	That which cannot be imitated	**Inimitable**
405	That which cannot be rubbed out or blotted out	**Ineffaceable, indelible**
406	Incapable of making errors	**Infallible**
407	Incapable of being destroyed	**Indestructible**
408	Incapable of being redeemed from evil, i.e., beyond correction	**Incorrigible**
409	Incapable of being burnt	**Incombustible**
410	That which cannot be avoided or prevented	**Inevitable**
411	That which cannot be made plain or understood	**Inexplicable**
412	Enduring for all times	**Imperishable**
413	Not admitting the passage or entrances of water, etc.	**Impervious**
414	Not endowed with animal life	**Inanimate**
415	Absolutely necessary, cannot be dispensed with	**Indispensable**
416	Not to the point	**Irrelevant**
417	Someone or something that will live or last forever.	**Immortal**
418	That which cannot be moved	**Immovable**
419	That which cannot be heard	**Inaudible**
420	That which cannot be seen	**Invisible**
WORDS PERTAINING TO THE FIELD OF LITERATURE		
421	A book in which the events of each day are recorded	**Diary**
422	A book containing the words of a language with their definitions, in alphabetical order	**Dictionary**
423	A book of names and addresses	**Directory**
424	A book of accounts showing debits and credits	**Ledger**
425	A book containing information on all branches of knowledge	**Encyclopaedia**
426	A book with blank pages for putting autographs, pictures, stamps, etc.	**Album**
427	A list of books in a library	**Catalogue, Bibliography**
428	A list of explanations of rare, technical, or obsolete words	**Glossary**

429	A written account, usually in book form, of the interesting and memorable experiences of one's life	**Memoirs**
430	The trade mark of the maker seen on paper when it is held up to the light	**Watermark**
431	One who pretends to have a great deal of knowledge	**Wiseacre**
432	A brief summary of a book	**Epitome**
433	An extract or selection from a book of writing	**Excerpt**
434	The heading or short description of a newspaper article, chapter of a book, etc.	**Caption**
435	A statement which is accepted as true without proof	**Axiom**
436	A list of the headings of the business to be transacted at a meeting	**Agenda**
437	Language which is confused and unintelligible	**Jargon**
438	A declaration of plans and promises put forward by a candidate for election, a political party or a sovereign	**Manifesto**
439	To remove the offensive portions of a book	**Expurgate**
440	Still in use (of books published long ago)	**Extant**
441	A picture facing the title of a book	**Frontispiece**
442	The exclusive right of an author or his heirs to publish or sell copies of his writings	**Copyright**
443	An error or misprint in printing, or writing	**Erratum**
444	An exact copy of handwriting, printing, or of a picture	**Facsimile**
445	A principle or standard by which anything is, or can be judged	**Criterion**
446	Delivered (of a speech) without previous preparation	**Extempore, Impromptu**
447	A short speech by a player at the beginning of a play	**Prologue**
448	A short speech by a player at the end of a play	**Epilogue**
449	Passing off another author's work as one's own	**Plagiarism**
450	A writing or speech in praise of a person	**Eulogy, Encomium**
451	A person's own handwriting	**Autograph**
452	A record of one's life written by himself	**Autobiography**
453	The history of the life of a person	**Biography**
454	A humorous play, having a happy ending	**Comedy**
455	A play with a sad or tragic end	**Tragedy**
456	A mournful song (or poem) for the dead	**Dirge**
457	A poem of lamentation, especially for the dead	**Elegy**
458	A conversation between two persons	**Dialogue**
459	Speaking to oneself	**Soliloquy**
460	To write or study, especially at night	**Lucubrate**
461	A succession of the same initial letters in a passage	**Alliteration**

462	A note to help the memory	**Memorandum**
463	A list of articles and their description	**Inventory**
464	The concluding part of a speech	**Peroration**
465	A noisy or vehement speech intended to excite passions	**Harangue**
466	To make expressive gestures or motions while speaking	**Gesticulate**
467	Language that is very much used	**Hackneyed**
468	To pronounce words distinctly	**Enunciate**
469	One who writes plays	**Dramatist, Playwright**
470	Letters of each line, taken in order, form a name or a sentence	**Acrostic**
	OTHER ONE WORD SUBSTITUTES	
471	Fluent in two languages	**Bilingual**
472	Lasting only for a day	**Ephemeral**
473	Word for word	**Verbatim**
474	To change to stone	**Petrify**
475	To reduce to powder	**Pulverise**
476	Wasteful in spending	**Extravagant**
477	To learn by heart	**Memorise**
478	(Travelling) under a name other than one's own	**Incognito**
479	Capable of being drawn out	**Malleable, Ductile**
480	Consisting of several kinds	**Miscellaneous**
481	The exclusive right to buy or sell a commodity	**Monopoly**
482	Unable to pay one's debts	**Insolvent**
483	The outfit of a new-born baby	**Layette**
484	Easily broken	**Fragile**
485	Capable of being reduced to powder	**Friable**
486	Capable of being separated or torn asunder	**Discerptible**
487	Close at hand	**Imminent**
488	Serving for money	**Mercenary**
489	Irresistible craving for alcoholic drinks	**Dipsomania**
490	Excessive devotion to the female sex	**Gyneolatry**
491	A fence or railing of stakes, or iron, etc.	**Palisade**
492	A job for which one is paid, but which has few or no duties attached to it	**Sinecure**
493	An appendix to a will	**Codicil**
494	Correct spelling	**Orthography**
495	Bad spelling	**Cartography**
496	A line of people waiting for something	**Queue**

497	Steps to enable one to get over a fence	**Stile**
498	Loss of memory	**Amnesia**
499	Loss of voice	**Aphonia, Aphony**
500	A seat on the back of an elephant	**Howdah**
501	To turn a train, etc., on a side track	**Shunting**
502	The liquid which comes out from a sewerage tank	**Effluent**
503	To separate the husks from the grain	**Winnow**
504	A bar or pair of bars for confining cattle in a stall	**Stanchion**
505	The likeness or representation of a person, especially on coins or medals	**Effigy**
506	A forsaken or neglected child who has no home and spends most of its time on the streets	**Waif**
507	An iron ring placed at the end of a staff to prevent from splitting	**Ferrule**
508	Living on flesh	**Carnivorous**
509	Living on grass	**Herbivorous, Graminivorous Piscivorous**
510	Feeding on both animal and vegetable food, i.e., eating all kinds of food	**Omnivorous**
511	A chairman's hammer	**Gavel**
512	A stick used by a music conductor, or by a policeman	**Baton**
513	The yellow part of an egg	**Yolk**
514	The white part of an egg	**Albumen**
515	The stripes on the sleeves of policemen and non-commissioned officers in the services to denote their rank	**Chevron**
516	A bridge carrying a road or railway across a river or valley	**Viaduct**
517	A mixture of metals, especially when an inferior metal is mixed with one of richer value	**Alloy**
518	A rich covering over a throne or bed or carried over some dignitary in a procession	**Canopy**
519	To lay a ship on its sides in order to clean it	**Careen**
520	Home-sickness or a sentimental longing for the past	**Nostalgia**
521	A list of the various items of food to be served at a meal	**Menu**
522	Direction for preparing certain dishes, sweetmeats, pastries, etc.	**Recipe**
523	The part of milk from which cheese is made	**Casein**
524	Able to adapt oneself readily to many situations	**Versatile**
525	Goods thrown overboard in order to make a ship lighter	**Jetsam**
526	Goods found floating after a shipwreck	**Flotsam**
527	A rally of Boy Scouts or a joyful gathering of youth groups	**Jamboree**

528	A set of bells so arranged that tunes of songs or hymns can be played on them	**Carillon**
529	A picture of a person or thing drawn in such a highly exaggerated manner as to cause laughter	**Caricature**
530	A name taken on by a person but which is not his real name	**Alias**
531	A picture or pattern produced by putting together small pieces of coloured glass, marble, or stone	**Mosaic**
532	A leather for sharpening razors	**Strops**
533	A leather travelling-bag carried in the hand	**Valise**
534	A list showing the order in which a number of persons have to perform certain duties	**Roster**
535	One of a pair of baskets slung over the back of a donkey	**Pannier**
536	A thing worn by some persons as a charm against evil, witchcraft, sickness, etc.	**Amulet**
537	The bony framework of the body	**Skeleton**
538	The framework of a car	**Chassis**
539	A covering of canvas, tarpaulin, or other material to shade windows and doors from the sun	**Awning**
540	To put to one's own use the money of another with which one is entrusted	**Embezzle**
541	To be over-particular about spending of money	**Parsimonious**
542	The space which for safety is left unfilled in a cask or vessel before it is sealed	**Ullage**
543	A hollow space in a wall for a statue	**Niche**
544	To compensate for loss or damage	**Indemnify**
545	To bring a person before a court of law, to answer a charge	**Arraign**
546	An enclosure for prisoners in a courthouse	**Dock**
547	The whole rim (or one of the segments of the rim) of a wheel	**Felloe**

9 ONE WORD SUBSTITUTION – PRACTICE TEST (MCQs)

190 MCQs

Every sentence is followed by four options. You have to find out the one-word substitution for given sentences.

Q 1. A man who diagnoses sick people is called

(a) operator
(b) surgeon
(c) physician
(d) physiotherapist

Q 2. A book containing summarised information on all branches of knowledge is known as

(a) dictionary
(b) microscope
(c) periscope
(d) encyclopaedia

Q 3. An instrument for viewing objects at a distance is

(a) telescope (b) microscope
(c) periscope (d) kaleidoscope

Q 4. A hater of learning and knowledge is called

(a) illiterate (b) bibliophile
(c) misologist (d) misogynist

Q 5. A person who does not believe in any religion is known as

(a) atheist (b) philatelist
(c) pagan (d) rationalist

Q 6. A person who looks at the dark side of everything is called

(a) sadist (b) blind
(c) pessimist (d) optimist

Q 7. A man of lax moral is

(a) pirate (b) ruffian
(c) vagabond (d) licentious

Q 8. Animals who eat flesh of another animal are

(a) maneater (b) beast
(c) carnivorous (d) cannibal

Q 9. A government by the nobles is

(a) aristocracy (b) democracy
(c) bureaucracy (d) autocracy

Q 10. Animals that can live on land and water are

(a) aquatic (b) amphibians
(c) reptiles (d) gregarious

Q 11. Anything written in a letter after it is signed is called

(a) post diction (b) posterity
(c) corrigendum (d) postscript

Q 12. A woman having several husbands at the same time is practice of

(a) polygamy (b) polyandry
(c) polysexual (d) polyglot

Q 13. A person who has no money to pay off his debts is called

(a) insolvent (b) debtor
(c) pauper (d) beggar

Q 14. A person who hates women is

(a) intolerant (b) misogamist
(c) bigamist (d) gullible

Q 15. A sleeping room for many persons

(a) boarding (b) hostel
(c) dormitory (d) dwelling

Q 16. A process involving too much official formality is

(a) red–tapism (b) bureaucracy
(c) diplomacy (d) nepotism

Q 17. A large scale departure of people from a territory is known as

(a) migration (b) immigration
(c) exodus (d) aberration

Q 18. A post without remuneration is

(a) involuntary (b) voluntary
(c) sinecure (d) honorary

Q 19. A disease that spreads by means of germs carried in atmosphere is

(a) infectious (b) epidemic
(c) contagious (d) endemic

Q 20. A government run by a dictator is called

(a) autocracy (b) democracy
(c) theocracy (d) oligarchy

Q 21. A speech delivered without preparation is

(a) straightforward (b) extempore
(c) verbose (d) maiden

Q 22. A person who believes that pleasure is the chief good is called

(a) sensual (b) stoic
(c) hedonist (d) epicure

Q 23. A speech made by someone for the first time

(a) spontaneous (b) extempore
(c) maiden speech (d) sermon

Q 24. A physician who specialises in diseases of skin

(a) obstetrician (b) dermatologist
(c) cardiologist (d) none of these

Q 25. A person who is fond of sensuous enjoyment

(a) epicure (b) witty
(c) hedonist (d) humorous

Q 26. A disease that affects a large number of people in an area at the same time

(a) endemic (b) epidemic
(c) infectious (d) contagious

Q 27. A religious discourse is called

(a) preach (b) stanza
(c) sanctorum (d) sermon

Q 28. A place that provides refuge

(a) asylum (b) sanatorium
(c) shelter (d) orphanage

Q 29. A large dark grey cloud that brings rain or snow

(a) nimbus (b) blizzard
(c) hail (d) fog

Q 30. A person who makes love without being serious is known as

(a) Romeo (b) consort
(c) goon (d) philanderer

Q 31. A child of unusual or remarkable talent

(a) prodigy (b) scholar
(c) diligent (d) stupid

Q 32. A disease which ends in death

(a) cancerous (b) contagious
(c) incurable (d) lethal

Q 33. A person who does not believe in the existence of God

(a) theist (b) heretic
(c) atheist (d) fanatic

Q 34. A person who tries to deceive people by claiming to be someone else's identity

(a) trickster (b) impostor
(c) magician (d) mountebank

Q 35. A place for sick people who need long periods for recovery

(a) clinic (b) hospital
(c) sanatorium (d) asylum

Q 36. A sudden rush of wind

(a) gust (b) gale
(c) storm (d) typhoon

Q 37. A person who eats too much

(a) glutton (b) reveller
(c) sensualist (d) omnivore

Q 38. A person who is reserved in talks

(a) silent (b) reticent
(c) garrulous (d) mendicant

Q 39. A short stay at a place

(a) interlude (b) refuge
(c) sojourn (d) asylum

Q 40. A general pardon granted by the government to political offenders

(a) pardon (b) excuse
(c) honesty (d) amnesty

Q 41. A person who is out to destroy government

(a) anarchist (b) destroyer
(c) atheist (d) theist

Q 42. A person who looks on the bright side of things

(a) atheist (b) optimist
(c) cynic (d) agnostic

Q 43. A government that is carried on through officers

(a) bureaucracy (b) officiousness
(c) class–one (d) dictatorship

Q 44. A woman whose husband is dead

(a) widow (b) virgin
(c) spinster (d) wedlock

Q 45. A man of odd habits

(a) cynical (b) eccentric
(c) moody (d) introvert

Q 46. A statement that is absolutely clear
(a) clean (b) confused
(c) ambiguous (d) unequivocal

Q 47. Animals living on land and in water are known as
(a) ambivalent (b) ambiguous
(c) amphibians (d) amorphous

Q 48. A political leader who tries to stir people is called
(a) martinet (b) statesman
(c) demagogue (d) dictator

Q 49. A man who pays too much attention to his clothes and personal appearance
(a) duffer (b) snob
(c) licentious (d) dandy

Q 50. A person very hard to please
(a) obstinate (b) unconquerable
(c) fastidious (d) invincible

Q 51. A funny imitation of a poem
(a) dialogue (b) sonnet
(c) caricature (d) parody

Q 52. A person without manners or polish
(a) boorish (b) rude
(c) dandy (d) dude

Q 53. A speech by an actor at the end of a play
(a) prologue (b) epilogue
(c) monologue (d) duologue

Q 54. Act of taking one's own life
(a) homicide (b) suicide
(c) immolation (d) slaughter

Q 55. A person who brings goods illegally into the country
(a) importer (b) exporter
(c) imposter (d) smuggler

Q 56. A man who dances to the tunes of his wife
(a) chum (b) effeminate
(c) slave (d) henpecked

Q 57. A person who has just started learning
(a) accomplice (b) foreman
(c) apprentice (d) novice

Q 58. A woman of lax morals
(a) concubine (b) prostitute
(c) hostess (d) NOTA

Q 59. A slow-witted and incompetent person
(a) duffer (b) commoner
(c) simple (d) simpleton

Q 60. A person's first speech
(a) opener (b) maiden
(c) extempore (d) preface

Q 61. Virus is a biological entity which lives on another organism is called
(a) symbiotic (b) dependent
(c) plebiscite (d) parasite

Q 62. An old unmarried woman
(a) bachelor (b) virgin
(c) matron (d) spinster

Q 63. A written declaration made on oath in the presence of a magistrate
(a) dossier (b) voucher
(c) document (d) affidavit

Q 64. A physician who delivers babies
(a) psychiatrist (b) paediatrician
(c) obstetrician (d) gynaecologist

Q 65. A man who is having the qualities of a woman
(a) epicurean (b) loquacious
(c) celibate (d) effeminate

Q 66. A word no longer in use
(a) primitive (b) exotic
(c) ancient (d) obsolete

Q 67. A person 70 to 79 years old
(a) centenarian
(b) septuagenarian
(c) nonagenarian
(d) octogenarian

Q 68. A person who sneaks into a country
(a) invader (b) infiltrator
(c) aggressor (d) sniper

Q 69. A person who readily believes others
(a) sensible (b) credible
(c) sensitive (d) credulous

Q 70. A paper written in one's own handwriting
(a) parchment (b) manuscript
(c) transcript (d) scroll

Q 71. A small named group of fixed stars
(a) constellation (b) cluster
(c) coaster (d) galaxy

Q 72. Voluntarily giving up the throne by a king in favour of his son
(a) accession (b) abdication
(c) rejuvenation (d) resurrection

Q 73. A person who wishes to throw over all establishments
(a) terrorist (b) hooligan
(c) anarchist (d) rebel

Q 74. A person interested in reading books
(a) scholar (b) student
(c) book-keeper (d) book worm

Q 75. Unreasoning enthusiasm for the glorification of one's country

(a) chauvinism (b) communism
(c) patriotism (d) imperialism

Q 76. A person who collects coins

(a) numismatist (b) narcissist
(c) fatalist (d) philatelist

Q 77. A school for infants and young children

(a) infantile (b) school
(c) kindergarten (d) nursery

Q 78. A ride on someone else's back or shoulders

(a) kickback (b) piggyback
(c) cuddle (d) hunchback

Q 79. A cure for all diseases

(a) panacea (b) exorcism
(c) antibiotic (d) incantation

Q 80. A short walk for pleasure or exercise

(a) gallop (b) jog
(c) promenade (d) stroll

Q 81. A person who is more interested in himself rather than anything that is going on around him

(a) introvert (b) egotist
(c) eccentric (d) extrovert

Q 82. A sea abounding in islands

(a) ocean (b) strait
(c) gulf (d) archipelago

Q 83. A song sung at a burial

(a) dirge (b) elegy
(c) ballad (d) ode

Q 84. A soldier who fights for the sake of money cannot be branded as courageous and patriotic

(a) mercenary (b) sinecure
(c) equestrian (d) honorary

Q 85. A careful preservation and protection of wildlife is the need of the hour.

(a) conservation (b) embarkment
(c) enhancement (d) management

Q 86. Both Buddha and Mahavira lived at the same time

(a) coincident (b) simultaneous
(c) synchronised (d) contemporary

Q 87. Custom of having many wives

(a) matrimony (b) monogamy
(c) bigamy (d) polygamy

Q 88. Cessation of arms before a formal treaty is signed during war

(a) truce (b) stalemate
(c) cessation (d) retreat

Q 89. Child bereaved of one or both the parents

(a) lout (b) desolate
(c) orphan (d) destitute

Q 90. Contempt of god is called

(a) agnosticism (b) blasphemy
(c) nihilism (d) atheism

Q 91. Changing one's mind too quickly

(a) vacillation (b) adaptability
(c) instability (d) versatility

Q 92. Clumsy or ill-bred fellow

(a) dandy (b) boor
(c) dude (d) rural

Q 93. Code of diplomatic etiquette and precedence is called

(a) hierarchy (b) formalism
(c) statesmanship (d) protocol

Q 94. Destruction of unborn baby in mother's womb is known as

(a) foeticide (b) infanticide
(c) abortion (d) regicide

Q 95. Deriving pleasure from inflicting pain on others is called

(a) masochism (b) sadism
(c) malevolence (d) bigotry

Q 96. Elimination of a racial group by killing is called

(a) homicide (b) regicide
(c) genocide (d) patricide

Q 97. Government by a single person is known as

(a) autocracy (b) plutocracy
(c) aristocracy (d) monarchy

Q 98. Government by the representatives of the people is called

(a) socialism (b) autocracy
(c) democracy (d) diplomacy

Q 99. Habit of secretly listening to private conversation is

(a) spying (b) spelling
(c) condign (d) murmuring

Q 100. Handwriting that cannot be read

(a) illegible (b) unreadable
(c) dim (d) dull

Q 101. His father is a doctor who treats children and infants

(a) podiatrist (b) dermatologist
(c) paediatrician (d) gynaecologist

Q 102. Incapable of being explained

(a) nondescript (b) untold
(c) unexplained (d) inexplicable

Q 103. Indifference to pleasure or pain
(a) patience (b) docility
(c) reticence (d) stoicism

Q 104. Incapable of being explained or accounted for
(a) inexplicit (b) incredible
(c) inexpressible (d) inexplicable

Q 105. Incapable of being wounded
(a) infallible (b) invulnerable
(c) impregnable (d) invincible

Q 106. Joint sovereignty exercised over a country by two or more countries is known as
(a) pandemonium (b) condominium
(c) entente (d) colonialism

Q 107. Killing of a human being is called
(a) murder (b) suicide
(c) homicide (d) assassination

Q 108. Killing of one's own brother is
(a) murder (b) matricide
(c) fratricide (d) genocide

Q 109. Life history of a person written by another is known as
(a) biography (b) autobiography
(c) memoir (d) bibliography

Q 110. Likely to break apart easily
(a) hard (b) thin
(c) brittle (d) harsh

Q 111. Lack of enough blood
(a) allergy (b) amnesia
(c) insomnia (d) anaemia

Q 112. Land so surrounded by water as to be almost an island
(a) lagoon (b) archipelago
(c) isthmus (d) peninsula

Q 113. Mania for stealing articles
(a) hypomania (b) logomania
(c) nymphomania (d) kleptomania

Q 114. Man whose wife has been unfaithful to him is called
(a) cuckold (b) dandy
(c) bastard (d) concubine

Q 115. Murder of a new-born child
(a) infanticide (b) homicide
(c) regicide (d) fratricide

Q 116. Murder of a king
(a) homicide (b) matricide
(c) regicide (d) genocide

Q 117. Using of new words
(a) malapropism (b) coinage
(c) vocabulary (d) neologism

Q 118. One who eats everything
(a) carnivorous (b) gourmet
(c) omnivorous (d) omnipotent

Q 119. Murder of one's mother
(a) genocide (b) gamicide
(c) matricide (d) patricide

Q 120. One who loves all and sundry
(a) altruist (b) optimist
(c) philanthropist (d) humanist

Q 121. Official misconduct
(a) malefactor
(b) malfeasance
(c) maltreatment
(d) maladministration

Q 122. One who is interested in the welfare of women
(a) feminist (b) feminine
(c) flamboyant (d) effeminate

Q 123. One who takes delight in excessive cruelty
(a) sadist (b) anarchist
(c) nihilist (d) sophist

Q 124. One who deserts his religion is called
(a) turn-coat (b) deserter
(c) apostate (d) fanatic

Q 125. One who feels at home in every country
(a) metropolitan (b) cosmopolitan
(c) citizen (d) denizen

Q 126. One who totally abstains from alcoholic drinks
(a) vedant (b) teetotaller
(c) samaritan (d) puritan

Q 127. One who is honourably discharged from service
(a) sinecure (b) emeritus
(c) retired (d) honorary

Q 128. One who talks very little is called
(a) stoic (b) reticent
(c) mute (d) phlegmatic

Q 129. One who loves books is called
(a) bibliophagist (b) bibliophobe
(c) bibliographer (d) bibliophile

Q 130. One knowing everything
(a) omniscient (b) learned
(c) omnipresent (d) omnipotent

Q 131. One who is neither intelligent nor dull
(a) commoner (b) tolerable
(c) diligent (d) mediocre

Q 132. One who eats human flesh
(a) cannibal (b) beast
(c) carnivorous (d) savage

Q 133. One who sacrifices his life for a cause is a

(a) martyr (b) soldier
(c) patriot (d) revolutionary

Q 134. One who cannot be corrected is

(a) hardened (b) incurable
(c) invulnerable (d) incorrigible

Q 135. One who does not know how to save money

(a) lavish (b) reckless
(c) spendthrift (d) careless

Q 136. One who talks continuously is

(a) loquacious (b) impecunious
(c) avaricious (d) voracious

Q 137. One who can use either of his hands with ease is called

(a) ambidextrous (b) gluttonous
(c) expert (d) amateur

Q 138. One who speaks or understands many languages

(a) grammarian (b) scholar
(c) polyglot (d) linguist

Q 139. One who possesses many talents

(a) exceptional (b) versatile
(c) nubile (d) gifted

Q 140. One who believes that everything is pre-destined

(a) fatalist (b) pessimist
(c) astrologer (d) palmist

Q 141. One who resides in a country of which he is not a citizen

(a) foreigner (b) alien
(c) prodigal (d) native

Q 142. Practice of a married woman having extra marital relationship is

(a) adultery (b) polygamy
(c) puberty (d) lechery

Q 143. Person who brings an action at law is called

(a) deponent (b) defendant
(c) litigant (d) plaintiff

Q 144. Paying back injury with injury is called

(a) subjugation (b) vendetta
(c) reprisal (d) repression

Q 145. Person who believes that god is everything and everything is god.

(a) pantheist (b) agnostic
(c) pantechnicon (d) theist

Q 146. Perceptible to the ear

(a) audible (b) laudable
(c) praiseable (d) adorable

Q 147. People working in the same department or office are known as

(a) fellows (b) colleagues
(c) mates (d) companions

Q 148. Place where birds are kept

(a) apiary (b) zoo
(c) aviary (d) armoury

Q 149. Person who has long experience

(a) veteran (b) stalwart
(c) vedantic (d) itinerant

Q 150. Plain or self-evident truth

(a) truism (b) proverb
(c) formula (d) percept

Q 151. People in a riot are called

(a) mob (b) crowd
(c) congregation (d) rabble

Q 152. Policy of a political party is called

(a) report (b) manifesto
(c) circular (d) agenda

Q 153. Rainfall at irregular intervals or occasionally is called

(a) irregular (b) sporadic
(c) accidental (d) temporary

Q 154. Relationship by blood or birth is by

(a) consanguinity (b) parentage
(c) nepotism (d) affiliation

Q 155. Run away from home with lover

(a) vanquish (b) abscond
(c) elope (d) asylum

Q 156. Ravi impressed everyone with his persuasive and fluent speech.

(a) eloquence (b) discourse
(c) lecture (d) expression

Q 157. Strong and settled dislike between two

(a) animosity (b) antipathy
(c) hatred (d) apathy

Q 158. Something that becomes outdated

(a) old (b) ancient
(c) obsolete (d) useless

Q 159. Study of mankind

(a) philology (b) pathology
(c) anthropology (d) physiology

Q 160. Study of statistics of births, deaths, diseases to show the state of community is called

(a) anthropology (b) geography
(c) demography (d) topography

Q 161. Something shining brilliant and magnificent is called

(a) resplendent (b) cheerful
(c) grandiose (d) joyful

Q 162. Something which is not thorough or profound
(a) superstitious (b) superficial
(c) supernatural (d) superfluous

Q 163. Story told to illustrate a moral or spiritual truth is called
(a) paragon (b) paradigm
(c) parable (d) didactic

Q 164. The state of complete continence on the part of a woman
(a) celibacy (b) virginity
(c) unmarried (d) spinster

Q 165. The policy of extending a country's empire and influence is known as
(a) internationalism (b) communism
(c) capitalism (d) imperialism

Q 166. The study of ancient societies is called
(a) anthropology (b) archaeology
(c) history (d) ethnology

Q 167. To send an unwanted person out of the country
(a) deport (b) exclude
(c) expatriate (d) ostracise

Q 168. Killing for political reasons is called
(a) homicide (b) murder
(c) assassination (d) genocide

Q 169. The cessation of warfare before a treaty is signed
(a) amnesty (b) affidavit
(c) agreement (d) armistice

Q 170. Teetotaller means
(a) one who abstains from theft
(b) one who abstains from meat
(c) one who abstains from taking wine
(d) one who abstains from taking malice

Q 171. Through which light cannot pass
(a) dark (b) dull
(c) opaque (d) obscure

Q 172. To talk much without coming to the point
(a) circumlocution (b) loquacity
(c) garrulousness (d) verbosity

Q 173. The state of being unmarried
(a) single (b) celibacy
(c) lonely (d) aloofness

Q 174. That which can be interpreted in any way
(a) amphibious (b) ambient
(c) ambiguous (d) ambivalent

Q 175. To do away with a rule/ law
(a) erase (b) cancel
(c) repeal (d) obliterate

Q 176. The list of courses at a meal or of dishes that can be served in a restaurant
(a) menu (b) agenda
(c) catalogue (d) biodata

Q 177. The place where bricks are baked
(a) cemetery (b) foundry
(c) mint (d) kiln

Q 178. The act of violating the sanctity of a church is
(a) sedation (b) heresy
(c) sacrilege (d) desecration

Q 179. To atone for one's sins is known as
(a) expiate (b) apologise
(c) propitiate (d) ingratiate

Q 180. That which can be carried
(a) portable (b) handy
(c) bearable (d) potable

Q 181. To remove the skin of a potato or an orange
(a) remove (b) rinse
(c) peel (d) scrub

Q 182. To surround with armed forces
(a) attack (b) seize
(c) besiege (d) cease

Q 183. To move along with quick, short twisting
(a) wriggle (b) swagger
(c) crawl (d) stumble

Q 184. That which cannot be done without
(a) indispensable (b) irrevocable
(c) impossible (d) impracticable

Q 185. That which cannot be rectified or made good
(a) irreconcilable (b) irreparable
(c) irreplaceable (d) irrevocable

Q 186. Feeling of under self-importance is known as
(a) insanity (b) paroxysm
(c) braggart (d) megalomania

Q 187. That which is perceptible by touch
(a) contagious (b) tangible
(c) contingent (d) tenacious

Q 188. That which cannot be understood
(a) unknown (b) illegible
(c) undecipherable
(d) incomprehensible

Q 189. Tuberculosis is a disease which spreads by contact
(a) fatal (b) infectious
(c) contagious (d) contiguous

Q 190. The committee insisted on a total check on all social evils and he was the one who heralded the revolution
(a) renegade (b) harbinger
(c) apostle (d) apostate

ANSWERS - ONE WORD SUBSTITUTION – PRACTICE TESTS (MCQs)									
1	(c)	39	(c)	77	(c)	115	(a)	153	(b)
2	(d)	40	(d)	78	(b)	116	(c)	154	(a)
3	(a)	41	(a)	79	(a)	117	(d)	155	(c)
4	(c)	42	(b)	80	(d)	118	(c)	156	(a)
5	(c)	43	(a)	81	(b)	119	(c)	157	(a)
6	(c)	44	(a)	82	(d)	120	(c)	158	(c)
7	(d)	45	(b)	83	(a)	121	(b)	159	(c)
8	(d)	46	(d)	84	(a)	122	(a)	160	(c)
9	(a)	47	(c)	85	(a)	123	(a)	161	(a)
10	(b)	48	(c)	86	(d)	124	(c)	162	(b)
11	(d)	49	(d)	87	(d)	125	(b)	163	(c)
12	(b)	50	(a)	88	(a)	126	(b)	164	(a)
13	(a)	51	(c)	89	(c)	127	(c)	165	(d)
14	(b)	52	(a)	90	(b)	128	(b)	166	(a)
15	(c)	53	(b)	91	(a)	129	(d)	167	(c)
16	(a)	54	(b)	92	(b)	130	(a)	168	(c)
17	(c)	55	(d)	93	(d)	131	(d)	169	(d)
18	(d)	56	(d)	94	(a)	132	(a)	170	(c)
19	(a)	57	(d)	95	(b)	133	(a)	171	(c)
20	(a)	58	(b)	96	(c)	134	(d)	172	(a)
21	(b)	59	(a)	97	(d)	135	(c)	173	(a)
22	(c)	60	(b)	98	(c)	136	(a)	174	(c)
23	(c)	61	(d)	99	(a)	137	(a)	175	(c)
24	(b)	62	(d)	100	(a)	138	(c)	176	(a)
25	(a)	63	(d)	101	(c)	139	(b)	177	(d)
26	(b)	64	(d)	102	(d)	140	(a)	178	(c)
27	(d)	65	(d)	103	(d)	141	(b)	179	(a)
28	(a)	66	(d)	104	(d)	142	(a)	180	(a)
29	(a)	67	(b)	105	(b)	143	(d)	181	(c)
30	(d)	68	(b)	106	(b)	144	(b)	182	(c)
31	(a)	69	(d)	107	(c)	145	(a)	183	(d)
32	(d)	70	(b)	108	(c)	146	(a)	184	(a)
33	(c)	71	(a)	109	(a)	147	(b)	185	(b)
34	(b)	72	(b)	110	(c)	148	(c)	186	(d)
35	(d)	73	(c)	111	(d)	149	(a)	187	(b)
36	(a)	74	(d)	112	(d)	150	(a)	188	(d)
37	(a)	75	(a)	113	(d)	151	(a)	189	(c)
38	(b)	76	(a)	114	(a)	152	(b)	190	(b)

10 WORD CLARIFICATION

In the English language, some words are known to be confusing and are often mistaken to mean the same thing, or even used in place of another word. This chapter presents examples of such seemingly similar words, along with their meanings. The meaning of these words is further clarified here with the help of sentences.

	A
1	**Abstain, Refrain** Abstain – keep away from a habit • We must abstain from drinking and smoking. **Refrain** – avoid an act or action • You must refrain from coming late to the class. • You must refrain from poking your nose into others' affairs.
2	**Accept, Except** **Accept** – to agree, consent to receive a thing • Please accept my heartiest congratulations on your selection for IAS. **Except** – save, excluding • All the students, except Prabhat, were present in the class.
3	**Access, Excess** **Access** – approach • Even a common man had access to Jyoti Basu. • I have no access to the Prime Minister. **Excess** – more than, being over and above a limit. • Excess of anything is bad.
4	**Accede, Exceed** **Accede** – to agree • My uncle did not accede to my request. • I cannot accede to your request. **Exceed** – to be greater, surpass • Write an essay not exceeding four pages of your answer books.
5	**Able, Capable** **Able** – competent, having the means or power • He is an able administrator. • He is not able to attend the college as he cannot manage to travel for a long distance. **Capable** – having the capacity to do a thing • He is not capable of running this institution.

6	**Abate, Abet** **Abate** – become less intense • The storm has not yet abated. **Abet** – help, assist, encourage • Aiding and abetting in a crime is an offence.
7	**Abject, Object** **Abject** – low in kind or character, mean • Abject poverty is a slap on the face of India. **Object** – target • The object in your life should be clear to you.
8	**Accelerate, Expedite** **Accelerate** – to increase the speed of • Accelerate your pace lest you should lag behind. **Expedite** – to hasten • Please expedite the matter.
9	**Accident, Incident** **Accident** – a sudden event or chance • She died in a motor accident. **Incident** – an event or occurrence • He narrated an interesting incident from his life.
10	**Abstract, Extract** **Abstract** – summary • An abstract of the Prime Minister's speech is given in today's newspaper. **Extract** – a short passage taken from a text, etc. • An extract of the novel Anna Karenina was given as a comprehension exercise in the examination.
11	**Adapt, Adept, Adopt** **Adapt** – to fit, modify, alter • Every country must adapt itself to the changed conditions. • He adapted himself to the circumstances. **Adept** – expert, skilled, proficient • He is an adept designer. • I am adept at writing. **Adopt** – to use, legally take another's child and bring up as own • The principal had to adopt strict measures to check undesirable activities in the college. • He had no daughter, so he has adopted one.
12	**Adverse, Averse** **Adverse** – unfavourable, hostile • Due to adverse circumstances, he could not pay the college dues. • The boss passed some adverse remarks on the conduct of his subordinates. **Averse** – to dislike, opposed to, unwilling to do a thing • One should not be averse to new ideas. • I am averse to flattery.

13	**Advice, Advise** **Advice** – (noun) counsel • Students should act upon the advice of their teachers. • I gave him a piece of advice to work hard. **Advise** – verb form of 'advice' • He advised his son to work hard.
14	**Admission, Admittance** **Admission** – acknowledgement of a thing as true, entrance to a society or a class of things • Admission to the show was strictly according to passes. **Admittance** – permission to enter a place • Some students were not allowed admittance to the exhibition.
15	**Affect, Effect** **Affect** – to have an effect on, to produce a change in, to influence • The climate of this place has affected my health. **Effect** – to bring about, result, consequence • The policy of globalisation and liberalisation had far reaching effects on Indian economy.
16	**Apposite, Opposite** **Apposite** – proper • The prophet made very apposite remarks about the necessity of moral values for a healthy society. **Opposite** – in contrast to, contrary • My house is situated opposite the college. • Her views are the opposite of mine.
17	**Appreciate, Appreciable** **Appreciate** – admire • The teacher found an appreciative class. **Appreciable** – great • There is no appreciable difference between the opinions of both the brothers.
18	**Aught, Ought** **Aught** – anything at all • I do not care aught from him. **Ought** – must • The teacher said that the students ought to follow the rules of the school.
19	**Allusion, Illusion** **Allusion** – indirect reference • There are many allusions in this book. **Illusion** – deceptive appearance; false belief • Youngsters have so many illusions about their future.
20	**Altar, Alter** **Altar** – a place of worship (a holy table) • My grandfather sacrificed his life at the altar of freedom. • She made offerings to the gods at the altar. **Alter** – to change • I am sorry I cannot alter my program now.

21	**Alternate, Alternative** **Alternate** – by turn, one after the other • We hold mathematics classes on alternate days. **Alternative** – choice • The government had no alternative but to expel the Telecom Minister B. Raju for his alleged involvement in the scam.
22	**Alteration, Altercation** **Alteration** – change • Her dress requires some alterations. **Altercation** – verbal quarrel • They came to blows after an altercation.
23	**Affection, Affectation** **Affection** – love, emotion, disease • A mother's affection for her children has no substitute. **Affectation** – pretence, assuming what is not real or natural • The affectation in her mannerisms earned her the reputation of a snob.
24	**Amiable, Amicable** **Amiable** – lovable, agreeable, sweet • Suman is a woman of amiable disposition. **Amicable** – friendly • We have come to an amicable settlement.
25	**Avocation, Vocation** **Avocation** – hobby, pastime • Gardening is my avocation these days. **Vocation** – profession • Teaching is my vocation. • He found his vocation in the legal field.
26	**Assent, Ascent** **Assent** – to agree • They assented to my proposal. • Her father has not given his assent to this marriage. **Ascent** – climbing up • The ascent of Mount Everest is very steep.
27	**Avert, Revert** **Avert** – to ward off • A calamity has been averted. **Revert** – to send back, to reply • My friend has been reverted to his post.
28	**Avenge, Revenge** **Avenge** – to punish a wrong-doer justly for an injury done to someone else • She vowed to avenge her son's death by plotting to murder his killers. **Revenge** – to retaliate, to punish an evil-doer with vengeance for an injury or wrong-doing • Gopal took revenge by setting his enemy's house on fire.

29	**Apprehend, Comprehend** **Apprehend** – to fear, to catch hold of • I apprehend a great danger to my life. • The police apprehended the murderer. **Comprehend** – to understand • I cannot comprehend what you say. • She could not comprehend what he said.
30	**Ancient, Old, Obsolete** **Ancient** – which is not modern • War was not so horrible in ancient times. **Old** – which is not new • I like my old pen even better than the new one. • My father is an old man. **Obsolete** – outdated, extinct, antiquated • The words 'thou' and 'thee' are obsolete now a days. • Record players have become obsolete.
31	**Antic, Antique** **Antic** – a playful trick or prank, funny • The antics of the circus clown entertained the spectators. **Antique** – old-fashioned, of old times, an old and collectible thing • She wore an antique necklace at the wedding.
32	**A Few, Few, The few** **A few** – a small number • He gave me a few suggestions on the art of teaching. • I gave my friend a few suggestions on the art of teaching. **Few** – hardly any • I have few friends in this city. **The few** – a small number • He cannot offend the majority for sake of a few.
33	**Allow, Permit** **Allow** – to refrain from refusal, permit • The judge allowed the accused to cross- examine the witness. **Permit** – to give a decided assent, allow, formal permission document • Bars should have a liquor permit to serve alcoholic drinks.
34	**Attenuate, Extenuate** **Attenuate** – to weaken • Religion is very much attenuated in the world these days. **Extenuate** – to lessen the crime or mistake • I will try to extenuate his offences.
35	**Aptitude, Aptness** **Aptitude** – tendency, disposition • He has an aptitude for teaching. **Aptness** – fitness, suitability • The aptness of her answer pleased the principal.

36	**Apathy, Antipathy** **Apathy** – want of feeling, indifference • Citizens' apathy is one of the biggest reasons for the squalid situation prevailing in India. **Antipathy** – dislike • Most wise men have an antipathy towards flattery.
37	**Assay, Essay** **Assay** – to attempt something difficult • He assayed to scale the great heights of the Himalayas. **Essay** – a written composition • Essay-writing is a skill that can be honed by practice.
38	**Ambition, Aspiration** **Ambition** – goal, aim • He has an ambition to become a great chef. **Aspiration** – desire, target • The teacher had great aspirations for his students.
39	**All Ready, Already** **All ready** – all things or persons are ready • We are all ready to go for the excursion. **Already** – at the time of mention • The burglars had already left when the police reached the bank.
40	**Acquittal, Acquittance** **Acquittal** – to be set free from charges of an offence by a court of law. • The convict Charles Sobhraj was acquitted by the Indian court. **Acquittance** – a written receipt for the settlement of a fine or debt • He took a sigh of relief after his acquittance from all the debts.
41	**Aggravate, Aggregate** **Aggravate** – to increase, to make heavier • The government's stand on the Kashmir issue only aggravated the problem. **Aggregate** – collective total, collect together • She secured 57 percent marks in aggregate in her Board examination.
	B
42	**Bare, Bear** **Bare** – naked, uncovered • He walked bare-feet in the park. **Bear** – tolerate, carry, endure, an animal • I cannot bear separation from my son. • I cannot bear this ill treatment at his hands.
43	**Berth, Birth** **Berth** – a place to sleep in a train or on a ship • I reserved a first-class berth in *Shatabdi* for my father. **Birth** – coming into life • The birth of a male child is regarded as great fortune among the Hindus. • I congratulated my friend on the birth of his child.

44	**Borne, Born** **Borne** – carried, endured, sustained • I have borne many hardships. **Born** – given birth to, to come into existence • My son was born in Agartala. • Independent India was born of the sacrifice of many brave men and women.
45	**Beside, Besides** **Beside** – by the side of, outside of • He sat beside his classmate in the school bus. **Besides** – in addition to, apart from • I gave him some grains besides his regular wages.
46	**Bridal, Bridle** **Bridal** – relating to marriage • Her bridal gown did not fit to her satisfaction. **Bridle** – of a horse • The horse broke the bridle and rode away.
47	**Bale, Bail** **Bale** – bundle • He purchased five bales of cotton from the market. **Bail** – security, usually a sum of money, exchanged for the release of an arrested person • The court agreed to release him on bail.
48	**Beneficent, Beneficial, Benevolent** **Beneficent** – kind, merciful • The people considered themselves lucky to have such a beneficent king. **Beneficial** – useful, helpful, advantageous • A morning walk is beneficial for health. • This plan may prove beneficial to the unemployed. **Benevolent** – kind-hearted • I cannot help liking him for his benevolent disposition.
49	**Barbarism, Barbarity** **Barbarism** – uncivilised state, absence of culture or civilisation • Barbarism still prevails in many parts of the world. **Barbarity** – cruelty • The bombing of hospitals during a war is an act of barbarity.
50	**Between, Among** **Between** – a word used in the context of two things, people, etc. • There was no love lost between the two sisters. **Among** – a word used in the context of things, people, etc., which are more than two in number • The four robbers divided the booty among themselves.
51	**Blunder, Mistake, Error** **Blunder** – a serious mistake • Many believe that Hitler committed a blunder in invading Russia. **Mistake** – to take or choose wrongly • She forgave him for his mistake. **Error** – inaccuracy, a mistaken opinion, departure from what is correct • The auditor detected many errors in the accounts register of the college canteen.

<table>
<tr><td>52</td><td>Breach, Breech
Breach – an opening
• Excessive rainfall caused a breach in the Bhakra Dam.
Breech – the hind part of a gun
• The breech of his gun is clogged.</td></tr>
<tr><td>53</td><td>Bath, Bathe
Bath – the act of cleansing oneself
• Take a bath and then come for breakfast.
Bathe – (verb) the act of taking a bath
• Gopis would fear that Krishna would hide their clothes when they went to bathe in the Yamuna.</td></tr>
<tr><td colspan="2">C</td></tr>
<tr><td>54</td><td>Credulous, Credible, Creditable
Credulous – willing to believe or trust easily
• The innocent children are generally credulous by nature.
Credible – believable
• Tales of the Loch Ness monster are not credible.
Creditable – honourable, praiseworthy
• The conduct of frontline workers during the Covid pandemic is really creditable.</td></tr>
<tr><td>55</td><td>Contemptuous, Contemptible
Contemptuous – full of hatred, scornful
• She treats her servants in a contemptuous manner.
Contemptible – deserving contempt
• He is such a contemptible fellow that no one respects him.</td></tr>
<tr><td>56</td><td>Considerate, Considerable
Considerate – sympathetic, mindful of the feelings of others
• He is so considerate that he would never hurt the feelings of his friends.
Considerable – moderately large
• It takes a considerable amount of time and effort to qualify for the Civil Services Examination.</td></tr>
<tr><td>57</td><td>Casual, Causal
Casual – without any definite, serious or formal intent
• He is a casual student.
• He was whistling casually.
Causal – pertaining to a cause
• There is no causal explanation for this delay.</td></tr>
<tr><td>58</td><td>Caste, Cast
Caste – hereditary social class
• There are many castes and communities in India.
• My friend is a Khatri by caste.
Cast – to throw, a group of actors for a film, etc.
• I did not mean to cast aspersion on others.
• He cast a longing glance at her.
• The star cast of this film includes famous actors.</td></tr>
</table>

59	**Censor, Censure** **Censor** – To examine the content of films, books, plays, or other material so as to remove or suppress what is considered morally, politically or otherwise objectionable • Even the abusive dialogues in the film *No One Killed Jessica* were not censored. **Censure** – find fault with, condemn • Many people are always censuring the conduct of their friends. • There was a note of censure in the teacher's voice.
60	**Complacent, Complaisant** **Complacent** – satisfied, pleased • Indians are generally complacent in their outlook. • It is foolish to be complacent about your preparation for the I.A.S. examination. **Complaisant** – willing to please, agreeable, obliging • He liked that she had extremely complaisant manners. • Mr. Chopra's complaisance is truly unparalleled.
61	**Complement, Compliment** **Complement** – that which completes or makes perfect • The tie was an attractive complement to his shirt. • The young couple complemented each other. **Compliment** – an expression of regard or admiration • Please convey my compliments to your brother. • I shall take your appreciation as a compliment.
62	**Confidant, Confident** **Confidant** – one entrusted with secrets • Mr. Singh is my friend and confidant. **Confident** – sure, self-assured • He is very confident about passing his driving test.
63	**Council, Counsel** **Council** – an assembly • A council of five teachers was appointed to help the principal. • My friend has been elected to the Legislative Council. **Counsel** – advice • I shall act upon the counsel of my legal advisors.
64	**Check, Cheque** **Check** – control, examine to determine accuracy • He cannot check himself from smoking. • I should have checked the amount before paying the bill. **Cheque** – a written order for money to a bank • He gave me a cheque for one thousand rupees.
65	**Cite, Sight, Site** **Cite** – quote • She cited many examples from history to prove her point. **Sight** – view, scene • The little girl beamed at the sight of her mother. **Site** – local position, situation • This is the site for the new college building.

66	**Coarse, Course** **Coarse** – rough • It is a very coarse cloth. **Course** – direction taken or pursued, line of action • Most rivers often change their course. • He is yet to decide which course to pursue in college.
67	**Confirm, Conform** **Confirm** – to ratify • I was confirmed in my post after a year. **Conform** – to make one thing like another, to comply • You must conform to a high standard of morality. • I do not conform to your ideas.
68	**Collision, Collusion** **Collision** – the act of striking together • There was a head-on collision between a truck and a bus. **Collusion** – secret conspiracy • Both the opponent parties were in collusion against the ruling government.
69	**Corporal, Corporeal** **Corporal** – relating to body • Corporal punishment is not allowed in colleges. • Corporal punishment can also cause psychological harm to children. **Corporeal** – material, having a body • Gods are not corporeal beings. • Saints do not care for corporeal considerations. • The spirit of a human being is not corporeal.
70	**Childish, Childlike** **Childish** – like a child (negative connotation) • I do not like his childish way of eating food. • Her tantrums were quite childish. **Childlike** – innocent (positive connotation) • Everybody likes her childlike charm. • His speech and simplicity were childlike.
71	**Conscientious, Conscious, Consensus** **Conscientious** – doing what is right • We need more conscientious leaders to build a strong nation. **Conscious** – aware • She is always conscious of her reputation. **Consensus** – agreement of opinion • All the decisions in the constituent assembly were taken by consensus.
72	**Contagious, Contiguous,** **Contagious** – disease communicated by touching or contact • Smallpox is a contagious disease. **Contiguous** – adjoining • India and Pakistan are contiguous countries.

73	**Continual, Continuous** **Continual** – frequent, coming after intervals • She has been receiving continual attacks of paranoia. **Continuous** – without a pause or interval • He has been reading for four hours continuously.
74	**Capture, Captivate** **Capture** – seize • His fort was captured by the neighbouring king. **Captivate** – charm, fascinate • The scenic beauty of Kashmir captivated my mind.
75	**Core, Corps, Corpse** **Core** – inmost • I thank you from the core of my heart. **Corps** – division of an army • He has joined the National Cadet Corps. **Corpse** – a dead body • At the sight of a corpse, her heart skipped a beat.
76	**Comprehensive, Comprehensible** **Comprehensive** – wide, extensive • The author has written a very comprehensive book. • Your scheme is quite comprehensive. **Comprehensible** - understandable • His talk is not comprehensible to me. • Our English professor speaks so lucidly that every word is comprehensible.
77	**Ceremonial, Ceremonious** **Ceremonial** – relating to ceremony • The convocation is a ceremonial occasion for all college students. **Ceremonious** – showing great ceremony or formality • The office of the Governor is ceremonious.
78	**Cession, Session** **Cession** – act of giving up • Pakistan is demanding the immediate cession of Kashmir. **Session** – period of sitting • The Lok Sabha is in session these days.
79	**Consider, Regard** **Consider** – to think carefully, reflect on, contemplate • As the Covid cases surged, the corporates were urged to consider 'work from home' facility for their employees. **Note:** The word 'consider' does not require 'as' following it. **Regard** – to pay attention, to show respect or concern, to think highly of • Our History professor is regarded as an expert in his subject. • They hold his expertise in high regard.
80	**Custom, Habit** **Custom** – common practice • The religious customs of Hindus differ from those of Christians. **Habit** – settled tendency or practice • She is in the habit of abusing her maid- servants.

81	**Coma, Comma** **Coma** – unnatural heavy sleep, lethargy • This boy has been in a state of coma for the last eight hours. **Comma** – a punctuation mark • He put a comma at the end of the phrase.
82	**Contemn, Condemn** **Contemn** – despise, scorn • The rich should not contemn the poor. **Condemn** – to censure, blame • The public strongly condemned the conduct of their leader.
83	**Cue, Queue** **Cue** – hint • I need only a cue to solve the puzzle. **Queue** – a line of persons waiting for their turn • There is a long queue outside the theatre.
84	**Compare, Contrast** **Compare** – to look for points of similarity • They say that an apple and an orange cannot be compared. • He often compared her beautiful face with the moon. **Contrast** – to look for points of difference • The contrast between the two brothers is striking. • The question in the examination asked the students to contrast Shakespeare and Bernard Shaw as dramatists.
85	**Capital, Capitol** **Capital** – centre of administration, money invested in a business • New Delhi is the capital of India. • An entrepreneur needs capital to start a business. **Capitol** – the main building of the capital • The Raj Bhavan may be called the capitol of Lucknow.
86	**Career, Carrier** **Career** – profession • Jawaharlal Nehru achieved great success in his political career. **Carrier** – one who carries • Contemporary cinema is an ambassador as well as a carrier of the prevalent culture.
87	**Cease, Seize, Siege** **Cease** – stop, discontinue • He has ceased to be the manager of our college. **Seize** – catch, hold tightly • The police seized the boy by the collar. **Siege** – state of being surrounded • The town was sieged by the enemy.
88	**Conduct, Character** **Conduct** – behaviour • He was awarded a medal for good conduct. **Character** – the nature and qualities of a person • He is a man of flawless character.

89	**Congenial, Genial** **Congenial** – suitable, agreeable • Office work is not congenial to my nature. • The climate of Saharanpur is not congenial to my health. **Genial** – cheerful • She is of genial temper.
90	**Clamant, Claimant** **Clamant** – noisy • Gopal is very clamant for reform. **Claimant** – one who lays a claim • My brother is a claimant for this post.
91	**Concert, Consort** **Concert** – a musical performance • All the tickets for his concert were sold out. **Consort** – a wedded partner • In the epic *Ramayana*, *Ravana* abducted *Sita*, the consort of *Rama*.
D	
92	**Defy, Deify** **Defy** – to challenge • The teacher defied the principal to disprove the charges made against him. **Deify** – worship, treat or regard as God • Gandhi and Nehru are deified by the Indian masses.
93	**Defer, Differ** **Defer** – to postpone • Do not defer your training to next year. **Differ** – to disagree • She did not differ with me in this matter.
94	**Deference, Difference** **Deference** – respect • With deference, I say that the principal is absolutely in the wrong. • I always pay due deference to my teachers. **Difference** – dissimilarity, disagreement • There is a world of difference between experienced and inexperienced teachers. • Is there any marked difference between these two colours?
95	**Decease, Disease** **Decease** – death • The news of the sudden decease of his son came to him as a shock. **Disease** – illness, ailment • Tuberculosis is no more a fatal disease.
96	**Dissent, Descent** **Dissent** – disagreement • Debate, dissent and discussion are the lifelines of a healthy democracy. **Descent** – coming down, derivation • Many boys were injured during the rapid descent.

97	**Desert, Dessert** **Desert** – arid land with sparse vegetation, to abandon • Rajasthan is a desert. ▪ The sailor deserted the vessel. **Dessert** – sweet course served at the end of the meal • Mangoes are generally served as dessert.
98	**Divers, Diverse** **Divers** – those who dive • Skilled divers can stay under water for a long time. **Diverse** – different • The members expressed diverse opinions. • There are diverse ways of answering this question.
99	**Dose, Doze** **Dose** – the quantity of medicine to be taken at one time • Only one dose of the cough syrup cured him. **Doze** – sleep, a short nap • The student was caught dozing in the class.
100	**Draft, Draught, Drought** **Draft** – a rough outline of a letter, etc. • He was not satisfied with the first draft of his novel. **Draught** – as much as can be drunk at one time, a current of air • In the desert, a draught of water is as precious as gold. • His candle was extinguished by a draught. **Drought** – scarcity of rain • A long drought generally causes famine. • Many lives were lost due to the severe drought in Uttar Pradesh.
101	**Dual, Duel** **Dual** – double, containing two • China is following a dual policy these days. **Duel** – a fight or combat between two persons • In ancient times, people fought duels to settle their disputes.
102	**Deny, Refuse** **Deny** – to declare that a statement is not true • The accused denied the charge. **Refuse** – to decline something offered, not to do or take a thing • He refused to lend me his watch. • I refuse to take help from anybody. • The post of junior lecturer was offered to him, but he refused to accept it.
103	**Drown, Sink** **Drown** – to flood or inundate, to kill or die by submerging under water or any other liquid • Two persons drowned in the river. **Sink** – to fall, drop or descend gradually (usually under water) • The sinking of the Titanic was a vast tragedy. • My heart sank when I saw who was coming.

104	**Destiny, Destination** **Destiny** – fate • Man is the maker of his own destiny. **Destination** – goal • The army reached its destination after two days' struggle.
105	**Doubt, Suspect** **Doubt** – to be uncertain about the truth of a thing or a statement • Many scientists doubt the existence of God. **Suspect** – to think that a person is guilty or to disbelieve that a statement is true • I suspect his servant ate the food.
106	**Die, Dye** **Die** – to cease to live • My friend died of cholera. **Dye** – to colour • She has dyed her hair brown.
107	**Discreet, Discrete** **Discreet** – judicious, not rash (but prudent), unostentatious • The Intelligence officer was very discreet addressing the Press. **Discrete** – separate, distinct • Her make-up is very discrete.
108	**Dependent, Dependant** **Dependent** – depending on another for maintenance • The army dependents are also entitled to the benefits. **Dependant** – depending on another for maintenance • He has to support many dependants at home. **Note:** In this case, both the words have the same meaning, and the difference is only of spelling – British and American.
109	**Deprecate, Depreciate** **Deprecate** – to disapprove • The public deprecated the leader in these elections. **Depreciate** – (the opposite of appreciate), to dispraise, to fall in value • The value of diesel cars depreciates over time.
110	**Disinterested, Uninterested** **Disinterested** – unselfish, without a vested interest • A true social worker serves the society with disinterest. **Uninterested** – not interested • I am uninterested in this affair. • His son is uninterested in the family business.
111	**Discover, Invent** **Discover** – finding something that already existed but was not known earlier (i.e., before the discovery) • Columbus discovered America. **Invent** – to devise or originate a new method or instrument • Marconi invented the radio.

112	**Decry, Descry** **Decry** – to criticise as worthless, to condemn • Everyone is decrying the Hindu Marriage Act. **Descry** – to catch sight of, to succeed in discerning • On the fifth day, the shipwrecked sailors descried a sail.
113	**Deficient, Defective** **Deficient** – lacking • The doctor told him he had calcium deficiency. **Defective** – faulty • That car was defective from day one.
114	**Dominant, Dominate, Domineer** **Dominant** – prevailing, ruling • Black was the dominant colour in the film. **Dominate** – to command • By sheer force of character, the SSP was able to dominate the situation. **Domineer** – rule with violence • It is no more possible to domineer over the public by sheer use of force.
E	
115	**Eligible, Illegible** **Eligible** – fit or qualified to be chosen (meeting the criteria) • A graduation degree makes one eligible for several prestigious competitive examinations in India. **Illegible** – difficult to read • Her handwriting is illegible.
116	**Eminent, Imminent** **Eminent** – famous, distinguished • He is one of the most eminent lawyers in Varanasi. • He is an eminent personality in their community. **Imminent** – near, impending • She is in imminent danger of losing her job. • War between China and America is imminent. • Boys are working hard as their annual test is imminent.
117	**Economic, Economical** **Economic** – related to economics • What are the economic causes of war? • Why is there an economic crisis in the country? **Economical** – careful about spending any resource • Her shopping is anything but economical.

118	**Efficient, Effectual, Effective, Efficacious** **Efficient** – competent • The company needed a really efficient manager for its modernisation. • Our college has efficient and experienced lecturers. **Effectual** – adequate, effective • The government must adopt effectual steps to remove poverty and illiteracy from the country. • She could find no effectual remedy for her ailment. **Effective** – producing a marked effect • Your approach is not very effective. **Efficacious** – useful in effect • This medicine has proved very efficacious in the treatment of nervous diseases.
119	**Exceedingly, Excessively** **Exceedingly** – more than normal, necessary or usual (unusual) • I found him to be an exceedingly obliging boy. **Excessively** – more than required or necessary, and, sometimes, more than desirable (too much) • He is an excessively humble man.
120	**Expedient, Expeditious** **Expedient** – proper • It is not expedient on his part to use abusive language. **Expeditious** – prompt • He had to find the most expeditious means to reach the hospital.
121	**Elicit, Illicit** **Elicit** – to draw out • The police elicited a lot of information from the guilty man. • Her good behaviour elicits praise from everyone. **Illicit** – unlawful • This girl has an illicit relationship with that boy. • That shop sells liquor illicitly.
122	**Exceptional, Exceptionable** **Exceptional** – rare, uncommon • Nehru was a man of exceptional ability. **Exceptionable** – objectionable • His remarks are highly exceptionable.
123	**Emerge, Immerge** **Emerge** – to come out • India will surely emerge glorious from her ordeals. **Immerge** – immerse, to dip • She immerged (immersed) her hand in the water.
124	**Envious, Enviable** **Envious** – feeling envy • He is envious of my success. **Enviable** – which causes exciting envy • A chef's job is very enviable. • She has enviable beauty.

125	**Excursion, Incursion** **Excursion** – a trip • We enjoyed a pleasant excursion in the countryside. **Incursion** – sudden attack, a hostile entrance into a territory • The Chinese army made an incursion into Ladakh.
126	**Excite, Incite** **Excite** – to stir, arouse enthusiasm (the word has a positive connotation) • My success excited his envy. • He was very excited on his wedding day. **Incite** – encourage, to urge, to stimulate (the word has a negative connotation) • The enemy's agents are inciting Indians to rebellion.
127	**Expenditure, Expenses** **Expenditure** – amount spent • My expenditure exceeds my income. **Expenses** – cost, that which is spent • His office will reimburse his travel expenses.
128	**Empty, Vacant** **Empty** – not occupied or inhabited (opposite of 'full') • Empty vessels make more noise. **Vacant** – unfilled (opposite of 'occupied') • There is no vacant position in the office. • She sat alone in a vacant room.
129	**Eruption, Irruption** **Eruption** – breaking out, outbreak • Volcanic eruptions can bring about vast damage. **Irruption** – invasion • India could not check the irruption of the Chinese in 1962.
130	**Esteem, Estimate, Estimation** **Esteem** – regard, respect • The manager was held in high esteem by his colleagues. **Estimate** – calculation • The engineer made a rough estimate of the expenses. **Estimation** – opinion, judgment • In my estimation, the work will be complete today.
131	**Elder, Older** **Elder** – greater in age (usually used to refer to older members in the same family) • I have no elder brother. • We should respect our elders. **Older** – anyone who is more in age • Ravi and Rajat are classmates, yet Ravi is the older of the two.
132	**Exhausting, Exhaustive** **Exhausting** – tiring • Today's journey was very exhausting. **Exhaustive** – comprehensive, complete • The restaurant menu is elaborate and exhaustive.

133	**Elemental, Elementary** **Elemental** – pertaining to elements, of the powers of nature • Wordsworth's poems appeal to man at an elemental level. **Elementary** – introductory or rudimentary • His knowledge of Physics is rather elementary.
	F
134	**Fain, Feign** **Fain** – glad, very willing • I would fain go there to help you. • He was fain to obey his Lord. **Feign** – pretend to be affected by • He feigned a headache in order to stay at home. • Few could tell that she was feigning madness.
135	**Famous, Notorious** **Famous** – renowned, celebrated • Varanasi is famous for its sarees and mangoes. • His father is a famous banker. **Notorious** – infamous • He is a notorious rumour monger.
136	**Fair, Fare** **Fair** – moderately good, impartial, of light complexion, substantial, a fete • He is fairly expert in Arithmetic. • He has been quite fair to me. • A fair lady was standing there. • You will get a fair deal. • The *Tarnetar* fair is held every year. **Fare** – charges for conveyance, food, performance • Railway and bus fares have gone up. • Even simple fare was not available in the village. • How did you fare in the examination?
137	**Feet, Feat** **Feet** – a part of the body • Human beings have two feet and two hands. **Feat** – an act of skill • The *Bhakra Dam* is a wonderful feat of Indian engineering.
138	**Floor, Flour** **Floor** – ground of a house • This room has a marble floor. **Flour** – ground wheat or any other grain • Brown bread is made with wheat flour.
139	**Foul, Fowl** **Foul** – dirty, unfair • An honest man never plays foul. • He played foul in the game. • There is some foul play in this matter. **Fowl** – a bird • He brought home a sea-fowl for the evening meal.

140	**Fatal, Fateful, Fatalist** **Fatal** – deadly, mortal • Most types of cancer are fatal. **Fateful** – eventful, important • 1947 is a fateful year in the history of India. **Fatalist** – one who believes in fate • Most Indians are generally fatalists.
141	**Faculty, Facility, Felicity, Falsity** **Faculty** – inherent mental or physical power • Education is imparted for the harmonious development of our faculties. • She possesses natural faculties. **Facility** – opportunity, ease • Our college offers free boarding facility to the poor students. • I gave her every facility to improve her English. **Felicity** – a blessing, happiness • A murderer can never enjoy true felicity. • This state of felicity won't continue for long. **Falsity** – the quality or state of being false • The falsity of his proposition was thus proved.
142	**Forego, Forgo** **Forego** – to go before, to precede, abstain from • His suspension is a foregone conclusion. • This point has been explained in the foregone chapter. **Forgo** – abstain from • We should forgo our own comforts for the sake of our country.
143	**Forceful, Forcible** **Forceful** – possessing force • Vinod has a forceful personality. **Forcible** – done by force • The thief made a forcible entry into the house.
144	**Forbid, Prohibit** **Forbid** – refused to allow (used generally) • I was forbidden to drink wine. • The doctor forbade me to eat sweets. **Prohibit** – refused to allow (used officially) • Visitors are prohibited from smoking in the hall.
145	**Faint, Feint** **Faint** – to become unconscious, light, indistinct • She fainted at the very sight of the lion. • His voice was weak and faint. **Feint** – a mock blow or attack, pretension • Shivaji feinted once or twice to deceive his enemies.

G	
146	**Gait, Gate** **Gait** – manner or style of walking • She has an impressive gait. • Her gait is graceful. **Gate** – entrance • Parents are not allowed to enter the school gate during class hours.
147	**Gaol, Goal** **Gaol** – a correction institution, a jail • Three thieves escaped from the goal yesterday. **Goal** – destination • Money-making has become the goal of life these days.
148	**Gracious, Graceful** **Gracious** – courteous, kind, merciful, pleasant • She is always a gracious hostess. • Gandhi was always gracious to his opponents. • It is very gracious of you to help the poor. **Graceful** – elegant • Mahima is a graceful dancer.
149	**Genteel, Gentle** **Genteel** – fashionable, well-dressed, graceful, elegant, well-bred • Simran is very genteel in her manners. **Gentle** – well-born, mild • This boy is as gentle as a lamb. • The nurse gently cleansed his wounds.
150	**Ghastly, Ghostly** **Ghastly** – terrible, shocking • The thief had a ghastly appearance. • The ghastly murder proved too much for her nerves. **Ghostly** – pertaining to a ghost • The ghostly figure of his mother vanished suddenly.
151	**Gilt, Guilt** **Gilt** – covered with a thin layer of gold • His gilt watch shone in the sun. **Guilt** – crime • Confess your guilt and I will forgive you.
152	**Grate, Great** **Grate** – the recess of a fireplace, reduce to shreds • She is sitting beside the grate. • She grated the potatoes for the pie. **Great** – big, distinguished • Bernard Shaw was a great playwright.

<table>
<tr><td>153</td><td>Gamble, Gambol
Gamble – a game of chance
• Gambling is a vice.
• Rich men like to gamble.
Gambol – to leap, skip or dance in frolic
• The young girls were gambolling in the park.
• The lamb is gambolling.</td></tr>
<tr><td>154</td><td>Gage, Gauge, Gaze
Gage – security, pledge
• A bank does not advance money without gage.
• His house was given as a gage.
Gauge – to determine the exact dimension, measure, to estimate or judge
• I gauged that the food would not be enough.
Gaze – to look intently with curiosity, interest or wonder
• The hero and heroine gazed into each other's eyes.</td></tr>
<tr><td>155</td><td>Godly, God-like
Godly – pious, religious
• My mother led a godly life.
God-like – like God
• Many believed that Osho had God-like qualities.</td></tr>
<tr><td>156</td><td>Give, Grant
Give – to offer, to make a present
• I gave a necktie to my brother.
Grant – to bestow, donate or concede
• The principal granted his request for leave.
• I pray that God grants me my wish.</td></tr>
<tr><td>157</td><td>Glad, Merry
Glad – pleased
• I am glad to meet you.
Merry – shows the expression of joy into actions.
• Children were making merry.
• 'Eat, drink, and be merry' is the philosophy of epicureans.</td></tr>
<tr><td>158</td><td>Genius, Talent
Genius – exalted intellectual power, a person of exceptional intellectual ability, creativity, or originality.
• Albert Einstein was a genius.
Talent – a special natural ability or aptitude, capacity to achieve success
• No one can deny that Suman is a talented young officer.</td></tr>
<tr><td colspan="2">H</td></tr>
<tr><td>159</td><td>Human, Humane, Humanitarian
Human – of or pertaining to man
• To err is human, to forgive divine.
Humane – kind, merciful, benevolent
• Indians were not treated in a humane manner in South Africa.
Humanitarian – one who has concern for the welfare of mankind
• Buddha, Gandhi, and Nehru are some of the finest humanitarians of the world.</td></tr>
</table>

160	**Humility, Humiliation** **Humility** – modesty, meekness, humble condition • Humility is a virtue. • Treat others with humility. **Humiliation** – disgrace • Indians had to suffer great humiliation under the British rule. • I cannot pocket this humiliation.
161	**Hoard, Horde** **Hoard** – store • Capitalists are known to hoard money. • Hoarding of commodities to make a profit is illegal. **Horde** – a wandering tribe, gang • A horde of Pakistani raiders invaded Kashmir in 1948.
162	**Hail, Hale** **Hail** – welcome, frozen raindrop, belong to • I hailed my friend from a distance. • It hailed last night. • He hails from Lahore. **Hale** – free from disease, robust, healthy • He is hale and hearty.
163	**Historic, Historical** **Historic** – important • 26 January, 1950 is a historic day for all Indians. **Historical** – relating to history • The Taj Mahal of Agra is a historical monument.
164	**Honorary, Honourable** **Honorary** – serving without pay • Rai Bahadur Pritam Das has been appointed as an honorary magistrate. **Honourable** – respectable, worthy of honour • Rai Bahadur Pritam Das is an honourable man.
165	**Heir, Hair** **Heir** – a person who inherits or is entitled to inherit the rank, title, position, etc., of his predecessor • I am the sole heir to my father's property. **Hair** – part of body • He has curly hair, but his friend has straight hair.
166	**Habit, Custom** **Habit** – an acquired behaviour pattern • Smoking is a bad habit. **Custom** – the habitual practice of a community or country, made specially for individual customers • It is a custom among the Hindus to cremate their dead. • He only wears custom shoes to play golf.

167	**Hear, Listen** **Hear** – to perceive or sense through the ears • I heard her groan. • Can you hear me? **Listen** – to hear with attention • The judge listened to both parties before giving out his verdict. • I tried to listen but could not hear a word.
168	**Heal, Heel** **Heal** – to cure • My wound is healing quickly. **Heel** – the hind part of the foot (below the ankle) • She hurt her heel by a fall.
169	**Handsome, Beautiful** **Handsome** – good-looking (refers to a man) • He is a very handsome young boy. **Beautiful** – good-looking (refers to a woman), something that is pleasing to the eyes, ears or the mind • She is a very beautiful girl. • It is a beautiful poem.
170	**Home, House** **Home** – the place or the country of one's birth, having family ties • Going to one's home after the day long hard work in office, is a pleasant experience. • I wish to go home during the Diwali holidays. **House** – a building for human habitation, household • I am yet to find a suitable house to live in. • Many houses were bombed during the Second World War.
	I
171	**Idle, Idol, Ideal** **Idle** – lazy • An idle man can never become great. **Idol** – statue or image that is the object of worship, a hero figure • Hindus offer prayers to idols of gods and goddesses. • The youth consider Salman Khan their idol. **Ideal** – a standard of perfection or excellence, values • This is an ideal location for a picnic. • Gandhi was a man of high ideals.
172	**Industrial, Industrious** **Industrial** – relating to industry • Bhilai is an old industrial town in India. **Industrious** – hard-working • He is a very industrious student.
173	**Imaginative, Imaginary** **Imaginative** – full of imagination, creative • Poets are very imaginative souls. **Imaginary** – unreal, fictitious • Most of her fears are imaginary.

174	**Ill, Sick** **Ill** – of unsound health, unwell, poor, faulty • He has been ill for the last four days. • She is an ill-mannered person. **Sick** – tired, not well • I am sick of seeing this painting. • She is so sick that she cannot eat anything.
175	**Imperial, Imperious** **Imperial** – pertaining to an empire or an emperor • She belongs to an imperial family. • The imperial glory of the Mughals is unparalleled in Asian history. **Imperious** – haughty, powerful • The commander is very imperious. • The Maharajah was an imperious ruler.
176	**Informer, Informant** **Informer** – a person who informs especially for reward (e.g., a spy), a person who gives news • The police arrested the informer and put him in jail. **Informant** – a person who gives information in answer to a question or investigation • My informant told me that there were foreign spies in the town.
177	**Implicit, Explicit** **Implicit** – not obvious but implied always to be found in • His boss's tone carried an implicit threat. • We must have implicit faith in our parents. **Explicit** – clearly stated, outspoken • Our government has not given a very explicit statement of its China policy. • Nobody appreciated his explicit language.
178	**Intolerable, Intolerant** **Intolerable** – unbearable • This heat is intolerable. **Intolerant** – impatient, not tolerating or respecting beliefs, opinions, usages, manners, etc. • He is intolerant when it comes to impunctuality. • Dictators are the most intolerant rulers.
179	**Injection, Injunction** **Injection** – something that is injected especially for a medicinal purpose • The doctor gave an injection to the patient. **Injunction** – a command or an order • The Magistrate issued a temporary injunction in favour of the plaintiff.
180	**Ingenuous, Ingenious** **Ingenuous** – frank, simple, noble • I like her ingenuous manners. **Ingenious** – clever, skilful • I have thought of an ingenious method to earn money.

181	**Impossible, Impassable** **Impossible** – that which is not possible • It is impossible for man to fly like a bird. • Nothing is impossible for a man of determination. **Impassable** – which cannot be crossed • This river is impassable.
182	**Inflammable, Inflammatory** **Inflammable** – combustible, easily aroused, or excited • Petrol is an inflammable liquid. • His mother feared that his inflammable disposition would land him in trouble one day. **Inflammatory** – tending to arouse anger or hostility • The politician delivered an inflammatory speech.
183	**Indigent, Indigenous** **Indigent** – needy, poor • Most schools always help the indigent students. **Indigenous** – native, originating in and characteristic of a particular region or country, innate, inherent • The Government of India should encourage indigenous products. • Kindness is a feeling indigenous to human beings.
184	**Incite, Insight** **Incite** – to stir, encourage, or urge, to stimulate action • Terrorist groups try to incite the religious sentiment of young men. **Insight** – a clear perception • Shakespeare had remarkable insight into human nature. • His poems offer a thorough insight into his character.
185	**Intelligent, Intelligible** **Intelligent** – wise, sensible • She made an intelligent statement. • He is a very intelligent boy. **Intelligible** – clear and understandable • Her speech was not intelligible to many.
	J
186	**Judicial, Judicious** **Judicial** – pertaining to a judge or court of law • I can exercise judicial powers. • He is a judicial magistrate. **Judicious** – wise, prudent • You should choose your subjects judiciously. • Her advice is not only sound but also judicious.
187	**Jealous, Zealous** **Jealous** – envious • He is jealous of my success. **Zealous** – earnest, enthusiastic • Gandhi was a zealous reformer.

K	
188	**Knotty, Naughty** **Knotty** – tied up in knots, intricate, difficult • It was a knotty piece of wood. • This math sum seems to be quite knotty. **Naughty** – mischievous • He is a naughty boy.
189	**Knave, Nave** **Knave** – an unprincipled, untrustworthy, or dishonest person • Besides being a knave, he is also a traitor. **Nave** – the main longitudinal area of a church • The bride walked past all the guests seated in the nave.
190	**Kind, Kindly** **Kind** – tender, compassionate • She is kind to animals. • Women are generally very kind-hearted. **Kindly** – benevolently, graciously, obligingly • Kindly close the door behind when you leave. • I like to believe that Indians are a kindly people.
L	
191	**Lawyer, Liar** **Lawyer** – a person engaged in practice of law • My friend is a leading lawyer at the Allahabad High Court. **Liar** – one who tells lies • Liars are disliked by all.
192	**Lessen, Lesson** **Lessen** – to make less, to decrease • Good society lessens grief. • Pain lessens over time. **Lesson** – a part of a book, an exercise, etc., something to be learnt or studied • All the lessons are included in the syllabus. • He should learn a lesson from this incident.
193	**Lovable, Lovely** **Lovable** – worthy of love • Ravi is so lovable that everyone likes him. **Lovely** – beautiful • Mahima is a lovely girl. • He has two very lovely daughters.
194	**Lightening, Lightning** **Lightening** – making light • His help will go a long way in lightening my burden. **Lightning** – a brilliant electrical charge occurring between or in the clouds • Thunder and lightning are forecast for today.

<table>
<tr><td>195</td><td>Loose, Lose, Loss
Loose – not tight
• He is very notorious for making loose talk.
Lose – (verb) to come to be without, to suffer deprivation
• He is losing precious time.
• You will lose all your money in gambling.
Loss – (noun) detriment, disadvantage, or deprivation from failure to keep, have, or get
• My friend could not bear the heavy loss in his business.</td></tr>
<tr><td>196</td><td>Loathe, Loath
Loathe – to hate
• I loathe the very sight of a greedy and selfish man.
Loath – unwilling
• I am loath to help a mean and selfish man.</td></tr>
<tr><td>197</td><td>Later, Latter, Latest
Later – comparative degree of late
• A murderer will be caught sooner or later.
Latter – opposed to former, refers to position
• Vinod and Vijay are brothers, the latter is more sensible.
Latest – fresh, most modern
• What is the latest news of the day?
• His mobile phone has the latest technology.</td></tr>
<tr><td>198</td><td>Luxuriant, Luxurious
Luxuriant – rich in growth
• My garden boasts of luxuriant vegetation.
• He has glossy, luxuriant hair.
Luxurious – given to luxury
• Rich men lead a luxurious life.</td></tr>
<tr><td colspan="2">M</td></tr>
<tr><td>199</td><td>Male, Mail
Male – man and boy
• All the male members of the family go out to work.
Mail – post
• I received the phone bill in my mail today.</td></tr>
<tr><td>200</td><td>Memorial, Memorable
Memorial – something designed to preserve the memory of a person or an event
• It is a fitting memorial to honour our brave soldiers.
Memorable – worthy to be remembered
• He wanted to make their wedding anniversary a memorable day for his wife.</td></tr>
<tr><td>201</td><td>Momentary, Momentous
Momentary – short-lived
• Wise men do not care for momentary pleasures.
Momentous – important
• The Cabinet arrived at momentous decisions.
• Students should prepare themselves to perform momentous duties.</td></tr>
</table>

202	**Mysterious, Mystic** **Mysterious** – secret, obscure, inexplicable • Mysterious are the ways of God. **Mystic** – a person who claims to attain, or believes in divine and spiritual mysteries • Mirabai was a mystic.
203	**Metal, Mettle** **Metal** – any of the elementary substances such as gold, silver or copper • Gold is a precious metal. **Mettle** – spirit, courage • Sardar Patel was a man of mettle.
204	**Miner, Minor** **Miner** – one who works in a mine • The coal miners were trapped underground. **Minor** – an under-age person, inferior in degree of importance • A minor cannot cast his vote.
205	**Marry, Merry** **Marry** – to wed • I will not marry before I am twenty-five. **Merry** – to enjoy • Let us make merry.
206	**Mendacity, Mendicity** **Mendacity** – untruthfulness, the tendency to lie • His friends mistrusted him due to his mendacity. **Mendicity** – beggary • His servant has been reduced to mendacity.
207	**Mean, Mien** **Mean** – intend, unkind • What do you mean? • He is a mean fellow. **Mien** – bearing or behaviour showing character, feeling, etc. • He is a man of noble mien.
208	**Monetary, Monitory** **Monetary** – relating to money • He needs monetary help. • India should change its monetary policy. **Monitory** – giving warning or advice • We should not neglect the monitory counsels of our teachers.
209	**Memory, Memoirs** **Memory** – the faculty to remember, recollection • It is said that elephants have great memory. **Memoirs** – an account of life • Babar wrote his own memoirs known as *Tuzuk-i-Babri.*

<table>
<tr><th colspan="2">N</th></tr>
<tr><td>210</td><td>Necessaries, Necessities
Necessaries – those things that are necessary, essential or indispensable
• I am too poor to buy even the necessaries of life.
Necessities – requirements, wants
• Every man has a right to food, shelter and other necessities of daily life.</td></tr>
<tr><td>211</td><td>Negligent, Neglectful, Negligible
Negligent – careless
• You must not be negligent in the discharge of your duties.
Neglectful – one who neglects anything
• She is so neglectful that she seldom finishes her work in time.
Negligible – very little
• There is negligible difference between the two shoes.</td></tr>
<tr><td>212</td><td>Notable, Notorious
Notable – remarkable
• This a notable event.
Notorious – of bad fame
• Phoolan Devi was a notorious dacoit.</td></tr>
<tr><th colspan="2">O</th></tr>
<tr><td>213</td><td>Official, Officious
Official – (noun) pertaining to an office, an officer
• It is official that tomorrow is a holiday.
• You must perform your official duties strictly.
Officious – assertive of authority, intrusively enthusiastic in offering help
• His officious manners are not liked by all the employees.
• He was so officious in helping the girl students that he offended every one of them.</td></tr>
<tr><td>214</td><td>Observation, Observance
Observation – perception, remark
• My father is a man of quick observation.
• She made a significant observation on that occasion.
Observance – performance of law, duty, custom, ritual, etc.
• Hindus are very particular when it comes to observing religious rites and ceremonies.</td></tr>
<tr><th colspan="2">P</th></tr>
<tr><td>215</td><td>Practice, Practise
Practice – (noun) habit, custom
• Practice makes a man perfect.
Practise – (verb)
• Practise your lesson thoroughly.
• Practise what you preach.</td></tr>
<tr><td>216</td><td>Practical, Practicable
Practical – not theoretical
• The coach gave them some practical suggestions before the match.
Practicable – which can be put into practice
• His scheme is not practicable.</td></tr>
</table>

217	**Popular, Populous** **Popular** – liked or favoured by many or most • A sociable man is always popular. • Some film stars are very popular. **Populous** – thickly populated • Mumbai is one of the most populous cities in India.
218	**Prescribe, Proscribe** **Prescribe** – recommend • This book has been prescribed for B.A. students. • He bought the prescribed medicines according to the doctor's advice. **Proscribe** – to prohibit legally, to ban • The government has proscribed all the copies of this book as it preaches violence.
219	**Principal, Principle** **Principal** – main, chief, foremost, head of a school or college • The principal reprimanded the students. **Principle** – a law, a doctrine, a fundamental truth • Gandhi and Nehru were men of strict principles.
220	**Pitiful, Pitiable, Piteous** **Pitiful** – feeling pity, merciful • The patient's condition was pitiful. • Your meanness is really pitiful. **Pitiable** – that deserves, evokes or can be given pity • He displayed pitiable lack of character. **Piteous** – exciting pity or showing it, pathetic • Nobody responded to his piteous cries for help.
221	**Persecute, Prosecute** **Persecute** – to harass or oppress especially because of race, religion, etc. • The Jews were persecuted by the Nazis. **Prosecute** – to institute legal proceedings against a person • Trespassers will be prosecuted.
222	**Precede, Proceed** **Precede** – to go before, to be prior to • Her name precedes mine in the admission list. **Proceed** – to go on or forward • You may now proceed to the dining room.
223	**Petrol, Patrol** **Petrol** – oil • I want petrol for my scooter. **Patrol** – guard • The army is patrolling the border area.
224	**Pale, Pail** **Pale** – yellowish • She turned pale on hearing the news. **Pail** – a bucket (vessel) • Ram took a pail of water to the bathroom.

225	**Precedent, President** **Precedent** – a previous case taken as example • His deeds set a precedent for the reform of other men. **President** – chief, chairman, the head of a country • Dr. Rajendra Prasad was the first President of the Republic of India.
226	**Peace, Piece** **Peace** – rest or quiet • All of us want peace and harmony. **Piece** – a part, portion or fraction • The little sparrow was eating a piece of bread.
227	**Pray, Prey** **Pray** – to pay homage, beseech • She prays to God every morning. **Prey** – victim • My daughter fell prey to a fatal disease.
228	**Physic, Physique** **Physic** – medicine, drug • No physic can cure her of her madness now. **Physique** – physical or bodily structure, appearance, or development • He has the physique of an athlete.
229	**Prophecy, Prophesy** **Prophecy** – (noun) something foretold or predicted • The prophecy of the astrologer came true. **Prophesy** – (verb) to foretell or predict • Octopus Paul prophesied the winning teams during the FIFA World Cup.
230	**Plain, Plane** **Plain** – simple, non-fussy • She wore a plain dress and a matching bow in her hair. • Students learn best when the teacher uses plain and simple language. **Plane** – an aircraft, a flat or level surface • He boarded the plane just minutes before take-off. • In mathematics, a plane is any flat, two- dimensional surface.
231	**Personality, Personalty** **Personality** – distinctive personal character • He has such a pleasing personality. **Personalty** – the state of being a person, personal estate or property • Wilful and malicious destruction of other's personalty is against the law.
232	**Personal, Personnel** **Personal** – private, one's own • This is my personal affair, please do not interfere. **Personnel** – persons employed in the same office or business • These two compartments are reserved for military personnel.

233	**Precipitate, Precipitous** **Precipitate** – to hasten the occurrence of, to cast, plunge, or send, especially violently or abruptly • The rising oil prices can precipitate an international crisis. • He precipitated himself into the struggle. **Precipitous** – steep • The hiker had a tough time keeping up with the precipitous mountain trails.
234	**Primary, Primitive** **Primary** – first or initial, original • Better education is the primary requirement of India. **Primitive** – ancient • Primitive people used stone implements.
235	**Punctual, Punctilious** **Punctual** – regular • My brother is very punctual in arriving at the college. **Punctilious** – attentive • He is always very punctilious in the discharge of his duties.
236	**Perpetrate, Perpetuate** **Perpetrate** – commit • Ravi has perpetrated a serious crime. **Perpetuate** – to continue • A monument to perpetuate the memory of Mahatma Gandhi has been set up in South Africa.
237	**Perspicuous, Perspicacious** **Perspicuous** – clear • Paulo Coelho has a perspicuous style of writing. **Perspicacious** – having keen mental perception and understanding, discerning • Dr. Manmohan Singh displayed perspicacious judgment in dealing with the opposition.
238	**Pair, Pare** **Pair** – a set of two things • She wants a pair of gloves. **Pare** – to cut the outer layer or coating, to reduce or diminish • Please pare some apples for his breakfast. • She must pare her expenses.
239	**Peal, Peel** **Peal** – a loud sound of thunder, laughter or bells • I heard peals of laughter emerging from the children's room. **Peel** – to remove the skin • I peeled and cut some apples for the pie.
240	**Profit, Prophet** **Profit** – gain • He is making a huge profit in this business. **Prophet** – a person who speaks for God or a deity, or by divine inspiration • Moses was the greatest prophet of the Old Testament.

241	**Proffer, Prefer** **Proffer** – offer • She was proffered many proposals. **Prefer** – like or choose (better than) • I prefer mangoes to oranges.
242	**Politic, Political** **Politic** – wise, prudent, tactful • I expected you to give a politic reply. **Political** – pertaining to politics • India's political system is riddled with corruption.
243	**Prudent, Prudential, Prudentiality** **Prudent** – (noun) wise, intelligent • A prudent decision can help to avert trouble. **Prudential** – (adjective) of or pertaining to prudence • It pays to adopt the prudential approach to life. **Prudentialism** (adverb) • The Food Minister should resign in all prudentialism.
244	**Possible, Probable** **Possible** – that which may or can exist, happen or be done • It is possible that a poor man may become very rich. **Probable** – likely to occur • It is probable that it will rain today.
245	**Proposal, Proposition** **Proposal** – a scheme or design, that which is proposed • His proposal is absurd. **Proposition** – something offered for, consideration, statement • I am considering his proposition about partnership.
246	**Pain, Pane** **Pain** – physical suffering or distress • I have a shooting pain in my arm. **Pane** – a single plate of glass in a frame to form a division • The kids broke the window pane with their cricket ball.
	Q
247	**Quite, Quiet** **Quite** – completely, actually • It is quite dark at 8 p.m. • This room is quite small. • He is quite a social reformer. **Quiet** – silent • He is a quiet social reformer. • Keep quiet.

R	
248	**Respectful, Respectable, Respective** **Respectful** – full of, characterised by, or showing respect • Students should be respectful to their teachers. • It was a respectful reply. **Respectable** – worthy of respect or esteem, estimable • She belongs to a respectable family. • Her father is a very respectable man. **Respective** – relating to a particular person or thing • The players retired to their respective rooms after the match.
249	**Right, Rite** **Right** – correct in judgement, opinion or conduct, just, proper • Women are fighting for equal rights. • I am right. • You have no right to rebuke me. **Rite** – ceremony • The marriage rites will be performed this evening. • The priest insisted on performing all the rites.
250	**Resource, Recourse** **Resource** – means, a source of supply, support or aid • He is a very resourceful man. • We should not selfishly exploit our natural resources. **Recourse** – access or resort to a person or thing for help or protection • You will have to take recourse to the court of law.
251	**Rout, Route, Root** **Rout** – an overwhelming defeat, a defeat attended with disorderly flight • The Sri Lankan team faced a complete rout in the World Cup finals. **Route** – a road, course, way for passage or travel • Please tell me the shortest route to your house. **Root** – that part of a tree or plant which develops and anchors the plant under-ground, bottom, main • The roots supply nutrients to the tree. • Rani is the root cause of all the trouble in the office. • The prejudices of parents usually take root in their children.
252	**Rain, Rein, Reign** **Rain** – rainfall, shower • It rains heavily in July. • People rained flower petals on the married couple. **Rein** – bridle, curb, restrain, control • Draw the reins, otherwise the horse will throw you off. • Artists don't restrict their thoughts and give full rein to their imagination. **Reign** – control, rule or influence • The reign of the last Mughal king came to a close in 1857. • People are longing for a reign of justice and peace. • The situation will worsen if you do not reign in your temper.

253	**Raise, Raze** **Raise** – to bring or make to rise, to lift up • The lecturer raised several questions at the staff meeting. • She has raised herself in our eyes. • We should raise funds for the flood victims. **Raze** – to tear down, demolish, level to the ground • Mughal invaders would plunder and raze the temples. • In London, during the Second World War, many impressive buildings were razed to the ground.
254	**Reverend, Reverent** **Reverend** – a member of the clergy, worthy of reverence • The reverend doctor was not arguing for victory. • The chairman of the college managing committee is a reverend old gentleman of sixty-five. **Reverent** – submissive, showing reverence, deeply respectful • He is reverent in his attitude towards me. • They acknowledged the teacher with a reverent greeting.
255	**Righteous, Riotous, Rightful** **Righteous** – upright, moral, virtuous • Our leader is a righteous and godly person. • His lies were greeted with righteous indignation. **Riotous** – inciting or taking part in a riot, lawless, boisterous • The police were unable to control the riotous mob. • There was riotous laughter in the cinema. **Rightful** – having a just and legal claim • He is the rightful owner of this house.
256	**Remember, Recollect** **Remember** – recall, retain in memory (opposite of 'forget') • I do not remember your name. **Recollect** – to collect, gather or assemble again, to recall from memory • This book is a recollection of his youthful adventures. • Can you recollect my name?
257	**Rob, Steal** **Rob** – to take by force or threat, to plunder • Sushil was robbed on the way home. **Steal** – to take something without right, especially secretly, a bargain • Someone stole my fountain pen. • This shirt is a steal at Rs. 200.
258	**Revel, Reveal** **Revel** – make merry, noisy festivity • Christmas is a time of revelry and joy. • Students revelled in their victory. **Reveal** – to make known, disclose, display • She did not reveal her identity. • The clouds dispersed to reveal the sun.

259	**Rest, Wrest** **Rest** – to refresh oneself by sleeping, lying down or relaxing, remainder • The doctor has advised me to take rest. • The rest of the students have gone home. **Wrest** – take away by force, turn, twist, pull by force • She tried to wrest his watch. • It is very tricky to wrest a knife from a child.
260	**Regretful, Regrettable** **Regretful** – full of regret or sorrow • You should be regretful for your misbehaviour. • I am regretful for what I have done. **Regrettable** – causing regret or sorrow • It is regrettable that you gave up your favourite sport.
261	**Rap, Wrap** **Rap** – to strike with a quick, sharp blow, to knock smartly or lightly • All the naughty boys got a rap on their knuckles. • He rapped on the door with his cane. **Wrap** – to wind, fold, cover or enclose • She wrapped her head in a scarf. • His gift was wrapped in blue and golden paper.
	S
262	**Stationary, Stationery** **Stationary** – not moving • The sun is stationary, the earth rotates around its axis. **Stationery** – writing materials like paper, pencil, etc. • My brother has set up a stationery shop.
263	**Social, Sociable** **Social** – friendly, pertaining to society • Man is a social animal. • India needs social reforms. **Sociable** – affable, companionable • We had a sociable evening at her place. • As he is a man of sociable temperament, he is liked by all.
264	**Sensible, Sensitive** **Sensible** – having, using or showing good sense • Ram is a very sensible boy. • The government needs to bring about a sensible reduction in the price of fuel. **Sensitive** – endowed with perception, easily and acutely affected • Highly sensitive people cry very easily. • You have sensitive skin, so apply some sunscreen on your face.
265	**Sensuous, Sensual** **Sensuous** – perceived by or pertaining to the senses • His poetry is highly sensuous. • All great poetry is simple, sensuous, and passionate. **Sensual** – pertaining to, inclined to, or preoccupied with the gratification of the senses or appetites • Those who pursue only sensual pleasures come to grief. • He finds sensual delight in eating good food.

266	**Statue, Statute** **Statue** – image • A life-size statue of Tagore was presented to Nehru by an English sculptor. **Statute** – a law or an enactment, a rule established by an organisation, corporation, etc. • There is a statute in India that no man can marry two women. • According to the company statute, absentees will be fired.
267	**See, Look** **See** – observe, perceive • I see many deer grazing in the park. **Look** – to direct the eye so as to see, implies effort, attention • I looked at her face.
268	**Spiritual, Spirituous, Spirited** **Spiritual** – pertaining to the soul, relating to sacred things • Mahatma Gandhi was a spiritual leader. **Spirituous** – like spirit, containing spirit • I do not touch spirituous drinks as they are harmful. **Spirited** – bold, fiery • She is a very spirited girl.
269	**Salutary, Salubrious** **Salutary** – beneficial • His mother gave him some salutary advice. **Salubrious** – favourable to or promo-ting health, healthful • The climate of Gulmarg is salubrious.
270	**Sanguine, Sanguinary** **Sanguine** – hopeful • He is sanguine about human nature. • I am sanguine of his success in the examination. **Sanguinary** – bloody • A sanguinary battle is raging at the border between the two countries.
271	**Stimulus, Stimulant** **Stimulus** – something that incites or quickens act, thought or feeling • The approval of others is a potent stimulus at work. **Stimulant** – something that offers stimulus or incentive • Coffee is a great stimulant. • Performance bonus is a great stimulant for most employees.
	T
272	**Temporal, Temporary** **Temporal** – of or pertaining to the present time (opposite of 'eternal') • The temporal joys on earth are nothing compared to those in heaven. **Temporary** – not permanent, lasting for a short time • He has applied for a temporary job. • The medicine gave the patient only temporary relief.

273	**Team, Teem** **Team** – a side of players in a game • The Indian Hockey team is very strong. **Teem** – abound, overflow • This tank is teeming with fish.
274	**Tail, Tale** **Tail** – the hindmost part of an animal • The cow has a long tail. **Tale** – a story, a lie full of creative embellishments • His mother narrated an interesting tale about his childhood. • I do not believe his tall tales.
275	**Transient, Transitory, Transitional** **Transient** – passing quickly, not permanent, or stationary **Transitory** – momentary, continuing only for a short time • Earthly pleasures are transitory. • He does not care for transitory pleasures of life. **Transitional** – movement, passage or change from one position or stage to another • Teenage is the most transitional phase in one's life.
276	**Tamper, Temper** **Tamper** – to interfere with, to meddle • Somebody has tampered with the seals of ballot boxes. • The packaging of this product is tamper- proof. **Temper** – state or disposition of mind • You should not lose your temper. • She is a mild-tempered girl.
	U
277	**Umpire, Empire** **Umpire** – a referee • The umpire's decision is always final. **Empire** – area of domination • Ashoka succeeded in building a vast empire.
278	**Union, Unison, Unity** **Union** – combination, act of uniting • Union is strength. **Unison** – agreement of sounds • Nina and Veena sang in unison. **Unity** – oneness • People of all castes and creed should live in unity.
279	**Urban, Urbane** **Urban** – pertaining to city or town (opposite of rural) • The urban population of India is increasing. **Urbane** – polite, refined • Her husband is a suave and urbane man.

	V
280	**Verbal, Verbose** **Verbal** – relating to words • I have sent a verbal message to my friend. • He received a verbal message from his boss. **Verbose** – characterised by too many words, wordy • My teacher is so verbose it is tiring to listen. • His verbosity is his drawback.
281	**Vain, Vane, Vein, Wane** **Vain** – empty, idle, fruitless, conceited, boastful • She is often vain of her achievements. • He had vain hopes of support from his colleagues. • I dislike vain display of friends. **Vane** – a weathercock, a contrivance to show the direction of the wind • Students can know the direction of the wind by observing the wind vane. **Vein** – a blood vessel • Nehru had blue blood in his veins. **Wane** – fade, decrease • The moonlight is waning.
282	**Virtual, Virtuous** **Virtual** – in effect if not in fact • Noor Jahan was the virtual ruler of India. • Children like to play virtual games on the Internet. **Virtuous** – chaste, pure, extremely moral • She leads a virtuous life. • My mother was a virtuous lady.
283	**Variance, Variation** **Variance** – disagreement • His action is at variance with his profession. **Variation** – change, alteration • There is a slight variation in colour.
284	**Venial, Venal** **Venial** – excusable • Her fault is venial. **Venal** – mercenary, who may be bribed • These days when corruption is rampant, venal ministers are no rarity.
	W
285	**Waste, Waist** **Waste** – spend uselessly, a wilderness, or a desert region • Don't waste your precious time in silly pursuits. • The canal water has turned the waste land of Rajasthan into green fields. **Waist** – the part of human body between the ribs and the hips • His shirt falls a little below his waist.

286	**Womanly, Womanish** **Womanly** – befitting a woman • My mother possessed all the womanly qualities. • Modesty is a womanly virtue. **Womanish** – women-like, feminine, weak • He has womanish qualities.
287	**Wilful, Willing** Wilful – deliberate, conscious, obstinate • Satyendra is so wilful that he never acts upon the advice of his father. • I will not tolerate your wilfulness. **Willing** – ready, having no reluctance • Vinit is willing to marry Veena. • I am always willing to help my friends.
288	**Wave, Waive** **Wave** – to move back and forth or up and down, a surge, swell, or rush (e.g., in the sea) • She waved her hand as the train started. • He waved his handkerchief to the crowd. • Waves are striking against the shore. **Waive** – to forego, give up • He waived his claim in my favour. • The bank waived the interest on his loan.
289	**Whither, Wither** **Whither** – where, for what purpose (Old English word) • I do not understand whither the modern youth is going. **Wither** – fade • Flowers and leaves wither away in autumn.
290	**Wet, Whet** **Wet** – moist, soaked • His clothes became wet in the rain. • Please do not enter with wet feet. **Whet** – sharpen, stimulate • Hunters spend hours to whet their knives. • Wine and cheese often whet the appetite.
291	**Wreath, Wreathe** **Wreath** – a garland • The President placed a wreath on Mahatma Gandhi's *Samadhi*. **Wreathe** – encircle, adorn • Thick, black smoke wreathed above the buildings.
292	**Weather, Whether** **Weather** – climate, a state of atmosphere • Some fine weather is forecast for today. **Whether** – if • I do not know whether she will come or not.

11 WORD CLARIFICATION - PRACTICE TESTS

17 PRACTICE TESTS

Complete the sentences in the given practice tests by inserting the correct words from the bracketed hints and cross-check your answers provided with the answers key at the end of the chapter.

PRACTICE TEST – 1

1. All came __________ Tom. (accept, except)
2. We did not follow her __________ (advise, advice)
3. Have you considered all __________ of the question? (angels, angles)
4. We were asked to write an __________ (essay, assay)
5. Try to __________ naturally. (breath, breathe)
6. We shall __________ a chairman. (chose, choose)
7. Only linen __________ were used for the table. (cloths, clothes)
8. They were __________ of victory. (confidant, confident)
9. He was not __________ of his error. (conscience, conscious)
10. The horses were led into the __________ (coral, corral)

PRACTICE TEST – 2

1. He is a member of the U.S. Marine __________ (corpse, corps)
2. It is their __________ to dine at seven. (custom, costume)
3. Good advice is good __________ (consul, counsel)
4. A daily recording of one's personal experiences is a ______________ (diary, dairy)
5. Legal heirs of the __________ were notified. (diseased, deceased)
6. The __________ was hazardous). (decent, descent)
7. To object is to __________. (demure, demur)
8. What have we for lunch __________? (desert, dessert)
9. He constructed a safety __________ (device, devise)
10. The fog will soon __________ the town. (envelope, envelop)

PRACTICE TEST – 3

1. A distinctive period of time in history is an __________ (epoch, epic)
2. Costly and __________ are synonyms. (expensive, expansive)
3. Her __________ words were soothing. (gentle, gentile)
4. He is __________ unaware of his predicament. (holy, wholly)
5. Cruelty to animals is not __________ (human, humane)
6. She arrived __________ than usual. (later, latter)
7. There must be some means of __________ the work. (lightning, lightening)
8. Dialect adds __________ colour. (locale, local)
9. Do not __________ your patience. (lose, loose)
10. He walked with a __________ stride. (martial, marital)

PRACTICE TEST – 4

1. He was in a jovial __________ (mood, mode)
2. If one conforms to a standard of what is right, one is __________. (moral, morale)
3. Let us not become __________ in our remarks. (personal, personnel)
4. __________ with your plans. (Proceed, Precede)
5. I __________ your rapid rise to success. (prophesy, prophecy)
6. What is the __________ of this inquiry? (purpose, propose)
7. How __________ the room is! (quiet, quite)
8. I __________ that remark. (recent, resent)
9. The young folks accepted the older man's counsel __________. (respectively, respectfully)
10. A __________ was reserved at the hotel. (suite, suit)

PRACTICE TEST – 5

1. __________unfortunate for him. (It's, its)
2. __________ turns is it? (Who's, Whose)
3. Was __________ no mail today? (there, their)
4. How late are you __________ to stay? (aloud, allowed)
5. __________ going with you? (Who's, Whose)
6. __________ are your papers. (Here, Hear)
7. We were __________ late to __________ the opening number. (to, too, two) (here, hear)
8. I need more __________ to complete my letter. (stationary, stationery)
9. We were __________ along narrow paths. (lead, led)
10. No one is __________ bad. (altogether, all together)

PRACTICE TEST – 6

1. Have you __________ Tom your new car? (shone, shown)
2. __________ go my good friends. (They're, Their, There)
3. __________ entering the building. (They're, Their, There)
4. Have you finished, __________? (too, to, two)
5. Let us whistle __________ (altogether, all together)
6. The kitten lost __________ ball. (it's, its)
7. We were __________ through the museum. (shone, shown)
8. The freshly polished silver __________ brightly. (shone, shown)
9. Never board a train that is not __________. (stationery, stationary)
10. __________ not too late to turn back. (Its, It's)

PRACTICE TEST – 7

1. Use the centre __________ (aisle, isle).
2. He has __________ gone. (already, all ready)
3. We need to __________ our plans. (altar, alter)
4. He is __________ on time. (always, all ways)
5. The __________ is steep. (ascent, assent)
6. A large __________ is expected. (attendants, attendance)
7. We lolled on the sandy __________ (beech, beach)
8. The present __________ rate is high. (birth, berth)
9. Cars must have good __________ . (breaks, brakes)
10. Our horses followed the __________ path. (bridle, bridal)

PRACTICE TEST – 8

1. A house to house __________ was made. (canvas, canvass)
2. Each state has a __________ city. (capital, capitol)
3. The __________ of the play is small. (cast, caste)
4. The story ran as a __________ (cereal, serial)
5. It was necessary for the committee to have a long __________. (session, cession)
6. They have a beautiful __________ beside a lake for their new home. (site, cite)
7. I consider his remark a __________, not an insult. (complement, compliment)

8. The village __________ met to elect new officers. (council, counsel)
9. The capsized boat disappeared in the swift __________. (current, currant)
10. The __________ in this material is not fast. (dye, die)

PRACTICE TEST – 9

1. He has a __________ personality. (duel, dual)
2. A __________ is a mythological character. (faun, fawn)
3. The learning of the entire selection was a __________ of memory. (feet, feat)
4. A distress __________ was noticed. (flair, flare)
5. We went __________ with our plans. (foreword, forward)
6. __________ air is unhealthful. (Foul, Fowl)
7. See the colts __________ in the pasture. (gambol, gamble)
8. Rembrandt was a __________ artist. (grate, great)
9. Although old, he is still __________ (hale, hail)
10. One adversity often comes upon the __________ of another. (heal, heel)

PRACTICE TEST – 10

1. We discussed the __________ matter. (whole, hole)
2. Do not make money your __________ (idle, idol, idyll)
3. __________ years brought hardships. (Lean, Lien)
4. He has a dignified __________ (mean, mien)
5. He excelled at the tennis __________. (meet, mete, meat)
6. A youth under twenty-one is a __________. (minor, miner)
7. She is still __________ her loss. (mourning, morning)
8. Do not live in the __________. (passed, past)
9. __________ has its reward. (Patients, Patience)
10. We walked to the edge of the __________ (peer, pier)

PRACTICE TEST – 11

1. Her clothes are __________ but in good taste. (plain, plane)
2. Every good citizen goes to the __________. (polls, poles)
3. The chairman requested the __________ of every member. (presents, presence)
4. The __________ of the high school addressed the students. (principle, principal)
5. The King's __________ was of short duration. (rain, rein, reign)
6. The old building will be __________ and a new one will be built in its place. (razed, raised)
7. Parcels for mailing must be __________ carefully. (rapt, wrapped, rapped)
8. The __________ of this area petitioned for bus service. (residence, residents)
9. A benefit __________ was staged by the students. (review, revue)
10. The bell has a harsh __________. (wring, ring)

PRACTICE TEST – 12

1. __________ yourself for bad news. (Steel, Steal)
2. Come __________ to the point. (strait, straight)
3. It was hard to __________ ourselves away from the exciting discussion. (tare, tear)
4. We have no more room; __________ we must enlarge the building. (therefore, therefor)
5. He __________ away every opportunity. (threw, through)
6. The theatrical __________ travelled in trailers. (troop, troupe)
7. There is a __________ of sarcasm in his remarks. (vein, vane, vain)
8. He __________ all rights. (waived, waved)
9. You __________ blue well. (ware, wear)
10. I am __________ out. (warn, worn)

PRACTICE TEST – 13

1. Have you __________ the invitation? (excepted, accepted)

2. Please __________ me on the matter. (advice, advise)
3. This is easier __________ I thought. (than, then)
4. Are you __________ sure? (quite, quiet)
5. You must __________ between the two. (chose, choose)
6. __________ no time. (Lose, Loose)
7. I am not __________ to blame. (holy, wholly)
8. He spoke __________ to his elders. (respectfully, respectively)
9. After discussing every __________ of the problem, we arrived at no solution. (angle, angel)
10. The actors were attired in colourful __________ (customs, costumes)

PRACTICE TEST – 14

1. Have you decided on a __________ for your story? (local, locale)
2. His __________ of living was different from ours. (mood, mode)
3. He is __________ that he will be chosen. (confident, confidant)
4. What do you __________ that we do? (purpose, propose)
5. A __________ supplies us with milk. (diary, dairy)
6. Let your __________ be your guide. (conscious, conscience)
7. Do not __________ from the path. (wander, wonder)
8. After __________ the load, we proceeded. (lightning, lightening)
9. The __________ of the dejected man was restored by encouraging words. (moral, morale)
10. Mirages are often seen on __________. (deserts, desserts).

PRACTICE TEST – 15

1. __________ are __________ many errors __________. (There, Their, They're) (too, to, two) (here, hear)
2. __________ themes were read __________? (Who's, Whose) (allowed, aloud)
3. __________ __________ __________ late. (Its, It's) (all together, altogether) (to, two, too)
4. As we were __________ through the park, we were __________ unusual trees. (lead, led) (shone, shown)
5. __________ not to leave the car until it is __________. (Their, They're, There) (stationery, stationary)
6. He walked slowly __________ the room. (through, threw)
7. Their __________ was recently vacated. (residents, residence)
8. He is a man of high __________. (principals, principles)
9. Have you __________ the test? (passed, past)
10. Many __________ were waiting for the doctor. (patience, patients)

PRACTICE TEST – 16

1. His explanations were __________. (plane, plain)
2. He will __________ for votes. (canvas, canvass)
3. Paris is the __________ of France. (capital, capitol)
4. The two colours are __________. (compliments, complements)
5. __________ jelly is delicious. (Current, Currant)
6. The __________ of a book is in the introductory section. (forward, foreword)
7. __________ seated the audience. (Attendance, Attendants)
8. He looked __________ from overwork. (warn, worn)
9. The building was __________ by fire. (raised, razed)
10. He refused __________ from his elders. (council, counsel)

PRACTICE TEST – 17

1. The coal __________ struck the higher wages. (minors, miners)
2. The police could not __________ a confession from her. (ring, wring)

3. I was asked to play a __________ role. (duel, dual)
4. I attended a court __________ today. (cession, session)
5. Do not __________ the dish. (brake, break)
6. Can you __________ the lines? (cite, site)
7. With __________ attention the children gazed at him. (wrapped, rapped, rapt)
8. She __________ her inheritance. (waved, waived)
9. She has a __________ for dramatics. (flair, flare)
10. They were __________ when I arrived. (all ready, already)

ANSWERS – WORD CLARIFICATION – PRACTICE TETS (MCQs)

	P.T. – 1	*P.T. – 2*	*P.T. – 3*	*P.T. – 4*	*P.T. – 5*	*P.T. – 6*
1	except	corps	epoch	mood	it's	shown
2	advice	custom	expensive	moral	whose	there
3	angles	counsel	gentle	personal	there	they're
4	essay	diary	wholly	proceed	allowed	too
5	breathe	deceased	humane	prophesy	who's	all together
6	choose	descent	later	purpose	here	its
7	cloths	demur	lightening	quiet	too, hear	shown
8	confident	dessert	local	resent	stationery	shone
9	conscious	device	lose	respectfully	led	stationary
10	corral	envelop	martial	suite	altogether	it's

	P.T. – 7	*P.T. – 8*	*P.T. – 9*	*P.T. – 10*	*P.T. – 11*	*P.T. – 12*
1	aisle	canvass	dual	whole	plain	steel
2	already	capital	faun	idol	polls	straight
3	alter	cast	feat	lean	presence	tear
4	always	serial	flare	mien	principal	therefore
5	ascent	session	forward	meet	reign	threw
6	attendance	site	foul	minor	razed	troupe
7	beach	compliment	gambol	mourning	wrapped	Vein
8	birth	council	great	past	residents	waived
9	brakes	current	hale	patience	revue	wear
10	bridle	dye	heel	pier	ring	worn

	P.T. – 13	*P.T. – 14*	*P.T. – 15*	*P.T. – 16*	*P.T. – 17*
1	accepted	locale	There, too, here	plain	miners
2	advise	mode	Whose, were, aloud	canvass	wring
3	than	confident	It's, altogether, too	capital	dual
4	quite	propose	led, shown	complements	session
5	choose	dairy	They're, stationary	currant	break
6	lose	conscience	through	foreword	cite
7	wholly	wander	residence	attendants	rapt
8	respectfully	lightening	principles	worn	waived
9	angle	morale	passed	razed	flair
10	costumes	deserts	patients	counsel	all ready

PART B: REFRESH THE CONCEPTS OF GRAMMAR (130 PTs)

IMPORTANCE OF GRAMMAR

CUET ENGLISH paper is a compulsory paper for almost all the CUET aspirants. Assessment of level of grammar is an indispensable part of this paper. Though all the aspirants appearing in this paper must be soundly grounded in this section because all the aspirants, irrespective of streams, must have passed 10th and 12th standard English language papers. But still, in any competition, no one can take any section non seriously. In competitive exams, it doesn't matter what you do, but the thing which matters is what the other does. So, keeping in view the stiff competition, all necessary elements of grammar have been explained in detail under PART B, supported with examples and illustrations. 130 PTs would enable the students to reinforce their concepts.

Good grammar means writing or speaking in such a way that one's choice of words is understandable and follows the rudimentary rules of sentence construction, punctuation, and spellings. Good grammar helps to communicate clearly and get what one wants. ***'The better the grammar**, **the clearer the message, the most likelihood of understanding the message's intent and meaning'***, says author Huffington Bradshaw.

Grammar refers to the rules and regulations that govern spoken and written language. Good grammar is a key to effective communication, whereas bad grammar leads to undesirable effects. The purpose of grammar is to bridge the gap between what one means and what the others understand.

According to oxford dictionary, a comma (,) marks a slight break between different parts of a sentence. Used properly, commas make the meaning of sentences clear by grouping and separating words, phrases, and clauses. However, uncertainty about the use of commas and sprinkling of commas here and there where not required, and omission to place commas where required, lead to confusion, and convey an absolutely wrong meaning.

Here is a classic English grammar example from the book, ***'Eats, shoots, and leaves,' by Lynne Truss;*** If you were to say, 'let us eat, grandma', everyone would understand that you were inviting your loved one for a meal. If you were to write, 'let us eat grandma,' this expression would convey something nasty and undesirable.

Another example will highlight the importance of grammar and punctuation in particular. Mr. Roy finds inspiration in cooking his family and his dog. It conveys meaning that Mr. Roy finds inspiration when he cooks his family and dog. Just an omission of commas made the sentence extremely funny and hilarious. Correctly punctuated, it will be written as, Mr. Roy finds inspiration in cooking, his family, and his dog.

The PART B starts with an introduction about the building blocks of grammar which are the eight parts of speech.

Verbs express actions, events, or states of being.

Nouns name a person, place, animal, thing, or abstract ideas.

Pronouns take the place of nouns.

Adjectives modify nouns or pronouns by describing, qualifying, or quantifying them.

Adverbs modify a verb, adjective, another adverb and indicate manner, time, place, cause, or degree.

Prepositions link the words in a sentence.

Conjunctions link words, phrases, and clauses.

Interjections convey emotions.

The PART B of the book, at the outset, introduces students with parts of speech as building blocks of grammar. They are explained in detail under separate chapters, highlighting the rules governing the eight parts of speech. For clear and effective communication in writing and speaking, words also are no less important than a twin sister of grammar. Hence, PART A serves the purpose of building sound vocabulary. The use of grammar along with the selection of befitting words makes writing very impressive.

Part B, in addition to the parts of speech also deals in detail with use of articles, prepositions, determiners, modals, etc.

Part C has been designed with the twin purpose of checking the level of retention of words and understanding of conceptual clarity of grammar. It is the applied and functional section which has been made very exhaustive dealing with a variegated form of English usage. 170PTs AND 1000 MCQs would facilitate the students to strengthen their base.

Part E is meant to assess the overall understanding of the English language through comprehension.

PART D will introduce them with 1200 common errors being committed inadvertently.

Having gone through this book, the students will feel quite confident with intensive and extensive coverage of all the topics of vocabulary, grammar, usage, comprehension, and common errors. The material provided is practically class tested and tried and trusted by hundreds of Toppers qualifying various competitive exams, trained, and tutored by the author A P Bhardwaj himself.

12 PARTS OF SPEECH – AN INTRODUCTION

The skeletal bones of grammar are the eightparts of speech, and they are as given here:

1. ***Noun – a naming word for a name,place, animal, thing, feeling, or quality.*** Rita, Paris, cow, or string.
2. ***Pronoun – stands in place of a noun.*** 'He' for Ram, 'she' for Maya, 'it' for land.
3. ***Adjective – a describing word that describes a noun.*** Tall, hot, three, cotton, and brown.
4. ***Verb – a doing/being/possession word.*** 'Is reading', 'has come', 'took', 'will bring'.
5. ***Adverb – a word describing a verb, an adjective, or another adverb.*** Slowly, quickly, fast, or well.
6. ***Conjunction – a joining word that joins words or sentences.*** This or that, rich but humble, mother and father.
7. ***Preposition – a relationship word that shows position, time, and direction.*** 'At', 'from', 'to', or 'near' the station.
8. ***Interjection – words that exclaim orshow surprise.*** Alas! Oh! Wow!

REVIEW, REVISE AND REFRESH

A **noun** is a word which names or refers to a person, animal, place, thing, or idea. The words **student, Saroja, dog, city, Nagpur, computer, fridge, joy, truth,** and **beauty** are all nouns.

A **pronoun** is a word (such as **I, me, you, we, he, him, she,** and **they**) which is used in place of a noun,

A **verb** says what somebody or something does (e.g., **eat**) or what happens (e.g., **die, rain**). A few verbs like **be, remain,** and **have** describe astate or condition.

An **adjective** is a word which describes or says more about a noun or pronoun, e.g., **clever, tall, hungry, interesting.**

An **adverb** is a word that mainly describes or gives more information (**how, when, where,** etc.) about a verb (e.g., He writes **neatly**. He came **yesterday**. Sit **there.**). An adverb sometimes gives more information about an adjective (e.g., You are **quite** right.) or another adverb (e.g., He walks **very** slowly.).

A **preposition** is a word like **on, in, at, with, for, under, from,** and **to**, used before a noun or pronoun to show place, time, method, etc.

A **conjunction** is a joining word such as **and, but, yet, or, when, because,** and **though**. It joins words or groups of words.

An **interjection** is a word spoken suddenly to express a strong feeling. **Hurrah, hello, bravo, oh, ah, gosh, ouch, shh, wow,** etc. are interjections.

Some words belong to more than one-word class or part of speech. Study the following:

1. *(a)* Would you give me some **water**? (noun)
   (b) We **water** the plants daily. (verb)
2. *(a)* We saw the film on **video**. (noun)
   (b) They **video** such programmes. (verb)
3. *(a)* He fell **off** the ladder. (preposition)
   (b) The thief ran **off**. (adverb)
4. *(a)* This is a **fast** train. (adjective)
   (b) He walks **fast**. (adverb)
   (c) Muslims **fast** during Ramzan. (verb)
   (d) He broke his **fast** yesterday. (noun)

Further classification of nouns, pronouns, adjectives, and adverbs would facilitate to understand better.

Nouns can be broadly divided into these categories:

1. **Common nouns** (= names given in common to all people, places, and things of the same kind.)

   E.g., **boy, teacher, city, river, month**
2. **Proper nouns** (= names of particular people, places, or things.)

   E.g., Suresh, Mr. Brown, Allahabad, the Ganga, October
3. **Abstract nouns** (= names of feelings, ideas, or qualities.)

   E.g., love, anger, beauty, wisdom, kindness
4. **Collective nouns** (= names of groups of people or collections of things.)

   E.g., crowd, team, flock, bunch, fleet

There is another classification of nouns:**"countable nouns"** (= names of things which can be counted) and **"uncountable nouns"** (= names of things which cannot be counted). Nouns like **pen, chair, house,** and **tree** are countable. Nouns like **milk, sugar, rice, gold, freedom,** and **happiness** are uncountable.

Pronouns: There are seven kinds of pronouns:

1. Personal pronouns

   I, you, he, we, they, me, him, us, etc.
2. Possessive pronouns

   mine, his, hers, ours, yours, theirs
3. Reflexive pronouns

   myself, yourself, himself, herself, ourselves, yourselves, themselves
4. **Demonstrative pronouns** (used to 'point out' somebody or something)

   this, that, these, those
5. **Interrogative pronouns** (used in asking questions)

   what, which, who, whom, whose
6. **Relative pronouns** (used to introduce clauses as in: 'This is the boy who helped me.')

   that, which, who, whom
7. **Pronouns of quantity** (and number) **many, much, some, few, all, both, each, either, neither, etc.**

ADJECTIVES

There are mainly five kinds of adjectives:

1. **Adjectives of quality** (or Descriptive adjectives)

   They show the quality of a person orthing.

   a **kind** person, a **large** city, an **honest** man, **dirty** clothes
2. **Adjectives of quantity** (and number) They include all the numerals (**one, two,second, fifth,** etc.) and also many

   words like all, both, some, many, much, few, each, every, etc.

   six apples, all men, some books, every player
3. Demonstrative adjectives

   Like demonstrative pronouns, they 'point out'.

   this book, **these** pencils, **that** man, **those** houses
4. Possessive adjectives

   my, your, his, her, our, their
5. Interrogative adjectives

   which, what, whose (e.g., **Which** pen is yours?)

ADVERBS

An adverb is a word which modifies or adds to the meaning of a verb. Sometimes an adverb modifies an adjective or another adverb.

She types **quickly**. (modifies the verb 'types')

You are **quite** right. (modifies the adjective'right')

He spoke **very** well. (modifies the adverb 'well')

The commonest types of adverbs are:

1. **Adverbs of manner** (These answers the question 'How?')

   quickly, angry, carefully, fast, well, etc.
2. **Adverbs of place** (These answers the question 'Where?')

   here, there, near, everywhere, etc.
3. **Adverbs of time** (They answer thequestion 'When?')

   now, today, yesterday, soon, etc.
4. **Adverbs of frequency** (They answer the question 'How often?')

   often, sometimes, always, never, twice, etc.
5. **Interrogative adverbs** (question words)

   where, when, why, how, etc.

13 USE OF NOUNS

13 PRACTICE TESTS

(a) Nouns are the **names** of things around us. Nouns that are used to name general things (rather than a particular person or thing) are called **common nouns.** Examples:

Dog table car bottle

(b) Some nouns are the nouns of particularor special people or things. These are called **proper nouns** and are written with a capital letter at the beginning. Examples:

Michael Jackson stayed at the Hilton Hotel in Adelaide last July.

(c) Some nouns are the names we use for collections of things. These are called **collective nouns.** Examples:

a **flock** of birds a **herd** of cattle

a **bunch** of grapes a **smack** of jellyfish a **siege** of bears a **murder** of ravens an **army** of frogs a **charm** of finches

a **pod** of dolphins

Other collective nouns name a number of different things in the same class. Examples:

fruit tools luggage birds

Students often have difficulty deciding whether a collective noun is singular or plural.

I. Words that represent a number of different things in the same group always take a single verb. Examples:

furniture is luggage is linen is

II. Words that have a plural meaning, but no plural form, take a plural verb. Examples:

people arepolice are

III. Other collective nouns can take a plural verb if the context emphasis is on a groupof individuals. However, the singular is preferred. Examples:

The crowd is cheering. Parliament is sitting. The crew is ready.

The Olympic Games are in Sydney.

(d) Nouns can be **singular** or **plural.** The relevant plural constructions at this level are:

1. Many plurals are made by simply adding –s. Examples:

   dog/dogs girl/girls

2. If the noun ends in –s, –sb, –ch, or –x, make the plural by adding –es. Examples:

   bus/buses bush/bushes
   church/churches fox/foxes

3. If the noun ends in a –y before which there is a consonant, make the plural by changing –y to –i and adding –es. Examples:

   fairy/fairies city/ cities

4. If the noun ends in – y before which there is a vowel, (a, e, i, o, u) make the plural by simply adding – s. Examples:

   monkey/monkeys toy/toys

5. If the noun ends in –f, change the –f to –v and add –es. Examples:
   loaf/loaves leaf/leaves

6. However, some simply add – s. Examples:
   roof/roofs chief/chiefs

7. Some nouns have an irregular plural. Examples:
   foot/feet goose/geese
   man/men child/children

(e) **Possessive nouns** are especially difficult to grasp.

1. The possessive of a singular noun is formed by adding an apostrophe and –s at the end of the word. No letters are changed or left off the original words. Examples:

the **boy's** dog (the boy owns a dog)
the **lady's** car (the lady owns a car)

2. The possessive of a plural noun ending in –s is formed by adding an apostrophe. Examples:

horses/ horses' **manes/manes'**
ladies/ ladies' **cars/cars'**

3. The possessive of a plural noun not ending in –s formed by adding an apostrophe and – s. Examples:

children/ children's **men/men's**

(*f*) An **abstract noun** is the name of something that can't be recognised by the five senses – you can't touch, taste, hear, smell, or see it – it can only be recognised by the mind. Examples:

courage	**misery**
delight	**fear**
excitement	**distress**
hope	**possibility**

NOUNS (PRACTICE TESTS)

PRACTICE TEST-1

Use a collective noun from the box to fill each space.

brood fleet library litter turf flight batch bunch

(*a*) a_____________of aircraft
(*b*) a_____________of cakes
(*c*) a_____________of grass
(*d*) a_____________of grapes
(*e*) a_____________of ships
(*f*) a_____________of puppies
(*g*) a_____________of chickens
(*h*) a_____________of books

PRACTICE TEST-2

Add a collective noun of your own on eachline below.

(*a*) a_____________of footballers
(*b*) a_____________of eggs
(*c*) a_____________of sheep
(*d*) a_____________of sailors
(*e*) a_____________of hay
(*f*) a_____________of wool
(*g*) a_____________of trees
(*h*) a_____________of bananas

PRACTICE TEST-3

Write the plural of the word in brackets. Hint! If there is a vowel before the y, add s. If there is a consonant before the y, change the y to i and add es.

(*a*) All the children in our school were given________ (diary)
(*b*) There are lots of large________in Australia. (city)
(*c*) The__were making a lot ofnoise. (turkey)
(*d*) This supermarket has over five hundred________. (trolley)
(*e*) We ate all the____on the tree. (cherry)
(*f*) Lots of________gathered around therotten food. (fly)

PRACTICE TEST-4

Write the plural of each word. Hint! For some words that end in f, change the f to v and add es.

For others, simply add s.

(*a*) loaf ________
(*b*) chief ________
(*c*) knife ________
(*d*) half ________
(*e*) leaf ________
(*f*) handkerchief ________
(*g*) thief ________
(*h*) wolf ________

PRACTICE TEST-5

Write the plural of the word in brackets

(*a*) The two___decided to end thewar. (army)
(*b*) They read the story 'Snow White and the Seven________'. (Dwarf)
(*c*) When the box was dropped, all the________ broke. (glass)
(*d*) At the zoo we saw lots of__________. (monkey)
(*e*) Several________were needed to pull the wagon. (ox)
(*f*) The_____left their coats on thebed. (lady)

PRACTICE TEST-6

Write the plural of the word in brackets. Hint!Most nouns form the plural by adding s. Those that end in ch, sh, s, or x, add es.

(*a*) There are over seven________in ourtown. (church)

(*b*) There are lots of________growing in the playground. (tree)

(*c*) The frightened dog hid between the two ________. (bush)

(*d*) Jan put all the________on the table. (box)

(*e*) My brother ate three________for lunch. (peach)

(*f*) The six school________were in a line. (bus)

PRACTICE TEST-7

Write the plural of each of the following words. Hint! They are all irregular.

(*a*) goose ________

(*b*) man ________

(*c*) foot ________

(*d*) house ________

(*e*) tooth ________

(*f*) woman ________

(*g*) child ________

(*h*) mouse ________

PRACTICE TEST-8

Write the plural of the word in brackets

(*a*) We planted ____in the garden. (potato)

(*b*) On our holiday, Kyle took lots of __. (photo)

(*c*) South America has many________. (volcano)

(*d*) Hundreds of ________damaged the wheat crop. (kangaroo)

(*e*) The brave ________were all given medals. (hero)

(*f*) I sliced the three________to make asalad. (tomato)

PRACTICE TEST-9

Complete the sentence by making a nounfrom the verb in brackets.

(*a*) We placed an________in the newspaper. (advertise)

(*b*) The________took place in a nearby church. (marry)

(*c*) Our teacher asked for our complete ________. (attend)

(*d*) Ian's________has been much better this term. (behaved)

(*e*) They had to make an important ________. (decide)

PRACTICE TEST-10

Complete the sentence by making a nounfrom the adjective in brackets.

(*a*) It was with great ________ we said goodbye. (sad)

(*b*) The firefighter was awarded for her ________. (brave)

(*c*) We sat in the coolness of the ________. (shade)

(*d*) There was a lot of________between the two teams. (bitter)

(*e*) We gasped at the________of the mountains. (beautiful)

(*f*) We were not sure what________he was suffering from. (sick)

PRACTICE TEST-11

Rewrite the following to show possession.

(*a*) The dress of the girl ________

(*b*) The stripes of the tiger ________

(*c*) The pencil of the boy ________

(*d*) The handbags of the lady ________

(*e*) The leaves of the tree ________

(*f*) The petals of the flower ________

(*g*) The antics of the clown ________

(*h*) The uniform of the police officer ______

PRACTICE TEST-12

Now rewrite the following to showpossession.

(*a*) The dresses of the girls ________

(*b*) The ears of the donkeys ________

(*c*) The books of the men ________

(*d*) The saddles of the horses ________

(*e*) The houses of the women ________

(*f*) The pencils of the boys ________

(*g*) The nests of the birds ________

(*h*) The ship of the sailors ________

PRACTICE TEST-13

Add an abstract noun from the box to fill each space.

Use a collective noun from the box to fill each space.

excitement fun pain health length happiness care wealth

(*a*) We had lots of________at the show.

(*b*) After he fell over, Tom had a ________ in his leg.

(*c*) Although he has been ill, he is in good ________ now.

(*d*) There was a lot of________when the mouse escaped in the classroom.

(*e*) I am not sure of the of this rope.

(*f*) Mr. Richman thinks that________is important.

(*g*) The genie said that I would have health, wealth and________.

(*h*) Tim took a lot of________with his work.

ANSWERS (PRACTICE TESTS)

Q. No.	*TEST – 1*	*TEST – 2*	*TEST – 3*	*TEST – 4*	*TEST – 5*
1.	Flight	Team	Diaries	Loaves	Armies
2.	Batch	Dozen	Cities	Chiefs	Dwarfs
3.	Turf	Flock	Turkeys	Knives	Glasses
4.	Bunch	Crew	Trolleys	Halves	Monkeys
5.	Fleet	Stack	Cherries	Leaves	Oxen
6.	Litter	Bail	Flies	Handkerchiefs	Ladies
7.	Brood	Line		Thieves	
8.	Library	Comb		Wolves	

Q. No.	*TEST – 6*	*TEST – 7*	*TEST – 8*	*TEST – 9*	*TEST – 10*
1.	Churches	Geese	Potatoes	Advertisement	Sadness
2.	Trees	Men	Photos	Merriment	Bravery
3.	Bushes	Feet	Volcanoes	Attendance	Shadow
4.	Boxes	Houses	Kangaroos	Behaviour	Bitterness
5.	Peaches	Teeth	Heroes	Decision	Beauty
6.	Buses	Women	Tomatoes	Encouragement	Sickness
7.		Children			
8.		Mice			

Q. No.	*TEST – 11*	*TEST – 12*	*TEST – 13*
1.	Girl's dress	Girls' dresses	Fun
2.	Tiger's strips	Donkeys' ears	Pain
3.	Boy's pencil	Men's books	Health
4.	Lady's handbags	Horses' saddles	Excitement
5.	Tree's leaves	Women's houses	Length
6.	Flower's petals	Boys' pencils	Wealth
7.	Clown's antics	Birds' nests	Happiness
8.	Police officer's uniform	Sailors' ships	Care

14 USE OF PRONOUNS

2 PRACTICE TESTS

Pronoun – Pronoun stands in place of a **noun.**

Personal Pronouns: Number and Person

A pronoun that stands for a person or thing is called a personal pronoun.

There are three persons: first person, second person, and third person.

First person ... the person(s) speaking

Second person ... the person(s) spoken to

Third person ... the person(s) spoken about

If **I** speak to **you** about **Vijay, I** am the first person, **you** are the second person, and **Vijay** is the third person.

The various forms of a personal pronouns are given below:

	Person	*Used as a subject*	*Used as an object*	*Possessive form*	*Remarks*
I	(sing.) (plu.)	I We	me us	mine ours	used for both mas. and fem.
II	(sing.) (plu.)	you you	you you	yours yours	used for both mas. and fem.
III	(sing.) (sing.) (sing.) (plu.)	he sheit they	himher it them	his hers —— theirs	Masculine feminine neuter all genders

POSSESSIVE PRONOUNS

The following words are the **possessive forms** of personal pronouns:

mine, ours, yours, his, hers, theirs

They can be call as **possessive pronouns** also.

The words **my, our, your, his, her,** and **their** are **possessive adjectives** and not possessive pronouns.

her book (possessive adjective)

a book of **hers** (possessive pronoun)

The noun which a pronoun stands for is calledits **antecedent.**

A pronoun must agree with its antecedent inits number, gender, etc.

You should speak to **Renu. She** needs your help.

(**Both Renu** and **She** – singular number, feminine gender).

You should speak to these **boys. They** need your help.

Note: **I, you, he, she, it,** and **they** act as the subject of a verb. **Me, you, him, her, it,** and**them** act as the object of a verb:

I	believe	him
T	T	
Subject		object

You and **it** can act both as the **subject** and the **object** of a verb:

You did not attend the meeting. Everybody missed you.

TT

subject object

The Personal Pronoun 'It'

1. The personal pronoun **it** is used to referto an **animal, a thing,** or a **child**:

   The fox is a wild animal. **It** is very cunning.

2. **It** is often used as an **empty** or **meaningless** subject with expressions that refer to **time, weather, temperature,** or **distance:**

   It is 10 o'clock.

   It rained heavily last evening.

It ... used for an animal, a thing, or a child.

... used as an empty subject.

REFLEXIVE PRONOUNS

Pronouns like **myself, yourself,** and **himself,** when used as the receiver of an action, are called **reflexive pronouns.**

For example: I blamed **myself.**

A reflexive pronoun can also be the object ofa preposition.

For example: My aunt lives by **herself.**

The various forms of reflexive pronouns aregiven below:

	Singular		Plural	
	Personal	Reflexive	Personal	Reflexive
First person	I	myself	we	ourselves
Second person	you	yourself	you	yourselves
Third person	he she it	himself herself itself	they	themselves

EMPHASISING PRONOUNS

A pronoun used to convey emphasis is called an **emphasising pronoun.**

For example:

I **myself** locked the door.

You **yourself** asked for money.

Emphasising and **reflexive** pronouns have the same form: **myself, yourself,** etc.

A reflexive pronoun answers the question: Whom?

A blamed **myself** for my failure.

An emphasising pronoun lends emphasis:

I **myself** locked the room.

INDEFINITE PRONOUNS

Indefinite pronouns do not stand for any specific person or thing:

some of the books **much** of the work

something **everybody** **nobody**

much work (adjective)

much of the work (pronoun)

all the birds (adjective)

all of the birds (pronoun)

Kinds of indefinite pronouns

Indefinite pronouns may be of two kinds:

'of' pronouns ... **some** (of the books), **both** (of the children), **much** (of the work), **none** (of my eighbours)

compound pronouns ... everyone, everybody, somebody, anybody, nothing, something, no one, someone

all the books ... all is an adjective

all of the books ... all is a pronoun.

Singular ... somebody, something, anybody,

Plural	nobody, nothing, anyone, etc. … both, few, many,	Singular or Plural	Several … all, most, none, any, some

PRONOUNS (PRACTICE TESTS)

PRACTICE TEST-1

Fill in the blanks with suitable reflexivepronouns.

1. Mary controlled__________and kept quiet.
2. Gaurav availed__________of the opportunity.
3. Rohit dried__________with a towel.
4. Children don't feel shy. They help__________to cakes and biscuits.
5. They were angry with__________for that silly mistake.
6. The train came to a halt by__________.
7. We enjoyed__________in the park.
8. I slipped and hurt__________.
9. She admired__________as she stood in front of the mirror.
10. On the day of the cross-examination, they absented__________from the court.

PRACTICE TEST-2

Fill in the blanks with suitable indefinite pronouns.

1. I pressed the call bell several times but__________answered.
2. You look tired and hungry. Would you have __________to eat?
3. If there is__________you want, please let me know.
4. __________saw him entering the minister's house.
5. These facts are known to__________. There is nothing secret at all.
6. I don't think__________has the courage to act against the Principal's wishes.
7. Could__________of you accompany me to the market?
8. __________could have answered these questions. They are so easy.
9. ______wanted to say_______openly.
10. All the doors were closed. So, I heard absolutely__________.

ANSWERS (PRACTICE TESTS)

Q. No.	*TEST – 1*	*TEST – 2*
1.	Herself	No one
2.	Himself	Something
3.	Himself	Anything
4.	Themselves	Someone
5.	Themselves	Everyone
6.	Itself	Anyone
7.	Ourselves	Anyone
8.	Myself	Everyone
9.	Herself	Somebody, something
10.	Themselves	Nothing

15 USE OF VERBS

11 PRACTICE TESTS

Verb means doing, saying, action, being, and having words.

(a) ***Action verbs are words that express a concrete action.*** They are common in spoken language and in the writing.

Examples:

work run sit eat jump

(b) ***Saying verbs express a spoken action.***

Examples:

talk tell said suggested yelled

(c) ***Some verbs do not express a concrete action – they express actions that happen mentally, such as feelings, ideas, thoughts, or attitudes. These can be called thinking and feeling verbs.*** They are common in arguments, narratives, and descriptions (but not scientific description, which are objective).

Examples:

I like Sam.

Katy believed the story. I see the rabbit.

I think people should recycle.

(d) ***Some verbs tell us about what things are and what they have.*** These are being and having verbs. They are common in allkinds of descriptions.

Examples:

Ben is a good swimmer.Ali has the answer.

They are here.

(Is, are, has, and have can also act as auxiliaries, or helping verbs, for doing, thinking, and feeling verbs.

Example: Ben is swimming.)

Verbs can be finite or non-finite

(a) Finite verbs have a subject.

Example:

The dog bit my leg.

The verb is bit. To find the subject, ask 'Who or what bit?'. In this case there is an answer – the dog – so there is a subject.

Finite verbs can also stand alone withouta helping verb. For a sentence to be complete it must have a finite verb.

(b) Non-finite verbs cannot stand alone.

Examples:

To go to the dance

Non-finite verbs can be infinitives or participles.

- The infinitive usually consists of a verb before which is the word to.

  Examples:

  to jump to hop

  Often the ***'two'*** is not written or spoken.

  Examples:

  Fred made me do this.

  Let me go with Sam.

- ***Participles are parts of verbs. When they are used with helping verbs (auxiliaries), they form complete verbs.***

  Example:

  Jack is running across the lawn.

  The helping verb is ***'is'*** and the presentparticiple is running.

  Participles can be present or past.

  Examples:

present	swimming	skipping	hopping
past	swum	skipped	hopped

A participle must never be used on its own as a verb.

Correct	***Incorrect***
I have done.	***I done.***
I have seen.	***I seen.***

Verbs do not only express actions; they also tell us the time of the action.

The tense of a verb tells us when the action is, was, or will be carried out.

The three tenses are past, present, and future.

(a) Present tense refers to actions that are happening now, at this moment.

Example:

I like the chocolate flavour.

(b) Past tense refers to actions that happened in the past, a few seconds ago or years ago.

Example:

I liked the chocolate flavour.

Don't confuse the past tense with the past participle. Remember, the past participle always has a helping verb.

Example:

Past tense I rang.

Past participle I have rung.

(c) Future tense refers to actions which will happen in the future, in a few seconds or in a few years.

Example:

She will like the chocolate flavour.

There are different forms of the present, past, and future tenses.

(a) The examples above are in the simple or indefinite form.

(b) The other main form is the continuous form. It refers to an action that is, was, or will be continuing.

Present Tense	Continuous	He is walking alongthe road.
Past Tense	Continuous	He was walking along the road.
Future Tense	Continuous	He will be walkingalong the road.

Most verbs form their tenses in a regular way, according to the following table.

REGULAR VERBS

Present Tense	*Past Tense*	*Past Participle*
I watch	I watched	(I have) watched
He plays	He played	(He has) played
They use	They used	(They have) used

IRREGULAR VERBS

There are three types of irregular verbs:

1. ***Verbs in which all three parts (the base form, the past tense, and the past participle) are identical, e.g., cut – cut – cut.***
2. ***Verbs in which two of the three parts are identical, e.g., get – got – got.***
3. ***Verbs in which all three parts are different, e.g., see – saw – seen.***

Here the common irregular verbs are grouped into three types.

1. All the three parts are identical

Base Form	*Past Tense*	*Past Participle*
bet	bet/betted	bet/betted
bid	bid	bid
broadcast	broadcast	broadcast
burst	burst	burst
cast	cast	cast
cut	cut	cut
hit	hit	hit
hurt	hurt	hurt
knit	knit/knitted	knit/knitted
let	let	let
put	put	put
quit	quit/quitted	quit/quitted
read	read	read
set	set	Set
shut	shut	shut
split	split	split
spread	spread	spread
thrust	thrust	thrust

2. Two parts are identical

Base Form	*Past Tense*	*Past Participle*
beat	beat	beaten
become	became	become
bend	bent	bent
bring	brought	brought
build	built	built
burn	burnt/burned	burnt/burned
catch	caught	caught
creep	crept	crept
dream	dreamt/ dreamed	dreamt/ dreamed

feed	fed	fed
feel	felt	felt
find	found	found
flee	fled	fled
flow	flowed	flowed
get	got	got
grind	ground	ground
hang	hung hanged	hung (e.g., the picture was hung.)
		hanged (e.g., he was hanged for murder)
have	had	had
hold	held	held
keep	kept	kept
kneel	knelt/ kneeled	knelt/kneeled
lay	laid	laid
leap	leapt/leaped	leapt/leaped
learn	learnt/ learned	learnt/learned
lend	lent	lent
light	lit/lighted	lit/lighted
make	made	made
mean	meant	meant
mislay	mislaid	mislaid
overcome	overcame	overcome
run	ran	ran
seek	sought	sought
sell	sold	sold
shoot	shot	shot
sit	sat	sat
slide	slid	slid
smell	smelt/ smelled	smelt/smelled
spell	spelt/spelled	spelt/spelled
spend	spent	spent
spill	spilt/spilled	spilt
stick	stuck	stuck
strike	struck	struck
string	strung	strung
sweep	swept	swept
swing	swung	swung
tell	told	told
think	thought	thought
weep	wept	wept
win	won	won
wind	wound	wound
withhold	withheld	withheld
wring	wrung	wrung

3. All the three parts are different

Base Form	Past Tense	Past Participle
arise ***(a) wake***	arose (a) woke	arisen (a) woken/ (a) waked
be	was	been
begin	began	begun
bite	bit	bitten
blow	blew	blown
choose ***do***	chose did	Chosen done
draw	drew	drawn
drive	drove	driven
eat	ate	eaten
fall	fell	fallen
fly	flew	flown
forbid	forbade	forbidden
forget	forgot	forgotten
freeze	froze	frozen
give	gave	given
go	went	gone
grow	grew	grown
hide	hid	hid/hidden
lie	lay	lain
mistake	mistook	mistaken
ride ***rise***	rode rose	Ridden risen
see	saw	seen
shake	shook	shaken
show	showed	showed/shown
sink	sank	sunk
speak	spoke	spoken
steal	stole	stolen
swear	swore	sworn
take	took	taken
tear	tore	torn
undergo	underwent	undergone
wear	wore	worn
weave	wove	woven
withdraw	withdrew	withdrawn
write	wrote	written

VERBS (PRACTICE TESTS)

PRACTICE TEST-1

Use a verb from the box to fill each space.

pounced	scowled
searched	pruned
wiped	gushed

(*a*) When we turned the tap, the water________ out.

(*b*) The angry lady________at me.

(*c*) The hungry cat________on the mouse.

(*d*) After he finished the ice-cream, he ________ his face.

(*e*) The farmer________the fruit trees.

(*f*) We________everywhere but couldnot find the missing watch.

PRACTICE TEST-2

Use a verb from the box to fill each space.

quench	comb	burst
throw	draw	obey

(*a*) to________a picture

(*b*) to________an order

(*c*) to________a ball

(*d*) to________your thirst

(*e*) to________your hair

(*f*) to________a balloon

PRACTICE TEST-3

Change each of the words in the box to the part tense verb. Then use the past tense verbs to complete the sentences. Hint! Some words add – ed to make the past tense.

delight_______	defeat_________
bark_________	thank_________
start_________	walk_________

(*a*) I ________the teacher for helping me throughout the year.

(*b*) The dog________ loudly at the stranger.

(*c*) Our football team________the other team ten goals to three.

(*d*) I was________when I was told I had won the prize.

(*e*) We________over three kilometres to the nearest house.

(*f*) The concert________right on time.

PRACTICE TEST-4

Change each of the words in the box to the part tense verb. Then use the past tense verbs to complete the sentences. Hint! If the word ends in –e, add –d to make the past tense.

whistle_______	refuse_______
waste_______	describe_______
capture_______	continuc_______

(*a*) The hunters________the leopard in the net.

(*b*) The soldier________to obey the orders of her sergeant.

(*c*) The children________a lot of good food on the camp.

(*d*) He________loudly to call his dog.

(*e*) The witness________the thief to the police officer.

(*f*) Although her leg had hurt badly Freya________the race.

PRACTICE TEST-5

Write the past tense verbs on the lines. Hint! If the word ends in –y, change the –y to –i and add –ed to make the past tense.

(*a*) study________

(*b*) deny________

(*c*) multiply________

(*d*) bury________

(*e*) terrify________

(*f*) tidy________

(*g*) copy________

(*h*) hurry________

PRACTICE TEST-6

Use the past tense verbs from previous questionto complete the sentence.

(*a*) The dog________its bone in the garden.

(*b*) When I________two by four I got eigh.

(*c*) The thief________stealing the jewels.

(*d*) Sally_____hard to pass her spelling test.

(*e*) The savage dog________the young child.

(*f*) I______up the lounge room for my mother.

(*g*) Mike________the answers from Peter.

(*h*) Joanne________to school because she thought she was late.

PRACTICE TEST-7

Complete the sentences by writing the past tense of the verb in brackets Hint! Some verbs form the past tense by doubling the final letter and adding –ed.

(*a*) The car_____across the greasy road. (skid)

(*b*) The old man________for money for food to eat. (beg)

(*c*) The glass broke when he________it on the floor. (drop)

(*d*) The thieves_____the hotel last night. (rob)

(*e*) Peter________his sister a woolen jumper. (knit)

(*f*) I________the sugar before I drank the tea. (stir)

(*g*) The class___to Melbourne by train. (travel)

(*h*) The leaking tap________all night. (drip)

PRACTICE TEST-8

Use the past tense verbs of the words in the box to complete the story. Hint! Some verbs change their spelling to make the past tense. You might need to say the verb aloud to see if it sounds right.

ride	speak
tell	bring
ring	teach
get	eat
go	fly

PRACTICE TEST-9

Circle the subject. Then choose the correct word from the brackets.

(*a*) This dog________friendly. (is are)

(*b*) These dogs________friendly. (is are)

(*c*) We________going to the zoo. (am are)

(*d*) I________going to the zoo. (am are)

(*e*) She________faster than me. (runs run)

(*f*) They________faster than me. (runs run)

PRACTICE TEST-10

Choose the correct word from the brackets.

(*a*) A new pack of cards________opened. (was were)

(*b*) The swarm of bees ________approaching. (is are)

(*c*) A school of whales ________sighted off the coast. (was were)

(*d*) The party of climbers________returned from the mountain. (has have)

(*e*) The football team________tonight. (practices practice)

(*f*) A sack of potatoes________on the road. (is are)

PRACTICE TEST-11

Choose the correct word from the brackets.

(*a*) Mum and Dad______on their way. (is are)

(*b*) Here___the bride and groom. (comes come)

(*c*) Sarah and Zoe__going away today. (is are)

(*d*) The parents and teachers________every month. (meets meet)

(*e*) Jack and Freya___very hard. (works work)

(*f*) This is where Ned and Max________to meet me. (was were)

ANSWERS (PRACTICE TESTS)

Q. No.	TEST – 1	TEST – 2	TEST – 3	TEST – 4
1.	Gushed	Draw	Thanked	Captured
2.	Scowled	Obey	Barked	Refused
3.	Pounced	Throw	Defeated	Wasted
4.	Wiped	Quench	Delighted	Whistled
5.	Pruned	Comb	Walked	Described
6.	Searched	Burst	Started	Continued

Q. No.	TEST – 5	TEST – 6	TEST – 7	TEST – 8
1.	Studied	Buried	Skidded	Rode
2.	Denied	Multiplied	Begged	Spoke
3.	Multiplied	Denied	Dropped	Told
4.	Buried	Studied	Robbed	Rang
5.	Terrified	Terrified	Knitted	Got
6.	Tidied	Tidied	Stirred	Went
7.	Copied	Copied	Travelled	Brought
8.	Hurried	Hurried	Dripped	Taught
9.				Ate
10.				Flew

Q. No.	TEST – 9	TEST – 10	TEST – 11
1.	Is	Was	Are
2.	Are	Is	Comes
3.	Are	Was	Are
4.	Am	Has	Meet
5.	Runs	Practices	Work
6.	Run	Is	Were

16 USE OF ADVERB

7 PRACTICE TESTS

An adverb is a word that adds meaning to a verb, an adjective or another adverb.

There are many types of adverbs.

(a) **Adverbs of Place-** These are used to show where something happens.

I told him to come **here**.

Other examples:

above behind below
upstairs outside near
everywhere

(b) **Adverbs of Time-** These are used to show when something happens.

He played **yesterday**.

Other examples:

soon later yesterday
today often seldom
never already nowthen

(c) **Adverbs of Manner-** These are used to show how something happens.

The child cried **loudly**.

Other examples:

quietly furiously helpfully
softly gently noisily

(d) **Interrogative Adverbs-** These ask questions.

How are you?

Other examples:

when whence where
whither why

(e) **Negative or Modal Adverbs-** These make sentences negative, agree, orexpress doubt.

He is **not** coming.

Other examples:

never no not at all
perhaps possibly probably
yes

Like adjectives, adverbs can change their form to indicate degrees of comparison. The three degrees are:

- ***Positive Degree-*** This refers to one person or thing. Example: Tom can play **hard.**
- ***Comparative Degree-*** This compares two people or things. Example: Tom can play **harder.**
- ***Superlative Degree-*** This compares more than two people or things. Example: Of the three children, Tom plays the **hardest.**

Things to remember:

- To adverbs of one syllable, add –er and –est to form the comparative and superlative.
  Examples:
  hard harder hardest
- Adverbs that end in –ly have more and most placed before them to form the comparative and superlative.
  Examples:
  silently more silently most silently
- Some adverbs are irregular and must be learnt individually.
  Examples:
  badly worse worst
  well better best
  much more most

ADVERBS OF PLACE

above	behind	below
downstairs	elsewhere	everywhere
here	inside	near
nowhere	outside	somewhere
upstairs	within	yonder

ADVERBS OF TIME

already	immediately	instantly
late	lately	meanwhile
never	now	often
presently	recently	seldom
shortly	soon	then
today	yesterday	Yet
tomorrow		

ADVERBS OF MANNER

anxiously	carefully	desperately
furiously	helpfully	jauntily
loudly	nervously	noisily
powerfully	quietly	rapidly
skillfully	tearfully	trustingly
urgently	vigorously	well

INTERROGATIVE ADVERBS

how	When	Whence
Where	Whither	Why

ADVERB (PRACTICE TESTS)

PRACTICE TEST-1

Select the best adverb to complete the sentence.

gracefully	neatly
busily	angrily
brightly	tightly
softly	carefully

(a) We should cross a busy street_________.
(b) We tie parcels_________.
(c) Lights can shine_________.
(d) We should write_________in our books.
(e) The children worked_________.
(f) The lion roared_________.
(g) We should whisper_________.
(h) A swan swims_________.

PRACTICE TEST-2

Select the best adverb telling where to complete each sentence.

out	everywhere
there	here
inside	nowhere
below	somewhere

(a) Put the boxes_________.
(b) The lost pens were_________to be found.
(c) I can't find it, but I must have put it________.
(d) Let's sit right_________.
(e) They stayed on the top deck, but I went____.
(f) When she dropped the bottle, the water spilled_________.
(g) He was so angry he stormed__________.
(h) Tim went outside but I stayed_________.

PRACTICE TEST-3

Add an adverb telling how to each verb.

politely	swiftly
softly	loudly
heavily	happily
slowly	sweetly

(a) fell _________
(b) whispered _________
(c) sang _________
(d) ran _________
(e) yelled _________
(f) limped _________
(g) spoke _________
(h) played _________

PRACTICE TEST-4

Write an adverb to replace the words inbrackets:

(a) The old man was sleeping (in peace).
(b) Our teacher left the room (in a hurry).
(c) Lisa jumped the fence (with ease).
(d) We are going to leave (in a short time).
(e) Tim arrived (after the expected time).
(f) He gazed (with pride) at his good writing.

PRACTICE TEST-5

Add an adverb from the box to complete each sentence.

wearily	here
upstairs	now
noisily	tomorrow
tonight	punctually

(*a*) We must leave right_________.
(*b*) Put it_________.
(*c*) Paul arrived_________.
(*d*) Ben yawned_________.
(*e*) The stars are shining brightly_________.
(*f*) The match will be played_________.
(*g*) There was a party_________.
(*h*) The monkeys chattered_________.

PRACTICE TEST-6

Write the adverb that has a similar meaning.

tidily	feebly
glumly	foolishly
abruptly	gently
gladly	rapidly

(*a*) weakly _________
(*b*) happily _________
(*c*) neatly _________
(*d*) stupidly _________
(*e*) softly _________
(*f*) sadly _________
(*g*) suddenly _________
(*h*) quickly _________

PRACTICE TEST-7

Write the adverb that has the opposite meaning.

swiftly	angrily
politely	neatly
bravely	suddenly
later	yesterday

(*a*) untidily _________
(*b*) slowly _________
(*c*) happily _________
(*d*) cowardly _________
(*e*) rudely _________
(*f*) tomorrow _________
(*g*) gradually _________
(*h*) immediately _________

ANSWERS (PRACTICE TESTS)

Q. No.	*TEST – 1*	*TEST – 2*	*TEST – 3*	*TEST – 4*
1.	Carefully	There	Heavily	Peacefully
2.	Tightly	Nowhere	Softly	Hurriedly
3.	Brightly	Somewhere	Sweetly	Easily
4.	Neatly	Here	Swiftly	Shortly
5.	Busily	Below	Loudly	Lately
6.	Angrily	Everywhere	Slowly	Proudly
7.	Softly	Out	Politely	
8.	Gracefully	Inside	Happily	

Q. No.	*TEST – 5*	*TEST – 6*	*TEST – 7*
1.	Now	Feebly	Neatly
2.	Here	Gladly	Swiftly
3.	Punctually	Tidily	Angrily
4.	Noisily	Foolishly	Bravely
5.	Tonight	Gently	Politely
6.	Tomorrow	Glumly	Yesterday
7.	Upstairs	Abruptly	Suddenly
8.	Wearily	Rapidly	Later

17 USE OF ADJECTIVES

10 PRACTICE TESTS

Adjectives tell us more about nouns. They are called describing words.

They describe the number, colour, size, texture, quality, quantity, and characteristics: two, red, big, silky, strong, some, stubborn.

Example:

A big fat cat; an old tattered shirt; a deep dark cave; a menacing mean ghost; a fierce fiery battle.

Adjectives can be identified by their endings. Adjectives usually end in –ual, -ic, -ing, -ous, -al, -ive, -ine, -ant, -ent, -ful, -ish, -ible, -able, -ial, -less, -ar.

Example: unusual, perpetual; basic, manic; dancing, fading; courageous; monstrous; banal, fatal; explosive, passive; canine, divine; dormant, pliant; obedient, patient; boastful, careful;' childish, selfish; sensible, visible; eatable, bearable; proverbial, jovial; careless, painless; angular, singular.

We can identify an adjective by putting a common noun after it like 'man', 'city', 'cake', 'feeling' or 'situation'.

Example: sensible man, massive city, expensive cake, unusual feeling, terrible situation

Adjective can be grouped into categories.

Categories of adjectives are given in the table below.

The table also shows the order of adjectives in a sentence when more than one adjective is used to describe a noun.

Example:

My large, two-year-old, brown, teak, Chinese dining table has been sold.

Adjective word order in sentences.

Note: Not all these categories will be used in a single sentence.

Word order of adjectives	*Adjective Category*	*Adjectives*
1.	Possession words	my, yours,his
2.	Demon-stration words	this, that,these
3.	Number	twenty, three, first,second
4.	Size	big, small,short, tall
5.	Nature	frisky, quiet, bored, annoying
6.	Age	two-year- old, of fouryears, new, young, aged
7.	Shape	round, square, triangular
8.	Colour	red, green,violet
9.	Origin	Indian, American, Chinese
10.	Material	cotton,plastic, rubber
11.	Texture	smooth, rough, sandy
12.	Purpose (adjectives underlined)	frying pan, rest room, service life

Example:

My two, little, frisky new puppies have a ***round, red, Persian wool*** sleeping bag to sleepin during winter.

The above sentence has the adjectives in bold italics and the nouns underlined. Four adjectives the noun 'puppies' and five adjectives describe the noun 'bag'.

Adjectives bring nouns to life.

They add important information to the noun. The more adjectives there are describing the noun, the better we see the complete picture.

The girl waited at the bus stop.

Girl – common noun (no adjectives)

The tall, well-dressed, pretty girl waited at the bus stop.

OR

The sloppy, fidgeting, worried girl waited at the bus stop.

Depending on the words that we use to describe the girl, the picture changes almost completely in the two sentences. the original sentence which has no adjectives to describe the girl, so it tells us nothing about her. Adjectives are called ***'modifiers'*** because they modify or change the information we have about a noun.

TYPES OF ADJECTIVES

The word demonstrative means to demonstrateor show.

Example: This, that, those + noun

The word interrogative means to interrogate or question.

Example: which, whose + noun

The word ***possessive*** means to possess or to own.

Example: my, your, his, her, our, their + noun The word ***comparative*** means to compare one thing to something else.

Better, worse, adjective + er, adjective + est The word ***distributive*** means to distribute and show definite and indefinite number.

Each, every, some, many, few, no, all, none + noun

Adjectives are of the following kinds:

Demonstrative: this house. Q: Which house? A:this

Interrogative: which dog? Q: this dog or that dog? A: which one?

Possessive: my hen Q: your hen or my hen? A:my hen

Comparative: better box Q: compared to this?A: better

Distributive: each student Q: how many? A: each

Note how each adjective has a noun attached.

If there was no noun, the word would not be an adjective but a pronoun.

Example:

This house is spacious.

'This' in the sentence above is a demonstrative adjective because it demonstrates or shows whichhouse – this house.

This is spacious house.

'This' in the sentence above is a pronoun. It refers to the house, so it is a demonstrative pronoun because the word 'this' stands in place of the word 'house'.

Adjectives can come before or after the noun. A lovely painting.

A painting which is lovely.

His shoes were new and shining. His new, shining shoes.

The dress was pink and embroidered.The pink, embroidered dress.

Adjectives are used to describe people andplaces powerfully.

The man had a leathery, pock-marked face. A large, deep scar ran across his fleshy, bulbous nose to the top of his thick, upper lip. This gave him a scowling, fierce look.

The sea was stormy. The gigantic waves rose like steep mountains and crashed on the sandy shore. The ferocious roar of the mighty ocean made the frightened fishermen run for shelter to the high cliff nearby.

Adjectives make comparisons.

The comparative adjective compares one thing with another by adding 'er' to the word.

If the word is a long one, then the words 'more'/'less' are used before the word to make the comparison.

Examples:

Short – shorter; long – longer; sweet – sweeter; tall – taller

Intelligent – more intelligent; beautiful – more beautiful; fortunate – more fortunate; important – more important

Adjectives that end in a 'e' only add an 'r' in the comparative.

Example: 'nice' becomes 'nicer'.

Adjectives that end in 'y' normally change to 'i' when they are compared, so 'happy' changes to 'happier'.

The superlative adjective compares all nouns and declares one the most superior.

This is done by adding 'est' for short words and 'most' before longer words.

Examples:

Short – shortest; long – longest; sweet – sweetest; tall – tallest

Intelligent – most intelligent; beautiful – most beautiful; fortunate – most fortunate; important –most important

Some adjectives change completely when compared.

Good – better – best

Many – more – most

Ill – worse – worst

Bad – worse – worst

Little – less – least

ADJECTIVES (PRACTICE TESTS)

PRACTICE TEST-1

Choose a word from the box to complete each sentence.

circular	fragile
broad	careful
perilous	stupid

(a) A river that is wide is________.

(b) Something easily broken is________.

(c) If something is round it is________.

(d) A foolish person is________.

(e) If something is dangerous it is________.

(f) If a person is cautious, he or she is_____.

PRACTICE TEST-2

Choose the most suitable describing adjective from the box.

delicious	rusty	sunny
savage	interesting	woolen
ripe	clever	

(a) ________story

(b) ________student

(c) ________knife

(d) ________food

(e) ________jumper

(f) ________weather

(g) ________apple

(h) ________watchdog

PRACTICE TEST-3

Rewrite the story replacing each underlined adjective with one of a similar meaning from the box.

big	minute
scared	thick
strong	high
sour	fat

As we walked through the <u>dense</u> forest, we saw a <u>plump</u> bird eating some <u>bitter</u> fruit that grew on a <u>tall</u> tree. My brother Sam, a <u>sturdy</u> lad,threw a <u>tiny</u> pebble at the bird. The <u>frightened</u> bird flew to the safety of a <u>gigantic</u> bush.

PRACTICE TEST-4

Choose the describing adjective from the box that has the opposite meaning to the adjective in the brackets.

plump	foolish
dangerous	false
fresh	deep

(a) This loaf of bread is________. (stale)

(b) This is a________spot to swim. (safe)

(c) The pool is very________here. (shallow)

(d) I knew his statement was________.(true)

(e) This pig is quite________. (thin)

(f) Tom is a________boy. (wise)

PRACTICE TEST-5

Choose the describing adjective from the box that has a similar meaning to the adjective in the brackets.

careful	sudden
peculiar	serious
sharp	sacred

(a) I found her to be a________person.(odd)

(b) Paul is a very________boy. (cautious)

(*c*) We were startled by the______movement. (abrupt)

(*d*) It was a________breach of rules. (grave)

(*e*) She felt a________pain in her arm.(acute)

(*f*) We entered the_____temple quietly. (holy)

PRACTICE TEST-6

Choose an adjective from the box to complete each sentence.

twelve	three
two	ten
eight	four
fourteen	one hundred

(*a*) There are________eggs in a dozen.

(*b*) A bicycle has________wheels.

(*c*) There are________years in a decade.

(*d*) A tricycle has________wheels.

(*e*) A century is________years.

(*f*) There are________days in a fortnight.

(*g*) A square has________sides.

(*h*) An octopus has________tentacles.

PRACTICE TEST-7

Complete each sentence by forming an adjective from the noun in brackets.

(*a*) I fell asleep in the_______chair. (comfort)

(*b*) The________animal was captured by the park rangers. (danger)

(*c*) It was a_day when the________children left. (storm)

(*d*) Mr. Smith is a very_____person.(patience)

(*e*) This is an extremely_____painting. (value)

(*f*) The________film star visited our town recently. (fame)

PRACTICE TEST-8

Complete these sentences by writing the correct degree of the adjective in brackets.

(*a*) This is the_____building in thecity. (old)

(*b*) My puppy is__than your puppy. (young)

(*c*) My brother is________than me. (short)

(*d*) Today is________than yesterday. (cold)

(*e*) Katy bought the___toy in the shop. (dear)

(*f*) Tim's mouse was the________pet ofall the pets at our show. (small)

PRACTICE TEST-9

Complete these sentences by writing the correct degree of the adjective in brackets. Hint! If the adjective ends in –y, change the –y to –i before adding –er or –est.

(*a*) Mike must be the________boy in the whole school. (busy)

(*b*) This box is much_________than that one. (heavy)

(*c*) You always seem to be________than I am. (lucky)

(*d*) This kitten is the________of the whole litter. (noisy)

PRACTICE TEST-10

Circle the correct adjective. Hint! Some adjectives have irregular forms.

(*a*) He is (gooder, better) than me atmarbles.

(*b*) This is the (worst, baddest) day I've hadall year.

(*c*) Joanne has (littler, less) cherries that I have.

(*d*) Tom is the (morest, most) reliable boy in the grade.

ANSWERS (PRACTICE TESTS)

Q. No.	TEST – 1	TEST – 2	TEST – 3	TEST – 4	TEST – 5
1.	Broad	Interesting	Thick	Fresh	Peculiar
2.	Fragile	Clever	Fat	Dangerous	Careful
3.	Circular	Rusty	Sour	Deep	Sudden
4.	Stupid	Delicious	High	False	Serious
5.	Perilous	Woolen	Strong	Plump	Sharp
6.	Careful	Sunny	Minute	Foolish	Sacred
7.		Ripe	Scared		
8.		Savage	Big		

Q. No.	TEST – 6	TEST – 7	TEST – 8	TEST – 9	TEST – 10
1.	Twelve	Comfortable	Oldest	Busiest	Better
2.	Two	Dangerous	Younger	Heavier	Worst
3.	Ten	Stormy	Shorter	Luckier	Less
4.	Three	Patient	Colder	Noisiest	Most
5.	Hundred	Valuable	Dearest		
6.	Fifteen	Famous	Smallest		
7.	Four				
8.	Eight				

18 USE OF ARTICLES

12 PRACTICE TESTS

THE USE OF ARTICLES

A, an, and the are called Articles. They are in fact, demonstrative adjective which point out to the noun that comes after them.

Functionally, they are Determiners because they determine, fix, restrict, or define the noun coming after them.

1. Rahul wrote ***a*** letter to his sister.

2. ***The*** book is lying on the table.

3. Take ***an*** umbrella with you as it is raining.

In sentence 1, the article ***a*** modifies the noun letter by referring to it in a general way.

In sentence 2, ***the*** used before the noun book makes it a particular or specific book. The second ***'the'*** in this sentence modifies the noun table and makes it a particular or specific table.

In sentence 3, the article ***an*** refers, in a general way, to the noun after it: ***umbrella***. In all these sentences, the articles are used to determine, fix, or specify the nouns coming after them.

An article can also be used before an adjective if this adjective is followed by a noun. Consider the following examples.

4. Shivani is ***a*** beautiful girl.

5. Rahul is ***an*** intelligent boy.

6. ***The*** scenery of Shimla is ***a*** charming one.

In sentence 4, the article ***a*** comes before the adjective beautiful.

So do the articles ***an*** in sentences 5, and ***a*** in sentence 6.

But these articles are because of the nouns and not because of the adjective. This fact can be easily verified by removing the intervening adjectives.

Conversely, we can rewrite these sentences without using the adjectives and the nouns modified by them, but then we shall have to remove the articles also.

4. *(a)* Shivani ***is*** beautiful.

5. *(a)* Rahul ***is*** intelligent.

6. *(a)* The scenery of Shimla ***is*** charming.

Secondly, if an adverb comes before an adjective which is followed by a noun, the article is placed before the adverb:

4. *(b)* Shivani is a very beautiful girl.

5. *(b)* Rahul is a very intelligent boy.

6. *(b)* The scenery of Shimla is an extremely charming one.

In these examples too, though the articles come before adverbs, they are there because of the nouns and not because of the adverbs.

THE INDEFINTE AND THE DEFINITE ARTICLES

Articles are of two kinds: ***Definite and Indefinite.***

A and an are called Indefinite Articles because they refer in a general and indefinite way to the nouns that come after them.

1. A man was sitting in the shade of a tree.

2. An umbrella was lying on a bench in the park.

3. Give me an inkpot.

In sentences 1-3, the articles ***'a and an'*** refer to singular nouns in a general way. That is to say, all that the article ***'a'*** tells about the man in sentence 1 is that ***this man is only one.*** Apart from this, there is nothing specific about this man. This is also true of a tree in this sentence. ***It is one tree,*** but we do not know if there is anything specific about it.

In sentence 2, the noun umbrella is proceeded by ***'an', which suggests one umbrella.*** Here again, there is nothing specific about this umbrella. Any umbrella will do. Again, in sentence 3 ***an inkpot*** virtually ***means any one inkpot.***

4. Where is the present that he brought for me?

5. What happened to the book I gave you?

6. The girl in blue jeans is my fiancés.

You note that the article ***'the'*** in sentence 4 refers to a particular present – ***the one that he brought for me.*** It is not any or every present.

In sentence 5, ***'the'*** refers to a ***specific book – the book I gave you.***

Again, in sentence 6, ***'the'*** refers to a specific girl and not any or every girl: she is my fiancée.

The second thing to note about the definite article is that it can be used with both the singular and the plural nouns, while a and an can be used only with singular nouns. Compare the following sentences.

7. Where is the pen that I gave you?

8. Where are the pens that we bought from the market yesterday?

9. I am thankful to you for the gift you have brought.

10. I am thankful to you all for the gifts that you have brought.

THE USE OF 'A' AND 'AN'

As already mentioned, ***a*** and ***an*** are indefinite articles. They are used before singular nouns, and they refer to these nouns in a general way. The choice between ***a/an*** is determined by the initial sound of the noun before which the indefinite article is used.

When the initial sound of a noun is a vowel sound (a, e, i, o, and u are all vowels), we use an.

The indefinite article a is used when the initial sound is that of a consonant (all sounds except those created by a, e, i, o, u are consonant sounds).

THE USE OF THE INDEFINITE ARTICLE 'AN'

Rule 1. As mentioned above, ***'an'*** is used before a noun beginning with a vowel sound (a, e, i, o, u or any variant of their sounds).

1. She gave me an umbrella as it was raining.

2. An egg a day is good for health.

3. I have bought an inkpot from the store.

4. Suman is an accomplished woman.

Note: If the noun requiring an article is preceded by an adjective or an adverb and adjective, the choice of ***'a or an'*** is made on the basis of the initial sound of that adjective or adverb.

1. He has bought an elegant car.

2. Rohit is an extremely hardworking boy.

3. Sudha is an unreliable woman.

Rule 2. If a noun requiring an article begins with a consonant but that initial consonant is either silent or unstressed, we use ***'an'*** before it.

1. Abhay is an honest worker. (Honest is pronounced as onest.)

2. He was late by an hour. (Hour is pronounced as our.)

3. The rich old man is looking for an heir. (Heir is pronounced as air.)

THE USE OF THE INDEFINITE ARTICLE 'A'

Rule 1. The indefinite article a is used before nouns which begin with a consonant sound (All letters except a, e, i, o, u are consonants and have consonant sounds if the initial consonant is silent or unstressed).

1. I found a novel lying on the table of his bedroom.

2. A bird in hand is worth two in the bush.

3. There was a woman behind the whole episode.

Note: If a noun taking an indefinite article is proceeded by an adjective or an adverb + adjective, the article is used according to the initial sound of that adjective or adverb and not that of the noun. In case of '***a***', the adjective or the adverb + adjective combination must begin with a consonant sound.

1. This is a costly inkpot.

2. Prakash gave him a spoiled egg.

3. Ravi is a very honest man.

If the above sentences did not have adjectives/adverbs before them, all of them would take an and not a:

1. This is an inkpot.

2. Prakash gave him an egg.

3. Ravi is an honest man.

Rule 2. If a noun begins with a vowel but the sound of that vowel is that of a consonant, we use '***a***' before it.

1. A university is a place of higher learning (University is pronounced as ***y university***).

2. A one-eyed man was staring at Shalini. (One-eyed is pronounced as ***won-eyed***).

3. This may prove to a be a useful plan. (Useful is pronounced as ***youseful***).

The definite article the, unlike the indefinite articles a and an, can be used before both singular and plural nouns. The main consideration is that there must be something specific about the noun which follows the, ***the*** definite article.

Rule 1. ***To refer to specific persons, places and things:***

1. Put the book on the table. ***(A specific book and a specific table; not any book and any table)***

2. The girl in blue jeans is my fiancée. ***(one specific girl, the one in blue jeans)***

3. The boys who are sitting in the lawn have been detained. (Not all boys ***but only those sitting in the lawn,*** which is also a specific lawn.

Rule 2. ***To refer to a single noun when it is meant to represent the whole class:***

1. The rose smells sweet. ***(All roses smell sweet.)***

2. The cow is a very useful animal. ***(All cows are useful animals.)***

3. The whale yields huge quantities of oil. ***(All whales do so.)***

4. Child is the father of man.

Rule 3. Before a common noun which is unique, i.e., one of its own kind:

The sun, the moon, the earth, the universe, etc.

Rule 4. ***With names of rivers, canals, gulfs, straits, seas, oceans, groups of islands, deserts, bays, etc.***

1. ***The*** Ganga, ***The*** Nile, ***The*** Godavari (all rivers)

2. ***The*** Persian Gulf, ***The*** Palk Straits, ***The*** Bay of Bengal (gulfs, bays, and straits)

3. ***The*** Arabian Sea, ***The*** Red Sea, ***The*** Indian Ocean, ***The*** Atlantic Ocean, etc. (all seas and oceans)

4. ***The*** Andamans, ***The*** Maldives, ***The*** Nicobars (all islands)

5. ***The*** Suez Canal, ***The*** Sirhind Canal, ***The*** Upper Bari Doab Canal (all canals)

6. ***The*** Thar Desert, ***The*** Kalahari Desert, ***The*** Sahara Desert (all deserts)

7. ***The*** Himalayas, ***The*** Vindhyan, ***The*** Alps (all mountain ranges)

Rule 5. ***With places which derive their names from geographical, historical, or political factors:***

1. ***The*** Punjab, ***The*** Deccan Plateau, ***The*** USA, ***The*** United Kingdom, etc.

Rule 6. ***Before the names of epics and religious books:***

1. ***The*** Iliad, ***The*** Mahabharata, ***The*** Ramayana (all epics)

2. ***The*** Bible, ***The*** Quran, ***The*** Gita, ***The*** Vedas (all holy books)

Note: But when the name of the author precedes such a book, an epic or a holy book, no article is used:

1. Valmiki's Ramayana, Jerome's Bible

2. Homer's Iliad, Milton's Paradise Lost

Rule 7. ***Before the names of newspapers, Journals, magazines, weeklies, etc.:***

1. ***The*** Times of India, ***The*** Tribune, ***The*** Statesman, etc.

2. ***The*** Readers' Digest, ***The*** Eve's Weekly, ***The*** Punjab Journal of History, ***The*** Quest, etc.

Rule 8. ***Before adjectives in their superlative degree:***

1. This is ***the best*** book on history I have got.

2. Manish is ***the most*** intelligent boy in this class.

3. Suman is ***the rarest*** of the rarest blend of beauty and brain.

Rule 9. ***Before adjectives in the Comparative Degree when used in the following kind of constructions:***

1. ***The*** more, ***the*** merrier.

2. ***The*** higher you go, ***the*** cooler it is.

3. ***The*** more he earns, ***the*** more his wife spends.

Rule 10. ***Before adjectives in their comparative degree when one of the two is referred to:***

1. Suman is more beautiful of ***the*** two Godara sisters.

2. Rohit is better of ***the*** two students.

3. Karina is the more charming of ***the*** two actresses.

Rule 11. ***Before an adjective which is used as a plural noun and stands for a class, section, or group.***

1. ***The*** educated should help ***the*** illiterate.

2. ***The*** rich often detest ***the*** poor.

3. We should think of ***the*** welfare of ***the*** handicapped.

Rule 12. ***Before a proper noun when it is used as a common noun to indicate some special quantity associated with that proper noun:***

1. Kalidas is said to be ***the*** Shakespeare of India. (the greatest dramatist)

2. He boasts to ***the*** Sachin Tendulkar of his club.

3. Martin Luther king was described as ***the*** Gandhi of America.

Rule 13. ***Before a material noun when it is used as a common noun:***

1. ***The*** wheat of the Punjab is superior to that of Haryana.

2. ***The*** milk of this cow is richer in quality than that of the black one.

3. ***The*** gold mine in India is very expensive.

Rule 14. ***Before a proper noun if it is modified by an adjective:***

1. ***The*** great Gavaskar

2. ***The*** match-winning Tendulkar

3. ***The*** mercurial Sehwag

4. ***The*** sober Suman

5. ***The*** sweet Ruchika

6. ***The*** innocent Navjot

7. ***The*** stylish Kanni

8. ***The*** pure Anvi Singh

Rule 15. ***Before an abstract noun when it is used as a common noun:***

1. ***The*** beauty of Kashmir cannot be compared with the beauty of any other valley.

2. ***The*** performance of Kapil Dev as a world-class bowler remains still unbeaten.

3. ***The*** integrity of Suman is just like the integrity of Caesar's wife.

Rule 16. ***Before numbers indicating order or position:***

1. He was ***the last*** man in the queue.

2. You are ***the first*** person to call me dishonest.

3. You will find this information in ***the ninth*** chapter of this book.

Rule 17. ***Before a noun to give it the force or emphasis of a superlative:***

1. Philosophy is ***the subject*** to study.

2. Sushmita is ***the beautiful*** woman in this city.

Rule 18. ***Before the names of a community, nation, or race:***

1. ***The Jews*** are a well-knit race no matter where they live.

2. ***The Hindus***, like the Greeks, believe in many gods and goddesses.

3. ***The Rajputs*** consider themselves a martial race.

Rule 19. ***Before a common noun to give it the sense of an abstract noun:***

1. ***The best*** in him enjoyed the sight.

2. ***The mother*** in her was moved to tears on the sight of the orphan.

3. ***The soldier*** in him could not remain a silent spectator to foul play.

OMISSION OF THE ARTICLE

It is very important to know the use of articles. But it is no less important to know when or where articles are not used. There are, in fact, many words which do not take any article before them.

Rule 1. ***No article is used before a proper, material, and abstract noun when such a noun is used in its own form and not as a common noun:***

1. Mohit was hurt in an accident (No article before 'Mohit' which is a proper noun.)

2. Beauty is said to be nine days wonder. (No articles before 'beauty' which is an abstract noun, 'health' is an abstract noun.)

Rule 2. No article is used before the names of subjects, languages, arts, and sciences:

1. Physics, chemistry, philosophy, mathematics, economics, political science, etc. ***(All subjects)***

2. English, Punjabi, Hindi, Sanskrit, Greek, Latin, Persian, etc. ***(All languages)***

3. Music, sculpture, painting, poetry, etc. ***(All arts)***

Rule 3. ***No article is used before the names of relations:***

Mother, father, brother, sister, cousin, wife, husband, etc.

Rule 4. ***No article is used before 'school', 'college', 'hospital', 'bed', 'church', 'prison/ jail', 'gas', etc. when they are used or visited for the purpose for which they are meant:***

1. She is still lying-in bed.

2. The patient has been taken to hospital.
3. I go to church every Sunday.

Note: But when these places/things are used for other purposes, they take an article:

1. I went to the school to deposit my son's fee.
2. He went to the prison to see his brother, who is a jailer there.
3. The mason went to the church to repair its damaged parts.

***Rule 5.* No article is used before plural nouns if there is nothing specific about them:**

1. Women who drink make bad mothers.
2. Scientists believe in rational thinking.
3. Men, women, and children were passing through the streets.

***Rule 6.* No article is used before certain nouns which figure in certain propositional phrases:**

At home, at night, by day, by train, by bus, at sunset, on earth, in jest, on horseback, underground, in debt, by day and night, etc.

***Rule 7.* No article is used before certain singular nouns when they form a part of phrase or consists of a transitive verb:**

To set foot, to bring word, to lay siege, to set sail, to lose heart, to take offence, etc.

***Rule 8.* No article is used before 'man', 'woman', and 'child' even when they refer to the whole class.**

1. Man is the maker of his own destiny.
2. Woman belongs to the fairer but the weaker sex.
3. Child is the father of man.

***Rule 9.* No article is used before nouns acting as subject complements when they denote a position held by only one man at time:**

1. Dr. A.P.J. Abdul Kalam was elected President.
2. Rohit became principal of this school two years ago.

USE OF ARTICLES - CATEGORY – 1 (PRACTICE TESTS)

Fill in the blanks with suitable articles in all the following sets.

PRACTICE TEST-1

1. I saw _______ snake in _______ grass.
2. _______ boy ran across _______ street.
3. I have waited for _______ hour.
4. It is _______ old house.
5. _______ moon is shining in sky.
6. I need _______ book of verse.
7. There is _______ big tree in front of _______ house.
8. Delhi is _______ capital of India.
9. It is _______ airy room.
10. ______ book on _______ table is new.

PRACTICE TEST-2

1. _______ Asia is a big continent.
2. _______ Deccan is in the South of India.
3. _______ Punjab is ____ land of five rivers.
4. _______ Times has _______ high reputation for reliable news.
5. _______ Narmada and _______ Tapti flow into _______ Arabian Sea.
6. _______ Vindhyas separate _______ Gangetic plain from _______ Deccan.
7. _______ Ravi left Singapore.
8. They stared at _______ Pacific from _______ top of _______ mountain.
9. _______ West Wind wakens _______ Mediterranean from its summer dream.
10. Do you read _______ Times of India?

PRACTICE TEST-3

1. If _______ gold rusts, what will _______ iron do?
2. She has _______ endurance, _______ foresight, _______ strength, and _______ skill.
3. Keats tried to be _______ Milton of _______ Romantic age.
4. _______ tiger is _______ wild animal.
5. _______ milk in that bottle has become sour.

6. _______ coal of Jharia belt is very rich.
7. Beware of _____fury of _____patient man.
8. You should come here by___shortest route.
9. _____donkeys are _______ stupid animals.
10. ____ girls do not often wear ____ hats.

PRACTICE TEST-4

1. _______ young man was sent to _______ prison for hitting _______ old man on _______ head.
2. _______ youngest brother went to _______ school in _______ morning. I will go to _______ school now to fetch him home.
3. If _____rich grow richer and _______ poor poorer, the country will go to_______ dogs.
4. _____ ship has come to ______ port. ______ port has been recently repaired.
5. Not always is ____ race to _____ swift or _______ battle to _______ strong.
6. My mother went to _______ market and bought _______ pound of _______ sugar.
7. We should help _______ needy and not _______ affluent.
8. You should take _______ umbrella when you go _______ office because it may rain today.
9. _______ young and _______ old rejoiced at his success.
10. _____crack troops went into_______ battle.

PRACTICE TEST-5

1. There is_____garden behind______ house.
2. _______ dog ran across _______ street.
3. We choose _______ knave or _______ eunuch to rule over us.
4. April is _______ cruelest month.
5. _______ eye for _______ eye and _______ tooth for _______ tooth, that was _______ old law.
6. Have you seen _______ Pope?
7. _______ people of _____Deccan are hardy.
8. The cavalry rode into _______ battle.
9. I am going ____ market to buy _____ book.
10. I shall visit _______ prison to see _______ prisoner.

PRACTICE TEST-6

1. Life is _____ tale told by ______ idiot.
2. _______ sun rises in _______ east and sets in _______ west.
3. You should be kind to _______ old and _______ sick.
4. Drink ______ plenty of _______ water.
5. _______ water of _______ Caspian Sea is blackish.
6. How is _______ circle different from _______ ellipse?
7. We were on board _______ Maharajah.
8. Read _______ Times of India regularly.
9. I travelled in _______ third-class carriage in _______ company of some Americans who could speak _______ French.
10. _______ clouds over _______ sea are lovely in _______ morning.

USE OF ARTICLES - CATEGORY – 2 (PRACTICE TESTS)

Fill in the blanks with suitable articles in all the following sets.

PRACTICE TEST-1

1. I saw _______ snake in _______ grass.
   (a) in, the (b) the, in
   (c) a, the (d) a, in
2. _______ boy ran across _______ street.
   (a) the, to (b) the, at
   (c) a, to (d) a, the
3. I have waited for _______ hour.
   (a) an (b) to
   (c) in (d) none of these
4. It is _______ old house.
   (a) an (b) to
   (c) in (d) at
5. _______ moon is shining in sky.
   (a) a (b) the
   (c) an (d) none of these

6. I need _______ book of verse.
(a) the (b) a
(c) few (d) to

7. There is _______ big tree in front of _______ house.
(a) an, the (b) the, an
(c) to, an (d) a, the

8. Delhi is _______ capital of India.
(a) the (b) a
(c) an (d) none of these

9. It is _______ airy room.
(a) a (b) an
(c) the (d) none of these

10. _______ book on _______ table is new.
(a) the, a (b) a, the
(c) an, the (d) the, an

PRACTICE TEST-2

1. _______ old horse stumbles and nods.
(a) an (b) a
(c) the (d) none of these

2. Here I am _______ old man being read to by_______ boy.
(a) an, the (b) the, an
(c) an, a (d) a, an

3. _______ old man is like _______ tattered coat upon _______ stick.
(a) an, the, the (b) on, an, the
(c) an, on, the (d) the, on, with

4. _______ shepherd in _______ field is playing on_______ pipe.
(a) a, the, the (b) on, the, an
(c) an, on, the (d) the, on, the

5. He gave me _______ guava and _______orange.
(a) a, an (b) an, an
(c) an, the (d) the, an

6. _______ Asia is a big continent.
(a) the (b) a
(c) an (d) none of these

7. _______ Deccan is in the South of India.
(a) the (b) an
(c) a (d) none of these

8. _______ Punjab is _______ land of five rivers.
(a) the, the (b) a, a
(c) the, a (d) none of these

9. _______ Times has _______ high reputation for reliable news.
(a) the, the (b) the, a
(c) a, the (d) none of these

10. _______ Narmada and _______ Tapti flow into_______ Arabian Sea.
(a) the, the, a (b) the, a, the
(c) a, the, a (d) the, the, the

PRACTICE TEST-3

1. _______ Vindhyas separate _______ Gangetic plain from _______ Deccan.
(a) a, the, the (b) the, a, the
(c) the, the, a (d) the, the, the

2. _______ Ravi left Singapore.
(a) the (b) a
(c) an (d) none of these

3. They stared at _______ Pacific from _______top of _______ mountain.
(a) the, the, the (b) the, a, the
(c) an, an, the (d) none of these

4. _______West Wind wakens _______ Mediterranean from its summer dream.
(a) the, an (b) the, the
(c) a, the (d) none of these

5. Do you read _______ Times of India?
(a) the (b) a
(c) an (d) none of these

6. If _______ gold rusts, what will _______ iron do?
(a) the, the (b) the, a
(c) an, the (d) a, an

7. She has _______ endurance, _______ foresight, _______ strength, and _______ skill.
(a) the, an, a, the (b) the, a, an, the
(c) an, a, the, a (d) the, the, the, the

8. Keats tried to be _______ Milton of _______Romantic age.
(a) the, the (b) a, an
(c) a, the (d) the, a

9. _______ tiger is _______ wild animal.
(a) the, the (b) a, the
(c) the, a (d) the, an

10. ______milk in that bottle has become sour.

(a) an (b) the
(c) a (d) none of these

PRACTICE TEST-4

1. _______ coal of Jharia belt is very rich.

(a) the (b) a
(c) an (d) none of these

2. Beware of______fury of_____patient man.

(a) the, the (b) a, an
(c) the, a (d) the, an

3. You should come here by _______ shortest route.

(a) the (b) a
(c) an (d) none

4. _______ donkeys are _______ stupidest animals.

(a) the, the (b) the, a
(c) a, the (d) the, an

5. _____girls do not often wear _______ hats.

(a) the, the (b) an, the
(c) the, an (d) none of these

6. ____few students who read for ____ knowledge do not care for _______ results.

(a) a, the, the (b) the, the, the
(c) the, an, the (d) a, an, the

7. Only _______ few books should be chewed and digested.

(a) a (b) the
(c) little (d) none of these

8. _______ memory is _______ fond deceiver.

(a) the, the (b) a, the
(c) the, a (d) a, a

9. This is _______ finest song I have ever heard.

(a) the (b) a
(c) an (d) none of these

10. _______ happiness is _______ inner state of mind.

(a) the, the (b) a, the
(c) the, a (d) none of these

PRACTICE TEST-5

1. _____young man was sent to______ prison for hitting______old man on _______ head.

(a) a, the, the, a (b) a, the, a, the
(c) the, the, a, a (d) a, the, an, the

2. _______ youngest brother went to _______school in ______morning. I will go to _______school now to fetch him home.

(a) a, the, a, the (b) the, a, the, a
(c) a, an, the, a (d) the, the, the, the

3. If______rich grow richer and _______ poor poorer, the country will go to_______ dogs.

(a) the, the, the (b) a, an, the
(c) the, a, an (d) the, an, a

4. _______ ship has come to _______ port. _______port has been recently repaired.

(a) a, an, the, the (b) the, the, a, a
(c) a, an, the, the (d) a, the, the

5. Not always is _______ race to _______ swift or_______ battle to _______ strong.

(a) a, an, the, a (b) the, a, an, the
(c) the, an, the, a (d) a, the, a, the

6. My mother went to _______ market and bought_______ pound of _______ sugar.

(a) the, the, a (b) a, the, the
(c) the, a, the (d) none of these

7. We should help _______ needy and not _______affluent.

(a) the, the (b) a, a
(c) a, the (d) the, a

8. You should take _______ umbrella when you go_______ office because it may rain today.

(a) the, a (b) a, the
(c) an, the (d) the, a

9. _______ young and _______ old rejoiced at his success.

(a) the, the (b) a, a
(c) a, the (d) the, a

10. _______ crack troops went into _______ battle.

(a) a, a (b) the, a
(c) a, the (d) none of these

PRACTICE TEST-6

1. There is _______ garden behind _______ house.

(a) a, an (b) a, the
(c) an, the (d) the, an

2. _______ dog ran across _______ street.
(a) the, the (b) the, a
(c) a, the (d) a, a

3. We choose _______ knave or _______ eunuch to rule over us.
(a) a, the (b) the, a
(c) the, the (d) a, a

4. April is _______ cruellest month.
(a) the (b) a
(c) an (d) none of these

5. _______ eye for _______ eye and _______ tooth for _______ tooth, that was _______ old law.
(a) the, the, a, an, the (b) the, the, an, an, a
(c) the, an, an, a, the (d) an, an, a, a, an

6. Have you seen _______ Pope?
(a) a (b) the
(c) an (d) none of these

7. _______ people of _______ Deccan are hardy.
(a) the, the (b) a, the
(c) the, a (d) none of these

8. The cavalry rode into _______ battle.
(a) a (b) the
(c) an (d) none of these

9. I am going to_______ market to buy _______book.
(a) a, an (b) the, a
(c) a, a (d) none of these

10. I shall visit _______ prison to see _______prisoner.
(a) a, an (b) the, the
(c) the, an (d) the, a

ANSWERS – CATEGORY – 1 (PRACTICE TESTS)

Q. No.	TEST – 1	TEST – 2	TEST – 3	TEST – 4
1.	a, the	the	the, the	a, the, an, the
2.	a, the	the	the, the, the, the	the, the, the, the
3.	an	the, the	the, the	the, the, the
4.	an	the, the	the, a	a, the, the
5.	the	the, the, the	the	a, the, a, the
6.	a	the, the, the	the	the, a, the
7.	a, the	the	the, a	the, the
8.	the	the, the, the	the	an, the
9.	an	the, the	the, the	the, the
10.	the, a	the	the, the	the, a

Q. No.	TEST – 5	TEST – 6
1.	a, the	a, an
2.	a, the	the, the, the
3.	a, a	an, the
4.	the	none of these
5.	an, an, a, a, an	the, the
6.	the	a, an
7.	the, the	the
8.	a	the
9.	the, a	a, the, the
10.	the, a	the, the, the

ANSWERS – CATEGORY – 2 (PRACTICE TESTS)

Q. No.	*TEST – 1*	*TEST – 2*	*TEST – 3*	*TEST – 4*	*TEST – 5*	*TEST – 6*
1.	c	a	d	a	d	b
2.	d	a	a	c	d	c
3.	a	a	a	a	a	d
4.	a	a	b	a	d	a
5.	b	a	a	a	d	d
6.	b	a	a	a	c	b
7.	d	a	d	a	a	a
8.	a	a	a	c	c	a
9.	b	b	c	a	a	b
10.	a	d	b	a	b	d

19 PREPOSITIONS

32 PRACTICE TESTS

A preposition is a word used to show the way in which other words are connected to each other.It is used to express basic relationships between words. You can express relationships of time andplace by using a preposition. For example:

- I can see you on Friday/in October/at 7 pm/for an hour, etc.
- I'll meet you at the university/in Delhi/outside the library/on the Delhi college campus, etc.

Besides the relationships of time and place, you can use prepositions to express many other different kinds of relationships. For example:

- means - She came by train/on foot/in a motorcar, etc.
- manner - She spoke with a smile/in a sweet tone.
- reaction - I was shocked at his sudden death/by his cruel joke.
- reason - I did for my country/out of duty /because of my countrymen.

A preposition is, then, a link in the chain of a sentence. It ties a noun or pronoun to the rest of the sentence. For example:

- Write your address in the notebook.
- There is a rat under the bed.
- This piece of chalk is for you.
- This letter is from him.

Preposition can be used in a sentence to show space, or time, or direction, or agency, or association, etc. For example:

- A few books have been placed on thedesk. (showing space)
- He arrived before lunch. (showing time)
- I walked to the town/towards the farm. (showing direction)

It was done by the night watchman with aknife. (showing agency)

- He left without hope. (showing association)

The use of different prepositions in a sentence gives us different shades of meaning. For example:

- Suman danced for Govinda. (for the sakeof Govinda)
- Suman danced with Govinda. (They danced together)
- Suman danced after Govinda. (after Govinda had finished dancing)
- Suman danced behind Govinda. (with Govinda in the front)

A particular preposition can often be used to express different shades of meaning. For example:

- We will meet you after 2 o'clock. (later than)
- Put the direct object after the verb. (nextin order to, following)
- It is a painting after Picasso. (in the style of)
- The police ran after the thief. (in pursuit of, in search of)
- She enquired after your health. (regarding)
- A son takes after his father. (resembles)
- After all my care, it was broken. (in spite of)
- Shut the door after you, when you leave the room. (behind)
- I shall never speak to him after what he has said about me. (in view of, as a result of)

Sometimes the same word requires different prepositions to express various situations. Take, for example, the words 'die' and 'divide':

- He died of cancer. He died from the loss of blood.
- He died through neglect. He died in atrain accident.
- He died by his own hand. He died for his country.
- Divide this mango in half. Divide this mango into four parts.

- Divide forty by eight. Divide these apples between the two children.
- Let me divide the property among my four sons.

Also note the following examples:

- Alive in every nerve; alive to every noble impulse; alive with fervor, hope, resolve; alive through all his being.
- Alliance with a neighbouring people; against the common enemy; for offence and defence; alliance of, between, or among nations.
- Agree in opinion with the speaker; to the terms proposed; persons agree on or upon a statement of principles, rules, etc.; we must agree among ourselves.

A particular preposition can often be used to express more than one kind of relationship. For example:

- time - by next month;
  - on the appointed hour;
- place - by the window;
  - on the tree top;
- means - by working overtime;
  - on a bicycle.

Time: at, by, between, before, after, during, in, on, to, from for, since, throughout, till, until	*Place/position: at, above, across, against, before, behind, in, on, over, under*
He came at 7 o'clock.	He is at home.
He will start after lunch.	He has no roof above his head.
It has rained for a week.	There is a cap on his head.
He will come by 7 o'clock.	The thief stood before the judge.
He will go out during pujas.	He is sitting under a tree.
He came on Monday.	He is in his room.
She will return before dinner.	There is an umbrella over his head.
It has been raining since Monday.	He will come before Rajesh.
He was here throughout summer.	
Direction: above, into, on, to, towards, up, down	*Relative position: between, among, amongst*
He is above me in rank.	There is friendship between him and me.
He fell into a river.	There is unity among the people.
He is kind towards the poor.	There is a village among the hills.
He climbed up a tree.	There is no difference amongst us.
He fired on the enemy.	
Destination: to, from	*State/conditions: at, in, on, under Change of state: at, in, on, under*
He is going to the market.	He is at work.
He is coming from the school.	That house is under repair.
Boys are at play.	He is in good health.
	He died in misery.
	Translate into English.
	Love turned into hatred.
Aim/goal/purpose/ target: for	*Origin/source: from, of*
He bought a pen for 10 rupees.	This road runs from Patna to Gaya.
He died for his society.	He comes of a rich family.

He has started for Bombay.	I borrowed a book from the library.
He lives for others.	It is a poem of Dinkar.
Separation: from, of, off	***Relation/possession: of***
Leaves are falling from the tree.	This is the house of my friend.
He is off duty now.	He is a servant of my uncle.
He is away from home.	
The dog jumped off the chair.	
He was robbed of his money.	
Material/ingredient: of, from	***Part/portion: of***
This chair is made of wood.	This is the window of this house.
We make butter from milk.	This is the horn of my car.
	Give me a piece of chalk.
Means/instrument: by, in, with, without	***Manner: like, with***
He came here by car.	He is like his father.
He was struck by lightning.	I look upon this work with pride.
It is written in ink.	He treated me with kindness.
Means/instrument: by, in, with, without	***Manner: like, with***
He speaks in English.	He heard me with sympathy.
We see with our eyes.	
This play was written by Mohan.	
The house was destroyed by fire.	
It is written in pencil.	
She writes in Hindi.	
We can't see without eyes.	
Cause: from, of, for, with	***Accompaniment: with, without***
He died from loss of blood.	I played with them.
He died of cholera.	He came without his wife.
He will suffer for his bad habits.	
He is sick with tears.	
Measurement/standard: at, by, for, to	
Rice sells at INR 41/- a kilo.	
It is 10 by my watch.	
He is good at painting.	
She is good at cooking.	
Mangoes sell two to a rupee.	
He is clever at games.	
Support/opposition: for, against	***Subject/matter: on, about***
I stand for my friend.	I am reading a book on English grammar.
He is against me.	I told him about my school.

PREPOSITIONS IN DAILY USE	
Abide by	You must abide by your promise.
Abound in, with	The tank abounds in fish.
Absent from	She is absent from the school today.
Abstain from	He should abstain from drinking.
Absorbed in	Pranav is absorbed in his work.
Access to	I have no access to the minister.
Act upon	He did not act upon his teacher's advice.
Accede to	The Principal did not accede to my request.
Account for	How do you account for your failure?
Accused	He was accused of theft.
Accomplished in	She is accomplished in painting.
Accustomed to	The farmer is accustomed to hard labour.
Accompanied by	When I went there, I was accompanied by my brother.
Acquit of	The judge acquitted him of all the charges.
Admit into	He was admitted into the 7th class.
Admit to	He was admitted to the college.
Addicted to	His father is addicted to gambling.
Advantage of	She took advantage of my leniency.
Advantage over	India gained an advantage over Pakistan in Lahore sector.
Affection for	I have great affection for her.
Affectionate to	She is affectionate to her parents.
Agree with	I do not agree with you in this matter.
Agree to	Mahima did not agree to my proposal.
Aim at	The hunter aimed at the tiger.
Alarmed at	We were alarmed at the news.

PREPOSITIONS IN DAILY USE	
Alive to	I'm alive to my duties.
Alive with	The street is alive with people.
Ambition of	He is ambitious of honour.
Amazed at	I was amazed at his behaviour.
Amused with	Day amused us with many jokes.
Angry with	It appears that he is angry with me.
Angry at	I'm angry at his rude behaviour.
Annoyed at	She felt annoyed at my remarks.
Anxious for	He is anxious for the health of his son.
Apologies to (aperson)	He apologised to me for his misconduct.
Aptitude for	Suchita has special aptitude for music.
Appeal to, for	He appealed to the government for help.
Appoint to	Mr. Chopra has been appointed to the post of the headmaster.
Apply to	He applied to the principal for free concession.
Apply for	Did you apply for this post?
Arrive at	The train arrived at the station.
Arrive in	The British Prime Minister arrived in India.
Ashamed of	You should be ashamed of your conduct.
Assent to (agree)	He readily assented to my proposal.
Assure of	I assured him of my help.
Astonished at	I was astonished at his failure.
Associate with	You should not associate with bad boys.
Attend to	Please attend to the work.
Attend upon	Many servants attend upon her.
Attachment to	I have a sentimental attachment to Shimla.
Attention to	Pay attention to what I say.
Avail of	She did not avail herself of the opportunity.

PREPOSITIONS IN DAILY USE	
Averse to	He is averse to hard work.
Avenge on	We must avenge ourselves on the Chinese.
Award to	The prize was awarded to the best speaker.
Aware of	I am aware of my short-comings.
Bark at	The dog barked at the passer-by.
Beg of	He begged a favour of me.
Beg for	The criminal begged for mercy.
Believe in	I believe in god.
Belong to	Does this book belong to you?
Beware of	Beware of pickpockets.
Bent on	He is bent on disturbing the class.
Blessed with	He has been blessed with a son.
Blind of	He is blind of one eye.
Blind to	He is blind to his weaknesses.
Born to	A son was born to him.
Born of	He was born of poor parents.
Blame for	I do not blame you for my loss.
Boast of	Do not boast of your riches.
Bound for	This ship is bound for Japan.
Borrow from	He borrowed a book from me.
Break into	The thief broke into his house last night.
Bear with (tolerate)	I cannot bear with such insulting remarks.
Break down	He broke down in the middle of his speech.
Begin with	The function began with a song.
Beset with	Life is beset with difficulties.
Blush at	She blushed at his remark.
Burst into	She burst into tears.
Certain of	I am certain of my success in the examination.
Confidence of	We are confident of our ultimate victory.
Confident in	My confidence in him has been shaken.
Care for	Nobody cares for a poor man.

PREPOSITIONS IN DAILY USE	
Care of	You should take care of your health.
Connive at	Do not connive at the faults of your son.
Charged with	He was charged with murder.
Capable of	He is capable of doing anything.
Compare with	The teacher compared Kashmir with Switzerland.
Cure of	The doctor cured him of the disease.
Confide in	I confide in him.
Confide to	He confided his secrets to me.
Comply with	I am sorry I cannot comply with your request.
Conscious of	He is conscious of his weakness.
Complain to	He complained to the teacher against me.
Content with	One should be content with one's lot.
Consist of	This class consists of eighty girls.
Convict of	He was convicted of murder.
Convince of	She was convinced of my sincerity.
Control over	He has no control over his children.
Congratulate on	I congratulated her on her brilliant success.
Count on	You can surely count on my help.
Correspond with	He corresponded with me on this matter.
Call on	I shall call on you tomorrow.
Call at	I called at her place, but she was not there.
Call for	Such conduct calls for punishment.
Contrary to	He worked contrary to my wishes.
Cheat of	He cheated me of ten rupees.
Come of	He comes of a noble family.
Conceal from	He concealed many facts from me.

PREPOSITIONS IN DAILY USE	
Cruel to	We should not be cruel to animals.
Cling to	The child clings to its mother.
Commence on	Our examination commences on the 17th of April.
Confer on	Many titles were conferred on him.
Confer with	He conferred with his father.
Consent to	She consented to my pro-posal.
Consist in	Happiness consists in content-ment.
Cope with	He could not cope with the heavy rush of work.
Crowned with	His efforts were crowned with success.
Courteous to	We should be courteous to all people.
Crave for	A hungry man craves for food.
Depend on	I depend on my brother for help.
Deal in	His father deals in sugar.
Deal with	He deals with his servants nicely.
Deaf to	He was deaf to my request.
Deprive of	I was deprived of my share.
Desirous of	He is desirous of helping me.
Devoid	This news is devoid of truth.
Demand for	There is a great demand for this book.
Die of	He died of cholera.
Die from	He died from overwork.
Differ with	I differ with him on this point.
Dispense with	He dispensed with his services.
Deficient in	He is deficient in common sense.
Devote to	She is devoted to her husband.
Doubtful of	We are doubtful of his success.
Derive from	He did not derive any benefit from this scheme.
Desire for	He has no desire for wealth.
Deter from	Nothing can deter me from performing my duty.
Different from	His plan is quite different from

PREPOSITIONS IN DAILY USE	
	mine.
Disgusted with	He is thoroughly disgusted with his life.
Dissuade with	I dissuaded him from going there.
Drive out	He must drive out the invaders.
Dull of	This boy is dull of under-standing.
Duty to	We must do our duty to our country.
Dedicate to	We should dedicate our lives to the service of the national cause.
Eat into	Rust eats into iron.
Eligible for	You are not eligible for this post.
Elate with	He was elated with the news.
Employ in	She is employed in the office.
Enquire of	She enquired of me about my health.
Enquire into	You must enquire into the matter.
Enquire after	I went to enquire after Renu's health.
Fail in	He failed in the examination.
Feed on	Cows feed on grass.
Entrust to	Can I entrust the task to you?
Escape from	The prisoner escaped from the jail.
Faith in	Have faith in god and do the right thing
Fail in	He failed in the examination.
Familiar with	I am not familiar with him.
Familiar to	Her face is familiar to me.
Fatal to	The accident proved fatal to him.
Gifted with	She is gifted with common sense.
Glad at	I am glad at your arrival.
Good at	He is good at mathematics.
Good for	Exercise is good for health.
Guilty of	He was found guilty of urder.
Hard of	The old man is hard of hearing.

PREPOSITIONS IN DAILY USE	
Hanker after	Why should you be always hankering after wealth?
Hinder from	I did not hinder her from going there.
Honest in	I always find him honest in his dealings.
Impertinent to	The servant was impertinent to his master.
Indulge in	Do not indulge in tall talk.
Insist in	He insisted on seeing her personally.
Jealous of	I am not jealous of his fame.
Jump at	She jumped at the conclusion soon.
Junior to	He is junior to me by two years.
Jeer at	Do not jeer at the poor.
Key to	Industry is the key to success in life.
Kind to	You should be kind to the poor.
Keen on	I am very keen on getting this job.
Keep to	Please keep to the left.
Lead to	This road leads to Shimla.
Lament for	He lamented for the loss of his property.
Listen to	Please listen to what I say.
Liable to	Everybody is liable to make a mistake.
Laugh at	Do no laugh at the poor man.
Look after	My son will look after the business in my absence.
Malice against	I bear no malice against anybody.
Moved by	He was not moved by my entreaties.
Mad with	He was mad with rage.
Match for	She is not a match for you.
Meet with	He met with an accident.
Need of	He is badly in need of money.
Necessary for	Exercise is necessary for health.
Negligent in	This boy is negligent in his work.

PREPOSITIONS IN DAILY USE	
Neglectful	He is neglectful of his duties.
Obedient to	Children should be obedient to their parents.
Obliged to	I am obliged to you for this kindness.
Object to	I strongly object to your proposal.
Opposed to	He is opposed to my plans.
Overwhelmed with	She was overwhelmed with grief.
Offence at	She took offence at my remarks.
Part with	He cannot part with money.
Part from	He parted from his son.
Participate in	You must participate in games.
Partial to	You should be partial to none.
Prepare for	I am preparing for the examination.
Qualified for	I don't think he is qualified for this job.
Quarrel with, over	It is foolish to quarrel with anybody over a trifle matter.
Quick of	She is quick of understanding.
Quick at	He is quick at figures.
Recover from	He has recovered from his illness.
Rejoice in	He rejoiced in his own success.
Refer to	We should refer this matter to the Principal.
Reconcile to	She reconciled herself to her fate.
Rely on	You cannot rely on that selfish fellow.
Repent of	I repented of my folly.
Satisfied with	The teacher is satisfied with his behaviour.
Sensitive to	She is very sensitive to cold.
Send for	Please send for the doctor at once.
Shocked at	We are shocked at the news.
Sick of	He is sick of her dull life.
Taste for	He has no taste for music.
Tide over	Try to tide over your difficulties.

PREPOSITIONS IN DAILY USE	
Take after	Bindu takes after her mother.
Teem with	This tank teems with fish.
True to	He is true to his word.
Unfit for	He is unfit for service.
Useful to	This book is really useful to me.
Vain of	She is vain of her beauty.
Versed in	She is well-versed in domestic chores.
Vexed with, at	I am vexed with him at his rude behaviour.
Vote for	He voted for the Congress candidate.
Vote against	Ten members voted against the bill.
Variance with	His views are at variance with mine.
Vouch for	I cannot vouch for the truth of his statement.

PREPOSITIONS IN DAILY USE	
Wait for	I waited for her but she did not turn up.
Wait on	The deputation waited on the minister.
Warm against	The teacher warned the class against making a noise.
Wanting in	He is wanting in common sense.
Worthy of	Our professor is worthy of praise.
Yearn for	He yearns for her love.
Yield to	He yielded to my entreaties.
Zeal for	I have a great zeal for work.
Zealous for	He is zealous for fame in the world.

PREPOSITIONS (PRACTICE TESTS)

Fill in the blanks with suitable prepositions:

PRACTICE TEST-1

The dowry system degenerated (1)_______ an evil custom. It becomes necessary (2)________ the parents (3)________ girls to give good dowry (4) _______their daughters. The married life (5) _______a girl depends (6)________the size (7) _______the dowry (8) _______their daughters. A successful and happy married life becomes impossible (9)________the absence (10)_______a handsome dowry. Newspapers are full (11) _______reports carrying tales (12) _______brides being burnt (13)________death or driven (14) _______hang themselves because (15)________constant nagging by their in-laws.

PRACTICE TEST-2

Cricket is a game known (1)_________its wonderful glories. It is popular (2)________ men and women (3)_________all ages. People used to go to see a cricket test match (4) ________thousands. They used to see a match (5) ________five days. Many a times, the match would end (6)_________a draw. But things have changed (7)________ the introduction (8)________one-day matches. This kind (9)___________cricket has certainly caught the fancy (10)_______the people. There is no need to wait (11)________ five days. Now (12)________ the outcome (13)________ the match is now decided the same day.

PRACTICE TEST-3

In modern times, books are being published (1) ______very large numbers (2)________ all subjects under the sun. It is not possible (3)_________a man to read all (4)_________them. Reading gives us a lot (5)__________pleasure. Books delight and educate (6)_________the same time. They give us a message (7)___________universal brotherhood. They tell us that a man should go on doing his work without worrying (8)________ the results.

PRACTICE TEST-4

It is (1)________ the very nature (2)_________ adversity to bring out the best (3)_________man, develop his latent abilities and lead him (4) _______a path (5)_________ prosperity and progress. The history (6)________ the world is the story (7)_____the survival (8)_____the fittest. In the course of time, man, through his heroic struggle against the adverse circumstances, came out (9)________ the forest, changed the face (10) ____the universe and landed (11)_______the moon.

PRACTICE TEST-5

I was astonished to see his capabilities as a journalist. I just had a look (1)________his face. He was trying to prove his position. He was really a man (2)________letters but unfortunately, he was blind (3)_________ one eye. I looked (4) _______the portrait (5)______a lady hanging (6) _______the wall. I went to take a round (7) _______his houseand I saw a family photograph. Mr. Blacksmithwas sitting (8)_______his wife and son (9) _______the photograph. After spending some time (10)________ him, I came back home.

PRACTICE TEST-6

Life is not a bed (1) _______thorn. Those who understand the reality (2) _______ life are winners, not losers. One has to go (3) _______ a lot (4) _______ trials and tribulations (5) _______taking a right decision or (6) _______ making a right choice. God has given us tremendous power to think and decide. But most (7) _______ us are ignorant (8) _______our capabilities. Move (9) _______ the destination (10) _______ any doubts or fear. This behavior will lead us (11) _______ greater heights. people (12) _______ norms (13) _______our culture. These days a lot (14) _____social organisations are coming forward to settle the disputes (15) ____husbands and wives.

PRACTICE TEST-7

Translation is an art. Good translation is the result (1)________practice and patience. It requires the skill to translate word and ideas (2)________ one language (3)_________ another. Literal translation (4)__________a sentence sometimes spoils the spirit (5)_________the language and sounds funny. One should translate words and ideas (6)________ precision. It is essential to be equally well versed (7)_______both the languages.

PRACTICE TEST-8

Positive thoughts are the wings (1) _______success. One should always look (2) _______the positive side (3)________life. We should not let negative thoughts come (4) _______our mind. Everybody should have this approach (5)__________life. Always hope (6) ________the best and believe (7)________God. He is always there to take care (8)__________his children. God is too great to ask (9)_____the price (10)_____the gifts hehas bestowed (11)________us.

PRACTICE TEST-9

First and foremost, (1)_________the blessings of civilisation are order and safety. We should not quarrel (2) _______each other. In disputes (3) _______man and man, right has taken the place (4) _______might. Law protects us (5)________ robbery and violence. Nobody can come and break (6)_________our house, steal our goods or run off (7)______our children. Many of us act (8)_thinking. This habit has injured the feelings (9)______many and has turned friends (10)________enemies.

PRACTICE TEST-10

The secret (1) _______a successful marriage is how we understand and believe each other. Those who involve themselves (2)________litigations are far (3) _______understanding the true meaning (4) _______marriage. As the time is changing, the divorce ratio is (5) _______the rise. Divorce is looked (6) _______as an evil (7) _______our society. Successful marriage depends (8)_______ cooperation and adjustment. The Government should take strict action (9) _______those who deliberately try to spoil the happiness (10) ______their better halves. The need (11) _______the hour is to acquaint the people (12) _______ norms (13)_________our culture. These days a lot (14)_________social organisations are coming forward to settle the disputes (15) _______husbands and wives.

PRACTICE TEST-11

Paul's family led a life (1)________ tension and anxiety. It was because the family always tried to keep a high standard (2) _______life. Paul wanted to bring luck (3)________the family. Once he thought (4)________a plan to help his mother. He borrowed some money (5)________a friend. But he had to go on borrowing as the expense also went up. There is no end (6) _______expenditure. We cannot have control (7)________expenditure. The evil has to come (8)________an end.

PRACTICE TEST-12

We belong (1) _______a country which is known (2)_________traditions and cultures. Ours isa country (3)_______Buddha, Guru Nanak and Mahatma Gandhi. It is (4) _______record that several people sacrificed their lives to save the honour (5)_______their country. We cannot forget their sacrifice and the way they fought manybattles (6)_______the sake (7)_______their country. We should also come forward and be ready to do anything (8) _______our country. We must love our country (9)_______the bottom (10) _______our heart

PRACTICE TEST-13

Once there lived a hermit (1) _______a forest. He was very kind (2) _______others. He lived alife away (3) _______worldly pleasure. Anybody who came (4)_______him (5)_______his help was always greeted (6) _______a smile. He triedhis best of help the needy. All the people felt grateful (7)_______him (8)_______his kindness.

PRACTICE TEST-14

The position and status of women(1) _______ society has been changing (2) _______time_______time. Today the woman has broken out (4)_______four walls (5) _______her house and has started marching ahead (6) _______life. She is certainly (7) _______the march. Now women are conscious (8) _______their position society. They compete (9) _______men (10) _______every field. They no longer depend (11) _______others.

PRACTICE TEST-15

The dog ran (1)_______the road. The river flows (2)_______the bridge. The work was done (3)_______haste. He is afraid (4)_______the dog. I am fond (5)_______music.He goes (6) _______Sunday (7)_______church. He died (8) _______his country. The steam-engine was invented (9)_______James Watt. The burglar jumped (10)_______the compound wall. The village was destroyed by fire. What is that (11)_______me? It cannot be done (12) _______offence. He spoke (13)_______me (14) _______Urdu. They live (15)_______the same roof.

PRACTICE TEST-16

I have not seen him (1)_______Wednesday last. I have known him (2) _______a long time. The moon does not shine (3) _______its own light. This is a matter (4)_______little importance. I am tired (5)_______walking. He has not yet recovered (6) _______his illness. I shall do it (7) _______pleasure. God is good (8)_______me. I will sit (9)_______my desk to do my lesson. I am sorry (10)_______what I have done. O God! Keep me (11)_______from sin. I bought it (12) _______fifteen rupees. He broke the jug (13) _______a hundred pieces. It has been raining (14) _______yesterday. I have been working hard (15) _______arithmetic.

PRACTICE TEST-17

We suffered (1)_______your neglect. The question set was written (2)_______me (3) _______a Camlin pen. 'Will you walk (4) _______my parlour?' said the spider (5) _______the fly. It is ten o'clock (6)_______my watch. There is nothing new (7)_______the sun. Do not cry (8)_______spilt milk. You boys must settle it (9) _____yourselves. The public are cautioned (10)_______pickpockets. They drove (11) _______Mumbai (12)_______Pune.

PRACTICE TEST-18

He lives (1)_______Hyderabad. He lives (2) _______48, Tilak Street. We started (3)_______ (4) _______the morning. He hanged himself (5) _______a piece of cloth. The portrait was painted (6)_______a famous artist who flourished (7) _______the sixteenth century. I must start (8) _______dawn to reach the station in time. I hope to reach the station (9)_______an hour at the outside. The child has been missing (10) _______yesterday. The caravan must reach its destination (11) _______the sunset. The mail train is due (12) _______3 P.M. He travelled thirty kilometres (13) _______panting for breath. He does not leave his house (15)_______9 o'clock.

PRACTICE TEST-19

The Express departs (1)_______3 P.M. (2) _______Delhi. Human sacrifices were practiced (3) _______the Nagas. I received his message (4) _______eight o'clock (5) _______the morning. (6)_______this month I had seen him but once. (7) _______rice they had curry. The fever has taken a turn for the better (8) _______yesterday. He has spent his life (9) _______Kolkata. I saw him felling a big tree (10) _______a hatchet. Come and sit (11) _______me. Nobody (12)_______you knows the truth. While I was (13)_______Delhi, he was (14) _______Mumbai.

PRACTICE TEST-20

He was killed (1)_______the robber (2)_______a hatchet. We shall stay three months (3)_______ America. (4) _______Rustom and Sohrab, there were three other boys present. (5) _______a Ford he has a Fiat car.

PRACTICE TEST-21

The Nizam subscribed a handsome sum (1) _______the Flood Relief Fund. His friends condoled him (2)_______his bereavement. He quarreled (3) _______me (4) _______a trifle issue. He readily complied (5)_______my request. He dispensed (6)_____the services of his dishonest clerk. He yielded (7)_______superior force. He despaired (8)_______success. He supplies the poor 9)_______clothing. His friends disagreed (10) _______him on that point. He acceded (11) _______my request. He abstains (12) _______liquor. He was found guilty (13)_______ manslaughter. He is incapable (14) _______ doing good work. He is married (15)_______my cousin.

PRACTICE TEST-22

He is sensible (1)_______your kindness. He is true (2)_______his king. He is involved (3) _______ difficulties. The auditor is entitled (4) _______his remuneration. I prefer tea (5) _______coffee. I don't concur (6)_______you (7) _______that opinion. There is no exception (8) _______this rule. I am obliged (9) _______you (10) _______your kindness. I am not envious (11) _______his success. I am convinced (12) _______ the necessity for prudence. We should rely (13)_______our own efforts. I inquired (14)_______the servant if his master was at home. I purposely refrained (15)_______saying more.

PRACTICE TEST-23

I insisted (1) _______going. I exchanged (2) _______him my calculator (3)_______a camera. I assented (4)_______his proposal. I am not satisfied (5)_______your explanation. You must confirm (6)_______the regulations. He did not profit (7) _______experience. We should all aim (8)_______excellence. Alcohol is injurious (9) _______ health. He is innocent (10)_______ the crime. The stories in that book are full (11) _______interest. Don't associate (12) _______disreputable people. Do not indulge (13) _______strong language. He is grateful (14)_______his master (15)_______many favours.

PRACTICE TEST-24

He is dependent (1) _______his parents. He is abstemious (2) _______eating and drinking. He is prompt (3) _______carrying out orders. He is vain (4) _______his attainments. He is deficient (5) _______common sense. He is vexed (6) _______me. He is indifferent (7) _______his own interest. He is proficient (8) _______mathematics. He is not ashamed (9) _______his neighbours. He is devoid (10) _______sense. He is suspicious (11) _______all his neighbours. He has a passion (12) _______arguing. Recently there has been a reduction (13) _______the price of milk. He proved false (14) _______his friend. A square may be equivalent (15) _______a triangle.

PRACTICE TEST-25

The avaricious man is greedy (1)_______gain. He is very different (2)_______his brother. The head-dress of the Cossacks is similar (3) _______that of the ancient Persians. He was born (4) _______humble parents in Nasik. His views donot accord (5)_____________mine.

PRACTICE TEST-26

Temperance and employment are conducive (1) _______health. A policeman rescued the child (2) _______danger. Dogs have antipathy (3)_______ cats. He promised not to do anything repugnant (4) _______ the wishes of his parents. He is not the man to allow anyone to encroach (5)_______his rights. Some of the members of the Assembly complained (6)__________increased military expenditure. Even the enemies admit that he is en_______owed (7)_______rare talents. He inspires respect (8)_______his friends. Our path is beset (9) _______difficulties. He was not able to give a satisfactory explanation (10)_______his absence. His illness is a mere pretext (11) _______ his absence. He has been very much indulgent_______ (12)_______his children. This discussion is hardly relevant (13)____the subject. Contentment is essential (14)_______happiness. Early rising is beneficial (15)_______health.

PRACTICE TEST-27

He is not likely to do anything detrimental (1) _______our interests. His benefactions must rebound (2)_______his credit. Only graduates are eligible (3) _______the post. He is capable as a leader, but intolerant (4)________opposition. Boys over sixteen are debarred (5) _______competing. Father Damien consecrated his life (6) _______ameliorating the lot of lepers. That rule is not applicable (7)________your case. A public man should be tolerant (8) _______criticism. He is willing to make a concession (9) _______the demand of his employees. I often find him absorbed (10) _______thought. The accommodation is adequate (11) _______our needs. The hotel is adjacent (12) _______the station. The authorship of the book is wrongly ascribed (13) _______him. Never do anything that is not compatible (14) _______public safety. His father often connives (15)_______his follies.

PRACTICE TEST-28

Some public men are very sensitive (1)_______criticism. He is addicted (2) _______ gambling. You need not be afraid (3) _______being late. Death is preferable (4) _______disgrace. Cats are tenacious (5) _______life It is not true that the study of science tends (6) _______atheism. Some films are an incitement (7) _______crime. He was angry (8) _______me, because he thought my remark was aimed (9) _______him. The climate of Rangoon does not agree (10) _______him. His plans are adverse (11) _______my interests. The question of unemployment bristles (12) _______difficulties. Although he was bred (13) _______the law, hebecame a successful journalist. Generally, the rich are more covetous (14) _______ money thanthe poor. He is still smarting (15)_______rebuke.

PRACTICE TEST-29

He scoffed (1) _______the idea of revolution. He has reverted (2) _______his former post. The battle resulted (3) _______a victory for the Allies. He restored the article (4) _______its rightful owner. The whole theory rests (5) _______no firmer foundation than mere conjecture. The ultimate decision rests (6) _______the board of directors. Only when persuasions failed, the police resorted (7) _______force. Superstitious fears preyed (8) _______his mind and made him miserable. He prides himself (9) _______his artistic taste. They now jeered (10) _______him whom they had once acclaimed as their hero. His followers now began to intrigue (11) _______his adversary. She interceded (12) _______her husband on behalf of the people. It is not easy to infer (13) _______his account the real state of affairs. He died without imparting (14) _______anyone the secret of his process. His statement was tantamount (15) _____ a confession.

PRACTICE TEST-30

The facts point (1)_________a different explanation. His friends prevailed (2) _______him to withdraw his resignation. A few boys are not amenable (3)_______discipline.

PRACTICE TEST-31

Silkworms feed (1)_________mulberry trees. Pavlova excels (2)________dancing. The wild boar abounds (3)______some parts of Europe. He has no special liking (4) _______ mathematics. Asoka is worthy (5)________remembrance. The godown is infested (6)________rats. There is no exception (7) ____this rule. Nothing conduces (8) ____happiness so much as contentment. Alcohol is injurious (9) _______health. Oil is good (10)________burns. Invalids are not capable (11) _______continued exertion. The British Parliament is composed (12) _______two Houses. Do not confide your secrets (13)________everyone. He is abstemious (14) _______his habits. He is ignorant (15) _______what he pretends to know.

PRACTICE TEST-32

My brother is weak (1) _______mathematics. He has conceived an aversion (2) _______all kinds of profitable labour. Birbal is celebrated (3) _______his witty sayings. The avaricious man is greedy (4) _______gain. The Atlantic separates Europe (5) _______America. Adam assigned (6) _______every creature a name peculiar (7) _______its nature. Temperance and employment are conducive (8) _______health. A brave boy rescued the child (9) _______danger. Industry is the key (10) _______success. The customs were searching (11) _______drugs at the airport. Elizabeth knew how to inspire her soldiers (12) _______hope. Long indulgence (13) _______vice impaired his once robust constitution. Early rising is beneficial (14) _______health. We should live in a style suited (15)_______our condition.

ANSWERS (PRACTICE TESTS)

Q. No.	TEST – 1	TEST – 2	TEST – 3	TEST – 4	TEST – 5
1.	into	for	in	in	at
2.	for	among	on	of	of
3.	of	of	for	in	in
4.	to	for	of	on	upon
5.	of	of	of	of	of
6.	on	in	at	of	on
7.	of	since	of	of	of
8.	of	of	about	of	with
9.	in	of		of	in
10.	of	of		of	with
11.	of	for		on	
12.	of	for			
13.	to	of			
14.	to				
15.	of				

Q. No.	TEST – 6	TEST – 7	TEST – 8	TEST – 9	TEST – 10
1.	of	of	of	amongst	of
2.	of	from	at	with	in
3.	through	into	of	between	from
4.	of	of	in	over	of
5.	before	of	towards	from	on
6.	for	with	for	into	at
7.	of	in	in	with	in
8.	of		of	without	on
9.	towards		for	of	against
10.	without		of	into	of
11.	to		upon		of
12.					with
13.					in
14.					of
15.					between

Q. No.	TEST – 11	TEST – 12	TEST – 13	TEST – 14	TEST – 15
1.	of	to	in	in	on
2.	of	for	to	from	under
3.	to	of	from	to	in
4.	of	on	to	of	of
5.	from	of	for	of	of
6.	to	for	with	in	every
7.	over	of	to	on	to
8.	to	for	for	of	for
9.		from		with	by
10.		of		in	over
11.				upon	against
12.					with
13.					to
14.					in
15.					under

Q. No.	TEST – 16	TEST – 17	TEST – 18	TEST – 19	TEST – 20
1.	since	from	in	before	by
2.	for	by	at	at	with
3.	of	with	at	for	in
4.	of	to	in	by	besides
5.	of	to	by	at	along with
6.	from	by	by	in	
7.	with	about	in	last	
8.	to	over	at	with	
9.	on	amongst	within	since	
10.	for	about	since	in	
11.	away	to	before the	with	
12.	for	from	at	beside	
13.	into		in	but	
14.	since		into	in	
15.	in			in	

Q. No.	TEST – 21	TEST – 22	TEST – 23	TEST – 24	TEST – 25
1.	for	of	upon	on	for
2.	on	to	with	of	from
3.	with	in	for	in	to
4.	over	to	to	of	to
5.	with	to	with	in	with

6.	with	with	for	at	
7.	to	on	from	to	
8.	for	to	at	in	
9.	with	to	to	of	
10.	with	for	of	of	
11.	to	of	of	of	
12.	from	of	with	for	
13.	for	on	into	in	
14.	of	from	to	to	
15.	to	from	for	to	

Q. No.	*TEST – 26*	*TEST – 27*	*TEST – 28*	*TEST – 29*	*TEST – 20*
1.	to	to	to	at	towards
2.	from	to	to	to	up
3.	to	for	of	in	to
4.	to	of	to	to	
5.	upon	from	in	upon	
6.	against	by	to	with	
7.	with	to	to	to	
8.	among	of	with	on	
9.	with	on	at	with	
10.	for	into	with	at	
11.	to	to	to	with	
12.	with	to	with	with	
13.	to	to	in	from	
14.	for	to	of	to	
15.	for	with	from	to	

Q. No.	*TEST – 31*	*TEST – 32*
1.	upon	in
2.	in	to
3.	in	for
4.	for	for
5.	of	from
6.	with	to
7.	to	to
8.	to	to
9.	to	from
10.	for	to
11.	of	for
12.	of	with
13.	to	into
14.	of	for
15.	of	to

20 DETERMINERS

5 PRACTICE TESTS

Determiners signal or determine that a noun will follow. Unlike adjectives–which are also followed by a noun— see after adjectives in the previous sentence. Determiners cannot add the inflectional morphemes '*-er*' and '*-est*'. In addition, because they are functional words, determiners do not have other forms or synonyms. Their 'meaning' is their function: to signal that a noun will follow. For example:

- You take *an* apple every day.
- I have *little* money to help you.
- Our team *won* the match.
- *Each* boy got a packet of sweets.
- I do not see *any* sense in going there now.

Determiners are used before nouns to indicate whether you are referring to something specific or something of a particular type. Singular nouns always need a determiner. In plural nouns, the determiner is optional. Determiners may or may not be used with uncountable nouns depending on the context.

Basically, determiners are used to:

- State the unit (number of people, things, or other nouns).
- State possessives.
- Specify someone or something.
- State how things or people are distributed.
- State the difference between nouns.

TYPES OF DETERMINERS

Determiners can be classified as follows:

Type of Determiners	*Examples (in words)*	*Examples (in sentences)*
Multipliers	double, twice, three times, etc.	We want double portions.
Fractions	half, a third, two fifths, etc.	I drove at half speed.
Intensifiers	what, such, etc.	Such impudence.
Quantifiers	all, both, most, etc.	I like most people.
Articles	a, an, the, etc.	Get a book from the shelf.
Demonstratives	this, that, these, those, other, etc.	That tree is in another garden.
Distributives	each, every, either, neither, etc.	I have a gift for each person.
Possessives Pronominal Nominal	my, your, their, our, his, her, its, etc.Reena's, Aditya's, people's, etc.	You can borrow Karan's video. You can borrow my video.
Interrogatives	what, which, whose, etc.	Whose book is that?
Quantifiers	some, any, no, etc.	I have no problem with them.
Cardinal Numbers	one, two, three hundred, etc.	Two heads are better than one.
Ordinal Numbers	first, fewer, much, more, least, etc.	It was my first tennis match.
Quantifiers Simple Compound	few, fewer, much, more, less, etc. a little, a lot of, a great deal of, etc.	I have few pals, but Karan has more. I have lots of time to spare.

Type of Determiners	*Examples (in words)*	*Examples (in sentences)*

POSSESSIVE DETERMINERS

Possessive determiners are personal pronouns in their possessive case. They indicate the relationship or possession of the noun with which they are used. For example:

- *My* name is Ranav Chopra.
- *His* parents live in the US.
- I do not know *which* book he will pick up.
- *Your* name is difficult to pronounce.
- *Her* house is just across this garden.
- *Their* names have been struck off the rolls.
- *Its* price is five hundred rupees.
- *One* should always remember one's duty.
- *His* conduct has displeased his parents.
- *Our* sole purpose is to help you.

Note: Possessive determiner (italicised in the given examples) is a pronoun. As such, its antecedent (the noun which it replaces) must be quite clear.

Listed here are some possessive determiners: my, our, your, his, her, its, their, everybody's, nobody's, of which, whose, someone's, everyone's, somebody's, etc.

NUMERAL DETERMINERS

Numeral determiners are primarily adjectives of numbers. They denote the number of persons, places, or things before which they are used. They also indicate the order or degree of relation of a person, place, or thing *vis-a-vis* another. Forexample:

- She has given me *many* favours.
- You have not seen her for *several* days.
- I borrowed a *hundred* rupees from him.
- Only a *few* people attended the poet's funeral.
- All men desire happiness but *very few* getit.

NUMERAL DETERMINERS ARE OF THREE KINDS:

Definite	*Indefinite*	*Distributive*
five, ten, twenty, etc.	many, several, a few, most, any, some, all, etc.	each, every, either, neither, etc.
fifth, tenth, last, etc.		

Definite Numeral Determiners

Definite numeral determiners refer to a definite or exact number (e.g., one, thirty, last, next, etc.)

For example:

- She has *five* hundred rupees in her purse.
- There are *fifty* students in this class.
- She has stood *first* in the university.
- Her house is the *last* in this row.
- Your name figures *next* in the list.

(1) I deposited one thousand rupees in thebank.	(1) She was the last person to enter thehall.
(2) Simmi has two brothers and three sisters.	(2) I have secured the first division in my M.A.
(3) We walked forfive kilo- meters.	(3) She has stood second in his class.

Definite numeral determiners belong to two categories:	
(i) Cardinals	*(ii) Ordinals*
A Cardinal numeral determiners point out how many persons, places, or things are meant.	Ordinal numeral determiners point out the order, rank, or position of a person, place, or thing before which they are used.

Indefinite numeral determiners

Indefinite numeral determiners refer toindefinite or vague numbers such as many, several, any, and some, etc.

For example:

- I have only a *few* good friends.
- *Some* girls are sitting in the common room.
- Are there *any* boys, too?

- She spent *several* weeks in Switzerland.
- We have bought *many* books for the library.

Distributive numerals

Distributive numerals refer to each one of a group of persons, places, or things, such as each, either, neither, and every.

For example

- *Each* girl has to sing a song here.
- *Every* guest must be well looked after.
- *Neither* party is happy with compromise.
- *Either* book will serve my purposeequally well.
- *Every* word that I have uttered is true.

Quantitative determiners

Quantitative determiners are like a quantitative adjective. It refers to the quantity of athing which cannot be otherwise counted. It answers the question 'How much?'. For example: some, any, little, a little, a good (great) deal of, the little, no, enough, much, a lot of, etc.

Some more examples:

- There is *enough* money in the house.
- I would love to have *some* coffee.
- The *little* milk there was in the house has turned sour.
- Not *much* effort was needed.
- Can you give me a *little* help in this matter?
- Is there *any* tea in the kettle?
- Dr. A.P.J. Abdul Kalam enjoys *a lot* of good will.
- *A great deal* of discussion took place in the conference hall.

Some of the determiners which serve as numerals can also serve as quantitative determiners when used to refer to quantity or mass of a thing. Study the difference between the two with the helpof the following table. For ex

Numeral determiners	*Quantitative determiners*
1. Some girls are absent today.	There is some milk inthe jug.
2. She gifted all her books.	She has gifted all her money.
4. She has no friendsin this room.	She has no money leftwith her.
5. Have you any supporters in this constituency?	She does not have anymoney in the bank.

Note: Here is a simple method to decide whether a determiner is numeral or quantitative. A numeral determiner is used before a countable form (pen, pencil, man, woman, girl, etc.); a quantitative determiner is used before an uncountable noun referring to mass or weight.

Demonstrative determiners

Demonstrative determines are, as pointed out earlier, demonstrative adjectives. They point out to the persons, places, or things before which theyare used. For example: this, that, these, and those.

Some more examples:

- Have you read this book?
- I did not like that picture.
- We bought these oranges in the market.
- Those days really belonged to us.
- No one is happy in this world.
- She did not like that sari.

These girls are just waiting for their marriage. It is to be remembered that only demonstrative adjectives are determiners, while demonstrative pronouns are not. The difference between a demonstrative adjective (determiner) and demonstrative pronoun is this: whereas a demonstrative determiner or adjective must be followed by a noun, a demonstrative pronoun can stand on its own and is therefore not followed by a noun. Study the following table carefully.

Demonstrative adjective	*Demonstrative pronoun*
1. This pen is mine.	This is my pen.
2. These girls are beautiful.	These are the girls who are beautiful.
3. That book on history is interesting.	That is an interesting book on history.
4. This book deals with writing.	This is a book about writing.
5. These toys are for the children.	These are children's toys.

DETERMINERS (PRACTICE TESTS)

PRACTICE TEST-1

Fill in the blanks using appropriate possessive determiners:

1. ______house is just across this park.
2. ______beauty is the talk of the town.
3. ______business is nobody's business.
4. This is pen ______price is Rs. 5/-
5. I don't know______book this is.
6. What you do is none of______business.
7. ______brother is now past thirty.
8. Maya did not like______husband's brothers and sisters.
9. She says that______girlfriend has betrayed him.
10. Our brave soldiers know______duty towards the motherland.

PRACTICE TEST-2

Fill in the blanks with suitable numeral determiners:

1. I have only______friends. But theyare all reliable.
2. _____words the old man spokewere true.
3. How______books did he borrowfrom you?
4. Are there______boys who were absent yesterday?
5. There are only______girls in this class.
6. Anil and Pankaj are friends.______of them is reliable.
7. There are trees on______side of theroad.
8. I gave him______rupees that I hadin my pocket.
9. She is very intelligent. She stood______in the university.
10. You must account for______rupee that I have given you.

PRACTICE TEST-3

Fill in the blanks with suitable quantitative determiners:

1. There is______sense in what hesays.
2. She drank the______milk that was there in the jug.
3. ______work and______play makes Jack a dull boy.
4. Does he have______sense of shame left?
5. She offered a lot but actually gave ______help.
6. ______money was spent on themarriage of his daughter.
7. I have given him only______help.
8. There is not______money in youraccount.
9. There is not______truth in what she says.
10. Could you give me______money asloan?

PRACTICE TEST-4

Fill in the blanks with 'this', 'that', 'these', or 'those' (whichever is suitable):

1. Look at______boy. He is runningafter the bus.
2. ______picture is selling like hot cake.
3. ______boys will never mend themselves.
4. ______days prices were not so high.
5. She is going to visit______place in a few days.
6. ______boys are hardworking.
7. ______book is interesting to read.
8. Do you see____cloud shaped likea camel?
9. ______days girls used to wear tight dresses.
10. ______pen does not write well.

PRACTICE TEST-5

Fill in the blanks with 'a' or 'an' (whichever is suitable):

1. Urvashi is______untidy girl.
2. Iron is______useful metal.
3. ______University is______ temple of learning.
4. ______apple a day keeps the doctor away.
5. Sushma is______honour to herschool.
6. Set the clock back. It is____hourtoo fast.
7. Brutus was______honourable man.
8. The river has______iron bridge overit.
9. ______honest man is the greatest work or God.

ANSWERS (PRACTICE TESTS)

Q. No.	TEST – 1	TEST – 2	TEST – 2
1.	my	a few	no
2.	her	many	little
3.	our	many	(i) all (ii) no
4.	(i) my (ii) it's	many	any
5.	whose	few	little
6.	my	none	a lot of
7.	her	both	Little
8.	her	hundred	Enough
9.	his	first	much
10.	their	every	some

Q. No.	TEST – 4	TEST – 5
1.	that	an
2.	this	a
3.	these	(i) a (ii) a
4.	those	an
5.	that	an
6.	these	an
7.	this	an
8.	that	an
9.	those	an
10.	this	

21 CONJUNCTION

13 PRACTICE TESTS

A conjunction is a sentence connector. It connects words, clauses, or sentences, or shows relations between sentences.

Study the following sentences:

1. I went home *and* took my food.
2. Give her a pen *or* a pencil.
3. He is hard-working *but* not intelligent.
4. I could not contact him *because* he was ill.

In all these sentences, the italicised words join words or sentences. They are linking words and are, therefore, called conjunctions (or connectors). Conjunctions can be classified into three types: (1) Coordinative; (2) Subordinative; and (3) Correlative conjunctions.

COORDINATIVE CONJUNCTIONS

The simple, little conjunctions are called coordinative conjunctions. They join words,phrases or clauses of equal rank. For example:

1. Ram and Shyam went to the market.
2. I did go there but I did not participate in the discussion.
3. Sonu is a coward, but his brother is very brave.

SUBORDINATIVE CONJUNCTIONS

A subordinating conjunction comes at the beginning of a subordinate (or dependent) clause and establishes the relationship between the dependent clause and the rest of the sentence. It also turns the clause into something that depends on the rest of the sentence for its meaning.

For example, study the following sentences:

1. (a) The thief was caught red-handed.
   (b) He was stealing a jewellery box.
   (c) The thief was caught red-handed *while* hewas stealing a jewellery box. (Time.)
2. (a) She is extremely happy today.
   (b) She has been engaged to a boy of her choice.
   (c) She is extremely happy today *because* she has been engaged to a boy of her choice. (Reason)
3. (a) He continued gambling.
   (b) He lost all his money.
   (c) He continued gambling *till* he lost all his money. (Time)

Sentences marked '(b)' depend upon or are subordinate to the sentences marked '(a)'. They have been joined (refer sentences marked) '(c)' with the help of some conjunctions (in italics). Such conjunctions are called subordinative conjunctions.

CORRELATIVE CONJUNCTIONS

Some conjunctions combine with other words to form what are called correlative conjunctions. They always travel in pairs, joining various sentence elements that should be treated as grammatically equal.

For example, study the following sentences:

1. No sooner did he reach the station, than the train steamed off.
2. Neither Sham nor his brother committed this crime.
3. He is so weak that he cannot walk.
4. She is not only beautiful but intelligent also.

In all these sentences, conjunctions are seen to occur in pairs such as no sooner … than; neither …nor; so … that; and not only … but also. Such conjunctions are correlative conjunctions.

CONJUNCTION (PRACTICE TESTS)

PRACTICE TEST-1

(1)_____I was young, I used to travel a lot. (2) _____now I am old (3) _____it is difficult for me to show as much zeal (4) _____I had in my youth. (5) _____ I can still do many things, there are certain things (6) _____ are beyond my reach now.

PRACTICE TEST-2

(1)_____ did I reach the station (2) _____the train left. I do not know (3) _____ it happened with me. (4) _____I narrated the incident to my mother, she was disappointed to hear it. (5) _____I was coming back to my house. I met a stranger (6) _____was carrying a basket with him. I tried to talk to him, (7) _____he gave no response.

PRACTICE TEST-3

Music is said to be food for the soul. (1) _____ does it give relaxation to our mind (2) _____ help us to forget our sorrows and worries of day-to-day life? There is no aspect of life (3) _____we do not find it. There is hardly any party or function (4) _____music is not played. (5) _____ we must enjoy it to forget our pains for some time.

PRACTICE TEST-4

Education has become a part of everybody's life. There is not even a single field (1) _____education has not left its mark. The day is not far (2) _____everybody would like to drink deep in its ocean. (3) _____the need of the hour is to spread education in every nook and corner (4) _____nobody is left without its mark.

PRACTICE TEST-5

One day (1) _____I went to my friend's house, I was surprised to see a man (2) _____ was wearing nothing. (3) _____ I asked him the reason, he tried to avoid me, (4) _____ I did not stop and asked him again. (5) _____ some time he told me the reason behind it. (6) _____ he was telling me a sad episode (7) _____ had happened with him two days (8) ___ I started weeping (9) _____ I heard his woeful tale.

PRACTICE TEST-6

The economic condition of a country depends on the resources available in the country (1) _____on its population. (2) _____ the population increases, resources start decreasing. (3) _____ there is a need to control population (4) _____ we want our country to move towards the path of development.

PRACTICE TEST-7

I was pained to hear about your problem. (1) _____ you should not worry. (2) _____ I am always there to help you. (3) _____ my means are limited, I will try to help you (4) much (5) _____I can. (6) _____ you want to progress in life you should have faith in your capabilities (7) aspirations.

PRACTICE TEST-8

(1) _____my knowledge is concerned, I only say (2) _____nowadays, it has become difficult to make both ends meet. I was seven years old (3) _____my mother died. I tried to put a lot of efforts (4) _____I may get (5) _____I desired in my life. My sister (6) _____I started running a shop (7) _____was situated near my house. My sister (8) _____I managed the shop (9) _____we had limited means. We were honest.

PRACTICE TEST-9

(1) _____I was nine years old, my parents told me (2) _____we originally belonged to Kashmir. (3) _____I grew up, I began to watch T.V. (4) _____I learnt about the happenings in Kashmir. (5) _____I saw some beautiful shots of the heavenly valley on the T.V., in movies, I would remember Kashmir.

PRACTICE TEST-10

My friend had been suffering from cholera (1) _____Monday. Today he did not come to school (2) _____he was not well again. (3) _____I reached his house, his family had left for the hospital. I hurriedly rushed towards the hospital (4) _____he had been admitted. The doctor came (5) _____assured us about his quick recovery. We heaved a sigh of relief (6) _____ we heard the news of his recovery.

PRACTICE TEST-11

I feel lonely (1) _____I prefer to enjoy the beauty of nature. Wordsworth was a famous poet (2) _____wrote poems on the beautiful objects of nature. Some of his poems show the zeal (3) _____ he had in his veins. (4) _____I was at school, my English teacher used to tell me about some of Wordsworth's poems (5) _____were worth reading.

PRACTICE TEST-12

(1) _____you do not get success despite your repeated efforts, you should not lose heart. Only those people get success (2) _____have an optimistic approach towards life. (3) _____you want to win the lost game, you should not feel exhausted. You can go up in life (4) _____you persist in your efforts.

PRACTICE TEST-13

(1) _____did we step out of the house (2) _____the rain started. I love rainy season (3) _____in that season my grandmother prepares lovely dishes for the whole family. I enjoy sitting alone (4) _____it is raining. (5) _____somebody comes to my house on a rainy day, I feel disturbed.

ANSWERS (PRACTICE TESTS)

Q. No.	TEST – 1	TEST – 2	TEST – 3	TEST – 4	TEST – 5
1.	when	hardly	however	where	when
2.	but	when	and	when	who
3.	and	how	where	hence	when
4.	as	when	where in	so that	but
5.	through	while	hence		after
6.	that	who			when
7.		but			that
8.					ago
9.					when

Q. No.	TEST – 6	TEST – 7	TEST – 8	TEST – 9	TEST – 10
1.	and	but	as far as	when	since
2.	when	as	that	that	as
3.	hence	though	when	while	when
4.	if	as	so that	and	where
5.		as	what	whenever	and
6.		if	and		when
7.		and	that		
8.			and		
9.			though		

Q. No.	TEST – 11	TEST – 12	TEST – 13
1.	but	when	no sooner
2.	who	who	than
3.	that	if	and
4.	when	if	while
5.	which		when

22 Non-Finite Verbs

14 PRACTICE TESTS

Verbs can be divided into two types — non-finite and finite verbs.

A verb that changes its form according to person, tense, mood, etc., is called a finite verb. For example:

- Mohan works hard.
- They worked hard.
- She is working hard.
- We have worked hard.
- How I wish we worked hard.

The *italicised words in the examples* are finite verbs because they change according to person, number, and tense. Now note the following examples:

- He *wants* to be rich.
- She *wanted* to be rich.
- They *want* to be rich.
- She *makes* me understand everything.
- She *made* me understand everything.
- We will *make* you understand science.

In these examples, the verbs 'be' and 'understand' do not change according to tense, number, and person. Such verbs are called non- finite verbs.

TYPES OF NON-FINITE VERBS

A. The Infinitive

The infinitive verb has two forms:

(i) Use of 'to + infinitive'

The to + infinitive is used in the followingways:

As a noun

- To err is human.
- To criticise others is very easy. (Subject)
- We want to learn French. (Object of thetransitive verb 'want')
- I know how to cook rice. (Object)
- The best thing is to do the work yourself. (Complement to the linking verb 'is')
- Her aim was to become a doctor. (Complement to the linking verb 'was')
- It is easier to preach than to practice. (After the dummy subject 'it')

As an adverb to modify a verb or an adjective

- He went to meet the President. (modifies the verb 'went')
- I stood up to speak. (modifies the verb 'stood')
- She is anxious to leave. (modifies the adjective 'anxious')
- You are difficult to please. (modifies the adjective 'difficult' as an adjective to qualify a noun)
- It is time to leave. (qualifies the noun 'time')
- We have nothing to offer. (qualifies'nothing')

As an object complement or an object toa preposition

- He is about to resign.
- We saw him go.
- This shop is about to close.
- I felt something fall on my foot.

As an adjunct

- He was the first to arrive.
- Please give me something to eat.

As part of 'too + adjective/adverb + infinitive' (enough + infinitive)

- The patient is too weak to walk.

As an absolute to modify the whole sentence.

- I don't have enough money to buy a car.

- To be honest with you, I hate you.
- To cut a long story short, he cheated everybody.

(ii) Use of the bare infinitive

After some verbs (e.g., watch, bid, see, let, make, help, hear, feel, etc.)

- She bade me to come.
- She helped me do my homework.
- The director made me wait.
- Let me ask a question.

With 'had better', 'had rather'

- I had better stay where I am.
- You had rather spoken to her.

With some prepositions (e.g., except, but, than, etc.)

- He does nothing except complain.
- I would rather die than beg.

Passive form of the infinitive (to + be + pastparticiple)

- It is an insult to be treated like that.
- She likes to be flattered.

B. The Gerund

A gerund is that form of the verb which ends in '-ing' and has the force of a noun. Therefore, the gerund is called a verbal noun.

Use of the gerund:

As a subject

- Swimming is good for health.
- Seeing is believing.
- Reading makes a complete man.

As an object

- We like painting.
- She likes eating rice.

As a complement to the linking verb

- My first love is dancing.

As an object of a preposition

- I am fond of fishing.
- The police prevented her from going.

As part of a noun phrase

- Playing on this field is enjoyable.
- Watching the snowfall was a real treat.

C. The Participle

Participles can be divided into two types:

(i) Use of the present participle As an adjective

- I will buy a jumping doll.
- This building has no running water.

As an object complement

- We found the terms tempting.
- I found the child sleeping.

As an adverb

- She went away crying.
- She went out of the house singing.
- The boy sat whistling.

Note: The following sentences show the difference between a participle and a gerund.

- Throwing a bomb there, he ran away.(Present participle)
- Throwing bombs in a street is againstlaw. (Gerund)
- Swimming in the canal, Mohan saved the life of a child. (Present participle)
- Swimming in the canal is a good exercise. (Gerund)
- I like the girls having long hair. (Presentparticiple)
- I like having long hair. (Gerund)

(ii) Use of the past participleAs an adjective

- The wounded man was taken to a hospital.
- He is a spoilt child.

As an object complement

- We found the door locked.
- The news left us shocked.

As an adverb

- The man left the hospital completelycured.
- Excited, he kept moving here and there.

As part of a participle phrase

- We saw a bird caught in a net.
- She found the door painted on both sides.

NON-FINITE VERBS (PRACTICE TESTS)

Complete the following sentences using the Infinitive form (with or without 'to') of the verb given in brackets:

PRACTICE TEST-1

1. You are requested_______me. (help) 2. She made us_____away. (go) 3. I find the word 'psychology' difficult____ (spell) 4. Please make me______why the stars twinkle. (understand) 5. The medicine is too bitter_______ (take)

PRACTICE TEST-2

Fill in the blanks with suitable non-finites (Infinitive, Gerund, or Participle):

1. I am afraid of_______in the court. (appear) 2. _______thieves in her house, she started _______ (see, shout) 3. He decided_______ his income by_______a private tuition. (increase, take) 4. I noticed your friend_______with a gambler. (sit) 5. _______is easier than_______ (say, do) 6. Do you want_______my address? (know) 7. Every miser hates_______money. (spend) 8. They were eager_______the game. (start) 9. This rent is quite reasonable for a well_______house. (furnish) 10. The children seemed_______on seeing the giant. (frighten)

PRACTICE TEST-3

Fill in the blanks with non-finites:

(1)_______ (know) little about Gorillas we want (2) _______ (know) a great deal more about them. Travelers have seen a male gorilla_______ (3) (help) a female climb up a steep rock. According to the observers, they make love in the same way as humans do. (4)_______ (make) a pile of their food they sit down (5) _______ (eat) it in a group.

PRACTICE TEST-4

Gorillas have good eyesight but are deficient in both (1) _______ (hear) and (2) _______ (smell). In the face of danger, the male gorilla prefers (3) _______ (stay) behind while his family members get away. At this time the male gorilla is used (4) _______ (make) a (5) _______(terrify) roar.

PRACTICE TEST-5

We should ask students (1) _______ (play) outdoor games. (2) _______ (play) outdoor games involves physical exercise. When children play such games, they sweat and lose the unwanted elements from the body. Children should be asked (3) _______ (be) regular, as it is through (4) _______ (play) regularly, that they can achieve full results. (5) _______ (play) and (6) _______ (study) should go hand in hand. After all (7) _______ (study), we need physical fitness and to gain physical fitness we need (8) _______ (play) regularly.

PRACTICE TEST-6

The signboards of No (1) _______ (Park) are usually seen on the roads which is a message for the people not (2) _______ (park) at certain places. Nowadays (3) _______ (drive) has become a tough job. It has become essential for the people (4)_______ (follow) all the rules and regulations of traffic. Generally, people don't remember (5) _______ (park) vehicles at right fixed place. They are in the habit of (6) _______ (overtake) other vehicles in a rash manner. We must have strict laws (7) _______ (compel) people (8) _______ (observe) the traffic rules.

PRACTICE TEST-7

When I reached home, my father had gone for (1) _______ (swim), because a few days back an uncle had advised him that (2) _______ (swim) is good for health. Following this, yesterday, I went (3) _______ (see) him at the swimming pool. To see my father (4) _______ (swim), but I am afraid of going into the pool because I do not know how (5) _______ (swim).

PRACTICE TEST-8

(1) _______ (enter) the theatre I read on the door '(2) _______ (smoke) is bad for health'. Many a time I had tried (3) _______ (give up) smoking but the temptation was too much. (4) _______ (remind) of my grand-mother's advice, I once again thought of (5) _______ (leave) it. I consoled myself (6) _______ (think) that (7) _______ (err) is human, I left the theatre (8) _______ (determine) not to smoke again. It (9) _______ (be) a rainy day, it took me some time (10) _______ (reach) home.

PRACTICE TEST-9

(1) _______ (walk) down the stairs I stumbled and one of the eggs broke. I kept the (2) _______

(break) an egg. I began (3) _______ (cry). (4) _______ (see) me weeping, my father scolded my mother.

PRACTICE TEST-10

Group life made the task of (1) _______ (collect) food easier, (2) _______ (Hunt) wild and fast (3) _______ (run) animals with weapons. Care of (4) _______ (bring up) the young also became possible in a group. Mothers could stay at home, (5) _______ (look) after the children.

PRACTICE TEST-11

(1) _______ (collect) stamps is an (2) _______ (interest) hobby. Children all over the world want (3)_______ (learn) about different countries. Stamps (4) _______ (carry) beautiful pictures of sports, nature, wildlife, etc. are issued by different nations from time to time. The stamps, thus, help them (5) _______ (know) about those countries. Children love (6) _______ (collect) them.

PRACTICE TEST-12

(1) _______ (have) become a saint, Ananda started (2) _______ (wear) saffron robes, soon he became very learned. His fame spread far and wide. (3) _______ (Attract) by his personality, several young men came (4) _______ (become) his disciples. (5) _______ (help) the poor became his mission. He taught his followers (6) _______ (help) the needy.

PRACTICE TEST-13

Last night, I heard someone (1) _______ (knock) at the gate. It is not my habit (2) _______ (keep) someone out for long. It is always decent (3) _______ (give) a warm welcome to visitors. Therefore, I opened the door and I was surprised (4) _______ (see) my old friend (5) _______ (carry) a basket of flowers in his hand. He wanted (6) _______ (greet) me on my birthday.

PRACTICE TEST-14

If you want (1) _______ (lose) your extra weight, start (2) _______ (follow) the sound medical advice. You have (3) _______ (try) small tricks and exercises as (4) _______ (tell) by your doctor. Once you start (5) _______ (do) the tricks, you will become fit and healthy.

ANSWERS (PRACTICE TESTS)

Q. No.	TEST – 1	TEST – 2	TEST – 3	TEST – 4	TEST – 5
1.	to help	appearing	knowing	hearing	to play
2.	go	on seeing, shouting	to know	smelling	playing
3.	to spell	to increase, taking	helping	to stay	to be
4.	understand	sitting	making	to making	playing
5.	to take	saying doing	to eat	terrifying	playing
6.		to know			studying
7.		spending			to study
8.		to start			to play
9.		furnished			
10.		frighten			

Q. No.	TEST – 6	TEST – 7	TEST – 8	TEST – 9	TEST – 10
1.	parking	swimming	having entered	walking	collecting
2.	to park	swimming	smoking	breaking	hunting
3.	driving	to see	to give up	crying	running
4.	to follow	swimming	reminded	seeing	bringing up
5.	to park	to swim	leaving		looking
6.	overtaking		by thinking		
7.	to compel		to err		
8.	to observe		determined		
9.	swimming		was		
10.	to see		to reach		
11.	swimming				
12.	to swim				

Q. No.	TEST – 11	TEST – 12	TEST – 13	TEST – 14
1.	collecting	having	knocking	to lose
2.	interesting	wearing	to keep	following
3.	to learn	attracted	to give	to try
4.	carrying	to become	to see	told
5.	know	helping	carrying	doing
6.	collecting	to help	to greet	

23 MODAL VERBS

11 PRACTICE TESTS

A modal is an auxiliary verb (generally termedas helping verb) which is used with a main verb to indicate a particular attitude (e.g., possibility, obligation, prediction, etc.). For example: can, could, may, might, will, would, shall, should, must, ought to, dare, need, used to, etc., sometimes, modals are also referred to as modal verbs or modal auxiliaries. **Auxiliary verbs are of two types:**

(a) Those that help form tenses, as well as interrogative and negative sentences.

(i) As main verbs

For example:

- The book is on the table.
- We are brothers.
- I have a pen.
- I do my duty.

(ii) As helping verbs

USE OF MODALS

For example:

- She is playing a match.
- I am not writing a letter.
- I did not hit him.

(b) Modal auxiliaries or modals

- Modal auxiliaries (or modals) cannot be used as main verbs or as independent primary auxiliaries.
- Modals are never used alone. They are used to help the main (principal) verb.
- They do not have the infinitive, present participle, or past participle form.
- They cannot be used in all tenses.

Note: Modals are mainly used to indicate one's attitude towards what one is saying or when one is concerned about the effect of one's speech on the other person in the communication channel

The ways in which modal verbs can be used can be mainly classified as follows:

'Can'	'Could'	'May'	'Might'
Concept/mode/ attitude	**Concept/mode/ attitude**	**Concept/mode/attitude**	**Concept/mode/ attitude**
(a) Ability/capacity	(a) Ability/capacity in the past	(a) Formal permission	(a) Permission in past
I can lift this box.	We couldn't get the tickets.	May I go home now? Yes, you may.	He might go anywhere whenever he liked.
Can you use a personal computer?	I could swim across this river when I wasyoung.	May I use your telephone?	She might marry anyone she wanted to.
I am sorry I cannot lendyou any money.		Teachers may parktheir cars here.	
(b) Informal permission	(b) Purpose in the past	(b) Possibility	(b) Purpose in that past

'Can'	'Could'	'May'	'Might'
You can go home now.	I ran fast so that I could catch the train.	She may have been unwell.	I left early so that I might reach home in time.
You can use any telephone whenever you like.	He worked so hard that he could stand first.	It may rain in a few days.	He helped her so that she might reciprocate.
(c) Permission granted by rules	(c) Possibility in the present/future	(c) Wish	(c) Possibility in the past
The referee can show you the yellow.	I could go there if you so desire.	May you live long and prosper!	You might have been robbed on the way.
You cannot park your car here.	I could get you a new book if you want one.	May you live long and do well in life!	If you had helped him, he might have thanked you.
No wires can be moved from here.			
(d) Doubt (usually in question form)	(d) Polite requests	(d) Purpose	(d) Polite request for permission
Can he still be alive?	Could you lend me some money?	Come closer so that I may see you.	Might I come in?
Can he be really true?	Could you post this letter for me?	Help him so that hemay help you.	Might I go home and have some rest now?
Can he help you with money?			
(e) Surprise (in question form)	(e) Suggestion that one should behave in a certain way.	(e) Hope/fear	(e) Suggestion to behave in a way
Can she be so foolish?	You could at least have informed me in time.	He hopes that he may get the ticket.	You might at least thank him for his nice gift.
Can he contest election against his father?	He could at least speak politely to his teacher.	He may not appear in the examination at all.	She might at least be nice to her mother.
(f) Actions of the senses		(f) Too strong likelihood	(f) Humour or pomposity
You can see the view from here.		He may well accept the job.	What might his wisdom tell him now?
You can hear the sound of the siren clearly.		He may well marry his girlfriend.	What news might he bring this time?
(g) Sporadic action; a mere possibility			(g) A past likelihood with well
You too can commit mistakes.			We might as well have won the match.
A driver can at times lose concentration.			You might just as well have informed us.

'Shall'	'Should'	'Will'	'Would'
Concept/mode/ attitude	**Concept/mode/ attitude**	**Concept/mode/ attitude**	**Concept/mode/ attitude**
(a) Simple futurity with I and we	(a) Past tense of shall	(a) Un-coloured futures with all subjects except I and We	(a) An idea of future when used in the past in reported speech
I shall inform you as soon as I can.	I said that I should be able to manage the show.	It is clear that they will come here in a few days.	She said that she would be ready in ten minutes.
I shall lend you money when I have enough.	We hoped that we should be able to help her.	If he goes to Delhi, he will stay with his aunt.	He said that he would accept the new offer.
(b) Polite suggestion in a question form	(b) In hypothetical past	(b) Strong intention, promise, threat, or expectation with I and We	(b) Imaginary or hypothetical past tense in conditions.
Shall I bring a chair for you?	If I were you, I should not live in that house.	I will not spare him, even if the worst happens.	The plants would wither if it did not rain soon.
Shall I type this letter for you?	If we could, we should leave this place at once.	We will not let him escape so cheaply.	She would leave this house if she could.
(c) Strong intention	(c) Humour or surprise	(c) Likelihood	(c) Unreal past
He shall do whatever he is told to.	Who should be there if not Mani?	The boy you mentioned will be Rajan.	She would have joined us if you had approved.
He shall marry the girl his mother chooses.	Who should convey the news if not Anu?	The boy she married will be her college friend.	I would have helped him if you had been decent.
(d) Threat (with subject other than I/we)	(d) In combination with some verbs	(d) Expectation, even certainty	(d) Habitual action in the past
You shall not speak a word more.	I desire that you should come personally.	This experiment will bring stability.	She would sit in the park and watch the show.
You shall not leave this place till I allow you.	I insist that you should leave at once.	Your friend will win the Presidential election.	He would go for a walk whenever he was free.
(e) Command in a formal/legal sense	(e) Likelihood in the present/future	(e) Suitability, capacity, power, etc.	(e) Politeness
	The reforms should show their result soon.	The provisions will last at least another month.	The lady you talked about would be her aunt.
	The monsoon should be plentiful this year.	A thousand rupees will serve the present need.	The girl you mentioned would be his cousin.
	(f) Unlikely future possibility		(f) Polite questions in the present

'Shall'	'Should'	'Will'	'Would'
	Should he fail, we will give him another chance.		Would you mind moving to the next chair?
	If you should miss the bus, hire a taxi.		Would you give her a helping hand?
	(g) Obligation in the present or future		(g) Preference when used with rather
	You should honour your word now.		What would he not do to get or this job?
	We all should respect our elders.		He would do everything to make his wife happy.

'Must'	*'Ought to'*	*'Need'*
Concept/mode/attitude	**Concept/mode/attitude**	**Concept/mode/attitude**
(a) necessity felt by the speaker	(a) moral duty or obligation	(a) absence of obligation or necessity in negatives and interrogatives
We must do everything for this noble cause.	We ought to respect our elders.	I have paid this bill, so you needn't pay it.
I must go home now; it is rather late.	You ought to help him in his hour of need.	You needn't go to office. It is a holiday.
(b) duty, obligation, compulsion	(b) logical necessity, expectation, etc.	(b) expectation of a negative answer when
We must respect our parents and teachers.	They ought to be here by now.	Need you go there in such a cold weather?
We must do whatever we can to help her.	He ought to reach Amritsar by this time.	Need you lend money to that rascal?
(c) Probability or certainly		(c) to suggest that something which was not necessary done.
He must be fully aware of the situation.		You needn't have paid the bill as I had paid it.
This must be in the knowledge of her father.		He needn't have gone to office; it was a holiday.
(d) the speaker's determination		
		'Need' as a lexical verb
I must help my friend in his hour of distress.		Need can also be used as lexical or principal verb. When it is used as such, it behaves like other lexical verbs. For example:
(e) prohibition negative statements		You need not go there right now. (modal verb)

'Must'	'Ought to'	'Need'
You mustn't walk on the right side.		You did not need to pay the bill. (lexical verb)
You must not park your car here.		If you want to go on leave, you will need to inform your boss. (lexical verb)
		You need not come to the office tomorrow; it is a holiday. (modal verb)

'Dare'	'Used to'	'Have/has/had to'
• How dare you say so to my face? (modal verb)	• She used to sit at the window and watch the people going down the street.	• I have to go there early tomorrow morning.
• Who dares me to prove him wrong. (lexical verb)	• He used to talk very highly of her before his marriage.	• She had to resign her job because of her marriage. (I may not like it, but I have no choice in the matter.)
• He dare not open his mouth before his father. (modal verb)	• She used to prepare delicious dishes for him.	• He has to commute from Jalandhar to Ludhiana every day.
• He dared his boss to take him to court. (lexical or full verb)	• She used to visit her friends and tell them about what her daughter- in-law said about them.	• He has to play a second fiddle to his wife; otherwise, she won't allow him any peace of mind.
		• I have to get up at five in the morning; otherwise, I cannot reach my office in time.

MODAL VERBS (PRACTICE TESTS)

PRACTICE TEST-1

1. ……. I see my wife now, doctor? (can/could) (not very sure)
2. ……. I smoke here? (may/might)
3. He …… help you if you ask him. (will/shall)
4. Rahul ……. attend school. (can/must)
5. This ……. be a Satyajit Ray film. (can/may) (not very sure)
6. He ……. be hiding. (can/may) (doubt but rather sure)
7. Ram ……. come today. (can/might/may) (very uncertain)
8. ……. I take your leave? (can/may) (asking permission)
9. It ……. rain today. (can/may) (greater possibility)
10. As he tried his best, he ……. easily win the game. (can/could)

PRACTICE TEST-2

1. You ……. complete your homework now. (should/must) (compulsory)
2. You ……. be in the school by 8 o'clock. (should/must) (order)
3. Rita ……. Speak English fluently. (can/would) (showing ability)

4. He told me that he .... return to his native land soon. (will/would)
5. Mohan .... still be lying in bed. (will/must)
6. That .... be the postman. (will/must) (prediction)
7. I .... smell a fire burning. (can/will) (showing ability)
8. Diana .... have suffered badly after the car crash. (must/shall) (supposition)
9. I .... like to have a cup of coffee. (will/would) (wish)
10. I ....that I were rich! (will/would) (a wish)

PRACTICE TEST-3

1. Duty .... be done. (should/must)(greater determination)
2. I wish he .... stand first. (will/would) (to express a wish)
3. We ...respect our elders. (should/must) (to express duty in a more determinedsense)
4. I .... to clear the exam this year. (need/dare)
5. How .... you do it! (dare/need) (challenge)
6. Your headache .... also be due to some other problem. (can/could) (not very dure)
7. I am sure it .... be cured. (can/may) (not very sure)
8. It .... be Jaya. (can/may) (not very sure)
9. I .... go to the bazaar today. (may/can)
10. Ram .... take exercise daily. (must/should)(less determination)

PRACTICE TEST-4

1. We .... serve our country. (ought to/should) (not so forceful)
2. You .... not waste your time. (should/must)
3. If wishes were horses, beggars .... ride. (will/would)
4. .... I take her out, mother? (can/could)
5. .... I come in sir? (may/can). (more formal)
6. It .... rain today. (may/might). (less uncertain)
7. The sun .... rise in the east. (will/shall) (to express general facts)
8. Had you worked hard, you .... have passed. (would/should)
9. I .... rather die than go. (will/would) (toexpress a preference)
10. Walk fast lest you .... miss the train. (shall/should)

PRACTICE TEST-5

1. I told him that he .... take the test. (can/could)
2. You .... leave now. (may/might) (permission in a less formalmanner)
3. The teacher .... be busy at this time. (can/must) (to express a greaterpossibility)
4. She told me that he .... go. (will/would)
5. I .... teach him a lesson. (will/would) (to express a threat)
6. She .... marry Shyam. (will/must) (insistence)
7. You .... attend the evening class. (must/will) (greater compulsion)
8. .... you give me a glass of water, please? (can/could) (request in a more formal manner)
9. You .... reach there in time. (must/should) (order in a mare determined sense)
10. .... I answer your question? (should/need) (requirement)

PRACTICE TEST-6

1. It .... be true. (may/might) (very unsure)
2. I wish I .... help you, but I have my own problems. (can/could)
3. .... that I were a king! (will/would)
4. If I were the Prime Minister, I .... fight corruption. (will/would)
5. Had I reached the station in time, I .... have caught the train. (will/would)
6. This is a film you .... not avoid. (must/can)
7. I .... do/perform Bharatanatyam. (can/may) (ability)
8. You .... not leave without my permission. (will/shall) (threat)
9. He was so weak that he .... not walk. (could/would)
10. I told him that he .... leave. (can/could)

PRACTICE TEST-7

1. He .... like to spend an evening with you. (will/would)
2. The headmaster .... check all these accounts. (should/dare)
3. .... you like to take coffee? (can/would)
4. If you meet him you .... tell him about it. (might/must)
5. He ... be rich, but he is very cruel. (will/may)
6. We .... show respect to our elders. (oughtto/can)
7. The doctor told me that I .... not smokeany more. (must/will)
8. .... you possibly lend me a thousand rupees? (could/will)
9. You .... not enter my class, I forbid it. (must/will)
10. We .... keep our neighbours as happy aswe can. (may/should)

PRACTICE TEST-8

1. I .... help him with money before I leave for London. (will/would)
2. The children asked if they .... have ice cream. (can/could)
3. We .... do as we are told. (can/should)
4. Work hard lest you .... fail. (may/should)
5. You ... respect your elders. (ought to/can)
6. .... I come in? I am sorry to be late. (may/shall)
7. He has been absent for a fortnight, he .... be ill. (must/will)
8. You .... not see him, just write a letter. (need/dare)
9. We .... go to the station by taxi, it is getting late. (may/should)
10. I .... not come yesterday since I was toobusy. (would/could)

PRACTICE TEST-9

1. You .... clean your teeth every morning. (shall/should)
2. It .... rain today. (very little possibility)(may/might)
3. This box is very heavy, I .... not lift it.(should/may)
4. You .... take a taxi or you will miss thetrain. (shall/should)
5. ......you like to read this book? (will/would)
6. .... you lift this elephant? (can/will)
7. It is getting late; we .... go home. (should/can)
8. I .... run five miles in an hour. (can/shall)
9. You .... go out for a walk every day. (must/may)
10. Why didn't you inform me? I .... have lentyou the money. (can/could)

PRACTICE TEST-10

1. .... you finish your work in two hours? (can/may)
2. .... his soul rest in peace!(may/might)
3. The doctor says that I .... eat anything Ilike. (can/may)
4. Walk carefully lest you .... sprain your foot. (may/should)
5. You .... not take this trouble, I'll do that. (need/may)
6. The door of his room is not locked, he .... be in. (may/shall)
7. Forty years ago, only the rich .... think of owning a radio set. (can/could)
8. .... you like to get rid of thattroublesome fellow? (would/can)
9. You .... not hurry; there is plenty of time. (need/may)
10. You .... have returned these books last week. (should/shall)

PRACTICE TEST-11

1. You .... do as you are told. (should/ shall)
2. I...certainly see you next week.(can/may)
3. You ......respect your parents. (should/can)
4. You .... not violate traffic regulations. (must/may)
5. Walk fast lest you .... miss the train. (may/should)
6. It is a serious matter, you .... consult a lawyer before you do anything. (must/shall)
7. The children asked if they .... have chocolates. (can/could)
8. None...question the ways of God. (can/could)
9. .... you run so fast? (can/may)
10. How .... you abuse your elder brother? (could/should)

ANSWERS (PRACTICE TESTS)

Q. No.	TEST – 1	TEST – 2	TEST – 3	TEST – 4
1.	could	must	must	ought to
2.	may	must	would	must
3.	will	can	must	would
4.	must	would	need	can
5.	may	will	dare	may
6.	may	will	could	may
7.	might	can	can	will
8.	may	must	may	would
9.	may	would	may	would
10.	could	would	should	shall

Q. No.	TEST – 5	TEST – 6	TEST – 7	TEST – 8
1.	could	might	would	will
2.	may	could	should	could
3.	must	would	would	should
4.	would	would	must	should
5.	will	would	may	ought to
6.	must	must	ought to	may
7.	must	can	must	must
8.	could	shall	could	need
9.	must	could	must	should
10.	need	could	should	could

Q. No.	TEST – 9	TEST – 10	TEST – 11
1.	should	can	shall
2.	might	may	can
3.	should	may	should
4.	should	should	must
5.	would	need	should
6.	can	may	must
7.	should	could	could
8.	can	would	can
9.	must	need	can
10.	could	should	could

PART C: TEST OF USAGE OF ENGLISH LANGUAGE (164 PTs AND APPROX 2000 MCQs)

24 TEST OF USAGE OF WORDS - SYNONYMS

300 MCQs

Directions: ***In the following sentences given below, a word, or phrase is written in the bold italicised letter. For each bold italicised word, four words/phrases are listed below each sentence. Choose the word nearest in meaning to the italicised word.***

PRACTICE TEST-1

Q 1. He had a ***penchant*** for fine phrases.
(a) bias (b) liking
(c) training (d) desire

Q 2. The parade route was down the main ***boulevard***.
(a) alley (b) high way
(c) avenue (d) drive way

Q 3. Your master will like you if you are ***diligent***.
(a) conscientious (b) obedient
(c) meticulous (d) hard working

Q 4. ***Incensed*** by his rude behaviour, the manager suspended the work.
(a) enthused (b) enraged
(c) inflamed (d) excited

Q 5. In the existing circumstances her success is ***out of the question***.
(a) impossible (b) possible
(c) unquestionable (d) certain

Q 6. The five experiments gave ***disparate*** results.
(a) similar (b) encouraging
(c) strange (d) different

Q 7. Though he is a teacher, his speed lacks ***distinctness***.
(a) clarity (b) precision
(c) distinction (d) fluency

Q 8. On account of the ***paucity*** of the funds, the plan remained incomplete.
(a) lack (b) scarcity
(c) abundance (d) excess

Q 9. We walked down a ***precipitous*** slope.
(a) precarious (b) steep
(c) precise (d) gradual

Q 10. The ***indiscriminate*** demand for mass consumption goods is deplorable.
(a) desperate (b) undifferentiated
(c) discreet (d) insensitive

Q 11. ***Malice*** is a feeling that we should always avoid.
(a) Ill–will (b) Spite
(c) Cruelty (d) Every

Q 12. It is discouraging to find educated people being *taken in* ***easily*** by the lies of religious charlatans.
(a) creditable (b) credulous
(c) credible (d) creative

Q 13. Outside I am nothing but a ***frolicsome*** little goat who is broken loose.
(a) happy (b) playful
(c) gay (d) delightful

Q 14. Due to the long ***lapse*** of time, I could not recognise my old friend.
(a) delay (b) passage
(c) duration (d) movement

Q 15. How I ***envy*** the man who can always produce his reading glasses at a moment's notice.
(a) begrudge (b) desire
(c) crave (d) covet

Q 16. The communal politics has done ***imponderable*** loss to the unity of India.
(a) incalculable (b) invaluable

(c) irreparable (d) invulnerable

Q 17. Wealth acquired through ***dishonourable*** means lead to moral downfall.

(a) incredulous (b) discreditable
(c) incredible (d) disgraceful

Q 18. Some satirists are known of their ***trenchant*** style.

(a) sharp (b) critical
(c) aggressive (d) incisive

Q 19. I am filled with ***remorse*** for my failure to help the young man.

(a) despair (b) regret
(c) anger (d) hatred

Q 20. ***Sanguine*** as he is in his attitude to life and its problems, he cannot but be noticed wherever he goes.

(a) optimistic (b) enthusiastic
(c) realistic (d) dispassionate

Q 21. Our Prime Minister is young and ***dynamic***.

(a) belligerent (b) explosive
(c) energetic (d) intelligent

Q 22. Quite ***unabashed***, he began his scholarly lecture on what was obvious to everyone.

(a) unashamed (b) unimpressed
(c) unnerved (d) unchecked

Q 23. He ***hardly*** works.

(a) arduously (b) mostly
(c) scarcely (d) strenuously

Q 24. The maid servant left the police station ***contrite***.

(a) penitent (b) sore
(c) angry (d) remorseless

Q 25. Would you please ***rectify*** the mistake?

(a) correct (b) clarify
(c) condone (d) regularise

PRACTICE TEST-2

Q 1. He had ***insidiously*** wormed his way into her affections.

(a) in a polite manner (b) in a secret manner
(c) in ugly way (d) in a forceful manner

Q 2. His close friend, who was senior to him in the office, did not hesitate to ***reprimand*** him when he misplaced one important file.

(a) demote (b) rebuke
(c) suspend (d) penalise

Q 3. One must not be ***callous*** to womenfolk.

(a) kind (b) hard hearted
(c) arrogant (d) proud

Q 4. Last fortnight the rains came to the parched soils of India after the merciless drought that had already ***sapped*** the vitality and livelihood of millions of peasants.

(a) decreased (b) demolished
(c) destroyed (d) drained away

Q 5. That young man is quite ***sanguine*** about the result of his competitive examination.

(a) optimistic (b) anxious
(c) depressed (d) pessimistic

Q 6. He tried to ***cajole*** her, but it was in vain.

(a) rejoice (b) inspire
(c) enjoin (d) coax

Q 7. The new government decided to ***rescind*** most of the decisions of its predecessor.

(a) re-consider (b) impose
(c) modify (d) repeal

Q 8. He had the ***nerve*** to suggest that I was cheating.

(a) strength (b) capacity
(c) audacity (d) courage

Q 9. Even today many people are guided by ***abstruse*** moral values.

(a) dangerous (b) impracticable
(c) obscure (d) irrational

Q 10. Millionaires become ***eccentric*** in their old age.

(a) miserly (b) dull
(c) peculiar (d) irritable

Q 11. The performance of the candidates was ***deplorable***.

(a) horrible (b) contentious
(c) laughable (d) lamentable

Q 12. Indian economy has always shown enough ***resilience*** in crisis.

(a) diversity (b) strength
(c) elasticity (d) adjustment

Q 13. Whatever the ***verdict*** of history may be, Chaplin will occupy a unique place in its pages.

(a) prediction (b) outcome
(c) judgement (d) voice

Q 14. Poonam is ever ready to ***lend a hand.***
(a) assist (b) obstruct
(c) praise (d) hand over

Q 15. She is very ***discreet***.
(a) mannered (b) mild
(c) proud (d) prudent

Q 16. The judge asked the contending parties to state their position ***unequivocally***.
(a) adequately (b) completely
(c) effectively (d) plainly

Q 17. If a leader wants to be popular he should master the art of being ***civil*** to everyone.
(a) polite (b) civilised
(c) friendly (d) obedient

Q 18. We have witnessed an ***inexorable*** march of progress by the organisation.
(a) inexhaustible (b) relentless
(c) comprehensive (d) sluggish

Q 19. Indian cricketers were ***brimming*** over with confidence after their English tour.
(a) overflow (b) blow over
(c) flow over (d) overspill

Q 20. His ***adulatory*** remarks surprised us.
(a) discreet (b) insulting
(c) flattering (d) funny

Q 21. The great dancer impressed the appreciative crowd by her ***nimble*** movements.
(a) subtle (b) clear
(c) quickening (d) arrhythmic

Q 22. He whirled round in a ***trice*** with a revolver in his hand.
(a) a trifle (b) a triangle
(c) an instant (d) a circle

Q 23. He used to ***regale*** us with anecdotes.
(a) flatter (b) bore
(c) tire (d) entertain

Q 24. Many of his acquaintances avoid him because he is so ***garrulous.***
(a) unreasonable (b) quarrelsome
(c) talkative (d) proud

Q 25. He spent his whole life caught up in ***mundane*** matters.
(a) inconsequential (b) foolish
(c) criminal (d) worldly

PRACTICE TEST-3

Q 1. It is the Prime Minister's ***prerogative*** to appoint or dismiss a Minister.
(a) monopoly (b) authority
(c) mastery (d) privilege

Q 2. Some people are extremely ***fastidious*** in their choice of dress.
(a) careless (b) pompous
(c) careful (d) discriminating

Q 3. A ***posthumous*** award was given to the poet.
(a) postal (b) after death
(c) creditable (d) literary

Q 4. The ***antidote*** to these problems is hard to find.
(a) result of (b) cause for
(c) consequence of (d) remedy for

Q 5. Before I could ***expostulate*** he had spoken again.
(a) explain (b) disclose
(c) protest (d) postulate

Q 6. Ramnath is such a ***sham*** that it is difficult to get along with him.
(a) pretender (b) unnatural
(c) blunt (d) unfair

Q 7. Whatever opinion he gives is ***sane***.
(a) arrogant (b) wild
(c) obscure (d) rational

Q 8. The early monsoon have brought ***respite*** to the people.
(a) despite (b) inspite of
(c) interval of relief (d) rest

Q 9. Such conduct deserves ***reprimand***.
(a) praise (b) punishment
(c) rebuke (d) reward

Q 10. Businessmen who lack ***acumen*** cannot be expected to be very successful.
(a) smartness (b) sharpness
(c) keenness (d) cleverness

Q 11. The journey to Siliguri is quite ***tedious***.
(a) diverting (b) wearisome
(c) lively (d) resolute

Q 12. The navy gave ***tactical*** support to the marines.

(a) sensitive (b) strategic
(c) expedient (d) expert

Q 13. The poets are known to ***fly*** in their thoughts more than a practical man.
(a) sore (b) soar
(c) sour (d) soare

Q 14. The ***facade*** of our school building got a face lift recently.
(a) basement (b) floor
(c) top (d) front

Q 15. Peace keeping for the United Nations is, at best of times, an ***arduous*** task.
(a) laborious (b) inconvenient
(c) difficult (d) delicate

Q 16. Before I could ***make out anything*** he had spoken again.
(a) find out (b) apprehend
(c) explain (d) reveal

Q 17. I won't go out of my way to ***placate*** him.
(a) please (b) pacify
(c) serve (d) satisfy

Q 18. He has traveled all over the continent by ***hitchhiking*** most of the time.
(a) free ride (b) ride
(c) drive (d) drive freely

Q 19. He is notorious for his ***voracious*** appetite.
(a) acute (b) haughty
(c) gluttonous (d) strong

Q 20. He kept his eyes peeled and his ears pricked for some important ***clue.***
(a) point (b) inkling
(c) intimation (d) signal

Q 21. I wrote to him as ***lately*** as last week.
(a) immediately (b) early
(c) recently (d) late

Q 22. Timely first aid ***resuscitated*** the patient.
(a) soothed (b) rescued
(c) revived (d) cured

Q 23 The eyewitness testimony was ***incontrovertible***.
(a) debatable (b) unquestionable
(c) unacceptable (d) disputable

Q 24. A careful ***preservation*** of wild life is the need of the hour.
(a) conservation (b) management
(c) promotion (d) enhancement

Q 25. She is not seen even smiling these days; she is rather ***pensive***.
(a) sad (b) thoughtful
(c) gloomy (d) black

PRACTICE TEST–4

Q 1. He displayed a distinct tendency to ***long–winded*** speeches when asked how he was.
(a) boring (b) repetitive
(c) circumlocutory (d) hyperbolic

Q 2. The man lives long through his ***good deeds*** after he had died.
(a) beneficial (b) benevolent
(c) beneficient (d) benediction

Q 3. In ***exasperation*** she railed at the shopkeeper.
(a) irritation (b) fear
(c) astonishment (d) disappointment

Q 4. The prisoner has been ***languishing*** in the jail for the last many years.
(a) enjoying (b) avoiding
(c) suffering (d) convicted

Q 5. Buoyed by these visions of the future of his son, the artist ***soldiered*** on.
(a) continued bravely (b) stopped further
(c) struggled hard (d) fought on

Q 6. He did not succeed in his ***endeavour***.
(a) enterprise (b) effort
(c) trick (d) plan

Q 7. He does not know how to ***husband*** his resources.
(a) manage (b) govern
(c) rule (d) watch

Q 8. The number of ***aboriginal*** inhabitants in Australia is considerable.
(a) unoriginal (b) irrational
(c) primitive (d) ancient

Q 9. The guests were offended with his ***uncouth*** manners.
(a) wasteful (b) uncultured
(c) undesirable (d) ungracious

Q 10. He does ***unpaid*** work for the Red Cross.
(a) honourable (b) honorary
(c) honest (d) honorific

Q 11. We did not expect such a ***judicious*** remark from him.

(a) legal (b) shrewd
(c) rational (d) sagacious

Q 12. It was pure fabrication with an ***eye*** for a sensation.

(a) observation (b) wish
(c) desire (d) aim

Q 13. His ***judicious*** handling of the matter saved the situation from going out of control.

(a) sensible (b) nervous
(c) cautious (d) helpful

Q 14. ***Furtive*** glances were exchanged between the lovers at the feast.

(a) unknown (b) secret
(c) unsuspecting (d) clandestine

Q 15. She purchased ***gimcrack*** ornaments from the market.

(a) expensive (b) worthless
(c) rare (d) smuggled

Q 16. The villagers offered us an excellent ***repast***.

(a) pass time (b) a good meal
(c) entertainment (d) fate

Q 17. The ***unlawful*** activities of the terrorists need to be dealt with an iron hand.

(a) lugubrious (b) salubrious
(c) nefarious (d) deleterious

Q 18. We will carry out the enquiry as ***expeditiously*** as possible.

(a) fairly (b) speedily
(c) timely (d) justifiably

Q 19. Don't entertain any ***misgivings*** about his conduct.

(a) distrust (b) doubt
(c) suspicion (d) impression

Q 20. He could rise to this stature because of his ***invincible*** courage.

(a) inviolable (b) unmanageable
(c) unbeatable (d) immeasurable

Q 21. Many educationists think that the classroom instruction should be made more ***vigorous***.

(a) serious (b) brisk
(c) lively (d) active

Q 22. What meaning have you ***drawn*** from her tongue in cheek remarks.

(a) deduced (b) induced
(c) conduced (d) deducted

Q 23. The Collector has yet not ***relinquished*** his charge.

(a) give up (b) abdicate
(c) leave (d) renounce

Q 24. Even though Akshay does not study hard, he always ***comes*** first in his class.

(a) scores (b) stands
(c) arrives (d) completes

Q 25. We should abstain from ***bullying*** our colleagues.

(a) silly jokes (b) frightening
(c) passing remarks (d) compliments

PRACTICE TEST-5

Q 1. His ***trite*** remarks failed to cut any ice with the audience.

(a) hackneyed (b) sharp
(c) illogical (d) bitter

Q 2. The prince fell in love with a ***comely*** young maiden.

(a) elegant (b) homely
(c) pretty (d) delightful

Q 3. My philosophy lecturer is unfailingly ***bombastic***.

(a) sensitive in the use of words
(b) impressionistic
(c) impressive
(d) pompous

Q 4. Inspite of their efforts, the team of scientists could not make much ***headway*** to solve the problem.

(a) results (b) start
(c) efforts (d) progress

Q 5. John Milton wrote 'Paradise Lost' to ***vindicate*** the ways of God to man.

(a) explain (b) support
(c) justify (d) criticise

Q 6. Some satirists are known for their ***trenchant*** style.

(a) critical (b) sharp
(c) aggressive (d) incisive

Q 7. The newspapers are ***clamouring*** against the injustice to the landless labourers.

(a) protesting (b) noising

(c) complaining (d) demonstrating

Q 8. The ***inexorable*** demands of the workers brought the company to a closure.

(a) unreasonable (b) relentless
(c) monetary (d) violent

Q 9. It is ***exasperating*** to listen to the suggestions of the minister about the educational reforms of which he knows nothing.

(a) irritating (b) amusing
(c) disappointing (d) boring

Q 10. The ***surreptitious*** movements of a long figure among the dunes filled the villagers with curiosity and awe.

(a) invisible (b) nocturnal
(c) secret (d) concealed

Q 11. ***Forthrightness*** in speech may not always be a desirable quality.

(a) outspokenness (b) obliqueness
(c) mendacity (d) equivocation

Q 12. The courage shown by the soldiers at this moment of crisis is ***exemplary***.

(a) admirable (b) clear
(c) elementary (d) suitable

Q 13. During the short stay in India, he had quite a few ***frustrating*** experiences.

(a) repulsive (b) humiliating
(c) disappointing (d) disenchanting

Q 14. His ***lascivious*** habits brought him nothing but bad name.

(a) vicious (b) lustful
(c) erotic (d) treacherous

Q 15. Some army units were ***decimated*** during the surprise attack

(a) defamed (b) captured
(c) destroyed (d) denounced

Q 16. The travel agent will ***confirm*** my reservation for the next week's flight to London.

(a) approve (b) obtain
(c) verify (d) ratify

Q 17. Everybody laughed at the ***puerility*** of his statement.

(a) insincerity (b) falsehood
(c) childishness (d) inaccuracy

Q 18. Reading of poetry is not ***congenial*** to his taste.

(a) preferable (b) helpful
(c) beneficial (d) suited

Q 19. The committee did not find him ***fit*** for the job.

(a) genuine (b) correct
(c) suitable (d) selected

Q 20. The novel was so interesting that I was ***oblivious*** of my surroundings.

(a) indifferent (b) watchful
(c) unmindful (d) precarious

Q 21. He is very much interested in the ***study of mankind***.

(a) anthropology (b) philology
(c) physiology (d) pathology

Q 22. The five day week in Government Offices is bound to benefit the ***jaded*** office goers.

(a) refreshed (b) routine
(c) fatigued (d) vigorous

Q 23. He is a good looking but ***insipid*** young man.

(a) arrogant (b) unscrupulous
(c) sick (d) lacking in spirit

Q 24. A genius tends to ***deviate*** from the routine way of thinking.

(a) dispute (b) differ
(c) disagree (d) distinguish

Q 25. Her evidence totally ***refuted*** the charges.

(a) refused (b) denied
(c) disproved (d) repelled

PRACTICE TEST-6

Q 1. Honest officers find it difficult to ***attune*** themselves to corrupt bureaucracy.

(a) tune (b) adapt
(c) harmony (d) accusation

Q 2. He mentioned in the ***postscript*** that he might need some money, soon.

(a) end of the letter after signature
(b) manuscript
(c) after the address
(d) post diction

Q 3. When youngsters do not have good role-models to ***emulate,*** they start searching for them among sportsmen or film stars.

(a) inhabit (b) imitate
(c) mollify (d) modify

Q 4. A ***rupture*** in the relationship of the two brothers is quite apparent.
(a) gap (b) damage
(c) break (d) breach

Q 5. ***Defection*** is quite common in our present day political life.
(a) desertion (b) disobedience
(c) disloyalty (d) indiscipline

Q 6. His conscience ***pricked*** him.
(a) soothed (b) cut
(c) hurt (d) pinched

Q 7. A person unrestrained by the rules of morality or tradition is called a ***licentious*** person.
(a) libertine (b) loafer type
(c) criminal (d) freelance

Q 8. I don't see why he should be so ***obsequious*** to his brother just because the latter is rich.
(a) unfriendly (b) unusually kind
(c) offensive (d) excessively respectful

Q 9. He was ***admonished*** for the delay.
(a) admired (b) warned
(c) censured (d) dismissed

Q 10. ***Hybrid*** variety of plants generally yield better crops.
(a) combined (b) transplanted
(c) complex (d) mixed

Q 11. The people welcomed the budget as there was ***judicious*** allocation of funds to all the sectors.
(a) legal (b) indiscriminate
(c) generous (d) sensible

Q 12. The poem is written in a very ***lucid*** style.
(a) intricate (b) noble
(c) elaborate (d) clear

Q 13. All the characters in the novel are ***fictitious***.
(a) unreliable (b) unbelievable
(c) unreal (d) imaginative

Q 14. Elsie is seventy years old and a ***fanatical*** gardener.
(a) crazy
(b) fantastic
(c) excessively enthusiastic
(d) obsessed

Q 15. It is so ***gratifying*** to know that there are not many cases of small pox these days.
(a) pleasing (b) surprising
(c) satisfying (d) happy

Q 16. India has not yet been able to ***harness*** her domestic resources in full.
(a) complete (b) utilise
(c) produce (d) bridle

Q 17. She ***upbraided*** the little girl who got frightened.
(a) make tails (b) make up
(c) scolded (d) handed

Q 18. The two opposing parties have reached a ***stalemate***.
(a) dilemma (b) deadlock
(c) exhaustion (d) settlement

Q 19. Rich people often have ***sycophants*** around them.
(a) pilots (b) sadists
(c) flatterers (d) servants

Q 20. The obstacles seem to be ***insurmountable***, but no one should doubt what this fearless woman can accomplish.
(a) too tall and too high
(b) too trivial to attract attention
(c) too easy to achieve
(d) too difficult to overcome

Q 21. Everybody in the assembly shouted and there was ***pandemonium*** in the hall.
(a) disorderly scene (b) noise
(c) laughter (d) crowd

Q 22. She looked ***gorgeous*** in her new dress.
(a) great (b) fantastic
(c) silly (d) splendid

Q 23. The ***aberration*** in the Indian Economy can be attributed to short sightedness of its political masters.
(a) deviation (b) steadfastness
(c) privilege (d) procrastination

Q 24. Sunlight and shadow made the landscape a ***kaleidoscope*** of colour.
(a) tube containing mirrors and loose pieces of coloured glass
(b) frequently changing pattern of bright scenes
(c) a mixture of black and white

(d) resembling the seven colours of rainbow

Q 25. My neighbour is an ***extravagant*** person.
(a) pompous (b) reckless
(c) unreasonable (d) wasteful

PRACTICE TEST-7

Q 1. He is so ***garrulous*** that all sober persons avoid his company.
(a) quarrelsome (b) talkative
(c) domineering (d) foolish

Q 2. Mumbai is the ***terminus*** of the Western Railways.
(a) last stop (b) termination
(c) junction (d) tenure

Q 3. Our fates seemed ***intertwined***.
(a) complicated (b) destined
(c) complex (d) linked

Q 4. The Prime Minister delivered an ***impromptu*** speech to the students.
(a) important (b) impressive
(c) inspiring (d) extempore

Q 5. The *honesty* of the king's minister was ***above board*** and the king was fond of him.
(a) propinquity (b) polarity
(c) beyond suspicion (d) posterity

Q 6. The treaty was later ***ratified***.
(a) charged (b) confirmed
(c) reformed (d) updated

Q 7. The District Collector made it clear that the Government cannot ***sustain*** for long the support for such a scheme.
(a) pay (b) succeed
(c) manage (d) continue

Q 8. The invasion forces had no artillery and were completely ***annihilated***.
(a) reduced (b) destroyed
(c) dismembered (d) split

Q 9. Our talks with the foreign delegation were really ***productive***.
(a) growing (b) efficient
(c) fruitful (d) lengthy

Q 10. Dr. S. Radha Krishnan has written an ***erudite*** commentary on the Bhagawad Gita.
(a) scholarly (b) inspiring
(c) effective (d) perfect

Q 11. Scientific knowledge is an intoxicating ***draught***, and it may be one which the human race is unable to sustain.
(a) process (b) product
(c) drink (d) disease

Q 12. The story is ***embellished*** with amusing put perhaps undue details.
(a) adorned (b) balanced
(c) sprinkled (d) filled

Q 13. In so far as his research is concerned, he is very ***meticulous***.
(a) alert to improve technique
(b) slovenly and inexact
(c) about to start
(d) stupendous

Q 14. ***Weird*** noises came from the haunted houses.
(a) beastly (b) unpleasant
(c) frightening (d) unnatural

Q 15. Something should be done about the ***insanitary*** conditions of our parks.
(a) poor (b) dingy
(c) ugly (d) unhygienic

Q 16. He had to ***curtail*** his leave as a lot of work was pending in his office.
(a) cancel (b) extend
(c) shorten (d) postpone

Q 17. True religion does not require one to ***proselytise*** through guile or force.
(a) convert (b) attack
(c) hypnotise (d) translate

Q 18. We should always try to maintain and promote communal ***amity***.
(a) understanding (b) bondage
(c) friendship (d) contention

Q 19. He displayed a distinct tendency to ***long winded*** speeches when asked how he was.
(a) circumlocutory (b) hyperbolic
(c) repetitive (d) boring

Q 20. English conversation means the learning of many ***catchy*** phrases.
(a) easily remembered (b) easily spoken
(c) easily understood (d) lucid

Q 21. This is a ***lucrative*** business.
(a) profitable (b) dangerous
(c) challenging (d) questionable

Q 22. We are happy that the two countries are trying to find an ***amicable*** solution to their disputes.

(a) a just (b) an appropriate
(c) a durable (d) a friendly

Q 23. A man of unsound mind, he was ***exone-rated*** from all responsibility for his actions.

(a) exculpated (b) prevented
(c) excused (d) liberated

Q 24. The coach followed a ***devious*** course to its destination.

(a) difficult (b) short–cut
(c) straight (d) winding

Q 25. The millions of the poor ***hapless*** Indians' future does not hold any promise.

(a) unhappy (b) unfortunate
(c) helpless (d) adverse

PRACTICE TEST-8

Q 1. He tried to ***alleviate*** the sufferings of his neighbours.

(a) abate (b) dissipate
(c) remove (d) relieve

Q 2. The ***disgruntled*** members of a party are constant source of tension to the party leader.

(a) disloyal (b) dishonest
(c) discontented (d) dispirited

Q 3. The young girl appeared ***self-possessed*** in front of TV cameras.

(a) shy (b) confident
(c) introvert (d) extrovert

Q 4. He ended his speech on a ***supercilious*** note which was quite unexpected of a person of balanced and stable temperament.

(a) defamatory (b) contemptuous
(c) superfluous (d) irrelevant

Q 5. Factory workers are ***restive*** as the company has not declared any bonus this year.

(a) restful (b) restless
(c) resting (d) satisfied

Q 6. She cannot tolerate ***exceptionable*** remarks about her parents.

(a) exceptional (b) objectionable
(c) exception (d) humility

Q 7. His ***forthright*** behaviour shows that he is honest but he seems rude to some people.

(a) courteous (b) correct
(c) straightforward (d) tactful

Q 8. It is amazing how such a ***motley*** group could get along 50 well.

(a) heterogeneous (b) assorted
(c) promiscuous (d) confused

Q 9. She leaned back, feeling ***enervated***.

(a) disheartened (b) confused
(c) saddened (d) weakened

Q 10. He was accused of ***graft***.

(a) corruption (b) inefficiency
(c) favouritism (d) negligence

Q 11. We didn't believe in his statement but ***subsequent*** events proved that he was right.

(a) latter (b) many
(c) few (d) conclusive

Q 12. He has been able to ***unearth*** a secret.

(a) suppress (b) discover
(c) disclose (d) decade

Q 13. It is difficult to ***authenticate*** these old manuscripts.

(a) elucidate
(b) illustrate
(c) establish genuinence
(d) edit properly

Q 14. Corruption ***stalks*** every sphere of national life.

(a) pervades (b) poisons
(c) pollutes (d) penetrates

Q 15. The rebels returned home under an ***amnesty.***

(a) general pardon
(b) financial assistance
(c) police security
(d) literary

Q 16. He is being treated for his ***somnolence.***

(a) sleepiness
(b) weakness
(c) intoxication
(d) severe pain in the joints

Q 17. The recent acts of ***vandalism*** in the country cannot be ignored.

(a) disturbance (b) ravage

(c) provocation (d) violence

Q 18. A bone got stuck in his ***gullet***.
(a) throat (b) chest
(c) molars (d) stomach

Q 19. For quick promotion, he hit on a plan to ***propitiate*** the Manager.
(a) evict (b) incite
(c) praise (d) conciliate

Q 20. He tried to ***mollify*** my hurt feelings.
(a) arouse (b) ignore
(c) soften (d) suppress

Q 21. The boy gave a ***vivid*** description of all that happened.
(a) brilliant (b) fresh
(c) explanatory (d) picturesque

Q 22. A ***conscientious*** worker is always admired by his employers.
(a) obedient (b) sinecure
(c) skilful (d) careful

Q 23. Few teachers have been spared the problem of an ***obstreperous*** pupil in the class.
(a) awkward (b) lazy
(c) unruly (d) sullen

Q 24. The ***deployment*** of para–military forces in Punjab has helped the provincial government a lot.
(a) activated (b) employment
(c) use (d) spreading out

Q 25. His boss's criticism left him feeling rather ***abashed***.
(a) annoyed (b) arrogant
(c) embarrassed (d) awakened

PRACTICE TEST-9

Q 1. Leaders of some political parties make ***fiery*** speeches.
(a) fantastic (b) inflammatory
(c) passionate (d) eloquent

Q 2. It was an ***astute*** move to sell the property at that stage.
(a) shrewd (b) unwise
(c) dishonest (d) inexplicable

Q 3. There is a ***tacit*** agreement between the superpowers not to engage themselves in armed conflict.
(a) unspoken (b) speechless
(c) silent (d) introvert

Q 4. No one expects a ***facile*** solution to the Punjab Problem.
(a) satisfactory (b) easy
(c) satisfying (d) difficult

Q 5. When I visited him he was in a ***retrospective*** mood.
(a) thoughtful (b) thinking of past
(c) pensive (d) introspective

Q 6. Plants that grow and exist in deserts have highly specialised means of adapting themselves to the ***arid*** environment.
(a) reproductive (b) useless
(c) withering (d) dry

Q 7. The arguments of the lawyer of the accused were so ***persuasive*** that the judge acquitted him.
(a) convincing (b) clever
(c) eloquent (d) logical

Q 8. He was sad that his seniority had been ***overlooked***.
(a) rejected (b) neglected
(c) confused (d) sidestepped

Q 9. He delivered a lengthy speech in which he committed several ***ludicrous*** mistakes.
(a) glaring (b) funny
(c) absurd (d) serious

Q 10. ***Eventually*** vision is affected and the patient is able to see only if light is present.
(a) primarily (b) initially
(c) gradually (d) ultimately

Q 11. It is ***futile*** to argue with a person who does not want to understand.
(a) unnecessary (b) useless
(c) dangerous (d) infuriating

Q 12. People of different ***persuasions*** have met on the same platform.
(a) taste (b) personalities
(c) convictions (d) qualifications

Q 13. He is believed to be a very ***industrious*** worker.
(a) successful (b) punctual
(c) sensible (d) diligent

Q 14. He found it an ***arduous*** task to perform.
(a) boring (b) ardent
(c) ordinary (d) difficult

Q 15. Lack of occupation is not necessarily revealed by ***manifest*** idleness.
(a) easily perceived (b) easily acquired
(c) easily infected (d) easily deflected

Q 16. He did his job with ***scrupulous*** care.
(a) exact (b) marvelous
(c) great (d) inattentive

Q 17. She is really a ***fantastic*** girl.
(a) wonderful (b) charming
(c) beautiful (d) intelligent

Q 18. He ***corroborated*** the statement of his brother.
(a) condemned (b) confirmed
(c) seconded (d) disproved

Q 19. There must be lively discussion of Indian authors if we are to ***foster our*** knowledge.
(a) promote (b) cherish
(c) nourish (d) nurture

Q 20. He wrote a ***scathing*** review of the prize–winning novel.
(a) biased (b) scornful
(c) unbalanced (d) subjective

Q 21. The library was built with donations from the ***munificent*** citizens of this city.
(a) generous (b) respectable
(c) learned (d) well–to–do

Q 22. As a speaker, he was an ***utter*** failure.
(a) total (b) partial
(c) completely (d) relative

Q 23. Mohinder Amarnath had ***penchant*** for hook shots.
(a) art (b) inclination
(c) strength (d) desire

Q 24. After he came back from his evening walk, he felt ***famished***.
(a) exhausted (b) hungry
(c) peevish (d) relaxed

Q 25. Medical science is yet to come out with a ***panacea*** for cancer.
(a) remedy (b) medicine
(c) treatment (d) drug

PRACTICE TEST-10

Q 1. The new volume provides substantial critical ***excerpts*** and biographical information on eight to ten major poets from all eras.
(a) sources (b) explanation
(c) extracts (d) substances

Q 2. The chairman conducted the meeting with ***aplomb***.
(a) arrogance (b) annoyance
(c) poise (d) authority

Q 3. Even the most careful researcher cannot predict the possible future ***ramifications*** of his findings.
(a) uses (b) developments
(c) consequences (d) conclusions

Q 4. There was no ***ostensible*** reason for her being angry at her husband's remarks.
(a) hidden (b) covert
(c) apparent (d) secret

Q 5. Ritu asked Rashmi not to ***meddle*** in her affairs.
(a) intercede (b) impose
(c) cross (d) interfere

Q 6. A pervading sense of ***ennui*** grips Gaurav.
(a) anger (b) anxiety
(c) weariness (d) melancholy

Q 7. We don't know how we are to ***recompense*** you for the trouble you have taken.
(a) reward (b) help
(c) praise (d) thank

Q 8. Most of the politicians these days have a large number of ***toadies*** around them.
(a) followers (b) professional assistants
(c) servants (d) sycophants

Q 9. The small boy was able to give a ***graphic*** description of the thief.
(a) vague (b) vivid
(c) drawing (d) picture

Q 10. The secret of good style is to avoid ***redundant*** words.
(a) repetitive (b) unwilling
(c) wrong (d) retarded

Q 11. Dowry is a ***pernicious*** social practice.
(a) traditional (b) prevalent
(c) painful (d) injurious

Q 12. I ***stood up for him*** when everyone else was criticising him.

(a) tolerated him
(b) opposed him insistently
(c) supported him energetically
(d) faced him boldly

Q 13. He is quite ***parsimonious*** by nature.

(a) cruel (b) haughty
(c) prodigal (d) miserly

Q 14. ***Sporadic*** rise in his temperature caused us much worry.

(a) scattered (b) occasional
(c) irksome (d) frequent

Q 15. I gave a shout when I sighted an ***oasis*** in the desert.

(a) waterfall
(b) a patch of grass
(c) a place with water and trees
(d) waterway

Q 16. He was warned at the ***outset*** of his career.

(a) end (b) beginning
(c) middle (d) entrance

Q 17. On scrutiny the police officer found out that the documents provided by the landlord were totally ***fabricated***.

(a) historical (b) genuine
(c) forged (d) prepared

Q 18. Most of the staff is ***restive*** under the new manager's rule.

(a) relaxed (b) friendly
(c) obstinate (d) discontented

Q 19. Grandfather has been getting ***feeble*** of late.

(a) tall (b) weak
(c) diseased (d) small

Q 20. His visit to foreign countries brought about a ***sea change*** in his outlook and his attitude to the people.

(a) favourable change
(b) complete change
(c) unfavourable change
(d) partial change

Q 21. Being a sociable bird she was ***conspicuous*** by her absence in the club last evening.

(a) important (b) prominent
(c) ignorant (d) apparent

Q 22. There seems to be ***perpetual*** war going on between the rich and the poor.

(a) never ending (b) regular
(c) always (d) intermittent

Q 23. The flat has been ***refurbished*** recently.

(a) white–washed (b) painted
(c) renovated (d) repaired

Q 24. The officer gave a ***lucid*** explanation of the company's course of action.

(a) vague (b) unconvincing
(c) long (d) clear

Q 25. ***Temperance*** in eating is conducive to health.

(a) discipline (b) caution
(c) moderation (d) care

PRACTICE TEST-11

Q 1. One's ***remonstration*** against social ills has to be consistent to be fruitful.

(a) outrage (b) demonstration
(c) protest (d) criticism

Q 2. It would be ***impertinent*** to suggest that he was generally wrong.

(a) fair (b) correct
(c) rude (d) impartial

Q 3. The opposition criticised the ruling party for the ***deteriorating*** law and order situation in the state.

(a) disrupting (b) worsening
(c) crumbling (d) eroding

Q 4. One of the ***salient*** features of your proposal is a stress on self employment.

(a) prominent (b) silent
(c) loud (d) important

Q 5. Man has to ***encounter*** many hardships in life.

(a) solve (b) face
(c) bear (d) overcome

Q 6. After the ***dismal*** performance of the team in the series concluded yesterday the captain offered his resignation to the President of the club.

(a) poor (b) miserly
(c) short (d) sorrowful

Q 7. Some of the discoveries of modern science are simply ***marvellous***.

(a) praiseworthy (b) commendable
(c) amazing (d) admirable

Q 8. The scheme failed for want of ***adequate*** funds.
(a) required (b) recommended
(c) sufficient (d) necessary

Q 9. The Border Security Force ***intercepted*** yesterday a truck carrying arms and ammunition.
(a) found (b) stopped
(c) met (d) interrupted

Q 10. Because of a family ***feud***, he never spoke to his wife's parents.
(a) trouble (b) crisis
(c) quarrel (d) problem

Q 11. Everyone turned to stare at the visitor and his ***preposterous*** dress.
(a) strange (b) vague
(c) pompous (d) absurd

Q 12. Mulberry plantation is a prerequisite for ***sericulture***.
(a) growing soft grass
(b) breeding silk worms
(c) growing trees for timber
(d) breeding shrimps

Q 13. I found his crude manners ***abominable***.
(a) detestable (b) flattering
(c) attractive (d) sloppy

Q 14. The international community may begin to doubt the ***credentials*** of the largest democracy in the world.
(a) principles
(b) credibility
(c) capacity to return loans
(d) trustworthiness

Q 15. It is a ***scandal*** that the murderer was declared innocent.
(a) rumour (b) silly notion
(c) talk (d) disgraceful action

Q 16. The prisoner made an ***abortive*** attempt to escape from the jail.
(a) courageous (b) futile
(c) illegal (d) furtive

Q 17. A million cinemas a year bring the same stale ***balderdash***.
(a) adventure (b) nonsense
(c) thriller (d) romance

Q 18. His speech was nothing but a string of ***platitudes***.
(a) grand statements
(b) stereo–typed statements
(c) noble sentiments
(d) humorous anecdotes

Q 19. The opposition made a ***strident*** demand for putting the bill to vote.
(a) courageous (b) brave
(c) vociferous (d) powerful

Q 20. He soon got fed up with his ***sedentary*** job.
(a) involving much sitting (b) routine
(c) roving (d) drab

Q 21. Though long, your essay is ***vague*** on the point.
(a) doubtful (b) eloquent
(c) indistinct (d) lucid

Q 22. The field was ***even*** enough for the joggers to have their practice.
(a) plane (b) plain
(c) plan (d) plaine

Q 23. On public occasions, she was very ***punctilious*** about forms and manners.
(a) serious (b) careful
(c) artificial (d) casual

Q 24. This library was built with donations from the ***munificent*** citizens of the city.
(a) well-to-do (b) generous
(c) respectable (d) learned

Q 25. The ***perspicuity*** of the lawyer's arguments was remarkable.
(a) logic (b) precision
(c) lucidity (d) profundity

PRACTICE TEST-12

Q 1. The import of technology as an alternative to ***indigenous*** technology has not been discussed fully.
(a) aboriginal (b) indigent
(c) terrestrial (d) native

Q 2. The ***ascending*** temperature in many parts of the world confirms global warming which is an environmental hazard.
(a) mounting (b) shooting
(c) falling (d) rising

Q 3. Reading fiction is an ***absorbing***, creative and entertaining hobby.
(a) a concentrating (b) an engrossing

(c) a fascinating (d) an enriching

Q 4. The data is ***misleading***.

(a) illusory (b) deceptive
(c) misplaced (d) misinformative

Q 5. Graduation day is a ***momentous*** day for most students.

(a) memorable (b) melancholy
(c) important (d) hectic

Q 6. There was a major ***split*** in the Congress Party in 1969.

(a) breach (b) division
(c) break (d) unity

Q 7. Her views are not *in* ***consonance*** with her husband's.

(a) in disagreement (b) in conflict
(c) in agreement (d) contradictory

Q 8. The claims of students look hollow when they ***attribute*** their poor performance to difficulty of examination.

(a) inundate (b) inhere
(c) impute (d) infer

Q 9. It is ***compulsory*** for all the students to join this tour.

(a) regular (b) necessary
(c) dutiful (d) obligatory

Q 10. The old man shows no sign of ***infirmity*** even though he is eighty years old.

(a) indolence (b) fickleness
(c) feebleness (d) lack of firmness

Q 11. The defendant was grateful for the judge's ***clemency***.

(a) patience (b) mercy
(c) relaxed attitude (d) politeness

Q 12. Pakistan has been vigorously pursuing a ***clandestine*** nuclear weapons programme.

(a) secretive (b) systematic
(c) progressive (d) nefarious

Q 13. He likes his friend inspite of his little ***frailties***.

(a) frenzy (b) timidness
(c) oddities (d) weakness

Q 14. I doubt the ***veracity*** of your statement.

(a) tenacity (b) wisdom
(c) truthfulness (d) reliability

Q 15. We should abstain from ***casting aspersions*** on the character of our colleagues.

(a) passing critical remarks
(b) paying left handed compliments
(c) cracking silly jokes
(d) passing slanderous remarks

Q 16. We should encourage ***indigenous*** industries.

(a) foreign (b) cottage
(c) big (d) native

Q 17. The number of ***aboriginal*** inhabitants in Australia is considerable.

(a) primitive (b) ancient
(c) unoriginal (d) irrational

Q 18. The leader's ***charisma*** attracted many followers.

(a) humility (b) power
(c) magnetic appeal (d) candour

Q 19. The teacher felt that the student lacked ***discrimination*** in the study of his data.

(a) imagination (b) good taste
(c) objectivity (d) good judgement

Q 20. The ***intrepid*** mountaineers who scaled the peak in winter should be specially congratulated.

(a) bold (b) courageous
(c) vigorous (d) brave

Q 21. The inspector was a ***vigilant*** young man.

(a) smart (b) watchful
(c) ambitious (d) intelligent

Q 22. The resignation of the Chief Minister is ***intriguing***.

(a) gripping (b) interesting
(c) secret (d) diplomatic

Q 23. India has made ***spectacular*** progress in science and technology.

(a) remarkable (b) great
(c) formidable (d) super

Q 24. The ***acerbic*** remarks of the manager were unwarranted.

(a) bitter (b) furious
(c) arrogant (d) childish

Q 25. In modern hospitals, computers ***check*** the patients before they see the doctor.

(a) stop (b) protect
(c) cover (d) screen

ANSWERS – USE OF WORDS – SYNONYMS – PRACTICE TESTS (MCQs)

Q. No.	*TEST – 1*	*TEST – 2*	*TEST – 3*	*TEST – 4*	*TEST – 5*	*TEST – 6*
1.	liking	in ugly way	privilege	circumlocutory	hackneyed	adapt
2.	drive way	rebuke	careful	benevolent	pretty	end of the letter after signature
3.	hard working	hard hearted	after death	irritation	impressive	imitate
4.	enraged	destroyed	remedy for	convicted	progress	break
5.	unquestionable	optimistic	explain	struggled hard	justify	desertion
6.	different	coax	pretender	effort	critical	pinched
7.	distinction	repeal	rational	manage	noising	libertine
8.	scarcity	courage	interval of relief	primitive	relentless	excessively respectful
9.	steep	obscure	rebuke	ungracious	irritating	warned
10.	undifferentiated	peculiar	sharpness	honorary	secret	mixed
11.	Ill–will	lamentable	wearisome	sagacious	outspokenness	sensible
12.	credulous	elasticity	strategic	aim	admirable	clear
13.	delightful	judgement	soar	cautious	disappoint-ting	imaginative
14.	passage	assist	front	secret	lustful	obsessed
15.	covet	proud	difficult	rare	destroyed	pleasing
16.	incalculable	completely	find out	pass time	verify	utilise
17.	disgraceful	polite	pacify	nefarious	childishness	scolded
18.	critical	relentless	free ride	speedily	suited	deadlock
19.	regret	overflow	gluttonous	suspicion	suitable	flatterers
20.	optimistic	flattering	inkling	unbeatable	unmindful	too difficult to overcome
21.	energetic	clear	recently	lively	anthropology	disorderly scene
22.	unashamed	a circle	revived	deducted	fatigued	splendid
23.	scarcely	entertain	unquestion - able	abdicate	lacking in spirit	deviation
24.	penitent	talkative	conser-vation	stands	differ	frequently changing pattern of bright scenes
25.	correct	worldly	thoughtful	frightening	denied	wasteful

Q. No.	TEST – 7	TEST – 8	TEST – 9	TEST – 10	TEST – 11	TEST – 12
1.	talkative	Abate	inflame-matory	extracts	outrage	native
2.	junction	discontented	shrewd	poise	rude	rising
3.	linked	confident	silent	consequences	worsening	an engros-sing
4.	extempore	defamatory	easy	apparent	important	misplaced
5.	beyond suspicion	restful	pensive	interfere	face	memorable
6.	confirmed	objection-able	dry	weariness	poor	division
7.	continue	straight-forward	convincing	help	amazing	in agree-ment
8.	destroyed	hetero-geneous	neglected	sycophants	sufficient	impute
9.	fruitful	weakened	absurd	drawing	interrupted	obligatory
10.	scholarly	corruption	ultimately	repetitive	problem	feebleness
11.	disease	latter	useless	injurious	absurd	mercy
12.	adorned	discover	convictions	supported him energetically	breeding silk worms	secretive
13.	stupendous	establish genuinence	diligent	miserly	detestable	weakness
14.	beastly	pervades	difficult	occasional	credibility	truthfulness
15.	unhygienic	general pardon	easily perceived	a place with water and trees	disgraceful action	passing slanderous remarks
16.	shorten	sleepiness	great	beginning	futile	native
17.	convert	ravage	wonderful	forged	nonsense	primitive
18.	friendship	stomach	confirmed	discontented	stereo–typed statements	magnetic appeal
19.	circumlocutory	conciliate	nourish	weak	vociferous	objectivity
20.	easily remembered	soften	scornful	complete change	involving much sitting	bold
21.	profitable	brilliant	generous	apparent	doubtful	watchful
22.	a friendly	careful	total	never ending	plain	gripping
23.	exculpated	sullen	inclination	renovated	artificial	remarkable
24.	winding	employment	exhausted	clear	generous	bitter
25.	unfortunate	embarrassed	remedy	moderation	precision	screen

25 TEST OF USAGE OF WORDS - ANTONYMS

300 MCQs

Directions: ***The following sentences consist of a word or a phrase which is written in bold italicised letter. Each of them is followed by four words or phrases. Select the word or the phrase which is closest to the opposite in meaning of the italicised word or phrase.***

PRACTICE TEST-1

Q 1. India will have to cultivate all her ***barren*** land to meet with her food requirements.

(a) arid (b) simple
(c) sterile (d) productive

Q 2. The members of the opposition made ***derogatory*** remarks about the policies of government.

(a) praise worthy (b) laudatory
(c) respectable (d) admirable

Q 3. The area is known of its ***plentiful*** rain.

(a) poor (b) impoverished
(c) scarce (d) miserly

Q 4. We were surprised by the ***hostile*** attitude of the villagers.

(a) gentle (b) friendly
(c) self (d) forgiving

Q 5. Old people are usually more ***conservative*** than young people.

(a) modern (b) old fashioned
(c) dynamic (d) liberal

Q 6. Lucy is a ***smart*** girl.

(a) lazy (b) active
(c) indecent (d) casual

Q 7. Of all the companions of our joyous ***ascent***, there were only the two of us left.

(a) descant (b) descendant
(c) descent (d) decent

Q 8. I was deeply affected by his ***urbane*** behavior.

(a) rural (b) indifferent
(c) rude (d) unsympathetic

Q 9. We went to the first floor through the ***rickety*** wooden stairs.

(a) stable (b) old
(c) narrow (d) uncomfortable

Q 10. Those in ***distress*** should not be laughed at because they deserve our sympathy.

(a) trouble (b) prosperity
(c) affluence (d) adversity

Q 11. His face bore ***a blank*** look all the time while I was telling him about that exciting incident.

(a) a passive (b) an expressive
(c) a passionate (d) a mysterious

Q 12. ***Counterfeit*** coins are in circulation because of negligence on the part of police authorities.

(a) spurious (b) genuine
(c) truthful (d) fake

Q 13. Though generous and ***benevolent***, he did not meet with success in his career.

(a) beneficent (b) malevolent
(c) goodwill (d) liberal

Q 14. The town has been experiencing ***incessant*** rains since 4 o' clock.

(a) continual (b) continuous
(c) uninterrupted (d) irregular

Q 15. Many snakes are ***innocuous***.

(a) poisonous (b) harmless
(c) deadly (d) ferocious

Q 16. It was universally characterised as ***progressive*** measure.

(a) regressive (b) obstructive

(c) retrograde (d) abhorrent

Q 17. His business ***acumen*** led him to the zenith of his career.

(a) imbecility (b) mental alertness
(c) enterprise (d) shrewdness

Q 18. The mountains present a ***bleak*** sight at night.

(a) warm (b) desolate
(c) dense (d) deserted

Q 19. The speaker has a ***superficial*** knowledge of the subject.

(a) artificial (b) deep
(c) fictitious (d) overt

Q 20. They made a ***profligate*** use of scarce resources.

(a) proper (b) extravagant
(c) effective (d) thrifty

Q 21. The outgoing Chairman has a number of ***laudable*** achievements to his credit.

(a) noble (b) disreputable
(c) glorious (d) praiseworthy

Q 22. His ***meanness*** is proverbial.

(a) generosity (b) pragmatism
(c) timidity (d) kindness

Q 23. Her dress was too ***slovenly*** for that kind of interview.

(a) gaudy (b) tidy
(c) formal (d) old–fashioned

Q 24. He was in a ***dejected*** mood.

(a) jubilant (b) rejected
(c) irritable (d) romantic

Q 25. Have you seen that ***timid*** child.

(a) tender (b) tall
(c) brave (d) big

PRACTICE TEST-2

Q 1. He glanced through the letter ***perfunctorily***.

(a) nicely (b) ceremoniously
(c) carefully (d) particularly

Q 2. She paid special attention to those women who had ***succumbed*** to adversity.

(a) surrendered (b) given up
(c) overcome (d) demanded

Q 3. Throughout the evening, Rahul looked very ***doleful***.

(a) aggressive (b) cheerful
(c) tired (d) involved

Q 4. ***Genuine*** jewellery is available only in this shop.

(a) false (b) cheap
(c) imitation (d) duplicate

Q 5. An honest person need not ***hesitate*** to take bold steps.

(a) shirk (b) demur
(c) act willingly (d) malinger

Q 6. Nothing has been organised properly and confusion seems ***inevitable***.

(a) uncertain (b) ineligible
(c) inevident (d) inefficient

Q 7. There is something ***repulsive*** about the way he handles people's complaints.

(a) lovely (b) delightful
(c) attractive (d) distinctive

Q 8. His ***vindictive*** nature often came up for comment among his friends.

(a) timid (b) obedient
(c) forgiving (d) forgetful

Q 9. ***Misogynists*** are not applauded in society.

(a) Philanthropists (b) Philologists
(c) Philogynists (d) Philanderers

Q 10. Every self–respecting circus needs at least one ***dwarf***.

(a) pigmy (b) undersized
(c) giant (d) human

Q 11. The new government has ***abolished*** the gold control act.

(a) removed (b) approved
(c) passed (d) restored

Q 12. It was a very ***dreary*** day.

(a) drab (b) dangerous
(c) beautiful (d) bright

Q 13. He appears to be a ***phony*** person.

(a) beautiful (b) unread
(c) genuine (d) ugly

Q 14. The revised pay scale is ***uniform***.

(a) equal (b) opposite
(c) varied (d) different

Q 15. We had a ***delectable*** meal yesterday.

(a) heavy (b) unsavoury
(c) tasty (d) nice

Q 16. The two friends were ***distinct*** in everything, dress, manners, hair–style and food habits.
(a) similar (b) uniform
(c) opposite (d) different

Q 17. The last show of the concert at the Ritz Theatre was a ***fiasco***.
(a) triumph (b) victory
(c) fruitful (d) success

Q 18. Everybody called it a ***lavish*** party.
(a) expensive (b) frugal
(c) wasteful (d) big

Q 19. Her ***adamant*** attitude brought her on the verge of divorce.
(a) flexible (b) inflexible
(c) hard (d) abrasive

Q 20. Even a ***lunatic*** person sometimes talk intelligently.
(a) sane (b) insane
(c) insensible (d) mad

Q 21. He is ***zealous*** only in the initial stages of a project.
(a) absent–minded (b) distraught
(c) inattentive (d) indifferent

Q 22. The politician was ***flummoxed*** by the questions put to him.
(a) comfortable (b) annoyed
(c) delighted (d) disconcerted

Q 23. The state government for its part can identify ***vulnerable*** villages where these forces can be stationed.
(a) important (b) famous
(c) remote (d) invincible

Q 24. In facing adverse situations, he was very ***stoical***.
(a) tactless (b) flinching
(c) awkward (d) assured

Q 25. Professors are generally ***serious*** about what they say.
(a) jolly (b) thoughtful
(c) smug (d) insincere

PRACTICE TEST-3

Q 1. There was ***dismal*** atmosphere in the dressing room of the defeated team.
(a) cheerful (b) dreadful
(c) gloomy (d) jovial

Q 2. What he tells me ***confirms*** my ideas.
(a) verifies (b) contradicts
(c) opposes (d) strengthens

Q 3. There are no permanent ***adversaries*** in politics.
(a) associates (b) allies
(c) collaborators (d) partners

Q 4. There is not a trace of ***vanity*** in her behavior.
(a) humility (b) selflessness
(c) modesty (d) dignity

Q 5. All the employees of this organisation want to have an officer who is ***lenient***.
(a) capable (b) strict
(c) strong (d) conservative

Q 6. A ***fortuitous*** combination of circumstan-ces led to the discovery of his lineage.
(a) unfortunate (b) accidental
(c) planned (d) ludicrous

Q 7. He made several attempts to ***placate*** his opponents.
(a) infuriate (b) defeat
(c) discourage (d) deceive

Q 8. The ***feebleness*** of mind is the greatest hurdle to success in life.
(a) sound (b) infirm
(c) imbecility (d) strength

Q 9. ***Formidable*** obstacles have to be overcome before success is achieved.
(a) indomitable (b) facile
(c) dangerous (d) invincible

Q 10. He has been accorded a ***lukewarm*** welcome.
(a) cordial (b) trepid
(c) stately (d) grand

Q 11. He liked the ***pungent*** sauce prepared by his mother.
(a) gentle (b) mild
(c) insipid (d) unsavoury

Q 12. The deliberate ***suavity*** of Dev's behavior made the emotions of the audience volatile.
(a) politeness (b) impetuosity
(c) stupidity (d) pleasant

Q 13. We should not ***belittle*** other's achievement.
(a) recommend (b) praise
(c) encourage (d) inspire

Q 14. Everything about him, especially his talkative nature, proclaims his ***effeminacy***.
(a) aggressiveness (b) attractiveness
(c) manliness (d) boorishness

Q 15. He has a weakness for ***foreign*** goods.
(a) exported (b) indigenous
(c) fashionable (d) exotic

Q 16. Everybody was astonished when he used such a ***profane*** language.
(a) high (b) pure
(c) profound (d) sacred

Q 17. I liked the poem for its ***literal*** meaning.
(a) deep (b) complex
(c) fictitious (d) figurative

Q 18. I like his ***friendly*** attitude.
(a) jealous (b) envious
(c) hostile (d) vicious

Q 19. She handled the machine with ***deft*** fingers.
(a) delicate (b) sturdy
(c) quick (d) clumsy

Q 20. At the beginning of the novel we see the hero in all the fresh ***vivid*** detail in which he would appear to be a curios stranger from Spain.
(a) obscure (b) unintelligible
(c) hazy (d) inanimate

Q 21. ***Genuine*** drugs are available in most of the medical shops.
(a) spurious (b) dubious
(c) wrong (d) harmful

Q 22. Her ***impetuous*** behavior was attributed to her upbringing.
(a) poised (b) hash
(c) quiet and gentle (d) sluggish

Q 23. The committee set about making ***provisional*** arrangements for the annual conference.
(a) unconditional (b) abiding
(c) permanent (d) lasting

Q 24. I thought about her a lot during the ***following*** months.
(a) receding (b) preceding
(c) proceeding (d) succeeding

Q 25. His failure in this venture may be attributed to his ***lackadaisical*** approach.
(a) enthusiastic (b) insufficient
(c) indifferent (d) reckless

PRACTICE TEST-4

Q 1. The Board of Directors showered ***encomium*** on the Chairman for his liberal policies.
(a) denunciation (b) generosity
(c) tribute (d) praise

Q 2. The minister was accused of indulging in ***nepotism***.
(a) impartiality (b) hatred
(b) condemnation (d) indifference

Q 3. Their arrival ***defiled*** the atmosphere.
(a) purified (b) polluted
(c) disturbed (d) glorified

Q 4. He has translated the play into English with ***fidelity***.
(a) difficulty (b) insincerity
(c) carelessness (d) inaccuracy

Q 5. The consultant analysed the proposal carefully before he decided to ***jettison*** it.
(a) abandon (b) strengthen
(c) accept (d) modify

Q 6. I am in a rather ***precarious*** position in my place of work.
(a) comfortable (b) senior
(c) privileged (d) secure

Q 7. How dare you ***desecrate*** an idol of this temple.
(a) defile (b) pollute
(c) deify (d) impious

Q 8. ***Bereft*** of his support he died poor.
(a) deprived (b) invested
(c) enjoying (d) disinvested

Q 9. He was ***dejected*** when he heard the news.
(a) elated (b) impressed
(c) hilarious (d) gleeful

Q 10. He proved utterly ***capricious*** in his dealings with his friends.
(a) helpful (b) steadfast
(c) understanding (d) obstinate

Q 11. The General Manager is quite ***tactful*** and handles the workers' union very effectively.
(a) relaxed (b) strict
(c) naïve (d) disciplined

Q 12. His style was ***smooth***, but there was no mistaking his determination.
(a) hard (b) dense
(c) harsh (d) rough

Q 13. His family has ***accumulated*** wealth over the years.
(a) amassed (b) collected
(c) drained (d) squandered

Q 14. Her ***debonair*** manners were noticed by everyone present in the party.
(a) pleasant (b) courteous
(c) cheerless (d) stiff

Q 15. We received a ***cordial*** welcome from our host.
(a) indifferent (b) distrustful
(c) cold (d) official

Q 16. Silence in this place is ***mandatory***.
(a) optional (b) compulsory
(c) imperative (d) irritating

Q 17. India is a ***heterogeneous*** country.
(a) strange (b) homogeneous
(c) complex (d) vast

Q 18. She used to ***disparage*** her neighbours every now and then.
(a) please (b) praise
(c) belittle (d) denigrate

Q 19. In ancient days, a ***fragile*** glass jar was considered to be more valuable than a human slave.
(a) broad (b) tall
(c) strong (d) heavy

Q 20. Sanjay's point of view was correct but his behaviour with his father was quite ***impertinent***.
(a) impressive (b) smooth
(c) healthy (d) respectful

Q 21. Water scarcity is a ***perennial*** problem in that village
(a) transitory (b) ephemeral
(c) momentary (d) temporary

Q 22. Why do you ***disparage*** him all the time?
(a) abuse (b) criticise
(c) encourage (d) glorify

Q 23. He stood gazing at the ***serene*** expanse of the sea.
(a) scenic (b) clear
(c) tranquil (d) ruffled

Q 24. The timely action ***foiled*** his evil designs.
(a) checked (b) opposed
(c) succeeded (d) avert

Q 25. The ***fetters*** of slavery are hard to shake off.
(a) bondage (b) shackles
(c) freedom (d) irons

PRACTICE TEST-5

Q 1. Born in ***squalid*** surroundings of the slums, she rose to stardom overnight.
(a) dirty (b) clean
(c) disorderly (d) mean

Q 2. ***Modesty*** is a virtue but it must not be allowed to be exploited.
(a) reserve (b) boldness
(c) mildness (d) humility

Q 3. The speaker recalled the deceased leader's ***benevolent*** deeds.
(a) unpopular (b) unkind
(c) unbecoming (d) unplanned

Q 4. He walked in ***ungainly*** strides.
(a) quick (b) short
(c) awkward (d) graceful

Q 5. Some of the needs of a modern man are surely ***dispensable***.
(a) desirable (b) acceptable
(c) relevant (d) essential

Q 6. It was ***fortuitous*** that I met her in that party.
(a) unlucky (b) bad
(c) distressing (d) abominable

Q 7. After a day's toil he was feeling ***fatigue***.
(a) energy (b) listlessness
(c) exertion (d) tiredness

Q 8. Manuscripts of Shakespeare's plays are still ***extant*** in the British Museum.
(a) existing (b) extinct
(c) present (d) alive

Q 9. Drinking proved to be the ***bane*** of his otherwise spotless career.

(a) evil (b) boon
(c) joy (d) stigma

Q 10. Overeating can often be ***detrimental*** to health.
(a) beneficial (b) injurious
(c) useful (d) destructive

Q 11. ***Feasibility*** of the project is under study.
(a) unsuitability (b) impracticability
(c) impropriety (d) cheapness

Q 12. In all places, and at all times, there is a ***profusion*** of talents.
(a) plenty (b) scarcity
(c) aversion (d) generosity

Q 13. He has been ***acquitted*** of the charge of theft.
(a) convicted (b) exonerated
(c) released (d) punished

Q 14. We have no doubt about the ***veracity*** of his statement.
(a) truthfulness (b) propriety
(c) falsity (d) morality

Q 15. The criminal was ***detained*** by the policc.
(a) deterred (b) released
(c) dismissed (d) protected

Q 16. He made an ***exhaustive*** list of the items his secretary should attend to.
(a) short (b) incomplete
(c) interesting (d) meticulous

Q 17. That man is known for his ***elegance***.
(a) awkwardness (b) indelicacy
(c) clumsiness (d) savagery

Q 18. Sherlock Holmes is ***fictitious*** character.
(a) foreign (b) imaginative
(c) fancy (d) real

Q 19. His was ***sulky*** disposition.
(a) kind (b) loving
(c) cheerful (d) mild

Q 20. That was a ***dauntless*** action.
(a) cowardly (b) secret
(c) subtle (d) devious

Q 21. Under the circumstances, such ***pejorative*** comments should have been avoided.
(a) soothing (b) sporting
(c) appreciative (d) critical

Q 22. His partners felt that it was a ***viable*** business proposition.
(a) impracticable (b) inviolable
(c) unavailable (d) enviable

Q 23. She used to ***deprecate*** her neighbour's conduct every now and then.
(a) denigrate (b) disparage
(c) praise (d) please

Q 24. He was asked to ***accelerate*** the pace of work.
(a) check (b) control
(c) slacken (d) supervise

Q 25. He ***endeavoured*** hard to reach the top of his career.
(a) shirked (b) strove
(c) undertake (d) laboured

PRACTICE TEST-6

Q 1. Like poverty, ***affluence*** can sometimes create its own problems.
(a) sorrow (b) indigence
(c) exuberance (d) opulence

Q 2. There is an ***obscure*** cave on the other side of the hill.
(a) admired (b) notorious
(c) infamous (d) well known

Q 3. The visit of the Vice Chancellor has been ***deferred*** indefinitely.
(a) expedited (b) dissolved
(c) postponed (d) put off

Q 4. Sometimes it is necessary to ***retreat*** in a battle.
(a) retrograde (b) march
(c) advance (d) go back

Q 5. However hard you may try to ***mitigate*** his problems, you will not succeed.
(a) augment (b) increase
(c) expand (d) enlarge

Q 6. The forwards of their football team made ***sporadic*** raids into the opponent's territory.
(a) rare (b) frequent
(c) sharp (d) coordinated

Q 7. The officer had issued ***explicit*** instructions to his staff.
(a) inadequate (b) elusive

(c) ambiguous (d) queer

Q 8. Some people always drive their cars ***recklessly***.

(a) slowly (b) regularly
(c) carefully (d) patiently

Q 9. Some have the habit of ***disparaging*** the success of their friend because of jealously.

(a) belittling (b) esteeming
(c) lauding (d) castigating

Q 10. You will have to learn to gloss over the ***trivial*** mistakes of the youngsters.

(a) important (b) pardonable
(c) insignificant (d) futile

Q 11. There has always been a feeling of ***rancour*** between the two families.

(a) rivalry (b) competition
(c) friendliness (d) suspicious

Q 12. ***Adversity*** teaches man to be humble and self reliant.

(a) prosperity (b) curiosity
(c) animosity (d) sincerity

Q 13. We ***solicit*** your co–operation.

(a) acknowledge (b) reject
(c) refute (d) cherish

Q 14. He is a very ***timid*** person.

(a) chivalrous (b) bold
(c) outgoing (d) dashing

Q 15. They took note of the ***humility*** of the visiting dignitary.

(a) grandeur (b) arrogance
(c) friendliness (d) decency

Q 16. He is quite ***industrious***.

(a) indisposed (b) hard working
(c) indifferent (d) lazy

Q 17. It is ***obligatory*** for a common citizen to follow the rules.

(a) advisable (b) unnecessary
(c) superfluous (d) optional

Q 18. The principal hardly managed to give the papers a ***cursory*** glance.

(a) curious (b) thorough
(c) through (d) superficial

Q 19. It was ***voluntary*** gesture.

(a) valuable (b) violent
(c) compulsory (d) deliberate

Q 20. Your term is full of ***delinquent*** children.

(a) law abiding (b) uncivil
(c) quarrelsome (d) jealous

Q 21. Unlike the other candidates, his manner was entirely ***languid***.

(a) energetic (b) lazy
(c) liquid (d) slow

Q 22. The two girls are always together. There is a great ***affinity*** between them.

(a) apathy (b) empathy
(c) antipathy (d) sympathy

Q 23. His principles are ***flexible***.

(a) accurate (b) rigid
(c) distinct (d) strict

Q 24. Every move I make seems to affect him ***adversely***.

(a) deeply (b) favourably
(c) badly (d) internally

Q 25. The actor is well known both for his ***humility*** and courage.

(a) gentleness (b) honesty
(c) determination (d) pride

PRACTICE TEST-7

Q 1. Many an ***abortive*** attempts to scale the mountains disappointed him.

(a) fruitless (b) successful
(c) futile (d) useless

Q 2. ***Hectic*** arrangements are on for the coming visit of the Minister.

(a) unhurried (b) unhindered
(c) feverish (d) fast

Q 3. ***Reunion*** was overwhelming as he returned home after long time.

(a) meeting (b) parting
(c) division (d) home coming

Q 4. He produced ***cogent*** reasons for the change of policy.

(a) flimsy (b) unconvincing
(c) improper (d) simple

Q 5. The booking–clerk looked very ***grumpy***.

(a) surly (b) pleasant
(c) efficient (d) honest

Q 6. Some democratic countries believe in racial ***segregation***.

(a) subordination (b) integration
(c) inferiority (d) domination

Q 7. Though aware of his crimes, he remained ***impenitent*** throughout.
(a) repentant (b) sorrowful
(c) hot–headed (d) pertinent

Q 8. The facts of the case were ***obscured*** by the speech of the defence counsel.
(a) reflected (b) illustrated
(c) clarified (d) exhibited

Q 9. None but his ***sycophants*** were impressed by his haughtiness.
(a) detractors (b) flatterers
(c) benefactors (d) officious

Q 10. Twenty point programme is aimed at ***alleviating*** the sufferings of the poor.
(a) aggravating (b) mitigating
(c) eradicating (d) appeasing

Q 11. The leader was ***pragmatic*** in his approach to the problems facing the country.
(a) optimistic (b) idealistic
(c) indefinite (d) vague

Q 12. The influence of political broadcasts on elections is ***considerable***.
(a) immense (b) influential
(c) negligible (d) insignificant

Q 13. ***Recession*** causes unemployment.
(a) poverty (b) computerisation
(c) education (d) inflation

Q 14. They have not been eating ***nourishing*** food.
(a) unhygienic (b) undercooked
(c) poor (d) heavy

Q 15. Nothing has been organised properly and confusion seems ***inevitable***.
(a) inevident (b) inefficient
(c) ineligible (d) uncertain

Q 16. That police officer is known to be ***humane*** in his approach.
(a) uncivilised (b) uncultured
(c) unsympathetic (d) uncompromising

Q 17. The decision was ***delayed*** because of him.
(a) expedited (b) advanced
(c) released (d) triggered

Q 18. There was a marked ***deterioration*** in his condition
(a) improvement (b) revision
(c) reformation (d) amendment

Q 19. He has a passion for ***indigenous*** goods.
(a) native (b) foreign
(c) silly (d) cheap

Q 20. His ***frivolous*** remarks provoked no comments.
(a) fanciful (b) frantic
(c) momentous (d) serious

Q 21. His friends liked everything about him except his ***frugality***.
(a) punctuality (b) shabbiness
(c) extravagance (d) short temper

Q 22. People who are actually running the system often take a ***myopic*** view of the situation.
(a) farsighted (b) visionary
(c) blind (d) glassy

Q 23. The students ***assembled*** in the meeting hall.
(a) removed (b) diffused
(c) dispersed (d) eliminated

Q 24. The minster gave a public speech on the controversial subject to ***precipitate*** the matter.
(a) pull (b) push
(c) defer (d) create

Q 25. The usual ***adulation*** of the officers must end.
(a) back–biting (b) flattery
(c) condemnation (d) praise

PRACTICE TEST-8

Q 1. His health has been ***deteriorating*** since he returned from trekking expedition.
(a) ameliorating (b) amending
(c) undertaking (d) worsening

Q 2. You are advised to show ***clemency*** to the defeated enemy.
(a) callousness (b) mercy
(c) leniency (d) kindness

Q 3. Guerillas ***infiltrated*** into the region during the severe winter of 1997.
(a) entered (b) expelled
(c) penetrated (d) filtered

Q 4. While facing that situation he turned out to be ***dauntless***.
(a) tactful (b) stoical
(c) bashful (d) cowardly

Q 5. The judge thought that the offence was ***deliberate***.
(a) negligible (b) casual
(c) unintentional (d) legitimate

Q 6. He gave the reply written in a ***terse*** style.
(a) pleasant (b) verbose
(c) rude (d) concise

Q 7. The professor had to share a hotel room with a ***garrulous*** tax collector.
(a) dumb (b) speechless
(c) tongue–tied (d) silent

Q 8. A lady of a few words, she is given to ***laconic*** answers.
(a) copious (b) lingering
(c) terse (d) brief

Q 9. She is known for her ***frugality*** in household expenditure.
(a) economy (b) extravagance
(c) miserliness (d) niggardliness

Q 10. ***Ambivalence*** on his part caused the ruin of all his aspirations.
(a) firmness (b) clarity of thoughts
(c) confusion (d) ambiguity

Q 11. His ***amiable*** nature has won him many admirers.
(a) surly (b) pleasing
(c) amicable (d) complaisant

Q 12. It was a ***revolting*** sight.
(a) comfortable (b) pleasant
(c) delicious (d) remarkable

Q 13. He was the most ***eccentric*** and difficult patron.
(a) normal (b) sober
(c) genial (d) sociable

Q 14. The momentum of the movement ***slackened*** in course of time.
(a) stopped (b) quickened
(c) multiplied (d) recovered

Q 15. He is well known for coming up with ***impracticable*** solutions.
(a) easy (b) possible
(c) feasible (d) alternate

Q 16. There is a great deal of ***spurious*** family affection.
(a) genuine (b) obvious
(c) fictitious (d) authentic

Q 17. His ***servility*** makes him detestable.
(a) slavery (b) insolence
(c) prudence (d) bravery

Q 18. Philosophers say that the world is an ***illusion***.
(a) a fact (b) a reality
(c) an actuality (d) a truth

Q 19. The drug will have ***pernicious*** effect on your health.
(a) pornographic (b) ruinous
(c) prolonged (d) beneficial

Q 20. There is only the most ***tenuous*** evidence for it.
(a) enough (b) reasonable
(c) less (d) abundant

Q 21. Mala was often teased as ***corpulent*** by her friends.
(a) fat (b) belligerent
(c) garrulous (d) gaunt

Q 22. Let us not ***aggravate*** the sufferings of the poor.
(a) advocate (b) appreciate
(c) alleviate (d) abbreviate

Q 23. The principal ***deprecated*** the attitude of some student leaders.
(a) appreciated (b) tolerated
(c) derided (d) ignored

Q 24. He directed a couple of ***mediocre*** films.
(a) noble (b) successful
(c) outstanding (d) famous

Q 25. The director had a ***derisive*** attitude towards some of the members of the committee.
(a) enthusiastic (b) respectful
(c) deprecatory (d) encouraging

PRACTICE TEST-9

Q 1. The climate in the north of Europe is really ***dreadful***.
(a) pleasant (b) amiable
(c) comfortable (d) gratifying

Q 2. There are many anecdotes about his sister who is an ***imperious*** personality.
(a) characterless (b) pious
(c) arrogant (d) submissive

Q 3. Arrangements were made to handle the ***mammoth*** gathering tactfully.

(a) quiet (b) significant
(c) huge (d) small

Q 4. He is showing signs of ***senility***.
(a) virility (b) laziness
(c) maturity (d) exhaustion

Q 5. The young business executive was very ***perspicacious***.
(a) banal (b) clever
(c) humble (d) unreliable

Q 6. The task assigned to him was ***arduous***.
(a) absorbing (b) good
(c) plain (d) easy

Q 7. His speech was full of frequent ***facetious*** remarks.
(a) stupid (b) grave
(c) dull (d) sarcastic

Q 8. A character without a ***blemish*** is a virtue of a leader.
(a) stigma (b) adornment
(c) strength (d) blot

Q 9. ***Apathy*** for the poor is common to officials of every cadre.
(a) indifference (b) sympathy
(c) eagerness (d) antipathy

Q 10. She is ***exquisite*** in figure.
(a) strong (b) well–built
(c) clumsy (d) slim

Q 11. All these measures will ***augment*** employment opportunities.
(a) constrain (b) restrain
(c) diminish (d) circumscribe

Q 12. After meeting the holy man his nagging mood of ***diffidence*** suddenly changed.
(a) confusion (b) self assurance
(c) contentment (c) consternation

Q 13. It is surprising to find ***condoning*** such an act.
(a) disparaging (b) condemning
(c) disliking (d) forbidding

Q 14. Many of the incidents in the autobiography appear to be ***fictitious***.
(a) imaginary (b) real
(c) creative (d) boring

Q 15. Many people try to ***resist*** reforms in the society.
(a) repel (b) welcome
(c) accept (d) fight

Q 16. The leader was ***pragmatic*** in his approach to the problems facing the country.
(a) indefinite (b) vague
(c) idealistic (d) optimistic

Q 17. The new officer is a ***brash*** young man.
(a) handsome (b) arrogant
(c) kind (d) polite

Q 18. His ***timidity*** proved to be costly.
(a) self confidence (b) self assertion
(c) arrogance (d) boldness

Q 19. It used to be said that travel ***broadens*** ones outlook.
(a) narrows (b) shrinks
(c) contracts (d) restricts

Q 20. She is ***slender*** in figure.
(a) slim (b) stout
(c) well built (d) strong

Q 21. Unsettled conditions in the land led to the ***exodus*** of hundreds of its citizens.
(a) invasion (b) intrusion
(c) immigration (d) expulsion

Q 22. Her ***vivacity*** attracted everybody.
(a) lethargy (b) truthfulness
(c) beauty (d) apathy

Q 23. The author has ***perspicuity*** in his style.
(a) frankness (b) bluntness
(c) obstruseness (d) vivacity

Q 24. The club meets on the last Thursday of every month in a ***dilapidated*** palace.
(a) furnished (b) renovated
(c) neglected (d) regenerated

Q 25. His books are well known for their ***progressive*** ideas.
(a) useless (b) old–fashioned
(c) complex (d) reactionary

PRACTICE TEST-10

Q 1. The research showed that the drug has ***pernicious*** effect on the health of the patients.
(a) fair (b) advantageous
(c) beneficial (d) satisfactory

Q 2. At his success in the examination he felt ***elated***.

(a) exultant (b) dejected
(c) resting (d) jubilant

Q 3. Mrs. Nisha made a ***fervent*** appeal to the members of the club to maintain unity.

(a) active (b) impassive
(c) cold (d) passionate

Q 4. He was charged with ***abetting*** the murder of an innocent child.

(a) baffle (b) instigate
(c) promote (d) support

Q 5. The ***indignation*** of the retreating troops resulted in large scale killings.

(a) displeasure (b) happiness
(c) orderliness (d) anger

Q 6. His ***servility*** makes him detestable.

(a) bravery (b) prudence
(c) insolence (d) slavery

Q 7. She had nothing but ***scorn*** for my ideas.

(a) admiration (b) encouragement
(c) appreciation (d) agreement

Q 8. The hall was packed with people, who came to hear the ***celebrated*** author.

(a) obscure (b) well-known
(c) ordinary (d) up-coming

Q 9. The chairman ***initiated*** the proceedings with a brief speech.

(a) complicated (b) started
(c) closed (d) confused

Q 10. The plantation workers were on ***collision*** course before the labour officer intervened.

(a) retaliatory (b) perfunctory
(c) conciliatory (d) circuitous

Q 11. Athletes tend to ***conceal*** their disappointment when they lose.

(a) hide (b) show
(c) ignore (d) accept

Q 12. He was the most ***fanatic*** person.

(a) tolerable (b) genial
(c) sober (d) tolerant

Q 13. The government empowered itself to ***attach*** the assets of all the scam suspects.

(a) release (b) return
(c) donate (d) detach

Q 14. His ***appointment*** was confirmed last month.

(a) disappointment (b) suspension
(c) dismissal (d) discharge

Q 15. The room was filled with a ***delicious*** odour.

(a) bitter (b) repulsive
(c) strange (d) unpalatable

Q 16. He tried to ***conceal*** the secret that they were already married.

(a) announce (b) reveal
(c) declare (d) state

Q 17. She was ***sceptical*** about the safety of the new drug.

(a) doubtful (b) certain
(c) hopeful (d) sanguine

Q 18. It was ***altercation*** throughout and there was no discussion.

(a) consonance (b) alternative
(c) inconsistency (d) resonance

Q 19. She is beautiful as well as ***frivolous***.

(a) indecent (b) serious
(c) insane (d) rude

Q 20. ***Miscellaneous*** items were discussed at the meeting.

(a) minor (b) unrelated
(c) mixed (d) classified

Q 21. High School students generally take pleasure in asking ***puerile*** questions.

(a) sensible (b) pleasing
(c) sure (d) familiar

Q 22. The ***tranquil*** surroundings of Shimla are healthful.

(a) noisy (b) peaceful
(c) healthy (d) congenial

Q 23. A crowd ***gathered*** quickly when the police came.

(a) collected (b) dispersed
(c) spread (d) disappeared

Q 24. Though ***novice*** in art he shows great promise.

(a) tyro (b) inexperienced
(c) veteran (d) green horn

Q 25. I was ***disgusted*** at the manner he was flattering the party leader.

(a) revolting (b) pleased
(c) sickening (d) irritated

PRACTICE TEST-11

Q 1. At least some students are in the habit of doing their exercises in a ***slovenly*** manner.

(a) neat (b) proper
(c) decent (d) correct

Q 2. The error in the newspaper article is ***accidental***.

(a) permissible (b) usual
(c) conventional (d) intentional

Q 3. He is a man of ***mellow*** temper.

(a) fickle (b) hot
(c) irrational (d) excitable

Q 4. ***Crestfallen*** he returned as he had never faced such humiliation in the whole of his life.

(a) vainglorious (b) indignant
(c) triumphant (d) disturbed

Q 5. The explosion and the plane's take off occurred ***simultaneously***.

(a) cotemporary (b) coincident
(c) separately (d) momentarily

Q 6. She was surprised by his ***amiability***.

(a) petulance (b) sincerity
(c) prudence (d) pessimism

Q 7. We should not ***belittle*** the value of small things.

(a) extol (b) praise
(c) inflate (d) expand

Q 8. Self reliance has been ***adopted*** as an important objective of economic planning in modern India.

(a) refused (b) forsaken
(c) denied (d) discarded

Q 9. The leader might have had some ***covert*** reason for the change of his political affiliations.

(a) unjustifiable (b) obvious
(c) inexplicable (d) flimsy

Q 10. Thousands of people died of ***spurious*** liquor in Baroda this year.

(a) diluted (b) genuine
(c) poisonous (d) illicit

Q 11. There is a ***dearth*** of dedicated workers in our party.

(a) scarcity (b) affluence
(c) prosperity (d) abundance

Q 12. Our knowledge of the past is still largely a matter of ***conjecture***.

(a) certainty (b) guess
(c) position (d) form

Q 13. The commission took two years to go through the ***massive*** collection of files and documents before preparing its reports.

(a) ugly (b) short
(c) light (d) meagre

Q 14. He is known for his ***arrogance***.

(a) honesty (b) cheerfulness
(c) generosity (d) humility

Q 15. James had the habit of ***running down*** his colleagues.

(a) deriding (b) pushing down
(c) praising (d) supporting

Q 16. He is quite ***industrious***.

(a) hard working (b) indifferent
(c) lazy (d) indisposed

Q 17. The children are playing in the ***nearby*** park.

(a) different (b) close
(c) separate (d) distant

Q 18. The plane lay burnt in ***fragments***.

(a) whole (b) parts
(c) scraps (d) pieces

Q 19. Their family ***feud*** has taken an ugly turn lately.

(a) brotherhood (b) dispute
(c) fraternal (d) quarrel

Q 20. You are advised not to ***dissipate*** your energy on impracticable schemes.

(a) conserve (b) reform
(c) waste (d) utilise

Q 21. He has always been ***fastidious*** while examining answer scripts.

(a) amiable (b) discriminating
(c) critical (d) judicious

Q 22. The speaker made some very ***cogent*** remarks.

(a) flattering (b) unconvincing
(c) superfluous (d) vociferous

Q 23. He ***despises*** classical music.

(a) appreciates (b) respects
(c) comprehends (d) endures

Q 24. His ***magnanimous*** gesture came to his employees as a surprise.
(a) small (b) cruel
(c) thoughtless (d) mean

Q 25. His ***urbane*** attitude won him many friends.
(a) indifferent (b) violent
(c) rustic (d) rude

PRACTICE TEST-12

Q 1. This offer has come as a great ***boon*** to me.
(a) curse (b) blemish
(c) trouble (d) misfortune

Q 2. The treaty was ***ratified*** by the Heads of States.
(a) annulled (b) destroyed
(c) unsettled (d) set aside

Q 3. The painting is full of ***radiant*** colours.
(a) rare (b) bright
(c) dull (d) delicate

Q 4. In the interest of one's reputation one should avoid ***ostentation*** while entertaining friends.
(a) miserliness (b) simplicity
(c) purity (d) innocence

Q 5. His was a ***delicate*** constitution.
(a) fit (b) strong
(c) rugged (d) ungainly

Q 6. The inhabitants of the island were ***barbarians***.
(a) bad (b) uncivilised
(c) cruel (d) civilised

Q 7. They had an ***insipid*** conversation.
(a) curious (b) loud
(c) argumentative (d) lively

Q 8. The minister is ***optimistic*** about the new project just launched.
(a) stoical (b) dubious
(c) pessimistic (d) cynical

Q 9. The principal is popular with students for his ***benign*** attitude.
(a) malignant (b) kindly
(c) generous (d) liberal

Q 10. It is a ***Herculean*** task for me.
(a) indecent (b) puny
(c) ponderous (d) big

Q 11. Her ***candid*** confession of the crime earned her reprieve.
(a) frank (b) crafty
(c) simple (d) ambiguous

Q 12. Indian economy is basically dependent on ***fickle*** monsoons.
(a) unsteady (b) benign
(c) stable (d) capricious

Q 13. You must put up the facts ***straight*** before me and don't try to befool me.
(a) distort (b) candid
(c) soften (d) direct

Q 14. He is very ***fastidious*** about his choice of food.
(a) sloppy (b) thoughtless
(c) careless (d) indiscreet

Q 15. The Prime Minister's radio broadcast ***galvanised*** the people's spirit.
(a) frightened (b) pacified
(c) dampened (d) distracted

Q 16. They approached the stranger ***warily***.
(a) suspiciously (b) cautiously
(c) carefully (d) carelessly

Q 17. He received the news ***coldly***.
(a) angrily (b) enthusiastically
(c) gratefully (d) bravely

Q 18. He is showing signs of ***senility***.
(a) virility (b) laziness
(c) maturity (d) exhaustion

Q 19. This officer is noted for his ***zeal***.
(a) intolerance (b) inefficiency
(c) insensibility (d) indifference

Q 20. Due to his excessive ***craftiness*** he achieved success but lost friends.
(a) simplicity (b) sincerity
(c) straight forwardness (d) innocence

Q 21. One usually feels ***languid*** on summer noons.
(a) brisk (b) fussy
(c) drowsy (d) listless

Q 22. There exists ***rancour*** between the two brothers.
(a) animosity (b) harmony
(c) devotion (d) enmity

Q 23. We must realise the ***futility*** of wars.

(a) urgency (b) usefulness
(c) value (d) importance

Q 24. In such difficult times it ***behoves*** all of us to remain united.
(a) becomes (b) discredits
(c) suits (d) creditable

Q 25. The police tried to find out the ***rightful*** owner of the ornaments left in the train.
(a) indefinite (b) mistaken
(c) unlawful (d) claimant

USE OF WORDS – ANTONYMS – PRACTICE TESTS (MCQs)

Q. No.	*TEST – 1*	*TEST – 2*	*TEST – 3*	*TEST – 4*	*TEST – 5*	*TEST – 6*
1.	productive	ceremo-niously	cheerful	denunciation	clean	indigence
2.	admirable	overcome	contradicts	indifference	boldness	well known
3.	scarce	cheerful	partners	purified	unkind	expedited
4.	friendly	duplicate	humility	insincerity	graceful	advance
5.	liberal	act willingly	strict	strengthen	essential	augment
6.	indecent	uncertain	ludicrous	secure	unlucky	frequent
7.	descent	delightful	infuriate	deify	energy	ambiguous
8.	rude	forgiving	strength	invested	extinct	carefully
9.	stable	Philogynists	facile	hilarious	boon	esteeming
10.	prosperity	giant	grand	helpful	beneficial	important
11.	an expressive	restored	mild	naïve	Impractical-bility	friendliness
12.	genuine	bright	impetuosity	rough	scarcity	prosperity
13.	malevolent	genuine	encourage	squandered	convicted	reject
14.	irregular	varied	manliness	cheerless	falsity	chivalrous
15.	ferocious	unsavoury	indigenous	indifferent	released	grandeur
16.	regressive	uniform	sacred	optional	short	lazy
17.	imbecility	victory	figurative	homogeneous	awkwardnes s	optional
18.	dense	frugal	hostile	praise	real	thorough
19.	deep	flexible	clumsy	strong	cheerful	compulsory
20.	thrifty	sane	obscure	respectful	cowardly	law abiding
21.	disreputable	indifferent	spurious	temporary	appreciative	energetic
22.	generosity	comfortable	poised	glorify	enviable	antipathy
23.	tidy	invincible	permanent	ruffled	praise	rigid
24.	jubilant	awkward	preceding	succeeded	slacken	favourably
25.	brave	insincere	enthusiastic	freedom	shirked	pride

Q. No.	TEST – 7	TEST – 8	TEST – 9	TEST – 10	TEST – 11	TEST – 12
1.	Successful	ameliorating	gratifying	beneficial	decent	misfortune
2.	unhurried	callousness	pious	dejected	intentional	annulled
3.	parting	expelled	small	impassive	hot	dull
4.	unconvincing	tactful	maturity	baffle	triumphant	simplicity
5.	pleasant	uninten-tional	humble	happiness	separately	ungainly
6.	integration	verbose	easy	bravery	petulance	civilised
7.	repentant	tongue–tied	dull	admiration	extol	lively
8.	illustrated	copious	adornment	ordinary	denied	pessimistic
9.	detractors	extravagance	eagerness	closed	obvious	malignant
10.	aggravating	clarity of thoughts	clumsy	conciliatory	genuine	puny
11.	idealistic	surly	diminish	show	affluence	crafty
12.	insignificant	pleasant	self assurance	tolerant	certainty	stable
13.	inflation	normal	condemning	release	meagre	distort
14.	poor	quickened	real	dismissal	humility	careless
15.	uncertain	feasible	accept	unpalatable	supporting	dampened
16.	unsympathetic	genuine	idealistic	reveal	lazy	cautiously
17.	advanced	bravery	kind	sanguine	distant	enthusiasti-cally
18.	improvement	a reality	boldness	consonance	whole	maturity
19.	foreign	beneficial	narrows	serious	brotherhood	inefficiency
20.	serious	reasonable	well built	classified	conserve	simplicity
21.	extravagance	gaunt	intrusion	sensible	discriminating	brisk
22.	farsighted	alleviate	lethargy	noisy	unconvincing	harmony
23.	dispersed	appreciated	bluntness	dispersed	appreciates	usefulness
24.	defer	outstanding	renovated	veteran	mean	discredits
25.	condemnation	respectful	old–fashioned	pleased	rustic	unlawful

26 TEST OF CORRECT USAGE

62 PRACTICE TESTS

SECTION I

In the paragraphs here, there are sentences with italicised words and phrases. The respective substitutes for all such italicised words are given in the box at the head of each paragraph. Choose the word nearest in meaning to the italicised word.

PRACTICE TEST-1

1. misplaced 2. in agreement 3. Mercy 4. obligatory 5. impute 6. weakness 7. truthfulness 8. native 9. passing slanderous remarks 10. an engrossing 11. division 12. feebleness 13. memorable 14. secretive 15. rising

1. The import of technology as an alternative to *indigenous* technology has not been discussed fully. **2.** The ascending temperature in many parts of the world confirms global warming which is an environmental hazard. **3.** Reading fiction is *an absorbing*, creative and entertaining hobby. **4.** The data is *misleading*. **5.** Graduation day is a *momentous* day for most students. **6.** There was a major *split* in the Congress party in 1969. **7.** Her views are not in consonance with her husband's. **8.** The claims of students look hollow when they *attribute* their poor performance to difficult examination. **9.** It is *compulsory* for all the students to join this tour. **10.** The old man shows no sign of *infirmity* even though he is eighty years old. **11.** The defendant was grateful for the judge's *clemency*. **12.** Pakistan has been vigorously pursuing a *clandestine* nuclear weapons programme. **13.** He likes his friend inspite of his little *frailties*. **14.** I doubt the *veracity* of your statement. **15.** We should abstain from *casting aspersions* on the character of our colleagues.

PRACTICE TEST-2

1. bold 2. rude 3. remarkable 4. native 5. screen 6. worsening 7. magnetic appeal 8. watchful 9. primitive 10. face 11. outrage 12. bitter 13. objectivity 14. curious 15. important

1. We should encourage *indigenous* industries. **2.** The number of *aboriginal* inhabitants in Australia is considerable. **3.** The leader's *charisma* attracted many followers. **4.** The teacher felt that the student lacked *discrimination* in the study of his data. **5.** The *intrepid* mountaineers who scaled the peak in winter should be specially congratulated. **6.** The inspector was a *vigilant* young man. **7.** The resignation of the Chief Minister is *intriguing*. **8.** India has made *spectacular* progress in Science and technology. **9.** The *acerbic* remarks of the manager were unwarranted. **10.** In modern hospitals, computers *check* the patients before they see the doctor. **11.** One's *remonstration* against social ills has to be consistent to be fruitful. **12.** It would be *impertinent* to suggest that he was generally wrong. **13.** The opposition criticised the ruling party for the *deteriorating* law and order situation in the state. **14.** One of the *salient* features of your proposal is a stress on self-employment. **15.** Man has to *encounter* many hardships in life.

PRACTICE TEST-3

1. necessary 2. vague 3. brave 4. disgraceful action 5. nonsense 6. dependability 7. stereotyped statements 8. involving much sitting 9. problem 10. amazing 11. met 12. breeding silk worms 13. poor 14. futile 15. detestable

1. After the *dismal* performance of the team in the series concluded yesterday, the captain offered his resignation to the President of the club. **2.** Some of the discoveries of modern science are simply *marvellous*. **3.** The scheme failed for want of *adequate* funds. **4.** The Border Security Force *intercepted* yesterday a truck carrying arms and am munition. **5.** Because of a family *feud*, he never spoke to his wife's parents. **6.** Everyone turned to stare at the visitor and his *preposterous* dress. **7.** Mulberry plantation is a prerequisite for *sericulture*. **8.** I found his crude manners *abominable*. **9.** The international community may begin to doubt the *credentials* of the largest democracy in the world. **10.** It is a *scandal* that the murderer was declared innocent. **11.** The prisoner made an *abortive* attempt to escape from the jail. **12.** A million cinemas a year bring the same stale *balderdash*. **13.** His speech was nothing but a string of *platitudes*. **14.** The opposition made a *strident* demand for putting the bill to vote. **15.** He soon got fed up with his *sedentary* job.

PRACTICE TEST-4

1. precision 2. interfere 3. poise 4. sycophants 5. artificial 6. help 7. plain 8. repetitive 9. drawing 10. consequences 11. weariness 12. generous 13. doubtful 14. extracts 15. apparent

1. Though long, your essay is *vague* on the point. **2.** The field was *even* enough for the joggers to have their practice. **3.** On public occasions, she was very *punctilious* about forms and manners. **4.** This library was built with donations from the *munificent* citizens of the city. **5.** The *perspicuity* of the lawyer's arguments was remarkable. **6.** The new volume provides substantial critical *excerpts* and biographical information on eight to ten major poets from all eras. **7.** The chairman conducted the meeting with *aplomb*. **8.** Even the most careful researcher cannot predict the possible future *ramifications* of his findings. **9.** There was no *ostensible* reason for her being angry at her husband's remarks. **10.** Ritu asked Rashmi not to *meddle* in her affairs. **11.** A pervading sense of *ennui* grips Gaurav. **12.** We don't know how we are to *recompense* you for the trouble you have taken. **13.** Most of the politicians these days have a large number of *toadies* around them. **14.** The small boy was able to give a *graphic* description of the thief. **15.** The secret of good style is to avoid *redundant* words.

PRACTICE TEST-5

1. frequent 2. renovated 3. weak 4. forged 5. clear 6. beginning 7. Injurious 8. complete change 9. never ending 10. miserly 11. discontented 12. moderation 13. a place with water and trees 14. apparent 15. supported him energetically

1. Dowry is a *pernicious* social practice. **2.** I *stood up for him* when everyone else was criticising him. **3.** He is quite *parsimonious* by nature. **4.** *Sporadic* rise in his temperature caused us much worry. **5.** I gave a shout when I sighted an *oasis* in the desert. **6.** He was warned at the *outset* of his career. **7.** On scrutiny, the police officer found out that the documents provided by the landlord were totally *fabricated*. **8.** Most of the staff is *restive* under the new manager's rule. **9.** Grandfather has been getting *feeble* of late. **10.** His visit to foreign countries brought about a *sea change* in his outlook and his attitude to the people. **11.** Being a sociable bird she was *conspicuous* by her absence in the club last evening. **12.** There seems to be *perpetual* war going on between the rich and the poor. **13.** The flat has been *refurbished* recently. **14.** The officer gave a *lucid* explanation of the company's course of action **15.** *Temperance* in eating is conducive to health.

PRACTICE TEST-6

1. silent 2. dry 3. ultimately 4. difficult 5. absurd 6. pensive 7. neglected 8. bombastic 9. easily perceived 10. shrewd 11. convictions 12. convincing 13. diligent 14. useless 15. easy

1. Leaders of some political parties make *fiery* speeches. **2.** It was an *astute* move to sell the property at that stage. **3.** There is a *tacit* agreement between the superpowers not to engage themselves in armed conflict **4.** No one expects a *facile* solution to the Punjab Problem. **5.** When I visited him he was in a *retrospective* mood. **6.** Plants that grow and exist in deserts have highly specialised means of adapting themselves to the *arid* environment. **7.** The arguments of the lawyer of the accused were so *persuasive* that the judge acquitted him. **8.** He was sad that his seniority had been *overlooked.* **9.** He delivered a lengthy speech in which he committed several *ludicrous* mistakes. **10.** *Eventually* vision is affected and the patient is able to see only if light is present. **11.** It is *futile* to argue with a person who does not want to understand. **12.** People of different *persuasions* have met on the same platform. **13.** He is believed to be a very *industrious* worker. **14.** He found it an *arduous* task to perform. **15.** Lack of occupation is not necessarily revealed by *manifest* idleness.

PRACTICE TEST-7

1. generous 2. nourish 3. discontented 4. restless 5. confident 6. defamatory 7. wonderful 8. remedy 9. scornful 10. great 11. total 12. abate 13. inclination 14. exhausted 15. confirmed

1. He did his job with *scrupulous* care. **2.** She is really a *fantastic* girl. **3.** He *corroborated* the statement of his brother. **4.** There must be lively discussion of Indian authors if we are to *foster our* knowledge. **5.** He wrote a *scathing* review of the prize-winning novel. **6.** The library was built with donations from the *munificent* citizens of this city. **7.** As a speaker he was an *utter* failure. **8.** Mohinder Amarnath had *penchant* for hook shots. **9.** After he came back from his evening walk, he felt *famished.* **10.** Medical science is yet to come out with a *panacea* for cancer. **11.** He tried to *alleviate* the sufferings of his neighbours. **12.** The *disgruntled* members of a party are constant source of tension to the party leader. **13.** The young girl appeared *self-possessed* in front of TV cameras. **14.** He ended his speech on a *supercilious* note which was quite unexpected of a person of balanced and stable temperament. **15.** Factory workers are *restive* as the company has not declared any bonus this year.

PRACTICE TEST-8

1. latter 2. soften 3. corruption 4. exceptional 5. heterogeneous 6. sleepiness7. establish genuineness 8. discover 9. straightforward 10. weakened 11. conciliate 12. pervades 13. general pardon 14. ravage 15. stomach

1. She cannot tolerate *exceptionable* remarks about her parents. **2.** His *forthright* behavior shows that he is honest but he seems rude to some people. **3.** It is amazing how such a *motley* group could get along well. **4.** She leaned back, feeling *enervated.* **5.** He was accused of *graft.* **6.** We didn't believe in his statement but *subsequent* events proved that he was right. **7.** He has been able to *unearth* a secret. **8.** It is difficult to *authenticate* these old manuscripts. **9.** Corruption *stalks* every sphere of national life. **10.** The rebels returned home under an *amnesty.* **11.** He is being treated for his *somnolence.* **12.** The recent acts of *vandalism* in the country cannot be ignored. **13.** A bone got stuck in his *gullet.* **14.** For quick promotion, he hit on a plan to *propitiate* the Manager. **15.** He tried to *mollify* my hurt feelings.

PRACTICE TEST-9

1. sullen 2. inked 3. succeed 4. scholarly 5. fruitful 6. reformed 7. brilliant 8. junction 9. employment 10. embarrassed 11. destroyed 12. probity 13. offhand 14. careful 15. talkative

1. The boy gave a *vivid* description of all that happened. **2.** A *conscientious* worker is always admired by his employers. **3.** Few teachers have been spared the problem of an *obstreperous* pupil in the class. **4.** The *deployment* of para-military forces in Punjab has helped the provincial government a lot. **5.** His boss' criticism left him feeling rather *abashed.* **6.** He is so *garrulous* that all sober persons avoid his company. **7.** Mumbai is the *terminus* of the Western Railways. **8.** Our fates seemed *intertwined.* **9.** The Prime Minister delivered an *impromptu* speech to the students. **10.** The *honesty* of the king's minister was above board and the king was fond of him. **11.** The treaty was later *ratified.* **12.** The District Collector made it clear that the Government cannot *sustain* for long the support for such a scheme. **13.** The invasion forces had no artillery and were completely *annihilated*. **14.** Our talks with the foreign delegation were really *productive*. **15.** Dr. S. Radha Krishnan has written an *erudite* commentary on the 'Bhagawad Gita'.

PRACTICE TEST-10

1. unfortunate 2. beastly 3. friendship 4. disease 5. winding 6. friendly 7. convert 8. profitable 9. unhygienic 10. easily understood 11. adorned 12. exculpated 13. shorten 14. circumlocutory 15. stupendous

1. Scientific knowledge is an intoxicating *draught*, and it may be one which the human race is unable to sustain. **2.** The story is *embellished* with amusing but perhaps undue details. **3.** In so far as his research is concerned, he is very *meticulous*. **4.** *Weird* noises came from the haunted houses. **5.** Something should be done about the *insanitary* conditions of our parks. **6.** He had to *curtail* his leave as a lot of work was pending in his office **7.** True religion does not require one to *proselytise* through guile or force. **8.** We should always try to maintain and promote communal *amity*. **9.** He displayed a distinct tendency to *long winded* speeches when asked how he was. **10.** English conversation means the learning of many *catchy* phrases. **11.** This is a *lucrative* business. **12.** We are happy that the two countries are trying to find an *amicable* solution to their disputes. **13.** A man of unsound mind, he was *exonerated* from all responsibility for his actions. **14.** The coach followed a *devious* course to its destination. **15.** The future of millions of poor *hapless* Indians does not hold any promise.

PRACTICE TEST-11

1. pleasing 2. obsessed 3. imaginative 4. clear 5. sensible 6. mixed 7. advised 8. excessively respectful 9. libertine 10. pinched 11. desertion 12. break 13. imitate 14. end of the letter after signature 15. adapt

1. Honest officer find it difficult to *attune* themselves to corrupt bureaucracy. **2.** He mentioned in the *postscript* that he might need some money, soon. **3.** When youngsters do not have good role-models to *emulate* they start searching for them among sportsmen or film stars. **4.** A *rupture* in the relationship of the two brothers is quite apparent. **5.** *Defection* is quite common in our present day political life. **6.** His conscience *pricked* him. **7.** A person unrestrained by the rules of morality or tradition is called a *licentious* person. **8.** I don't see why he should be so *obsequious* to his brother just because the latter is rich. **9.** He was *admonished* for the delay. **10.** *Hybrid* variety of plants generally yield better crops. **11.** The people welcomed the budget as there was *judicious* allocation of funds to all the sectors. **12.** The poem is written in a very *lucid* style. **13.** All the characters in the novel are *fictitious*. **14.** Elsie is seventy years old and a *fanatical* gardener. **15.** It is so *gratifying* to know that there are not many cases of small pox these days.

PRACTICE TEST-12

1. deviation 2. pretty 3. too difficult to overcome 4. scolded 5. frequently changing pattern of bright scenes 6. impressive 7. flatterers 8. disorderly scene 9. progress 10. wasteful 11. deadlock 12. justify 13. utilise 14. hackneyed 15. splendid

1. India has not yet been able to *harness* her domestic resources in full. **2.** She *upbraided* the little girl who got frightened. **3.** The two opposing parties have reached a *stalemate*. **4.** Rich people often have *sycophants* around them. **5.** The obstacles seem to be *insurmountable*, but no one should doubt what this fearless woman can accomplish. **6.** Everybody in the assembly shouted and there was *pandemonium* in the hall. **7.** She looked *gorgeous* in her new dress. **8.** The *aberration* in the Indian Economy can be attributed to short sightedness of its political masters. **9.** Sunlight and shadow made the landscape a *kaleidoscope* of colour. **10.** My neighbour is an *extravagant* person. **11.** His *trite* remarks failed to cut any ice with the audience. **12.** The prince fell in love with a *comely* young maiden. **13.** My philosophy lecturer is unfailingly *bombastic*. **14.** Inspite of their efforts, the team of scientists could not make much *headway* to solve the problem. **15.**

John Milton wrote 'Paradise Lost' to *vindicate* the ways of God to man.

PRACTICE TEST-13

1. lustful 2. outspokenness 3. unmindful 4. noising 5. disappointing 6. approve 7. destroyed 8. critical 9. secret 10. irritating 11. suited 12. suitable 13. childishness 14. admirable 15. relentless

1. Some satirists are known for their *trenchant* style. **2.** The newspapers are *clamouring* against the injustice to the landless labourers. **3.** The *inexorable* demands of the workers brought the company to a closure. **4.** It is *exasperating* to listen to the suggestions of the minister about the educational reforms of which he knows nothing. **5.** The *surreptitious* movements of a long figure among the dunes filled the villagers with curiosity and awe. **6.** *Forthrightness* in speech may not always be a desirable quality. **7.** The courage shown by the soldiers at this moment of crisis is *exemplary*. **8.** During the short stay in India, he had quite a few *frustrating* experiences. **9.** His *lascivious* habits brought him nothing but bad name. **10.** Some army units were *decimated* during the surprise attack. **11.** The travel agent will *confirm* my reservation for the next week flight to London. **12.** Everybody laughed at the *puerility* of his statement. **13.** Reading of poetry is not *congenial* to his taste. **14.** The committee did not find him *fit* for the job. **15.** The novel was so interesting that I was *oblivious* of my surroundings.

PRACTICE TEST-14

1. denied 2. lacking in spirit 3. irritation 4. struggled hard 5. manage 6. circumlocutory 7. anthropology 8. honorary 9. ungracious 10. primitive 11. effort 12. differ 13. benevolent 14. fatigued 15. convicted

1. He is very much interested in the *study of mankind*. **2.** The five day week in Government Offices is bound to benefit the *jaded* office goers. **3.** He is a good looking but *insipid* young man. **4.** A genius tends to *deviate* from the routine way of thinking. **5.** Her evidence totally *refuted* the charges. **6.** He displayed a distinct tendency to *long-winded* speeches when asked how he was. **7.** The man lives long through his *good deeds* after he had died. **8.** In *exasperation* she railed at the shopkeeper. **9.** The prisoner has been *languishing* in the jail for the last many years. **10.** Buoyed by these visions of the future of his son, the artist *soldiered* on. **11.** He did not succeed in his *endeavour*. **12.** He does not know how to *husband* his resources. **13.** The number of *aboriginal* inhabitants in Australia is considerable. **14.** The guests were offended with his *uncouth* manners. **15.** He does *unpaid* work for the Red Cross.

PRACTICE TEST-15

1. nefarious 2. stands 3. speedily 4. wish 5. secret 6. abdicate 7. deduct 8. lively 9. frightening 10. suspicion 11. sagacious 12. rare 13. cautious 14. pass time 15. unbeatable

1. We did not expect such a *judicious* remark from him. **2.** It was pure fabrication with an *eye* for a sensation. **3.** His *judicious* handling of the matter saved the situation from going out of control. **4.** *Furtive* glances were exchanged between the lovers at the feast. **5.** She purchased *gimcrack* ornaments from the market. **6.** The villagers offered us an excellent *repast*. **7.** The *unlawful* activities of the terrorists need to be dealt with an iron hand. **8.** We will carry out the enquiry as *expeditiously* as possible. **9.** Don't entertain any *misgivings* about his conduct. **10.** He could rise to this stature because of his *invincible* courage. **11.** Many educationists think that the classroom instruction should be made more *vigorous*. **12.** What meaning have you *drawn* from her tongue in cheap remarks. **13.** The Collector has yet not *relinquished* his charge. **14.** Even though Akshay does not study hard, he always *comes* first in the class. **15.** We should abstain from *bullying* our colleagues.

PRACTICE TEST-16

1. remedy for 2. strategic 3. rational 4. rebuke 5. after death 6. front 7. pretender 8. difficult 9. monopoly 10. sore. 11. wearisome 12. postulate 13. careful 14. interval of relief 15. sharpness

1. It is the Prime Minister's *prerogative* to appoint or dismiss a Minister. **2.** Some people are extremely *fastidious* in their choice of dress. **3.** A *posthumous* award was given to the poet. **4.** The *antidote* to these problems is hard to find **5.** Before I could *expostulate* he had spoken again. **6.** Ramnath is such a *sham* that it is difficult to get along with him **7.** Whatever opinion he gives is *sane*. **8.** The early monsoon have brought *respite* to the people. **9.** Such conduct deserves *reprimand*. **10.** Businessmen who lack *acumen* cannot be expected to be very successful. **11.** The journey to Siliguri is quite *tedious*. **12.** The navy gave *tactical* support to the marines. **13.** The poets are known to *fly* in their thoughts more than a practical man. **14.** The *facade* of our school building got a face lift recently. **15.** Peace-keeping for the United Nations is, at best of times, an *arduous* task.

PRACTICE TEST-17

1. gluttonous 2. conservation 3. optimistic 4. rebuke 5. in ugly way 6. destroyed 7. recently 8. find out 9. unquestionable 10. hard hearted 11. free ride 12. thoughtful 13. pacify 14. inkling 15. revived

1. Before I could *make out anything* he had spoken again. **2.** I won't go out of my way to *placate* him. **3.** He has travelled all over the continent by *hitchhiking* most of the time. **4.** He is notorious for his *voracious* appetite. **5.** He kept his eyes peeled and his ears pricked for some important *clue*. **6.** I wrote to him as *lately* as last week. **7.** Timely first aid *resuscitated* the patient. **8.** The eyewitness testimony was *incontrovertible*. **9.** A careful *preservation* of wild life is the need of the hour. **10.** She is not seen even smiling these days; she is rather *pensive*. **11.** He had *insidiously* wormed his way into her affections. **12.** His close friend, who was senior to him in the office, did not hesitate to *reprimand* him when he misplaced one important file. **13.** One must not be *callous* to womenfolk. **14.** Last fortnight the rains came to the parched soils of India after the merciless drought had already *sapped* the vitality and livelihood of millions of peasants. **15.** That young man is quite *sanguine* about the result of his competitive examination.

PRACTICE TEST-18

1. peculiar 2. relentless 3. judgement 4. completely 5. polite 6. courage 7. repeal 8. strength 9. overflow 10. assist 11. flattering 12. lamentable 13. obscure 14. coax 15. proud

1. He tried to *cajole* her, but it was in vain. **2.** The new government decided to *rescind* most of the decisions of its predecessor. **3.** He had the *nerve* to suggest that I was cheating. **4.** Even today many people are guided by *abstruse* moral values. **5.** Millionaires become *eccentric* in their old age. **6.** The performance of the candidates was *deplorable*. **7.** Indian economy has always shown enough *resilience* in crisis. **8.** Whatever the *verdict* of history may be, Chaplin will occupy a unique place in its pages. **9.** Poonam is ever ready to *lend a hand*. **10.** She is very *discreet*. **11.** The judge asked the contending parties to state their position *unequivocally*. **12.** If a leader wants to be popular he should master the art of being *civil* to everyone. **13.** We have witnessed an *inexorable* march of progress by the organisation. **14.** Indian cricketers were *brimming* over with confidence after their English tour. **15.** His *adulatory* remarks surprised us.

PRACTICE TEST-19

1. liking 2. entertain 3. distinction 4. enraged 5. unquestionable 6. different 7. scarcity 8. undifferentiated 9. drive way 10. talkative 11. clear 12. a circle 13. hard working 14. steep 15. worldly

1. The great dancer impressed the appreciative crowd with her *nimble* movements. **2.** He whirled round in a *trice* with a revolver in his hand. **3.** He used to *regale* us with anecdotes. **4.** Many of his acquaintances avoid him because he is so *garrulous*. **5.** He spent his whole life caught up in *mundane* matters. **6.** He had a *penchant* for the phrases **7.** The parade route was down the main *boulevard*. **8.** Your master will like you if you are *diligent*. **9.** *Incensed* by his rude behaviour the manager suspended the work. **10.** In the existing circumstances her success is *out of the question*. **11.** The five experiments give *disparate* results. **12.** Though he is a teacher, his speed lacks *distinctness*. **13.** On account of the *paucity* of funds the plan remained incomplete. **14.** We walked down a *precipitous* slope. **15.** The *indiscriminate* demand for mass consumption goods is deplorable.

PRACTICE TEST-20

1. disgraceful 2. passage 3. scarcely 4. credulous 5. penitent 6. critical 7. regret 8. incalculable 9. correct 10. energetic 11. ill-will 12. covet 13. delightful 14. optimistic 15. unashamed

1. *Malice* is a feeling that we should always avoid. **2.** It is discouraging to find educated people being *taken in easily* by the lies of religious charlatans. **3.** Outside I am nothing but a *frolicsome* little goat who is broken loose. **4.** Due to the long *lapse* of time, I could not recognise my old friend. **5.** How I *envy* the man who can always produce his reading glasses at a moment's notice. **6.** The communal politics has done *imponderable* loss to the unity of India. **7.** Wealth acquired through *dishonourable* means leads to moral downfall. **8.** Some satirists are known for their *trenchant* style. **9.** I am filled with *remorse* for my failure to help the young man. **10.** *Sanguine* as he is in his attitude to life and its problems, he cannot but be noticed wherever he goes. **11.** Our Prime Minister is young and *dynamic*. **12.** Quite *unabashed*, he began his scholarly lecture on what was obvious to everyone. **13.** He *hardly* works. **14.** The maid servant left the police station *contrite*. **15.** Would you please *rectify* the mistake?

SECTION II

In the paragraphs here, there are sentences with italicised words and phrases. The respective substitutes for all such italicised words are given in the box at the head of each paragraph. Choose the word opposite in meaning to the italicised word.

PRACTICE TEST-21

1. simplicity 2. puny 3. strong 4. misfortune 5. distort 6. cautiously 7. careless 8. enthusiastically 9. crafty 10. lively 11. dull 12. pessimistic 13. dampened 14. maturity 15. annulled 16. benign 17. malignant 18. inefficiency 19. civilised 20. simplicity

1. This offer has come as a great *boon* to me. **2.** The treaty was *ratified* by the Heads of States. **3.** The painting is full of *radiant* colours. **4.** In the interest of one's reputation one should avoid *ostentation* while entertaining friends. **5.** His was a *delicate* constitution. **6.** The inhabitants of the island were *barbarians*. **7.** They had an *insipid* conversation. **8.** The minister is *optimistic* about the new project just launched. **9.** The principal is popular with students for his *benign* attitude. **10.** It is a *Herculean* task for me. **11.** Her *candid* confession of the crime earned her reprieve. **12.** Indian economy is basically dependent on *fickle* monsoons. **13.** You must put up the facts *straight* before me and don't try to befool me. **14.** He is very *fastidious* about his choice of food. **15.** The Prime Minister's radio broadcast *galvanised* the people's spirit. **16.** They approached the stranger *warily*. **17.** He received the news *coldly*. **18.** He is showing signs of *senility*. **19.** This officer is noted for his *zeal*. **20.** Due to his excessive *craftiness* he achieved success but lost friends.

PRACTICE TEST-22

1. hot 2. denied 3. praising 4. petulance 5. extol 6. triumphant 7. brisk 8. obvious 9. humility 10. decent 11. unlawful 12. separately 13. discredits 14. harmony 15. intentional 16. meagre 17. genuine 18. certainty 19. importance 20. affluence

1. One usually feels *languid* on summer noons. **2.** There exists *rancour* between the two brothers. **3.** We must realise the *futility* of wars. **4.** In such difficult times it *behoves* all of us to remain united. **5.** The police tried to find out the *rightful* owner of the ornaments left in the train. **6.** At least some students are in the habit of doing their exercises in a *slovenly* manner. **7.** The error in the newspaper article is *accidental*. **8.** He is a man of *mellow* temper. **9.** *Crestfallen* he returned as he had never faced such humiliation in the whole of his life. **10.** The explosion and the plane's take off occurred *simultaneously*. **11.** She was surprised by his *amiability*. **12.** We should not *belittle* the value of small things. **13.** Self-reliance has been *adopted* as an important objective of economic planning in modern India. **14.** The leader might have had some *covert* reason for the change of his political affiliations. **15.** Thousands of people died of *spurious* liquor in Baroda this year. **16.** There is a *dearth* of dedicated workers in our party. **17.** Our knowledge of the past is still largely a matter of *conjecture*. **18.** The commission took two years to go through the *massive* collection of files and documents before preparing its reports. **19.** He is known for his *arrogance*. **20.** James had the habit of *running down* his colleagues.

PRACTICE TEST-23

1. brotherhood 2. appreciates 3. rustic 4. bravery 5. dejected 6. baffle 7. admiration 8. close 9. closed 10. impassive 11. unconvincing 12. conserve 13. lazy 14. retaliatory 15. ordinary 16. advantageous 17. whole 18. mean 19. discriminating 20. happiness

1. He is quite *industrious*. **2.** The children are playing in the *nearby* park. **3.** The plane lay burnt in *fragments*. **4.** Their family *feud* has taken an ugly turn lately. **5.** You are advised not to *dissipate* your energy on impracticable schemes. **6.** He has always been *fastidious* while examining answer scripts. **7.** The speaker made some very *cogent* remarks. **8.** He *despises* classical music. **9.** His *magnanimous* gesture came to his employees as a surprise. **10.** His *urbane* attitude won him many friends. **11.** The research showed that the drug has *pernicious* effect on the health of patients. **12.** At his success in the examination he felt *elated*. **13.** Mrs. Nisha made *fervent* appeal to the members of the club to maintain unity. **14.** He was charged with *abetting* the murder of an innocent child. **15.** The *indignation* of the retreating troops resulted in large scale killings. **16.** His *servility* makes him detestable. **17.** She had nothing but *scorn* for my ideas. **18.** The hall was packed with people, who came to hear the *celebrated* author. **19.** The chairman *initiated* the proceedings with a brief speech. **20.** The plantation workers were on *collision* course before the labour officer intervened.

PRACTICE TEST-24

1. unpalatable 2. sensible 3. sanguine 4. pleased. 5. classified 6. veteran 7. dismissal 8. tolerant 9. small 10. noisy 11. gratifying 12. pious 13. humble 14. maturity 15. release 16. show 17. consonance 18. dispersed 19. serious 20. reveal

1. Athletes tend to *conceal* their disappointment when they lose. **2.** He was a most *fanatic* person. **3.** The government empowered itself to *attach* the assets of all the scam suspects. **4.** His *appointment* was confirmed last month. **5.** The room was filled with a *delicious* odour. **6.** He tried to *conceal* the secret that they were already married. **7.** She was *sceptical* about the safety of the new drug. **8.** It was *altercation* throughout and there was no discussion. **9.** She is beautiful as well as *frivolous*. **10.** *Miscellaneous* items were discussed at the meeting. **11.** High School students generally take pleasure in asking *puerile* questions. **12.** The *tranquil* surroundings of Shimla are healthful. **13.** A crowd *gathered* quickly when the police came. **14.** Though *novice* in art, he shows great promise. **15.** I was *disgusted* at the manner in which he was flattering the party leader. **16.** The climate in the north of Europe is really *dreadful*. **17.** There are many anecdotes about his sister who is an *imperious* personality. **18.** Arrangements were made to handle the *mammoth* gathering tactfully. **19.** He is showing signs of *senility*. **20.** The young business executive was very *perspicacious*.

PRACTICE TEST-25

1. idealistic 2. condemning 3. old–fashioned 4. diminish 5. kind 6. lethargy 7. self-confidence 8. dull 9. easy 10. renovated 11. bluntness 12. clumsy 13. real 14. self-assurance 15. narrows 16. adornment 17. accept 18. well-built 19. intrusion 20. eagerness

1. The task assigned to him was *arduous*. **2.** His speech was full of frequent *facetious* remarks. **3.** A character without a *blemish* is a virtue of a leader. **4.** *Apathy* for the poor is common to officials of every cadre. **5.** She is *exquisite* in figure. **6.** All these measures will *augment* employment opportunities. **7.** After meeting the holy man his nagging mood of *diffidence* suddenly changed. **8.** It is surprising to find someone *condoning* such an act. **9.** Many of the incidents in the autobiography appear to be *fictitious*. **10.** Many people try to *resist* reforms in the society. **11.** The leader was *pragmatic* in his approach to the problems facing the country. **12.** The new officer is a *brash* young man. **13.** His *timidity* proved to be costly. **14.** It used to be said that travel *broadens* one's outlook. **15.** She is *slender* in figure. **16.** Unsettled conditions in the land led to the *exodus* of hundreds of its citizens. **17.** Her *vivacity* attracted everybody. **18.** The author has *perspicuity* in this style. **19.** The club meets on the last Thursday of every month in a *dilapidated* palace. **20.** His books are well-known for their *progressive* ideas.

PRACTICE TEST-26

1. confusion 2. tongue-tied 3. verbose 4. callousness 5. surly 6. quickened 7. pleasant 8. feasible 9. bravery 10. unintentional 11. ameliorating 12. genuine 13. a reality 14. reasonable 15. tactful 16. miserliness 17. beneficial 18. normal 19. expelled 20. copious

1. His health has been *deteriorating* since he returned from trekking expedition. **2.** You are advised to show *clemency* to the defeated enemy. **3.** Guerillas *infiltrated* into the region during the severe winter of 1997. **4.** While facing that situation he turned out to be *dauntless*. **5.** The judge thought that the offence was *deliberate*. **6.** He gave a reply written in a *terse* style. **7.** The professor had to share a hotel room with a *garrulous* tax collector. **8.** A lady of a few words, she is given to *laconic* answers. **9.** She is known for her *frugality* in household expenditure. **10.** *Ambivalence* on his part caused the ruin of all his aspirations. **11.** His *amiable* nature has won him many admirers. **12.** It was a *revolting* sight. **13.** He was the most *eccentric* and difficult patron. **14.** The momentum of the movement *slackened* in course of time. **15.** He is well-known for coming up with *impracticable* solutions. **16.** There is a great deal of *spurious* family affection. **17.** His *servility* makes him detestable. **18.** Philosophers say that the world is an *illusion*. **19.** The drug will have *pernicious* effect on your health. **20.** There is only the most *tenuous* evidence for it.

PRACTICE TEST-27

1. respectful 2. unconvincing 3. unhurried 4. repentant 5. aggravating 6. detractors 7. gaunt 8. appreciated 9. uncertain 10. idealistic 11. insignificant 12. poor 13. outstanding 14. integration 15. inflation 16. alleviate 17. pleasant 18. illustrated 19. successful 20. parting

1. Mala was often teased as *corpulent* by her friends. **2.** Let us not *aggravate* the sufferings of the poor. **3.** The principal *deprecated* the attitude of some student leaders. **4.** He directed a couple of *mediocre* films **5.** The director had a *derisive* attitude towards some of the members of the committee. **6.** Many an *abortive* attempts to scale the mountains disappointed him. **27.** *Hectic* arrangements are on for the coming visit of the Minister. **8.** *Reunion* was overwhelming as he returned home after a long time. **9.** He produced *cogent* reasons for the change of policy. **10.** The booking-clerk looked very *grumpy*. **11.** Some democratic countries believe in racial *segregation*. **12.** Though aware of his crimes, he remained *impenitent* throughout. **13.** The facts of the case were *obscured* by the speech of the defence counsel. **14.** None but his *sycophants* were impressed by his haughtiness. **15.** Twenty point programme is aimed at *alleviating* the sufferings of the poor. **16.** The leader was *pragmatic* in his approach to the problems facing the country. **17.** The influence of political broadcasts on elections is *considerable*. **18.** *Recession* causes unemployment. **19.** They have not been eating *nourishing* food. **20.** Nothing has been organised properly and confusion seems *inevitable*.

PRACTICE TEST-28

1. foreign 2. farsighted 3. indigence 4. frequent 5. expedited 6. defer 7. carefully 8. important 9. augment 10. improvement 11. unsympathetic 12. advance 13. extravagance 14. dispersed 15. ambiguous 16. esteeming 17. well-known 18. condemnation 19. advance 20. serious

1. That police officer is known to be *humane* in his approach. **2.** The decision was *delayed* because of him. **3.** There was a marked *deterioration* in his condition. **4.** He has a passion for *indigenous* goods. **5.** His *frivolous* remarks provoked no comments. **6.** His friends liked everything about him except his *frugality*. **7.** People who are actually running the system often take a *myopic* view of the situation. **8.** The students *assembled* in the meeting hall. **9.** The minster gave a public speech on the controversial subject to *precipitate* the matter. **10.** The usual *adulation* of the officer must end. **11.** Like poverty, *affluence* can sometimes create its own problems. **12.** There is an obscure cave on the other side of the hill. **13.** The visit of the Vice Chancellor has been *deferred* indefinitely. **14.** Sometimes it is necessary to *retreat* in a battle. **15.** However hard you may try to *mitigate* his problems, you will not succeed. **16.** The forwards of their football team made *sporadic* raids into the opponent's territory. **17.** The officer had issued *explicit* instructions to his staff. **18.** Some people always drive their cars *recklessly*. **19.** Some have the habit of *disparaging* the success of their friend because of jealousy. **20.** You will have to learn to gloss over the *trivial* mistakes of the youngsters.

PRACTICE TEST-29

1. chivalrous 2. favourably 3. pride 4. thorough 5. unkind 6. compulsory 7. graceful 8. prosperity 9. essential 10. rigid 11. clean 12. grandeur 13. friendliness 14. boldness 15. antipathy 16. lazy 17. energetic 18. reject 19. law abiding 20. optional

1. There has always been a feeling of *rancour* between the two families. **2.** *Adversity* teaches man to be humble and self-reliant. **3.** We *solicit* your cooperation. **4.** He is a very *timid* person. **5.** They took note of the *humility* of the visiting dignitary. **6.** He is quite *industrious*. **7.** It is *obligatory* for a common citizen to follow the rules. **8.** The principal hardly managed to give the papers a *cursory* glance. **9.** It was a *voluntary* gesture. **10.** Your team is full of *delinquent* children. **11.** Unlike the other candidates, his manner was entirely *languid*. **12.** The two girls are always together. There is a great *affinity* between them. **13.** His principles are *flexible*. **14.** Every move I make seems to affect him *adversely*. **15.** The actor is well-known both for his *humility* and courage. **16.** Born in *squalid* surroundings of the slums she rose to stardom overnight. **17.** *Modesty* is a virtue but it must not be allowed to be exploited. **18.** The speaker recalled the deceased leader's *benevolent* deeds. **19.** He walked in *ungainly* strides. **20.** Some of the needs of a modern man are surely *dispensable*.

PRACTICE TEST-30

1. scarcity 2. beneficial 3. falsity 4. awkwardness 5. short 6. critical 7. cheerful 8. unlucky 9. extinct 10. praise 11. slacken 12. enviable 13. convicted 14. real 15. shirked 16. boon 17. impracticability 18. cowardly 19. released 20. energy

1. It was *fortuitous* that I met her at that party. **2.** After a day's toil he was feeling *fatigued*. **3.** Manuscripts of Shakespeare's plays are still *extant* in the British Museum. **4.** Drink proved to be the *bane* of his otherwise spotless career. **5.** Overeating can often be *detrimental* to health. **6.** *Feasibility* of the project is under study. **7.** In all places, and at all times, there is a *profusion* of talent. **8.** He has been *acquitted* of the charge of theft. **9.** We have no doubt about the *veracity* of his statement. **10.** The criminal was *detained* by the police. **11.** He made an *exhaustive* list of the items his secretary should attend to. **12.** That man is known for his *elegance*. **13.** Sherlock Holmes is a *fictitious* character. **14.** His was a *sulky* disposition. **15.** That was a *dauntless* action. **16.** Under the circumstances, such *pejorative* comments should have been avoided. **17.** His partners felt that it was a *viable* business proposition. **18.** She used to *deprecate* her neighbour's conduct every now and then. **19.** He was asked to *accelerate* the pace of work. **20.** He *endeavoured* hard to reach the top of his career.

PRACTICE TEST-31

1. insincerity 2. homogeneous 3. rough 4. understanding 5. invested 6. purified 7. denunciation 8. indifferent 9. respectful 10. optional 11. squandered 12. praise 13. secure 14. hilarious 15. strengthen 16. strong 17. deify 18. cheerless 19. naïve 20. indifference

1. The Board of Directors showered *encomium* on the Chairman for his liberal policies. **2.** The minister was accused of indulging in *nepotism*. **3.** Their arrival *defiled* the atmosphere. **4.** He has translated the play into English with *fidelity*. **5.** The consultant analysed the proposal carefully before he decided to *jettison* it. **6.** I am in a rather *precarious* position in my place of work. **7.** How dare you *desecrate* an idol of this temple! **8.** *Bereft* of his support he died poor. **9.** He was *dejected* when he heard the news. **10.** He proved utterly *capricious* in his dealings with his friends. **11.** The General Manager is quite *tactful* and handles the workers' union very effectively. **12.** His style was *smooth*, but there was no mistaking his determination. **13.** His family has *accumulated* wealth over the years. **14.** Her *debonair* manners were noticed by everyone present in the party. **15.** We received a *cordial* welcome from our host. **16.** Silence in this place is *mandatory*. **17.** India is a *heterogeneous* country. **18.** She used to *disparage* her neighbours every now and then. **19.** In ancient days a *fragile* glass jar was considered to be more valuable than a human slave. **20.** Sanjay's point of view was correct but his behaviour with his father was quite *impertinent*.

PRACTICE TEST-32

1. humility 2. contradicts 3. strength 4. temporary 5. ludicrous 6. trepid 7. infuriate 8. aggressiveness 9. mild 10. facile 11. freedom 12. indigenous 13. ruffled 14. impetuosity 15. encourage 16. partners 17. strict 18. succeeded 19. jovial 20. glorify

1. Water scarcity is a *perennial* problem in that village. **2.** Why do you *disparage* him all the time? **3.** He stood gazing at the *serene* expanse of the sea. **4.** The timely action *foiled* his evil designs. **5.** The *fetters* of slavery are hard to shake off. **6.** There was *dismal* atmosphere in the dressing room of the defeated team. **7.** What he tells me *confirms* my ideas. **8.** There are no permanent *adversaries* in politics. **9.** There is not a trace of *vanity* in her behaviour. **10.** All the employees of this organisation want to have an officer who is *lenient*. **11.** A *fortuitous* combination of circumstances led to the discovery of his lineage. **12.** He made several attempts to *placate* his opponents. **13.** The *feebleness* of mind is the greatest hurdle to success in life. **14.** *Formidable* obstacles have to be overcome before success is achieved. **15.** He has been accorded *lukewarm* welcome. **16.** He liked the *pungent* sauce prepared by his mother. **17.** The deliberate *suavity* of Dev's behaviour made the emotions of the audience volatile. **18.** We should not *belittle* other's achievement. **19.** Everything about him especially his talkative nature proclaims his *effeminacy*. **20.** He has a weakness for *foreign* goods.

PRACTICE TEST-33

1. clumsy 2. permanent 3. Ceremoniously 4. delightful 5. cheerful 6. giant7. overcome 8. sacred 9. obscure 10. wrong 11. uncertain 12. cheap13. act willingly 14. forgiving 15. figurative 16. preceding 17. enthusiastic 18. philogynists 19. hostile 20. poised

1. Everybody was astonished when he used such *profane* language. **2.** I liked the poem for its *literal* meaning. **3.** I like his *friendly* attitude. **4.** She handled the machine with *deft* fingers. **5.** At the beginning of the novel we see the hero in all the fresh *vivid* detail in which he would appear to be a curious stranger from Spain. **6.** *Genuine* drugs are available in most of the medical shops. **7.** Her *impetuous* behaviour was attributed to her upbringing. **8.** The committee set about making *provisional* arrangements for the annual conference. **9.** I thought about her a lot during the *following* months. **10.** His failure in this venture may be attributed to his *lackadaisical* approach. **11.** He glanced through the letter *perfunctorily*. **12.** She paid special attention to those women who had *succumbed* to adversity. **13.** Throughout the evening, Rahul looked very *doleful*. **14.** *Genuine* jewellery is available only in this shop. **15.** An honest person need not *hesitate* to take bold steps. **16.** Nothing has been organised properly and confusion seems *inevitable*. **17.** There is something *repulsive* about the way he handles people's complaints. **18.** His *vindictive* nature often came up for comment among his friends. **19.** *Misogynists* are not applauded in society. **20.** Every self-respecting circus needs at least one *dwarf*.

PRACTICE TEST-34

1. bright 2. invincible 3. uniform 4. awkward 5. sane 6. admirable 7. frugal 8. productive 9. comfortable 10. restored 11. scarce 12. insincere 13. varied 14. flexible 15. genuine 16. liberal 17. indifferent 18. friendly 19. unsavoury 20. victory

1. The new government has *abolished* the gold control act. **2.** It was a very *dreary* day. **3.** He appears to be a *phony* person. **4.** The revised pay scale is *uniform*. **5.** We had a *delectable* meal yesterday. **6.** The two friends were *distinct* in everything, dress, manners, hair-style, and food habits. **7.** The last show of the concert at the Ritz Theatre was a *fiasco*. **8.** Everybody called it a *lavish* party. **9.** Her *adamant* attitude brought her on the verge of divorce. **10.** Even a *lunatic* person sometimes talks intelligently. **11.** He is *zealous* only in the initial stages of a project. **12.** The politician was *flummoxed* by the questions put to him. **13.** The state government for its part can identify *vulnerable* villages where these forces can be stationed. **14.** In facing adverse situations, he was very *stoical*. **15.** Professors are generally *serious* about what they say. **16.** India will have to cultivate all her *barren* land to meet with her food requirements. **17.** The members of the opposition made *derogatory* remarks about the policies of the government. **18.** The area is known for *plentiful* rain. **19.** We were surprised by the *hostile* attitude of the villagers. **20.** Old people are usually more *conservative* than young people.

PRACTICE TEST-35

1. stable 2. irregular 3. disreputable 4. regressive 5. genuine 6. extravagant 7. deep 8. generosity 9. indecent 10. rural 11. old–fashioned 12. romantic 13. malevolent 14. prosperity 15. dense 16. harmless 17. imbecility 18. big 19. decent 20. an expressive

1. Lucy is a *smart* girl. **2.** Of all the companions of our joyous *ascent*, there were only the two of us left. **3.** I was deeply affected by his *urbane* behaviour. **4.** We want to the first floor through the *rickety* wooden stairs. **5.** Those in *distress* should not be laughed at because they deserve our sympathy. **6.** His face bore *a blank* look all the time while I was telling him about that exciting incident. **7.** *Counterfeit* coins are in circulation because of negligence on the part of police authorities. **8.** Though generous and *benevolent*, he did not meet with success in his career. **9.** The town has been experiencing *incessant* rains since 4 o'clock. **10.** Many snakes are *innocuous*. **11.** It was universally characterised as a *progressive* measure. **12.** His business *acumen* led him to the zenith of his career. **13.** The mountains present a *bleak* sight at night. **14.** The speaker has a *superficial* knowledge of the subject. **15.** They made a *profligate* use of scarce resources. **16.** The outgoing Chairman has a number of *laudable* achievements to his credit. **17.** His *meanness* is proverbial. **18.** Her dress was too *slovenly* for that kind of interview. **19.** He was in a *dejected* mood. **20.** Have you seen that *timid* child?

SECTION III

Find out the substitutes given in the boxes and fill in the blank given in the paragraphs. The word must be a substitute for the whole sentence.

PRACTICE TEST-36

1. encyclopedia 2. pessimist 3. amphibians 4. cannibal 5. surgeon 6. licentious 7. misologist 8. pagan 9. telescope 10. aristocracy

1. A man who operates on sick people __________. **2.** A book containing summarised information on all branches of knowledge __________. **3.** An instrument for viewing objects at a distance __________. **4.** A hater of learning and knowledge __________. **5.** A person who does not believe in any religion __________. **6.** A person who looks at the dark side of everything __________. **7.** A man of lax moral __________. **8.** Animals who eat flesh of another animal _______ **9.** A government by the nobles __________. **10.** Animals that can live on land and water __________.

PRACTICE TEST-37

1. insolvent 2. dormitory 3. honorary 4. exodus 5. postscript 6. autocracy 7. infectious 8. red tapism 9. misogynist 10. polyandry

1.Anything written in a letter after it is signed __________. **2.** A woman having several husbands at the same time__________. **3.** A person who has no money to pay off his debts ___________. **4.** A person who hates women __________. **5.** A sleeping room for many persons__________. **6.** A process involving too much official formality __________. **7.** A large scale departure of people from a territory__________. **8.** A post without remuneration __________. **9.** A disease that spreads by means of germs carried in atmosphere_______. **10.** A government run by a dictator _______.

PRACTICE TEST-38

1. dermatologist 2. asylum 3. epicure 4. extempore 5. sermon 6. nimbus 7. epidemic 8. maiden speech 9. philanderer 10. epicure

1. A speech delivered without preparation __________. **2.** A person who believes that pleasure is the chief good __________. **3.** A speech made by someone for the first time __________. **4.** A physician who specialises in diseases of skin __________. **5.** A person who is fond of sensuous enjoyment __________. **6.** A disease that affects a large number of people in an area at the same time __________. **7.** A religious discourse __________. **8.** A place that provides refuge __________. **9.** A large dark grey cloud that brings rain or snow __________. **10.** A person who makes love without being serious _________.

PRACTICE TEST-39

1. magician 2. gust 3. sojourn 4. reticent 5. amnesty 6. glutton 7. atheist 8. freak 9. asylum 10. lethal

1. A child of unusual or remarkable talent__________. **2.** A disease which ends in death __________. **3.** A person who does not believe in the existence of God__________. **4.** A person who tries to deceive people by claiming to be able to do wonderful things__________. **5.** A place for sick people who need long periods for recovery__________. **6.** A sudden rush of wind __________. **7.** A person who eats too much__________. **8.** A person who is reserved in talks _______. **9.** A short stay at a place ______. **10.** A general pardon granted by the government to political offenders ____.

PRACTICE TEST-40

1. optimist 2. dandy 3. unequivocal 4. ambiguous 5. widow 6. demagogue 7. obstinate 8. anarchist 9. bureaucracy 10. eccentric

1. A person who is out to destroy government __________. **2.** A person who looks on the bright side of things __________. **3.** A Government that is carried on through Officers________ **4.** A woman whose husband is dead __________. **5.** A man of odd habits __________. **6.** A statement that is absolutely clear__________. **7.** Animals living on land and in water __________. **8.** A political leader who tries to stir people __________. **9.** A man who pays too much attention to his clothes and personal appearance __________. **10.** A person very hard to please__________.

PRACTICE TEST-41

1. epilogue 2. smuggler 3. brittle 4. henpecked 5. duffer 6. novice 7. caricature 8. boorish 9. prostitute 10. suicide

1. A funny imitation of a poem__________. **2.** A person without manners or polish __________. **3.** A speech by an actor at the end of a play __________. **4.** Act of taking one's life __________. **5.** A person who brings goods illegally into the country __________. **6.** A man who dances to the tunes of his wife __________. **7.** A person who has just started learning__________. **8.** A woman of lax moral conduct __________. **9.** A slow-witted and incompetent person________. **10.** A thing liable to be easily broken __________.

PRACTICE TEST-42

1. effeminate 2. obsolete 3. affidavit 4. hedonist 5. septuagenarian 6. infiltrator 7. credulous 8. maiden 9. pediatrician 10. spinster

1. A person's first speech__________ **2.** A person who is very fond of sensuous enjoyments _____. **3.** An old unmarried woman__________. **4.** A written declaration made on oath in the presence of a magistrate __________. **5.** A physician who delivers babies__________. **6.** A man who is having the qualities of woman __________. **7.** A word no longer in use__________. **8.** A person 70 to 79 years old __________. **9.** A person who sneaks into a country__________. **10.** A person who readily believes others__________.

PRACTICE TEST-43

1. unsocial 2. misogamist 3. piggyback 4. kindergarten 5. panacea 6. constellation 7. manuscript 8. book worm 9. philatelist 10. anarchist

1. A paper written in one's own handwriting __________. **2.** A small named group of fixed stars__________**3.** A person who lives alone and avoids other people__________. **4.** A person who wishes to throw over all establishments __________. **5.** A person interested in reading books and __________. **6.** A person who hates women __________. **7.** A person who collects coins __________. **8.** A school for infants and young children__________. **9.** A ride on someone else's back or shoulders __________. **10.** A cure for all diseases __________.

PRACTICE TEST-44

1. egoist 2. mercenary 3. contemporary 4. polygamy 5. stroll 6. truce 7. orphan 8. elegy 9. conservation 10. archipelago

1. A short walk for pleasure or exercise __________. **2.** A person who is more interested in himself rather than anything that is going on around him __________. **3.** A sea abounding in islands __________. **4.** A song sung at a burial __________. **5.** A soldier who fights for sake of money cannot be branded as courageous and patriotic __________. **6.** A careful preservation and protection of wildlife is the need of the hour. __________. **7.** Both Buddha and Mahavira lived at the same time __________. **8.** Custom of having many wives __________. **9.** Cessation of arms before a formal treaty is signed during war __________. **10.** Child bereaved of one or both the parents __________.

PRACTICE TEST-45

1. boor 2. monarchy 3. foeticide 4. genocide 5. vacillation 6. protocol 7. blasphemy 8. sadism 9. democracy 10. spying

1. Contempt of god __________. **2.** Changing one's mind too quickly __________. **3.** Clumsy or ill-bred fellow __________. **4.** Code of diplomatic etiquette and precedence __________. **5.** Destruction of unborn baby in mother's womb__________. **6.** Deriving pleasure from inflicting pain on others __________. **7.** Elimination of a racial group by killing__________. **8.** Government by a single person __________. **9.** Government by the representatives of the people __________. **10.** Habit of secretly listening to private conversation_______.

PRACTICE TEST-46

1. inexplicable 2. condominium 3. stoicism 4. invulnerable 5. illegible 6. homicide 7. biography 8. fratricide 9. inexplicable 10. pediatrician

1. Handwriting that cannot be read__________. **2.** His father is a doctor who treats children and infants__________. **3.** Incapable of being explained__________. **4.** Indifference to pleasure or pain __________. **5.** Incapable of being explained or accounted for __________. **6.** Incapable of being wounded __________. **7.** Joint sovereignty exercised over a country by two or more countries __________. **8.** Killing of human beings__________. **9.** Killing of one's own brother__________. **10.** Life history of a person written by another __________.

PRACTICE TEST-47

1. infanticide 2. cuckold 3. extempore 4. regicide 5. exodus 6. omnivorous 7. peninsula 8. anaemia 9. kleptomania 10. brittle

1. Large scale departure of people __________. **2.** Likely to break apart easily__________. **3.** Lack of enough blood __________. **4.** Land so surrounded by water as to be almost an island __________. **5.** Mania for stealing articles __________. **6.** Man whose wife has been unfaithful to him __________. **7.** Murder of a new-born child __________. **8.** Murder of a king __________. **9.** Not many people were impressed by a speech delivered without previous preparation. __________. **10.** One who eats everything__________.

PRACTICE TEST-48

1. maladministration 2. cosmopolitan 3. demagogue 4. matricide 5. apostate 6. nihilist 7. teetotaller 8. retired 9. humanist 10. feminist

1. One who murder one's mother __________. **2.** One who loves all and sundry __________. **3.** Official misconduct__________ **4.** One who is interested in the welfare of women __________. **5.** One who takes delight in excessive cruelty __________. **6.** One who deserts his religion__________. **7.** One who feels at home in every country __________. **8.** One who totally abstains from alcoholic drinks__________. **9.** One who stirs people for personal politics or profit__________ **10.** One who is honourably discharged from service __________.

PRACTICE TEST-49

1. omniscient 2. incorrigible 3. cannibal 4. ambidextrous 5. reserved 6. spendthrift 7. martyr 8. loquacious 9. bibliophile 10. mediocre

1. One who talks very little __________. **2.** One who loves books __________. **3.** One knowing everything __________. **4.** One who is neither intelligent nor dull __________. **5.**_One who eats human flesh _______. **6.** One who sacrifice his life for a cause _______. **7.** One who cannot be corrected _______. **8.** One who does not know how to save money ________. **9.** One who talks continuously __________. **10.** One who can use either of his hands with ease __________.

PRACTICE TEST-50

1. alien 2. commandos 3. versatile 4. stoic 5. polyglot 6. pantheist 7. vendetta 8. adultery 9. plaintiff 10. fatalist

1. One who speaks or understands many languages __________. **2.** One who possesses many talents __________. **3.** One who believes that everything is pre-destined __________. **4.** One who resides in a country of which he is not a citizen __________. **5.** Practice of a married woman having extra marital relationship __________. **6.** Person who brings an action at law __________. **7.** Person who is indifferent to both pleasure and pain __________. **8.** Paying back injury with injury _______. **9.** Person who believes that god is everything and everything is god. __________. **10.** Policemen riding on motorcycles as guards of VIP__________.

PRACTICE TEST-51

1. veteran 2. manifesto 3. sporadic 4. aviary 5. consanguinity 6. mob 7. audible 8. colleagues 9. elope 10. truism

1. Perceptible to the ear __________. **2.** People working in the same department or office_______**3.** Place where birds are kept

__________. **4.** Person who has long experience __________. **5.** Plain or self evident truth __________. **6.** People in a riot __________. **7.** Policy of a political party __________. **8.** Rainfall at irregular intervals or occasionally__________. **9.** Relationship by blood or birth __________. **10.** Run away from home with lover __________.

PRACTICE TEST-52

1. animosity 2. anthropology 3. resplendent 4. parable 5. imperialism 6. celibacy 7. superficial 8. demography 9. obsolete 10. eloquence

1. Ravi impressed everyone with his persuasive and fluent speech__________**2.** Strong and settled dislike between two __________. **3.** Something that becomes outdated__________. **4.** Study of mankind __________. **5.** Study of statistics of births, deaths, diseases to show the state of community ________. **6.** Shining brilliant and magnificant ______________**7.** Something which is not thorough or profound __________. **8.** Story told to illustrate a moral or spiritual truth __________. **9.** The state of complete continence on the part of a woman_______. **10.** The policy of extending a country's empire and influence____.

PRACTICE TEST-53

1. assassination 2. anthropology 3. single 4. opaque 5. circumlocution 6. armistice 7. expatriate 8. ambiguous 9. obliterate 10. one who abstains from taking wine

1. The study of ancient societies __________. **2.** To send an unwanted person out of the country __________. **3.** To kill someone for political reasons__________. **4.** The cessation of warfare before a treaty is signed __________. **5.** Teetotaler means__________. **6.** Through which light cannot pass __________. **7.** To talk much without coming to the point __________. **8.** The state of being unmarried__________. **9.** That which can be interpreted in any way ______. **10.** To do away with a rule _______.

PRACTICE TEST-54

1. portable 2. propitiate 3. expiate 4. kiln 5. stumble 6. seize 7. menu 8. indispensable 9. peel 10. sacrilege

1. The list of courses at a meal or of dishes that can be served in a restaurant __________. **2.** The place where bricks are baked __________. **3.** The act of violating the sanctity of church __________. **4.** To atone for one's sins__________. **5.** That which can be carried __________. **6.** To remove the skin of a potato or an orange __________. **7.** To atone for one's sins __________. **8.** To surround with armed forces __________. **9.** To move along with quick, short twisting __________. **10.** That which cannot be done without __________.

PRACTICE TEST-55

1. tangible 2. harbinger 3. neologism 4. irreparable 5. parasite 6. abdication 7. chauvinism 8. unintelligible 9. megalomania 10. contagious

1. that which cannot be rectified or made good __________. **2.** The form of madness which gives a person the idea that his importance is very great __________. **3.** That which is perceptible by touch __________. **4.** That which cannot be understood __________. **5.** Tuberculosis is a disease which spreads by contact. __________. **6.** The committee insisted on a total check on all social evils and he was the one who heralded the revolution. __________. **7.** Using of new words __________. **8.** Unreasoning enthusiasm for the glorification of one's country __________. **9.** Voluntarily giving up throne by king in favour of his son __________. **10.** Virus is a biological entity which lives on another organism. __________.

SECTION IV

Fill in the blanks from the words given in the boxes and make a sentence which makes a complete IDIOMATIC sentence and make proper sense.

PRACTICE TEST-56

1. smoke 2. fair 3. done 4. wane 5. offing 6. burning 7. fiddle 8. add 9. eleventh hour 10. pell–mell

1. A movement for the world unity is in the ____________. **2.** As our army attacked, the enemy retreated __________. **3.** A hen pecked husband plays second ____________to his wife. **4.** All his schemes to murder the king ended in ______________. **5.** At the___________, Mridul arrived and saved him from the crisis. **6.** By ___________ means or foul. **7.** Caesar was _________ to death by the conspirators. **8.** Dowry is a _____________ question of the day. **9.** Do not __________ ____ __ ___ _ ___ **10.** Discipline is on the _________ in schools and colleges these days.

PRACTICE TEST-57

1. loggerheads 2. fishing 3. mark 4. by 5. fair 6. nerves 7. premium 8. Spade 9. bonnet 10. cold

1. Dishonesty is at a __________ in almost all spheres of public life. **2.** Do you know why I avoid this man? He has a bee in his/the __________. **3.** His voice gets on my __________. **4.** He works__________ fit and starts. **5.** He threw __________ water over the project that the secretary had prepared. **6.** He is a plain, simple, and sincere man. He will always call a __________ a spade. **7.** He is at __________ with his assistants about the management of the concern. **8.** He is in the habit of __________ in troubled waters. **9.** His father advised him to be __________ and square in his dealings lest he should fall into trouble. **10.** He has made his __________ in pclitics.

PRACTICE TEST-58

1. cuts 2. make 3. wrong 4. lurch 5. after 6. cool 7. hard 8. phenomenal 9. herculean 10. ill

1. He is a person __________ my own heart. **2.** He felt __________ at ease after receiving the letter from his son. **3.** His___________-earned money has gone down the drain. **4.** He was __________ as a cucumber. **5.** He always __________ both ends. **6.** He left his friend in __________. **7.** He has accomplished a __________ task. **8.** His ___________ success shows that he has got the midas touch. **9.** He is on the ___________ ____________**10.** He cannot __________ both ends meet.

PRACTICE TEST-59

1. piece 2. oily 3. eat 4. salt 5. candles 6. wolf 7. buttered 8. cards 9. accord 10. prodigal

1. He gave his erring son a __________ of his mind. **2.** His __________ tongue has won him promotion. **3.** He had to __________ a humble pie owing to his misdeeds. **4.** He is really worth his __________. **5.** He blew out all the __________ at one go. **6.** He finds no difficulty in keeping the__________ away from the door. **7.** He knows what side his bread is ___________. **8.** His promotion is on the___________. **9.** He resigned the post of his own ___________. **10.** His __________ son was a constant source of trouble to him.

PRACTICE TEST-60

1. feather 2. cats 3. chicken 4. tables 5. blues 6. sang 7. dealing 8. flesh 9. dogs 10. harness

1. He has turned the __________ on his enemy. **2.** I won't mind even if he goes to __________. **3.** If you pass this difficult examination, it will be a __________ in your cap. **4.** In the Armed Forces, it is considered a great privilege to die in __________. **5.** It has been raining __________ and dogs. **6.** I have been betrayed by my own __________ and blood. **7.** Kishan is a __________-hearted fellow. **8.** Mrs. Khanna has been in the __________ for the last several weeks. **9.** Please do not indulge in double __________. **10.** She exhibited remarkable __________ froid during the crisis.

PRACTICE TEST-61

1. corner 2. ducks 3. lock 4. hard 5. wane 6. intents 7. no 8. lip 9. wee 10. casting

1. Some people now wonder whether we just pay __________ service or genuinely subscribe to democracy. **2.** Seema is a little __________ of hearing. **3.** To all __________ and purposes he is a good man. **4.** The __________ vote of the chairman clinched the issue. **5.** The doctor says the patient has turned the__________. **6.** The robbery was committed in the __________ hours of the day. **7.** The popularity of the yester years superstar is on the __________. **8.** The young heir to his father's huge estate made __________ and drakes of his patrimony. **9.** There is __________ love lost between the two neighbours. **10.** There company has been handed over to new masters__________, stock, and barrel.

PRACTICE TEST-62

1. flesh 2. white 3. tenterhooks 4. moot 5. devil 6. hard 7. gift 8. bird's 9. unturned 10. bury

1. The sailor found himself between the __________ and the deep sea. **2.** The sight of the accident made my __________ creep. **3.** The sworn enemies have decided to __________ the hatchet. **4.** The politician was able to sway the mob with his __________ of the gab. **5.** The speaker gave a __________ eye view of the political conditions in the country. **6.** The detective left no stone __________ to trace the culprit. **7.** They sold their house because it was a real __________ elephant. **8.** The captors of the kidnapped kept his family on __________. **9.** There is no __________ and fast rule regarding this subject. **10.** The question of abolition of private property is still a __________ point.

ANSWERS (PRACTICE TESTS)

SECTION-I

Q. No.	TEST–1	TEST –2	TEST –3	TEST –4
1.	native	native	poor	doubtful
2.	rising	primitive	amazing	plain
3.	an engrossing	magnetic appeal	necessary	artificial
4.	misplaced	objectivity	met	generous
5.	memorable	bold	problem	precision
6.	division	watchful	vague	extracts
7.	in agreement	curious	breeding silk worms	poise
8.	impute	remarkable	detestable	consequences
9.	obligatory	bitter	dependability	apparent
10.	feebleness	screen	disgraceful action	interfere
11.	mercy	outrage	futile	weariness
12.	secretive	rude	nonsense	help
13.	weakness	worsening	stereo-type statements	sycophants
14.	truthfulness	important	brave	drawing
15.	passing slanderous remarks	face	involving much sitting	repetitive

Q. No.	TEST –5	TEST –6	TEST –7	TEST –8
1.	injurious	bombastic	great	exceptional
2.	supported him energetically	shrewd	wonderful	straightforward
3.	miserly	silent	confirmed	heterogeneous
4.	frequent	easy	nourish	weakened
5.	a place with water and trees	pensive	scornful	corruption
6.	beginning	dry	generous	latter
7.	forged	convincing	total	discover
8.	discontented	neglected	inclination	establish genuineness
9.	weak	absurd	exhausted	pervades
10.	complete change	ultimately	remedy	general pardon
11.	apparent	useless	abate	sleepiness
12.	never ending	convictions	discontented	ravage
13.	renovated	diligent	confident	stomach
14.	clear	difficult	defamatory	conciliate
15.	moderation	easily perceived	restless	soften

Q. No.	TEST –9	TEST –10	TEST –11	TEST –12
1.	brilliant	disease	adapt	utilise
2.	careful	adorned	end of the letter after signature	scolded
3.	sullen	stupendous	imitate	deadlock
4.	employment	beastly	break	flatterers
5.	embarrassed	unhygienic	desertion	too difficult to overcome
6.	talkative	shorten	pinched	disorderly scene
7.	junction	convert	libertine	splendid
8.	inked	friendship	excessively respectful	deviation
9.	offhand	circumlocutory	advised	frequently changing pattern of bright scenes
10.	probity	easily understood	mixed	wasteful
11.	reformed	profitable	sensible	hackneyed
12.	succeed	a friendly	clear	pretty
13.	destroyed	exculpated	imaginative	impressive
14.	fruitful	winding	obsessed	progress
15.	scholarly	unfortunate	pleasing	justify

Q. No.	TEST –13	TEST –14	TEST –15	TEST –16
1.	critical	anthropology	sagacious	monopoly
2.	noising	fatigued	wish	careful
3.	relentless	lacking in spirit	cautious	after death
4.	irritating	differ	secret	remedy for
5.	secret	denied	rare	postulate
6.	outspokenness	circumlocutory	pass time	pretender
7.	admirable	benevolent	nefarious	rational
8.	disappointing	irritation	speedily	interval of relief
9.	lustful	convicted	suspicion	rebuke
10.	destroyed	struggled hard	unbeatable	sharpness
11.	approve	effort	lively	wearisome
12.	childishness	manage	deduct	strategic
13.	suited	primitive	abdicate	sore
14.	suitable	ungracious	stands	front
15.	unmindful	honorary	frightening	difficult

Q. No.	TEST –17	TEST –18	TEST –19	TEST –20
1.	find out	coax	clear	ill-will
2.	pacify	repeal	a circle	credulous
3.	free ride	courage	entertain	delightful
4.	gluttonous	obscure	talkative	passage
5.	inkling	peculiar	worldly	covet
6.	recently	lamentable	liking	incalculable
7.	revived	strength	drive way	disgraceful
8.	unquestionable	judgement	hard-working	critical
9.	conservation	assist	enraged	regret
10.	thoughtful	proud	unquestionable	optimistic
11.	in ugly way	completely	different	energetic
12.	rebuke	polite	distinction	unashamed
13.	hard hearted	relentless	scarcity	scarcely
14.	destroyed	overflow	steep	penitent
15.	optimistic	flattering	undifferentiated	correct

SECTION II

Q. No.	TEST –21	TEST –22	TEST –23	TEST –24
1.	misfortune	brisk	lazy	show
2.	annulled	harmony	close	tolerant
3.	dull	importance	whole	release
4.	simplicity	discredits	brotherhood	dismissal
5.	strong	unlawful	conserve	unpalatable
6.	civilised	decent	discriminating	reveal
7.	lively	intentional	unconvincing	sanguine
8.	pessimistic	hot	appreciates	consonance
9.	malignant	triumphant	mean	serious
10.	puny	separately	rustic	classified
11.	crafty	petulance	advantageous	sensible
12.	benign	extol	dejected	noisy
13.	distort	denied	impassive	dispersed
14.	careless	obvious	baffle	veteran
15.	dampened	genuine	happiness	pleased
16.	cautiously	affluence	bravery	gratifying
17.	enthusiastically	certainty	admiration	pious
18.	maturity	meager	ordinary	small
19.	inefficiency	humility	closed	maturity
20.	simplicity	praising	retaliatory	humble

Q. No.	TEST –25	TEST –26	TEST –27	TEST –28
1.	easy	ameliorating	gaunt	unsympathetic
2.	dull	callousness	alleviate	advanced
3.	adornment	expelled	appreciated	improvement
4.	eagerness	tactful	outstanding	foreign
5.	clumsy	unintentional	respectful	serious
6.	diminish	verbose	successful	extravagance
7.	self-assurance	tongue-tied	unhurried	farsighted
8.	condemning	copious	parting	dispersed
9.	real	miserliness	unconvincing	defer
10.	accept	confusion	pleasant	condemnation

Q. No.	TEST –25	TEST –26	TEST –27	TEST –28
11.	idealistic	surly	integration	indigence
12.	kind	pleasant	repentant	well-known
13.	self confidence	normal	illustrated	expedited
14.	narrows	quickened	detractors	advance
15.	well built	feasible	aggravating	augment
16.	intrusion	genuine	idealistic	frequent
17.	lethargy	bravery	insignificant	ambiguous
18.	bluntness	a reality	inflation	carefully
19.	renovated	beneficial	poor	esteeming
20.	old-fashioned	reasonable	uncertain	important

Q. No.	TEST –29	TEST –30	TEST –31	TEST –32
1.	friendliness	unlucky	denuniciation	temporary
2.	prosperity	energy	indifference	glorify
3.	reject	extinct	purified	ruffled
4.	chivalrous	boon	insincerity	succeeded
5.	grandeur	beneficial	strengthen	freedom
6.	lazy	impracticability	secure	jovial
7.	optional	scarcity	deify	contradicts
8.	thorough	convicted	invested	partners
9.	compulsory	falsity	hilarious	humility
10.	law abiding	released	understanding	strict
11.	energetic	short	naïve	ludicrous
12.	antipathy	awkwardness	rough	infuriate
13.	rigid	real	squandered	strength
14.	favourably	cheerful	cheerless	facile
15.	pride	cowardly	indifferent	trepid
16.	clean	critical	optional	mild
17.	boldness	enviable	homogeneous	impetuosity
18.	unkind	praise	praise	encourage
19.	graceful	slacken	strong	aggressiveness
20.	essential	shirked	respectful	indigenous

Q. No.	TEST –33	TEST –34	TEST –35
1.	scared	restored	indecent
2.	figurative	bright	decent
3.	hostile	genuine	rural
4.	clumsy	varied	stable
5.	obscure	unsavoury	prosperity
6.	wrong	uniform	an expressive
7.	poised	victory	genuine
8.	permanent	frugual	malevolent
9.	preceding	flexible	irregular
10.	enthusiastic	sane	harmless
11.	ceremoniously	indifferent	regressive
12.	overcome	comfortable	imbecility
13.	cheerful	invincible	dense
14.	cheap	awkward	deep
15.	act willingly	insincere	extravagant
16.	uncertain	productive	disreputable
17.	delightful	admirable	generosity
18.	forgiving	scarce	old-fashioned
19.	philogynists	friendly	romantic
20.	giant	liberal	big

SECTION III

Q. No.	TEST –36	TEST –37	TEST –38	TEST –39
1.	physician	postscript	extempore	freak
2.	encyclopedia	polyandry	epicure	lethal
3.	telescope	insolvent	maiden speech	atheist
4.	misologist	misogamist	dermatologist	magician
5.	pagan	dormitory	epicure	asylum
6.	pessimist	red-tapism	epidemic	gust
7.	licentious	exodus	sermon	glutton
8.	cannibal	honorary	asylum	reticent
9.	aristocracy	infectious	nimbus	sojourn
10.	amphibians	autocracy	philanderer	amnesty

Q. No.	TEST –40	TEST –41	TEST –42	TEST –43
1.	anarchist	caricature	maiden	manuscript
2.	optimist	boorish	hedonist	constellation
3.	bureaucracy	epilogue	spinster	unsocial
4.	widow	suicide	affidavit	anarchist
5.	eccentric	smuggler	pediatrician	book worm
6.	unequivocal	henpecked	effeminate	misogamist
7.	ambiguous	novice	obsolete	philatelist
8.	demagogue	prostitute	septuagenarian	kindergarten
9.	dandy	duffer	infiltrator	piggyback
10.	obstinate	brittle	credulous	panacea

Q. No.	TEST –44	TEST –45	TEST –46	TEST –47
1.	stroll	blasphemy	illegible	exodus
2.	egoist	vacillation	pediatrician	brittle
3.	archipelago	boor	inexplicable	anaemia
4.	elegy	protocol	stoicism	peninsula
5.	mercenary	foeticide	inexplicable	kleptomania
6.	conservation	sadism	invulnerable	cuckold
7.	contemporary	genocide	condominium	infanticide
8.	polygamy	monarchy	homicide	matricide
9.	truce	democracy	fratricide	extempore
10.	orphan	spying	biography	omnivorous

Q. No.	TEST –48	TEST –49	TEST –50	TEST –51
1.	matricide	reserved	polyglot	audible
2.	humanist	bibliophile	versatile	colleagues
3.	maladministration	omniscient	fatalist	aviary
4.	feminist	mediocre	alien	veteran
5.	nihilist	cannibal	adultery	truism
6.	apostate	martyr	plaintiff	mob
7.	cosmopolitan	incorrigible	stoic	manifesto
8.	teetotaler	spendthrift	vendetta	sporadic
9.	demagogue	loquacious	pantheist	consanguinity
10.	retired	Ambidextrous	commandos	elope

Q. No.	TEST –52	TEST –53	TEST –54	TEST –55
1.	eloquence	anthropology	menu	irreparable
2.	animosity	expatriate	foundry	megalomania
3.	obsolete	assassination	sacrilege	tangible
4.	anthropology	armistice	propitiate	unintelligible
5.	demography	one who abstains from taking wine	portable	contagious
6.	resplendent	opaque	peel	harbinger
7.	superficial	circumlocution	expiate	neologisme
8.	parable	single	seize	chauvinism
9.	celibacy	ambiguous	stumble	abdication
10.	imperialism	obliterate	indispensable	parasite

SECTION IV

Q. No.	TEST –56	TEST –57	TEST –58	TEST –59
1.	offing	premium	after	piece
2.	pell-mell	bonnet	ill	oily
3.	fiddle	nerves	hard	eat
4.	smoke	sby	cool	salt
5.	eleventh	cold	cuts	candles
6.	fair	spade	lurch	wolf
7.	done	loggerheads	herculean	buttered
8.	burning	fishing	phenomenal	cards
9.	add	fair	wrong	accord
10.	wane	mark	make	prodigal

Q. No.	TEST –60	TEST –61	TEST –62
1.	tables	lip	devil
2.	dogs	hard	fresh
3.	feather	intents	bury
4.	harness	casting	gift
5.	cats	corner	bird’s
6.	flesh	wee	unturned
7.	chicken	wane	white
8.	blues	ducks	tenterhooks
9.	dealing	no	hard
10.	sang	lock	moot

27 TEST OF UNDERSTANDING OF ENGLISH LANGUAGE

48 PRACTICE TESTS

The paragraphs given here are basically meant to check your level of understanding of the English language, your word power and its usage. Fill in the blanks with appropriate words, prepositions, determiners, modals, and other options given in the boxes at the head of each paragraph.

Note: The blanks in each of the paragraphs have been numbered. Also given are some words, each of which fits a particular blank appropriately. Select the appropriate word (with its assigned number) for each blank.

PRACTICE TEST-1

1. deteriorating 2. budget 3. significant 4. under 5. resources 6. gap 7. obviously 8. impact 9. outlay 10. curtail

This … (1) … balance of payment situation must be seen along with an equally … (2) … problem of deficits in the government's own budget. A growing … (3)… exists between the government's total …(4) … And sum of its current revenue and capital receipts. This gap, which has to be met through either external assistance or ... (5) … deficit finance has grown over the years. The government … (6) … cannot resort to indefinitely growing volumes of external assistance of deficit finance to meet the increasing gap between its total … (7) … and total receipts. …. (8)…. these conditions, there has been strong pressure on government to … (9) … various development programmes, outlay in money terms are not actually cut, the … (10)… of these programmes may be reduced in real terms or their rate of expansion at least brought down.

PRACTICE TEST-2

1. writings 2. fall 3. consist 4. addressed 5. personal 6. editor 7. objective 8. content 9. personal 10. lucid

Broadly speaking, letters may be said to …. (1) …. into two classes: the formal and ….. (2) … Formal letters … (3) …… of official or business matters and are …. (4) …. to an employer, officials of a department or institutions. Letters to the …. (5) … of a newspaper also belong to this class. In fact all …. (6) …. using formal pattern is of this category. The …. (7) … has to be precisely stated. It must be … (8) …. in style and quite …. (9) ….. No ….. (10) ….. has any place in it.

PRACTICE TEST-3

1. glorified 2. eldest 3. like 4. deeply 5. retracted 6. over 7. importance 8. pretention 9. blinded 10. attractive

Dhritrashtra, the elder brother of Pandu, was blind by birth. When he grew up, he was married to Gandhari. She loved him so …. (1) …. that she …. (2) …. her own eyes with a cloth. A hundred sons were born to Dhritrashtra and Gandhari. They were called Kauravas. Duryodhana was the …. (3) ….. son of Dhritrashtra, who was quite obstinate by nature. When Kunti …. (4) …. to Hastinapur with her five sons, Duryodhana did not …. (5) …. it. He wanted that the Pandavas should live in the forest with their mother, Kunti. In fact, he wanted to rule … (6) Hastinapur without any interference in his affairs, although outwardly he made a .... (7) ... of happiness. His mother Gandhari consoled Kunti but her son Duryodhana did not like it. Pandavas were so good and .... (8) ..... that everyone who saw them ... (9) ..... them with greater ... (10) .... to the Pandavas thanto the Kauravas.

PRACTICE TEST-4

1. to 2. is 3. last 4. had 5. but 6. make 7. of 8. know 9. from lips10. goes

I want to avoid violence. Non-violence also ... (1) ... the first article of my faith. It is also the ... (2) ..... article of my creed. But I had to .... (3) .... my choice.I had either to submit ... (4) .... a system which I considered ... (5) ... done irreparable harm to my country ... (6) ...... incur the risk of the mad fury ..... (7) .... my people bursting forth, when they .... (8) .... the truth from my lips. I ..... (9) .... that my people have sometimes .... (10) ..... mad. I am deeplysorry for it.

PRACTICE TEST-5

1. do 2. hire 3. talented 4. usually 5. willing 6. better 7. protest 8. hike 9. unreasonably 10. lower

New industries supported by foreigninterests ... (1) .... offer .... (2) .... salaries to their employees at all levels of responsibility than ... (3) .... locally owned industries. They need ... (4) .... people and are .... (5) .... to pay high wages to .... (6) ..... them. Local industries often ... (7) .... the high salaries offered by foreign supported industries, arguing that this will .... (8) ..... raise all wages to an excessive level. Workers in local industries, seeing the sharp ... (9) .... in job-pay, will agitate for an improvement in their salaries. This eventually will drain the resources and ... (10) ... their profitability.

PRACTICE TEST-6

1. over 2. at 3. deaf 4. declared 5. strange 6. red 7. eats. 8. effectively 9. to 10. efficacy

It is not proper to damn a system without understanding it. The Indian bureaucracy may be as bad after all, as it is made outto be. Times without number, it has been ... (1) that our bureaucrat is a ... (2) ..... creature who has the habit of sitting .... (3) .... the files and also happens to sleep ... (4) .... the remainders. What is worse is ..... (5) ..... his own word. He turns a .... (6) .... ear to the visitor's request and binds his hands and feet with .... (7) .... tape. However, in all fairness .... (8) .... the bureaucracy, it is necessary to note that a major reason for its ..... (9) ..... to discharge its functions ....(10)..... throughout has been the concentration of power in the hands of the politicians. The bureaucrat may be a devil, but because he has his own share of difficulties, we would not deny him his due.

PRACTICE TEST-7

1. couples 2. method 3. whether 4. undertaking 5. group 6. always 7. care 8. approved 9. executed 10. occasionally

Some people believe that marriages are made in heaven. One cannot say ... (1) ... this is true or not. However, in America now many ... (2) ....who get married seek to evolve a fool proof ... (3) ... to ensure that the marriage survives. However, the idea of married persons ... (4) ... the burden of domestic chores, instead of all the dirty work being dumped on the woman has ... (5)... been propagated by the feminist ... (6) .... And it has gradually, if grudgingly, been ... (7).... This arrangement may work on a temporary basis but talking ... (8) ... of a particular domestic work on a permanent basis will pose problems of its own. For instance, taking out the rubbish may ... (9) .... make a refreshing change from washing baby's nappies. However, a contract is a contract and must be ... (10) ... You may not like it but this what life is coming out to be in the most modern of the countries in the world.

PRACTICE TEST-8

1. setback 2. decision 3. community 4. war 5. learnt 6. for 7. disaster 8. grow 9. defence 10. atmosphere

We will be crushed if civil ... (1) .... is started. It will be a ... (2) ... to the clock. The technique of ... (3) ... against it has been

... (4) .... We may have to wait .... (5) .... a year or more, for a suitable ... (6)... to be created. Any hasty ... (7) ... may result in complete ... (8) ... Labour troubles will ... (9) ... to violence and there will be ... (10) ... discord.

PRACTICE TEST-9

1. at 2. where 3. as 4. beautiful 5. were 6. happy 7. tattered 8. hands 9. chosen 10. denied

It looks like the trail that leads to a magical land. The path climbs out of the forest .... (1) .... White and yellow butterflies flutter .... (2) .... the hanging creepers. It emerges on a ... (3) ..... meadow basking in the sun .... (4) .... This is no fairy-tale country. The .... (5) .... inhabitants of the meadows .... (6) .... Barely living human skeletons, with sunken, fevered .... (7) .... and clothed infilthy and ... (8) .... rags. They are the refugees who have .... (9) .... To flee deeper into Thailand, and have ... (10) ..... instead to stay close to their Cambodian homeland, inspite of all the dangers and hardships they face every day.

PRACTICE TEST-10

1. population 2. imagine 3. gross 4. fringes 5. mount 6. transformation 7. brave 8. shortage 9. growing 10. suffers

The cities are ... (1) .... up and urban unemployment steadily grows. Very probably there is an equal measure of ... (2).... in the countryside. The poorest quarter of the population in developing lands. .... (3) ... being left almost entirely behind in the vast .... (4) .... of the modern technological society. The 'marginal men', the ... (5) ... strugglers for survival on the .... (6) .... of farm andcity, may .... (7) ... more than two billion. Can we ... (8) .... any human order surviving with so .... (9) .... a mass of .... (10) .... piling up at its base?

PRACTICE TEST-11

1. completely 2. expected 3. moment 4. my 5. its 6. right 7. had 8. pleasantly 9. solid 10. stood

After an absence of thirty years, I decidedto visit my old school again. I had .... (1).... to find changes but not a .... (2) .... different building. As I walked up .... (3) .... school driveway, I wondered for a .... (4) .... if I had come to the .... (5) .... address. The grimy, red-brick fortress with ... (6) .... tall windows that had looked down .... (7) .... on the playground and playing fields .... (8) .... been swept away. In its place .... (9) ....a bright, modern block raised from .... (10) .... ground on great concrete stilts.

PRACTICE TEST-12

1. sleep 2. thief 3. probably 4. desist 5. ignore 6. toll 7. mount 8. prolong 9. rest 10. viewing

Most experts agree that even people who think they are sleeping enough would ... (1) .... be better off with more .... (2) .... as evidence of a general sleep deficit, they ... (3) .... the use of the bedside alarm clock used by people to .... (4) .... their waling hours, The most relentless robbery of .... (5) .... is the complexity of everyday life. Whenever pressures from work, family, and community .... (6).... many people .... (7) .... with sleep. another .... (8) .... of sleep is the shift work. The .... (9) ..... of round-the-clock entertainment, especially all-night television, also takes its ... (10)....

PRACTICE TEST-13

1. reduced 2. fighting 3. boon 4. commited 5. evoke 6. blatant 7. demand 8. because 9. blunt 10. demoralise

The feeling of insecurity among the people has increased even though there is ... (1) .... use of the para-military and themilitary. The excesses .... (2) .... by the two forces, particularly by the first, donot .... (3) .... the type of anger it should because they are seen .... (4) .... those who are trying to disintegrate the country.Even a .... (5) .... for more say in the administration is shouted down. Human rights organisations and civil libertyactivists are considered a .... (6) ...., if not unpatriotic. Even the .... (7) .... cases of cruelty are not pursued by the government .... (8) ..... the inquiry should .... (9) .....

the forces and .... (10) ..... the instrument on which it has come to depend.

PRACTICE TEST-14

1. discharge 2. will be 3. progress 4. towards 5. their 6. how

A university stands for humanism, reason, and the adventure of ideas. It stands for the onward ... (1) .... of the human race ... (2) .... higher objectives. If the universities .... (3) ... their duty adequately, then it .... (4) .... well with the nation and ... (5) .... people. But if the temple of learning itself becomes a home of narrow bigotry and petty objectives... (6) .... will the nation prosper?

PRACTICE TEST-15

1. through 2. nor 3. of 4. in 5. being 6. of 7. on 8. shower 9. little 10. bad

Children are loved by all human beings. But ... (1) .... this world of human ... (2) ... there is no .... (3) .... nuisance than a boy .... (4) .... (5) .... useful. It is impossible to .... (6) .... affection on himas on a .... (7) ... boy and he is always getting .... (8) ..... the ways. If he talks with a childish lips he is called a baby, and if he answers in a grown up way he is called impertinent. Then he is .... (9) .... the unattractive, growing age. He grows out.... (10) .... his clothes, with indecent haste. His voice begins to break and losesits childish charm.

PRACTICE TEST-16

1. selfish 2. arrived 3. result 4. preferable 5. sacrifice 6. decision 7. autocratic 8. inability 9. hesitate 10. substantial

Decisions may be ... (1) .... at either through initiative or through inertia. Many misfortunes in the world come across the bridge of indecision. Power corrupts but weakness also corrupts. The fruits of weakness like fear, bitterness and suspicion can ... (2) .... in a paralysisof decision. Inner division can produce indecision, and indecision results by weakness of character. An occasional wrong decision may be sometimes ... (3) .... to indecision. The ... (4) .... man is often self-centred. He fears making a .... (5) .... and the fear paralyses him. When indecision grips a nation, free men feel the need for an ... (6) .... ruler and they are prepared to ... (7) .... democracy overboard. In certain large democracies, the governments rule with a .... (8) .... majority. They often know what decisions would be overboard. In certain large democracies, the to take them lest they be unpopular. Their ... (10) .... to carry the opposition and to rally people to a larger purpose makes them ineffective rulers.

PRACTICE TEST-17

1. had 2. exciting 3. though 4. man 5. a 6. or 7. marvelous 8. since 9. that 10. within 11. would leave 12. worse 13. over 14. has become 15. can

Many of us believe that science is something modern ... (1) ... the truth is that .... (2) ..... has been using sciencefor .... (3) ..... very long time. However, it has .... (4) .... a greater effect on human lives in the last 25 .... (5) ..... 30 years than in the hundreds of years ... (6) .... the invention of the plough. The .... (7) .... gift of science has made modern life .... (8) .... and comfortable. But science has ... (9) .... the same time created new problems. One of these, which may become ... (10) .... in the years to come, is .... (11) of 'Jet-lag'.With the 900 kilometres an hour, the world .... (12) ... very small indeed. Today if you .... (13) .... New Delhi at 4:00 in the morning, you .... (14) ..... eat early breakfast in the sky ... (15) ..... Kabul, and be in London by about 1:00 p.m.

PRACTICE TEST-18

1. transfer 2. patriotism 3. threatened 4. elicited 5. gauged 6. anarchy 7. serious 8. inevitability 9. bondage 10. realise

'Quite India' came not from the lips but the aching hearts of millions. In this open rebellion, the Indian ... (1) ... reached its climax. The British were not only ... (2) ... by it, but also were obliged to quit unilaterally. The importance of Quit Indiacan be ... (3) ... from Lord Linlithgow's statement, 'I am engaged here, inmeeting by far the most .... (4) .... rebellion since that of 1857, the gravity and extent of which we have so far ... (5) ... from the world for reasons of military security'. Still more significant was Churchill's gloomy disclosure to the King Emperor that 'the idea of .. (6) ... of power had become an admitted ... (7) ... in the minds of British party leaders', although his public statements were diametrically opposite. The... (8) ... created by Quit India made the British ... (9) ... that they could no longer keep India in ... (10)...

PRACTICE TEST-19

1. worsens 2. upon 3. into 4. deployed 5. reserve 6. out 7. control 8. mobilise 9. shortage 10. lag

Why is it that the CRP, BSF and the Army give a better account of themselves than the state police? It is the structure of the state police that needs to be looked ... (1) .... In a district or city, where there is a separate police force, a majority of the policemen are .... (2) .... in police stations. The police station staff is often over-extended and no .... (3) .... is available at that level. It is the state force that has to be called .... (4) .... But it takes time to ... (5).... forces. If the law and order situation ... (6) .... simultaneously at many places, there is manpower .... (7) ..... Thus once rioting breaks .... (8) .... it takes time to bring it under control so that there is a time .... (9) .... between the first incident and the appearance of the adequate force to ... (10).... the situation. The public hue and cry about the delayed arrival of the police force is not unjustified.

PRACTICE TEST-20

1. actions 2. men 3. possible 4. humanity 5. stands 6. longer 7. them 8. men 9. cease 10. organisation

To change the hearts of .... (1) .... in such a way as to make it .... (2) .... for them to indulge in these .... (3) .... without changing the .... (4) .... of the government that rule over .... (5) .... is an impossibility. When .... (6) ..... reaches that point it will .... (7) .... To behuman; it will become an .... (8) ... of supermen of gods and it will no .... (9) ... need the guidance of .... (10) .... ofthe type of Mahatma Gandhi.

PRACTICE TEST-21

1. shortage 2. encouraging 3. tested 4. in 5. results 6. as 7. is 8. widespread 9. produce 10. quality

During World War I, penicillin was ... (2) .... on six patients. The .... (2) ... were very much .... (3) .... but unfortunately due to the .... (4) of penicillin two patients died. This tragic incident proved that it ... (5) ... essential to .... (6) ... the medicine ... (7) ... larger quantities. After many months of tireless efforts, a flawless ... (8) ... of extracting penicillin in larger quantities was evolved. ...(9) ... the manufacture and use of it became ... (10)....

PRACTICE TEST-22

1. tremendous 2. categories 3. hundreds 4. rivals 5. alongside 6. about 7. uniting 8. followed 9. lie 10. sites

The Ganga all through its route in filled with innumerable points of interest. Its inspiring beauty, its spiritual value, its purity has no ... (1) ... But what distinguishes it so much as the .... (2) ..... help it has been in bringing .... (3) .... a sense of unity among the .... (4) .... .. and thousands of people who live ... . it. For, from ancient times, the river has been a bond ... (6) .... the provinces that ... (7) .... on its banks. The people who lived in these ... (8) .... spoke different languages, ... (9) .... Different customs and ate different .... (10) .... of food. All this should have made them strangers to one another. Butit did not.

PRACTICE TEST-23

1. that 2. help 3. commercial 4. intelligent 5. traits 6. contribution 7. valuable 8. reservoir 9. probably 10. recognise

'One thing scientists have discovered', notes Thomas Dreier, 'is ... (1).... often- praised children become more ... (2) .... than often-blamed ones. There's creative element in praise'. Good leaders know that. Fundamentally, their job is to ... (3) .... others make the most of themselves. Viewed in strictly ... (4) .... terms, that is their greatest .... (5) .... to their companies.

People employees, are a great untapped ... (6) .... of energy. Leaders who can tap this source are ... (7) .... to any organisation. It doesn't elaborate ... (8) ... to bring, out the best in people. If you ... (9) .... their work, they'll .... (10) .... give you the best that's in them.

PRACTICE TEST-24

1. treated 2. duration 3. begin 4. encounter 5. advantages 6. maintaining 7. persons 8. mutually 9. repressed 10. manifest

First .... (1) .... in all human relationships is crucially important. If ... (2) .... well, they can .... (3) .... the process of .... (4) .... social relationships between ... (5) ... and, at the same time, lay the foundation for future productive and .... (6) .... beneficial .... (7) ... Equally important is the business of closing an encounter. The .... (8) ... of social relationships, even if only temporary, can ... (9) .... strong emotions, since participants have usually ... (10) ... some of their most inner feelings and thoughts to each other.

PRACTICE TEST-25

1. halt 2. initiated 3. flucturates 4. frustrated 5. positively

Nations which have .... (1) .... upon programmes of economic development often run into unsuspected barriers which threaten, and often ... (2) ... the .... (3) .... needed growth of the economy. Industrialisation .... (4) .... and productivity fails to respond and the nation's goals of a rising standard of living for its people are .... (5) ....

PRACTICE TEST-26

1. shortage 2. encouraging 3. tested 4. in 5. results 6. as 7. is 8. widespread 9. produce 10. quality

It is difficult to find a person who would put in a good word for the kind of bureaucracy we have in India. Incidentally, things may now be seen as coming to a head. .... (1) .... the attainment of Independence, India .... (2) ... from time to time several ... (3) .... Power Committees or Commissions to ... (4) .... administration, Inspite of all this, the impression ... (5) .... that the Indian variety of bureaucracy has been slow and slothful. Fact is that the .... (6).... of bureaucracy happens to be .... (7) .... the same all over the world. Even in the U.S.A. presidents have .... (8) .... a great deal of concern. .... (9) .... the manner in which bureaucracy has been functioning at various levels. Inspite of all this, not much change can be .... (10) .... in the near future. One may feel like hanging one's head to despair unless one believes in some superhuman power that looks after our universe.

PRACTICE TEST-27

1. project 2. essential 3. first 4. strategies 5. electricity 6. construction 7. irrigation 8. ingredient 9. major 10. modern

The first problem to be tackled was that of feeding the huge population of the country after Independence. It became ..... (1) ..... to adopt .... (2) ..... for agricultural development. The ... (3) .... of multi-purpose .... (4) .... with the development of .... (5) ..... as one of its ..... (6) ...... components was the ..... (7) ..... step towards the provision of ..... (8) ..... infrastructure. It was realised that ..... (9) ..... is the basic .... (10) ..... in developing agricultural. The total irrigation potential was, therefore, increased.

PRACTICE TEST-28

1. not 2. being 3. announcing 4. compels 5. entitled 6. performance 7. expect 8. endangers 9. unrealistic 10. incentives

Motivating employees with traditional authority and financial .... (1) .... has become increasingly ..... (2) ..... as employees become economically secure and their dependency on any one particular organisation ..... (3).... According to expectancy theorists, the motivation to .... (4) .... increases when an employee feels his ..... (5) ..... is an instrument for obtaining desired rewards. Nevertheless, in many organisations, today employeesare ..... (6).... to organisational rewards just by being employed. Unions, governmental regulations, and the nature of the job itself in some cases .... (7) .... management from .... (8) .... financial rewards performance. People may be attracted to join and remain in organisations to receive organisational rewards, but ..... (9) ..... motivated tojoin an organisation is ..... (10) ..... the same as being motivated to exert effort in an organisation.

PRACTICE TEST-29

1. move. 2. ancient 3. stars. 4. modern 5. and 6. bodies 7. stay 8. Frigid 9. resembles 10. planets

The Earth is one of the known planets that circles the sun. In ... (1) ... times,the men who studied the ... (2) ... noticed that while certain heavenly ... (3) ... seemed fixed in the latter they named planets or wanderers. .... (5) ....astronomers have discovered that the four planets, Jupiter, Saturn, Uranus, ... (6) .... Neptune, are surrounded by poisonous gases and are so ..... (7) .... that any living thing attempting to .... (8) .... on them would instantly be frozen to death. Of the five remaining .... (9) ...., Venus most closely .... (10) ..... the Earth in size.

TEST YOUR VOCABULARY

The paragraphs given here are basically meant to check your level of understanding of the English language, your word power and its usage. Fill in the blanks with appropriate words, prepositions, determiners, modals, and other options given in the boxes at the head of each paragraph.

Note: The blanks in each of the paragraphs have been numbered. Also given in the adjacent box are some words, each of which fits a particular blank appropriately. Select the appropriate word (with its assigned number) for each blank.

PRACTICE TEST-30

1. enter 2. weight 3. from 4. Held 5. solve

Jawaharlal Nehru was probably the first important public leader to realise that if India were to (1) its problems, it would have to (2) .... the age of science. The Government of free Indiawas one of the first in the world to set up a department of science and technology The (3) .... the Government has attached to science is also clear (4) .... The fact that the portfolio of science and technology has always been (5) ...... by the Prime Minister himself.

PRACTICE TEST-31

1. change 2. resilience 3. subject 4. unproductive 5. sincerity 6. resilience 7. dynamics 8. fiercely 9. faith

Human nature has an extraordinary power of (1) .... Social and political institutions are (2) to the same laws of (3) ....to which all other things in the world are subject. If we have (4) .... in the (5) .... of human nature, the healing power of time, the (6)of social and political institutions and above all the (7) .... of the people, the problems which divide us so (8) today may appear to be purely (9) ....after some time.

PRACTICE TEST-32

1. bloodless 2. lesson 3. attaining 4. notwithstanding 5 to 6. bring 7. squeezes 8. means 9. conformity 10. but

Perhaps, we Americans do not yet fully understand the great (1)... that India has to teach in thus (2) .... her freedom. (3) .... her mightytriumph of a (4) revolution our War of Independence (5) .... in size and concept. India has taughthumanity a lesson, and it is (6) .... our peril if we do not learn it. The lesson? That war and killing (7) ....nothing (8) loss, and that a noble end is assured only if the (9) ....to attain it are of a (10) ....with it and also noble.

PRACTICE TEST-33

1. intellect 2. religious 3. Society 4. species 5. relegated 6. hostil

Within the (1) ....we are more friendly to each other than are many (2) ....of animals but in our attitude towards those outside the herd, in spite of all that has been done by moralists and (3)... teachers, our emotions are as (4) as those of any animal, and our (5) enables us to give them a scope which is (6)..............to eventhe most savage beast.

PRACTICE TEST-34

1. hollow 2. quack 3. human 4. affects 5. applications 6. oval 7. carriage 8. killed 9. lineage 10. Place

Science (1) .... the average men and women in two ways already. He or she benefits by its (2)..........driving in a motor-car or omnibus instead of a horse-drawn (3)..........being treated for disease by a doctor or surgeon rather than a priest or a (4) .... being (5).......... with an automatic pistol or a shell in (6) of a dagger or battle-axe. It also affects his or her opinions. Almost everyone believes that the earth is (7)... , and the heavens nearly (8)................, instead of solid. And we are beginning to believe in our animal (9) and the possibility of vast improvements in (10) ....nature by biological methods.

PRACTICE TEST-35

1. collapse 2. generated 3. on 4. supplement 5. depends 6. propels 7. infinitely 8. principal 9. aplenty

Every society depends on energy (1) ....from one source or another to supply its needs. In the past the energy of beasts and water power from water-mills was used to (2)... what man could not do alone. Modern society (3)..............above all on heat-based energy. This produces electricity, cooks food and (4) .... motor cars, ships and planes. The (5) .... source is oil. Without it the industry would (6) ...., standard of living would drop. Oil is no longer so cheap and (7).................. as it was. Existing supplies will not last (8) .... yet world energy demand goes (9) ....increasing.

PRACTICE TEST-36

1. continual 2. body 3. union 4. partners 5. spirituality 6. rapport 7. for 8. procreation

Human society is a (1) ....growth, an unfoldment in terms of (2) .... If so, it must be based on ever-increasing restraint upon the demands of the (3) ....

Thus marriage must be considered to be a (4) ....imposing discipline upon the (5)..........restricting them to the physical (6) ....only among themselves and for the purpose only of (7) .... when both the partners desire and are prepared (8) ....it.

PRACTICE TEST-37

1. disappear 2. actually 3. company 4. in 5. minds 6. thoughts 7. preserved 8. voice 9. enigma 10. around 11. enjoy

Books introduce to us the best (1) ....they bring us (2) ....the presence of the greatest (3) .... that have ever lived. We hear what they said and did; we see them as if they were (4) alive; we share their (5) ...., we sympathise with them, (6)... with them in the scenes which they describe. The great and the good do not (7).............even in this world. (8)................in books, their spirits walk (9)............ the book is a living (10)..............., it is an (11)................ to which one still listens.

PRACTICE TEST-38

1. playthings 2. pride 3. perish 4. on 5. silent 6. opportunity 7. choice 8. Loses 9. venture 10. beckons

India is (1) ....the move and the old order passes. Too long have we been (2) ....spectators of events and the (3)of others. The (4) ....comes to our people now and we shall make the history of our (5)... Let us all join in this mighty (6) ....and make India, the (7).................. Of our heart, great among nations, foremost in the arts of peace and progress. The door is open and destiny (8)to all. There is no question of who wins and who (9)..............., for we have to go forward and together as comrades and either all of us win or we all (10) .... together.

PRACTICE TEST-39

1. aggravating 2. destroy 3. vivify 4. raze 5. mitigate 6. wasteland 7. leaders 8. into

9. jaws 10. multiply 11. escalate 12. possibility 13. prevent 14. recoil from

The chief business of war is to (1) …………… human life, to (2)………….. down and burn cities, to turn fruitful fields into (3) …………………… to scourge means (4) ………….. famine, to (5)………….. widows and orphans. Are these honourable deeds? Grant that a (6)… for them may exist; it is a dreadful necessity, such as good man must (7)… , and though it may (8)………………….. these deeds from guilt, it cannot turn them into glory. We have thought that it was honourable to heal, to save, to (9)…….pain, to snatch the sick from the (10)… of death. We have placed among the revered (11)………….of the human race, the discoverers of arts which (12)……….human sufferings, which prolong comfort, (13)… and cheer human life, and if these arts are honourable, where is the glory of multiplying and (14) …………….. tortures and death?

PRACTICE TEST-40

1. man's 2. saddest 3. unhappy 4. sorrow 5. aspires 6. want 7. back 8. heart 9. into 10. happily 11. Pre-occupation

In (1)……….life there is always a feeling of want. It is this which makes man (2) ………….. man (3) ……………………of things which he cannot get and feels sad looking (4) …………..upon the past, and looking forward (5) ………………future. This (6)… with the past and future does not allow man to live (7)……………..in the present. Thus, there is always pain in man's (8) …………., always a sense of (9) ………………in the moment of enjoyment. That is why the best poetry of man is the poetry of (10) ………….. Our sweetest songs are those that tell of (11)…… thoughts', has been rightly said.

PRACTICE TEST-41

1. known 2. gainer 3. gains 4. dull 5. contest 6. continous 7. is 8. enthusiasm 9. contest 10. contested 11. adversary

In life there are no (1)… without pains. Life indeed would be (2) ………….. if there (3) …………… no difficulties. Games lose their (4) ………….. if there is no real (5) ……………. if the result is a (6) ………. conclusion. Both (7) …………….and loser enjoy a game most if it is closely (8) to the last. No victory is a real triumph unless the (9)…………………..is worthy of the (10) ……….. whether we like it or not, life is one (11) ……………. competitive examination.

PRACTICE TEST-42

1. adversity 2. anything 3. generous 4. rainbow 5. shallow 6. fairly 7. like 8. prosperity 9. fallow 10. vegetables

It is not god for man that his life should be all joy and (1) ………… the lands which only know sunshine and never rain become (2) …………… the most beautiful countries are those which are (3)……………… visited by both sunshine and rain. It is in these lands that (4)……….. and fruits grow and sweet birds sing. There is nothing more beautiful than a (5) ………..if life is to be rounded and many-coloured (6)………………the rainbow, both joy and sorrow must come to it. Those who have never known (7) ………………… but prosperity and pleasure become hard and (8) ……….. but those whose prosperity has been mixed with (9) ……………… become kind and (10)………

PRACTICE TEST-43

1. decay 2. empires 3. romans 4. weakness 5. ceased 6. on 7. spectacle 8. down 9. upon 10. downfall 11. spot

Civilisation, like (1) ……………. fall, not so much because of the (2) …………….of the enemy outside, as through the weakness and (3) ……………..within. Rome fell not because of the (4) ……………. they merely knocked (5) ………… something that was already dead. The heart of Rome had (6) ……………. beating when the arms and legs were cut (7) ……………… we see something of this (8) ……………… in India and China and in the case of the Arabs. The (9)…………..of Arabian civilisation was sudden even as their rise had been. In India and China, the process is long-drawn (10) ....and it is not easy to (11) .... it.

PRACTICE TEST-44

1. push 2. attained 3. goal 4. bear 5. distinguish 6. dungeon 7. tolerate 8. habituate 9. twilight 10. dazzle 11. bondage

There is only one cure for the evils which newly (1) .... Freedom produces; and that cure is freedom. When a prisoner first leave his (2)..........he cannot (3) ....the light of day; he is unable to (4) ....colours or recognise faces. But the remedy is not to (5)..........him into his (6)..................but to (7) ....him to the (8) ....of the sun. The blaze of truth and liberty may at first (9).................. and bewilder nations which have become half blind in the house of (10) ....but let them gaze on, and they will soon be able to (11) ....it. In a few years men will learn to reason.

PRACTICE TEST-45

1. ascends 2. labour 3. treasure 4. down 5. proportionate 6. will 7. self–indulgence 8. powerful 9. competence 10. progeny 11. work–culture 12. for

It is not luck but (1) .... that makes men. Luck, says an American writer, is ever waiting for something to turn (2) .... ; labour with keen eye and strong (3) ..... always turns up something. Luck lies in bed and wishes the postman would bring him news of a (4) ......; labour turns out at six and with busy pen and (5) ..... hammer lays the foundation of a (6) ...... Luck relies on chance; labour on (7) ...... Luck slips downwards to (8) .....; labour (9) ...... upwards and aspires (10) .... Independence. The conviction, therefore, is extending that diligence is the (11) ..... of good luck; in other words, that a man's success in life will be (12) ..... to his efforts, to his industry, to his attention to small things.

PRACTICE TEST-46

1. averse 2. affair 3. at 4. obligation 5. bare 6. interests 7. choose 8. concern

Liberty is not a personal (1) .... only, but a social (2) .... It is an accommodation of (3) .... In matters which do not (4) .... anybody else's liberty, of course, I may be as free as I like. If I (5) .... to go down the strand in a dressing–gown, with long hair and (6) .... feet, who shall say me nay? You have the liberty to laugh (7) .... me, but I have the liberty to be (8) .... to you.

PRACTICE TEST-47

1. diversity 2. inculcates 3. limits 4. principles 5. varied 6. underlies

But if travel brings a conviction of human (1)...., it brings an equally strong conviction of human unity. It (2) ..... tolerance, but it also shows the (3) ..... of possible toleration. Religious and moral (4)...., forms of government and of society are almost endlessly (5) ....., and each has a right to its separate existence. But a oneness (6) .... this diversity.

PRACTICE TEST-48

1. pale 2. streaked 3. wonderful 4. rested 5. pink 6. earthly 7. shaggy 8. curls 9. rickety 10. motionless

At the table a man, unlike ordinary people, was sitting (1) ..... he was a (2) ..... with the skin drawn tight over his bones, with long (3) .... Like a woman's and a (4) .... beard. His face was yellow with an (5) .... tint, in it, his checks were (6).... , his back long and narrow, and the hand on which his shaggy head was (7) ...... was so thin and delicate that it was (8) .... to look at it. His head was already (9) ..... with silver, and seeing his (10) ...., aged–looking face, no one would have believed that he was only forty.

ANSWERS (PRACTICE TESTS)

Q. No.	P.TEST–1	P.TEST –2	P.TEST –3	P.TEST –4
1.	deteriorating	fall	deeply	is
2.	significant	personal	blinded	last
3.	gap	consist	eldest	make
4.	resources	addressed	retracted	to
5.	budget	printer	like	had
6.	obviously	writings	over	but
7.	outlay	content	pretention	of
8.	under	lucid	attractive	listen
9.	curtail	objective	glorified	know
10.	impact	personal	importance	goes

Q. No.	P.TEST –5	P.TEST –6	P.TEST –7	P.TEST –8
1.	usually	declared	whether	war
2.	better	strange	couples	setback
3.	do	at	method	defence
4.	talented	over	undertaking	learnt
5.	willing	eats	always	for
6.	hire	deaf	group	atmosphere
7.	protest	red	approved	decision
8.	unreasonably	to	care	disaster
9.	hike	efficacy	occasionally	grow
10.	lower	effectively	executed	community

Q. No.	P.TEST –9	P.TEST –10	P.TEST –11	P.TEST –12
1.	where	growing	expected	probably
2.	at	shortage	completely	rest
3.	beautiful	suffers	my	ignore
4.	as	transformation	moment	prolong
5.	happy	brave	right	sleep
6.	were	fringes	its	mount
7.	hands	mount	pleasantly	desist
8.	tattered	imagine	had	thief
9.	denied	gross	stood	viewing
10.	chosen	population	solid	toll

Q. No.	P.TEST –13	P.TEST –14	P.TEST –15	P.TEST –16
1.	reduced	progress	in	arrived
2.	committed	towards	beings	result
3.	evoke	discharge	bad	preferable
4.	fighting	will be	of	selfish
5.	demand	their	nor	decision
6.	boon	how	shower	autocratic
7.	blatant		little	sacrifice
8.	because		through	substantial
9.	demoralise		on	hesitate
10.	blunt		of	inability

Q. No.	P.TEST –17	P.TEST –18	P.TEST –19	P.TEST –20
1.	though	patriotism	into	men
2.	man	threatened	deployed	possible
3.	a	gauged	reserve	actions
4.	had	serious	upon	stands
5.	or	elicited	mobilise	them
6.	since	transfer	worsens	humanity
7.	marvelous	inevitability	shortage	cease
8.	exciting	anarchy	out	organisation
9.	within	realise	lag	longer
10.	worse	bondage	control	men
11.	that			
12.	has become			
13.	would leave			
14.	can			
15.	over			

Q. No.	P.TEST –21	P.TEST –22	P.TEST –23	P.TEST –24
1.	tested	rivals	that	encounter
2.	results	tremendous	intelligent	treated
3.	encouraging	about	help	begin
4.	shortage	hundreds	commercial	maintaining
5.	is	alongside	contribution	persons
6.	produce	uniting	reservoir	mutually
7.	in	lie	valuable	advantages
8.	quality	sites	traits	duration
9.	as	followed	recognise	manifest
10.	widespread	categories	probably	repressed

Q. No.	P.TEST –25	P.TEST –26	P.TEST –27	P.TEST –28
1.	initiated	since	essential	incentives
2.	halt	appointed	strategies	unrealistic
3.	positively	multiple	construction	endangers
4.	fluctuates	transform	projects	expect
5.	frustrated	persists	irrigation	performance
6.		structure	major	entitled
7.		structurally	first	compels
8.		asserted	modern	announcing
9.		at	electricity	being
10.		expected	ingredient	not

Q. No.	P.TEST –29	P.TEST –30	P.TEST –31	P.TEST –32
1.	ancient	solve	resilience	lesson
2.	stars	enter	subject	attaining
3.	bodies	weight	change	notwithstanding
4.	move	from	faith	bloodless
5.	modern	held	resilience	squeezes
6.	and		dynamics	to
7.	frigid		sincerity	bring
8.	stay		fiercely	but
9.	planets		unproductive	means
10.	resembles			conformity

Q. No.	P.TEST –33	P.TEST –34	P.TEST –35	P.TEST –36
1.	society	affects	generated	continual
2.	species	applications	supplement	spirituality
3.	religious	carriage	depends	body
4.	hostile	quack	propels	union
5.	intellect	killed	principal	partners
6.	relegated	place	collapse	rapport
7.		oval	aplenty	procreation
8.		hollow	infinitely	for
9.		lineage	on	
10.		human		

Q. No.	P.TEST –37	P.TEST –38	P.TEST –39	P.TEST –40
1.	company	on	sadestroy	man's
2.	in	silent	raze	unhappy
3.	minds	playthings	wasteland	aspires
4.	actually	opportunity	into	back
5.	thoughts	choice	multiply	into
6.	enjoy	venture	possibility	preoccupation
7.	disappear	pride	recoil from	happily
8.	preserved	beckons	prevent	heart
9.	around	loses	escalate	want
10.	voice	perish	jaws	sorrow
11.	enigma		leaders	saddest
12.			mitigate	

Q. No.	P.TEST –41	P.TEST –42	P.TEST –43	P.TEST –44
1.	gains	prosperity	empires	attained
2.	dull	fallow	weakness	gaol
3.	is	fairly	decay	bear
4.	enthusiasm	vegetables	romans	distinguish
5.	contest	rainbow	on	push
6.	known	like	ceased	dungeon
7.	gainer	anything	down	habituate
8.	contested	shallow	spectacle	twilight
9.	adversary	adversity	downfall	dazzle
10.	contest	generous	upon	bondage
11.	continous		spot	tolerate

Q. No.	P.TEST –45	P.TEST –46	P.TEST –47	P.TEST –48
1.	labour	affair	diversity	motionless
2.	down	obligation	inculcates	rickety
3.	will	interests	limits	curls
4.	distinguish	concern	principles	shaggy
5.	powerful	choose	varied	earthly
6.	competence	bare	underlies	pink
7.	work–culture	at		rested
8.	self–indulgence	averse		wonderful
9.	ascends			streaked
10.	for			pale
11,	progeny			
12.	proportionate			

28 SENTENCE SEQUENCING OR REORDERING OF JUMBLED SENTENCES

Sentence Sequencing or Reordering of Jumbled sentences is a very tough exercise. It requires to flex muscles to read the sentences carefully and fetch the central idea and correlation between different sentences. Reordering of jumbled sentences requires you to read the sentences, re-read them and re-read them, before making sense out of it.

Directions for Question 1 to 8: In each questions a set of six sentences of a continuous paragraph are provided. The sentence numbered 1 starts the paragraph and the sentence numbered 6 ends it. Arrange statements A, B, C, D between 1 and 6 to form a coherent paragraph.

Q 1.

1. What does the state do in a country where tax morality is very low?

(A) It ties to spy upon the tax payers.

(B) It investigates income sources and spending patterns.

(C) Exactly what the tax authority tries to do now, even if inconsistently.

(D) It could also encourage people to denounce to the tax authorities any conspicuously prosperous neighbours who may be suspected of not paying their taxes properly.

6. The ultimate solution would be an Orwellian system.

(a) BACD (b) DBAC

(c) ABCD (d) DCBA

Q 2.

1. The fragile Yugoslav state has an uncertain future.

(A) Thus, there will surely be chaos and uncertainty if the people fail to settle their differences.

(B) Sharp ideological differences already exist in the country.

(C) Ethnic, regional, linguistic, and material disparities are profound.

(D) The country will also lose the excellent reputation it enjoyed in the international arena.

6. At worst, it will once more become vulnerable to international conspiracy and intrigue.

(a) BCAD (b) ADCB

(c) ACBD (d) DBCA

Q 3.

1. India's experience of industrialisation is characteristic of the difficulties faced by a newly independent developing country.

(A) In 1947, India was undoubtedly an under-developed country with one of the lowest per capita incomes in the world.

(B) Indian industrialisation was the result of a conscious deliberate policy of growth by an indigenous political elite.

(C) Today India ranks fifth in the international community of nations if measured in terms of purchasing power.

(D) Even today, however, the benefits of Indian industrialisation since independence have not reached the masses.

6. Industrialisation in India have thus been a limited success: One more example of growth without development.

(a) CDAB (b) DCBA
(c) CABD (d) BACD

Q 4.

1. The New Economic Policy comprises the various policy measures and changes introduced since July 1991.

(A) There is a common thread running through all these measures.

(B) The objective is simple – to improve the efficiency of the system.

(C) The regulatory mechanism involving multitude of controls has fragmented the capacity and reduced competition even in the private sector.

(D) The thrust of the new policy is towards creating a more competitive environment as a means to improving the productivity and efficiency of the economy.

6. This is to be achieved by removing the barriers and restrictions on the entry and growth of firms.

(a) DCAB (b) ABCD
(c) BDAC (d) CDBA

Q 5.

1. It is significant that one of the most common objections to competition is that it is blind.

(A) This is important because in a system of free enterprise based on private property, chances are not equal and there is indeed a strong case for reducing that inequality of opportunity.

(B) Rather it is a choice between a system where it is the will of a few persons that decides which is to get what and one where it depends at least partly, on the ability and the enterprise of the people concerned.

(C) Although competition and justice may have little else in common, it is as much as commendation of competition as of justice that it is no respecter of persons.

(D) The choice today is not between a system in which everybody will get what he deserves according to some universal standard and one where individual shares are determined by chance or goodwill.

6. The fact that opportunities open to the door in a competitive society are much more restricted than those open to the rich, does not make it less true that in such a society, the poor are more free than a person commanding much greater material comfort in a different type of society.

(a) CDBA (b) DCBA
(c) ABCD (d) BADC

Q 6.

1. The necessity for regional integration in South Asia is underlined by the very history of the last 45 years since the liquidation of the British Empire in this part of the world.

(A) After the partition of the Indian subcontinent, Pakistan was formed in that very area which the imperial powers had always marked out as the potential base for operations against the Russian power in Central Asia.

(B) Because of the disunity and ill-will among the South Asian neighbours, particularly India and Pakistan, great powers from outside the area could meddle into their affairs and thereby keep neighbours apart.

(C) It needs to be added that it was the bountiful supply of sophisticated arms that emboldened Pakistan to go for warlike bellicosity toward India.

(D) As part of the cold war strategy of the US, Pakistan was sucked into Washington's military alliance spreading over the years.

6. Internally too, it was the massive induction of American arms into Pakistan which empowered the military junta of that country to snuff out the civilian government and destroy democracy in Pakistan.

(a) ACBD (b) ABDC
(c) CBAD (d) DCAB

Q 7.

1. Commercial energy consumption shows an increasing trend and poses the major challenge for the future.

(A) The demand, for petroleum, during 1996-97 and 2006-07 is anticipated to be 81 million tonnes and 125 million tonnes respectively.

(B) According to the projections of the 14th Power Survey Committee Report, the electricity generation requirements from utilities will be about 416 billion units by 1996-97 and 824 billion units by 2006-07.

(C) The production of coal should reach 303 million tonnes by 1996-97 to achieve plan targets and 460 million tonnes by 2006-07.

(D) The demand for petroleum products has already rapidly outstripped indigenous production.

6. Electricity is going to play a major role in the development of infrastructural facilities.

(a) DACB (b) CADB
(c) BADC (d) ABCD

Q 8.

1. The success of any unit in a competitive environment depends on prudent management of resources.

(A) In this context, it would have been more appropriate if the concept of accelerated depreciation, together with additional incentives towards capital allowances for recouping a portion of the cost of replacements out of the current generations had been accepted.

(B) Added to this are the negligible retention of profits because of inadequate capital allowances and artificial disallowances of genuine outflows.

(C) One significant cause for the poor generation of surpluses is the high cost of capital and its servicing cost.

(D) The lack of mechanism in Indian tax laws for quick recovery of capital costs has not received its due attention.

6. While this may apparently look costly from the point of view of the exchequer, the ultimate cost to the Government and the community in the form of losses suffered through poor viability will be prohibitive.

(a) ADBC (b) BCDA
(c) CBDA (d) DBAC

Directions for Question 9 to 14: A number of sentences are given below which, when properly sequenced form a coherent paragraph. Each sentence is labeled with a letter. Choose the most logical order of sentences from among the four given choices to construct a coherent paragraph.

Q 9.

(A) Realists believe that there is an object reality out there independent of ourselves.

(B) This reality exists solely by virtue of how the world is, and it is in principle discoverable by application of the methods of science.

(C) They believe in the possibility of determining whether or not a theory is indeed really true or false.

(D) I think it is fair to say that this is the position to which most working scientists subscribe.

(a) ABCD (b) CDBA
(c) DCBA (d) BCAD

Q 10.

(A) There is a strong manufacturing base for a variety of products.

(B) India has come a long way on the technology front.

(C) But the technology adopted has been largely of foreign origin.

(D) There are, however, areas such as atomic energy, space, agriculture and defence where significant strides have been made in evolving relevant technologies within the country.

(a) ADCB (b) DBAC
(c) BACD (d) CBAD

Q 11.

(A) In emission trading, the government fixes the total amount of pollution that is acceptable to maintain a desired label to air quality.

(B) Economists argue that this approach makes air pollution control more cost effective than the current practice of fixing air pollution standards and expecting all companies to pollute below these standards.

(C) USA uses emission trading to control air pollution.

(D) It then distributes emission permits to all companies in the region, which add up to the overall acceptable level of emission.

(a) BADC (b) ACBD
(c) CBAD (d) DBAC

Q 12.

(A) The individual companies vary in size, from the corner grocery to the industrial giant.

(B) Policies and management methods within firms range from formal, well-planned organisations, and controls to slipshod day-to-day operations.

(C) Various industries offer a wide array of products or services through millions of firms largely independent of each other.

(D) Variation in the form of ownership contributes to diversity in capital investment, volume of business, and financial structure.

(a) DBCA (b) CADB
(c) BADC (d) ADCB

Q 13.

(A) All levels of demand, whether individual, aggregate, local, national, or international are subject to change.

(B) At the same time, science and technology add new dimensions to products, their uses and the methods used to market them.

(C) Aggregate demand fluctuates with changes in the level of business activity, GNP, and national income.

(D) The demand of individuals tend to vary with changing need and rising income.

(a) CBDA (b) DCAB
(c) BCAD (d) ADCB

Q 14.

(A) Secret persons shall strike with weapons, fire or poison.

(B) Clans, mutually supporting each other, shall be made to strike at the weak points.

(C) He shall destroy their caravans, herds, forests, and troop reinforcements.

(D) The conqueror shall cause enemy kingdom to be destroyed by neighbouring kings, jungle tribes, pretenders, or unjustly treated princes.

(a) DCBA (b) ABCD
(c) ABDC (d) ADCB

Directions for Questions 15 to 17: Arrange the sentences A, B, C, and D to form a logical sequence between sentences 1 and 6.

Q 15.

1. That was the day that Walter Alva made the boldest decision of his career.

(A) He had believed that somehow the situation would resolve itself.

(B) First, he apologised to his teammates for putting them in danger.

(C) He now encouraged anyone who wished to leave to do so without delay.

(D) Until recently, he explained, his fascination with the tomb had blinded him to the peril of their position.

6. None did.

(a) BACD (b) DBAC
(c) BDAC (d) DABC

Q 16.

1. During this summer, I spent blissfully long days with my friend.

(A) In the afternoons, we would retire to the cottage, and she would talk about her husband – what a fine man he'd been.

(B) I discovered she made the finest shortbread (a kind of biscuit) in the universe.

(C) Once or twice she seemed about to cry and left the room quickly to make more tea.

(D) We could explore Bear Wood, munching happily and discussing the books she had lent me.

6. But she always came back smiling.

(a) BCAD (b) ADCB
(c) ACBD (d) DABC

Q 17.

1. The chainsaw howled as I finished cutting through the branch.

(A) The branch crashed to the ground, taking my spectacles with it.

(B) I almost dropped the saw as I shielded my face from the twigs that brushed by.

(C) Howard retrieved my glasses and handed them up to me.

(D) I pulled the saw away, and my husband tugged against the other end of the rope that I had tied just above the cut.

6. Are you okay? He asked.

(a) BCAD (b) DBAC
(c) DCAB (d) BDAC

Directions for Questions 18 to 19: Sentences given in each question, when properly sequenced form a coherent paragraph. Each sentence is labeled with a letter. Choose the most logical order of sentences from among the four given choices to construct a coherent paragraph.

Q 18.

(A) One reason can be that the total investment allocated to power was deficient.

(B) However, it may also be that the demand for power was based on incorrect information.

(C) The question arises as to why the planning of the power sector in Indian plans turned out to be faulty, as widely alleged.

(D) In that case, obviously the plan was bad even on paper.

(a) DABC (b) CBAD
(c) CADB (d) DBAC

Q 19.

(A) Children need to be loved, and in a sense they cannot have too much of it.

(B) She herself doesn't want to grow up and attempts to make time stand still.

(C) Fortunately, she cannot succeed.

(D) But it is not because of love that a mother prevents her child from growing up.

(a) ACDB (b) DABC
(c) CADB (d) ADBC

Directions for Questions 20 to 22: Arrange the sentences A, B, C, and D to form a logical sequence between sentences 1 and 6.

Q 20.

1. The market mechanism is the natural coordinator of private sector activities.

(A) It is also linked to the centrality of the notion of a free contract for both the operation of the market mechanism and the safeguarding of private property.

(B) This is linked to the autonomy of the decision maker under the market mechanism.

(C) It is futile to expect the State unit to behave as if it were privately owned.

(D) It is time to get rid of this vain hope once and for all.

6. There is no reason to be astonished by the fact that the State ownership permanently recreates the bureaucracy because it is but an organic part of the bureaucratic hierarchy.

(a) BADC (b) ACDB
(c) DCBA (d) BACD

Q 21.

1. A manager is faced with innumerable situations in which he has to make a choice.

(A) These are not the only kind of decisions that managers take.

(B) As a seller, he has to decide what to sell.

(C) As a producer, he has to decide what to produce, how to produce, how much to produce, and where to produce.

(D) As a buyer, he has to decide what to buy.

6. They generally face a wide range of situations involving choice.

(a) ABCD (b) DCBA
(c) CDBA (d) BDAC

Q 22.

1. Operating a small motel, I tried to avoid answering the doorbell before 6:30 a.m.

(A) One morning at about 5 o'clock, the doorbell rang.

(B) So I had a box put up next to the door and placed a sign on it saying, deposit keys here.

(C) But some guests continued to summer me as early as 4:30 a.m.

(D) Customers were told me to leave their keys in the rooms when checking out.

6. When I opened the office door, a smiling guest greeted me with: I just wanted you to know, I put my key in the box.

(a) DCBA (b) DACB
(c) BADC (d) ABDC

Directions for Questions 23 to 27: Sentences given in each question, when properly sequenced form a coherent paragraph. Each sentences is labeled with a letter: Choose the most logical order of sentences from among the four given to construct a coherent paragraph.

Q 23.

(A) Widely publicised tables of income levels of all countries indicate that when incomes are higher, the greater is the contribution made by the manufacturing industry.

(B) Countries which have little or no industry are almost invariably poor.

(C) The lesson is clear: to overcome poverty and backwardness, a country must industrialise.

(D) Industrialisation is seen as the key to growth and a prerequisite for development.

(a) CBAD (b) DCBA
(c) DABC (d) CABD

Q 24.

(A) A wife may not be sure that what her husband is saying means the end.

(B) She has found that people's voices often get higher or shriller when they lie, and they are more likely to stumble over words.

(C) According to De Paulo, changes in voices can be significant.

(D) She should listen closely, not only to what he says, but how he says it.

(a) ADCB (b) ACDB
(c) ADBC (d) ABCD

Q 25.

(A) He pulled popcorn dipped in ketchup out of her mouth with a pair of pliers.

(B) Soon Steven was making horror pictures, using his sisters as victims.

(C) A few years later, Steven borrowed hid dad's eight-millimeter movie camera to film 'The Last Train Wreck' using his own electric train set.

(D) In one, he played a dentist, with his sister Ann as the patient.

(a) CBAD (b) DACB
(c) DABC (d) CBDA

Q 26.

(A) In bulk processing, a set of standard prices typically emerge.

(B) Competing therefore means keeping products flowing, trying to improve quality, getting costs down.

(C) Let us look at the two cultures of competition.

(D) Production tends to be repetitive – much the same from day to day or even from year to year.

(a) CDBA (b) ABDC
(c) CADB (d) DCBA

Q 27.

(A) A moment later, my prospective fiancée reappeared and shoved a ticket to Jiuquan through the hatch.

(B) The queue gazed at me dumbstruck, then broke into a little ripple of applause.

(C) The station master and clerk retreated into the back room.

(D) I lifted it like a trophy.

(a) CABD (b) ACDB
(c) ACBD (d) CADB

Directions for Questions 28 to 30: Arrange the sentences A, B, C, and D to form a logical sequence between sentences 1 and 6.

Q 28.

1. So now, let's sum it up.

(A) We can call this the material of knowledge.

(B) According to Kant, there are two elements that contribute to man's knowledge of the world.

(C) The other is the internal conditions in man himself.

(D) One is the external conditions that we cannot know of before we have perceived them though the sense.

6. We can call this the form of knowledge.

(a) BDAC (b) BADC
(c) CADB (d) CBDA

Q 29.

1. I may have a strong desire for a fresh ripe peach, but no peaches may be available.

(A) I am about to take a bite when news arrives of an accident injuring someone dear to me.

(B) The hay fever passes.

(C) One the other hand, I buy some preaches but a sudden track of hay fever prevents me from enjoying their fragrance or taste.

(D) My interest in the peach vanished.

6. I no longer have any appetite.

(a) DCBA (b) CBAD
(c) ABCD (d) ACBD

Q 30.

1. A national like an individual, has many personalities and many approaches to life.

(A) If there is a strong organic bond between different possibilities, it is well.

(B) Otherwise, this could lead to disintegration and trouble.

(C) Normally, some kind of equilibrium is eventually established.

(D) If normal development is arrested, then conflict arises between different personalities.

6. In the mind and spirit of India, there has been this fundamental conflict due to a long period of arrested growth.

(a) ABCD (b) BDCA
(c) CABD (d) DBCA

Directions for Questions 31 to 33: Sentences given in each question, when properly sequenced form a coherent paragraph. Each sentence is labeled with a letter. Choose the most logical order of sentences from among the four given choices to construct a coherent paragraph.

Q 31.

(A) Because negotiations had been delayed until the last moment, he was at a tremendous disadvantage.

(B) Only then did the truth dawn on him.

(C) He broke off talks and returned home.

(D) My friend was under intense pressure to make concessions.

(a) DBAC (b) ACBD
(c) ABCD (d) DBCA

Q 32.

(A) 'Son, why are you reading this sissy magazine'? he asked.

(B) 'There's an article that tells women where to meet men', I responded, pointing to the magazine's cover.

(C) 'I need to know where I'm supposed to be'.

(D) When I was a teenager, my father caught me reading one of my older sister's magazines.

(a) DCAB (b) ADCB
(c) DABC (d) DACB

Q 33.

(A) 'Actually', Ronnie replied, 'I asked my wife'.

(B) One day, a man named Ronnie answered a difficult one correctly to put the men in front.

(C) Impressed, the host kept Ronnie on the line and asked how he knew the answer to such a tough question.

(D) Occasionally, a local radio station airs 'Battle of the sexes', in which listeners phone in to answer trivial questions.

(a) BCAD (b) ACDB
(c) CABD (d) DBCA

Directions for Questions 34 to 36: Arrange the sentences A, B, C, and D to form a logical sequence between sentences 1 and 6.

Q 34.

1. Why are horses the same?

(A) It may be old and lame, and in time, it will die.

(B) A particular horse 'flows', naturally.

(C) But there is something all horses have in common.

(D) You probably don't think they are at all.

6. But the 'form' of the horse is eternal and immutable.

(a) DCAB (b) CABD
(c) CBDA (d) DCBA

Q 35.

1. Buddhism is a way to salvation.

(A) But Buddhism is more severely analytical.

(B) In the Christian tradition, there is also a concern for the fate of human society conceived as a whole, rather than merely as a sum or network of individuals.

(C) Salvation is a property, or achievement, of individuals.

(D) Not only does it dissolve society into individuals; the individual in turn is dissolved into component parts and instants, a stream of events.

6. In modern terminology, Buddhist doctrine is reductionism.

(a) BCAD (b) ADBC
(c) CBAD (d) CDAB

Q 36.

1. Matrilineal systems of land inheritance advantaged women in many respects, especially in granting them economic and social security.

(A) Women, in particular, were profoundly affected by these changes.

(B) The large joint family estates came to be partitioned, there was an increasing penetration of market forces and patriarchal ideologies spread in influence.

(C) These systems, however, did not remain fixed over time.

(D) Interventions by the colonial and post-colonial states, and the processes of social change which these set in motion, eroded customary practices.

6. At the same time, their customary exclusion from major authority in public bodies meant that they were unlikely to be the ones directing the changes.

(a) BDCA (b) CDBA
(c) CDAB (d) CADB

Directions for Questions 37 to 39: Sentences given in each question, when properly sequenced form a coherent paragraph, each sentence is labelled with a letter. Choose the most logical order of sentences from among the four given choices to construct a coherent paragraph.

Q 37.

(A) However, the real challenge today is unlearning, which is much harder.

(B) But the new world of business behaves differently from the world in which we grew up.

(C) Learning is important for both people and organisations.

(D) Each of us has a 'mental model' that we've used over the years to make sense.

(a) DBCA (b) CADB
(c) DACB (d) CBDA

Q 38.

(A) A large number of intellectuals believe that the North is using its military and economic powers to force unequal contracts on the South.

(B) The make-believe ethical issue of the sanctity of law camouflages the unethicality of the entire transaction, which is a travesty of the ethical concept of the greatest good for the greatest number.

(C) Once these contracts are made, the North uses the façade of legality and ethics to pin down the South.

(D) Thus, it suffers from the flaw that the flaw – one of the useful means to implement ethics – has fouled the ethicality of the ends.

(a) DACB (b) CBDA
(c) ACBD (d) BDAC

Q 39.

(A) The fact that he could find absolutely nothing to substantiate their wild claims made no difference.

(B) We always gave the poor man a cup of tea, and he grew quite fond of some of the animals.

(C) The neighbours, now thoroughly indignant, kept bombarding the local health authorities.

(D) On an average, twice a week, the poor inspector was forced to come up to the house.

(a) DBAC (b) CDAB
(c) ADBC (d) CADB

Directions for Questions 40 to 44: Sentences given in each question, when properly sequenced form a coherent paragraph. Each sentence is labeled with a letter. Choose the most logical order of sentences from among the four given choices to construct a coherent paragraph.

Q 40.

(A) In rejecting the functionalism in positivist organisation theory, either wholly or partially, there is often a move towards a political model of organisation theory.

(B) Thus the analysis would shift to the power resources possessed by different groups in the organisation and the way they use these resources in actual power plays to shape the organisational structure.

(C) At the extreme, in one set of writings, the growth of administration in the organisation is held to be completely unrelated to the work to be done and to be caused totally by the political pursuit of self-interest.

(D) The political model holds that individual interests are pursued in organisational life through the exercise of power and influence.

(a) ADBC (b) CBAD
(c) DBCA (d) ABDC

Q 41.

(A) Group decision making, however, does not necessarily fully guard against arbitrariness and anarchy, for individual capriciousness can get substituted by collusion of group members.

(B) Nature itself is an intricate system of checks and balances, meant to preserve the delicate balance between various environmental factors that affect our ecology.

(C) In institution also, there is a need to have in place a system of checks and balances which inhibits the concentration of power in only some individuals.

(D) When human interventions alter this delicate balance, the outcome have been seen to be disastrous.

(a) CDAB (b) BCAD
(c) CABD (d) BDCA

Q 42.

(A) He was bone-wary and soul-weary, and found himself muttering, 'either I can't manage this place, or it's unmanageable'.

(B) To his horror; he realised that he had become the victim of an amorphous, unwitting, unconscious conspiracy to immerse him in routine work that had no significance.

(C) It was one of those nights in the office when the office clerk was moving towards four in the morning and Bennis was still not through with the incredible mass of paper stacked before him.

(D) He reached for his calendar and ran his eyes down each hour, half-hour, and quarter hour, to see where his time had gone that day, the day before, the month before.

(a) ABCD (b) CADB
(c) BDCA (d) DCBA

Q 43.

(A) With that I swallowed the shampoo, and obtained most realistic results almost on the spot.

(B) The man shuffled away into the back regions to make up a prescription, and after a moment, I got through on the shop-telephone to the Consulate, intimating my location.

(C) Then, while the pharmacist was wrapping up a six-ounce bottle of the mixture, I groaned and inquired whether he could give me something for acute gastric cramp.

(D) I intended to stage a sharp gastric attack, and entering an old-fashioned pharmacy, I asked for a popular shampoo mixture, consisting of olive oil and flaked soap.

(a) DCBA (b) DACB
(c) BDAC (d) BCDA

Q 44.

(A) Since then, intelligence tests have been mostly used to separate dull children in school from average or bright children, so that special education can be provided to the dull.

(B) In other words, intelligence tests give us a norm for each age.

(C) Intelligence is expressed as intelligence quotient, and tests are developed to indicate what an average child of a certain age can do – what a 5-year old can answer, but a 4-year old cannot, for instance.

(D) Binet developed the first set of such tests in the early 1900s to find out which children in school needed special attention.

(E) Intelligence can be measured by tests.

(a) CDABE (b) DECAB
(c) EDACB (d) CBADE

Directions for Questions 45 to 49: Sentences given in each question, when properly sequenced form a coherent paragraph. The first and last sentences are 1 and 6, and the four in between are labeled A, B, C, and D. Choose the most logical order of these four sentences from among the four given choices to construct a coherent paragraph from sentences 1 to 6.

Q 45.

1. Security inks exploit the same principle that causes the vivid and constantly changing colours of a film of oil on water.

(A) When two rays of light meet each other after being reflected from these difference surfaces, they have each traveled slightly different distances.

(B) The key is that the light is bouncing off two surfaces, that of the oil and that of the water layer below it.

(C) The distance the two rays travel determines which wavelengths, and hence colours, interface constructively and look bright.

(D) Because light is an electromagnetic wave, the peaks and troughs of each ray then interface either constructively, to appear bright, or destructively, to appear dim.

6. Since the distance the rays travel changes with the angle as you look at the surface, different colours look bright from different viewing angles.

(a) ABCD (b) BADC
(c) BDAC (d) DACB

Q 46.

1. Commercially reared chicken can be unusually aggressive, and are often kept in darkened sheds to prevent them pecking at each other:

(A) The birds spent far more of their time – up to a third – pecking at the inanimate objects in the pens, in contrast to birds in other pens which spent a lot of time attacking others.

(B) In low light conditions, they behave less belligerently, but are more prone to ophthalmic disorders and respiratory problems.

(C) In an experiment, aggressive head pecking was all but eliminated among birds in the enriched environment.

(D) Altering the bird's environment, by adding bales of wood – shavings to their pens, can work wonders.

6. Bales could diminish aggressiveness and reduce injuries; they might even improve productivity, since a happy chicken is a productive chicken.

(a) DCAB (b) CDBA
(c) DBAC (d) BDCA

Q 47.

1. The concept of a 'nation-state' assumes a complete correspondence between the boundaries of the nation and the boundaries of those who live in a specific state.

(A) Then there are members of national collectivities who live in other countries, making a mockery of the concept.

(B) There are always people living in particular states who are not considered to be (and often do not consider themselves to be) members of the hegemonic nation.

(C) Even worse, there are nations which never had a state or which are divided across several states.

(D) This, of course, has been subject to severe criticism and is virtually everywhere, a fiction.

6. However, the fiction has been, and continues to be, at the basis of nationalist ideologies.

(a) DBAC (b) ABCD
(c) BACD (d) DACB

Q 48.

1. In the sciences, even questionable examples of research fraud are harshly punished.

(A) But no such mechanism exists in the humanities – much of what humanities researchers call research does not lead to results that are replicable by other scholars.

(B) Given the importance of interpretation in historical and literary scholarship, humanities researchers are in a position where they can explain away deliberate and even systematic distortion.

(C) Mere suspicion is enough for funding to be cut off, publicity guarantees that careers can be effectively ended.

(D) Forgeries, which take the form of practices in which the forger intersperses fake and real parts can be defended as mere mistakes or aberrant misreading.

6. Scientists fudging data have no such defenses.

(a) BDCA (b) ABDC
(c) CABD (d) CDBA

Q 49.

1. Horses and communism were, on the whole, a poor match.

(A) Fine horses bespoke the nobility the party was supposed to despise.

(B) Communist leaders, when they visited villages, preferred to see cows and pigs.

(C) Although a working horse was just about tolerable, the communists were right to be wary.

(D) Peasants from Poland to the Hungarian Puszta preferred their horses to party dogma.

6. 'A farmer's pride is his horse, his cow may be thin but his horse must be fat', went a Slovak saying.

(a) ACDB (b) DBCA
(c) ABCD (d) DCBA

Directions for Questions 50 to 54: The sentences given in each questions, when properly

sequenced form a coherent paragraph. Each sentence is labeled with a letter. Choose the most logical order of sentences from among the four given choices to construct a coherent paragraph.

Q 50.

(A) If caught in the act, they were punished, not for the crime, but for allowing themselves to be caught, with another lash of the whip.

(B) The bellicose Spartans sacrificed all the finer things in life military expertise.

(C) Those fortunate enough to survive babyhood were taken away from their mothers at the age of seven to undergo rigorous military training.

(D) This consisted mainly of beatings and deprivations of all kinds like going around barefoot in winter, and worse, starvation so that they would be forced to steal food to survive.

(E) Male children were examined at birth by the city council and those deemed too weak to become soldiers were left to die of exposure.

(a) BECDA (b) ECADB
(c) BCDAE (d) ECDAB

Q 51.

(A) This very insatiability of the photographing eye changes the terms of confinement in the cave, our world.

(B) Humankind lingers unregenerately in Plato's cave, still reveling, its age-old habit, in mere image of truth.

(C) But being educated by photographs is not like being educated by older images drawn by hand; for one thing, there are a great many more images around, claiming our attention.

(D) The inventory started in 1839 and since then, just about everything has been photographed, or so it seems.

(E) In teaching us a new visual code, photographs alter and enlarge our notions of what is worth looking at and what we have a right to observe.

(a) EABCE (b) BDEAC
(c) BCDAE (d) ECDAB

Q 52.

(A) To be culturally literate is to possess the basic information needed to thrive in the modern world.

(B) Nor is it confined to one social class; quite the contrary.

(C) It is by no means confined to 'culture', narrowly understood as an acquaintance with the arts.

(D) Cultural literacy constitutes the only sure avenue of opportunity for disadvantaged children, the only reliable way of combating the social determinism that now condemns them.

(E) The breadth of that information is great, extending over the major domains of human activity from sports to science.

(a) AECBD (b) DECBA
(c) ACBED (d) DBCAE

Q 53.

(A) Both parties use capital and labour in the struggle to secure property rights.

(B) The thief spends time and money in his attempt to steal (he buys wire cutters) and the legitimate property owner expends resources to prevent the theft (he buys locks).

(C) A social cost of theft is that both the thief and the potential victim use resources to gain or maintain control over property.

(D) These costs may escalate as a type of technological arms race unfolds.

(E) A bank may purchase more and more complicated and sophisticated safes, forcing safecrackers to invest further in safecracking equipment.

(a) ABCDE (b) CABDE
(c) ACBED (d) CBEDA

Q 54.

(A) The likelihood of an accident is determined by how carefully the motorist drives and how carefully the pedestrian crosses the street.

(B) An accident involving a motorist and a pedestrian is such a case.

(C) Each must decide how much care to exercise without knowing how careful the other is.

(D) The simplest strategic problem arises when two individuals interact with each other and each must decide what to do without knowing what the other is doing.

(a) ABCD (b) ADCB
(c) DBCA (d) DBAC

Directions for Questions 55 to 59: Arrange sentences A, B, C, and D to form a logical sequence between sentences 1 to 6.

Q 55.

1. Making people laugh is tricky.

(A) At times, the intended humour may simply not come off.

(B) Making people laugh while trying to sell them something is a tougher challenge, since the commercial can fell flat on two grounds.

(C) There are many advertisements which do amuse, but do not even begin to set the cash tills ringing.

(D) Again, it is rarely sufficient for an advertiser simply to amuse the target audience in order to reap the sales benefit.

6. There are indications that in substituting the hard sell for a more entertaining approach, some agencies have rather thrown out the baby with the bath water.

(a) CDBA (b) ABCD
(c) BADC (d) DCBA

Q 56.

1. Picture a termite colony, occupying a tall mud hump on an African Plain.

(A) Hungry predators often invade the colony and unsettle the balance.

(B) The colony flourishes only if the proportion of soldiers to workers remains roughly the same, so that the queen and workers can be protected by the soldiers, and the queen and soldiers can be serviced by the workers.

(C) Bit its fortunes are presently restored, because the immobile queen, walled in well below ground level, lays eggs not only in large enough numbers, but also in the varying proportions required.

(D) The hump is alive with worker termites and soldier termites going about their distinct kinds of business.

6. How can we account for her mysterious ability to respond like this to events on the distant surface?

(a) BADC (b) DBAC
(c) ADCB (d) BDCA

Q 57.

1. According to recent research, the critical period of developing language skills is between the ages of three and five and a half hears.

(A) The read-to child already has a large vocabulary and a sense of grammar and sentence structure.

(B) Children who are read to in these years have a far better chance of reading well in school, indeed, of doing well in all their subjects.

(C) And the reason is actually quite simple.

(D) This correlation is far and away the highest yet found between home influences and school success.

6. Her comprehension of language is therefore very high.

(a) DACB (b) ADCB
(c) ABCD (d) BDCA

Q 58.

1. High-powered outboard motors were considered to be one of the major threats to the survival of the Beluga whales.

(A) With these, hunters could approach Belugas within hunting range and profit from its inner skin and blubber.

(B) To escape an approaching motor, Belugas have learned to dive to the ocean bottom and stay there for up to 20 minutes, by which time the confused predator has left.

(C) Today, however, even with much powerful engines, it is difficult to come close, because the whales seem to disappear suddenly just when you thought you had them in your sights.

(D) When the first outboard engines arrived in the early 1930s, one came across 4 and 8 HP motors.

6. Belugas seem to have used their well-known sensitivity to noise to evolve an 'avoidance' strategy to outsmart hunters and their powerful technologies.

(a) DACB (b) CDAB
(c) ADBC (d) BDAC

Q 59.

1. The reconstruction of history by post-revolutionary science texts involves more than a multiplication of historical misconstructions.

(A) Because they aim quickly to acquaint the student with what the contemporary scientific community thinks it knows, textbooks treat the various experiments, concepts, law, and theories of the current normal science as separately and as nearly seriatim as possible.

(B) Those misconstructions render revolutions invisible; the arrangement of the still visible material in science texts implies a process that, if it existed, would deny revolutions a function.

(C) But when combined with the generally unhistorical air of science writing and with the occasional systematic misconstruction, one impression is likely to follow.

(D) As pedagogy, this technique of presentation is unexceptionable.

6. Science has reached its present state by a series of individual discoveries and inventions that, when gathered together, constitute the modern body of technical knowledge.

(a) BADC (b) ADCB
(c) DACB (d) CBDA

Directions for Questions 60 to 64: The sentences given in each question, when properly sequenced form a coherent paragraph. Each sentence is labeled with a letter: Choose the most logical order of sentences from among the given choices to construct a coherent paragraph.

Q 60.

(A) Although there are large regional variations, it is not infrequent to find a large number of people sitting here and there and doing nothing.

(B) Once in office, they receive friends and relatives who feel free to call any time without prior appointment.

(C) While working, one is struck by the slow and clumsy actions and reactions, indifferent attitudes, pro-cedure rather than outcome orien-tation, and the lack of consideration for others.

(D) Even those who are employed often come late to the office and leave early, unless they are forced to be punctual.

(E) Work is not intrinsically values in India.

(F) Quite often, people visit ailing friends and relatives or go out of their way to help them in their personal matters even during office hours.

(a) ECADBF (b) EADCFB
(c) EADBFC (d) ABFCBE

Q 61.

(A) But in the industrial era, destroying the enemy's productive capacity means bombing the factories which are located in the cities.

(B) So in the agrarian era, if you need to destroy the enemy's productive capacity, what you want to do is burn his fields, or if you're really vicious, salt them.

(C) Now in the information era, destroying the enemy's productive capacity means destroying the information infrastructure.

(D) How do you battle with your enemy?

(E) The idea is to destroy the enemy's productive capacity, and depending upon the economic foundation, that productive capacity is different in each case.

(F) With regard to defence, the purpose of the military is to defend the nation and be prepared to do battle with its enemy.

(a) FDEBAC (b) FACBED
(c) DEBACF (d) DFEBAC

Q 62.

(A) Michael Hofmann, a poet and translator, accepts this sorry fact without approval or complaint.

(B) But thanklessness and impossibility do not daunt him.

(C) He acknowledges too – in fact he returns to the point often that best translators of poetry always fail at some level.

(D) Hofmann feels passionately about his work, and this is clear from his writings.

(E) In terms of the gap between worth and rewards, translators come somewhere near nurses and street-cleaners.

(a) EACDB (b) ADEBC
(c) EACBD (d) DCEAB

Q 63.

(A) Passivity is not, of course, universal.

(B) In areas where there are no lords or laws, or in frontier zones where all men go armed, the attitude of the peasantry may well be different.

(C) So indeed, it may be on the fringe of the unsubmissive.

(D) However, for most of the soil-bound peasants, the problem is not whether to be normally passive or active, but when to pass from one state to another.

(E) This depends on an assessment of the political situation.

(a) BEDAC (b) CDABE
(c) EDBAC (d) ABCDE

Q 64.

(A) The situation in which violence occurs and the nature of that violence tends to be clearly defined at least in theory, as in the proverbial Irishman's question: 'Is this a private fight or can anyone join in'?

(B) So the actual risk to outsiders, though no doubt higher than our societies, is calculable.

(C) Probably the only uncontrolled applications of force are those of social superiors to social inferiors and even here, there are probably some rules.

(D) However, binding the obligation to kill, members of feuding families engaged in mutual massacre will be genuinely appalled if by some mischance, a bystander or outsiders is killed.

(a) DABC (b) ACDB
(c) CBAD (d) DBAC

Directions for Questions 65 to 72: The sentences given in each questions, when properly sequenced form a coherent paragraph. Each sentence is labeled with a letter. Choose the most logical order of sentences from among the given choices to construct a coherent paragraph.

Q 65.

(A) The wall does not simply divide Israel from a putative Palestinian state on the basis of the 1967 borders.

(B) A chilling omission from the road map is the gigantic 'separation wall' now being built in the West Bank by Israel.

(C) It is surrounded by trenches, electric wire, and moats; there are watchtowers at regular intervals.

(D) It actually takes in new tracts of Palestinian land, sometimes five or six kilometers at a stretch.

(E) Almost a decade after the end of South African apartheid, this ghastly racist wall is going up with scarcely a peep from Israel's American allies, who are going to pay for most of it.

(a) EBCAD (b) BADCE
(c) AEDCB (d) ECADB

Q 66.

(A) Luckily, the tide of battle moved elsewhere after the American victory at Midway and an Australian victory over Japan at Milne Bay.

(B) It could have been no more than a delaying tactic.

(C) The Australian military, knowing the position was homeless, planned to fall back to the south-east in the hope of defending the main cities.

(D) They had captured most of the Solomon Islands and much of New Guinea, and seemed poised for an invasion.

(E) Not many people outside Australia realise how close the Japanese got.

(a) EDCBA (b) ECDAB
(c) ADCBE (d) CDBAE

Q 67.

(A) Call it the third wave sweeping the Indian media.

(B) Now, they are starring in a new role, as suave dealmakers who are in a hurry to strike alliances and agreements.

(C) Look around and you will find a host of deals that have been inked or are ready to be finalised.

(D) Then the media barons wrested back control from their editors, and turned marketing warriors with the brand as their missile.

(E) The first came with those magnificent men in their mahogany chambers who took on the world with their mighty fountain pens.

(a) ACBED (b) CEBDA
(c) CAEBD (d) AEDBC

Q 68.

(A) The celebrations of economic recovery in Washington may be as premature as that 'Mission Accomplished' banner hung on the USS Abraham Lincoln to hail the end of the Iraq war.

(B) Meanwhile, in the real world, the struggles of families and communities continue unabated.

(C) Washington responded to the favourable turn in economic news with enthusiasm.

(D) The celebrations and high-fives up and down Pennsylvania Avenue are not to be found beyond the Beltway.

(E) When the third quarter GDP showed growth of 7.2% and the monthly unemployment rate dipped to 6%, euphoria gripped the US capital.

(a) ACEDB (b) CEDAB
(c) ECABD (d) ECBDA

Q 69.

(A) To much of the Labour movement, it symbolises the brutality of the upper classes.

(B) And to everybody watching, the current mess over fox hunting symbolises the government's weakness.

(C) To fox hunting's supporters, Labour's 1991 manifesto commitment to ban it, symbolises the party's metropolitan roots and hostility to the countryside.

(D) Small issues sometimes have large symbolic power.

(E) To those who enjoy thundering across the countryside in red coats after foxes, foxhunting symbolises the ancient roots of rural lives.

(a) DEACB (b) ECDBA
(c) CEADB (d) DBAEC

Q 70.

(A) In the case of King Merolchazzar's courtship of the Princess of the Outer Isles, there occurs a regrettable hitch.

(B) She acknowledges the gifts, but no word of a meeting date follows.

(C) The monarch, hearing good reports of a neighbouring princess, dispatches messengers with gifts to her court, beseeching an interview.

(D) The princess names a date, and a formal meeting takes place; after that everything buzzes along pretty smoothly.

(E) Royal love affairs in olden days were conducted on the correspondence method.

(a) ACBDE (b) ABCDE
(c) ECDAB (d) ECBAD

Q 71.

(A) Who can trace to its first beginnings, the love of Damon for Pythias, of

David for Jonathan, of Swan for Edgar?

(B) Similarly with men.

(C) There is about great friendships between man and man a certain inevitability that can only be compared with the age-old association of ham and eggs.

(D) One simply feels that it is one of the things that must be so.

(E) No one can say what was the mutual magnetism that brought the deathless partnership of these wholesome and palatable foodstuffs about.

(a) ACBED (b) CEDBA
(c) ACEBD (d) CEABD

Q 72.

(A) Events intervened, and in the late 1930s and 1940s, Germany suffered from 'over-branding'.

(B) The British used to be fascinated by the home of Romanticism.

(C) But reunification and the federal government's move to Berlin have prompted Germany to think again about its image.

(D) The first foreign package holiday was a tour of Germany organised by Thomas Cook in 1855.

(E) Since then, Germany has been understandably nervous about promoting itself abroad.

(a) ACEBD (b) DECAB
(c) BDAEC (d) DBAEC

Directions for Questions 73 to 77: The sentences given in each question, when properly sequenced form a coherent paragraph. Each sentence is labeled with a letter. Choose the most logical order of sentences from among the given choices to construct a coherent paragraph.

Q 73.

(A) He felt justified in bypassing Congress altogether, on a variety of moves.

(B) At times, he was fighting the entire Congress.

(C) Bush felt he had a mission to restore power to the presidency.

(D) Bush was not fighting just the democrats.

(E) Representative democracy is a messy business, and a CEO of the White House does not like a legislature of second guessers and time wasters.

(a) CAEDB (b) DBAEC
(c) CEADB (d) ECDBA

Q 74.

(A) The two neighbours never fought each other.

(B) Fights involving three male fiddler crabs have been recorded, but the status of the participants was unknown.

(C) They pushed or grappled only with the intruder.

(D) We recorded 17 cases in which a resident that was fighting an intruder, was joined by an immediate neighbor, an ally.

(E) We therefore tracked 268 intruder males until we saw them fighting a resident male.

(a) BEDAC (b) DEBAC
(c) BDCAE (d) BCEDA

Q 75.

(A) In the west, Allied Forces had fought their way through southern Italy as far as Rome.

(B) In June 1944, Germany's military position in World War Two appeared hopeless.

(C) In Britain, the task of amassing the men and materials for the liberation of northern Europe had been completed.

(D) The Red Army was poised to drive the Nazis back through Poland.

(E) The situation on the eastern front was catastrophic.

(a) EDACB (b) BEDAC
(c) BDECA (d) CEDAB

Q 76.

(A) But this does not mean that death was the Egyptians' only preoccupation.

(B) Even papyri come mainly from pyramid temples.

(C) Most of our traditional sources of information about the Old Kingdom are monuments of the rich like pyramids and tombs.

(D) Houses in which ordinary Egyptians lived have not been preserved, and when most people died, they were buried in simple graves.

(E) We know infinitely more about the wealthy people of Egypt that we do about the ordinary people, as most monuments were made for the rich.

(a) CDBEA (b) ECDAB

(c) EDCBA (d) DECAB

Q 77.

(A) Experts such as Larry Burns, head of research at GM, reckon that only such a full hearted leap will allow the world to cope with the mass motorisation that will one day come to China or India.

(B) But once hydrogen is being produced from biomass or extracted from underground coal or made from water, using nuclear or renewable electricity, the way will be open for a huge reduction in carbon emissions from the whole system.

(C) In theory, once all the bugs have been sorted out, fuel cells should deliver better total fuel economy than any existing engines.

(D) That is twice as good as the internal combustion engine, but only five percentage points better than a diesel hybrid.

(E) Allowing for the resources needed to extract hydrogen from hydrocarbon, oil, coal or gas, the fuel cells has an efficiency of 30%.

(a) CEDBA (b) CEBDA

(c) AEDBC (d) ACEBD

ANSWERS – REORDERING OF JUMBLED SENTENCES

1	c	*16*	d	*31*	b	*46*	d	*61*	d
2	a	*17*	b	*32*	d	*47*	a	*62*	c
3	d	*18*	a	*33*	d	*48*	c	*63*	d
4	c	*19*	d	*34*	d	*49*	c	*64*	b
5	a	*20*	a	*35*	c	*50*	a	*65*	b
6	b	*21*	c	*36*	b	*51*	d	*66*	a
7	a	*22*	c	*37*	a	*52*	a	*67*	d
8	d	*23*	b	*38*	c	*53*	b	*68*	d
9	a	*24*	d	*39*	b	*54*	d	*69*	a
10	c	*25*	d	*40*	a	*55*	c	*70*	c
11	c	*26*	c	*41*	d	*56*	b	*71*	b
12	d	*27*	c	*42*	b	*57*	d	*72*	c
13	d	*28*	a	*43*	a	*58*	a	*73*	d
14	c	*29*	d	*44*	c	*59*	a	*74*	a
15	c	*30*	a	*45*	b	*60*	c	*75*	b
		76	b			*77*	a		

29 SENTENCE COMPLETION – PRACTICE TESTS (MCQS)

15 PRACTICE TESTS

Sentence Completion demands precise understanding of the words and their usage. It is possible only and only if one is well-versed with copious vocabulary, its understanding and usage as various forms of speech.

Choose the correct option:

PRACTICE TEST-1

Q 1. George Bernard Shaw said that the contemporary social values could be flippant and __________ at some times.

(a) important (b) profound
(c) inane (d) riveting
(e) absurd

Q 2. __________ the general had been told by the field staff that continuing warfare would be __________ to his soldiers, he insisted on deploying more battle tanks.

(a) Although ….. detrimental
(b) Because ….. instrumental
(c) Although ….. formidable
(d) Because ….. immediate
(e) Because ….. incremental

Q 3. The Senate warned the Prime Minister that if he did not accept their advice, the differences between the Legislative and the Executive arms of the Government would be __________.

(a) eliminated (b) eroded
(c) exacerbated (d) exemplified
(e) exasperated

Q 4. Most journalistic writing could do with __________ of paragraphs to make the prose more __________.

(a) suppression ….. legible
(b) removal ….. argumentative
(c) simplification ….. abstruse
(d) deletion ….. succinct
(e) exemplification ….. incoherent

Q 5. Varun has been accused of murdering his wife, and though he was never __________, he never recovered from the shame and the scandal.

(a) charged (b) booked
(c) indicted (d) acquitted

Q 6. The earthquake warning and the fragility of our houses make us certain that disaster is __________.

(a) available (b) imminent
(c) forthcoming (d) catastrophic

Q 7. The television serials are characterised by an __________ story line and __________ plots and sub-plots.

(a) unending ….. convoluted
(b) infantile ….. simple
(c) uniform ….. emotional
(d) extempore ….. routine
(e) erratic ….. forthcoming

Q 8. The __________ transformation of the former Soviet Union of Russia as it was popularly known, remains one of the biggest stories of the decade.

(a) smooth (b) singular
(c) tumultuous (d) prophetic
(e) traumatic

Q 9. If mankind has to survive for long, it must __________ and deliberately renounce the fruits of __________ and whirling technology.

(a) willfully ….. wild
(b) honestly ….. responsible
(c) sincerely ….. labor
(d) effectively ….. sliding
(e) knowingly ….. impending

Q 10. Although similar to moth in many ways, butterflies may be __________ moths by the beauty of their wings.

(a) akin to (b) in comparison with
(c) listed as (d) distinguished from
(e) equal to the

Q 11. Renu saw no __________ in the exercises that had been set for her and worked at them in a __________ manner.

(a) reason ….. organised
(b) point ….. desultory
(c) strength ….. careless
(d) meaning ….. doubtful
(e) sense ….. painful

Q 12. Mother Teresa was __________ about her achievements and unwilling to __________ them before anyone.

(a) modest ….. discuss
(b) proud ….. promote
(c) unsure ….. reveal
(d) ignorant ….. eulogise
(e) immodest ….. play

Q 13. Martin Luther strived for justice and fought against attempts to __________ ignorant peasants in the medieval ages.

(a) influence (b) change
(c) exploit (d) corrupt
(e) discharge

Q 14. The instruction manual that came with the computer is not a masterpiece of __________ prose because its instructions are so __________ that we still do not know how to set up the computer.

(a) clear ….. garbled
(b) valuable ….. intelligent
(c) worthless …. Clear
(d) confused ….. varied
(e) worth ….. muffled

Q 15. The strike will not end because both the management and the workers are ______.

(a) insipid (b) intransigent
(c) intricate (d) inexplicable
(e) saddened

PRACTICE TEST-2

Q 1. Book lovers who think of Gone With The Wind as a Southern romance miss its underlying __________ important.

(a) democratic (b) novelistic
(c) thematic (d) exceptional
(e) argumentative

Q 2. The professors at Lucknow University have a permanent __________ on their positions and do not have to look for more secure __________ in.

(a) fixture ….. jobs
(b) tenure ….. employment
(c) security ….. means
(d) right ….. employees
(e) eye ….. seats

Q 3. It is very difficult to overcome the __________ of habits such as smoking and taking drugs.

(a) stupidity (b) tenacity
(c) insecurity (d) insistence

Q 4. The __________ and __________ happenings in many talk shows annoy many viewers.

(a) aggravating ….. irritating
(b) trite ….. predictable
(c) happy ….. playful
(d) dramatic ….. eventful
(e) ranting ….. jocular

Q 5. Slander and libel laws stand as a protection of a person's reputation against the __________ dissemination of falsehood.

(a) inferential (b) inevitable
(c) incontestable (d) irresponsible
(e) semblance

Q 6. Most of the settlements that grew up near the logging camps were __________ affairs, thrown together in a hurry because people needed to live on the job.

(a) nomadic (b) protracted
(c) unobtrusive (d) rickety
(e) uncouth

Q 7. Pipes are not a safer __________ to cigarettes because, though pipe smokers do not inhale, they are still __________ higher rates of lung and mouth cancers than nonsmokers.

(a) preference ….. free from

(b) answer ….. responsible for
(c) alternative ….. subject to
(d) rejoinder ….. involved in
(e) offer ….. involved with

Q 8. Author Anjali Agarwal was a rare phenomenon, a single woman who maintained and even __________ a respectable reputation while earning a living by her pen.

(a) impaired (b) decimated
(c) avoided (d) enhanced
(e) evacuated

Q 9. Because Sherry is so __________, we can never predict what he will do at any moment.

(a) old (b) immature
(c) capricious (d) lazy
(e) dormant

Q 10. Paper money is merely a representation of wealth; therefore unlike gold or any other precious metal, it has no __________ value.

(a) financial (b) fiscal
(c) inveterate (d) intrinsic

Q 11. The law cannot and should not pardon such __________ act of violence.

(a) a flagrant (b) a lavish
(c) a cautious (d) a dull
(e) condemn

Q 12. As many students know, a/(an) __________ response, if skillfully worded, can imply at least a superficial __________ of knowledge about the subject.

(a) ambiguous ….. veneer
(b) garbled ….. ignorance
(c) inarticulate ….. piece
(d) elegant ….. lack
(e) wrong ….. lack

Q 13. There are too many __________ and not enough serious students.

(a) dilettantes (b) hunky dory
(c) lay-men (d) novices
(e) nascent

Q 14. Her parents were __________ when, despite losing the first three games, Sandy __________ to win the set by a 6 – 3 score.

(a) surprised ….. failed
(b) relieved ….. came back
(c) puzzled ….. refused
(d) alarmed ….. attempted
(e) shocked ….. failed

Q 15. The reviews of Deepak Chopra's latest literary work were enjoyed by many of his readers, but the subjects dreaded Mr. Chopra's comments; he was scathing, bitter, irritating and never __________.

(a) logical (b) constructive
(c) uncharitable (d) controversial
(e) acidic

PRACTICE TEST-3

Q 1. In poor and under developed countries, trucks are the only means of getting about town, the public transportation being virtually __________ .

(a) indecipherable (b) ubiquitous
(c) inadequate (d) nonexistent
(e) negligent

Q 2. Given the __________ state of published evidence, we cannot conclude here that exposure to low-level microwave energy is either hazardous or safe.

(a) inconclusive (b) indulging
(c) descriptive (d) immaculate
(e) descriptive

Q 3. The clothes Nafees, the famous designer, designs for men are conservative, but her fashions for women are more __________.

(a) subtle (b) flamboyant
(c) tasteful (d) expensive
(e) open

Q 4. The equipments that were being used in the survey were __________, and because of the below-zero temperature, it was feared they would freeze and __________.

(a) icy ….. capsize
(b) frosty ….. shield
(c) fragile ….. shatter
(d) frozen ….. dehydrate
(e) useless ….. capsize

Q 5. Because of its tendency to __________, most Indian art is __________ Japanese art, where symbols have been minimised and meaning has been conveyed by using the method of the merest suggestion.

(a) imitate ..... superior to
(b) understate ..... reminiscent of
(c) overdraw ..... similar to
(d) sentimentalise ..... supportive of
(e) synergise ..... half

Q 6. Irony can sometimes become a mode of escape; to laugh at the terrors of life is, in a way, to __________ them.

(a) bolster (b) approve
(c) evade (d) foster
(e) avail

Q 7. The negotiations for the deal were often surprisingly __________, deteriorating at times into a volley of accusations and counter-accusations.

(a) insouciant (b) sedate
(c) acrimonious (d) propitious
(e) adequate

Q 8. A __________ student is unlikely to gain admission to a top level institution.

(a) mediocre (b) putative
(c) mendacious (d) vicarious
(e) commerce

Q 9. Either Japanese dishes are __________, or the one I had was a poor example.

(a) delicious (b) overrated
(c) underestimated (d) unpopular

Q 10. A person who is __________ is slow to adapt to a new way of life.

(a) intractable (b) furious
(c) insolent (d) valiant
(e) constructive

Q 11. Amit, who refrained from excesses in his personal life, differed markedly from Nirmal, who __________ notorious drinking bouts with his buddies.

(a) minimised (b) indulged in
(c) shunned (d) compensated for
(e) specialised

Q 12. The library in charge proposed a new schedule of fines for overdue books with the __________, if not the outright encouragement, of the faculty library committee.

(a) cynosure (b) acquiescence
(c) scorn (d) applause
(e) management

Q 13. Maya's remarks were so __________ that Arun could not decide which possible meaning was correct.

(a) congruent (b) impalpable
(c) ambiguous (d) facetious
(e) incorrigible

Q 14. By nature, Rahul was __________, given to striking up casual conversation with strangers he encountered at bus stops or check-out stands.

(a) gregarious (b) reticent
(c) casual (d) diffident
(e) indulgent

Q 15. In the absence of native predators, to stop the spread of their population, the imported goats __________ to such an inordinate degree that over grazed the country side and __________ the native vegetation.

(a) propagated ..... cultivated
(b) suffered ..... abandoned
(c) thrived ..... threatened
(d) dwindled ..... eliminated
(e) outnumbered ..... cultivated

PRACTICE TEST-4

Q 1. Jayashree was habitually so docile and __________ that her friends could not understand her sudden __________ her employers.

(a) accommodating ..... outburst against
(b) erratic ..... envy of
(c) truculent ..... virulence toward
(d) hasty ..... annoyance toward
(e) apologetic ..... hostile

Q 2. That Amitabh's newest film is No. 1 at the box office this week is a testament to the star's __________ power and not the reviews, which were __________ at best.

(a) increasing ..... matchless
(b) ongoing ..... glowing
(c) drawing ..... modest
(d) waning ..... indifferent
(e) super ..... dismal

Q 3. The __________ background music hinted of the dangers threatening the movie's protagonist.

(a) loud (b) sardonic
(c) ebullient (d) portentous
(e) icy

Q 4. In order to ensure that she passed the exam, Asha __________ outlined every chapter of her course book, painstakingly noting the most obscure points.

(a) carefully (b) playfully
(c) jokingly (d) superficially
(e) cursory

Q 5. Mr. Purty hastily __________ all the warnings of his friends. And now, he finds it difficult to complete the task within its time and budget __________.

(a) accepted ….. amounts
(b) ignored ….. amounts
(c) listened to ….. problems
(d) disregarded ….. constraints
(e) acknowledged …… schedule

Q 6. Lacking confidence in his skills in English, Pervez was __________ when called on to speak in class.

(a) horrified (b) reticent
(c) impolite (d) sartorial
(e) shocked

Q 7. The castle has been __________, we cannot even be sure exactly where it stood.

(a) obliterated (b) burned down
(c) ruined (d) debilitated
(e) spoilt

Q 8. Being a bit hesitant about __________ the man as the complete fraud he suspected him to be, Bill close to attack the weaker points of his theory, __________ them one by one.

(a) denouncing ….. debunking
(b) ridiculing ….. proving
(c) castigating ….. strengthening
(d) mocking ….. destroying
(e) mistrusting ….. telling

Q 9. The analysis of the coach's report was anything but __________, but those of us who have learned to discount such dismal __________ are optimistic.

(a) pessimistic ….. confusion
(b) sanguinary ….. traps
(c) malicious ….. benefits
(d) pleasant ….. prognostications
(e) sugary ….. performances

Q 10. Angered by the bureaucrat's __________ comments, the reporter insisted for a more __________ response.

(a) redundant ….. repetitive
(b) tactless ….. immediate
(c) phlegmatic ….. lackadaisical
(d) circumlocutions ….. direct
(e) sarcastic ….. beneficial

Q 11. Raman's __________ record collection included everything from Bach to rock.

(a) effusive (b) rhapsodic
(c) eclectic (d) inherent
(e) refulgent

Q 12. My grandparents were such __________ followers of the soap opera that they taped every episode.

(a) avid (b) skillful
(c) flagrant (d) retentive
(e) hopeless

Q 13. __________ the finger points of etiquette in high society, Devesh simply watched his host and followed his actions.

(a) Arguing for (b) Unaware
(c) Ignorant of (d) Saddened by
(e) Looking at

Q 14. This book of Covey creates a mood of _____, a (n) _____of tranquility and calm.

(a) somberness ….. atmosphere
(b) serenity ….. ambience
(c) melancholy ….. oasis
(d) formality ….. feeling
(e) tranquility ….. sea

Q 15. Although they seem amateurish, primitive art has become more sophisticated as its creator becomes increasingly __________.

(a) infamous (b) aged
(c) jaded (d) impotent
(e) ignorant

PRACTICE TEST-5

Q 1. Though a __________ of four campaigns, Bush had never seen such demonstrations.

(a) watchman (b) veteran
(c) volunteer (d) witness
(e) follower

Q 2. Carried away by the __________ effects of the experimental medication, the patients __________ his desire to continue as a subject for as long as he could.

(a) supplementary ..... announced
(b) noxious ..... proclaimed
(c) frantic ..... repeated
(d) salutary ..... reiterated
(e) painful .... undermined

Q 3. Confused and __________, Hogwarts fumbled to make sense of seemingly inconsistent statements, __________ the impatience of his listeners.

(a) prostrate ..... listening to
(b) muddled ..... aware of
(c) philosophical ..... overlooking
(d) incoherent ..... oblivious to
(e) agitated ..... following

Q 4. One of the most productive research __________ in contemporary neuroscience is devoted to __________ maps of human consciousness.

(a) trajectories ..... reconnoitering
(b) designs ..... enunciating
(c) paradigms ..... elucidating
(d) declensions ..... obfuscating
(e) terminologies ..... newal

Q 5. Today computers can __________ information from a number of sources, then automatically create a picture of their data manipulations.

(a) collate (b) inculcate
(c) extrapolate (d) adjudicate
(e) execute

Q 6. Just as a highway automobile accident leaves lasting marks of spilled coolant, __________ and oil, the smashing together of gigantic land masses releases and redirects fluids that flow, heat, __________, and deposit, leaving an enduring record of their presence.

(a) petrol ..... disappear
(b) fuel ..... evaporate
(c) paint ..... mark
(d) anti-freeze ..... drip
(e) gases ..... electric

Q 7. Although publicity has been __________ the film itself is intelligent, well-acted, handsomely produced, and altogether __________.

(a) tasteless ..... respectable
(b) extensive ..... moderate
(c) sophisticated ..... amateur
(d) perfect ..... spectacular
(e) useless ..... extraneous

Q 8. Ironically, his normally __________ speaker became shy and __________ when confronted with the approbatory stares of her eager audience.

(a) quiet ..... passionate
(b) garrulous ..... reticent
(c) dispassionate ..... passionate
(d) humble ..... supercilious
(e) soft ..... remorseful

Q 9. Although the whole team acted in unison, each member was __________ for a (n) __________ of the production process.

(a) reliable ..... source
(b) responsible ..... element
(c) appointed ..... article
(d) agreeable ..... felony
(e) agreeable ..... amount

Q 10. The studies of the children were __________ and __________ was the result of it.

(a) neglected ..... ignorance
(b) interrupted ..... incongruence
(c) off tracked ..... alienation
(d) instructed ..... genius
(e) ignored ..... negligence

Q 11. The US has shown little __________ to go after the terrorist or help India get him.

(a) inclination (b) urgency
(c) importance (d) alacrity
(e) endeavour

Q 12. Most young children are highly conformist and will __________ a classmate whose appearance or manners are __________.

(a) ostracise ….. conventional
(b) emulate ….. different
(c) shun ….. unusual
(d) deride ….. ordinary
(e) choose ….. deriding

Q 13. The royal astrologers had to determine the most __________ date for the coronation ceremony.

(a) propitious (b) sacred
(c) approximate (d) resplendent
(e) expected

Q 14. A satirical poem is often venom-filled, __________ with scorn.

(a) contained (b) filled up
(c) dripping (d) sardonic
(e) acidic

Q 15. The __________ rites in the Black Magic cult were kept secret by the members and were never __________ to outsiders.

(a) eclectic ….. delegated
(b) esoteric ….. divulged
(c) inscrutable ….. introduced
(d) elusive ….. prescribed
(e) exclusive ….. delegated

PRACTICE TEST-6

Q 1. Mr. Sharma, the critic was __________ enough to praise an author he detested.

(a) magnanimous (b) loquacious
(c) parsimonious (d) surreptitious
(e) verbose

Q 2. The goodwill of its clients is a genuine __________ asset for any business.

(a) redolent (b) dismissive
(c) intangible (d) vigilant
(e) indolent

Q 3. Though the law's __________ purpose is to curtail false advertising, its actual result is to __________ free speech.

(a) erroneous ….. eschew
(b) ostensible ….. characterise
(c) illicit ….. reconcile
(d) recalcitrant ….. repress
(e) elusive ….. contain

Q 4. __________ by her children, Radha Devi ultimately agreed to sell the house.

(a) Decimated (b) Importuned
(c) Interpolated (d) Designated
(e) Apportioned

Q 5. There was a __________ all about the palace, and the __________ concerned the security guards.

(a) gift ….. distribution
(b) silence ….. quiet
(c) tranquil ….. temper
(d) feast ….. circulation
(e) commotion ….. quiet

Q 6. Giuliana Benetton __________ a small neighbourhood business into a worldwide chain of stores.

(a) renovated (b) infused
(c) parlayed (d) blessed
(e) decimated

Q 7. The football team was once __________ by injuries; of 11 members, only 5 were fit to play.

(a) decimated (b) isolated
(c) boycotted (d) heckled
(e) ambushed

Q 8. Displeased with the __________ of the novel, the writer abandoned the idea of a film to be made on his writings.

(a) adaptation (b) transfer
(c) transfusion (d) resurgence
(e) imagination

Q 9. Because of his indecisive nature, Mr. Bhushan has a reputation for __________.

(a) impartiality (b) tenacity
(c) prevarication (d) vacillation
(e) wandering

Q 10. The conspirators met __________ in order to plot a (n) __________ against the oppressive governance of Julius Ceaser.

(a) clandestinely ….. revolt
(b) wickedly ….. invocation
(c) craftily ….. referendum
(d) wittily ….. ban
(e) aggressively ….. crime

Q 11. Vinay is much too __________ in his writings: he writes a paragraph when a sentence should suffice.

(a) benevolent (b) skilled
(c) verbose (d) lucid
(e) crafted

Q 12. With one __________ motion, Rakesh disarmed his assailant.

(a) swift (b) ponderous
(c) superficial (d) boisterous
(e) levitations

Q 13. The patient put up with the pain __________, neither wincing, nor whimpering when the surgeon made an incision to drain the pus of his abscess.

(a) surprisingly (b) miserably
(c) logically (d) stoically
(e) enduringly

Q 14. In relation to the interrelationships among a number of the Indo-Pakistani stalwarts treated in this compilation there is surely a certain amount of __________ in some of the essays presented here.

(a) overlap (b) indulgence
(c) exaggeration (d) subjectivity
(e) complacency

Q 15. Being an advocate of consumer rights, Sharad has spent much of his career trying to __________ the fraudulent claims of the businessmen of his home-town Patna.

(a) reprove (b) debunk
(c) immortalise (d) import
(e) improve

PRACTICE TEST-7

Q 1. The report was __________ since the information on which it was based was erroneous, but it was brilliantly presented.

(a) intelligent (b) wonderful
(c) worthless (d) verbose
(e) elegant

Q 2. Pretending not to notice the toys in the shop, Aryan the small boy, acted in a __________ manner.

(a) doleful (b) nonchalant
(c) convincing (d) ordinary
(e) indulgent

Q 3. As several shops have __________ across the street, the old directory is __________.

(a) relocated ..... obsolete
(b) reversed ..... enticing
(c) transferred ..... dismantled
(d) vanished ..... beautiful
(e) transferred ..... upto date

Q 4. The __________ room in this apartment has not been used for a long time.

(a) derelict (b) contractual
(c) bereaved (d) crowded
(e) interpolated

Q 5. Salman, the superstar, felt that certain incidents in his life were too __________ to be divulged.

(a) intriguing (b) derivative
(c) private (d) rudimentary
(e) incremental

Q 6. Distressed at an increasing __________ for books, Amrita, the famous novelist, has turned to painting.

(a) disregard (b) imagination
(c) panacea (d) prominence
(e) derelict

Q 7. The bank is negotiating with Group 4 security to devise a system to provide __________ security to account holders.

(a) accurate (b) prompt
(c) reliable (d) tough
(e) proactive

Q 8. As the rate of life expectancy has increased due to tremendous progress in medical science, the over-population problem has __________.

(a) aggravated (b) minimised
(c) distorted (d) encouraged
(e) unfazed

Q 9. The story of the novel, *The Deranged*, is very __________. It shows how a man cut off from the world for a long time because he was a mad man.

(a) absorbing (b) irritating
(c) controversial (d) useless
(e) derived

Q 10. Although Agatha is arguably as good a mystery writer as Grundy, she is clearly far less __________ than Grundy, having written only six books in comparison to Grundy's sixty.

(a) prolific (b) equivocal
(c) verbose (d) gripping
(e) astronomical

Q 11. Being cynical, Ashish was reluctant to __________ the __________ of any kind act until he had ruled out all possible secret, uncharitable motives.

(a) acknowledge ..... wisdom
(b) accept ..... unselfishness
(c) endure ..... loss
(d) witness ..... outcome
(e) uncover ..... outcome

Q 12. A golden rule which should always be followed by an investor is that: never invest on sentiment or on a tip; look for stocks with promising __________ potential for growth.

(a) fast (b) long-term
(c) higher (d) quick
(e) string

Q 13. At the world's finest educational institutes, only students with the __________ to succeed are selected.

(a) luck (b) drive
(c) resources (d) experience
(e) reliable

Q 14. Jamshedji Tata, the founder of the Tata Group in India, knew that only dedication and __________ could ensure that the customer gets the very best.

(a) commitment (b) money
(c) perception (d) supervision
(e) perception

Q 15. Parveen fascinated the world with her beauty and her charm, and her life mixed public spectacle with private anguish; her tragic death __________ a flood of grief on every continent.

(a) brought (b) prompted
(c) called (d) managed
(e) revoked

PRACTICE TEST-8

Q 1. As Shyam __________ retirement, he became more intelligent and active.

(a) awarded (b) withdrew
(c) derived (d) neared
(e) recollected

Q 2. As a steadfast __________ of our right to liberty time, Mishra had few __________.

(a) defender ..... equals
(b) opponent ..... enemies
(c) follower ..... enemies
(d) advocate ..... defenders
(e) leader ..... unequals

Q 3. A careful __________ of the premises revealed some useful clues.

(a) autopsy (b) incarceration
(c) examination (d) incineration
(e) emphases

Q 4. Almost everyone was __________ by the cheerful, lively sound of the dance music.

(a) revived (b) tired
(c) fired (d) bored
(e) withdrawn

Q 5. The __________ of the air crash could have been avoided if more safety __________ had been taken.

(a) sad event ..... preservers
(b) disasters ..... reservations
(c) scientist ..... measures
(d) tragedy ..... precautions
(e) aftermath ..... steps

Q 6. They were disappointed to see the armed guards. It __________ them from doing anything disruptive.

(a) inspired (b) prevented
(c) encouraged (d) irritated

Q 7. The __________ politicians thought that all bureaucrats should be polite to him.

(a) insolent (b) merciless
(c) civilised (d) docile
(e) amateur

Q 8. The newspapers accused the politician of __________ for making promises he knew he could not __________.

(a) revulsion ..... condone
(b) liability ..... improve

(c) impunity ..... reprise
(d) hypocrisy ..... fulfill
(e) forgery ..... overcome

Q 9. Paula was __________ as a child, accepting without a question, everything she was told.

(a) reticent (b) taciturn
(c) recalcitrant (d) credulous
(e) impatient

Q 10. Cautioned by an anonymous phone call that an explosion was __________, the anti bomb police squad __________ the building immediately.

(a) expected ..... filled
(b) ubiquitous ..... purged
(c) imminent ..... evacuated
(d) eminent ..... checked
(e) eminent ..... entered

Q 11. The route between the two cities has always been known to wind its __________ way through steep mountain passes and coarse terrain.

(a) easy (b) smooth
(c) elusive (d) tortuous
(e) trajectory

Q 12. As there were not enough seats to __________ so many people at the venue of the address, they had to put up a big tent outside.

(a) entertain (b) ascertain
(c) welcome (d) accommodate

Q 13. This _____ old stone farmhouse has been a landmark since before the Independence.

(a) fragile (b) sturdy
(c) ramshackle (d) flimsy
(e) rickety

Q 14. The Chief Minister was __________ in his commitment to __________ the rise of crime and unemployment among his constituents.

(a) uncertain ..... staunch
(b) headstrong ..... stem
(c) faltering ..... identity
(d) firm ..... uphold
(e) sturdy ..... counter

Q 15. Sahil's clear __________ of the situation kept the meeting from breaking up into __________.

(a) idea ..... humor
(b) notion ..... anarchy
(c) understanding ..... chaos
(d) wit ...... tumult
(e) report ..... tumult

PRACTICE TEST-9

Q 1. In the past, the coach had always viewed Kapil's ideas with __________, but today he surprised the team by enthusiastically __________ his proposal.

(a) disdain ..... rejecting
(b) empathy ..... considering
(c) objectivity ..... forgetting
(d) skepticism ..... adopting
(e) temerity ..... dissuading

Q 2. The embarrassed host felt that the uninvited guest's rude comments and offensive jokes were __________.

(a) steadfast (b) reactionary
(c) intolerable (d) partisan
(e) alarming

Q 3. The celebrated trainer's __________ for helping his trainees to learn and achieve their goals was highly __________.

(a) propensity ..... commendable
(b) distinction ..... enigmatic
(c) predilection ..... reprehensible
(d) derision ..... admissible
(e) decisiveness ..... desired

Q 4. A few decades ago, __________ about gender roles made it somewhat difficult for a woman to study veterinary science, but today, female veterinarians are quite __________.

(a) diatribes ..... affluent
(b) preconception ..... prevalent
(c) mindsets ..... poor
(d) lectures ..... negligent
(e) analysis ..... prominent

Q 5. Greg Chappell was impressed by the __________ of the youthful Railways team.

(a) ardor (b) corpulence

(c) languor (d) impertinence
(e) turbulence

Q 6. In the plots of most Bollywood movies, there is/are a character/s with __________ intentions, whose primary role is to try to __________ the handsome hero in his noble mission.

(a) furtive ….. abet
(b) malevolent ….. thwart
(c) unsavory ….. depict
(d) inappropriate ….. derail
(e) benevolent ….. obstruct

Q 7. After a natural spring was discovered in the arid region, the family's old, abandoned farm was quickly __________ into a profitable private business, centered around a state-of-the-art well that __________ valuable water.

(a) turned ….. expiates
(b) configured ….. manipulates
(c) transformed ….. emanates
(d) expropriated ….. eradicates
(e) transpired ….. exhaled

Q 8. The young boy's __________ attempts to explain to his girlfriend why he had failed to show for their movie date did little to ease her __________ feelings.

(a) impassioned ….. disconsolate
(b) veracious ….. vacuous
(c) unbelievable ….. gluttonous
(d) chronic ….. vicarious
(e) immeasurable ….. vacuous

Q 9. For some politicians, charm is a mere ______ adopted to get votes and ______ criticism.

(a) prerequisite ….. distort
(b) affectation ….. alleviate
(c) tool ….. inflict
(d) ruse ….. condone
(e) contender ….. earn

Q 10. Although the food in the hostel mess was barely __________, after six months, the residents of the hostel had become __________ to it.

(a) edible ….. immune
(b) edible ….. inured
(c) palatable ….. immune
(d) palatable ….. inured
(e) affordable ….. attuned

Q 11. During childhood and adolescence, individuals acquire habits that are __________ to good health: which include having a sedentary lifestyle, frequently eating fatty and fast foods, and developing poor sleep patterns.

(a) dangerous (b) harmful
(c) inimical (d) unsuitable
(e) despicable

Q 12. Divyansh's disciplined and __________ study habits resulted in his earning numerous honors and awards which also included an academic scholarship.

(a) painstaking (b) sedulous
(c) unhealthy (d) taciturn
(e) pecuniary

Q 13. The old miser's __________ did him little good when he died without heir or friend, and all his precious money was __________ to the state.

(a) frugality ….. escheated
(b) miserliness ….. ordained
(c) exemplariness ….. given
(d) frugality ….. ordained
(e) indulgence ….. willed

Q 14. To most modern day readers, the language in Shakespeare's plays seems obscure and inaccessible, lacking the __________ of modern day authors.

(a) elegance (b) impertinence
(c) perspicuity (d) perceptibility
(e) diligence

Q 15. Unlike the other photojournalists, Rochelle despised the __________ nature of the newspaper business because she craved __________.

(a) permutable ….. habitude
(b) flexible …. chaos
(c) permutable ….. chaos
(d) flexible ….. stable
(e) heinous ….. posterity

ANSWERS – SENTENCE COMPLETION – PRACTICE TESTS (MCQs)

Q. No.	TEST – 1	TEST – 2	TEST – 3	TEST – 4	TEST – 5
1.	inane	thematic	nonexistent	accommo-dating ….. outburst against	veteran
2.	Although ….. detrimental	thematic	inconclusive	drawing ….. modest	salutary ….. reiterated
3.	exacerbated	tenure ….. employment	flamboyant	portentous	incoherent ….. oblivious to
4.	deletion ….. succinct	tenacity	fragile ….. shatter	carefully	paradigms ….. elucidating
5.	indicted	trite ….. predictable	understate ….. reminiscent of	disregarded ….. constraints	collate
6.	imminent	irresponsible	evade	horrified	fuel ….. evaporate
7.	unending ….. convoluted	rickety	acrimonious	obliterated	extensive… moderate
8.	tumultuous	alternative ….. subject to	mediocre	denouncing ….. debunking	garrulous ….. reticent
9.	willfully ….. wild	enhanced	overrated	pleasant ….. progno-stications	responsible ….. element
10.	equal to the	capricious	intractable	Circumlo-cutions ….. direct	neglected ….. ignorance
11.	point ….. desultory	intrinsic	indulged in	effusive	inclination
12.	modest ….. discuss	a flagrant	acquiescence	avid	shun ….. unusual
13.	exploit	ambiguous ….. veneer	ambiguous	ignorant of	propitious
14.	clear ….. garbled	dilettantes	gregarious	sombreness… atmosphere	dripping
15.	intransigent	relieved ….. came back constructive	thrived ….. threatened	jaded	esoteric ….. divulged

Q. No.	TEST – 6	TEST – 7	TEST – 8	TEST – 9
1.	magnanimous	worthless	neared	skepticism ….. adopting
2.	intangible	nonchalant	defender ….. equals	intolerable
3.	recalcitrant ….. repress	relocated ….. obsolete	examination	propensity ….. commendable
4.	Importuned	derelict	revived	preconception ….. prevalent
5.	silence ….. quiet	private	tragedy ….. precautions	ardor
6.	parlayed	disregard	prevented	malevolent ….. thwart
7.	decimated	reliable	insolent	transformed ….. emanates
8.	adaptation	aggravated	hypocrisy ….. fulfill	impassioned …. disconsolate
9.	vacillation	absorbing	credulous	affectation ….. alleviate
10.	clandestinely ….. revolt	prolific	imminent ….. evacuated	palatable ….. inured
11.	verbose	accept ….. unselfishness	tortuous	inimical
12.	swift	long-term	accommodate	sedulous
13.	stoically	drive	sturdy	frugality ….. escheated
14.	overlap	commitment	headstrong ….. stem	perspicuity
15.	debunk	prompted	understanding ….. chaos	permutable ….. habitude

30 CLOZE TEST

15 PRACTICE TESTS

Innumerable questions have been provided throughout the book to test vocabulary along with other aspects of language proficiency. Cloze Test is one of them. Here a passage is taken and words are deleted at intervals. These could be words of a particular class like nouns, verbs, adjectives, adverbs, or prepositions. Four or five words are generally given. You have thus a number of options, only one of which is correct (the answer), the others (the detractors) being wrong. You have to supply the missing words to fill in the blanks by choosing them from the words listed.

PRACTICE TESTS

Directions: In the following passage there are blanks, each of which has been numbered. These numbers are printed below the passage and against each, four or five words are suggested, one of which fits the blank appropriately. Find out the appropriate words.

PRACTICE TEST – 1

Jawaharlal Nehru was probably the first important public leader to realise that if India were to ***(1)*** __________ its problems, it would have to ***(2)*** __________ the age of science. The ***(3)*** __________ the Government has attached to science is also clear ***(4)*** __________ the fact that the portfolio of science and technology has always been ***(5)*** _________ by the Prime Minister himself.

1.

(a) usher (b) work
(c) solve (d) face
(e) raise

2.

(a) enter (b) come
(c) continue (d) direct
(e) evolve

3.

(a) depth (b) weight
(c) budget (d) policy
(e) importance

4.

(a) for (b) when
(c) above (d) from
(e) to

5.

(a) offered (b) held
(c) charged (d) appointed
(e) regarded

PRACTICE TEST – 2

Human nature has an extraordinary power of ***(1)*** __________. Social and political institutions are ***(2)*** __________ to the same laws of ***(3)*** __________ to which all other things in the world are subject. If we have ***(4)*** __________ in the ***(5)*** __________ of human nature, the healing power of time, the ***(6)*** __________ of social and political institutions and above all the ***(7)*** __________ of the people, the problems which divide us so ***(8)*** __________ today may appear to be purely ***(9)*** _____ after some time.

1.

(a) resistance (b) resilience
(c) patience (d) toleration

2.

(a) set (b) tuned
(c) subject (d) equal

3.

(a) gravitation (b) mutation
(c) acceleration (d) change

4.

(a) confidence (b) belief
(c) trust (d) faith

5.
(a) resilience (b) patience
(c) perseverance (d) toleration

6.
(a) working (b) mutability
(c) flexibility (d) dynamics

7.
(a) generosity (b) magnanimity
(c) goodwill (d) sincerity

8.
(a) foolishly (b) fiercely
(c) acutely (d) powerfully

9.
(a) academic (b) intellectual
(c) unproductive (d) inane

PRACTICE TEST – 3

Perhaps, we Americans do not yet fully understand the great *(1)* __________ that India has to teach in thus *(2)* __________ her freedom. *(3)* __________ her mighty triumph of a *(4)* __________ revolution, our War of Independence *(5)* __________ in size and concept. India has taught humanity a lesson, and it is *(6)* __________ our peril if we do not learn it. The lesson? That war and killing *(7)* __________ nothing *(8)* __________ loss, and that a noble end is assured only if the *(9)* __________ to attain it are of a *(10)* __________ with it and also noble.

1.
(a) message (b) lesson
(c) moral (d) instruction

2.
(a) attaining (b) obtaining
(c) getting (d) winning

3.
(a) beside (b) besides
(c) despite (d) notwithstanding

4.
(a) bloody (b) blood-free
(c) bloodless (d) non-violent

5.
(a) pales (b) shrinks
(c) squeezes (d) reduces

6.
(a) to (b) for
(c) in (d) on

7.
(a) bring (b) get
(c) achieve (d) secure

8.
(a) except (b) beside
(c) besides (d) but

9.
(a) measures (b) means
(c) technique (d) method

10.
(a) piece (b) peace
(c) harmony (d) conformity

PRACTICE TEST – 4

Within the *(1)* __________ we are more friendly to each other than are many *(2)* __________ of animals but in our attitude towards those outside the herd, inspite of all that has been done by moralists and *(3)* __________ teachers, our emotions are as *(4)* __________ as those of any animal, and our *(5)* __________ enables us to give them a scope which is *(6)* __________ to even the most savage beast.

1.
(a) society (b) caste
(c) herd (d) institution

2.
(a) species (b) kinds
(c) types (d) specimens

3.
(a) college (b) school
(c) religious (d) social

4.
(a) uncontrolled (b) hostile
(c) wild (d) ferocious

5.
(a) intellect (b) intelligence
(c) knowledge (d) exuberance

6.
(a) relegated (b) denial
(c) denied (d) conceded

PRACTICE TEST – 5

Science *(1)* __________ the average man and woman in two ways already. He or she benefits by its *(2)* __________, driving in a motor-car or omnibus instead of a horse-drawn *(3)* __________, being treated for disease by a doctor or surgeon rather than a priest or a *(4)* __________, being *(5)* __________ with an automatic pistol or a shell in *(6)* __________ of a danger or battle-axe. It also affects is or her opinions. Almost everyone believes that the earth is *(7)* __________, and the heavens nearly *(8)* __________, instead of solid. And we are beginning to believe in our animal *(9)* ________ and the possibility of vast improvements in *(10)* __________ nature by biological methods.

1.
(a) effects (b) affects
(c) helps (d) alienate

2.
(a) implication (b) applications
(c) use (d) admission

3.
(a) automobile (b) carriage
(c) vehicle (d) cart

4.
(a) quack (b) magician
(c) swindler (d) witch

5.
(a) hacked (b) killed
(c) murdered (d) gagged

6.
(a) lieu (b) spite
(c) place (d) want

7.
(a) flat (b) oval
(c) opaque (d) round

8.
(a) hollow (b) empty
(c) vacant (d) fallow

9.
(a) ancestry (b) progeny
(c) lineage (d) association

10.
(a) humane (b) human
(c) animal (d) basic

PRACTICE TEST – 6

Every society depends on energy *(1)* __________ from one source or another to supply its needs. In the past the energy of beasts and water power from water-mills was used to *(2)* __________ what man could not do alone. Modern society *(3)* __________ above all on heat-based energy. This produces electricity, cooks food and *(4)* __________ motor cars, ships and planes. The *(5)* __________ is oil. Without it the industry would *(6)* __________, standard of living would drop. Oil is no longer so cheap and *(7)* __________ as it was. Existing supplies will not last *(8)* __________. Yet world energy demand goes *(9)* __________ increasing.

1.
(a) got (b) obtained
(c) generated (d) derived

2.
(a) compliment (b) complement
(c) supplement (d) augment

3.
(a) draws (b) bases
(c) depends (d) stands

4.
(a) moves (b) drives
(c) propels (d) pushes

5.
(a) principal (b) principle
(c) only (d) main

6.
(a) ruin (b) collapse
(c) wreck (d) perish

7.
(a) available (b) aplenty
(c) plentiful (d) luxuriant

8.
(a) infinitely (b) indefinitely
(c) eternally (d) always

9.
(a) by (b) from
(c) on (d) none of these

PRACTICE TEST – 7

Human society is a *(1)* __________ growth, an unfoldment in terms of *(2)* __________. If so, it must be based on ever-increasing restraint upon the demands of the *(3)* __________. Thus, marriage must be considered to be a *(4)* __________ imposing discipline upon the *(5)* __________, restricting them to the physical *(6)* __________ only among themselves and for the purpose only of *(7)* __________ when both the partners desire and are prepared *(8)* ________ it.

1.

(a) perennial (b) continual
(c) ceaseless (d) continuing

2.

(a) spirit (b) spiritual
(c) spirituous (d) spirituality

3.

(a) body (b) flesh
(c) sex (d) ego

4.

(a) sacrament (b) contract
(c) contact (d) union

5.

(a) couples (b) partners
(c) set (d) duo

6.

(a) union (b) contact
(c) penetration (d) rapport

7.

(a) creation (b) procreation
(c) multiplication (d) adjustment

8.

(a) in (b) about
(c) for (d) no word

PRACTICE TEST – 8

Books introduce to us the best *(1)* __________; they bring us *(2)* __________ the presence of the greatest *(3)* __________ that have ever live. We hear what they said and did; we see them as if they were *(4)* __________ alive; we share their *(5)* __________; we sympathise with them, *(6)* __________ with them in the scenes which they describe. The great and the good do not *(7)* __________ even in this world.

1.

(a) social (b) society
(c) company (d) atmosphere

2.

(a) before (b) in
(c) into (d) through

3.

(a) man (b) minds
(c) intellect (d) scholars

4.

(a) actually (b) really
(c) decidedly (d) indeed

5.

(a) thoughts (b) ideas
(c) feelings (d) observations

6.

(a) enjoy (b) grieve
(c) exult (d) sorrow

7.

(a) die (b) dye
(c) disappear (d) eclipse

PRACTICE TEST – 9

India is *(1)* __________ the move and the old order passes. Too long have we been *(2)* __________ spectators of events and the *(3)* __________ of others. The *(4)* __________ comes to our people now and we shall make the history of our *(5)* __________. Let us all join in this mighty *(6)* __________ and make India, the *(7)* __________ of our heart, great among nations, foremost in the arts of peace and progress. The door is open and destiny *(8)* __________ to all. There is no question of who wins and who *(9)* __________, for we have to go forward and together as comrades and either all of us win or we all *(10)* ______________ together.

1.

(a) for (b) on
(c) in (d) at

2.

(a) passive (b) silent
(c) detached (d) impartial

3.

(a) toys (b) hireling
(c) playthings (d) subordinates

4.

(a) initiative (b) charge
(c) opportunity (d) offer

5.

(a) desire (b) need
(c) dream (d) choice

6.

(a) work (b) venture
(c) task (d) project

7.
(a) heaven (b) pride
(c) cynosure (d) seat

8.
(a) calls (b) beckons
(c) summons (d) reiterates

9.
(a) loses (b) falls
(c) fails (d) stumbles

10.
(a) fall down (b) lie down
(c) perish (d) go down

PRACTICE TEST – 10

Put all your knowledge, learning and *(1)* _______ in one scale and truth and *(2)* _________ in the other and the *(3)* _________ will by far *(4)* _________ the former. The *(5)* _________ of moral impurity has today spread among our school-going children and like a hidden *(6)* _________ is causing *(7)* _________ among them. I, therefore, appeal to you, boys and girls, to keep your minds and bodies *(8)* _________. All your scholarship, all your study of the *(9)* _________ will be in vain if you fail to translate their teachings *(10)* _________ your daily life.

1.
(a) showmanship (b) thoughts
(c) scholarship (d) experiences

2.
(a) honesty (b) purity
(c) sincerity (d) falsehood

3.
(a) later (b) latter
(c) least (d) last

4.
(a) outweigh (b) outsmart
(c) outsource (d) outshine

5.
(a) evil (b) filth
(c) virus (d) stink

6.
(a) epidemic (b) disease
(c) cancer (d) pestilence

7.
(a) harm (b) vengeance
(c) havoc (d) discord

8.
(a) free (b) pious
(c) pure (d) healthy

9.
(a) Bible (b) Ramayan
(c) arts (d) scriptures

10.
(a) in (b) into
(c) on (d) for

PRACTICE TEST – 11

In *(1)* _________ life there is always a feeling of want. It is this which makes man *(2)* _________. Man *(3)* _________ for things which he cannot get and feels sad looking *(4)* _________ upon the past, and looking forward *(5)* _________ future. This *(6)* _________ with the past and future does not allow man to live *(7)* _________ in the present. Thus, there is always a pain in man's *(8)* _________ always a sense of *(9)* _________ in the moment of enjoyments. That is why the best poetry of man is the poetry of *(10)* ___________. 'Our sweetest songs are those that tell of *(11)* ___________ thoughts', has been rightly said.

1.
(a) man's (b) our
(c) human (d) humane

2.
(a) sad (b) disappointed
(c) unhappy (d) mundane

3.
(a) looks (b) pines
(c) hankers (d) aspires

4.
(a) on (b) for
(c) back (d) No word

5.
(a) into (b) to
(c) the (d) for

6.
(a) preoccupation (b) engagement
(c) connection (d) relation

7.
(a) carelessly (b) blissfully
(c) happily (d) honourably

8.

(a) laugh (b) smile
(c) laughter (d) heart

9.

(a) want (b) loss
(c) fulfilment (d) scarcity

10.

(a) pain (b) dejection
(c) sorrow (d) joy

11.

(a) saddest (b) loftiest
(c) happiest (d) sorrowful

PRACTICE TEST – 12

In life there are no ***(1)*** __________ without pains. Life indeed would be ***(2)*** __________ if there ***(3)*** __________ no difficulties. Games lose their ***(4)*** __________ if there is no real ***(5)*** __________, if the result is a ***(6)*** __________ conclusion. Both ***(7)*** __________ and loser enjoy a game most if it is closely ***(8)*** __________ to the last. No victory is a real triumph unless the ***(9)*** __________ is worthy of the ***(10)*** __________. Whether we like it or not, life is one ***(11)*** __________ competitive examination.

1.

(a) earning (b) profit
(c) gains (d) relief

2.

(a) dull (b) stale
(c) colourless (d) cheerful

3.

(a) is (b) are
(c) was (d) were

4.

(a) zest (b) enthusiasm
(c) charm (d) attraction

5.

(a) fight (b) contest
(c) struggle (d) obstacle

6.

(a) known (b) foregone
(c) expected (d) predictable

7.

(a) victor (b) victorious
(c) winner (d) gainer

8.

(a) fought (b) contested
(c) watched (d) balanced

9.

(a) rival (b) adversary
(c) foe (d) enemy

10.

(a) prize (b) steal
(c) steel (d) contest

11.

(a) regular (b) continuous
(c) continual (d) severe

PRACTICE TEST – 13

It is not good for man that his life should be all joy and ***(1)*** __________. The lands which only know sunshine and never rain become ***(2)*** __________. The most beautiful countries are those which are ***(3)*** __________ visited by both sunshine and rain. It is in these lands that ***(4)*** __________ and fruits grow and sweet birds sing. There is nothing more beautiful than a ***(5)*** __________. If life is to be rounded and many-coloured ***(6)*** __________ the rainbow, both joy and sorrow must come to it. Those who have never known ***(7)*** __________ but prosperity and pleasure become hard and ***(8)*** __________ but those whose prosperity has been mixed with ***(9)*** __________ become kind and ***(10)*** __________.

1.

(a) adversity (b) pain
(c) prosperity (d) sorrow

2.

(a) deserts (b) garbage
(c) marshy (d) fallow

3.

(a) regularly (b) interminably
(c) occasionally (d) fairly

4.

(a) flowers (b) hedges
(c) vegetables (d) bowers

5.

(a) sky (b) flower
(c) rainbow (d) rain

6.

(a) like (b) so

(c) as (d) by

7.

(a) nothing (b) something
(c) anything (d) no word

8.

(a) cruel (b) harsh
(c) shallow (d) stern

9.

(a) adversity (b) hardship
(c) poverty (d) tragedy

10.

(a) gracious (b) meek
(c) gentle (d) generous

PRACTICE TEST – 14

Civilisation, like ***(1)*** __________, fall, not so much because of the ***(2)*** __________ of the enemy outside, as through the weaknesses and ***(3)*** __________ within. Rome fell not because of the ***(4)*** __________; they merely knocked ***(5)*** __________ something that was already dead. The heart of Rome had ***(6)*** __________ beating when the arms and legs were cut ***(7)*** __________. We see something of this ***(8)*** __________ in India and China and in the case of the Arabs. The ***(9)*** __________ of Arabian Civilisation was sudden even as their rise had been. In India and China, the process is long-drawn ***(10)*** __________ and it is not easy to ***(11)*** __________ it.

1.

(a) states (b) kingdom
(c) empires (d) buildings

2.

(a) weakness (b) strength
(c) power (d) tenacity

3.

(a) disease (b) decease
(c) decay (d) fortitude

4.

(a) barbarity (b) barbarous
(c) barbarians (d) Romans

5.

(a) off (b) on
(c) down (d) no word

6.

(a) seized (b) rotated
(c) ceased (d) started

7.

(a) down (b) off
(c) up (d) no word

8.

(a) process (b) procedure
(c) spectacle (d) scene

9.

(a) downfall (b) death
(c) collapse (d) dismemberment

10.

(a) out (b) up
(c) upon (d) no word

11.

(a) find (b) single
(c) spot (d) pick

PRACTICE TEST – 15

It is not luck but ***(1)*** __________ that makes men. Luck, says an American writer, is ever waiting for something to turn ***(2)*** __________; labour with keen eye and strong ***(3)*** __________ always turns up something. Luck lies in bed and wishes the postman would bring him news of a ***(4)*** __________; labour turns out at six and with busy pen and ***(5)*** __________ hammer lays the foundation of a ***(6)*** __________. Luck relies on chance; labour on ***(7)*** __________. Luck slips downwards to ***(8)*** __________; labour ***(9)*** __________ upwards and aspires ***(10)*** __________independence. The conviction, therefore, is extending that diligence is the ***(11)*** ______ of good luck; in other words, that a man's success in life will be ***(12)*** __________ to his efforts, to his industry, to his attention to small things.

1.

(a) work (b) diligence
(c) labour (d) experience

2.

(a) on (b) up
(c) down (d) off

3.

(a) will (b) power
(c) resourcefulness (d) grit

4.

(a) windfall (b) treasure
(c) legacy (d) wealth

5.
(a) swinging (b) ringing
(c) moving (d) powerful

6.
(a) competence (b) knowledge
(c) skill (d) learning

7.
(a) work-culture (b) character
(c) honesty (d) integrity

8.
(a) self-indulgence (b) self-effacement
(c) selfishness (d) self-gratification

9.
(a) jumps (b) strides
(c) climbs (d) ascends

10.
(a) after (b) for
(c) to (d) on

11.
(a) progeny (b) father
(c) offspring (d) mother

12.
(a) equal (b) proportionate
(c) subject (d) match

ANSWERS – CLOZE TEST – (PRACTICE TESTS)

Q. No.	P.TEST – 1	P.TEST – 2	P.TEST – 3	P.TEST – 4	P.TEST – 5
1.	solve	resilience	lesson	herd	affects
2.	enter	subject	winning	species	applications
3.	importance	mutation	Beside	religious	vehicle
4.	from	faith	bloodless	ferocious	witch
5.	held	resilience	pales	intelligence	killed
6.		mutability	to	denied	place
7.		goodwill	achieve		round
8.		fiercely	but		hollow
9.		inane	means		ancestry
10.			peace		animal

Q. No.	P.TEST – 6	P.TEST – 7	P.TEST – 8	P.TEST – 9	P.TEST – 10
1.	derived	ceaseless	society	on	scholarship
2.	supplement	spirituality	into	passive	purity
3.	depends	A body	minds	playthings	latter
4.	propels	sacrament	rally	opportunity	outweigh
5.	principal	partners	thoughts	choice	virus
6.	collapse	contact	grieve	task	epidemic
7.	plentiful	procreation	die	pride	havoc
8.	indefinitely	for		beckons	pure
9.	on			loses	scriptures
10.				go down	into

Q. No.	P.TEST – 11	P.TEST – 12	P.TEST – 13	P.TEST – 14	P.TEST – 15
1.	human	gains	prosperity	empires	labour
2.	unhappy	dull	deserts	strength	up
3.	pines	were	regularly	decay	will
4.	back	charm	flowers	barbarians	windfall
5.	into	contest	rainbow	down	powerful
6.	engagement	predictable	like	ceased	competence
7.	happily	winner	anything	off	character
8.	heart	contested	shallow	process	self-indulgence
9.	want	adversary	adversity	collapse	strides
10.	sorrow	steel	gracious	out	for
11.	saddest	continuous		spot	mother
12.					proportionate

PART D:
COMPREHENSION (16 PTs)

COMPREHENSION

What is Comprehension?

Comprehension means 'understanding'. Not a superficial understanding but an understanding in depth with all the ramifications of thoughts (both expressed and implied). Sometimes thoughts are so embedded in the cobweb of words that it becomes rather difficult to follow, at first glance, the drift of thought. An average student may read the passage and yet fail to grasp the main ideas. Mere skimming over the surface is not of much help. For language is the art of concealing thought. A proper understanding of the given passage, therefore, requires, among other things, a fairly good command over English, a keen power of observation, a quick understanding of the central idea, a knack to detect error in logic, a quick reading habit, a sufficient stock of words and a little bit of imagination.

Method of Comprehension

- Read the given passage with purpose and imagination. A careful reading will help you enter into the spirit of the passage.
- Read the passage once again, concentrating on the drift of thought. Notice the key words and see how the passage is developed.
- Read with an open mind, with purposeful concentrated attention even if the topic is new or not to your liking.
- Read all the questions carefully lest you should miss the spirit of any question.
- When you have read all the questions, read through the passage, bearing the questions in mind.
- Answer the questions methodically, one by one. If you are bogged down by a particular question, don't waste your time over it. Switch over to another question, leaving the space for questions unanswered. Sometimes the question that appears tricky at first attempt becomes easier as you answer other questions.

31 COMPREHENSION

16 PRACTICE TESTS

Directions: *The questions in this section are based on what is stated or implied in the passages given below. For each question, choose the option that most accurately and completely answers the question.*

COMPREHENSION

PRACTICE TEST – 1

The words invention and innovation are closely linked, but they are not interchangeable. The inventor is a genius who uses his intellect, imagination, time and resources to create something that does not exist. But this invention may or may not be of utility to the masses. It is the enterprising innovator who uses various resources, skills and time to make the invention available for use. The innovator might use the invention as it is, modify it or even blend two or more inventions to make one marketable product. A great example is that of the iPhone which is a combination of various inventions.

If an invention is the result of countless trials and errors, so can be the case with an innovation. Not every attempt to make an invention is successful. Not every innovation sees the light of day. Benjamin Franklin had the belief that success doesn't come without challenge, mistake, and in a few cases failure.

One of the world's most famous innovators, Steve Jobs says, 'Sometimes when you innovate, you make mistakes. It is best to admit them quickly and get on with improving your other innovations'.

Thus, inventors and innovators have to be intrepid enough to take risks; consider failures as stepping stones and not stumbling blocks.

Some inventions are the result of a keen observation or a simple discovery. The inventor of Velcro, also called the zipless zipper, is the Swiss engineer George de Mestral. He was hiking in the woods when he found burrs clinging to his clothes and his dog's fur. Back at home, he studied the burrs. He discovered that each burr was a collection of tiny hooks which made it cling on to another object. A few years later, he made and patented the strips of fabric that came to us as Velcro.

The world of inventions and innovations is a competitive one. But the race does not end here; it is also prevalent in the case of getting intellectual property rights. There have been inventors who failed to get a single patent while there have been some who managed to amass numerous patents in their lifetime. Thomas Edison had 1,093 patents to his credit!

We relate the telephone with Alexander Graham Bell. It is believed that around the same time, Antonio Meucci had also designed the telephone, but due to lack of resources and various hardships, he could not proceed with the patent of his invention. It is also believed that Elisha Gray had made a design for the telephone and applied for the patent at the U.S. patent office on the same day as Graham Bell did. By sheer chance, Graham's lawyer's turn to file the papers came first. Hence, Graham was granted the first patent for the telephone.

It is not easy, and at times almost impossible, for an inventor to be an innovator too. There are very few like Thomas Edison who graduated from being an incredible inventor to a successful manufacturer and businessman with brilliant marketing skills.

While innovations that have helped to enhance the quality of life are laudable, equally laudable are the inventions that laid the foundation of these very innovations.

Q 1. The text in the passage can be best termed as
(a) narrative (b) descriptive
(c) persuasive (d) expository

Q 2. The main idea of the author is to
(a) highlight the difficulties faced by innovators
(b) focus on the hardships of patent-seekers
(c) compare innovators to inventors
(d) reveal the importance of inventors

Q 3. The author believes that
(a) innovators enhance the utility of inventions
(b) innovators face fewer challenges than inventors do
(c) every inventor has a patent for the invention
(d) invention is the same as innovation

Q 4. Benjamin Franklin and Steve Jobs, believe that
(a) there is no place for mistakes in the process of making an innovation
(b) making a mistake before finding success is not unusual
(c) failure is a permanent stumbling block
(d) all innovators have to go through failure

Q 5. Velcro can be best described as
(a) a highly-planned and deeply researched invention
(b) the fruit of failure
(c) the need of the hour
(d) an accidental invention

Q 6. It is believed that Graham Bell became the first patent holder of the telephone because of
(a) his ingenuity and good fortune
(b) the carelessness of Elisha's lawyer
(c) the clever trick played by his lawyer
(d) the biased officials in the patent office

Q 7. Which of the following is Untrue?
(a) Inventors may not be innovators
(b) Innovators are not expected to be enterprising
(c) To get a patent, the applicant has to follow a legal process
(d) Intellectual property rights are not always easy to get

Q 8. Which of the following texts from the passage clearly indicates failure?
(a) The world of inventions and innovations is a competitive one
(b) Not every innovation sees the light of day
(c) Thus, inventors and innovators have to be intrepid enough to take risks
(d) None of the above

Q 9. Which of these words can replace the word intrepid?
(a) hasty (b) intellectual
(c) daring (d) rich

Q 10. Which of these words is the antonym of laudable?
(a) praiseworthy (b) challenging
(c) tiring (d) disgraceful

COMPREHENSION

PRACTICE TEST – 2

IOT has had an impact across all fields, be it industries, government, small or large businesses and even for Personal Consumption.

What is IOT (Internet of things) you might ask. It's been a growing topic of conversation for some time now. Put in the simplest term it means anything that has an on and off button and is connected to the internet for receiving, analysing, storing or sending data. This could mean anything, from the watch that you wear to airplanes that can be controlled from a remote location. According to the analyst firm Gartner, by the year 2020 we'll have over 26 billion connected devices. That could mean people to people, people connected to things and things connected to things. The new rule of the future is going to be 'Anything that can be connected will be connected'. Take for example that when you set an alarm to wake up and that alarm goes off, it not only wakes you up but also brews your coffee, sets the right temperature of water for your bath, puts on the television to bring you the latest updates from around the globe and all this before you even put a foot out of your bed. This is all done by simply getting the network of interconnected things/devices that have embedded sensors, network connectivity, software and necessary electronics that collect and exchange data. To show how far we have come with technology and connectivity, we have smart watches such as Fitbit, Garmin to name a few that have changed the way we look at time. We have one device that not only tells us the time but also tracks the number of steps, calories and our heart rate. This watch is actually connected to our phone so with just one turn of the wrist one can tell who is calling or what messages have been received without having to dig through pockets or handbags.

IOT is making its presence felt in health care as well. Doctors can now remotely monitor and communicate with their patients, and health care providers can benefit from this. Whether data comes from foetal monitors, electrocardiograms, temperature monitors or blood glucose levels, tracking this information is vital for some patients. Many of this requires follow-up interaction with healthcare professionals. With smarter devices that deliver more valuable data, it can reduce the need for direct patient- physician interaction.

Take for instance in the sporting field, minute chips are being attached to balls and bats which will transmit information of how fast the ball is travelling and a batsman's moves, the time, the angles, the pressure on the bat at different positions, data of the muscle stretch if he's hit a six, so on and so forth. Formula one cars are also being fitted with these sensors which relays information on the minute moves being made by the driver. Chips are also being put into wearable devices of sportsmen to detect sub-optimal action of any body parts to show signs of stress or strain which will help in the early detection of injuries and take preventive measures.

IOT has had an impact across all fields, be it industries, government, small or large business and even for personal consumption. IBM, Google, Intel, Microsoft and Cisco are some of the top players in the IOT spectrum.

With billions of devices connected, security becomes a big issue. How can people make sure that their data is safe and secure? This is one of the major concerns in the IOT that becomes a hot topic. Another issue is with all these billions of devices sharing data, companies will be faced with the problem of how to store, track, analyse and make vast sense of the information being generated. Companies are monitoring the network segment to identify anomalous traffic and to take action if necessary.

Now that we have a fair understanding of IOT let's see what impact it's had on the education sector. The only constant in our lives is change and learning. From the get go we learn, be it to walk, talk or run. We adapt to the changing times and constantly learn from it. Education or learning as we know it in the broader sense is the most important of all and the one that decides which way we handle those changes to impact us and the world.

Today's world is fast paced and to keep up with this we need an infusion of speed with learning. From the classroom assignments, lectures, blackboards and chalk we have come a long way to what is now known as e-learning (electronic learning) or m-learning (mobile learning). With the GenNext, it is imperative to provide the right kind of education.

The rise of technology and IOT allows schools to improve the safety of their campuses, keep track of resources and enhance access to information. It ensures data quality being the top priority but also facilitates development of content allowing teachers to use this technology to create smart lesson plans and ensuring the reach of this content to any corner of the world.

Q 1. How is IOT a concept of connecting?
- (a) It is the internet in a different form
- (b) It is the internet but connected to anything
- (c) It is an analysing machine
- (d) It is a data collection term

Q 2. It is said that we look at time differently now, why?
- (a) It is connected to different devices
- (b) It is in a different format
- (c) It is connected to the aeroplane
- (d) It connects people

Q 3. IOT will help in simplifying patient-physician interaction because
- (a) It helps reduce data
- (b) Doctors can remotely connect to patients
- (c) It improves connectivity
- (d) It is a simple process

Q 4. How will IOT work in the sporting field?
- (a) Through sport fields with chips
- (b) Through a special machine
- (c) Through minute wearable chips which are connected
- (d) Through special moves by the sportsmen

Q 5. Preventive measure is imperative because
- (a) It can detect anything
- (b) It identifies treatment needed
- (c) It keeps them in touch
- (d) It helps to identify stress and strain

Q 6. One of the major concerns of IOT is
- (a) Security and privacy, data loss and tracking data
- (b) Only security and privacy
- (c) Only data loss
- (d) Only tracking data

Q 7. Technology and IOT has benefited education considerably because it has
(a) Helped in improving the lesson
(b) Helped keep track of all resources
(c) Helped teachers to track
(d) Helped with keeping up with the change in learning

Q 8. Teachers can use this data
(a) Only to teach with more resources
(b) Only to create a smart classroom
(c) Only to reach out to the world
(d) To teach with more resources, create a smart classroom and reach out to the world

Q 9. Select a title that is most suitable for the passage
(a) IOT curse or boon
(b) IOT and our life tomorrow
(c) IOT is changing the way we learn
(d) IOT is all pervading

Q 10. To conclude, IOT has an impact on
(a) Education, sports, medicine and our daily lives
(b) Education and sports only
(c) Education only
(d) Education and medicine only

COMPREHENSION

PRACTICE TEST – 3

The World Trade Organisation (WTO) was created in the early 1990s as a component of the Uruguay Round negotiation. However, it could have been negotiated as part of the Tokyo Round of the 1970s, since negotiation was an attempt at a 'constitutional reform' of the General Agreement on Tariffs and Trade (GATT). Or it could have been put off to the future, as the US government wanted. What factors led to the creation of the WTO in the early 1990s? One factor was the pattern of multilateral bargaining that developed late in the Uruguay Round. Like all complex international agreements, the WTO was a product of a series of trade-offs between principal actors and groups. For the United States, which did not want a new organisation, the disputed settlement part of the WTO package achieved its longstanding goal of a more effective and more legal dispute settlement system. For the Europeans, who by the 1990s had come to view GATT dispute settlement less in political terms and more as a regime of legal obligations, the WTO package was acceptable as a means to discipline the resort to unilateral measures by the United States. Countries like Canada and other middle and smaller trading partners were attracted by the expansion of a rule-based system and by the symbolic value of a trade organisation, both of which inherently support the weak against the strong. The developing countries were attracted due to the provisions banning unilateral measures. Finally, and perhaps most important, many countries at the Uruguay Round came to put a higher priority on the export gains than on the import losses that the negotiation would produce, and they came to associate the WTO and a rule-based system with those gains. This reasoning – replicated in many countries – was contained in U.S. Ambassador Kantor's defence of the WTO, and it announced to recognise that international trade and its benefits cannot be enjoyed unless trading nations accept the discipline of a negotiated rule-based environment. A second factor in the creation of the WTO was pressure from lawyers and the legal process. The dispute settlement system of the WTO was seen as a victory of legalists but the matter went deeper than that. The GATT, and the WTO are contract organisations based on rules, and it is inevitable that an organisation creating a further rule will in turn be influenced by legal process. Robert Hudee has written of the 'momentum of legal development', but what is this precisely? Legal development can be defined as promotion of the technical legal values of consistency, clarity (or certainty) and effectiveness; these are values that those responsible for administering any legal system will seek to maximise. As it played out in the WTO, consistency meant integrating under one roof, the whole lot of separate agreements signed under GATT auspices; clarity meant removing ambiguities about the powers of contracting parties to make certain decisions or to undertake waivers; and effectiveness meant eliminating exceptions arising out of grandfather-rights and resolving defects in dispute settlement procedures and institutional provisions. Concern for these values is inherent in any rule-based system of co-operation, since without these, value rules would be meaningless in the first place, therefore, create their own incentive for fulfilment. The moment of legal development has occurred in other institutions besides the GATT, most notably in the European Union (EU). Over the past two decades the European Court of Justice (ECJ) has consistently rendered decisions that have expanded incrementally the EU's internal market, in which the doctrine of 'mutual recognition' handed down in Cassis de Dijon case in 1979 was a key turning point. The court is now widely recognised as a major player in European integration, even though arguably such a strong role was not originally envisaged in the Treaty of Rome, which initiated the current European Union. One means the court used to expand integration was the 'teleological method of interpretation', whereby the actions of member states were evaluated against the accomplishment of the most elementary goals set forth in the Preamble to the (Rome) treaty. The teleological method represents an effort to keep current policies consistent with slated goals, and it is analogous to the effort in GATT to keep contracting party trade practices consistent with slated rules. In both cases legal concerns and procedures are an independent force for further co-operation.

In the large part, the WTO was an exercise in consolidation. In the context of a trade negotiation that created a near-revolutionary expansion of international trade rules, the formation of the WTO was a deeply conservative act needed to ensure that the benefits of the new rules would not be lost. The WTO was all about institutional structure and dispute settlement: these are the concerns of conservatives and not revolutionaries, that is why lawyers and legalists took the lead on these issues. The WTO codified the GATT institutional practice that had developed by custom over three decades, and it incorporated a new dispute settlement system that was necessary to keep both old and new rules from becoming a sham. Both the international structure and the dispute settlement system were necessary to preserve and enhance the integrity of the multilateral trade regime that had been built incrementally from the 1940s to the 1990s.

Q 1. In the statement '... it amounted to a recognition that international trade and its benefits cannot be enjoyed unless trading nations accept the discipline of a negotiated rule-based environment', it refers to

(a) The export gains many countries came to associate with a rule-based system
(b) The higher priority on export gains placed by many countries at the Uruguay Round
(c) The provision of a rule-based system by the WTO
(d) Ambassador Kantor's defence of the WTO

Q 2. What would be the closest reason why WTO was not formed in 1970s?

(a) The US government did not like it
(b) Important players did not find it in their best interest to do so
(c) Lawyers did not work for the dispute settlement system
(d) The Tokyo Round negotiations was an attempt at constitutional reform

Q 3. In the method of interpretation of the European Court of Justice

(a) Actions against member states needed to be evaluated against the said community goals
(b) Enunciation of the most elementary community goals needed to be emphasised
(c) Current policies need to be consistent with stated goals
(d) Contracting party trade practices need to be consistent with stated rules

Q 4. According to the passage, WTO promoted the technical legal values partly through

(a) Integrating under one roof the agreements signed under GATT
(b) Rules that create their own incentive for fulfillment
(c) Ambiguities about the powers of contracting parties to make certain decisions
(d) Grandfather-rights exceptions and defects in dispute settlement procedures

Q 5. The most likely reason for the acceptance of the WTO package by nations was that

(a) It has the means to prevent the US from taking unilateral measures
(b) Its rule-based system leads to export gains
(c) It settles disputes more legally and more effectively
(d) They recognised the need for a rule-based environment to protect the benefits of increased trade

COMPREHENSION

PRACTICE TEST – 4

1. Often, we passionately pursue matters that in the future appear to be contradictory to our real intention or nature; and triumph is followed by remorse or regret. There are numerous examples of such a trend in the annals of history and contemporary life.

2. Alfred Nobel was the son of Immanuel Nobel, an inventor who experimented extensively with explosives. Alfred too carried out research and experiments with a large range of chemicals; he found new methods to blast rocks for the construction of roads and bridges; he was engaged in the development of technology and different weapons; his life revolved around rockets and cannons and gun powder. The ingenuity of the scientist brought him enough wealth to buy the Bofors armament plant in Sweden.

3. Paradoxically, Nobel's life was a busy one yet he was lonely and as he grew older, he began suffering from guilt of having invented the dynamite that was being used for destructive purposes. He set aside a huge part of his wealth to institute Nobel Prizes. Besides honouring men and women for their extraordinary achievements in physics, chemistry, medicine and literature, he wished to honour people who worked for the promotion of peace.

4. It's strange that the very man whose name was closely connected with explosives and inventions that helped in waging wars willed a large part of his earnings for the people who work for the promotion of peace and the benefit of mankind. The Nobel Peace Prize is intended for a person who has accomplished the best work for fraternity among nations, for abolition or reduction of war and for promotion of peace.

5. Another example that comes to one's mind is that of Albert Einstein. In 1939, fearing that the Nazis would win the race to build the world's first atomic bomb, Einstein urged President Franklin D Roosevelt to launch an American programme on nuclear research. The matter was considered and a project called the Manhattan Project was initiated. The project involved intense nuclear research the construction of the world's first atomic bomb. All this while, Einstein had the impression that the bomb would be used to protect the world from the Nazis. But in 1945, when Hiroshima was bombed to end World War II, Einstein was deeply grieved and he regretted his endorsement of the need for nuclear research.

6. He also stated that had he known that the Germans would be unsuccessful in making the atomic bomb, he would have probably never recommended making one. In 1947, Einstein began working for the cause of disarmament. But, Einstein's name still continues to be linked with the bomb. Man's fluctuating thoughts, changing opinions, varying opportunities keep the mind in a state of flux. Hence, the paradox of life, it's certain that nothing is certain in life.

Q 1. The Manhattan Project was initiated ______.
(a) in honour of Einstein
(b) to protect the Nazis
(c) to bomb Hiroshima
(d) to carry out nuclear research

Q 2. Alfred established the Nobel Prizes to ______.
(a) remind people of his achievements
(b) ease his guilt and promote work for the betterment of mankind
(c) use his wealth for hard working people
(d) honor only those people who are intelligent

Q 3. In paragraph 4, the word 'accomplished' means _________.
(a) completed successfully
(b) worked hard
(c) won awards
(d) made an effort to do something

Q 4. In the fifth paragraph, the word 'endorsement' means:
(a) Expressing one's opposition
(b) Expressing one's approval or support
(c) Making a promise to do something
(d) Expressing one's regret

Q 5. Working with arms and ammunition helped Alfred to amass _______.
(a) enemies
(b) intelligence
(c) wealth
(d) popularity

Q 6. Immanuel's interest in dynamites influenced Alfred's inclination for working ___________.
(a) for humanity
(b) with explosives
(c) for the Nobel Peace Prize
(d) with contradiction

Q 7. One of the paradoxes in Alfred's life was that he was ___________.
(a) lonely yet rich
(b) hard working but a failure
(c) intelligent yet lonely
(d) occupied yet lonely

Q 8. Einstein had the impression that the Germans would __________.
(a) bomb Hiroshima
(b) be successful in making the world's first atomic bomb
(c) be unsuccessful in making the atomic bomb
(d) work for humanity

Q 9. The passage is ____________.
(a) an argumentative essay
(b) an expository essay
(c) a process essay
(d) a descriptive essay

Q 10. The paradox, 'it's certain that nothing is certain in life', indicates the writer's
(a) Hatred for scientists
(b) Analytical mind
(c) Scientific mind
(d) Persuasive nature

COMPREHENSION

PRACTICE TEST – 5

When talks come to how India has done for itself in 50 years of Independence, the world has nothing but praise for our success in remaining a democracy. On the other front, applause is less loud in absolute terms, India has not done too badly, of course, life expectancy has increased, so has literacy. Industry, which was barely a fledgling, has grown tremendously. And as far as agriculture is concerned, India has been transformed from a country perpetually on the edge of starvation into a success story held up for others to emulate. But these are competitive times when changes are rapid, and to walk slowly when the rest of the world is running is almost as bad as standing still or walking backwards.

Compared with large chunks of what was then the developing world South Korea, Singapore, Malaysia, Thailand, Indonesia, China and what was till lately a separate Hong Kong - India has fared abysmally. It began with a far better infrastructure than most of these countries had it suffered hardly or not at all during the Second World War. It had advantage like an English speaking elite, quality scientific manpower (including a Nobel laureate and others who could be ranked among the world's best) and excellent business acumen. Yet, today, when countries are ranked according to their global competitiveness, it is tiny Singapore that figures at the top. Hong Kong is an export powerhouse, so is Taiwan. If a symbol were needed to know how far we have fallen back, note that while Korean Cielos are sold in India, no one in South Korea is rushing to buy an Indian car. The reasons list themselves. Topmost is economic isolationism.

The government discouraged imports and encouraged self-sufficiency. Whatever the aim was, the result was the creation of a totally inefficient industry that failed to keep pace with global trends and, therefore, became absolutely uncompetitive. Only when the trade gates were opened a little did this become apparent. The years since then have been spent in merely trying to catch up. That the government actually sheltered its industrialists from foreign competition is a little strange. For in all other respects, it operated under the conviction that businessmen were little more than crooks who were to be prevented from entering the most important areas of the economy, who were to be hamstrung in as many ways as possible, who were to be tolerated in the same way as an in excisable wart. The high expropriatory rates taxation, the licensing laws, the reservation of whole swathes of industry for the public sector, and the granting of monopolies to the public sector firms were the principal manifestations of this attitude. The government forgot that before wealth could be distributed, it had to be created.

The government forgot it itself could not create, but only squander wealth. Some of the manifestations of the old attitude have changed. Tax rates have fallen. Licensing has been all but abolished. And the gates of global trade have been opened wide. But most of these changes were first by circumstances, partly by the foreign exchange bankruptcy of 1991 and the recognition that the government could no longer muster the funds to support the public sector, leave alone expand it. Whether the attitude of the government itself, or that of more than a handful of ministers, has changed one with. Business still has to negotiate a welter of negotiations. Transparency is still a long way off. And there is no exit policy. In defending the existing policy, politicians betray an inability to see beyond their noses. A no-exit policy for labour is equivalent to a no-entry policy for new business. If one industry is not allowed to retrench labour, other industries will think a hundred times before employing new labour. In other ways too, the government hurts industries.

Public sector monopolies like the Department of Telecommunication and Videsh Sanchar Nigam Ltd., make it possible for Indian business to operate only at a cost several times than that of their counterparts abroad. The infrastructure is in shambles partly because it is unable to formulate a sufficiently remunerative policy for private business, and partly because it does not have the stomach to change market rates for services. After a burst of activity in the early nineties, the government is dragging its feet. At the rate it is going, it will be another fifty years before the government realises that a pro-business policy is the best pro-people policy. By then of course, the world would have moved even farther ahead.

Q 1. The writer's attitude towards the Government is _______
- (a) critical
- (b) ironical
- (c) sarcastic
- (d) derisive

Q 2. The writer is surprised at the Government's attitude towards its industrialists because_______
- (a) the government did not need to protect its industries
- (b) the issue of competition was non-existent
- (c) the government looked upon its industrialists as crooks
- (d) the attitude was a conundrum

Q 3. The Government was compelled to open the economy due to _______
- (a) pressure from international market
- (b) pressure from domestic market
- (c) foreign exchange bankruptcy and paucity of funds with the government
- (d) All of the above

Q 4. The writer ends the passage on a note of _______
- (a) cautious optimism
- (b) pessimism
- (c) optimism
- (d) pragmatism

Q 5. According to the writer, India should have performed better than the other Asian nations because _______
- (a) it had adequate infrastructure
- (b) it had better infrastructure
- (c) it had better politicians who could take the required decisions
- (d) All of the above

Q 6. India was in a better condition than the other Asian nations because _______
- (a) it did not face the ravages of the Second World War
- (b) it had an English speaking populace and a good business sense
- (c) it had enough wealth through its exports
- (d) Both (a) and (b) above

Q 7. The major reason for India's poor performance is______
- (a) economic isolationism
- (b) economic mismanagement
- (c) inefficient industry
- (d) All of these

Q 8. One of the factors of the government's projectionist policy was _______
- (a) encouragement of imports
- (b) discouragement of imports
- (c) encouragement of exports
- (d) discouragement of exports

Q 9. The example of the Korean Cielo has been presented to highlight _______
- (a) India's lack of stature in the international market
- (b) India's poor performance in the international market
- (c) India's lack of credibility in the international market
- (d) India's disrepute in the international market

Q 10. According to the writer _______
- (a) India's politicians are myopic in their vision of the country's requirements
- (b) India's politicians are busy lining their pockets
- (c) India's politicians are not conversant with the needs of the present scenario
- (d) All of the above

COMPREHENSION

PRACTICE TEST – 6

The spread of education in society is at the foundation of success in countries that are latecomers to development. In the quest for development, primary education is absolutely essential because it creates the base. But higher education is just as important, for it provides the cutting edge. And universities are the life-blood of higher education. Islands of excellence in professional education, such as Indian Institutes of Technology (IITs) and Indian Institutes of Management (IIMs), are valuable complements but cannot be substitutes for universities which provide educational opportunities for people at large.

There can be no doubt that higher education has made a significant contribution to economic development, social progress and political democracy in independent India. It is a source of dynamism for the economy. It has created social opportunities for people. It has fostered the vibrant democracy in our polity. It has provided a beginning for the creation of a knowledge society. But it would be a mistake to focus on its strengths alone. It has weaknesses that are a cause for serious concern.

There is, in fact, a quiet crisis in higher education in India that runs deep. It is not yet discernible simply because there are pockets of excellence, an enormous reservoir of talented young people and an intense competition in the admission process. And, in some important spheres, we continue to reap the benefits of what was sown in higher education 50 years ago by the founding fathers of the Republic. The reality is that we have miles to go. The proportion of our population, in the age group 18–24 that enters the world of higher education is around 7 per cent, which is only one-half the average for Asia. The opportunities for higher education, in terms of the number of places in universities, are simply not enough in relation to our needs. What is more, the quality of higher education in most of our universities requires substantial improvement.

It is clear that the system of higher education in India faces serious challenges. It needs a systematic overhaul, so that we can educate much larger numbers without diluting academic standards. This is imperative because the transformation of economy and society in the 21st century would depend, in significant part, on the spread and the quality of education among our people, particularly in the sphere of higher education. It is only an inclusive society that can provide the foundations for a knowledge society.

The challenges that confront higher education in India are clear. It needs a massive expansion of opportunities for higher education, to 1500 universities nationwide, that would enable India to attain a gross enrolment ratio of at least 15 per cent by 2015. It is just as important to raise the average quality of higher education in every sphere. At the same time, it is essential to create institutions that are exemplars of excellence at par with the best in the world. In the pursuit of these objectives, providing people with access to higher education in a socially inclusive manner is imperative. The realisation of these objectives, combined with access, would not only develop the skills and capabilities we need for the economy but would also help transform India as a knowledge economy and society.

Q 1. The principal focus of the passage is
(a) Primary education
(b) Intermediate education
(c) Higher education
(d) Entire education system

Q 2. The style of the passage can be best described as
(a) Academic
(b) Critical and analytical
(c) Comparative
(d) None of the above

Q 3. What kind of society can provide the foundation for a knowledge society?
(a) Elite society
(b) Contracted society
(c) Exclusive society
(d) Inclusive society

Q 4. According to the passage, which of the following is INCORRECT?
(a) There arc no quality institutes providing excellent professional education in India
(b) Not many people go for higher education in India
(c) Education is the basis of success
(d) All the above options are correct

Q 5. According to the passage, the current state of affairs of higher education in India is
(a) Satisfactory
(b) Excellent, and there is no need of any expansion of opportunities for higher education
(c) Not good enough, and there is a need for expansion of opportunities for higher education, besides creating institutions and universities that are models of excellence
(d) Not explained in the passage

Q 6. According to the passage, which of the following is NOT a challenge that confronts higher education in India?
(a) Expanding opportunities for higher education
(b) Creating institutions and universities that are exemplars of excellence
(c) Substantial improvement in the quality of higher education in most of our universities
(d) Getting into World University Rankings

Q 7. According to the passage, which of the following is CORRECT?
(a) Primary education is very important
(b) Universities are the life-blood of higher education
(c) Transformation of economy and society in the 21st century would depend, in significant part, on the spread and the quality of education among our people, particularly in the sphere of higher education
(d) All the above propositions are correct

Q 8. Should the entire university system in India be modelled on premier institutes, such as IITs and IIMs, providing professional education?
(a) Yes
(b) For sure
(c) No
(d) The passage is silent on this question

Q 9. What is the antonym of the expression 'cutting edge'?
(a) Conventional (b) Avant-garde
(c) Advanced (d) Contemporary

Q 10. What is the meaning of the word 'discernible'?
(a) Unobtrusive
(b) Noticeable
(c) Unremarkable
(d) Inconspicuous

COMPREHENSION

PRACTICE TEST – 7

It is an old saying that knowledge is power. Education is an instrument which imparts knowledge and therefore, indirectly controls power. Therefore, ever since the dawn of our civilisation, persons in power have always tried to supervise or control education. It has been the handmaid of the ruling class. During the Christian era, the ecclesiastics controlled the institution of education and diffused among the people the gospel of the Bible and religious teachings. These gospels and teachings were none other than a philosophy for the maintenance of the existing society. It taught the poor man to be weak and to earn his bread with the sweat of his brow, while the priests and the landlords lived in luxury and fought duels for the slightest offence. During the Renaissance, education passed more from the clutches of the priest into the hands of the prince. In other words, it became more secular. Under the control of the monarch, education began to devise and preach the infallibility of its masters, the monarch or king. It also invented and supported fantastic theories like 'The Divine Right Theory' and that the king can do no wrong, etc. With the advent of the industrial revolution, education took a different turn and had to please the new masters. It now no longer remained the privilege of the baron class, but was thrown open to the new rich merchant class of the society. The philosophy which was in vogue during this period was that of laissez-faire restricting the function of the state to a mere keeping of laws and order while on the other hand, in practice the law of the jungle prevailed in the form of free competition and the survival of the fittest.

Q 1. What does the theory 'Divine Right of King' stipulate?
(a) The kings are God
(b) That the right of governing is conferred upon the kings by God
(c) They have the right to be worshipped like Gods by their subjects
(d) That the right of kings are divine and therefore sacred

Q 2. Who controlled education during the Renaissance?
(a) The common people
(b) The prince
(c) The church and the priests
(d) None of these

Q 3. What did the ruling class in the Christian era think of the poor man?
(a) That he is the beloved of God
(b) That he deserves all sympathy of the rich
(c) That he should be strong and lord over others
(d) That he is meant for serving the rich

Q 4. Who controlled the institution of education during the Christian era?
(a) The secular leaders of society
(b) The church and the priests
(c) The monarchs
(d) The common people

Q 5. What does the word 'infallibility' mean?
(a) That every man is open to error
(b) Sensitivity
(c) The virtue of not making mistake
(d) That some divine power is responsible for determining the fate of the man

Q 6. What do you mean by 'sweat of his brow'?
(a) Very hard work

(b) The tiny droplets of sweat on the forehead
(c) The wrinkles visible on the forehead
(d) The sign of innocence

Q 7. What does the policy of laissez-faire stand for?
(a) Individual freedom in the economic field
(b) Slate control over law and order in society
(c) Joint control of the means of production by the state and private enterprise
(d) Decontrol over law and order by the ruling class

Q 8. Which of the following describes the writer?
(a) Concerned (b) Unconcerned
(c) Aggressive (d) Frustrated

Q 9. Choose the correct synonym out of the four choices given:
Gospels
(a) Chit chat
(b) A teaching or doctrine of a religious teacher
(c) Rumour
(d) Guidance

Q 10. Choose the correct synonym out of the four choices given:
Vogue
(a) Uncertain
(b) Out-dated
(c) Prevailing fashion or style
(d) Journey

COMPREHENSION

PRACTICE TEST – 8

The work which Gandhiji had taken up was not only regarding the achievement of political freedom but also the establishment of a new social order based on truth and non-violence, unity and peace, equality and universal brotherhood and maximum freedom for all. This unfinished part of his experiment was perhaps even more difficult to achieve than the achievement of political freedom. In the political struggle, the fight was against a foreign power and all one could do was either join it or wish it success and give it his/her moral support. In establishing a social order on this pattern, there was a strong possibility of a conflict arising between diverse groups and classes of our own people. Experience shows that man values his possessions even more than his life because in the former he sees the means for perpetuation and survival of his descendants even after his body is reduced to ashes, A new order cannot be established without radically changing the mind and attitude of men towards property and, at some stage or the other, the 'haves' have to yield place to the 'have-nots'. We have seen, in our time, attempts to achieve a kind of egalitarian society and the picture of it after it was achieved. But this was done, by and large, through the use of physical force. In the ultimate analysis it is difficult, if not impossible, to say that the instinct to possess has been rooted out or that it will not reappear in an even worse form under a different guise. It may even be that, like a gas kept confined within containers under great pressure, or water held back by a big dam, once the barrier breaks, the reaction will one day sweep back with a violence equal in extent and intensity to what was used to establish and maintain the outward egalitarian form.

This enforced egalitarianism contains, in its bosom, the seed of its own destruction. The root cause of class conflict is possessiveness or the acquisitive instinct. So long as the ideal that is to be achieved is one of securing the maximum material satisfaction, possessiveness is neither suppressed nor eliminated but grows on what it feeds. Nor does it cease to be possessiveness, whether it is confined to only a few or is shared by many. If egalitarianism is to endure, it has to be based not on the possession of the maximum material goods by a few or by all but on voluntary, enlightened renunciation of those goods which cannot be shared by others or can be enjoyed only at the expense of others. This calls for substitution of material values by purely spiritual ones. The paradise of material satisfaction, which is sometimes equated with progress these days, neither spells peace nor progress. Mahatma Gandhi has shown us how the acquisitive instinct inherent in man can be transmuted by the adoption of the ideal of trusteeship by those who 'have' for the benefit of all those who 'have not' so that, instead of leading to exploitation and conflict, it would become a means and incentive for the amelioration and progress of society respectively.

Q 1. According to the passage, egalitarianism will not survive if
(a) it is based on voluntary renunciation
(b) it is achieved by resorting to physical force
(c) underprivileged people are not involved in its establishment

(d) people's outlook towards it is not radically changed

Q 2. According to the passage, why does man value his possessions more than his life?
(a) He has inherent desire to share his possession with others
(b) He is endowed with the possessive instinct
(c) Only his possession helps him earn love and respect from his descendants
(d) Through his possessions he can preserve his name even after his death

Q 3. According to the passage, which was the unfinished part of Gandhi's experiment?
(a) Educating people to avoid class conflict
(b) Achieving total political freedom for the country
(c) Establishment of an egalitarian society
(d) Radically changing the mind and attitude of men towards truth and non-violence

Q 4. Which of the following statements is 'not true' in the context of the passage?
(a) True egalitarianism can be achieved by giving up one's possessions under compulsion
(b) Man values his life more than his possessions
(c) Possessive instinct is a natural desire of human beings
(d) In the political struggle, the fight was against alien rule

Q 5. According to the passage, true egalitarianism will last only if
(a) it is thrust upon people
(b) it is based on truth and non-violence
(c) people inculcate spiritual values instead of material values
(d) 'haves' and 'have-nots' live together peacefully

Q 6. According to the passage, people ultimately overturn a social order
(a) which is based on coercion and oppression
(b) which does not satisfy their basic needs
(c) which is based upon conciliation and rapprochement
(d) which is not congenital to the spiritual values of the people

Q 7. According to the passage, the root cause of class conflict is
(a) The paradise of material satisfaction
(b) Dominant inherent acquisitive instinct in man
(c) Exploitation of the 'have-nots' by the 'haves'
(d) A social order where the unprivileged are not a part of the establishment

Q 8. Which of the following statements is 'not true' in the context of the passage?
(a) A new order can be established by radically changing the outlook of people towards it
(b) Adoption of the ideal of trusteeship can minimise possessive instinct
(c) Enforced egalitarianism can be the cause of its own destruction
(d) Ideal of new order is to secure maximum material satisfaction

Q 9. Which of the following conclusions can be deduced from the passage?
(a) A social order based on truth and non-violence alone can help the achievement of political freedom
(b) After establishing the social order of Gandhiji's pattern, the possibility of a conflict between different classes of society will hardly exist
(c) It is difficult to change the mind and attitude of men towards property
(d) In an egalitarian society, material satisfaction can be enjoyed only at the expense of others

Q 10. According to the passage, what does 'adoption of the ideal of trusteeship' mean?
(a) Equating peace and progress with material satisfaction
(b) Adoption of the ideal by the 'haves' for the benefit of 'have-nots'
(c) Voluntary enlightened enunciation of the possessive instinct by the privilege class
(d) Substitution of spiritual values by material ones by those who live in the paradise of material satisfaction

COMPREHENSION

PRACTICE TEST – 9

'The night I arrived in Delhi on a visit in January 1996, the elevator at the Maurya Sheraton took us up to the twelfth floor in a breath-taking six or seven seconds. 'Remarkable,' I commented admiringly to the friendly hotel employee in a maroon sari and business-like pageboy haircut, who had draped a three-kilogram marigold garland around my neck as I stepped across the threshold. 'We couldn't have ascended faster in the U.S.A.'

She took my praise in stride, as well she should have. Jet-lagged after an eighteen-hour journey from New York, I had failed to notice that this was not some superfast new elevator technology that the Maurya had brought to Delhi, but rather some highly creative labelling. When I finally woke up and looked out of my window, I realised that what the elevator buttons had called the twelfth floor was in fact the second. The gleaming Maurya elevator had merely taken me for a ride – and a shorter ride I'd imagined.

I couldn't help the accusatory tone out of my voice the next time I ran into the maroon sari. 'Twelfth-floor, huh?' I said pointedly. 'liberalisation meant being liberal with the facts.'

She was surprised that I had taken offense. 'Our foreign visitors much prefer to think of themselves as being on eleventh and twelfth floors than the first or second,' she replied with wide-eyed innocence. 'And they don't look out of the windows that much.'

Welcome, I thought, to the new India. An India I was discovering for the first time: an India of five-star hotels, welcoming garlands, and smooth-talking hotel staff, where nothing is quite what it seems (not even the elevator buttons), where windows are not meant to be opened and appearances are the only reality. [Shashi Tharoor, India : From Midnight to the Millennium and Beyond (Arcade Publishing, 1997) 275-276]

Q 1. After reading the last line of the first paragraph, 'We couldn't have ascended faster in the U.S.A.', which of the options do you think the author is most likely to agree with?
(a) India never fails to surprise
(b) Indians have been great innovators
(c) Foreigners are turning to India's technical advancement
(d) It's a fact that India hasn't made significant progress

Q 2. As used in the third paragraph, the underlined word 'accusatory' most nearly means all options, except
(a) denunciative (b) criminate
(c) eulogistic (d) censuring

Q 3. It can be inferred from the passage that the author's impression
(a) transgresses from being proud to being even prouder
(b) plummets from a sense of pride to a sense of disillusionment
(c) trends from a level of disappointment to a level of condemnation
(d) remains steadfast on the thought of being an Indian

Q 4. In the line, '...taken me for a ride–and a shorter ride I'd imagined', means
(a) the elevator had taken them very swiftly
(b) the hotel was treating its guests like royalties
(c) technology had advanced in third world countries
(d) people were being hoodwinked

Q 5. The tone of the passage could be summed up to be
(a) pensive and remorseful
(b) matter of fact and somber
(c) humorous and reflective
(d) fiery and critical

COMPREHENSION

PRACTICE TEST – 10

In order to understand the development of Gangetic Valley plains, scholars have traditionally relied primarily on evidence from historical documents. However, such documentary sources provide a fragmentary record at best. Reliable accounts are very scarce for many parts of Northern India prior to the fifteenth century, and many of the relevant documents from the fourteenth and fifteenth centuries focus selectively on matters relating to cultural or commercial interests.

Studies of fossilised pollens preserved in peats and lake muds provide an additional means of investigating vegetative landscape change. Details of changes in vegetation resulting from both human activities and natural events are reflected in the kinds and quantities of minute pollens that become trapped in sediments. Analysis of samples can identify which kinds of plants produced the preserved pollens and when they were deposited, and in many cases the findings can serve to supplement or correct the documentary record.

For example, analysis of samples from a bay in Jammu has revealed significant patterns of cereal-grain pollens beginning about the fourth century. The substantial clay content of the soil in this part of Jammu makes cultivation by primitive tools difficult.

Historians thought that such soils were not tilled to any significant extent until the introduction of the wooden plough to India in the seventh century. Because cereal cultivation would have required tilling of the soil, the pollens' evidence indicates that these soils must indeed have been successfully tilled before the introduction of the new plough.

Another example concerns flax cultivation in Jammu, one of the great linen-producing areas of India during the sixteenth century. Some aspects of linen production in Jammu are well documented, but the documentary record tells little about the cultivation of flax, the plant from which linen is made, in that area. The record of sixteenth century linen production in Jammu, together with the knowledge that flax cultivation had been established in India centuries before that time, led some historians to surmise that this plant was being cultivated in Jammu before the sixteenth century. But pollens' analyses indicate that this is not the case; flax pollens were found only in deposits laid down since the sixteenth century.

It must be stressed, though, that there are limits to the ability of the pollen record to reflect the vegetative history of the landscape. For example, pollen analysis cannot identify the species, but only the genus or family, of some plants. Among these is turmeric, a cultivated plant of medicinal importance in India. Turmeric belongs to a plant family that also comprises various native weeds, including Brahma Thandu. If turmeric pollen were present in a deposit, it would be indistinguishable from that of uncultivated native species.

Q 1. The phrase 'documentary record' (para 2 and 4) primarily refers to
- (a) articles, books, and other documents by current historians listing and analysing all the available evidence regarding a particular historical period
- (b) government and commercial records, maps, and similar documents produced in the past that recorded conditions and events of that time
- (c) documented results of analyses of fossilised pollen
- (d) the kinds and qualities of fossilised pollen grains preserved in peats and lake muds

Q 2. The passage indicates that pollen analyses have provided evidence against which one of the following views?
- (a) In certain parts of Jammu, cereal grains were not cultivated to any significant extent before the seventh century
- (b) Cereal grain cultivation began in Jammu around fourth century
- (c) In certain parts of India, cereal grains have been cultivated continuously since the introduction of the wooden plough
- (d) Cereal grain cultivation requires successful tilling of the soil

Q 3. The passage indicates that prior to the use of pollen analysis in the study of the history of the Gangetic Valley plains, at least some historians believed which one of the following?
- (a) Turmeric was not used as a medicinal plant in India until after the sixteenth century
- (b) Cereal grain was not cultivated in India until at least the seventh century
- (c) The history of the Gangetic Valley plains during the fourteenth and fifteenth centuries was well documented
- (d) The beginning of flax cultivation in Jammu may well have occurred before the sixteenth century

Q 4. Which of the following most accurately describes the relationship between the second paragraph and the final paragraph?
- (a) The second paragraph describes a view against which the author intends to argue, and the final paragraph states the author's argument against that view
- (b) The second paragraph proposes a hypothesis which the final paragraph offers a supporting example
- (c) The final paragraph qualifies the claim made in the second paragraph
- (d) The final paragraph describes a problem that must be solved before the method advocated in the second paragraph can be considered viable

Q 5. Which one of the following most accurately expresses the main point of the passage?
- (a) While pollen evidence can sometimes supplement other sources of historical information, its applicability is severely limited, since it cannot be used to identify plant species
- (b) Analysis of fossilised pollen is a useful means of supplementing and in

some cases correcting other sources of information regarding changes in the Gangetic Valley plains

(c) Analysis of fossilised pollen has provided new evidence that the cultivation of such crops as cereal grains, flax, and turmeric had a significant impact on the Gangetic Valley plains

(d) Analysis of fossilised pollen has proven to be a valuable tool in the identification of ancient plant species

COMPREHENSION

PRACTICE TEST – 11

Surajendu Kumar's study on the effect of the modernisation of a Government Printing Press on Press maintenance work and workers is a solid contribution to debate that encompasses two lively issues in the history and sociology of technology: technological determinism and social constructivism.

Kumar makes the point that the characteristics of a technology have a decisive influence on job skill and work organisation. Put more strongly, technology can be a primary determinant of social and managerial organisation. Kumar believes this possibility has been obscured by the recent sociological fashion, exemplified by Cravman, the analysis that emphasises the way machinery reflects social choices. For Cravman the shape of a technological system is subordinate to the manager's desire to wrest control of the labour process from the workers. Technological change is construed as the outcome of negotiations among interested parties who seek to incorporate their own interests into the design and configuration of the machinery. This position represents the new mainstream called the social constructivism.

The constructivists gain acceptance by misrepresenting technological determinism. The technological determinists are supposed to believe, for example, that machinery imposes appropriate forms of order society. The alternative to constructivism, in other words, is to view technology as existing outside society, capable of directly influencing skills and work organisation.

Kumar refutes the extremes of the constructivists by both theoretical and empirical arguments. Theoretically he defines 'technology' in terms of relationship between social and technical variables. Attempts to reduce the meaning of technology to cold, hard metal are bound to fail, for machinery is just scrap unless it is organised functionally and supported by appropriate system of operation and maintenance. At the empirical level, Kumar shows how a change at the Printing Press from maintenance-intensive electromechanical devices to semi-altered work tasks, skills, training opportunities, administration, and organisation of workers. Some changes Kumar attributes to the particular way in which management and labor union negotiated the introduction of the technology, whereas others are seen as arising from the capabilities and nature of the technology itself. Thus, Kumar helps answer the question: 'When is social choice decisive and when are concrete characteristics of technology more important?'

Q 1. The primary purpose of the passage is to

(a) challenge the position of advocates of technological determinism

(b) consider a successful challenge to the constructivist view of technological change

(c) suggest that the social causes of the technological change should be studied in real situation

(d) advocated a more positive attitude towards technological change

Q 2. Which of the following statements about the modernisation of the Printing Press is supported by the information provided in the passage?

(a) Some of the maintenance workers felt victimised by the new technology

(b) The modernisation was implemented without the consent of the employees directly affected by it

(c) The new technology reduced the role of managers in labour negotiations

(d) The modernisation had an impact that went significantly beyond maintenance routines

Q 3. Which of the following most accurately describes Kumar's opinion of Cravman's position?

(a) He is sympathetic to its concern about the impact of modern technology of workers

(b) He is concerned about its potential to impede the implementation of new technologies

(c) He disapproves if its misplaced emphasis on the influence of managers

(d) He admires the consideration it gives to the attitude of workers affected

Q 4. Which of the following statements from the passage suggest that the hypothetical sociological studies of change in industry most clearly exemplifies the social constructivists' version of technological determinism?

(a) It is the available technology that determines worker's skills, rather than worker's skill influencing the application of technology

(b) Some industrial technology eliminates jobs, but educated workers can create whole new skill areas by the adaptation of technology

(c) Most major technological advances in industry have been generated through research and development

(d) All progress in industrial technology grows out of a continuing negotiation between technological possibility and human need

Q 5. According to the passage, Kumar believes if social constructivism had not gained widespread acceptance, then which of the following would be true?

(a) Modernisation would have occurred at a slower rate

(b) Businesses would be more likely to modernise without considering the social consequences of their actions

(c) There would be greater understanding of the role played by technology in producing social change

(d) Businesses would be less likely to understand the attitudes of employees affected by modernisation

Q 6. According to the passage, constructivists employed which of the following to promote their argument?

(a) Construction of hypothetical situations that support their view

(b) Empirical studies of business situations involving technological change

(c) Descriptions of the breadth of impact of technological change

(d) Contrasts of their view with a misstatement of an opposing view

Q 7. The author of the passage uses the expression 'are supposed to' in third para (highlighted) primarily in order to

(a) Define the generally accepted position of determinists regarding the implementation of technology

(b) Engage in speculation about the motivation of determinists

(c) Suggest that a contention made by constructivists regarding determinists is inaccurate

(d) Lend support to a comment critical of the position of determinists

Q 8. Which of the following statements about Kumar's study of the Printing Press can be inferred from information in the passage?

(a) Kumar's study suggests that the implementation of technology should be discussed in the context of conflict between labour and management

(b) Kumar examined the impact of change in the technology at the Printing Press in terms of overall operations and organisation

(c) Kumar concluded that the implementation of new technology was equally beneficial to management and labour

(d) Kumar's reason for undertaking the study was to undermine Cravman's analysis of the function of technology

COMPREHENSION

PRACTICE TEST – 12

Rural manual workers comprise the single largest occupational category in India. In 1991, according to the National Commission on Rural Labour, 60 per cent of the workers in rural India were manual workers and they numbered more than 160 million. The changes in the working and living conditions of rural labourers are thus central to changes in the welfare of the rural population and of the country as a whole. The structure and working of rural labour markets in India is complex and it is well-known, there is a great diversity across regions and across segments of the labour market. This article brings together an interesting body of research that seeks to understand and explain the types of changes that have accrued in the structure of rural labour markets over the last few decades.

The 1980s were characterised by an explosion of the rural labour force, slow employment growth in agriculture and a rise in the share of non-agricultural employment. The decade was also characterised by a growing casualisation of the work force (for a relative rise in casual employment as opposed to regular employment).

At the same time, it was a period when agricultural wages increased in real terms and when income poverty declined. There was what may be called 'the tension between the estimated decline in poverty on the one hand, and the slow growth of agricultural employment and increased casualisation of the labour force on the other'. Some of the trends in the development of rural labour for this period are a source of concern. These include, as Radhakrishnan and Sharma note, the continuous widening of the gap between labour productivity in agricultural and non-agricultural occupations, the burgeoning mass of rural casual workers who have no social security safety net and the increasing number of women employed at very low wages in agriculture. Another matter for concern, one that emerges from a desegregation of data on rural unemployment by age groups is that the incidence of unemployment is higher for persons in the age group of 15-29 than for any other age group, in other words, unemployment is typically high among new entrants to the workforce.

In her review of trends in wages, employment and poverty, Sheila Bhalla shows that the real wages of agricultural labourers stagnated from the time of independence to the mid-1970s and then began to rise in all parts of the country. This was also the period in which the incidence of rural poverty began to decline. The rise in wages was not limited to the more prosperous agricultural zones, and Bhalla argues that the movement in real wages was co-related with the increase in the share of non-agricultural employment in total employment. As wages in non-agricultural work are typically higher than wages in agriculture, the expansion of non-farm work could also explain some of the decline in rural poverty. In the 1990s, the improvement in real wages and the decline in poverty were reversed while agricultural employment expanded. Economic development all over the world has been associated with a rise in the share of employment in the secondary and tertiary sectors of the economy and a fall in the share of the agricultural sector. In India, changes in the composition of the rural workforce in the 1990s points to a 'structural retrogression'.

Q 1. Give an appropriate title to the passage
- (a) The complex labour markets in India
- (b) Matters of concern in rural agriculture
- (c) The agricultural and non-agricultural sectors: changing perspective
- (d) The changing structure of rural labour market

Q 2. The author does not say
- (a) In 1991, about 3/5th of the workers in rural India were manual workers
- (b) The decade of 1980s was characterised by a relative rise in casual employment as opposed to regular employment
- (c) There is no gender bias among workers in agricultural sector
- (d) Wages in agricultural employment have been lesser than those in non-agricultural employment in the 1990s

Q 3. Why is the increasing gap between labour productivity in agricultural and non-agricultural occupations a cause of concern, according to Radhakrishnan and Sharma?
- (a) This would increase the wages of agricultural sector
- (b) This would lead to pressure on both the agricultural and non-agricultural sectors as whichever sector expands at the expense of the other; there would be increased labour pressure on that sector and lesser economic development in the other
- (c) This would indirectly mean a pressure on agricultural sector in terms of higher wages
- (d) This would indirectly mean a pressure on non-agricultural sector in terms of higher wages

Q 4. How does Bhalla explain the fact that the real wages of agricultural labourers began to rise in all parts of the country after mid-70s?
- (a) Economic development increased for both the sectors across the world
- (b) Economic liberalisation in India led to the development of the agricultural sector
- (c) The agricultural labourers became rich due to successive good crops during the time of Green Revolution
- (d) There was a mass outflow of agricultural labourers into the non-agricultural sectors and the remaining labourers, who were lesser in number, now apportioned the existing agricultural sector's wealth, getting richer individually

Q 5. What is the most important problem in understanding the condition of rural labour markets in India?
- (a) The rural labour markets are uneconomic in nature
- (b) The rural labour markets are very complex and there exists great diversity across regions and across segments of such markets
- (c) The rural labourers are a reticent lot; not forthcoming with their problems, not very open to suggestions on how to improve their lifestyle
- (d) They are lazy and want doles from the government without undertaking any viable productive activities

Q 6. What sort of tension exists between the decline of poverty and the slow growth of agricultural employment and the increased casualisation of the labour force?
- (a) A decline in rural poverty is only possible when there is increased agricultural employment and lower casualisation of the labour force
- (b) The tension exists in the fact that an increased casualisation of the labour force would increase poverty
- (c) When there is a decline in poverty there should be faster growth of agricultural employment and the decreased casualisation of the labour force
- (d) Both (b) and (c)

Q 7. What sort of passage is this?
- (a) Political
- (b) Social commentary
- (c) Economic
- (d) Philosophical

Q 8. The author does not say which of the following statements in the passage?
- (a) The National Commission on Rural Labour gives data on the activities of rural labourers in India
- (b) Economic development basically means a rise in the share of employment in the agricultural sector at the expense of the secondary and the tertiary sectors
- (c) In India, employment was higher among the new entrants to the workforce in the 1980s
- (d) Real wages of the agricultural labourers started showing an upward trend from the 1970s

Q 9. What are the changes in the working and living conditions of rural manual workers of utmost significance to the country as a whole?
- (a) Rural workers migrate a lot to the cities, adding to the already burgeoning population of these places and so any improvement in their living conditions which would stall this trend would benefit
- (b) The rural workers live in abject poverty and a change in their working and living conditions is therefore very crucial
- (c) They form the bulk of the rural workers and so any change in their living standards augurs well for the country as a whole
- (d) Both (a) and (b)

COMPREHENSION

PRACTICE TEST – 13

The Constitution of the United States protects both property rights and freedom of speech. At times these rights conflict. Resolution then requires a determination as to the type of property involved. If the property is private and not open to the general public, the owner may absolutely deny the exercise of the right of free speech thereon. On the other hand, if public land is at issue, the First Amendment protection of expression are applicable. However, the exercise of free speech thereon is not absolute. Rather it is necessary to determine the appropriateness of the forum. This requires that consideration be given to a number of factors including: character and normal use of the property, the extent to which it is open to the public, and the number and types of persons who frequent it. If the forum is clearly public or clearly private, the resolution of the greater of rights is relatively straight forward.

In the area of quasi-public property, balancing these rights has produced a dilemma. This is the situation when a private owner permits the general public to use his property. When persons seek to use the land for passing out handbills or picketing, how is a conflict between property right and freedom of expression resolved?

The precept that a private property owner surrenders his rights in proportion to the extent to which he opens up his property to the public is not new. In 1675, Lord Chief Justice Hale wrote that when private property is 'affected with a public interest, it ceases to be private.' Throughout the development of Anglo-American law, the individual has never possessed absolute dominion over property. Land becomes clothed with a public interest when the owner devotes his property to a use in which the public has an interest. In support of this position the chairman of the board of the Wilde Lake Shopping Centre in Columbia, Maryland said:

The only real purpose and justification of any of these centres is to serve the people in the area – not the merchants, not the developers, not the architects. The success or failure of a regional shopping centre will be measured by what it does for the people it seeks to serve.

These doctrines should be applied when accommodation must be made between a shopping centre owner's private property rights and the public's right to free expression. It is hoped that when the court is asked to balance these conflicting rights it will keep in mind what Justice Black said in 1945: 'When we balance the constitutional rights of owners of property against those of the people to enjoy (First Amendment) freedom(s). We remain mindful of the fact that the latter occupy a preferred position.'

Q 1. In which one of the following cases would the owner of the property probably be most free to restrict the freedom of speech?
- (a) an amusement park attended by five million people each year owned by a multinational company
- (b) a small grocery shopping mall owned by a husband and wife
- (c) an enclosed shopping mall owned by a single woman
- (d) an eight-unit residential apartment building owned by a large real company

Q 12. A conflict between property rights and freedom of speech might arise in all of the following situations, EXCEPT
- (a) protestors carrying signs outside a cinema in an enclosed shopping mall
- (b) a disgruntled employee passing out leaflets in front of a hairdresser's saloon
- (c) a religious order soliciting funds and converts in the swimming pool area of a condominium
- (d) a candidate for mayor handing out flyers in front of his opponent's headquarters

Q 3. According to the passage, an owner's freedom to deny freedom of speech on his property is determined by all of the following EXCEPT
- (a) whether or not the land is open to the public
- (b) the nature of and the usual use of the property
- (c) the type of persons who frequent the land
- (d) the nature and character of the owner

Q 4. We can infer from the passage that the author believes that shopping malls in America
- (a) should be in the service of the people who frequent them
- (b) have a right to prohibit distribution of advertising handbills
- (c) have a right to control any distributed materials
- (d) should permit any charitable solicitations

Q 5. According to the passage, the idea that a property owner's rights decline as the property is more used by the general public
- (a) is peculiar to recent Supreme Court decisions
- (b) is attested by a three-hundred-year-old opinion
- (c) conflicts with the idea that property affected with a public interest ceases to be private
- (d) is now universally accepted in Great Britain and in Canada

Q 6. All other things being equal, the courts must
- (a) favour First Amendment rights over property rights
- (b) favour property rights over First Amendment rights
- (c) treat property rights and First Amendment rights equally
- (d) protect property rights of the owners

COMPREHENSION

PRACTICE TEST – 14

Under very early common law, all felonies were punishable by death. The perpetrators of the felony were hanged whether or not a homicide had been committed during the felony. Later, however, some felonies were declared to be non capital offences. The common law courts, in need of a deterrent to the use of deadly force in the course of these non-capital felonies, developed the 'felony-murder' rule. The first formal statement of the rule stated: 'Any killing by one in the commission of a felony is guilty of murder'. The killing was a murder whether intentional or unintentional, accidental or mistaken. The usual requirement of malice was eliminated and the only criminal intent necessary was the intent to commit the particular underlying felony. All participants in the felony were guilty of murder - actual killer and non-killer confederates.

Proponents of the rule argued that it was justified because the felony demonstrated a lack of concern for human life by the commission of a violent and dangerous felony and that the crime was murder either because of a conclusive presumption of malice or simply by force of statutory definition.

Opponents of the rule describe it as a highly artificial concept and "an enigma wrapped in a riddle." They are quick to point out that the rule has been abandoned in England where it originated, abolished in India, severely restricted in Canada and a number of other commonwealth countries, is unknown in continental Europe, and abandoned in Michigan. In reality, the real strength of the opponents' criticism stems from the bizarre and of times unfair results achieved when the felony-murder rule is applied mechanically. Defendants have been convicted under the rule where the killing was purely accidental, or the killing took place after the felony during the later flight from the scene; or a third party killed another (police officer killed a citizen or vice versa; or a victim died of a heart attack 15 – 20 minutes after the robbery was over; or the person killed was an accomplice in the felony).

Attacks on the rule have come from all directions with basically the same demand – re-evaluate and abandon the archaic legal fiction; restrict and limit vicarious criminal liability; prosecute killers for murder, not non-killers; increase punishment for the underlying felony as a real deterrent; and initiate legislative modifications. With the unstable history of the felony-murder rule, including its abandonment by many jurisdictions in this country, the felony-murder rule is dying a slow but certain death.

Q 1. (a) The felony-murder rule should be abolished
(b) Some jurisdictions are about to abandon the felony- murder rule
(c) The felony-murder rule can be unfair
(d) Supreme Court of the United States

Q 2. The felony-murder rule was developed in order to
(a) deter felonies
(b) deter murders
(c) deter deadly force in felonies
(d) extend the definition of murder to any malicious act resulting in death

Q 3. Arguments in favour of the felony-murder rule may include all of the following EXCEPT
(a) We can infer that anyone undertaking a dangerous felony demonstrates an indifference to human life
(b) If the punishment for the use of deadly force whether intended or not is the same, criminals will be less likely to use deadly force
(c) Because a life has been taken, the crime is murder by force of statutory definition
(d) The victim of murder may be an accomplice of the felony

Q 4. According to the passage, opponents of the felony-murder rule have raised all of the following objections to the statute EXCEPT
(a) The felony-murder rule results in murder prosecutions of defendants who have not committed murder
(b) The felony-murder rule assigns a criminal liability vicariously
(c) The felony-murder rule is based upon a presumption of malice even if death is wholly accidental
(d) The felony-murder rule deters the use of deadly force in non-capital felonies

Q 5. In which of the following situations would the defendant NOT be liable to the charge of murder under the felony-murder rule?
(a) In escaping from an unsuccessful attempt to rob a bank, the defendant crashes his car, killing an innocent pedestrian in another city
(b) A bank security officer, pursuing the defendant after a robbery, falls down a flight of stairs and suffers serious permanent brain and spinal cord injuries
(c) The driver of the escape car, who has not entered the bank, crashes the

car killing the armed gunman who committed the robbery

(d) A bank teller, locked safely in' the bank vault by the robber, has a stroke and dies

Q 6. According to the passage, the decline of support for the felony-murder rule is indicted by the abandoning of the rule in all of the following locations EXCEPT

(a) Continental Europe
(b) India
(c) England
(d) Canada

Q 7. The author believes that the felony-murder rule is

(a) unconstitutional
(b) bizarre and unfair
(c) a serviceable rule unfairly attacked by the "intelligentsia"
(d) an unfair equating of intent to commit a felony and intent to commit murder

COMPREHENSION

PRACTICE TEST – 15

Although the legal systems of England and the United States are superficially similar, they differ profoundly in their approaches to and uses of legal reasons: substantive reasons are more common than formal reasons in the United States, whereas in England the reverse is true. This distinction reflects a difference in the visions of law that prevails in the two countries. In England, the law has traditionally been viewed as a system of rules; the United States favours a vision of law as an outward expression of community's sense of right and justice.

Substantive reasons, as applied to law, are based on moral, economic, political and other considerations. These reasons are found both 'in the law' and 'outside the law' so to speak. Substantive reasons inform the content of a large part of the law: constitutions, statutes, contracts, verdicts, and the like. Consider, for example, a statute providing that 'no vehicles shall be taken into public parks.' Suppose that no specific rationales or purposes were explicitly written into the statute, but that it was clear (from its legislative history) that the substantive purpose of the statute was to ensure quiet and safety in the park. Now suppose that a veterans' group mounts a World War II jeep (in running order but without a battery) as a war memorial on a concrete slab in the park, and charges are brought against its members. Most judges in the United States would find the defendants not guilty because what they did had no adverse effect on park's quiet and safety.

Formal reasons are different in that they frequently prevent substantive reasons from coming into play, even when substantive reasons are explicitly incorporated into the law at hand. For example, when a document fails to comply with stipulated requirements, the court may render the document legally ineffective. A Will requiring written witness may be declared null and void and, therefore, unenforceable for the formal reason that the requirement was not observed. Once the legal rule – that a Will is invalid for lack of proper witnessing – has been clearly established, and the legality of the rule is not in question, application of that rule precludes from consideration substantive arguments in favour of the Will's validity or enforcement.

Legal scholars in England and the United States have long bemused themselves with extreme examples of formal and substantive reasoning. On the one hand, formal reasoning in England has led to wooden interpretations of statutes and an unwillingness to develop the common law through judicial activism. On the other hand, freewheeling substantive reasoning in the United States has resulted in statutory interpretations so liberal that the texts of some statutes have been ignored.

Q 1. Which one of the following best describes the content of the passage as a whole?

(a) An analysis of similarities and differences between the legal systems of England and the United States
(b) A re-evaluation of two legal systems with the use of examples
(c) A contrast between the types of reasons embodied in the United States and English legal systems
(d) An explanation of how two distinct visions of the law shaped the development of legal reasoning

Q 2. It can be inferred from the passage that English judges would like to find the veterans' group discussed in the second paragraph guilty of violating the statute because

(a) not to do so would encourage others to act as the group did
(b) not to do so would be to violate the substantive reasons underlying the law

(c) the veterans failed to comply with the substantive purpose of the statute
(d) the veterans failed to comply with the stipulated requirements of the statute

Q 3. From the discussion of Wills in the third paragraph it can be inferred that substantive arguments as to the validity of a Will might be considered under which one of the following circumstances?
(a) The legal rule that a Will be witnessed in writing does not stipulate the format of the Will
(b) The legal rule requiring that a Will be witnessed stipulates that the Will must be witnessed in writing by two people
(c) The legal rule requiring that a Will be witnessed in writing stipulates that the witnessing must be done in the presence of a judge
(d) A judge rules that the law can be interpreted to allow for a verbal witness to a Will in a case involving a medical emergency

Q 4. Which one of the following best describes the function of the last paragraph of the passage?
(a) It presents the consequences of extreme interpretations of the two types of legal reasons discussed by the author
(b) It shows how legal scholars can incorrectly use extreme examples to support their views
(c) It corrects inaccuracies in legal scholars' view of the nature of two types of legal systems
(d) It suggests how characterisations of the two types of legal reasons can become convoluted and inaccurate

Q 5. The author of the passage suggests that in English law a substantive interpretation of a legal rule might be warranted under which one of the following circumstances?
(a) Social conditions have changed to the extent that to continue to enforce the rule would be to decide contrary to present day social norms
(b) The composition of the legislature has changed to the extent that to enforce the rule would be contrary to the views of the majority in the present legislative assembly
(c) The legality of the rule is in question and its enforcement is open to judicial interpretation
(d) Individuals who have violated the legal rule argue that application of the rule would lead to unfair judicial interpretations

Q 6. The author of the passage makes use of all of the following in presenting the discussion of the English and the United States legal systems except
(a) comparison and contrast
(b) generalisation
(c) explication of terms
(d) a chronology of historical developments

COMPREHENSION

PRACTICE TEST – 16

In principle, a cohesive group—one whose members generally agree with one another and support one another's judgments—can do a much better job at decision making than it could if it were non-cohesive. When cohesiveness is low or lacking entirely, compliance out of fear of recrimination is likely to be strongest. To overcome this fear, participants in the group's deliberations need to be confident that they are members in good standing and that the others will continue to value their role in the group, whether or not they agree about a particular issue under discussion. As members of a group feel more accepted by the others, they acquire greater freedom to say what they really think, becoming less likely to use deceitful arguments or to play it safe by dancing around the issues with vapid or conventional comments. Typically, then, the more cohesive a group becomes, the less its members will deliberately censor what they say out of fear of being punished socially for antagonising their fellow members. But group cohesiveness can have pitfalls as well: while the members of a highly cohesive group can feel much freer to deviate from the majority, their desire for genuine concurrence on every important issue often inclines them not to use this freedom. In a highly cohesive group of decision makers, the danger is not that individuals will conceal objections they harbour regarding a proposal favoured by the majority, but that they will think the proposal is a good one without attempting to carry out a critical scrutiny that could reveal grounds for strong objections. Members may then decide that any misgivings they feel are not worth pursuing—that the benefit of any doubt should be given to the group consensus. In this way, they may fall victim to a syndrome known as 'groupthink', which one psychologist concerned with collective decision making has defined as 'a deterioration of mental efficiency, reality testing, and moral judgment that results from in-group pressures'. Based on analyses of major fiascos of international diplomacy and military decision making, researchers have identified groupthink behaviour as a recurring pattern that involves several factors: overestimation of the group's power and morality, manifested for example, in an illusion of invulnerability, which creates excessive optimism; closed-mindedness to warnings of problems and to alternative viewpoints; and unwarranted pressures towards uniformity, including self-censorship with respect to doubts about the group's reasoning and a concomitant shared illusion of unanimity concerning group decisions. Cohesiveness of the decision-making group is an essential antecedent condition for this syndrome but not a sufficient one, so it is important to work towards identifying the additional factors that determine whether group cohesiveness will deteriorate into groupthink or allow for effective decision making.

Q 1. Why does the author think that the cohesive group can do a much better job at decision making than it could if it were non-cohesive?

(a) The members of a highly cohesive group can feel much freer to deviate from the majority
(b) Individuals will not conceal objections they harbour regarding a proposal favoured by the majority
(c) Participants in the group's deliberations are confident that they are members in good standing and that the others will continue to value their role in the group, whether or not they agree about a particular issue under discussion
(d) All of the above

Q 2. Which one of the following most accurately expresses the main point of the passage?

(a) Despite its value in encouraging frank discussions, high cohesion can lead to a debilitating type of group decision making called groupthink
(b) Group members can guard against groupthink if they have a good understanding of the critical role played by cohesion
(c) Groupthink is a dysfunctional collective decision-making pattern that can occur in diplomacy and military affairs
(d) Low cohesion in groups is sometimes desirable when higher cohesion involves a risk of groupthink behavior

Q 3. A group of closely associated colleagues has made a disastrous diplomatic decision after a series of meetings marked by disagreement over conflicting alternatives. It can be inferred from the passage that the author would be most likely to say that this scenario:

(a) provides evidence of chronic indecision, thus indicating a weak level of cohesion in general
(b) indicates that the group's cohesiveness was coupled with some other factor to produce a groupthink fiasco
(c) provides no evidence that groupthink played a role in the group's decision
(d) provides evidence that groupthink can develop even in some groups that do not demonstrate an 'illusion of unanimity'

Q 4. The passage mentions which one of the following as a component of group think?

(a) unjustified suspicions among group members regarding an adversary's intentions
(b) strong belief that the group's decisions are right
(c) group members working under unusually high stress, leading to illusions of invulnerability
(d) the deliberate use of vapid, cliched arguments

Q 5. It can be inferred from the passage that both the author of the passage and the researchers mentioned in the passage would be most likely to agree with which one of the following statements about group think?

(a) Groupthink occurs in all strongly cohesive groups, but its contribution to collective decision making is not fully understood
(b) The casual factors that transform group cohesion into groupthink are unique to each case
(c) The continued study of cohesiveness of groups is probably fruitless for determining what factors elicit group think
(d) On balance, groupthink cannot be expected to have a beneficial effect in a group's decision making

ANSWERS – COMPREHENSION PRACTICE TESTS

Q.No.	*P.T. – 1*	*P.T. – 2*	*P.T. – 3*	*P.T. – 4*	*P.T. – 5*	*P.T. – 6*	*P.T. – 7*	*P.T. – 8*
1	d	b	a	d	a	c	c	b
2	c	a	b	b	c	b	b	d
3	a	b	a	a	c	d	d	c
4	b	c	a	b	b	a	b	b
5	d	d	d	c	b	c	c	c
6	a	a		b	d	d	a	a
7	b	d		d	a	d	a	b
8	b	d		b	a	c	a	d
9	c	b		d	b	a	b	b
10	d	a		b	a	b	c	b

Q.No.	*P.T. – 9*	*P.T. – 10*	*P.T. – 11*	*P.T. – 12*	*P.T. – 13*	*P.T. – 14*	*P.T. – 15*	*P.T. – 16*
1	a	b	b	d	d	a	c	c
2	c	a	d	c	c	c	d	a
3	b	d	c	b	d	d	d	b
4	d	c	a	d	a	d	a	b
5	c	b	c	b	b	b	c	a
6			d	a	a	d	d	
7			c	c		d		
8			b	b				
9				c				

PART E:
SENTENCE CORRECTION
(1200 CE and 29 PTs)

32 SENTENCE CORRECTION (1200 COMMON ERRORS)

This is a part of verbal ability questions where you have to rewrite grammatically and structurally wrong sentences with correct grammar and vocabulary in English. At times, a sentence correction question will present you a combination of several errors at once. They mustall be corrected. Sentence correction questions test correctness and effectiveness of expression. In choosing your answer, follow the requirements of standard written English. In other words, pay attention to grammar, choice of words, and sentence construction. Choose the answer that provides the most effective sentence; your answer should be clear and exact, without awkwardness, ambiguity, redundancy, or grammatical error.

POINTS TO NOTE IN SENTENCE CORRECTION

1. Read the sentence. Do not read just the underlined part of the sentence. Read the complete sentence. Choice (A) will always be a copy of the original underlined part of the sentence. If you cannot find any errors in the original sentence, choose A. Don't worry about spelling, capitalisation, or punctuation; these corrections are not included in such questions.
2. Figure out what the question is testing. This is a multiple-choice exam, so you know that one of the answer choices must be right. Therefore, you may look at the different answer choices and see what the differences are to figure out the problem in the sentence.
3. Eliminate answer choices. The process of elimination is very important here. Eliminate a choice once you find one error in it. Gradually, you should be down to one or two choices, and you may make a reasonable guess. Use the process of elimination to scrap paper charts to narrow your choices.

SOME COMMON ERRORS

Incorrect sentence		Correct sentence	
1.	One of my friends are an engineer.	1.	One of my friends is an engineer.
2.	One of my dogs have disappeared.	2.	One of my dogs has disappeared.

Note: One of is followed by a plural nounphrase. It means 'one of them'.
It takes a singular noun.

3.	I don't know nothing about him.	3.	I don't know anything about him.
4.	He does not want none of that cake.	4.	He does not want any of that cake.
5.	I always like to closely examine every proposal.	5.	I always like to examine closely every proposal.

Note: The use of two negatives to express asingle negative idea is incorrect.
Two negatives lead to a positive (meaning). Therefore, one negative word should be used to express a negative idea (refer sentence nos. 3, 4, and 5).

6.	He plans to hurriedly complete this work.	6.	He plans to complete this work hurriedly.
7.	I wish I was as tall as my father.	7.	I wish I were as tall as my father.
8.	If he was alive, he would help me.	8.	If he were alive, he would help me.

9.	He is working hard with a view to win this match.	9.	He is working hard with a view to winning this match.
10.	I look forward to meet my old friend next months.	10.	I look forward to meeting my old friend next month.

Note: The verb that follows the phrase 'with a view to' or 'look forward to' is always to be in the '– ing' form. with a view to + V (ing) + ... or look forward to + V1 (ing) + ...
(refer sentence nos. 9 and 10).

Note: When verbs like absent, apply, acquit, enjoy, overreach, resign, and pride are used reflectively (that is, when the subject of the verb is also the receiver of the action, the action is 'reflected'), then a reflexive pronoun (I - myself; you - yourself; we – ourselves; they – themselves; he – himself; she – herself; one – oneself) is used after it (refer sentence nos. 12, 13, 14, and 15).

16.	I cut me shaving this morning.	16.	I cut myself shaving this morning.
17.	We got out of the swimming pool and dries us.	17.	We got out of the swimming pool and dried ourselves.
18.	I, you, and he are neighbours.	18.	You, he, and I are neighbours.

Note: When the same person is the subject and the object, it is necessary to use the reflexive pronouns: myself, yourself, herself, himself, itself, ourselves, themselves, oneself (refer sentence nos. 17 and 18).

19.	You, they, and we must work together.	19.	We, you, and they must work together.

Note: When first, second, and third-person singular pronouns (I, you, and he) are used together in the same sentence, they are placed in this order:

Second person (you), third person (he) and first person (I).

In the case of plural pronouns, 'we' is first, then 'you', and then 'they' (refer sentence no. 19)

20.	I have read Shakespeare's works who was a great dramatist.	20.	I have read the works of Shakespeare who was a great dramatist.
21.	Ravi's dog who is my friend has died.	21.	The dog of Ravi, who is my friend, has died.
22.	Let he do whatever he likes to do.	22.	Let him do whatever he likes to do.
23.	Let you and I solve this riddle.	23.	Let you and me solve this riddle.
24.	These books are for you and I.	24.	These books are for you and me.
25.	Between he and I there is an understanding.	25.	Between him and me there is an understanding.
26.	He is taller than me.	26.	He is taller than I.
27.	I love you more than him.	27.	I love you more than he. (loves you)
28.	I love you more than he.	28.	I love you more than (I love) him.
29.	The climate of Ranchi is better than Gaya.	29.	The climate of Ranchi is better than that of Gaya.
30.	The roads of Delhi are wider than Allahabad.	30.	The roads of Delhi are wider than those of Allahabad.

Note: The objects of comparison are 'the climate of Ranchi' and 'the climate of Gaya'; 'the roads of Delhi' and 'the roads of Allahabad' (refer sentence nos. 29 and 30).

To avoid the repetition of a noun in a sentence, use 'that' for singular noun and 'those' for plural noun.

31.	One of them has already given up one's studies.	31.	One of them has already given up his studies.
32.	One should not waste his time.	32.	One should not waste one's time.
33.	Either the Chief Minister or his cabinet colleagues have submitted his resignation.	33.	Either the Chief Minister or his cabinet colleagues have submitted their resignation.
34.	Neither the officer nor the clerks could get salary.	34.	Neither the officer nor the clerks could get their salary.
35.	The father and the son love one another.	35.	The father and the son love each other.
36.	Those three girls love each other.	36.	Those three girls love one another.
37.	Neither of the three boys came.	37.	None of the three boys came.

Note: When two nouns joined by 'either ...... or' or 'neither ...... nor' differ in number, the pronoun must agree with the plural noun which comes after 'or'/'nor' (refer sentence nos. 33, 34, 34, 36, and 37).

38.	None of the two boys came.	38.	Neither of the two boys came.
39.	Either of the four boys has done this work.	39.	None of the four boys has done this work.
40.	Any one of the two candidates is fit for this post.	40.	Either of the two candidates is fit for this post.

Note: The words 'either' and 'neither' are only used with reference to two. Similarly, the words 'anyone' and 'none' are used for more than two (refer sentence nos. 36, 37, 38, 39, and 40)

44.	It is not such a good book whichI expected.	44.	It is not as good a book as I expected. Or, The book is not as good as I expected.
45.	My problem is the same which is yours.	45.	My problem is the same as yours.

Note: The relative pronoun 'as' or 'that' should be used after 'same' or 'such'. Do not use 'who' or 'which' after 'same' or 'such' (refer sentence nos. 44 and 45).

46.	This is the same beggar who came yesterday.	46.	This is the same beggar that came yesterday.
47.	He is more wiser than his brother.	47.	He is wiser than his brother.
48.	He is the most wisest of all.	48.	He is the wisest of all.
49.	He is more wiser than brave.	49.	He is more wise than brave.
50.	You are wiser than old.	50.	You are more wise than old.
51.	He is braver than wise.	51.	He is more brave than wise.
52.	He is as wise, if not wiser than his brother.	52.	He is as wise as, if not wiser than his brother.
53.	This book is as good, if not better than that book.	53.	This book is as good as, if not better than that book.
54.	It is the best of the two books.	54.	It is the better of the two books.
55.	He is the better of the three boys.	55.	He is the best of the three boys.
56.	Which is the best: bread or butter?	56.	Which is better: bread or butter?
57.	Which is better – bread, butter, or fruit?	57.	Which is the best – bread, butter, or fruit?

Note: Do not use double comparatives and double superlatives.
(refer sentence nos. 54, 55, 56, and 57).

58.	Out of these two watches, this is the best.	58.	Out of these two watches, this is better.
59.	There are no less than twenty boys in this class.	59.	There are no fewer than twenty boys in this class.
60.	He takes no fewer than one kilo of milk.	60.	He takes no less than one kilo of milk.

Note: The word 'less' refers to quantity, whereas 'fewer' denotes a number. The former is used in the case of uncountable things and the latter to refer to countable things (refer sentence nos. 58 and 59).

Examples: fewer people, fewer houses, fewer boxes; less milk, less sunshine, less rice.

61.	It is a ten-miles walk.	61.	It is a ten-mile walk.
62.	It is a four-men committee.	62.	It is a four-man committee.
63.	It is a two-hours journey.	63.	It is a two-hour journey.

Note: When expressions of measurement, amount, and quantity are used as adjectives, they are usually singular. The noun occurring after the hyphen is always singular notwithstanding the fact that the preceding word indicates plurality (refer sentence nos. 61, 62, and 63).

64.	It took us one and a half hour.	64.	It took us one and a half hours.
65.	This box weighs one and a half pound.	65.	This box weighs one and a half pounds.
66.	It is 1.5 millimetre in length.	66.	It is 1.5 millimetres in length.
67.	Kapil is better than any bowler.	67.	Kapil is better than any other bowler.
68.	He is better than any student.	68.	He is better than any other student.
69.	He is senior than me.	69.	He is senior to me.
70.	I am junior than him.	70.	I am junior to him.
71.	This book is superior than that book.	71.	This book is inferior to that book.
72.	It is the most unique book.	72.	It is a unique book.

Note: The comparative adjectives, senior, junior, superior, inferior, posterior, anterior, prior are followed by 'to' instead of 'than' (refer sentence nos. 69, 70, and 71).

73.	It is the most ideal place.	73.	It is an ideal place.
74.	It is the most perfect answer.	74.	It is the perfect answer.

Note: Some adjectives are not compared because they denote meanings which do not admit of variation of degree or qualities already possessed by them, to the utmost possible extent (refer sentence nos. 72, 73, and 74). Examples: unique, ideal, perfect, extreme, chief, entire, complete, round, square, universal, impossible, golden, infinite, perpetual.

75.	The higher you go, the cool you feel.	75.	The higher you go, the cooler you feel.
76.	The older you get, the wise you grow.	76.	The older you get, the wiser you grow.
77.	Her house is better than my one.	77.	Her house is better than mine.
78.	His motor car is more expensive than Ravi's.	78.	His motor car is more expensive than Ravi's.
79.	The Victoria Memorial is a worth seeing building.	79.	The Victoria Memorial is a building worth seeing.
80.	This is a worth seeing sight.	80.	This is a sight worth seeing.
81.	Have they heard the last news?	81.	Have they heard the latest news?

82.	His last novel is being published next month.	82.	His latest novel is being published next month.
83.	'Edward II' was Marlowe's latest play.	83.	'Edward II' was Marlowe's last play.
84.	I am looking forward to his nearest visit.	84.	I am looking forward to his next visit.
85.	Excuse me. Where's the next railway station?	85.	Excuse me. Where's the nearest railway station?

Note: We usually use the word 'next' to denote time. It means 'nearest in the future'. It is generally used when we think of things coming one after another in a series.

'Nearest' is used to denote place; it means 'most near' or 'closest' (refer sentence nos. 84 and 85).

86.	There are not some books on the table.	86.	There are no books on the table.
	Or, There are not many books on the table.		
87.	Has he brought some books?	87.	Has he brought any books?
88.	He is not as tall as his brother.	88.	He is not as tall as his brother is.
89.	She is richer than you are.	89.	She is richer than you.
90.	He is my older brother.	90.	He is my elder brother.
91.	She is my oldest sister.	91.	She is my eldest sister.
92.	He is the eldest man of this place.	92.	He is the oldest man in this place.

Note: The words 'elder' and 'eldest' are used to compare the members of a family.

They are often used before words like 'brother', 'sister', 'son', 'daughter', 'grandson', and 'granddaughter'.

'Older' and 'oldest' are used with regard to age and family relationships (refer sentence nos. 91 and 92).

93.	Few politician can be relied on.	93.	A few politicians can be relied on.
94.	Little learning isa dangerous thing.	94.	A little learning is a dangerous thing.
95.	He has few interest in politics.	95.	He has little interest in politics.

Note: The word 'few' is usually used with plural nouns and 'little' with uncountable nouns (refer sentence nos. 94 and 95).

'Little' means 'not much/many'; it is rather negative.

Whereas, 'a little' is more positive; it means 'some'.

96.	He is enough bold to take up this challenge.	96.	He is bold enough to take on this challenge.
97.	He hasn't got enough good voice.	97.	He hasn't got a good enough voice.
98.	He is not driving enough fast.	98.	He is not diving fast enough.

Note: The word 'enough' can qualify an adjective or an adverb. It usually follows adjectives and adverbs (refer sentence nos. 97 and 98).

99.	His all books were burnt.	99.	All his books were burnt.
100.	His both hands are skinny.	100.	Both his hands are skinny.
101.	He is addicted to smoke.	101.	He is addicted to smoking.
102.	Raju's all hopes were gone.	102.	All Raju's hopes were gone.

Note: The noun of the possessive case (e.g. Raju's, Sheela's, etc.) or the pronoun of the possessive case (e.g. mine, ours, theirs, his, her, etc.) comes just before that noun for which it is used (refer sentence no. 102)

103.	He hit the ball hardly.	103.	He hit the ball hard.
104.	You have to work hardly.	104.	You have to work hard.
105.	He has got hard any money.	105.	He has got hardly any money.
106.	He is hardly pressed for time.	106.	He is hard- pressed for time.

Note: The word 'hard' is both an adjective and an adverb. Its meaning is quite different from 'hardly' which is also an adverb. 'Hardly' means 'almost no' or 'almost not'; here, the correct expression is 'hard-pressed' which means 'under pressure', or 'strained' (refer sentence nos. 103, 104, 105, and 106).

107.	The two first pages of this book are torn.	107.	The first two pages of this book are torn.
108.	The two first chapters of this book are good.	108.	The first two chapters of this book are good.
109.	He speaks well English.	109.	He speaks English well.
110.	I like very much skating.	110.	I like skating very much.
111.	I yesterday met him.	111.	I met him yesterday.
112.	They're tomorrow leaving for Paris.	112.	They're leaving for Paris tomorrow.
113.	You well organised that function.	113.	You organised that function well.
114.	She badly dances.	114.	She dances badly.
115.	She is very slower than Reena.	115.	She is much slower than Reena.
116.	You are very older than me.	116.	You are much older than me.

Note: When 'than' or 'as' is followed by third person pronoun, the verb is repeated. If 'than' or 'as' is followed by first and second person, then the verb is omitted (refer sentence nos. 115 and 116).

Note: The word 'later' denotes the comparative of 'late'. It means more late in time, or afterwards. But 'latter' is the opposite of 'former'; it means the second of the two people/things mentioned. 'Later' denotes time whereas 'latter' denotes position (refer sentence nos.).

117.	It is nothing else than pride.	117.	It is nothing else but pride.
118.	Call me anything else than a thief.	118.	Call me anything else but a thief.
119.	He seldom or ever goes to his village.	119.	He seldom — if ever (seldom or never) — goes to his village.
120.	It is no use to ask her – she is not interested in it.	120.	It is no use asking her — she is not interested in it.
121.	Is it any use to try to talk to him?	121.	Is it any use trying to talk to him?
122.	His mother kept on to encourage to study.	122.	His mother kept on encouraging him to study.
123.	Whatever happens, keep on to try.	123.	Whatever happens, keep on trying.
124.	She knows to sing and dance.	124.	She knows how to sing and dance.
125.	He know to prepare French toast.	125.	He knows how to prepare French toast.
126.	He has finished to mend the puncture.	126.	He has finished mending the puncture.
127.	I enjoy to travel.	127.	I enjoy traveling.
128.	Why is she appearing so sad?	128.	Why does she appear so sad?

129.	I am owing a great deal to my parents.	129.	I owe a great deal to my parents.
130.	I am not feeling well today.	130.	I am not well today.

An adjective of superlative degree is used when the noun it qualifies shows the possession of a quality to a higher degree than any other member of the same class.

131.	He is adoring that political leader.	131.	He adores that political leader.
132.	I have not and shall not bear this trouble.	132.	I have not borne and shall not bear this trouble.
133.	I have never and will never do such a thing.	133.	I have never done and shall never do such a thing.
134.	He hanged the lamp on the wall.	134.	He hung the lamp on the wall.
135.	He was hung for murder.	135.	He was hanged for murder.
136.	This book costed me half post twelve rupees.	136.	This book cost me rupees twelve and fifty paise.
137.	The hens have lain no eggs today.	137.	The hens have laid no eggs today.
138.	Let me lay on the bed.	138.	Let me lie on the bed.
139.	He has returned back from Delhi.	139.	He has returned (come back) from Delhi.
140.	I awaited for his arrival.	140.	I awaited (waited for) his arrival.

- A compound subject joined by the word 'generally' takes a plural verb.
- You and I are working.
- Four and four make eight.
- Are not your sister and brother ill?
- Wealth and happiness are all Ravi wants.
- Bed and table were both very costly.
- Rice and wheat, purchased a week before, were both rotten.

141.	He has repaid back his loan.	141.	He has repaid (paid back) his loan.
142.	The boat was drowned in the river.	142.	The boat was sunk in the river.
143.	A boy has been sunk in the river.	143.	A boy has drowned in the river.
144.	Who invented America?	144.	Who discovered America?
145.	Marconi discovered the wireless.	145.	Marconi invented the wireless.
146.	Neither his action was just nor unjust.	146.	His action was neither just nor unjust.
147.	I neither saw him nor her.	147.	I saw neither him nor her.
148.	Neither it is good nor it is bad.	148.	It is neither good nor bad.
149.	Ten students have passed and one failed.	149.	Ten students have passed and one has failed.
150.	One of the thieves escaped and two caught.	150.	One of the thieves escaped and two were caught.
151.	Tell me where are you going.	151.	Tell me where you are going.
152.	He asked me what was your name.	152.	He asked me what my name was.
153.	Tell me when are you leaving for New York.	153.	Tell me when you are leaving for New York.

154.	She finished her work when I met her.	154.	She had finished her work when I met her.
155.	The train started before he reached the station.	155.	The train had started before he reached the station.
156.	They will be delighted if you will welcome them.	156.	They will be delighted if you welcome them.
157.	I will tell you as soon as I will know about it.	157.	I will tell you as soon as I know about it.
158.	When I shall go to Paris, I shall inform you.	158.	When I go to Paris, I shall inform you.
159.	It is time you go to bed.	159.	It is time you went to bed.
160.	It is time you wash your face.	160.	It is time you washed your face.
161.	She knew that I am coming.	161.	She knew that I was coming.
162.	Both Raju as well as his brother were present.	162.	Both Raju and his brother were present.
163.	Tigers are both found in Asia and in Africa.	163.	Tigers are found both in Asia and in Africa.
164.	Will I turn the light on?	164.	Shall I turn the light on?
165.	Shall he come tomorrow?	165.	Will he come tomorrow?
166.	Will we attend the party?	166.	Shall we attend the party?
167.	Please excuse me being late.	167.	Please excuse my being late.

168.	She disliked me coming late.	168.	She disliked my coming late.
169.	Unless you do not work hard, you will cut a sorry figure.	169.	Unless you work hard, you will cut a sorry figure.
170.	Walk slowly lest you should not fall down.	170.	Walk slowly lest you should fall down.
171.	I thought of attending the party, but could not.	171.	I had thought of attending the party but could not.
172.	We hoped that you would solve this problem.	172.	We had hoped that you would solve this problem.
173.	I expected not such a turn of events.	173.	I had not expected such a turn of events.
174.	I had gone to Chandigarh.	174.	I went to Chandigarh. Or, I had been to Chandigarh.
175.	I had slept for hours.	175.	I slept for hours.
176.	He needs not seek my help.	176.	He need not seek my help.
177.	She dares not walk in the dark.	177.	She dare not walk in the dark.
178.	There is a HE school in my village.	178.	There is an HE school in my village.
179.	He is a NCC officer.	179.	He is an NCC officer.
180.	He has set up a X-ray plant.	180.	He has set up an X-ray plant.
181.	He is an university professor.	181.	He is a university professor.
182.	It is an unit of measurement.	182.	It is a unit of measurement.

183.	It is an universal truth.	183.	It is a universal truth.
184.	He plays violin.	184.	He plays the violin.
185.	Can you lay table?	185.	Can you lay the table?
186.	He has no knowledge and interest in music.	186.	He has no knowledge of and interest in music.
187.	He did not agree but differed from my opinion.	187.	He did not agree to but differed from my opinion.
188.	There is no end of troubles.	188.	There is no end to troubles.
189.	I am busy in my work.	189.	I am busy with my work.
190.	Send this letter on my address.	190.	Send this letter to my address.
191.	Entering the room, the boys were found quarrelling.	191.	Entering the room, he found the boys quarrelling.
192.	Walking in the garden, a snake bit him.	192.	While he was walking in the garden, a snake bit him.
193.	Barking furiously, I let the dog out of the compound.	193.	I let the dog, barking furiously, out of the compound.
194.	Going out of the room, the door was left open by her.	194.	Going out of the room, she left the door open.
195.	On examining the answer books, many silly mistakes were detected.	195.	On examining the answer books, we detected many silly mistakes.
196.	I saw her to go.	196.	I saw her go.
197.	I observed him to limp.	197.	I observed him limp.

198.	He insisted to go.	198.	He insisted ongoing.
199.	I am tired to sing and dance.	199.	I am tired of singing and dancing.
200.	He succeeded to win the match.	200.	He succeeded in winning the match.
201.	Avoid to go there.	201.	Avoid going there.
202.	Stop to worry.	202.	Stop worrying.
203	Keep on to try.	203.	Keep on trying.
204.	He is busy to write letters.	204.	He is busy writing letters.
205.	It is no good to cry over spilt milk.	205.	It is no good crying over spilt milk.
206.	There is no harm to do this work.	206.	There is no harm in doing this work.
207.	Death is more preferable than dishonour.	207.	Death is preferable to dishonour.
208.	I prefer swimming than walking.	208.	I prefer swimming to walking.
209.	He regards me his guardian.	209.	He regards me as his guardian.
210.	They portrayed Nehru is dictator.	210.	They portrayed Nehru as dictator.

- Plural words placed between a singular subject and its verb do not change the number of the subject.
- The sound of the bells was heard by everyone.
- One of the books is missing.
- The water of those streams was sweet.
- The trouble with all those cars was slow speed.

211.	She called me as a dullard.	211.	She called me a dullard.

212.	He was appointed as principal.	212.	He was appointed principal.
213.	She look as if she suspects foul play.	213.	She looks as if she suspected foul play.
214.	You act as though everything is in your hand.	214.	You act as though everything was in your hands.
215.	He did nothing but to play.	215.	He did nothing but play.
216.	She did nothing but to sing.	216.	She did nothing but sing.
217.	She did no more than to cry.	217.	She did no more than cry.
218.	She will wash up before she will go to bed.	218.	She will wash up before she goes to bed.
219.	You won't know how good pudding, is till you will have tasted it.	219.	You won't know how good the pudding is till you have tasted it.
220.	It is I who is responsible for this mistake.	220.	It is I who am responsible for this mistake.

- 'The two first' is a meaningless expression; it implies that two things may be first.
- It makes no sense. The correct expression is 'the first two'.
- Adverbs of definite time are put at the beginning or the end of a clause.
- They are not to be placed in the middle.
- 'Very' is used with adjectives and adverbs in the positive degree and with present participle whereas 'much' is used with adjectives and adverbs in the comparative degree, and with the past participle.

221.	It is you who is responsible for this mistake.	221.	It is you who are responsible for this mistake.
222.	I want an armchair for an old man with sliding back.	222.	I want an armchair with a sliding back for an old man.
223.	He shot himself dead after bidding his wife goodbye with a pistol.	223.	He shot himself dead with a pistol after bidding his wife goodbye.
224.	Nobody has ever helped you, has he?	224.	Nobody has ever helped you, have they?
225.	Don't do that anymore, do you?	225.	Don't do that anymore, will you?

- Ever usually means 'at any time'. It cannot go with seldom which means 'not often, rarely'. The correct expression is seldom or never, or seldom if ever.
- We usually use the adverb 'but' (not, 'than') after 'else'.

226.	I am taller than him, isn't I?	226.	I am taller than him, aren't I?
227.	Bring a cold glass of water.	227.	Bring a glass of cold water.
228.	He has purchased a fresh basket of apples.	228.	He has purchased a basket of fresh apples.
229.	I'd love to have a hot cup of tea.	229.	I'd love to have a cup of hot tea.
230.	He already left for Delhi.	230.	He has already left for Delhi.

Note: In expressions like these, use is followed by an '–ing' form.

The correct expression is, it or there is no use + '–ing' form of verb.

231.	He did not speak to me since that incident.	231.	He has not spoken to me since that incident.

232.	He did not receive any message up till now.	232.	He has not received any message up till now.
233.	So far he did not reach the station.	233.	So far he has not reached the station.
234.	This tragic incident has taken place last year.	234.	This tragic incident took place last year.
235.	She has gone to bed at 9 o'clock.	235.	She went to bed at 9 o'clock.
236.	I have met him yesterday.	236.	I met him yesterday.
237.	Reeta was married by Rakesh.	237.	Rakesh married Reeta.
238.	He married his youngest daughter.	238.	He got his youngest daughter married.
239.	His youngest daughter was married with an engineer.	239	His youngest daughter was married to an engineer.
240.	She comes to college by a bicycle.	240.	She comes to college by bicycle.
			Or, She comes to college on a bicycle.

- When words are added to a singular subjects using terms like 'with', 'together with', 'along with', 'in addition to', 'as well as', 'except', 'besides', 'and not', and 'no less than', then the number of the subject remains singular.
- The ship, with all its passengers, was drowned.
- The letter, together with other documents, was lost.
- He, along with his parents, is coming today.
- A watch, in addition to rupees fifty, was given to Hari.

241.	He came back by my car.	241.	He came back in my car.

242.	Supposing if he does not come, what will you do?	242.	Supposing he does not come, what will do?
			Or, If he does not come, what will you do?
243.	He informed that everybody had gone against him.	243.	He informed me (us, him, them, etc.) that everybody had gone against him.
244.	She told that she was interested in chess.	244.	She told me (us, him, them, etc.) that she was interested in chess.
245.	He assured that every help would be given.	245.	He assured me (us, him, them, etc.) of every help to be given.
249.	Flour is made of wheat.	249.	Flour is made from wheat.
250.	Your chair is not made from wood.	250.	Your chair is not made of wood.
251.	I think you haven't met my father.	251.	I do not think you have met my father.
252.	I believe you haven't seen the Taj Mahal.	252.	I don't believe you have seen the Taj Mahal.
253.	Do sit down, will you?	253.	Do sit down, won't you?
254.	Give me sufficient time, won't you?	254.	Give me sufficient time, will you?
255.	Shut up, can you?	255.	Shut up, can't you?
256.	He pays more attention to films than books.	256.	He pays more attention to films than to books.
257.	I can rely more on you than her.	257.	I can rely more on you than on her.

258.	He is declared to pass in the first division.	258.	He is declared to have passed in the first division.
259.	She is supposed to commit this murder.	259.	She is supposed to have committed this murder.

- When two subject are joined by 'as well as', the verb agrees in number and person with the first one.
- He, as well as they, is ready to jump.
- My comrades, as well as I, are visiting Delhi.
- When two or more nouns or pronouns in the singular are connected using 'or' 'nor', 'either…or', 'neither…nor', then they take a singular verb.
- Neither Dick nor his sister is to blame. Either the dog or the cat has been killed.
- When one of the subjects – joined with 'or', 'nor', 'either …or', 'neither…nor' – is plural, then the verb must be plural, and the plural subject should be placed close to the verb.
- Either the farmer or his sons reap harvest.
- Neither Satish nor his sons are honest.
- When the subjects joined by or, nor, either…. Or, neither.... nor are of different persons, the verb agrees with the nearer subject.
- Either he or you are guilty.
- Neither you nor I am to blame.
- Neither you nor he is willing to come.
- Neither he nor they are honest.

COMMON ERRORS MADE WHILE USING ONE WORD FOR ANOTHER:

Incorrect sentence		Correct sentence	
1.	His forefather were great men.	1.	His forefathers were great men.
2.	He is given free boarding and lodging.	2.	His is given free board and lodging.
3.	There is a bevy of boys.	3.	There is a bevy of girls.
4.	This house is made of brick.	4.	This house is made of bricks.
5.	There is a crowd of grapes.	5.	There is a bunch of grapes.
6.	He has not paid the fooding charge.	6.	He has not paid the food charge.
7.	I enjoy free-ship.	7.	I enjoy free studentship.
8.	He has applied for lecturer.	8.	He has applied for lectureship.
9.	He doesn't like teachery as a profession.	9.	He doesn't like teaching as a profession.
10.	A towny man gets a lot of comforts.	10.	A townsman gets a lot of comforts.
11.	The house is beyond repairs.	11.	This house is beyond repair.
12.	You are a man of words.	12.	You are a man of your word.
13.	He is true to his words.	13.	He is true to his word.
14.	I did all my works.	14.	I did all my work.
15.	I have sent a petition for casual leave.	15.	I have sent an application for casual leave.
16.	He is out of door.	16.	He is out of doors.
17.	I have placed order for a book.	17.	I have ordered a book.
18.	He is out of spirit.	18.	He is out of spirits.
19.	I am out of sort.	19.	I am out of sorts.
20.	I am a man of part.	20.	I am a man of parts.
21.	He applied himself to study.	21.	He applied himself to studies.
22.	I am resting the shadow of a tree.	22.	I am resting under the shade of a tree.

	Incorrect sentence		Correct sentence
23.	There is no place on this berth.	23.	There is no room on this berth.
24.	I have no rupees.	24.	I have no money.
25.	He walked on his cycle.	25.	He rode on his cycle.
26.	My salary is Rs. 400/- per month.	26.	My salary is Rs. 400 a month.
27.	My salary is Rs. 4800/- per year.	27.	My salary is Rs. 4800 a year.
28.	Please credit this amount to my name.	28.	Please credit this amount to my name.
29.	Good bye, Ram, I am glad to see you.	29.	Good evening Ram, I am glad to see you.
30.	Good night, sir, you are welcome.	30.	Good morning Sir, you are welcome.
31.	The weather of this place suits me.	31.	The climate of this place suits me.
32.	He is devoted to gambling.	32.	He is addicted to gambling.
33.	You are addicted to literature.	33.	You are devoted to literature.
34.	There is lack of poverty here.	34.	There is absence of poverty here.
35.	I gave him a cheque of Rs.500/-.	35.	I have him a cheque for Rs.500.
36.	This great poem is very artful.	36.	This great poem is very artistic.
37.	I like you childish nature.	37.	I like your childlike nature.
38.	Shakespeare was an imaginary poet.	38.	Shakespeare was an imaginative poet.
39.	As he is sick, he is absent.	39.	As he is ill, he is absent.

	Incorrect sentence		Correct sentence
40.	Please grant me ill leave.	40.	Please grant me sick leave.
41.	What's the cause for delay?	41.	What's the cause of delay?
42.	There is no cause of complain.	42.	There is no cause for complain
43.	She is somewhat tall for her age.	43.	She is too tall for her age.
44.	The great saint is notorious in the spiritual field.	44.	The famous saint is notorious in the spiritual field.
45.	You are a luxuriant man.	45.	You are a luxurious man.
46.	Please shut the tap.	46.	Please turn off the tap.
47.	Bread is made of flour.	47.	Bread is made from flour.
48.	He is very coward.	48.	He is a coward.
49.	He is our mutual friend.	49.	He is our common friend.
50.	He rose by dint of sheer merit.	50.	He rose by dint of great merit.
51.	They are fast enemies.	51.	They are fast friends.
52.	They are sworn enemies.	52.	They are avowed enemies.
53.	He highly deserves this punishment.	53	He rightly deserves this punishment.
54.	It is utterly right.	54.	It is wholly right.
55.	I have done good at the examination.	55.	I have done well at the examination.
56.	The thief stood in front of the judge.	56.	The thief stood before the judge.
57.	It is 4:30 in my watch.	57.	It is 4:30 by my watch.

Incorrect sentence		Correct sentence	
58.	It is totally clear to me.	58.	It is perfectly clear to me.
59.	It is totally right.	59.	It is all right.
60.	It is totally good.	60.	It is wholly good.
61.	The pot is vacant.	61.	The pot is empty.
62.	I admire her womanish virtues.	62.	I admire her womanly virtues.
63.	It is a historical event.	63.	It is a historic event.
64.	My tooth is paining.	64.	My tooth is aching.
65.	I took my admission.	65.	I was admitted Or, I got myself admitted.
66.	I took my birth in 1920.	66.	I was born in 1920.
67.	He invited me but I denied.	67.	He invited me but I declined.
68.	He denied to help me.	68.	He refused to help me.
69.	She gave a speech.	69.	She made a speech.
70.	A lot of men suspect the existence of God.	70.	A lot of men doubt the existence of God.
71.	I don't like that he should go out.	71.	I don't like him to go out.
72.	The ship was drowned in the sea.	72.	The ship sank in the sea.
73.	Fish float in the river.	73.	Fish swim in the river.
74.	A piece of wood is swimming.	74.	A piece of wood is floating.
75.	The picture was hanged.	75.	The picture was hung.

Incorrect sentence		Correct sentence	
76.	I cannot rise it.	76.	I cannot raise it.
77.	I will do it some way or another.	77.	I will do it in some or the other way.
78.	Please await me here.	78.	Please wait for me here.
79.	He jumped at a conclusion.	79.	He jumped to a conclusion.
80.	Neither of them saw each other.	80.	Neither of them saw the other.
81.	The cars followed each other.	81.	One car followed the other.
82.	My speech was broadcasted.	82.	My speech was broadcast.
83.	His words are as sweet as sugar.	83.	His words are as sweet as honey.
84.	I went there especially to see him.	84.	I went there specially to see him.
85.	I cannot stay here anymore.	85.	I cannot stay here any longer.
86.	He went with me so far as Bombay.	86.	He went with me as far as Bombay.
87.	She refused to look at me, much more speak to me.	87.	She refused to look at me, much more speak to me.

- If the subject is a title, the name of a book, a clause, a quotation, or other group of words expressing a single idea, then the verb is singular.
- Tales from Shakespeare makes interesting reading.
- Sparks is a well-known weekly.
- All men are created equal is a truth.
- The United States is a rich country.
- Hard Times has been written by Dickens.
- If the subject of a sentence – although plural in form - denotes a specific quality or distance, then it is considered as a single unit. In all such cases the verb is generally singular.

- Three thousand miles is a long distance.
- Ten pounds is enough for me.
- Ten years is sufficient to complete this project.
- Three mounds of coal has been consumed.
- Sixteen annas is equal to one rupee.
- Five hours is not much for outdoor work.
- Some nouns which are plural in form but singular in meaning, require a singular verb.
- This news is not correct.
- Economics is a difficult subject.
- Ethics deal with the problem of morality.
- Measles is a dangerous disease.
- The wages of sin is death.

88.	He was hung for murder.	88.	He was hanged for murder.
89.	The smoke is rising from huts.	89.	The smoke rising from huts.
90.	I didn't approve this marriage proposal.	90.	I didn't approve of this marriage proposal.
91.	Columbus invented America.	91.	Columbus discovered America.
92.	You enjoy bad health.	92.	You have bad health.
93.	This scheme has been approved of by the VC.	93.	This scheme has been approval by the V.C.
94.	I can't question his bona fide.	94.	I can't question his bon fides.
95.	Please excuse me coming late.	95.	Please excuse my coming late.
96.	Will you forego your holiday?	96.	Will you forego your holiday?
97.	I told him good morning.	97.	I wished him good morning.
98.	He tells me a fool.	98.	He calls me a fool.
99.	He stopped at my house for a week.	99.	He stayed at my house for a week.
100.	He saw my certificates.	100.	He looked into my certificates.
101.	The doctor saw my pulse.	101.	The doctor felt my pulse.

- If the subject of a sentence begins with a fraction, then the verb agrees with the noun or pronoun that comes after the preposition 'of'.
- Two-thirds of the book is interesting.
- Two-thirds of the books are interesting.
- A quarter of it is fresh.
- A quarter of them are on sale.
- Half of it is useful.
- Half of them are rotten.
- The same principle applies to phrases such as 'the rest of', 'majority of', 'heaps of', 'most of', and 'lots of'.

102.	Have you seen all the examination papers?	102.	Have you seen all the examined papers?
103.	See this word in the dictionary.	103.	Look up this word in the dictionary.
104.	The teacher told that the earth is round.	104.	The teacher said that the earth is round.
105.	Whom are you speaking to?	105.	Who are you speaking to?
106.	His dear half is ill.	106.	His better half is ill.
107.	The matter shook in the balance.	107.	The matter trembled in the balance.
108.	He is as gentle as a cow.	108.	He is as gentle as a lamb.
109.	He is as greedy as a cat.	109.	He is as greedy as a wolf.
110.	He is as faithful as a horse.	110.	He is as faithful as a dog.
111.	He turned every stone.	111.	He left no stone unturned.
112.	My friend tells that the Five-Year Plan is good.	112.	My friend says that the Five-Year Plan is good.

113.	It is as white as milk.	113.	It is as white as snow.
114.	I have given examination this year.	114.	I have appeared at examination this year.
115.	He broke the news of my grand success.	115.	He communicated the news of my grand success.
116.	I could not help to laugh.	116.	I could not help laughing.
117.	My parrot speaks.	117.	My parrot talks.
118.	It is as heavy as stone.	118.	It is as heavy as lead.
119.	He talks English well.	119.	He speaks English well.
120.	He is as firm as a hill.	120.	He is as firm as a rock.
121.	Do not speak a lie.	121.	Do not tell a lie.
122.	It is as soft as velvet.	122.	It is as soft as butter.
123.	It is a forgone conclusion.	123.	It is a forgoing conclusion.
124.	She is as busy as an ant.	124.	She is as busy as a bee.
125.	What to speak of helping, he did not even see me.	125.	What to speak of helping, he didn't even look at me.
126.	It is an apple of contention.	126.	It is an apple of discord.
127.	He shook my hand.	127.	He shook hands with me.
128.	Except for your help I would have been ruined.	128.	Without your help I would have been ruined.
129.	His name is full- known.	129.	His name is well- known.
130.	It is as clear as gold.	130.	It is as clear as crystal.
131.	He made goal.	131.	He made score.

COMMON ERRORS MADE WHILE USING SUPERFLUOUS WORDS

Incorrect sentence		Correct sentence	
1.	She is a mother of mine.	1.	She is my mother.
2.	He is my own father.	2.	He is my father.
3.	The fact is true.	3.	It is a fact.
4.	I am awaiting for your reply.	4.	I am waiting for your reply.
5.	He picked up a quarrel.	5.	He picked a quarrel.
6.	He died at the age of seventy years.	6.	He died at the age of seventy.
7.	I met a child of five years old.	7.	I met a five-year old child. Or, I met a child of five years.
8.	The clock has struck six hours.	8.	The clock has struck six.
9.	It is almost quite right.	9.	It is quite right.
10.	He is a man of good position.	10.	He is a man of position.

- Some nouns — e.g., abuse, advice, alarm, alphabet, bread, brick, bunting, clothing, folk, furniture, gossip, hair, information, issue, luggage, offspring, poetry, scenery thunder, etc. — are used only in the singular form and the verb that follows them is also singular.
- Incorrect: The sceneries of Darjeeling are very beautiful.
- Correct: The scenery of Darjeeling is very beautiful.
- Incorrect: Their informations are based on facts.
- Correct: Their information is based on facts.
- Incorrect: All my furnitures have been burnt.
- Correct: All my furniture has been burnt

11.	It is rather unique.	11.	It is unique.

12.	I am a man of good principle.	12.	I am a man of principle.
13.	I walked on my feet.	13.	I walked on foot.
14.	I think myself.	14.	I think.
15.	I forbade him not to smoke.	15.	I forbade him to smoke.
16.	This is just the right thing.	16.	This is just the thing.
17.	He is my cousin brother.	17.	He is my cousin.
18.	I ordered for his dismissal.	18.	I ordered his dismissal.
19.	He was a proved to be wrong.	19.	He was proved wrong.
20.	I consider it a good thing.	20.	Consider it a good thing.
21.	I think/consider him to be a good student.	21.	I consider him a good student.
22.	The train is behind due time.	22.	The train is behind time.
23.	You are my only one friend.	23.	You are my only friend.
24.	There is no other alternative.	24.	There is no alternative.
25.	She made a fine figure.	25.	She made a figure.
26.	The poet describes about nature.	26.	The poet describes nature.
27.	I saw him on last week.	27.	I saw him last week.
28.	I doubt as to whether he is honest.	28.	I doubt whether he is honest.
29.	Let us discuss about the problem.	29.	Let us discuss the problem.
30.	I am investigating into the case.	30.	I am investigating the case.
31.	I am contesting for a seat.	31.	I am contesting a seat.
32.	I recommended for him to the Principal.	32.	I recommended him to the Principal.
33.	Her face resembles to her mother.	33.	She resembles her mother.
34.	Wait here until I do not return.	34.	Wait here until I return.
35.	Unless you do not work hard, you will not pass.	35.	Unless you work hard, you will not pass.
36.	My watch is in proper order.	36.	My watch is in order.
37.	She is in a bad temper.	37.	She is in a temper.
38.	He is out of good temper.	38.	He is out of temper.
39.	I am forty years.	39.	I am forty years old.
40.	He will return back in a week.	40.	He will come back in a week.

COMMON ERRORS CAUSED BY THE OMISSION OF WORDS

Incorrect sentence		**Correct sentence**	
1.	This house is 200 years.	1.	This house is 200 years old.
2.	Please come to mine.	2.	Please come to my house.
3.	I find hard to doit.	3.	I find it hard to do.
4.	Suffice to say.	4.	Suffice it to say.
5.	I know him a good man.	5.	I know him to bea good man.
6.	His services were dispensed.	6.	His services were dispensed with.
7.	She does not listen my advice.	7.	She does not listen to my advice.

Incorrect sentence		Correct sentence	
8.	He does not know to read andwrite.	8.	He does not know how to read and write.
9.	It is regarded sacred.	9.	It is regarded as sacred.
10.	I took him a thief.	10.	I took him for a thief.
11.	I have a pen to write.	11.	I have a pen to write with.
12.	You have a house to live.	12.	You have a house to live in.
13.	He resides in a boarding.	13.	He resides in a boarding house.
14.	Open page 15.	14.	Open at page 15.

Incorrect sentence		Correct sentence	
15.	I wrote him to come.	15.	I wrote to him to come.
16.	I replied him.	16.	I replied to him.
17.	I pray God.	17.	I pray to God.
18.	Go there and enjoy.	18.	Go there and enjoy yourself.
19.	He met an accident.	19.	He met with an accident.
20.	She is five feet.	20.	She is five feet tall.
21.	When he grows he will enter a college.	21.	When he grows up he will enter a college.
22.	She avenged on her enemy.	22.	She avenged herself on her enemy.

If the subject begins with 'a number of', then the verb is always plural. This is because 'a number of' means 'many'.

- A number of children are playing in the field.
- A number of prisoners have escaped from the jail.

However, when the subject begins with 'the number of, then the verb is singular.

- The number of the persons present is very small.
- The number of students in this college has swelled.

Certain nouns – such as cattle, clergy, gentry, people, police, poultry, public, swine, vermin, etc. – though singular in form, are used as plural and they usually require a plural verb.

- The cattle are grazing in the field.
- The public were moved by this spectacle.
- The clergy were unanimous in their opinion.
- The vermin are harmful.

Phrases beginning with 'a band of', 'a chain of', 'a bouquet of', 'a galaxy of', 'a series of', 'a team of', 'a bevy of', 'a set of', 'a crowd of', 'a regiment of', 'a flock of', 'a class of', and 'a batch of' require a singular verb though the word following 'of' is plural.

- A band of musicians has come.
- A series of accidents has taken place.
- A team of doctors has been called in.
- A herd of cattle is in the field.
- A set of bangles has been purchased.

If the subject of a sentence begins with any of the following phrases - 'a good deal of', 'a great deal of', 'a lot of', 'most of', and 'some of', then the verb agrees with the subject of the preposition 'of'. • A good deal of time has been lost. • A good deal of efforts are needed. • Some of the music was boring. • Some of the children were hungry. • The class (as a unit) is marching into the hall.	Some collective nouns – such as 'class', 'cabinet', 'committee', 'board', 'army', 'jury', 'mob', 'government', 'team', etc. – require the verb in the singular or in the plural, depending on whether the speaker of that sentence thinks of the thing as a single whole or in terms of the individuals of which it is composed. • The team (as a unit) is winning. • The team (as individuals) are fighting for a win. • The class (as individuals) are debating this point. • The jury (as a single body) has given its verdict. • The jury (as individuals) were discussing this point. • The committee (as a single body) has issued its report. • The committee (as individuals) are divided in their opinion.	The words 'rage', 'temper', 'headache', 'rest', 'cold', etc. require an indefinite article preceding them when spoken of in connection with some person(s). However, both 'catch a cold' and 'catch cold' are acceptable in modern usage. We say, 'a bad cold' and 'a severe pain'.

23.	Will you take rest here?	23.	Will you take a rest here?
24.	The lady was in temper.	24.	The lady was in a temper.
25.	I have got headache.	25.	I have got a headache.
26.	He flew into rage.	26.	He flew into a rage.
27.	You may have cold if you go out.	27.	You may catch a cold if you go out.
28.	She prides on her beauty.	28.	She prides herself on her beauty.
29.	Students should avail of good opportunities.	29.	Students should avail themselves of good opportunities.

30.	I may absent tomorrow.	30.	I may absent myself tomorrow.

Following verbs are made meaningful by the prepositions that follow the verbs.

- In that sense, 'money to buy' means 'money that will buy' and 'chair to sit' means 'chair to sit on'.
- The word 'enjoy' is used to denote 'enjoy something', 'enjoy doing something', or 'enjoy oneself doing something'.
- The verb 'write' is one that can be used with two objects.
  Write me a letter soon.
- When there is no direct object, we usually use it with the indirect object. However, 'to' is often left out in conversational style, particularly in American English.
  Write me when you get back.

31.	I know him a sincere friend.	31.	I know him to be a sincere friend.
32.	I believe you a noble worker.	32.	I believe you to be a noble worker.
33.	He does not know to write.	33.	He does not know how to write.
34.	This book is useful as that.	34.	This book is as useful as that.
35.	He attends his duty punctually.	35.	He attends to his duty punctually.
36.	I have nothing to complain.	36.	I have nothing to complain of.
37.	He has no money to buy food.	37.	He has no money to buy food with.
38.	Here are two chairs to sit.	38.	Here are two chairs to sit on (or, in).
39.	I have no pen to write.	39.	I have no pen to write with.
40.	Open page twenty- five.	40.	Open at page twenty-five.
41.	India became free in nineteen hundred forty–seven.	41.	India became free in nineteen hundred and forty-seven.
42.	I enjoy from the fresh air.	42.	I enjoy myself from the fresh air.
43.	We enjoyed at the party.	43.	We enjoyed ourselves at the party.
44.	Write me when you get back.	44.	Write to me when you get back.

COMMON ERRORS INTRUSION OF WORDS

Incorrect sentence		Correct sentence	
1.	The clock has struck seven hours.	1.	The clock has struck seven. ('hours' is superfluous)
2.	This is a fine poetry.	2.	This is fine poetry. Or, This is a fine poem.

Note: Abstract nouns such as 'poetry', 'scenery', etc. require no article preceding them (refer sentence no. 476).

3.	He will go to school on his foot.	3.	He will go to school on foot.
4.	He will reach home in the time.	4.	He will reach home in time.

Note: Phrases such as 'go on foot', 'reach in time', etc. are idiomatic ways of expression (refer sentence nos. 3 and 4).

5.	Unless you do not labour hard you cannot be successful.	5.	Unless you labour hard, you cannot be successful.

Note: The word 'unless' means 'if not'; hence 'not' should never be used after 'unless' to make the sentence negative (refer sentence no. 5).

6.	He recommended for me to the S.D.O.	6.	He recommended me to the S.D.O.
7.	The Principal ordered for his expulsion.	7.	The Principal ordered his expulsion.
8.	Do not violate against the rule.	8.	Do not violate the rule.

Note: Transitive verbs like 'recommend', 'violate', 'ordered', etc. require no preposition preceding their objects (refer sentence nos. 6, 7, and 8).

9.	I am sixty years.	9.	I am sixty. Or I am sixty years old,
10.	Wordsworth describes about nature.	10.	Wordsworth describes nature.
11.	Don't discuss about politics here.	11.	Don't discuss politics here.

12.	The judge ordered for the execution of the murderer.	12.	The judge ordered the execution of the murderer.

- If the subject of a sentence begins with 'none of', then the verb is generally plural.
- None of the candidates have appeared for an interview.
- None of these scientists are willing to take up this challenge.

- If 'none' refers to an uncountable noun, the verb is singular.
- If it refers to a countable noun in its plural form, then the verb can be either singular or plural.
- I have been waiting for the sugar, but none (of it) has arrived.
- I have been waiting for my friends, but none (of them) has/have arrived.
- Certain adjectives are used with the definite article 'the' to denote a group of people in a particular condition: 'the blind', 'the sick', 'the deaf', 'the poor', 'the young', 'the old', 'the dead', 'the brave', 'the coward', 'the handicapped', 'the unemployed', etc.
- Certain expressions refer to a plural: the blind means 'the blind people', or 'all blind people', but not 'the blind man'. When such expressions form the subject of a sentence, the subject requires a plural verb: The blind are helpless; The rich are selfish; The poor are hungry; The unemployed are restless.

13.	This man resembles to his brother.	13.	This man resembles his brother.
14.	You should inform to the police officer.	14.	You should inform the police officer.
15.	He does not obey to my words.	15.	He does not obey my words.
16.	You should assist to him your best.	16.	You should assist him your best.
17.	The Police Inspector investigated into the case of theft.	17.	The Police Inspector investigated the case of theft.

18.	I shall combat with your views in the meeting.	18.	I shall combat your views in the meeting.

Note: Transitive verbs such as 'describe', 'discuss', 'resemble', 'inform', 'obey', 'order', 'assist', 'sign', 'investigate', 'combat', 'pervade', etc. do not require a preposition between them and their objects (refer sentence nos. 13, 14, 15, 16, 17, and 18).

19.	Have you signed on that contract?	19.	Have you signed that contract?
20.	Negative thoughts pervade through the mind of many persons.	20.	Negative thoughts pervade the mind of many persons.
21.	How much late was he?	21.	How late was he?

Some words indicating nationality and ending with '–sh' or '–ch' or '–ese' can also be used with a definite article: 'the British', 'the English', 'the French', etc.

- These expressions are plural: 'the British' means 'all (the) British people'.
- When the subject of a sentence is one such expression it requires a plural verb.
- The French love good food.
- The Japanese are hard-working.
- The British have a long history.
- The Chinese are strong-willed.

(a) When the article 'a' or 'an' is used after many, the noun that follows it is always singular and consequently the verb is also singular.

- Many a man comes and goes.
- Many an animal lives on grass.

(b) The collection more-than-one is treated as a compound of one.

As a singular noun it is followed by a singular verb.

- More than one passenger was killed.
- More than one examinee was expelled. Here, you cannot use 'passengers' or 'examiners' in place of 'passenger' and 'examinee'. Nor can you use 'were' in place of 'was'.

(c) In the sentences pattern, 'more + plural noun + than one', the verb is always plural.

- More principles than one were present.
- More books than one have been burnt.

COMMON ERRORS ARISING OUT OF THE ORDER OF WORDS

Incorrect sentence		Correct sentence	
1.	This is a quite different thing.	1.	This is quite a different thing.
2.	His both eyes are weak.	2.	Both his eyes are weak.
3.	The both men came.	3.	Both the men came.
4.	The all men came.	4.	All the men came.
5.	He lost his all book.	5.	He lost all his books.
6.	There is nothing such as luck.	6.	There is no such thing as luck.
7.	To whom you will give it?	7.	To whom will you give it?
8.	When he went to Patna?	8.	When did he go to Patna?
9.	Tell me how are you.	9.	Tell me how you are.
10.	He asked her what was the matter.	10.	He asked her what the matter was.
11.	Let me know why did you do it.	11.	Let me know why you did it.
12.	I, he, and you have been invited.	12.	You, he, and I have been invited.
13.	Silver and gold I have none.	13.	Silver and gold have I none.
14.	The more you labour hard the more you will learn.	14.	The more you labour hard, the more will you learn.
15.	The more men have, the more they desire.	15.	The more men have, the more do they desire.
16.	Neither Ram will come to my house nor his brother.	16.	Neither will Ram come to my house nor will his brother.
17.	Neither it is good nor it is bad.	17.	Neither is it good, nor is it bad.
18.	No sooner I had started than it began to rain.	18.	No sooner had I started than it began to rain.
19.	Scarcely the bell had rung before I reached school.	19.	Scarcely had the bell rung before I reached the school.

Note: When two clauses are joined by a pair of correlative conjunctions like 'no sooner…than' and 'scarcely...before', then the subject in the first clause is placed after its verb or auxiliary verb (refer sentence nos. 18 and 19).

20.	My some books were lost.	20.	Some of my books were lost.
21.	He would not lend me his any book.	21.	He would not lend me any of his books.

Note: The words 'some' and 'any' should not be placed between the possessive adjective and its noun.

'Some of his books' and 'any of his books' are correct; whereas 'his some men' or 'his any man' are incorrect (refer sentence nos. 20 and 21).

22.	Scarcely we had reached home before it began raining.	22.	Scarcely had we reached home before it began raining.
23.	A house stands on the road to let.	23.	A house to let stands on the road.
24.	A beautiful to look at girl was singing.	24.	A girl beautiful to look at was singing.
25.	He has made befitting his position gift.	25.	He has made a gift befitting his position.

Note: An adjective is generally placed before the noun it qualifies. However, if the adjective made up of an adjectival phrase, it is placed after the noun it qualifies e.g., a house to let; beautiful to look at; a gift befitting his position; a building three storeys high, places worth seeing, etc.

26.	Please examine the book carefully, sent herewith.	26.	Please examine carefully the book sent herewith.
27.	One table after another was brought, more or less damaged.	27.	One table after another, more or less damaged, was brought.
28.	I have a book at home named 'Three Giants'.	28.	I have a book named 'Three Giants' at home.
29.	He received a hurt in the arm of no consequence.	29.	He received in the arm a hurt of no consequence.
30.	The debate will not cease on this questions.	30.	The debate on this question will not cease.

- In expressions where the same singular noun is joined by a preposition (i.e., singular noun + preposition), the verb used is in the third form.
- When clauses are introduced by the relative pronouns 'who', 'whom', 'whose', 'which', or 'that', then the verb agrees with the antecedent of the relative pronoun in person and number.
- He made a list of things that were required.
- I like a boy who shows intelligence.
- I like people who are honest.

The book which is on the table is not mine.

31.	The reasons are not yet known for his failure.	31.	The reasons for his failure are not yet known.
32.	Hostile laws to the people were passed.	32.	Laws hostile to the people were passed.
33.	I have never seen a clever man at mathematics.	33.	I have never seen a man clever at mathematics.
34.	He jumped a ten feet wide ditch.	34.	He jumped a ditch ten feet wide.
35.	Bring me some fit fruit to eat.	35.	Bring me some fruit fit to eat.
36.	The horse could go no further being tired out.	36.	The horse being tired out could go no further.

37.	Ludhiana is further from Delhi than Ambala.	37.	Ludhiana is farther from Delhi than Ambala.
38.	Farther discussion on this topic is useless.	38.	Further discussion on this topic is useless.

Note: The word 'farther' means 'at' or 'to a great distance' or 'more distant point' (refer sentence no. 43).
Whereas, 'further' means 'more, additional'.

39.	Akbar ruled wisely over his kingdom.	39.	Akbar wisely ruled over his kingdom.
40.	He exactly came in time.	40.	He came exactly on time.
41.	He explained clearly the meaning of the sentence.	41.	He clearly explained the meaning of the sentence. Or, He explained the meaning of the sentence clearly.

- The word 'there' can never be the subject of a verb.
  So, look for the subject after the verb in a sentence beginning with 'there'.
- There were ten students in our group.
- There are always two sides to every story.
- There seem to be three lions in the den.
- There is a book on the table.

42.	He comes here often to see me.	42.	He often comes here to see me.
43.	I go out seldom before sunrise.	43.	I seldom go out before sunrise.
44.	He laughs always at my jokes.	44.	He always laughs at my jokes.
45.	Always I have been helping you.	45.	I have always been helping you.
46.	He weeps sometimes bitterly.	46.	He sometimes weeps bitterly.

In the case of denial, for a person, the words 'no one' are used as a singular, and 'none' as plural.

- Is there any servant in the house? No, there is no one.
- Are there any servants in the house? No, there are none.

47.	A good boy is loved generally by all his neighbour.	47.	A good boy is generally loved by all his neighbours.
48.	He comes rarely to this town.	48.	He rarely comes to this town.
49.	You have made surely a mistake.	49.	You have surely made a mistake.
50.	I shall punish all who disobey this severely.	50.	I shall severely punish all who disobey this.

Note: Adverbs, such as always, never, seldom, often, sometimes, generally, rarely, surely, etc. are placed before – and not after – the verb they qualify (refer sentence nos. 53, 54, and 55).

51.	I was enough pleased at his industry.	51.	I was pleased enough at his industry.
52.	He is enough strong to do the work.	52.	He is strong enough to do the work.
53.	He prepares thoroughly his lessons.	53.	He prepares his lessons thoroughly.
54.	I have decided to strongly support your proposal	54.	I have decided to support your proposal strongly.
55.	I confess openly my fault.	55.	I openly confess my fault.
56.	Often I have seen you in this house.	56.	I have often seen you in this house.
57.	What for has he come?	57.	What has he come for?
58.	Whom for are you looking?	58.	Whom are you looking for?
59.	I can't say what about he is taking.	59.	I can't say what he is talking about.
60.	What for did you go?	60.	What did you go for?
61.	Not only he tried to pass but also to secure position in the class.	61.	He tried not only to pass but also to secure position in the class.

When a sentence is built around a linking verb, then the verb must agree with the subject, not the complement. The most difficult thing is the adjectives.

62.	Either you shall have to stay here or go home.	62.	You shall either have to stay here or go home.
63.	English is not only difficult to read, but also to write.	63.	English is difficult not only to read but also to write.
64.	Neither I shall go to college nor to the market.	64.	I shall neither go to college nor to the market.
65.	This will not only interest children, but also good men.	65.	This will interest not only children but also good men.
66.	I neither know the name of the author, nor the bookseller.	66.	I know the name of neither the author nor the bookseller.
67.	This is both impracticable in theory and practice.	67.	This is impracticable both in theory and in practice.
68.	He was either educated at Bombay or at Madras.	68.	He was educated either in Bombay or in Madras.
69.	You will either do it or I shall beat you.	69.	You will do it or I shall beat you.
70.	Walking is good both for health and recreation.	70.	Walking is good for both health and recreation.
71.	Gandhiji was not only a maker of a nation but also of a religion.	71.	Gandhiji was a maker not only of a nation but also of a religion.

72.	I do not want to fight but only to get my right.	72.	I want not to fight but only to get my right.
73.	This is nice, is not it?	73.	This is nice, isn't it?
74.	He likes it, does not he?	74.	He likes it, doesn't he?

COMMON ERRORS MADE DUE TO THE USE OF INCORRECT WORDS

Incorrect sentence		Correct sentence	
1.	He was hung for murder.	1.	He was hanged for murder.

Note: When 'hang' means to 'suspend', its past participle is 'hung'; but when 'hang' means 'to kill by murder', its past participle is 'hanged'.

2.	I was tired; so I laid down.	2.	I was tired, so I lay down.

Note: The verb 'to lie' is an intransitive verb. Its meaning is 'to remain in a prostrate position' or 'to be prostrate' or 'to be in a resting position'. Its past tense is 'lay' and past participle form is 'laid' (refer sentence no. 2).

3.	The judge sentenced him to imprisonment for two years.	3.	The judge sentenced him to two years imprisonment.
4.	I saw a dead body, walking along the street.	4.	I saw a dead body, while walking along the street.
5.	Being the only candidate, I appointed him to the post.	5.	He being the only candidate, I appointed him to the post.
6.	Sitting here a very fine view can be seen.	6.	Sitting here one can see a very fine view.
7.	I was running because I was too late.	7.	I was running because I was very late.
8.	The milk of a cow is too nutritious.	8.	The milk of a cow is very nutritious.
9.	He spells too accurately.	9.	He spells very accurately.
10.	Mohan live in a boarding.	10.	Mohan lives in a boarding house.
11.	He made a blunder mistake.	11.	He made a blunder. Or, he made a serious mistake.
12.	The students require some blotting.	12.	The students require some blotting-paper.
13.	This room is more bigger than that.	13.	This room is much bigger than that.
14.	I worked out the sum with somewhat difficult.	14.	I worked out the sum with some difficulty.
15.	He is superior than me in learning.	15.	He is superior to me in learning.
16.	He took birth in Patna.	16.	He was born in Patna.
17.	He has taken admission in a law college.	17.	He has been admitted to a law college. Or, he has obtained admission in a law college.
18.	They left the office-room by and by.	18.	They left the office- room one by one.
19.	He feels very weak to walk.	19.	He feels too weak to walk.
20.	He seems as if dead.	20.	He seems as if he were dead.
21.	Until you remain inactive, you can't get money.	21.	So long as you remain inactive, you can't get money.
22.	The tide was so strong that the rope was torn.	22.	The tide was so strong that the rope broke.
23.	Some persons are devoted to drinking.	23.	Some persons are addicted to drinking.

24.	The boat was drowned.	24.	The boat sank.
25.	Please catch the stick.	25.	Please catch hold of the stick.
26.	He denied to leave the office.	26.	He refused to leave the office.
27.	He is a very long man.	27.	He is a very tall man.
28.	There were long trees on either side of the road.	28.	There were high/tall trees on either side of the road.
29.	He died by the accident.	29.	He was killed in an accident.
30.	Do you give the examination?	30.	Do you appear for the examination?

We 'take', 'sit for', or 'appear for' an examination, but we do not 'give' the examination.

31.	I have remained at Delhi for six years.	31.	I have lived in Delhi for six years.
32.	The judge ordered, 'He has committed theft, punished.'	32.	The judge ordered, 'He has committed theft, so he shall be punished.'
33.	Do it or you will be beaten.	33.	Do it or you shall be beaten.
34.	If they make noise, they will be fined.	34.	If they make a noise, they shall be fined.
35.	He is suffering from a strong cold.	35.	He is suffering from a bad cold.
36.	A friend of you came to my house yesterday.	36.	A friend of yours came to my house yesterday.
37.	Sir, have I got passable marks?	37.	Sir, have I got pass marks?
38.	He became a rich man by and by.	38.	He became a rich man in the course of time.
39.	This plant will be a big tree by and by.	39.	This plant will be a big tree in time.

COMMON ERRORS MADE WHILE USING SINGULAR AND PLURAL NOUNS

Incorrect sentence		Correct sentence	
1.	Cattle is grazing in the field.	1.	Cattle are grazing in the field.
2.	These cattles are mine.	2.	These cattle are mine.
3.	The gentry of this town does not like it.	3.	The gentry of this town do not like it.
4.	The police has arrested him.	4.	The police have arrested him.
5.	Vermin carries diseases.	5.	Vermin carry diseases.
6.	He gave me good advices.	6.	He gave me good advice.
7.	I saw his furnitures.	7.	I saw his furniture.
8.	I shall go to my quarter.	8.	I shall go to my quarters.
9.	The Indian force marched.	9.	The Indian forces marched.
10.	I stopped to admire the sceneries.	10.	I stopped to admire the scenery.
11.	Commander-in- chiefs get handsome pay.	11.	Commanders-in- chief get handsome pay.
12.	I have four son-in-laws.	12.	I have four sons- in-law.
13.	All the passer-bys saw her.	13.	All the passers-by saw her.
14.	I have got a summon today.	14.	I have got a summons today.
15.	Mathematic is an easy subject.	15.	Mathematics is an easy subject.

Incorrect sentence		Correct sentence	
16.	I shall spare no pain to make the function a success.	16.	I shall spare no pains to make the function a success.
17.	He had no issues.	17.	He had no issue.
18.	He gave me thank.	18.	He thanked me.
19.	He is a man of letter.	19.	He is a man of letters.
20.	Ram is a man of part.	20.	Ram is a man of parts.
21.	The Principal of a college is all in all in his college premise.	21.	The Principal is all in all in his college premises.
22.	My house is built of bricks.	22.	My house is built of brick.
23.	He ate all the breads.	23.	He ate all the bread.
24.	He is true to his words.	24.	He is true to his word.
25.	Let me buy some fruits.	25.	Let me buy some fruit.
26.	He eats fishes everyday.	26.	He eats fish everyday.
27.	The house is out of repairs.	27.	The house is out of repair.
28.	My hairs are black.	28.	My hair is black.
29.	Sad news were given to me.	29.	Sad news was given to me.
30.	His circumstance is not good.	30.	His circumstances are not good.

The words 'hair', 'repair', 'machinery', and 'news' are used as singular.

'Circumstances' means 'condition'. However, 'hair' can be used as a countable noun also.

We say, 'He found a hair in the cup.' And 'There are two grey hairs on his coat collar.'

In that sense, hair is used as a collective singular.

31.	I have three pairs of shoes.	31.	I have three pair of shoes.
32.	I have got four dozens of books.	32.	I have got four dozen books.
33.	I have got a few dozen of pencils and score of eggs.	33.	I have got a few dozens of pencils and scores of eggs.
34.	There are hundred of birds in the tree.	34.	There are hundreds of birds in the tree.

Note: The words 'pair', 'dozen', 'score', 'gross', 'hundred-weight', 'stone', 'hundred', 'thousand', etc. are used as a singular number after numerals (refer sentence nos. 31, 32, 33, and 34.

35.	I have got twelve-inches rule.	35.	I have got a twelve-inch rule.
36.	I have a ten years old dog.	36.	I have a ten-year old dog.
37.	Let us take a two-miles walk.	37.	Let us take a two-mile walk.

Note: Some nouns like 'a ten-rupee note', 'a ten- year-old dog', 'a three-foot rule', 'a two-mile walk', 'a ten-man committee', etc. retain the singular form to express some specific quantity or number (refer sentence nos. 35, 36, and 37).

38.	Bring a 50 centimetres rule.	38.	Bring a 50 centimetres rule.
39.	He stopped his study.	39.	He stopped his studies.
40.	He is in high spirit today.	40.	He is in high spirits today.
41.	He did three-fourth of the work.	41.	He did three-fourths of the work.
42.	She got full mark in Grammar.	42.	She got full marks in Grammar.
43.	I don't like those sorts of boys.	43.	I don't like boys of that sort.
44.	I have got two summons.	44.	I have got two summonses.

45.	He went to the picture to see Gandhi.	45.	He went to the cinema to see Gandhi.
46.	Our surrounding was pleasant.	46.	Our surroundings were pleasant.
47.	The rich is happier than the poor.	47.	The rich are happier than the poor.
48.	It is kind to give something to a poor.	48.	It is kind to give something to the poor.
49.	He gave me some informations.	49.	He gave me some information.
50.	He had to do several works.	50.	He had to do several pieces of work.
51.	There were many works that I had to do.	51.	There was a lot of work that I had to do.

COMMON ERRORS MADE WHILE USING INAPPROPRIATE WORDS

Incorrect sentence		**Correct sentence**	
1.	I saw a bad dream last night.	1.	I had a bad dream last night.
2.	This man always says the truth.	2.	This man always tells the truth.
3.	We tell or speak the truth, not say the truth.	3.	We tell a lie, not say a lie.
4.	I have no rupees.	4.	I have no money.
5.	There is no place for us.	5.	There is no room for us.
6.	There is no place for doubt.	6.	There is no room for doubt.
7.	He gave false witness.	7.	He gave false evidence.
8.	We enjoyed the theatre.	8.	We enjoyed the play.
9.	It is a nice poetry.	9.	It is a nice poem.

Incorrect sentence		**Correct sentence**	
10.	He was allowed free ship.	10.	He was allowed free studentship.
11.	I took insult at his words.	11.	I took offence at his words.
12.	There are three females.	12.	There are three women.
13.	Give me fooding and lodging.	13.	Give me food and lodging.
14.	Boarding and lodging.	14.	Board and lodging.
15.	It's a pleasant night, let us sit here.	15.	It's a pleasant evening; let us sit here.
16.	This meat is hard.	16.	This meat is tough.
17.	A little number of men are here.	17.	A small number of men are here.
18.	His head was open.	18.	His head was bare.
19.	I can talk English well.	19.	I can speak English well.
20.	Keep it on the table.	20.	Put it on the table.
21.	I heard his advice.	21.	I listened to his advice.
22.	The officer saw my certificates.	22.	The officer looked into my certificates.
23.	Have you taken admission?	23.	Have you been admitted?
24.	Inform this accident to the police.	24.	Inform the police of this accident.
25.	The tree was loaded with fruit.	25.	The tree was laden with fruit.
26.	I feel some better.	26.	I feel somewhat better.
27.	This is somewhat true.	27.	This is partially true.
28.	I am somewhat sure.	28.	I am pretty sure.

Incorrect sentence		Correct sentence	
29.	Take care of her until she is with you.	29.	Take care of her as long as she is with you.
30.	Are you feeling cold?	30.	Do you feel cold?
31.	I informed him against the danger.	31.	I warned him against the danger.
32.	I denied to help him.	32.	I refused to help him.
33.	My watch goes two minutes behind.	33.	My watch is two minutes slow.
34.	I am going to cut my hair.	34.	I am going to have my hair cut.
35.	The film will be played shortly.	35.	The film will be shown shortly.
36.	I have seen him today morning.	36.	I have seen him this morning.
37.	How do you call this in English?	37.	What do you call this in English?

COMMON ERRORS MADE WHILE USING NOUNS

Incorrect sentence		Correct sentence	
1.	These news are good.	1.	This news is good.
2.	Mathematics are a difficult subject.	2.	Mathematics is a difficult subject.
3.	Summons were issued against him.	3.	A summons was issued against him.
4.	The first innings were won by India.	4.	The first innings was won by India.
5.	Politics are dirty game.	5.	Politics is a dirty game.
6.	The gallows have been just erected.	6.	The gallows has been just erected.

Nouns like 'scenery', 'hair', 'machinery', 'furniture', 'poetry', 'luggage', fruit', vacation', 'bread', 'mischief', etc. are used only as singular.

- Nouns like 'sheep', 'deer', 'stone', (measure of weight), 'pair', 'poor', 'score', 'thousand' (when used after numerals), etc. are both singular and plural.
- Nouns like 'cattle', 'people', peasantry', 'poultry', 'gentry', 'folk', etc. are singular in form but plural in use.

7.	The wages of sin are death.	7.	The wages of sin is death.
8.	The sceneries of Kashmir are harming.	8.	The scenery of Kashmir is charming.
9.	My hairs have turned grey.	9.	My hair has turned grey.
10.	These machineries are out of order.	10.	This machinery is out of order.
11.	These furnitures are for sale.	11.	This furniture is for sale.
12.	He wrote fine poetries.	12.	He wrote fine poetry.
13.	He packed his luggages.	13.	He packed his luggage.
14.	He takes fruits after meals.	14.	He takes fruit after meals.
15.	I spent my vacations at Shimla.	15.	I spent my Vacation in Shimla.
16.	There are no breads in this shop.	16.	There is no bread in this shop.

- Nouns like 'spectacles', 'order', 'thanks', 'shoes', scissors', 'pains', alms', 'studies', and 'repairs', are used in their plural form.
- Generally, 's' is used for nouns indicating living beings, and 'of' is used in the case of lifeless things.
- When three different pronouns are used together for different persons, then the third person should come first, the second person next and the first person in the end.
- The pronoun 'one' must be accompanied by 'one' and not by 'his' or 'her' in the same sentence.

- When a pronoun is the object or a verb or a preposition it is in the objective case.

17.	He did many mischiefs.	17.	He did many acts of mischief.
18.	My father gave me many advices.	18.	My father gave me much advice.
19.	I keep many sheeps and deers.	19.	I keep many sheep and deer.
20.	I bought two dozens oranges.	20.	I bought two dozen oranges.
21.	He weighs about five stones.	21.	He weighs about five stone.
22.	I want two pairs of shoes.	22.	I want two pair of shoes.
23.	Shyam helped the poors.	23.	Shyam helped the poor.
24.	He has reached the age of three scores and five.	24.	He has reached the age of five.
25.	This house cost me fifty thousand rupees.	25.	This house cost me fifty thousand rupees.
26.	The cattles are gazing in the field.	26.	The cattle are grazing in the field.
27.	The peoples were happy to see their favourite leader.	27.	The people were happy to see their favourite leader.
28.	The peasantry was starving.	28.	The peasantry a starving.
29.	This poultry belong to Mohan Singh.	29.	This poultry belongs to Mohan Singh.
30.	The gentry was invited to the function.	30.	The gentry were invited to the function.
31.	The village folk is illiterate.	31.	The village folk are illiterate.
32.	His spectacle is very fine.	32.	His spectacles are very fine.
33.	The judge passed order for his arrest.	33.	The judge passed orders for his arrest.

34.	Will you accept my thank.	34.	Will you accept my thanks?
35.	His shoe is brown.	35.	His shoes are brown.
36.	His scissor is blunt.	36.	His scissors are blunt.
37.	No pain was spared.	37.	No pains were spared.
38.	The alm has been distributed.	38.	The alms have been distributed.
39.	I cannot continue my study.	39.	I cannot continue my studies.
40.	This road is under repair.	40.	This road is under repairs.
41.	His family members are here.	41.	The members of his family are here.
42.	This room's walls are dirty.	42.	The walls of this room are dirty.
43.	The chair's legs are broken.	43.	The legs of the chair are broken.
44.	The son of Tulsi Dass has been killed.	44.	Tulsi Dass's son has been killed.
45.	I have a ten-rupees note.	45.	I have a ten-rupee note.
46.	She stood first in the 400-metres race.	46.	She stood first in the 400-metre race.
47.	His three years old son died.	47.	His three-year old son died.
48.	We had a six-hours meeting.	48.	We had a six-hour meeting.
49.	An eight-men-committee was appointed.	49.	An eight-man-committee was appointed.
50.	She gave a four annas coin to the beggar.	50.	She gave a four anna coin to the beggar.
51.	There is no place for you in this compartment.	51.	There is no room for you in this compartment.

52.	Entry to the show will be by tickets.	52.	Entry to the show will be by ticket.
53.	Cities after cities were conquered by the army.	53.	City after city was conquered by the army.
54.	Keat's poetry are very beautiful.	54.	Keats' poems are very beautiful.
55.	March in four.	55.	March in fours.
56.	His ashes was taken to Haridwar.	56.	His ashes were taken to Haridwar.
57.	He bought a bag of rices.	57.	He bought a bag of rice.
58.	He showered abuses on me.	58.	He showered much abuse on me.
59.	She gave me a great deal of troubles.	59.	She gave me a great deal of trouble.
60.	He is a man of words.	60.	He is a man of his word.
61.	The jury is divided in this opinions.	61.	The jury are divided in their opinions.
62.	She has five grey hair.	62.	She has five grey hairs.
63.	I gave him many informations.	63.	I gave him much information.
64.	My aunt has no issues.	64.	My aunt has no issue.
65.	Your trouser is loose.	65.	Your trousers are loose.
66.	He is a tall gentleman.	66.	He is a tall man.
67.	India's Five-Years Plans have failed.	67.	India's Five-Year Plans have failed.
68.	He goes to his college on feet.	68.	He goes to his college on foot.
69.	One of my friends are an actor.	69.	One of my friends is an actor.
70.	Mankind are basically selfish.	70.	Mankind is basically selfish.
71.	If sent my servant to bring vegetable from market.	71.	If sent my servant to bring vegetables from the market.
72.	She lives in the boarding.	72.	She lives in the boarding-house.
73.	She is my cousin sister.	73.	She is my cousin.
74.	The fleet were destroyed by the enemy.	74.	The fleet was destroyed by the enemy.
75.	If have many works to do.	75.	If have much work to do.
76.	My house is built of bricks and stones.	76.	My house is built of brick and stone.
77.	If saw two females in the bazaar.	77.	If saw two women in the bazaar.
78.	If need a blotting.	78.	If need a piece of blotting paper.
79.	Good night, sir, you are welcome.	79.	Good evening, sir, you are welcome.
80.	Relate the story in details.	80.	Relate the story in detail.

COMMON ERRORS MADE WHILE USING PRONOUNS

Incorrect sentence		Correct sentence	
1.	I and you were present.	1.	You and I were present.
2.	I and he went to the college.	2.	He and I went to the college.
3.	He, you, and I were absent.	3.	You, he, and I were absent.
4.	One must do his duty.	4.	One must do one's duty.
5.	Let he and I go there.	5.	Let him and me go there.

Incorrect sentence		Correct sentence	
6.	Who are you speaking to?	6.	Whom are you speaking to?
7.	Distribute these sweets between the four brothers.	7.	Distribute these sweets among the four brothers.
8.	Distribute these mangoes among the two sisters.	8.	Distribute these mangoes between the two sisters.
9.	The two sisters quarrelled with one another.	9.	The two sisters quarrelled with each other.
10.	The four brothers quarrelled with each other.	10.	The four brothers quarrelled with one another.
11.	Each of the four brothers have eaten their sweets.	11.	Each of the four brothers has eaten his sweets.
12.	Everyone of them have eaten their sweets.	12.	Everyone of them has eaten his sweets.
13.	Nobody of them have eaten their sweets.	13.	Nobody of them has eaten his sweets.
14.	Every girl was in their best dress.	14.	Every girl was in her best dress.
15.	Everybody did their work.	15.	Everybody did his work.
16.	You can choose any of these two books.	16.	You can choose either of these two books.
17.	None of these two girls is good at studies.	17.	Neither of these two girls is good at studies.
18.	Neither of these six books is mine.	18.	None of these six books is mine.
19.	Either he or his sister have stolen my purse.	19.	Either he or his sister has stolen my purse.
20.	Neither he nor his brother do their duty.	20.	Neither he nor his brother does his duty.

Incorrect sentence		Correct sentence	
21.	He is one of those who does his duty.	21.	He is one of those who do their duty.
22.	Give me the share of goods that fall to my lot.	22.	Give me the share of the goods that falls to my lot.
23.	He is taller than me.	23.	He is taller than I.
24.	If I were him, I would have helped you.	24.	If I were he, I would have helped you.
25.	Between you and I, he is a fool.	25.	Between you and me, he is a fool.
26.	Nobody was present but I.	26.	Nobody was present but me.
27.	That could not be her.	27.	That could not be she.
28.	Let you and I do this.	28.	Let you and me do this.
29.	I did better than them.	29.	I did better than they.
30.	Whom do you think is suitable for the post?	30.	Who do you think is suitable for the post?
31.	Whom these men are, I cannot say.	31.	Who these men are, I cannot say.
32.	He absented from the college.	32.	He absented himself from the college.
33.	You must avail of this chance.	33.	You must avail yourself of this chance.
34.	He did not like you coming in this dress.	34.	He did not like your coming in this dress.
35.	I am yours humble servant.	35.	I am your humble servant.
36.	Her behaviour is such which cannot be tolerated.	36.	Her behaviour is such as cannot be tolerated.

Incorrect sentence		Correct sentence	
37.	The girl who stands first, she will get a gold medal.	37.	The girl who stands first, will get a gold medal.
38.	Are you the young man which got the first prize?	38.	Are you the young man who got the first prize?
39.	He married Sita's sister who is my friend.	39.	He married the sister of Sita who is my friend.
40.	All which glitters is not gold.	40.	All that glitters is not gold.
41.	What is it which pains you?	41.	What is it that pains you?
42.	This is the best book which we have ever seen.	42.	This is the best book that we have ever seen.
43.	She did not come to mine house.	43.	She did not come to my house.
44.	They who shirk work cannot get through the examination.	44.	Those who shirk work cannot get through the examination.
45.	Bring me one other glass of water.	45.	Bring me another glass of water.
46.	Your need is greater than that of mine.	46.	Your need is greater than mine.
47.	The climate of Ambala is hotter than Shimla.	47.	The climate of Ambala is hotter than that of Shimla.
48.	This is the bird who sings.	48.	This is the bird that sings.
49.	They have no books of their.	49.	They have no books of their own.
50.	Your's sincerely.	50.	Yours sincerely.

- 'Each other' is used for two persons; whereas 'one another' is used for more than two persons.
- 'Between' is used for two persons; whereas 'among' is used for more than two persons.

COMMON ERRORS MADE WHILE USING ADJECTIVES

Incorrect sentence		Correct sentence	
1.	I know no other person here but Mohan.	1.	I know no other person here than Mohan.
2.	She turned out to be no other but my old friend.	2.	She turned out to be no other than my old friend.
3.	This pen is superior than that.	3.	This pen is superior to that.
4.	I am senior than you.	4.	I am senior to you.
5.	I prefer milk than tea.	5.	I prefer milk to tea.
6.	This cloth is inferior than that.	6.	This cloth is inferior to that.
7.	This event happened prior than that.	7.	This event happened prior to that.
8.	Circle is the most perfect curve.	8.	Circle is a perfect curve.
9.	This is the most unique problem.	9.	This is a unique problem.
10.	This is of most universal application.	10.	This is of universal application.
11.	Shyam is his oldest son.	11.	Shyam is his eldest son.
12.	Ram is elder than you.	12.	Ram is older than you.
13.	She left Chandigarh by the latest bus.	13.	She left Chandigarh by the last bus.

Incorrect sentence		Correct sentence	
14.	He reached latter than I.	14.	He reached later than I.
15.	The latter novels of Hardy are better.	15.	The later novels of Hardy are better.
16.	He and his sister quarrelled. The later was at fault.	16.	He and his sister quarrelled. The latter was at fault.
17.	Rita, Anita, and Sunita quarrelled. The latest was at fault.	17.	Rita, Anita, and Sunita quarrelled. The last one was at fault.
18.	Ludhiana is further from Delhi than Ambala.	18.	Ludhiana is farther from Delhi than Ambala.
19.	Farther discussion on this topic is useless.	19.	Further discussion on this topic is useless.
20.	His house is nearest to ours.	20.	His house is next to ours.
21.	The injured were taken to the next hospital.	21.	The injured were taken to the nearest hospital.
22.	Few girls attended the class.	22.	A few girls attended the class.
23.	I lent him a few books I had.	23.	I lent him the few books I had.
24.	There is a little hope of her recovery.	24.	There is little hope of her recovery.
25.	She took the little rest.	25.	She took a little rest.
26.	I gave her little money I had.	26.	I gave her the little money I had.
27.	I will not buy some mangoes.	27.	I will not buy any mangoes.
28.	I have any money.	28.	I have some money.

Incorrect sentence		Correct sentence	
29.	She is rather very intelligent.	29.	She is very intelligent.
30.	He has strong headache.	30.	He has a headache.
31.	He has proved much useful than harmful.	31.	He has proved more useful than harmful.
32.	She is good than you.	32.	She is better than you.
33.	She wrote a best play.	33.	She wrote a very good play.
34.	I shall not go somewhere.	34.	I shall not go anywhere.
35.	This book is easier from that.	35.	This book is easier than that.
36.	What is the fresh news today?	36.	What is the latest news today?
37.	It was the most cruellest act.	37.	It was the cruellest act.
38.	Honour is preferable than money.	38.	Honour is preferable to money.
39.	He is the ablest and wise man.	39.	He is the ablest and the wisest man.
40.	He called the both girls.	40.	He called both the girls.
41.	No less than ten men died in the accident.	41.	No fewer than ten men died in the accident.
42.	This is the best book of the two.	42.	This is the better book of the two.
43.	It is the eldest school in the city.	43.	It is the oldest school in the city.
44.	He has a little sense.	44.	He has little sense.
45.	He gets a less salary.	45.	He gets a small salary.
46.	She is the better girl of the five.	46.	She is the best girl of the five.
47.	She is our mutual friend.	47.	She is our common friend.

Incorrect sentence		Correct sentence	
48.	A very little number of the students got through the examination.	48.	A very small number of the students got through the examination.
49.	It is much cold today.	49.	It is very cold today.
50.	Many a student have been placed in the first division.	50.	Many a student has been placed in the first division.

- The words 'each', 'every', 'everyone', 'everybody' and 'nobody' are always followed by verbs, pronouns, and adjectives in the singular.
- 'Either' and 'neither' are used for two persons or things, while 'any' and 'none' are used for more than two persons or things. The verb in both the cases is singular.
- When two or more than two singular nouns are joined by 'either…or' or 'neither …nor', then the verb and the pronouns that follow are singular.
- A pronoun must agree with the preceding noun both in person and in number.
- If a comparison is made using 'other', then 'than' is used instead of 'but'.

COMMON ERRORS MADE WHILE USING VERBS

Incorrect sentence		Correct sentence	
1.	One of my pencils were stolen.	1.	One of my pencils was stolen.
2.	Our only guide were the stars.	2.	Our only guide was the stars.
3.	The voice of the girls were beautiful.	3.	The voice of the girls was beautiful.
4.	If I was he, I would have helped Sita.	4.	If I were he, I would have helped Sita.
5.	Was he present, he would have helped us.	5.	Were he present, he would have helped us.
6.	God blesses you!	6.	God bless you.
7.	Two and two makes four.	7.	Two and two make four.
8.	He and I am friends.	8.	He and I are friends.
9.	Ignorance and idleness is the cause of many vices.	9.	Ignorance and idleness are the cause of vices.
10.	Our guide and philosopher have left us.	10.	Our guide and philosopher has left us.
11.	The musician and the poet has died.	11.	The musician and the poet have died.
12.	Man and woman are one flesh.	12.	Man and woman is one flesh.
13.	Rice and curry are his favourite food.	13.	Rice and curry is his favourite food.
14.	Bread and butter are ready.	14.	Bread and butter is ready.
15.	She as well as her friends were present.	15.	She as well as her friends was present.
16.	Deepak like his sisters are good for nothing.	16.	Deepak like his sisters is good for nothing.
17.	The leader besides his followers have been arrested.	17.	The leader besides his followers has been arrested.
18.	The number of students in our college have decreased.	18.	The number of students in our college has decreased.
19.	A number of students has migrated.	19.	A number of students have migrated.
20.	The majority are against the Congress.	20.	The majority is against the Congress.

Incorrect sentence		Correct sentence	
21.	The majority of cinema-goers are college students.	21.	The majority of cinema-goers is college students.
22.	The jury were unanimous in their decision.	22.	The jury was unanimous in its decision.
23.	The jury were divided in their opinions.	23.	The jury was divided in its opinion.

Note: Collective nouns like 'jury', 'majority', etc. require singular or plural verbs depending on the context.

24.	The Union of the Soviet Socialist Republic has prospered.	24.	The Union of the Soviet Socialist Republic have prospered.
25.	The Canterbury Tales are a collection of stories.	25.	The Canterbury Tales is a collection of stories.

Note: If one plural noun is a proper name for some collective unit or single object, it requires a singular verb.

26.	The brave never tastes of death but once.	26.	The brave never taste of death but once.
27.	The rich hates the poor.	27.	The rich hate the poor.

Note: If an adjective preceding with the article 'the' is used as a subject, then it requires a plural verb.

28.	I treated him my friend.	28.	I treated him as my friend.
29.	Mahatma Gandhi is called as the Father of the Nation.	29.	Mahatma Gandhi is called the Father of the Nation.
30.	She thinks you as a fool.	30.	She thinks you are a fool. Or, she thinks you to be a fool.

31.	Eighty miles are a long distance.	31.	Eighty miles is a long distance.
32.	The quality of these mangoes are not good.	32.	The quality of these mangoes is not good.
33.	Either you or he are at fault.	33.	Either you or he is at fault.
34.	A number of dancers has come.	34.	A number of dancers have come.

- The comparatives 'superior', 'senior', 'prefer', 'inferior', 'prior', etc. are followed by 'to' and not by 'than'.
- Adjectives like 'perfect', 'unique', 'universal', etc. do not allow for comparison because their meaning is already in the superlative.
- 'Elder' and 'eldest' apply to the members of the same family, whereas 'older' and 'oldest' are used when comparative age is in question.
- 'Later' and 'latest' refer to time; 'latter' and 'last' refer to position.
- 'Farther' means more distant; 'further' means additional.

35.	He refused the statement.	35.	He denied the statement.
36.	He denied to accompany me to the college.	36.	He refused to accompany me to the college.
37.	He was hung.	37.	He was hanged.
38.	Neither he nor I were called.	38.	Neither he nor I was called.
39.	The horse and the carriage are at the door.	39.	The horse and the carriage is at the door.
40.	He kept himself away from the college.	40.	He kept away from the college.
41.	She absented from the college.	41.	She absented herself from the college.
42.	Time and tide waits for no man.	42.	Time and tide wait for no man.
43.	He regards me his superior.	43.	He regards me as his superior.

44.	What are you speaking?	44.	What are you saying?
45.	My tooth is paining.	45.	My tooth is aching.
46.	The people was excited.	46.	The people were excited.
47.	The nation are progressing.	47.	The nation is progressing.
48.	The public know everything.	48.	The public knows everything.
49.	A hue and cry were raised.	49.	A hue and cry was raised.
50.	The senate has passed this rule.	50.	The senate have passed this rule.
51.	Greatness of mind and beauty of soul is the gift of nature.	51.	Greatness of mind and beauty of soul are the gift of nature.
52.	Five rupees are the price of this pen.	52.	Five rupees is the price of this pen.
53.	Her voice and manner was gentle.	53.	Her voice and manner were gentle.
54.	He did not know where he or the girl were.	54.	He did not know where he or the girl was.

COMMON ERRORS MADE DUE TO THE TENSE

Incorrect sentence		Correct sentence	
1.	I am writing him a letter every day.	1.	I write him a letter every day.
2.	She waits outside.	2.	She is waiting outside.

Note: The Present Indefnite tense should not be used for Present Continuous or Perfect tense, and vice versa.

3.	I am in bed for the last one week.	3.	I have been in bed for the last one week.
4.	I have passed my B.A. in 1973.	4.	I passed my B.A. in 1973.
5.	The patient has passed the night peacefully.	5.	The patient passed the night peacefully.
6.	I have received your letter yesterday.	6.	I received your letter yesterday.
7.	He had attended the class yesterday.	7.	He attended the class yesterday.

Note: Mark the wrong use of Present Perfect for Past Indefinite (refer sentence nos. 6 and 7).

8.	Before I reached the station, the train left.	8.	Before I reached the station, the train had left.
9.	I could foresee that he will fail.	9.	I could foresee that he would fail.
10.	Our teacher told us that honesty was the best policy.	10.	Our teacher told us that honesty is the best policy.
11.	I will see you tomorrow.	11.	I shall see you tomorrow.
12.	He shall see you tomorrow.	12.	He will see you tomorrow.
13.	I shall do or die.	13.	I will do or die.
14.	Come what may, we shall go on strike.	14.	Come what may, we will go on strike.
15.	I shall do good in future.	15.	I will do good in future.
16.	I shall beat you, if you make a noise.	16.	I will beat you, if you make a noise.
17.	You will get a reward for your loyal service.	17.	You shall get a reward for your loyal services.
18.	Shall you do it?	18.	Will you do it?

- 'Little' means 'hardly any'; 'a little' means 'some'; and 'the little' means 'not much but all that is'.

- 'Some' is used in affirmative sentences and 'any' in negative sentences.
- 'Few' means practically 'none'; 'a few' means 'some'; and 'the few' means 'not many yet all'.
- 'A verb must agree with its subject, both in number and in person.

19.	Shall he lend you money?	19.	Will he lend you money?
20.	He has been here an hour ago.	20.	He was here an hour ago.
21.	I am working since morning.	21.	I have been working since morning.
22.	The patient died before the doctor arrived.	22.	The patient had died before the doctor arrived.
23.	Where the battle was fought?	23.	Where was the battle fought?
24.	The robber was caught and his pockets searched.	24.	The robber was caught and his pockets were searched.
25.	I just finished my speech.	25.	I have just finished my speech.
26.	I have passed M.A. since ten years.	26.	I passed M.A. examination ten years ago.
27.	Can I look at your book?	27.	May I look at your book?
28.	We wish that I was dead.	28.	I wish that I were dead.
29.	We shall reach our house before the sun sets.	29.	We will reach our house before the sun sets.
30.	I shall stand by you through thick and thin.	30.	I will stand by you through thick and thin.
31.	Will I ever forget these happy days?	31.	Shall I ever forget these happy days?
32.	He astonished at the result.	32.	He was astonished at the result.
33.	Why you went there?	33.	Why did you go there?
34.	How many hours you require for this paper?	34.	How many hours do you require for this paper?
35.	He promised that he will be there.	35.	He promised that he would be there.
36.	This was happened yesterday.	36.	This happened yesterday.
37.	He speaks as if he is mad.	37.	He speaks as if he were mad.
38.	When the police went there, they found that the thief was disappeared.	38.	When the police went there, they found that the thief had disappeared.
39.	She told me that she read The Tempest.	39.	She told me that she had read The Tempest.
40.	When he will go to the bazaar, he will bring your book.	40.	When he goes to the bazaar, he will bring your book.
41.	She said that she saw this picture last year.	41.	She said that she had seen this picture last year.

COMMON ERRORS MADE WHILE USING ADVERBS

Incorrect sentence		Correct sentence	
1.	He sound slept.	1.	He slept soundly.
2.	Before and after we looks.	2.	We look before and after.
3.	He keeps his word always.	3.	He always keeps his word.
4.	He seldom is late for college.	4.	He is seldom late for college.
5.	He comes to me frequently.	5.	He frequently comes to me.
6.	He always is punctual.	6.	He is always punctual.

Incorrect sentence		Correct sentence	
7.	She is not enough strong to do this work.	7.	She is not strong enough to do this work.
8.	He was enough kind to lend me three hundred rupees.	8.	He was kind enough to lend me three hundred rupees.
9.	She sings good.	9.	She sings well.
10.	She is very fool.	10.	She is very foolish.
11.	He is very coward.	11.	He is very cowardly.
12.	He speaks much slowly.	12.	He speaks very slowly.
13.	The patient is very better today.	13.	The patient is much better today.
14.	I am very senior to him.	14.	I am much senior to him.
15.	This book is much interesting.	15.	This book is very interesting.
16.	They were very delighted to see me.	16.	They were much delighted to see me.
17.	Of course, she sings well.	17.	Certainly, she sings well.
18.	Of course, he is in the wrong.	18.	Certainly, he is in the wrong.
19.	I am quite sorry.	19.	I am very sorry.
20.	He tells very another story.	20.	He tells quite another story.
21.	We are rather very sad today.	21.	We are very sad today.
22.	No sooner I went out when it began to rain.	22.	No sooner did I go out than it began to rain.
23.	I shall see her just now.	23.	I shall see her presently.
24.	He has left for the station presently.	24.	He has left for the station just now.
25.	I cannot wait any more.	25.	I cannot wait any longer.
26.	I cannot eat any further.	26.	I cannot eat any more.
27.	He ran fastly.	27.	He ran fast.
28.	This boy is too strong.	28.	The boy is very strong.
29.	He is too clever.	29.	He is very clever.
30.	I have finished my work nearly.	30.	I have nearly finished my work.
31.	It is a much difficult sum.	31.	It is a very difficult sum.
32.	Honey is too sweet.	32.	Honey is very sweet.
33.	She is wonderful beautiful.	33.	She is wonderfully beautiful.
34.	He works very hardly.	34.	He works very hard.

COMMON ERRORS MADE WHILE USING CONJUNCTIONS

Incorrect sentence		Correct sentence	
1.	Though he is poor, but he is honest.	1.	Though he is poor he is honest.
2.	Although he is rich, but he is miserly.	2.	Although he is rich, yet he is miserly.
3.	She had scarcely left the college then her friend came.	3.	She had scarcely left the college when her friend came.
4.	Hardly she had left the college then her friend came.	4.	Hardly had she left the college when her friend came.
5.	No sooner he reached the station when the train left.	5.	No sooner did he reach the station than the train left.

Incorrect sentence		Correct sentence	
1.	Though he is poor, but he is honest.	1.	Though he is poor he is honest.
6.	Walk carefully lest you may not fall.	6.	Walk carefully lest you should fall.
7.	You should do like your father tells you to do.	7.	You should do as your father tells you to do.
8.	Unless you do not work hard, you cannot succeed.	8.	Unless you work hard, you cannot succeed.
9.	Until you do not mend your ways, you cannot succeed.	9.	Until you mend your ways, you cannot succeed.
10.	Wait here till I do not return.	10.	Wait here till I return.
11.	She brought neither her books or her notes.	11.	She brought neither her books nor her notes.
12.	Because he is honest, therefore he is liked by all.	12.	Because he is honest, he is liked by all.
13.	If she is intelligent, then she will solve this problem.	13.	If she is intelligent, she will solve this problem.
14.	While the cat will be away, the mice will play.	14.	While the cat is away, the mice will play.
15.	I shall wait until she will come.	15.	I shall wait until she comes.
16.	Before you will be appointed, you shall sign a bond	16.	Before you are appointed, you shall sign a bond.
17.	She has got through the examination, but I am happy.	17.	She has got through the examination and I am happy.

Incorrect sentence		Correct sentence	
1.	Though he is poor, but he is honest.	1.	Though he is poor he is honest.
18.	His uncle is a millionaire, and his father is a pauper.	18.	His uncle is a millionaire, but his father is a pauper.
19.	While in Rome, do like the Romans do.	19.	While in Rome, do as the Romans do.
20.	I asked him that why was he absent from the college.	20.	I asked him why he was absent from the college.
21.	Supposing if you fall, what will you do?	21.	Supposing you fail, what will you do?
22.	As you sow, that you will reap.	22.	As you sow, so shall you reap.
23.	He was much tired that he could not walk further.	23.	He was so tired that he could not walk further.
24.	The house is beautiful where he resides.	24.	The house where he resides is beautiful.
25.	He is such a man that no one likes.	25.	He is such a man as no one likes.
26.	Boys study because they may earn their livelihood.	26.	Boys study so that they may earn their livelihood.
27.	Such students will be allowed to appear at the interview who have passed B.A. examination.	27.	Such students as have passed B.A. examination will be allowed to appear at the interview.

- 'Very' is used before adjectives and adverbs in the positive degree; 'much' is used in the case of comparative degree.
- A singular subject joined to other words by 'as well as', 'like', or 'besides', takes a singular verb.

- When an adverb modifies, an Intransitive Verb it generally follows the same.
- Adverbs such as 'always', 'seldom', 'frequently', 'never', and 'sometimes' are generally used before the verb they modify; but are placed after the verb 'to be'.
- The adverb 'enough' is always placed after the word it modifies.
- 'Very' is generally used with the Present Participles and 'much' with the Past Participles. An exception is, 'I am much obliged to you'.

COMMON ERRORS MADE WHILE USING PREPOSITIONS

Incorrect sentence		Correct sentence	
1.	Shakespeare was born in Stratford-upon-Avon at England.	1.	Shakespeare was born at Stratford-upon-Avon in England
2.	The Prime Minister is coming in Ludhiana next month.	2.	The Prime Minster is coming to Ludhiana next month.
3.	She jumped in the well.	3.	She jumped into the well.
4.	We are sitting into our house.	4.	We are sitting in our house.
5.	She has been teaching here since five years.	5.	She has been teaching here for five years.
6.	She has been teaching here for 1970.	6.	She has been teaching here since 1970.
7.	Her father died ten years before.	7.	Her father died ten years ago.
8.	India and China were friends 1962 ago.	8.	India and China were friends before 1962.
9.	You have not answered to my question.	9.	You have not answered my question.
10.	She did not inform to me in time.	10.	She did not inform me in time.
11.	She assisted to me in my work.	11.	She assisted me in my work.
12.	You must obey to your teachers.	12.	You must obey your teachers.
13.	He left from the house at night.	13.	He left the house at night.
14.	She requested to me to help her.	14.	She requested me to help her.
15.	He ordered for a cup of coffee.	15.	He ordered a cup of coffee.
16.	She asked to me many questions.	16.	She asked me many questions.
17.	I cannot resist to the temptation of tea.	17.	I cannot resist the temptation of tea.
18.	She entered into the room without my permission.	18.	She entered the room without my permission.
19.	God pervades in the whole universe.	19.	God pervades the whole universe.
20.	China attacked on India in 1962.	20.	China attacked India in 1962.
21.	Ornaments add the beauty of women.	21.	Ornaments add to the beauty of women.
22.	Attend your roll call.	22.	Attend to your roll call.
23.	Do not knock my door at night.	23.	Do not knock at my door at night.
24.	I do not approve your laziness.	24.	I do not approve of your laziness.
25.	Listen what I say.	25.	Listen to what I say.
26.	I have disposed my old books.	26.	I have disposed of my old books.
27.	He acceded my request.	27.	He acceded to my request.
28.	She boasts her beauty.	28.	She boasts of her beauty.

Incorrect sentence		Correct sentence	
29.	She enquired me the way to the college.	29.	She enquired of me the way to the college.
30.	The mother always sides her son.	30.	The mother always sides with her son.
31.	The hunter aimed the tiger.	31.	The hunter aimed at the tiger.
32.	I have applied the Principal for leave.	32.	I have applied to the Principal for leave.
33.	She did not reply my letter.	33.	She did not reply to my letter.
34.	We must pray God for help.	34.	We must pray to God for help.
35.	He objected my marriage.	35.	He objected to my marriage.
36.	Has he enough of money?	36.	Has he enough money?
37.	You must stick up to your promise.	37.	You must stick to your promise.
38.	She resembles with her mother.	38.	She resembles her mother.
39.	Do not shirk from work.	39.	Do not shirk work.
40.	He has fallen down in her eyes.	40.	He has fallen in her eyes.
41.	I will fight the cause.	41.	I will fight for the cause.
42.	Trust God.	42.	Trust in God.
43.	Write with ink.	43.	Write in ink.
44.	He died from cholera.	44.	He died of cholera.
45.	The examination will begin from Monday.	45.	The examination will begin on Monday.
46.	He has no chance for getting the post.	46.	He has no chance of getting the post.
47.	He gave me a pen to write.	47.	He gave me a pen to write with.
48.	He enjoyed at the match.	48.	He enjoyed the match.
49.	He is desirous to go home.	49.	He is desirous of going home.
50.	I caught him from the ear.	50.	I caught him by the ear.

COMMON ERRORS MADE WHILE USING ARTICLES

Incorrect sentence		Correct sentence	
1.	Mohan is a Indian, but John is an European.	1.	Mohan is an Indian, but John is a European.
2.	He is a LLB.	2.	He is an LLB.
3.	A honest man is work of God.	3.	An honest man is the work of God.
4.	She is a M.A.	4.	She is an M.A.
5.	Her father is a S.P.	5.	Her father is an S.P.
6.	A egg is cheaper than a orange.	6.	An egg is cheaper than an orange.
7.	This is a boy who won the prize.	7.	This is the boy who won the prize.
8.	These are books that I have written.	8.	These are the books that I have written.
9.	Camel is the ship of the desert.	9.	The camel is the ship of the desert.
10.	Lion is the king of the jungle.	10.	The lion is the king of the jungle.
11.	Pt. Jawaharlal Nehru was greatest leader of India.	11.	Pt. Jawaharlal Nehru was the greatest leader of India.

Incorrect sentence		Correct sentence	
12.	Lata has sweetest voice.	12.	Lata has the sweetest voice.
13.	Moon rises when sun sets.	13.	The moon rises when the sun sets.
14.	Man wants to become the master of earth and sky.	14.	Man wants to become the master of the earth and the sky.
15.	Ganga and Jamuna meet at Allahabad.	15.	The Ganga and the Jamuna meet at Allahabad.
16.	Ganga comes from Himalayas.	16.	The Ganga comes from the Himalayas.
17.	Punjab is a rich state.	17.	The Punjab is a rich state.
18.	I have been to U.S.A.	18.	I have been to the U.S.A.
19.	Ramayana and Mahabharata are the holy books of Hindus.	19.	The Ramayana and The Mahabharata are the holy books of the Hindus.
20.	English are whiter than Indians.	20.	The English are whiter than the Indians.
21.	Tribune is the most popular paper in Punjab.	21.	The Tribune is the most popular paper in the Punjab.
22.	Rich should not hate poor.	22.	The rich should not hate the poor.
23.	Only brave deserve fair.	23.	Only the brave deserve the fair.
24.	Mother in her could not see the child burning live.	24.	The mother in her could not see the child burning alive.
25.	Beast in a man cannot kill angel in him.	25.	The beast in a man cannot kill the angel in him.

Incorrect sentence		Correct sentence	
26.	Older you grow, weaker you become.	26.	The older you grow, the weaker you become.
27.	Higher you go, cooler it is.	27.	The higher you go, the cooler it is.
28.	Deeper the well, sweeter is the water.	28.	The deeper the well, the sweeter is the water.
29.	The Shakespeare was born at the Stratford-upon-Avon.	29.	Shakespeare was born at Stratford- upon-Avon.

- The words 'unless', 'until', and 'till' are not followed by 'not' because they already convey a negative sense.
- 'No sooner' is followed by 'than'.
- The words 'just now' indicate action begun in the past and 'presently' is used in the case of action that is to begin in the future.
- 'Any longer', 'any further', and 'any more' refer to time, distance, and number respectively.

30.	The silver is more precious than the iron.	30.	Silver is more precious than iron.
31.	The virtue has its own reward.	31.	Virtue has its own reward.
32.	The cholera is a dangerous disease.	32.	Cholera is a dangerous disease.
33.	He loves the cricket but hates the hockey.	33.	He loves cricket but hates hockey.
34.	The man is mortal.	34.	Man is mortal.
35.	The crow is black.	35.	Crow is black.
36.	The men are taller than the women.	36.	Men are taller than women.
37.	Bible is a famous book.	37.	The Bible is a famous book.

38.	Do not make noise.	38.	Do not make a noise.
39.	What fool you are!	39.	What a fool you are!
40.	I never tell lie.	40.	I never tell a lie.
41.	Chandigarh is fine city.	41.	Chandigarh is a fine city.
42.	I saw an one-eyed man.	42.	I saw a one-eyed man.
43.	Ram was in hurry.	43.	Ram was in a hurry.
44.	He is a honorary magistrate.	44.	He is an honorary magistrate.

- (i) The words 'though' and 'although' are followed by 'yet' and not 'but'.
  (ii) 'Scarcely' and 'hardly' are followed by 'when' and not 'then'.
  (iii) Lest is followed by should.
  (iv) 'No sooner' is followed by 'than'.
- The preposition 'like' should not be used instead of the conjunction 'as.'
- 'Rather' means 'not very'.
  'Neither' is followed by 'nor' and not by 'or'.

45.	Krishna bought a umbrella.	45.	Krishna bought an umbrella.
46.	He is a honourable man.	46.	He is an honourable man.
47.	Two of trade seldom agree.	47.	Two of a trade seldom agree.
48.	The bird in hand is worth two in the bush.	48.	A bird in hand is worth two in the bush.
49.	Sun rises in the east.	49.	The sun rises in the east.
50.	Dog is a faithful animal.	50.	The dog is a faithful animal.
51.	Chandigarh is capital of the Punjab.	51.	Chandigarh is the capital of Punjab.
52.	More you get, more you desire.	52.	The more you get, the more you desire.
53.	The Delhi is the capital of India.	53.	Delhi is the capital of India.
54.	The mathematics is a difficult subject.	54.	Mathematics is a difficult subject.
55.	Do not make a fun of me.	55.	Do not make fun of me.
56.	He got an employment.	56.	He got employment.
57.	It is quarter to ten now.	57.	It is a quarter to ten now.
58.	The love begets love.	58.	Love begets love.
59.	The beauty attracts thieves sooner than the gold.	59.	Beauty attracts thieves sooner than gold.
60.	All that glitters is not the gold.	60.	All that glitters is not gold.

MISCELLANEOUS ERRORS

Incorrect sentence		Correct sentence	
1.	More tea? Thank you.	1.	More Tea? No, thank you. Or, More tea? Yes, thank you.

Note: The words 'thank you' imply neither the negative nor the affirmative.
Therefore, it is necessary to answer clearly with 'no, thank you 'or' 'yes, thank you'

2.	Good night, Hari; let us talk now.	2.	Good evening, Hari; let us talk now.

Note: At times, it is forgotten that 'good night' is a parting salutation, whereas is 'good evening' is the proper salutation to be used when two people meet for the first time in the evening (refer sentence no. 2). One cannot, therefore, make any further conversation after saying 'Good night'.

3.	He has already cheated me twice or thrice.	3.	He has already cheated me twice or three times.

Note: Whereas 'twice' is permissible, 'thrice' is old-fashioned English; always say 'three times' (refer sentence no. 3).

4.	A king's life is different from a Prime Minister.	4.	A king's life is different from a Prime Minister's.

Note: In a comparative statement, if the first noun is in the possessive case, then the second noun must be too.

5.	I gave him one and a half rupee.	5.	I gave him one and a half rupees.

Note: Anything greater than one, even by a fraction, should be considered as the plural form.

6.	Has your brother bought a new dress?	6.	Has your brother bought a new suit?

Note: Remember that men and boys wear 'suit', whereas women and girls wear 'dresses'.

However, 'evening dress' is a general term which refers to both sexes.

7.	When I entered the bedroom, I saw a snake on the ground.	7.	When I entered the bedroom, I saw a snake on the floor.

Note: The 'ground' is outside the house, whereas the 'floor' constitutes a part of the room.

8.	Read the two first chapters to this book.	8.	Read the first two chapter of this book.
9.	I have finished three-fourth of this book.	9.	I have finished three-fourths of this book.

Note: Three-fourths 'mean' three parts' out of 'four parts' Therefore use the plural form.

10.	He bought a radio and sold the same at a handsome profit.	10.	He bought a radio and sold it at a handsome profit.
11.	My brother and myself will go.	11.	My brother and I will go.

12.	They cannot endure my separation.	12.	They cannot endure separation from me.
13.	May I now take your leave?	13.	May I now take leave of you?
14.	Whom do you think will be dismissed first?	14.	Who, do you think, will be dismissed first?
15.	You are fairer than me.	15.	You are fairer than I.

Note: To better understand the correct sentence, read it as it is meant 'You are fairer than I am'.

16.	He is thirty years old, isn't it?	16.	He is thirty years old, isn't he?

Note: In the second part of the sentence, the subject of the verb 'is' is 'he' not 'it'.

17.	You must see him after the dinner.	17.	You must see him after dinner.

Note: Do not use definite articles preceding the name of a meal – namely supper, dinner, lunch, breakfast, etc.

18.	What kind of a friend are you?	18.	What kind of friend are you?

Note: Do not use indefinite article 'a' and 'an' after phrases such as 'sort of', 'kind of' and 'type of'.

19.	There is famine in the whole Bihar.	19.	There is famine in the whole of Bihar.

Note: Do not use 'the whole' with proper nouns. Write 'the whole of India', and not 'the whole India'.

20.	There are many a books you can choose from.	20.	There is many a book you can choose from.

Note: The words 'many a book' – meaning 'many books' – require a singular verb.

21.	One must learn to distinguish good from bad.	21.	One must learn to distinguish the good from the bad.

Note: When adjectives are used as nouns to denote an entire class of things or persons, use the definite article.

22.	I am certain that he is in right.	22.	I am certain that he is in the right.

Note: The correct phrases are 'in the right', 'in the wrong', 'in the negative', 'in the positive', etc.

23.	I am living in Delhi.	23.	I live in Delhi.

Note: Use simple present tense in such sentences.

24.	He walks as if the world belongs to him.	24.	He walks as if the world belonged to him.

Note: Expressions like 'as if', 'as though', etc. are always followed by the past tense.

25.	Kindly see my certificates.	25.	Kindly look at (or examine) my certificates.

Note: The word 'seeing' refers to the simple faculty of vision, without drawing attention to anything critical. We can 'see' a thing without looking at it. 'I am seeing this great painting' is incorrect; 'I am looking at this great painting' is correct.

26.	My sister always puts on a white sari.	26.	My sister always wears a white sari.

Note: The words 'to put on', implies a simple act; whereas 'to wear' denotes 'putting on' something more out of habit.

27.	He asked me where was I going.	27.	He asked me where I was going.

Note: When a statement is made in the reported speech ('he asked where'), it is wrong to retain the question form ('where was I going?') (refer sentence no. 27).

28.	Hundreds of people died by the earthquake.	28.	Hundreds of people were killed due to the earthquake.

Note: We 'die' of natural causes (illness, hear-failure, etc.); however, in the case of unexpected causes and calamities (fire, war, etc.), use the verb 'kill'.

29.	Will you please open the knot?	29.	Will you please untie the knot?

Note: We 'open' a door or a window, but not a 'knot'.

30.	I have to give another examination next year.	30.	I have to take another examination next year.

Note: An examiner 'gives' an examination or a test; a candidate 'takes' an examination or a test (refer sentence no. 30).

31.	Better revise this essay.	31.	You had better revise this essay.

Note: The correct structure is 'You had better do this first', or 'You had better sleep now' (refer sentence no. 31).

32.	Are you a vegetarian? Yes, I am not.	32.	Are you a vegetarian? No, I am not. Or, Are you a vegetarian? Yes, I am.

Note: When the answer is the affirmative, say 'yes' and drop the negative form 'not'.
If the answer is in the negative, say 'no'; you may also retain the negative 'not'.

33.	When he lost my book, I became very angry.	33.	When he lost my book, I felt very angry.

Note: Preferably, use 'feel' or 'get' with adjectives like 'angry', 'hungry', 'thirsty', 'tired', etc.

34.	I went there with a view to buy a book.	34.	I went there with a view to buying a book.

Note: The phrase 'with a view to' is always followed by a gerund and not an infinitive.

35.	I did nothing but cried.	35.	I did nothing but cry.

Note: One 'sharpens' a pencil, but 'mends' a pen (refer sentence no. 36).

36.	Will you kindly mend this pencil?	36.	Will you kindly sharpen this pencil?

Note: One 'sharpens' a pencil, but 'mends' a pen (refer sentence no. 36).

37.	The thief escaped before the police came.	37.	The thief had escaped before the police came.

Note: The former action (when a sentence comprises two actions) should always take on the past perfect verb (refer sentence no. 37).

38.	He bore cheerfully his sorrows.	38.	He bore his sorrows cheerfully.

Note: In the case of a transitive verb, use the adverb after the object (refer sentence no. 38).

39.	I shall be back just now.	39.	I shall be back presently.

Note: The words 'just now' refer either to the past or the present, but certainly not to the future. 'presently' means 'shortly' and refers to the future (refer sentence no. 39).

40.	Please write your name with ink.	40.	Please write your name in ink.

Note: Always say 'write in chalk', 'write in pencil', etc.; but 'write with a pen/pencil' (refer sentence no. 40).

41.	He caught the thief from hand.	41.	He caught the thief by the hand.

Note: The words 'catch', 'hold', 'seize' and 'take' always precede 'by the hand' (refer sentence no. 41).

42.	He is sitting on his table.	42.	He is sitting at his table.

Note: It is incorrect to say 'sitting on' while referring to a piano, table, etc.

However, 'to sit on a bench', 'to sit on a sofa', etc. are equally correct (refer sentence no. 42).

43.	Why do you repent from your misdeeds?	43.	Why do you repent your misdeeds?
44.	The Principal disposed my application.	44.	The Principal disposed of my application.

Note: It is correct to say 'dispose of', 'repent of, 'accuse of', etc. (refer sentence nos. 43 and 44).

45.	This book comprise of five chapters.	45.	This book comprises five chapters.

Note: Do not use a preposition after 'comprises' (refer sentence no. 45).

However, it is correct to say 'The book consists of five chapters.

46.	Let me congratulate you for your success.	46.	Let me congratulate you on your success.
47.	Ram's pen is different than his brother's.	47.	Ram's pen is different from his brother's.
48.	He is poor in English.	48.	He is poor at English.

Note: It is correct to say 'poor at', 'clever at', 'quick at', 'slow at', etc.

However, it is equally correct to say 'different from' (refer sentence nos. 47 and 48).

49.	Moti is married with Rekha.	49.	Moti is married to Rekha.
50.	Who will buy this car for such a price?	50.	Who will buy this car at such a price?

Note: Use 'for' only where a specific amount is mentioned (refer sentence no. 50).

For example, 'He sold his horse for Rs.700'.

51.	I shall return this book after a week.	51.	I shall return this book in a week. Or, I shall return this book in a week's time.

Note: At times, 'in' is used to indicate 'within' or 'at the end of' a duration/period (refer sentence no. 51).

52.	Open seventh page of this book.	52.	Open this book at page seven.
53.	Unless you do not work hard, you will not succeed.	53.	Unless you work hard, you will not succeed.

Note: The word 'unless' means 'if not'; in such cases do not use two negatives in the same sentence (refer sentence no. 53)

54.	Literature has no to her aim but entertainment.	54.	Literature has no other aim than entertainment.
55.	The book contains five hundred fifty pages.	55.	The book contains five hundred and fifty pages.

Note: The correct usage is 'other than', and not 'other but' (refer sentence no. 55).

56.	He asked that where I lived.	56.	He asked where I lived.
57.	What to speak of English, he can't even talk in Hindi.	57.	Not to speak of English, he can't even talk in Hindi.
58.	He can't make his both ends.	58.	He can't make both ends meet.

Note: Always recognise and retain the correct use of idioms.

For example, 'both ends meet' is an idiom (refer sentence no. 58)

SENTENCE CORRECTION (PRACTICE TESTS)

Correct the following sentences

PRACTICE TEST-1

1. I am working here for the last seven years.
2. He has no money nor land.
3. Work hard lest you should not get poor marks.
4. If you will help me I will feel thankful.
5. Mohan as well as Sohan were punished.
6. Neither of three was guilty.
7. I congratulate you for your success.
8. He asked me that why I had come.
9. He has ordered for a radio-set.
10. The river has over flown its banks.
11. His all sons are ugly.
12. This is a worth seeing film.
13. None of the students have learnt their lesson.
14. The murderer was tried and hung.
15. I am feeling unwell since day before yesterday.
16. He was one of the wisest man that has ever lived.
17. He is the youngest of the two brothers.
18. No sooner he saw a lion he began to cry.
19. Although he worked hard but he could not succeed.
20. I have neither known him nor his brother.

PRACTICE TEST-2

1. It is getting dark, please open the light.
2. He refused that he had broken the pen.
3. My friend is ill since six months.
4. There are good news for you in this letter.
5. Lions are both found in Asia and Africa.
6. Students, who shirk work, they suffer in the end.
7. This book is too interesting.
8. None of us have ever been England.
9. Tribune has the largest circulation than any newspaper in the Punjab.
10. Health is more preferable than riches.
11. My views are different than you.
12. The examination begins from Tuesday next.
13. Though he worked hard failed.
14. What to speak of English, he cannot even read Hindi.
15. I regard him my friend.
16. His services have dispensed.
17. Has both of you been to Calcutta?
18. Kamlesh is the youngest and most beautiful of my two sisters.
19. My companions as well as I was nicely entertained.
20. I cannot invite Mohan to this place without you agree.

PRACTICE TEST-3

1. He is confined to bed with bad cold for the last three days.

2. He is very weak to attend the office today.
3. He has been ill since the last two weeks.
4. He is incapable for hard work.
5. Sham is holding this post for the last six months.
6. No sooner he saw his father he began to cry.
7. It is no use finding fault at everything.
8. Who is the braver of these four brothers?
9. Though we invited him for dinner warmly, but he declined.
10. He was bent to do evil.
11. I avoid to go there.
12. Which is the best of these two books?
13. No sooner he entered the room there was a great noise.
14. Wait here until I do not come.
15. The patient died before the doctor arrived.
16. Your pen is in my suitcase, shall I bring.
17. He had a great number of money.
18. I wish he was with me today.
19. Gopal absented from the class.
20. None of them are helpful to me.

PRACTICE TEST-4

1. He turned a deaf ear to the advices of his teacher.
2. The sceneries of Kashmir beggars description.
3. His hairs have turned grey.
4. He has many grey hair on his head.
5. Second-hand furnitures were put to auction.
6. Alms is given to the poors.
7. He takes pain over his work.
8. I am well up in my study.
9. Heads of cattles were swept away in the storm.
10. How many son-in-laws have you?
11. Sushil's my neighbour's house was burgled last night.
12. I bought two dozens mangoes and four scores apples.
13. The wages of sin are death.
14. Some men possess means that is great.
15. He has no issues.
16. I have many works to do.
17. Road closed for repair.
18. My house is out of repairs.
19. Do not make friend with selfish people.
20. Circumstance influences a man's character.

PRACTICE TEST-5

1. Nobody was there but I.
2. Who is there? It is me.
3. Let you and I go to fetch the doctor.
4. Only you and me can admitted on this ticket.
5. Between you and I, Mr. Sharma is not to be trusted.
6. I am, your's sincerely.
7. You and I have revised your lessons.
8. You and Ashok have improved their chances of success.
9. Each of the two sisters were hardworking.
10. None of the two contestants was willing to withdraw.
11. One should keep his word.
12. Everyone present got one's pay.
13. He and myself went to get the seats reserved.
14. I did not like him disturbing me at that late hour.
15. Who do you think I met?

PRACTICE TEST-6

1. This is the best of the two books on this subject.
2. Solomon was wiser than all the Jewish kings.
3. Who is tallest, you or I?
4. It is more hotter today than yesterday.
5. Death is more preferable than dishonour.
6. I am junior than you by two years.
7. I have given you a most complete account of my travels in Italy.
8. Her command over the English language is the most excellent.
9. He has not some money with him.
10. I gave him a few books I had.
11. No less than fifty ships were destroyed by the storm.
12. Choose the least of the two evils.
13. I have visited the place many a times.
14. Whole the country is with the great leader.
15. Be respectful to the older members of the family.
16. Jagdish is elder than Inder.
17. What is the last score?
18. Of Kanti and Usha, the later is the more beautiful.
19. If he wants farther help, send him to me.
20. We went further than three miles.

PRACTICE TEST-7

1. I have ordered for dinner.
2. The younger brother resembles to the elder.
3. I want the police to investigate into the case.
4. He deeply loved with me.
5. I reached at Delhi only this morning.
6. The teacher has not yet entered in the classroom.
7. Why have you picked up a quarrel with him?
8. He asked from me if I was interested in a job,
9. He thought if he could cram a few important questions, he could pass in the examination.
10. Your name precede before mine and succeeds after Ashok's.
11. You will come to grief if you do not obey to my orders.
12. He should not have violated against the rules.
13. Let us discuss about the problem.
14. May I accompany with you to the railway station?
15. As he approached to his office, he was attacked by a stranger.
16. The teacher promised to the boys a holiday.
17. The Principal requested to the President to distribute the prizes.
18. He married with a rich widow.
19. He prevailed upon me to resign from my post.
20. Sign on this paper.
21. Fear from God.
22. Do you have enough of money?
23. A sense of gloominess pervades through the whole novel.
24. Please recommend for me to the officer.
25. Your advice will benefit to me much.

PRACTICE TEST-8

1. I hope you are keeping good health.
2. These days he is enjoying bad health.
3. There are many females in the bus.
4. The male members of my family are all employed.
5. Many homes are lying vacant. Are you going to your house straight from the office?
6. The roads of this town are narrow.
7. Let us sit in the shadow of the tree.
8. How many individuals were present in the meeting?
9. He made an interesting lecture.
10. My leg is paining.
11. The captain of our team made four goals.
12. See this word in the dictionary.
13. Please send the reply on the address given below.
14. Our parents may be resembled of a tree which gives cool shade.
15. He is enough educated.
16. Have you given the test?
17. Yesterday our teacher took your test.
18. Have you written him any letter?
19. A dog is very faithful to it's master.
20. I am your's affectionate son.
21. He asked from me that I had gone there or not.
22. He never hears my advice.
23. Please remind me this.
24. The train will arrive just now.
25. I can depend upon your help, can't it?

PRACTICE TEST-9

1. Cities after cities fell.
2. I have applied for leave of two days.
3. What is the use of Munir going there?
4. This water is good for drinking.
5. What to speak of fruit, they had not even food to eat.
6. He is boy of ten years old.
7. He is always ready to pick up quarrels.
8. He did many mischiefs.
9. You should return home before two hours.
10. All the patients have been admitted and received attention.
11. It is exact five in my watch.
12. I bow down to your will.
13. She is not as efficient and energetic now as she was five years before.
14. What to do?
15. I will dine with them on next Sunday?
16. Due to illness I cannot attend my office today.
17. His illness was owing to overwork.
18. He went to school but returned back immediately.
19. He worked for one and a half hours.
20. Supposing if he fails, what he will do?
21. One cannot be too careful about what he says.
22. Misfortunes when faced bravely and manly become less troublesome.
23. Not unoften I have asked him to speak truth.

24. Aeroplanes carry out letters and passengers from one place to another.
25. Who hanged this picture on the wall?

PRACTICE TEST-10

1. Slow and steady win the race.
2. He absented from college.
3. I know swimming.
4. We should fear from God.
5. I am tired from him.
6. I knocked the door twice.
7. He was accused with murder.
8. I caught her from the arm.

PRACTICE TEST-11

1. She feels sadly.
2. I have invited him on tea.
3. Wait here until I do not return.
4. He is a M.A.
5. Do not make noise here.
6. Do not write with ink.
7. Trust in God and do right.
8. He has many works to do.

PRACTICE TEST-12

1. Please call the doctor.
2. Until he does not study hard he will not pass.
3. He told me that he is a coward.
4. I have not met him since a week.
5. Two boys were sunk in the river.
6. He likes the sceneries of Kashmir.
7. Politics are a dirty game.
8. She does not resemble with her sister.

PRACTICE TEST-13

1. No sooner he passed the examination, he felt happy.
2. The jug is full with water.
3. He is living in this town for four years.
4. He died from cholera.
5. Do not make noise.
6. I read Tribune daily.
7. Politics are a dirty game.
8. I met him in the way.

PRACTICE TEST-14

1. The judge has passed order for his release.
2. I told the porter to carry my luggages.
3. One must keep one's words.
4. I want some blotting.
5. There is not place in compartment.
6. My house's roof is leaking.
7. Get me a copy of Wren's and Martin's grammar.
8. This picture of the king's is a very striking likeness of his.
9. He has completed two-third of his manuscript.
10. I have lost a ten-rupees note.

PRACTICE TEST-15

1. Here is the boy who he told me the teacher punished yesterday.
2. Who was it written by?
3. Such, men who have five year's teaching experience are eligible for this post.
4. He has a dog whom he loves very much.
5. Who is greater – Ashoka or Akbar?
6. You should avail this opportunity.
7. They enjoyed in the fair.
8. I, you and he will movies this evening.
9. Both you and I are equally to blame.
10. Those who came late they should stand.
11. He is one of those men who is always finding fault with other people.
12. I lost my way, which prevented me from reaching my destination in time.

PRACTICE TEST-16

1. India is the first peace-loving country in the World.
2. Even his next relations did not stand by him in his misfortunes.
3. Verbal instructions will not serve the purpose.
4. The climate of Bombay is more pleasant than Delhi.
5. The welfare of the soul is surely preferable than of the body.
6. I have read each book of this library.
7. He has been sick for a very long time.
8. This is one of the best and interesting novels that I have ever read.

9. I am leaving for Bombay by the 2:30 o'clock train.
10. I do not like these kind of novels.

PRACTICE TEST-17

1. It is bitter cold today.
2. I am feeling so lonely.
3. He is a much learned man.
4. He is very poorer than all of his friends.
5. He is rather very tired.
6. His son is working very hardly.
7. This hardly won liberty is to be defended at all costs.
8. He is presently at Chandigarh.
9. Last night you returned lately.
10. He went directly to his house.
11. I only engaged this servant for a week.
12. She was even blamed by her parents.
13. He is enough wise to understand the situation.
14. Our class will be tomorrow here.
15. I met him four weeks before.
16. He is seldom or ever to be seen at his shop.
17. No excuse is too slight not to be seized upon.
18. I will wait here until you do not go.
19. I care a straw for it.
20. I never remember having met him before.
21. Drinking is quite harmful for one's health.
22. Scarcely the water crossed the danger level, the warning signals were sounded.
23. Did you reach in time? Yes, I didn't. No, I did.
24. It is nothing else than pride.
25. Of course, you will get this job.
26. I have not been here too long to have many friends.
27. They haven't still spent all their money.
28. We yet have time to catch the train.
29. It is rather a good film.
30. She is accurate and neat but she is fairly slow.

HINTS (FOR ANSWERS TO PRACTICE TESTS)

Q. No.	*TEST-1*	*TEST-2*	*TEST-3*
1.	have been	switch on	has been
2.	neither, nor	denied	too weak
3.	lest, should	for six months	for
4.	help, shall feel	is, news	of
5.	was	both in	has been
6.	three accused	suffer in	no sooner, than
7.	on, success	very	with
8.	why	has	bravest, four
9.	ordered a	than any other	to dinner
10.	over flowed	preferable	bent on
11.	all his	from yours	going
12.	a film worth seeing	on	better of, two
13.	has learnt	yet he failed	no sooner, than
14.	hanged	not to speak of English	until I come
15.	have been feeling	as my friend	had died
16.	that have	have been dispensed with	should I bring
17.	younger of	have both of	amount of money
18.	than he	younger and more	he were
19.	yet he	were	himself
20.	know neither, nor	will not, unless	is

Q. No.	TEST-4	TEST-5	TEST-6
1.	advice	but me	better, two
2.	scenery	It is I	other Jewish kings
3.	hair	you and me	taller
4.	hairs	you and I	hotter
5.	furniture	you and me	preferable to
6.	are	yours sincerely	junior to
7.	pains	our	a complete account of my
8.	studies	your	is excellent
9.	head of cattle	each, was	not any money
10.	sons-in-law	neither, was	the few
11.	Sushil my neighbour's	one, one's	no fewer than
12.	dozen mangoes, four score	everyone, his	lesser of
13.	is	He and I	many times
14.	are	his disturbing	the whole country
15.	issue	whom	respectful to the elder
16.	much work to do	—	is older
17.	repairs	—	latest
18.	repair	—	the latter
19.	make friends	—	send him
20.	circumstances	—	farther

Q. No.	TEST-7	TEST-8	TEST-9
1.	ordered dinner	enjoying good health	city after city
2.	resembles the elder	keeping bad health	two days' leave
3.	to investigate the case	many women	Munir's going
4.	loved me	men in my family	good to drink
5.	reached Delhi	houses are lying	not to speak of fruit
6.	entered the classroom	streets of this town	boy of ten
7.	picked a quarrel	shade of the tree	to pick quarrels
8.	asked me	persons	much mischief
9.		delivered, lecture	within two hours
10.	precedes mine, succeeds Ashok's	feeling pain	have received attention
11.	obey my orders	scored goals	five by my watch
12.	violated the rules	look up	bow to your
13.	discuss the problem	to the address	five years ago
14.	accompany you to	may be compared	am I to
15.	as he approached his office	sufficiently educated	Sunday next

Q. No.	TEST-7	TEST-8	TEST-9
16.	promised the boys	taken the test	owing to illness
17.	Principal requested the President	gave us a test	due to overwork
18.	married a rich	written to him	returned immediately
19.	to resign my post	to its master	one hour and a half
20.	sign this paper.	your	supposing (or if) he fails
21.	Fear God	whether I	what one says
22.	enough money	listens to	bravely and manfully
23.	pervades the whole	remind me of	have I asked
24.	recommend me to	shortly	carry letters and passenger
25.	benefit me	can't I	hung

Q. No.	TEST-10	TEST-11	TEST-12
1.	Slow and steady wins the race.	She feels sad.	Please call a doctor.
2.	He was absent from the college.	I have invited him over tea.	Until he studies hard he will not pass.
3.	I know how to swim.	Wait here until I return.	He told me that he was a coward.
4.	We should have fear of God/We should fear God.	He is an M.A.	I have not met him for a week.
5.	I am tired of him.	Do not make a noise here.	Two boys were drowned in the river.
6.	I knocked at the door twice.	Do not write in ink.	He likes the scenery of Kashmir.
7.	He was accused of murder.	Trust in the God and do the right.	Politics is a dirty game.
8.	I caught her by the arm.	He has many things to do.	She does not resemble her sister.

Q. No.	TEST-13	TEST-14
1.	No sooner did he pass the examination, he felt happy.	The judge has passed an order of his release.
2.	The jug is full of water.	I told the porter to carry my luggage.
3.	He has been living in this town for four years.	One must keep one's word.
4.	He died of cholera.	I want some blotting paper.
5.	Do not make a noise.	There is no room in the compartment.
6.	I read the Tribune daily.	The roof of my house is leaking.

7.	Politics is a dirty game.	Get me a copy of Wren and Martin's grammar.
8.	I met him on the way.	This picture of the king has a very striking likeness of him.
9.	—	He has completed two–third of the manuscript.
10.	—	I have lost a ten–rupee note.

Q. No.	*TEST-15*	*TEST-16*
1.	Here is the boy who told me that the teacher had punished yesterday.	India is the most peace–loving country in the World.
2.	By whom was it written?	Even his nearest relations did not stand by him in his misfortunes.
3.	Men with five years' teaching experience are eligible for this post.	Oral instructions will not serve the purpose.
4.	He has a dog which he loves very much.	The climate of Bombay is more pleasant than that of Delhi.
5.	Who is greater – The Ashoka or The Akbar?	Welfare of the soul is surely preferable to that of the body.
6.	You should avail of this opportunity.	I have read every book in this library.
7.	They enjoyed the fair.	He has been sick since a very long time.
8.	You, he, and I will go to the movie this evening.	This is one of the best and the most interesting novel that I have ever read.
9.	Both you and I are equally to be blamed.	I am leaving for Bombay by train at 2:30 in the afternoon.
10.	Those who came late should stand.	I do not like these kind of novels.
11.	He is one of those men who are always finding fault with other people.	—
12.	Losing my ways prevented me from reaching my destination on time.	—

Q. No.	*TEST-17*
1.	It is bitterly cold today.
2.	I am feeling extremely lonely.
3.	He is a highly learned man.
4.	He is poorer than all of his friends.
5.	He is very tired.
6.	His son is working very hard.
7.	This hard-won liberty is to be defended at all costs.
8.	He is presently in Chandigarh.

9.	Last night you returned late.
10.	He went directly to his home.
11.	I engaged this servant only for a week.
12.	She was blamed even by her parents.
13.	He is wise enough to understand the situation.
14.	Our class will be here tomorrow.
15.	I met him four weeks ago.
16.	He is seldom or never to be seen at his shop.
17.	No excuse is too slight to be seized upon.
18.	I will wait here until you go.
19.	I care a damn for it.
20.	I do not remember having met him before.
21.	Drinking is quite harmful for health.
22.	Scarcely had the water crossed the danger level, the warning signals were sounded.
23.	Did you reach in time? Yes, I did. No, I didn't.
24.	It is nothing else but pride.
25.	Surely, you will get the job.
26.	I have not been here long enough to have any friends.
27.	They haven't yet spent all their money.
28.	We still have time to catch the train.
29.	It is a good film.
30.	She is accurate and neat but fairly slow.

PRACTICE TEST-18

1. Every man, woman, and child were rescued.
2. No sooner I am out, than the students make a noise.
3. Walk carefully lest you may not fall.
4. The patient died before the doctor arrived.
5. Time and tide waits for none.
6. Into what kind of mess have you got me into?
7. I learned the answer would come sooner than I expected.
8. Hardly he had stepped out than it began to rain.
9. Either of the five dancers will dance tonight.
10. My client was neither aware nor party to the plot.

PRACTICE TEST-19

1. My sister prefers dogs than cats.
2. I don't approve to your smoking in public.
3. One of my student has got the prestigious Commonwealth Scholarship this year.
4. The fresher the fruit, the best it tastes.
5. He questioned my motif behind meeting the director.

6. The director went and bidded goodbye to the composer.
7. His acceptance of your fancy story indicates his credible nature.
8. Are you invited for the office party?
9. When I will reach home, I will let you know the details of the event.
10. The University comprises of several Departments.

PRACTICE TEST-20

1. Have you brought some mangoes?
2. The Ganga is the sacred river.
3. I and Chetan did all the work.
4. He said it himself.
5. Blessed is he that has found a job.
6. He is much ill to do any work.
7. One of the boy was absent for a week.
8. Gopal came home lately.
9. She was sitting besides him.
10. Our hoard is small and our hearts are large.

PRACTICE TEST-21

1. The manager was angry upon the employee.
2. One of the answer was wrong.
3. You should buy new furnitures for your house.
4. They pitched the tent besides the lake.
5. The woodcutter was falling the trees in the forest.
6. The hens had stopped lying eggs.
7. The mother sings until the child does not go to sleep.
8. There was no one to look at the children in the hostel.
9. The reply is awaited for.
10. The chairman flew the flag.

PRACTICE TEST-22

1. He died with fever.
2. Ram acted with my proposal.
3. She quarreled against me over the property issue.
4. Be careful for your mother's health.
5. A Sikh, tall than any of his comrades, rushed forward.
6. They cheated each another.
7. Old father looks to his children.
8. Many a man have been ruined by speculation.
9. Let him and I go together.
10. The priest was very kind for all of us.

PRACTICE TEST-23

1. The older the wine, better it tastes.
2. You cannot cross the bridge until you do not come to it.
3. He asked me what was my profession.
4. Give me a pencil to write.
5. Netaji is one of the bravest patriot of the country.
6. I met an one-eyed beggar in the street.
7. The traders dealing with garments are jittery about the impact of GST.
8. His efficiency soon made him the boss's blue-eyes boy.
9. She does not know cooking doesn't she?
10. No sooner the bell rang than the children rushed out of their classrooms.

PRACTICE TEST-24

1. I request your favour to grant me leave.
2. He lived there for a day.
3. He is the fastest runner and he came last.
4. They know each other since January.
5. All the patients have been admitted and received attention.
6. They didn't see any movies since March.
7. We shall go on a tour as soon as the schools will close.
8. Each of the answers was not correct.
9. If we had had money we would go shopping.
10. I wanted that he should get leave.

PRACTICE TEST-25

1. He enjoyed during the holidays.
2. Whoever works hard he will win.
3. The man who knocked at the door was stranger.
4. I asked my colleague when was he going to his home town.
5. Besides clothes, the shopkeeper deals with cosmetics too.

6. He is desirous for joining the army.
7. The judge said that the truth always triumphed.
8. One should help his friend in difficulty.
9. Sachin Tendulkar is the best batsman India has produced, isn't it?
10. More you read less you understand.

PRACTICE TEST-26

1. School is very near my home.
2. They never fail who die in great cause.
3. It rained an hour before.
4. He wrote a most complete account of his travels.
5. Either of these three answers is incorrect.
6. You will be late until you hurry.
7. He is seldom or ever absent from school.
8. The colours so passed off one another that she could not distinguish them.
9. The general as well as his soldiers were killed in the battle.
10. The boat was drowned.

PRACTICE TEST-27

1. One must do what he thinks best.
2. He will surely not do that, did he?
3. Can I leave the room now, Sir?
4. My neighbour, along with two friends, was pushing his car which is stalled.
5. I thought to help him, but he did not welcome my suggestion.
6. When I was a child, I enjoyed to eat ice cream in the bench.
7. The Principal, along with the teachers, are planning to apply for a leave.
8. Do you have an idea who is that man?
9. Unemployment as well as poverty influence the votes.
10. When I woke up, the man already disappeared after committing murder in the running train.

PRACTICE TEST-28

1. The vehicular pollution causes serious harm to human beings.
2. Both Ashish and Smita came late to college today.
3. There is many problems relating to this matter.
4. Not only David passed but got a distinction.
5. We'd like some information about the types of cars available.
6. I prefer to pay by cash.
7. My uncle has proposed me a job in his company.
8. All of a sudden she burst in tears.
9. I enjoy this type of music still now.
10. The teacher said me to submit the assignment the next day.

PRACTICE TEST-29

1. Saints desire nothing to the society.
2. I regret at the delay in doing this.
3. I congratulate you for your success.
4. Ram as well as Mohan have gone.
5. He has passed order on my application.
6. He is more intelligent than any boy.
7. What will be ensued on this?
8. This is high time that we should change the bike.
9. I did nothing but laughed.
10. I informed him, 'Leave the room'.

ANSWERS

PRACTICE TEST-18

1. Every man, woman, and child was rescued.
2. No sooner am I out, than the students make a noise.
3. Walk carefully, lest you should fall.
4. The patient had died, before the doctor arrived.
5. Time and tide wait for none.
6. What kind of mess have you got me into?
7. I knew the answer would come sooner than I expected.
8. Hardly had he stepped out when it began to rain.
9. One of the five dancers will dance tonight.
10. My client was neither aware nor a party to the plot.

PRACTICE TEST-19

1. My sister prefers dogs to cats.
2. I don't approve of your smoking in public.
3. One of my students has got the prestigious Commonwealth Scholarship this year.
4. The fresher the fruit, the better it tastes.
5. He questioned my motive behind meeting the director.
6. The director went and bid goodbye to the composer.
7. His acceptance of your fancy story indicates his credulous nature.
8. Are you invited to the office party?
9. When I reach home, I will let you know the details of the event.
10. The University comprises of several Departments.

PRACTICE TEST-20

1. Have you brought any mangoes?
2. The Ganga is a sacred river.
3. Chetan and I did all the work.
4. He said it to himself.
5. Blessed is he who has found a job.
6. He is too ill to do any work.
7. One of the boys was absent for a week.
8. Gopal came home late.
9. She was sitting beside him.
10. Our hoard is little and our hearts are large.

PRACTICE TEST-21

1. The manager was angry with the employee.
2. One of the answers was wrong.
3. You should buy new furniture for your house.
4. They pitched the tent beside the lake.
5. The woodcutter was felling the trees in the forest.
6. The hens had stopped laying eggs.
7. The mother sings until the child goes to sleep.
8. There was no one to look after the children in the hostel.
9. The reply is awaited.
10. The chairman unfurled the flag.

PRACTICE TEST-22

1. He died of fever.
2. Ram acted on my proposal.
3. She quarreled with me over the property issue.
4. Be careful about your mother's health.
5. A Sikh, taller than any of his comrades, rushed forward.
6. They cheated each other.
7. An old father looks to his children.
8. Many men have been ruined by speculation.
9. Let him and me go together.
10. The priest was very kind to all of us.

PRACTICE TEST-23

1. The older the wine, the better it tastes.
2. You cannot cross the bridge until you come to it.
3. He asked me what my profession was.
4. Give me a pencil to write with.
5. Netaji is one of the bravest patriots of the country.
6. I met a one-eyed beggar in the street.
7. The traders dealing with garments are feeling jittery about the impact of GST.
8. His efficiency soon made him the boss's blue-eyed boy.
9. She does not know how to cook, does she?
10. No sooner did the bell ring than the children rushed out of their classrooms.

PRACTICE TEST-24

1. I request you to grant me leave.
2. He lived there for one day.
3. He is the fastest runner, but he came last.
4. They have known each other since January.
5. All the patients were admitted and received attention.
6. They haven't seen any movies since March.
7. We shall go on a tour as soon as the schools close.
8. Every answer was not correct.
9. If we had money, we would go shopping.
10. I wanted him to get leave.

PRACTICE TEST-25

1. He enjoyed himself during the holidays.
2. Whoever works hard will win.
3. The man who knocked at the door was a stranger.
4. I asked my colleague when he was going to his hometown.
5. Besides clothes, the shopkeeper deals in cosmetics too.
6. He is desirous of joining the army.
7. The judge said that the truth always triumphs.
8. One should help one's friend in difficulty.
9. Sachin Tendulkar is the best batsman India has produced, isn't he?
10. The more you read, the less you understand.

PRACTICE TEST-26

1. School is very near to my home.
2. They never fail who die for a great cause.
3. It has rained an hour before.
4. He wrote a complete account of his travels.
5. Anyone of these three answers is incorrect.
6. You will be late unless you hurry.
7. He is seldom or never absent from school.
8. The colours so matched that she could not distinguish them.
9. The general as well as his solders was killed in the battle.
10. The boat was sunk.

PRACTICE TEST-27

1. One must do what one thinks is best.
2. He will surely not do that, will he?
3. May I leave the room now, Sir?
4. My neighbour, along with two friends, was pushing his car which was stalled.
5. I thought of helping him, but he did not welcome my suggestion.
6. When I was a child, I enjoyed eating ice cream in the bench.
7. The Principal, along with the teachers, is planning to apply for a leave.
8. Do you have an idea who that man is?
9. Unemployment as well as poverty influences the votes.
10. When I woke up, the man had already disappeared after committing the murder in the running train.

PRACTICE TEST-28

1. Vehicular pollution causes serious harm to human beings.
2. Today, both Ashish and Smita came to college late.
3. There are many problems relating to this matter.
4. David not only passed but also got a distinction.
5. We'd like some information about the types of cars available.
6. I prefer to pay in cash.
7. My uncle has proposed to me a job in his company.
8. All of a sudden, she burst into tears.
9. I enjoy this type of music even now.
10. The teacher said to me to submit the assignment the next day.

PRACTICE TEST-29

1. Saints desire nothing from the society.
2. I regret the delay in doing this.
3. I congratulate you on your success.
4. Ram as well as Mohan has gone.
5. He has passed order against my application.
6. He is more intelligent than any other boy.
7. What will be ensued after this?
8. It is high time that we should change the bike.
9. I did nothing but laugh.
10. I told him to leave the room.

PART F:
MOCK PAPERS AND PREVIOUS YEAR QUESTION PAPERS

33 MOCK TEST - 1

M. Marks: 50 **Time Allowed: 45 Mins.**

Less than 25 – Poor; 25 to 30 – Average; 30 – 35 – Good; 35 – 40 – Very Good; 40 – 45 – Excellent; 45 – 50 – Outstanding

SENTENCE SEQUENCING OR REORDERING OF JUMBLED SENTENCES

Directions for Question 1 to 5: In each questions a set of six sentences of a continuous paragraph are provided. The sentence numbered 1 starts the paragraph and the sentence numbered 6 ends it. Arrange statements A, B, C, D between 1 and 6 to form a coherent paragraph.

Q 1.

1. What does the state do in a country where tax morality is very low?
   (A) It tries to spy upon the taxpayers.
   (B) It investigates income sources and spending patterns.
   (C) Exactly what the tax authority tries to do now, even if inconsistently.
   (D) It could also encourage people to denounce to the tax authorities any conspicuously prosperous neighbours who may be suspected of not paying their taxes properly.

6. ***The ultimate solution would be an Orwellian system***
   (a) BACD (b) DBAC
   (c) ABCD (d) DCBA

Q 2.

1. The fragile Yugoslav state has an uncertain future.
   (A) Thus, there will surely be chaos and uncertainty if the people fail to settle their differences.
   (B) Sharp ideological differences already exist in the country.
   (C) Ethnic, regional, linguistic, and material disparities are profound.
   (D) The country will also lose the excellent reputation it enjoyed in the international arena.

6. ***At worst, it will once more become vulnerable to international conspiracy and intrigue.***
   (a) BCAD (b) ADCB
   (c) ACBD (d) DBCA

Q 3.

1. India's experience of industrialization is characteristic of the difficulties faced by a newly independent developing country.
   (A) In 1947, India was undoubtedly an under-developed country with one of the lowest per capita incomes in the world.
   (B) Indian industrialisation was the result of a conscious deliberate policy of growth by an indigenous political elite.
   (C) Today India ranks fifth in the international community of nations if measured in terms of purchasing power.
   (D) Even today, however, the benefits of Indian industrialisation since independence have not reached the masses.

6. ***Industrialisation in India have thus been a limited success: One more example of growth without development.***
   (a) CDAB (b) DCBA
   (c) CABD (d) BACD

Q 4.

1. The New Economic Policy comprises the various policy measures and changes introduced since July 1991.
   (A) There is a common thread running through all these measures.

(B) The objective is simple – to improve the efficiency of the system.
(C) The regulatory mechanism involving multitude of controls has fragmented the capacity and reduced competition even in the private sector.
(D) The thrust of the new policy is towards creating a more competitive environment as a means to improving the productivity and efficiency of the economy.

6. ***This is to be achieved by removing the barriers and restrictions on the entry and growth of firms.***

(a) DCAB (b) ABCD
(c) BDAC (d) CDBA

Q 5.

1. It is significant that one of the most common objections to competition is that it is blind.

(A) This is important because in a system of free enterprise based on private property, chances are not equal and there is indeed a strong ca. e for reducing that inequality of opportunity.
(B) Rather it is a choice between a system where it is the will of a few persons that decides which is to get what and one where it depends at least partly, on the ability and the enterprise of the people concerned.
(C) Although competition and justice may have little else in common, it is as much as commendation of competition as of justice that it is no respecter of persons.
(D) The choice today is not between a system in which everybody will get what he deserves according to some universal standard and one where individual shares are determined by chance or goodwill.

6. ***The fact that opportunities open to the door in a competitive society are much more restricted than those open to the rich, does not make it less true that in such a society, the poor are freer than a person commanding much greater material comfort in a different type of society.***

(a) CDBA (b) DCBA
(c) ABCD (d) BADC

SENTENCE COMPLETION

Choose the correct option:

Q 6. In poor and under developed countries, trucks are the only means of getting about town, the public transportation being virtually __________.

(a) indecipherable (b) ubiquitous
(c) inadequate (d) non-existent
(e) negligent

Q 7. Given the __________ state of published evidence, we cannot conclude here that exposure to low-level microwave energy is either hazardous or safe.

(a) inconclusive (b) indulging
(c) descriptive (d) immaculate
(e) descriptive

Q 8. The clothes Nafees, the famous designer, designs for men are conservative, but her fashions for women are more __________.

(a) subtle (b) flamboyant
(c) tasteful (d) expensive
(e) open

Q 9. The equipments that were being used in the survey were __________, and because of the below-zero temperature, it was feared they would freeze and __________.

(a) icy ..... capsize
(b) frosty ..... shide
(c) fragile ..... shatter
(d) frozen ..... dehydrate
(e) useless ..... capsize

Q 10. Because of its tendency to __________, most Indian art is __________ Japanese art, where symbols have been minimised and meaning has been conveyed by using the method of the merest suggestion.

(a) imitate ..... superior to
(b) understate ..... reminiscent of
(c) overdraw ..... similar to
(d) sentimentalise ..... supportive of
(e) synergise ..... half

Q 11. Irony can sometimes become a mode of escape; to laugh at the terrors of life is, in a way, to __________ them.

(a) bolster (b) approve
(c) evade (d) foster
(e) avail

Q 12. The negotiations for the deal were often surprisingly __________, deteriorating at times into a volley of accusations and counter-accusations.

(a) insouciant (b) sedate

(c) acrimonious (d) propitious
(e) adequate

Q 13. A __________ student is unlikely to gain admission to a top level institution.
(a) mediocre (b) putative
(c) mendacious (d) vicarious
(e) commerce

Q 14. Either Japanese dishes are __________, or the one I had was a poor example.
(a) delicious (b) overrated
(c) underestimated (d) unpopular

Q 15. A person who is __________ is slow to adapt to a new way of life.
(a) intractable (b) furious
(c) insolent (d) valiant
(e) constructive

Q 16. Amit, who refrained from excesses in his personal life, differed markedly from Nirmal, who __________ notorious drinking bouts with his buddies.
(a) minimised (b) indulged in
(c) shunned (d) compensated for
(e) specialised

Q 17. The library in charge proposed a new schedule of fines for overdue books with the __________, if not the outright encouragement, of the faculty library committee.
(a) cynosure (b) acquiescence
(c) scorn (d) applause
(e) management

Q 18. Maya's remarks were so __________ that Arun could not decide which possible meaning was correct.
(a) congruent (b) impalpable
(c) ambiguous (d) facetious
(e) incorrigible

Q 19. By nature, Rahul was __________, given to striking up casual conversation with strangers he encountered at bus stops or check-out stands.
(a) gregarious (b) reticent
(c) casual (d) diffident
(e) indulgent

Q 20. In the absence of native predators, to stop the spread of their population, the imported goats __________ to such an inordinate degree that over grazed the country side and __________ the native vegetation.
(a) propagated ..... cultivated
(b) suffered ..... abandoned
(c) thrived ..... threatened
(d) dwindled ..... eliminated
(e) outnumbered ..... cultivated

CLOZE TEST

Directions: In the following passage there are blanks, each of which has been numbered. These numbers are printed below the passage and against each, four or five words are suggested, one of which fits the blank appropriately. Find out the appropriate words.

Put all your knowledge, learning, and ***(21)*** __________ in one scale and truth and ***(22)*** __________ in the other and the ***(23)*** __________ will by far ***(24)*** __________ the former. The ***(25)*** __________ of moral impurity has today spread among our school-going children and like a hidden ***(26)*** __________ is causing ***(27)*** __________ among them. I, therefore, appeal to you, boys and girls, to keep your minds and bodies ***(28)*** __________. All your scholarship, all your study of the ***(29)*** __________ will be in vain if you fail to translate their teachings ***(30)*** __________ your daily life.

21. (a) showmanship (b) thoughts
(c) scholarship (d) experiences

22. (a) honesty (b) purity
(c) sincerity (d) falsehood

23. (a) later (b) latter
(c) least (d) last

24. (a) outweigh (b) outsmart
(c) outsource (d) outshine

25. (a) evil (b) filth
(c) virus (d) stink

26. (a) epidemic (b) disease
(c) cancer (d) pestilence

27. (a) harm (b) vengeance
(c) havoc (d) discord

28. (a) free (b) pious
(c) pure (d) healthy

29. (a) Bible (b) Ramayana
(c) arts (d) scriptures

30. (a) in (b) into
(c) on (d) for

IDIOMS & PHRASES

DIRECTIONS: Every idiom/phrase provided in bold and italics is followed by four options. You have to find out the exact option from the given options. NOTA means none of the above given answers.

Q 31. To turn over a new leaf
- (a) to change the old habits and adopt new ones
- (b) to cover up one's faults by wearing new marks
- (c) to completely change one's course of action
- (d) to shift attention to new problems after having studied the old ones thoroughly

Q 32. To frame a person
- (a) to make one appear guilty
- (b) a narrow escape
- (c) to befool someone
- (d) to praise someone

Q 33. To cross swords
- (a) to defend
- (b) to fight
- (c) to rob
- (d) to kill

Q 34. To give up the ghost
- (a) to become rational
- (b) to suffer
- (c) to fight evil forces
- (d) to die

Q 35. Hobson's choice
- (a) feeling of strength
- (b) feeling of insecurity
- (c) excellent choice
- (d) accepts or leave the offer

ARTICLES

Fill in the blanks with suitable articles in all the following sets.

36. If _______ gold rusts, what will _______ iron do?

37. She has _______ endurance, _______ foresight, _______ strength, and _______ skill.

38. Keats tried to be _______ Milton of _______ Romantic Age.

39. _______ tiger is _______ wild animal.

40. _______ milk in that bottle has become sour.

41. _______ coal of Jharia belt is very rich.

42. Beware of _______ fury of _______ patient man.

43. You should come here by _______ shortest route.

44. _______ donkeys are _______ stupid animals.

45. ____ girls do not often wear ____ hats.

COMPREHENSION

Directions: For each question, choose the option that most accurately and completely answers the questions.

In principle, a cohesive group—one whose members generally agree with one another and support one another's judgments—can do a much better job at decision making than it could if it were non-cohesive. When cohesiveness is low or lacking entirely, compliance out of fear of recrimination is likely to be strongest. To overcome this fear, participants in the group's deliberations need to be confident that they are members in good standing and that the others will continue to value their role in the group, whether or not they agree about a particular issue under discussion. As members of a group feel more accepted by the others, they acquire greater freedom to say what they really think, becoming less likely to use deceitful arguments or to play it safe by dancing around the issues with vapid or conventional comments. Typically, then, the more cohesive a group becomes, the less its members will deliberately censor what they say out of fear of being punished socially for antagonising their fellow members. But group cohesiveness can have pitfalls as well: while the members of a highly cohesive group can feel much freer to deviate from the majority, their desire for genuine concurrence on every important issue often inclines them not to use this freedom. In a highly cohesive group of decision makers, the danger is not that individuals will conceal objections they harbour regarding a proposal favoured by the majority, but that they will think the proposal is a good one without attempting to carry out a critical scrutiny that could reveal grounds for strong objections. Members may then decide that any misgivings they feel are not worth pursuing—that the benefit of any doubt should be given to the group consensus. In this way, they may fall victim to a syndrome known as 'groupthink', which one psychologist concerned with collective decision making has defined as 'a deterioration of mental efficiency, reality testing, and moral judgment that results from in-group pressures'. Based on analyses of major fiascos of international diplomacy and military decision making, researchers have identified groupthink behaviour as a recurring pattern that involves several factors: overestimation of the group's power and morality, manifested, for example, in an illusion of invulnerability, which creates excessive optimism; closed-mindedness to warnings of problems and to alternative viewpoints; and unwarranted pressures toward uniformity, including self-censorship with respect to doubts about the group's reasoning and a concomitant shared illusion of unanimity concerning group decisions. Cohesiveness of the decision-making group is an essential antecedent condition for this syndrome but not a sufficient one, so it is important to work toward identifying the additional factors that determine whether group cohesiveness will deteriorate into groupthink or allow for effective decision making.

Q 46 Why does the author think that the cohesive group can do a much better job at decision making than it could if it were non-cohesive?

(a) The members of a highly cohesive group can feel much freer to deviate from the majority.
(b) Individuals will not conceal objections they harbour regarding a proposal favoured by the majority.
(c) Participants in the group's deliberations are confident that they are members in good standing and that the others will continue to value their role in the group, whether or not they agree about a particular issue under discussion.
(d) All of the above

Q 47. Which one of the following most accurately expresses the main point of the passage?

(a) Despite its value in encouraging frank discussions, high cohesion can lead to a debilitating type of group decision making called groupthink.
(b) Group members can guard against groupthink if they have a good understanding of the critical role played by cohesion.
(c) Groupthink is a dysfunctional collective decision-making pattern that can occur in diplomacy and military affairs.
(d) Low cohesion in groups is sometimes desirable when higher cohesion involves a risk of groupthink behaviour.

Q 48. A group of closely associated colleagues has made a disastrous diplomatic decision after a series of meetings marked by disagreement over conflicting alternatives. It can be inferred from the passage that the author would be most likely to say that this scenario,

(a) provides evidence of chronic indecision, thus indicating a weak level of cohesion in general.
(b) indicates that the group's cohesiveness was coupled with some other factor to produce a groupthink fiasco.
(c) provides no evidence that groupthink played a role in the group's decision.
(d) provides evidence that groupthink can develop even in some groups that do not demonstrate an 'illusion of unanimity'.

Q 49. The passage mentions which one of the following as a component of groupthink?

(a) unjustified suspicions among group members regarding an adversary's intentions.
(b) strong belief that the group's decisions are right.
(c) group members working under unusually high stress, leading to illusions of invulnerability.
(d) the deliberate use of vapid, cliched arguments.

Q 50. It can be inferred from the passage that both the author of the passage and the researchers mentioned in the passage would be most likely to agree with which one of the following statements about groupthink?

(a) Groupthink occurs in all strongly cohesive groups, but its contribution to collective decision making is not fully understood.
(b) The casual factors that transform group cohesion into groupthink are unique to each case.
(c) The continued study of cohesiveness of groups is probably fruitless for determining what factors elicit group think.
(d) On balance, groupthink cannot be expected to have a beneficial effect in a group's decision making.

MOCK TEST - 2

COMPREHENSION

Directions: For each question, choose the option that most accurately and completely answers the questions.

'The night I arrived in Delhi on a visit in January 1996, the elevator at the Maurya Sheraton took us up to the twelfth floor in a breath-taking six or seven seconds. 'Remarkable', I commented admiringly to the friendly hotel employee in a maroon sari and business-like pageboy haircut, who had draped a three-kilogram marigold garland around my neck as I stepped across the threshold. 'We couldn't have ascended faster in the U.S.A.'.

She took my praise in stride, as well she should have. Jet-lagged after an eighteen-hour journey from New York, I had failed to notice that this was not some superfast new elevator technology that the Maurya had brought to Delhi, but rather some highly creative labelling. When I finally woke up and looked out my window, I realised that what the elevator buttons had called the twelfth floor was in fact the second. The gleaming Maurya elevator had merely taken me for a ride – and a shorter ride I'd imagined.

I couldn't help the accusatory tone out of my voice the next time I ran into the maroon sari. 'Twelfth-floor, huh?', I said pointedly. 'I didn't think liberalisation meant being liberal with the facts'.

She was surprised that I had taken offense. 'Our foreign visitors much prefer to think of themselves as being on eleventh and twelfth floors than the first or second', she replied with wide-eyed innocence. 'And they don't look out of the windows that much'.

Welcome, I thought, to the new India. An India I was discovering for the first time: an India of five-star hotels, welcoming garlands, and smooth-talking hotel staff, where nothing is quite what it seems (not even the elevator buttons), where windows are not meant to be opened and appearances are the only reality'. [Shashi Tharoor, India: From Midnight to the Millennium and Beyond (Arcade Publishing, 1997) 275-276]

Q 1. After reading the last line of the first paragraph, 'We couldn't have ascended faster in the U.S.A.', which of the options do you think the author is most likely to agree with?
- (a) India never fails to surprise
- (b) Indians have been great innovators
- (c) Foreigners are turning to India's technical advancement
- (d) It's a fact that India hasn't made significant progress

Q 2. As used in the third paragraph, the underlined word 'accusatory' most nearly means all options, except
- (a) denunciative
- (b) criminate
- (c) eulogistic
- (d) censuring

Q 3. It can be inferred from the passage that the author's impression
- (a) transgresses from being proud to being even prouder
- (b) plummets from a sense of pride to a sense of disillusionment
- (c) trends from a level of disappointment to a level of condemnation
- (d) remains steadfast on the thought of being an Indian

Q 4. In the line, '...taken me for a ride–and a shorter ride I'd imagined', means
- (a) the elevator had taken them very swiftly
- (b) the hotel was treating its guests like royalties
- (c) technology had advanced in third world countries
- (d) people were being hoodwinked

Q 5. The tone of the passage could be summed up to be
- (a) pensive and remorseful

(b) matter of fact and somber
(c) humorous and reflective
(d) fiery and critical

PREPOSITION

Fill in the blanks with appropriate prepositions from the options given against each sentence.

6. Have you ever been _______ love?
(a) by (b) at
(c) in (d) to

7. My Greek friend reads English books _______ ease, but has some difficulty _______ understanding broadcast talk in English.
(a) with, in (b) in, with
(c) at, in (d) with, at

8. The part of the Thames called pool is _______ London Bridge.
(a) over (b) under
(c) in (d) on

9. Mr. Green has left London _______ Paris.
(a) in (b) at
(c) to (d) for

10. Trams disappeared _______ the streets of London several years ago.
(a) to (b) on
(c) from (d) for

11. He is in some way or other connected _______ journalism.
(a) with (b) to
(c) by (d) in

12. The boat trains _______ London to Dover run in connection _______ the steamers from Dover to Calais.
(a) with, from (b) from, to
(c) from, with (d) to, with

13. Scotland is to the north of England. Glasgow is _______ the river Clyde.
(a) in (b) on
(c) at (d) by

14. I have much experience _______ sickness, but none _______ curing them. He guesses _______ his answers: for he has genius for mathematics; in fact, he is not a genius _______ anything.
(a) of, at, in, to (b) of, at, in, in
(c) of, in, at, in (d) in, at, of, in

15. In old times an incursion was made _______ England _______ the Danes who at first were more than a match _______ the Saxon.
(a) by, for, into (b) into, for, by
(c) for, into, by (d) into, by for

SENTENCE COMPLETION

Choose the correct option:

Q 16. Though a _________ of four campaigns, Bush had never seen such demonstrations.
(a) watchman (b) veteran
(c) volunteer (d) witness
(e) follower

Q 17. Carried away by the _________ effects of the experimental medication, the patients _________ his desire to continue as a subject for as long as he could.
(a) supplementary ….. announced
(b) noxious ….. proclaimed
(c) frantic ….. repeated
(d) salutary ….. reiterated
(e) painful …. undermined

Q 18. Confused and _________, Hogwart fumbled to make sense of the seemingly inconsistent statements, _________ the impatience of his listeners.
(a) prostrate ….. listening to
(b) muddled ….. aware of
(c) philosophical ….. overlooking
(d) incoherent ….. oblivious to
(e) agitated ….. following

Q 19. One of the most productive research _________ in contemporary neuroscience is devoted to _________ maps of human consciousness.
(a) trajectories ….. reconnoitering
(b) designs ….. enunciating
(c) paradigms ….. elucidating
(d) declensions ….. obfuscating
(e) terminologies ….. newal

Q 20. Today, computers can _________ information from a number of sources, then automatically create a picture of their data manipulations.
(a) collate (b) inculcate
(c) extrapolate (d) adjudicate
(e) execute

Q 21. Just as a highway automobile accident leaves lasting marks of spilled coolant, _________, and oil, the smashing together of gigantic land masses releases and redirects fluids that flow, heat, _________, and deposit, leaving an enduring record of their presence.
(a) petrol ….. disappear
(b) fuel ….. evaporate
(c) paint ….. mark
(d) anti-freeze ….. drip
(e) gases ….. electric

Q 22. Although publicity has been __________, the film itself is intelligent, well-acted, handsomely produced, and altogether __________.
(a) tasteless ..... respectable
(b) extensive ..... moderate
(c) sophisticated ..... amateur
(d) perfect ..... spectacular
(e) useless ..... entraneous

Q 23. Ironically, his normally __________ speaker became shy and __________ when confronted with the approbatory stares of her eager audience.
(a) quiet ..... passionate
(b) garrulous ..... reticent
(c) dispassionate ..... passionate
(d) humble ..... supercilious
(e) soft ..... remorseful

Q 24. Although the whole team acted in unison, each member was __________ for a(n) __________ of the production process.
(a) reliable ..... source
(b) responsible ..... element
(c) appointed ..... article
(d) agreeable ..... felony
(e) agreeable ..... amount

Q 25. The studies of the children were __________ and __________ was the result of it.
(a) neglected ..... ignorance
(b) interrupted ..... incongruence
(c) off tracked ..... alienation
(d) instructed ..... genius
(e) ignored ..... negligence

Q 26. The US has shown little __________ to go after the terrorist or help India get him.
(a) inclination (b) urgency
(c) importance (d) alacrity
(e) endeavour

Q 27. Most young children are highly conformist and will __________ a classmate whose appearance or manners are __________.
(a) ostracise ..... conventional
(b) emulate ..... different
(c) shun ..... unusual
(d) deride ..... ordinary
(e) choose ..... deriding

Q 28 The royal astrologers had to determine the most __________ date for the coronation ceremony.
(a) propitious (b) sacred
(c) approximate (d) resplendent
(e) expected

Q 29. A satirical poem is often venom-filled, __________ with scorn.
(a) contained (b) filled up
(c) dripping (d) sardonic
(e) acidic

Q 30. The __________ rites in the Black Magic cult were kept secret by the members and were never __________ to outsiders.
(a) eclectic ..... delegated
(b) esoteric ..... divulged
(c) inscrutable ..... introduced
(d) elusive ..... prescribed
(e) exclusive ..... delegated

ONE WORD SUBSTITUTION

Every sentence is followed by four options. You have to find out the one-word substitution for the given sentences.

Q 31. Through which light cannot pass
(a) dark (b) dull
(c) opaque (d) obscure

Q 32. To talk much without coming to the point
(a) circumlocution (b) loquacity
(c) garrulousness (d) verosity

Q 33. The state of being unmarried
(a) single (b) celibacy
(c) lonely (d) aloofness

Q 34. That which can be interpreted in any way
(a) amphibious (b) ambient
(c) ambiguous (d) ambivalent

Q 35. To do away with a rule/law
(a) erase (b) cancel
(c) repeal (d) obliterate

IDIOMS & PHRASES

DIRECTIONS: Every idiom/phrase provided in bold, italics, and underlined is followed by four options. You have to find out the exact option from the given options.

Q 36. His promotion is on the cards.
(a) certain (b) due
(c) probable (d) evident

Q 37. He resigned the post of his own accord.
(a) voluntarily and willingly
(b) according to his judgement
(c) according to his convenience
(d) which he liked

Q 38. He faced the music for reaching home late.
(a) faced reprimand
(b) faced punishment
(c) faced pleasure
(d) faced entertainment

Q 39. He has too many irons in the fire.
(a) is very selfish and greedy
(b) wants to grab everything
(c) is engaged in too many enterprises simultaneously
(d) pokes his nose in every affair

Q 40. He is disliked because of his habit of making a mountain of a mole hill.
(a) taking undue advantage of a favourable opportunity
(b) giving great importance to trifles
(c) boasting
(d) exaggerating

CLOZE TEST

Directions: In the following passage there are blanks, each of which has been numbered. These numbers are printed below the passage and against each, four or five words are suggested, one of which fits the blank appropriately. Find out the appropriate words.

Perhaps, we Americans do not yet fully understand the great (41) __________ that India has to teach in thus (42) __________ her freedom (43). __________ her mighty triumph of a (44) __________ revolution our War of Independence (45) __________ in size and concept. India has taught humanity a lesson, and it is (46) __________ our peril if we do not learn it. The lesson? That war and killing (47) __________ nothing (48) __________ loss, and that a noble end is assured only if the (49) __________ to attain it are of a (50) __________ with it and also noble.

41. (a) message (b) lesson (c) moral (d) instruction
42. (a) attaining (b) obtaining (c) getting (d) winning
43. (a) Beside (b) Besides (c) Despite (d) Notwithstanding
44. (a) bloody (b) blood-free (c) bloodless (d) non-violent
45. (a) pales (b) shrinks (c) squeezes (d) reduces
46. (a) to (b) for (c) in (d) on
47. (a) bring (b) get (c) achieve (d) secure
48. (a) except (b) beside (c) besides (d) but
49. (a) measures (b) means (c) technique (d) method
50. (a) piece (b) peace (c) harmony (d) conformity

ANSWERS MOCK TEST - 1

1	c	**11**	evade	**21**	scholarship	**31**	c	**41**	the
2	a	**12**	acrimonious	**22**	purity	**32**	a	**42**	the, a
3	d	**13**	mediocre	**23**	latter	**33**	b	**43**	the
4	c	**14**	overrated	**24**	outweigh	**34**	b	**44**	the, the
5	a	**15**	intractable	**25**	virus	**35**	d	**45**	the, the
6	non-existent	**16**	indulged in	**26**	epidemic	**36**	the, the	**46**	c
7	inconclusive	**17**	acquiescence	**27**	havoc	**37**	the, the, the, the	**47**	a
8	flamboyant	**18**	ambiguous	**28**	pure	**38**	the, the	**48**	b
9	fragile .... shatter	**19**	gregarious	**29**	scriptures	**39**	the, a	**49**	b
10	understate .... reminiscent of	**20**	thrived .... threatened	**30**	into	**40**	the	**50**	a

ANSWERS MOCK TEST - 2									
1	a	**11**	a	**21**	fuel .... evaporate	**31**	c	**41**	lesson
2	c	**12**	c	**22**	extensive...moderate	**32**	a	**42**	winning
3	b	**13**	b	**23**	garrulous .... reticent	**33**	a	**43**	Beside
4	d	**14**	c	**24**	responsible .... element	**34**	c	**44**	bloodless
5	c	**15**	d	**25**	neglected .... ignorance	**35**	c	**45**	pales
6	c	**16**	veteran	**26**	inclination	**36**	b	**46**	to
7	a	**17**	salutary .... reiterated	**27**	shun .... unusual	**37**	a	**47**	achieve
8	b	**18**	incoherent .... oblivious to	**28**	propitious	**38**	a	**48**	but
9	d	**19**	paradigms .... elucidating	**29**	dripping	**39**	c	**49**	means
10	c	**20**	collate	**30**	esoteric .... divulged	**40**	b	**50**	peace

CUET UG - 2022 ENGLISH PAPER
18.08.2022 SLOT - 2

Read the passage carefully and answer questions from 1 to 6:

It was a dark autumn night. The old banker was pacing from corner to corner of his study, recalling to his mind the party he gave in autumn fifteen years before. There were many clever people at the party and much interesting conversation. They talked among other things of capital punishment. The guests, among them a few scholars and journalists, for the most part disapproved of capital punishment. They found it obsolete as a means of punishment, unfitted to a Christian State and immoral. Some of them thought that capital punishment should be replaced universally by life-imprisonment.

'I don't agree with you', said the host. 'I myself have experienced neither capital punishment nor life-imprisonment, but if one may judge a priori, then in my opinion capital punishment is more moral and more humane than imprisonment. Execution kills instantly, life-imprisonment kills by degrees. Who is the more humane executioner, one who kills you in a few seconds or one who draws the life out of you incessantly, for years'?

'They're both equally immoral', remarked one of the guests, 'because their purpose is the same, to take away life. The State is not God. It has no right to take away that which it cannot give back, if it should so desire'.

1. The season in which the narrator remembered the party he had given fifteen years ago was.
   (A) summer (B) spring
   (C) winter (D) autumn
2. Why did the banker feel that capital punishment is more moral than life imprisonment?
   (A) Execution brings an instantaneous end to the life of the offender and prevents prolonged suffering and trauma.
   (B) execution allows the offender to have a last sumptuous meal.
   (C) execution draws the attention of the society of the offender.
   (D) execution allows the offender to pray.
3. From the passage it becomes clear that the discussion and concern was primarily over the validity of
   (A) corporal punishment at schools
   (B) getting marooned in an island
   (C) capital punishment
   (D) punishment of any kind
4. Capital punishment is highly debated across the world because it
   (A) Takes away the property of the criminal.
   (B) Takes the criminal away from his family.
   (C) Denies the prisoner all his or her fundamental rights to education.
   (D) Denies and takes away from the criminal his or her fundamental right to live.
5. Why did a guest feel that both capital punishment and life-imprisonment are equally immoral?
   (A) Because the jury is often unfair.
   (B) The media does not allow the jury to pronounce a judgement at place.
   (C) Most democratic governments shelter hardened criminals.
   (D) Because the purpose of both the punishments is to deny the offender the right to live.
6. Match List-I with List-II.

	List-I		List-II
i.	The banker is	a.	disapproved of capital punishment.
ii.	The party was organised	b.	the host of the party.

iii.	Most of the guests who were scholars and journalists	c.	Is the pronouncement of a death sentence by a jury for an unaccusable crime.
iv.	Capital punishment	d.	In an autumn fifteen years ago.

Choose the CORRECT answer from the options given below:

(A) i– b, ii– d, iii– a, iv– c
(B) i– d, ii– b, iii– c, iv– a
(C) i– a, ii– b, iii–c, iv– d
(D) i– b, ii– c, iii– d, iv– a

[**Note:** *Question has been modified to get the answer.*]

Read the passage carefully and answer questions from 7 to 12:

The significance of William Shakespeare, 'To be or not to be' is one of William Shakespeare's most well-known quotes. It is part of his famous play Hamlet. Shakespeare is one of the most easily identified poem writers. He is known for his incredible writing style. He expressed this using iambic pentameter which would mean each line has 10 symbols, and they would all go in a pattern. He invented almost 1,700 common English words and phrases that we use today.

William Shakespeare was born on April 26, 1564, in the Shakespeare family home on Henley Street, Stratford-upon-Avon. Mary and John Shakespeare were William Shakespeare's mother and father. He was the third child of eight. However, the first two were daughters who died before he could remember. John Shakespeare sold farm products and wool. Both Mary and John Shakespeare had a high position in the community and had roles in their community. As a kid, William Shakespeare was sent to the highest level of elementary education at a school which was called Petty School. These schools were not like today's schools. Instead, they were usually held in someone's house and were taught by a very well-educated housewife. The children were also taught good behaviour and a Christian way of life. These were the most important part of the education. He then went to grammar school, where he had to attend school from 6 in the morning to 5 at night. In grammar school he was taught by a private usher. The grammar school used hornbook and the alphabet as a tool and for the basis of Elizabethan education. William's life was pretty strict. He had to be polite and do a lot of chores around the house. Shakespeare's school consisted of five full days and one-half day each week. He spent between 40 and 44 weeks of the year at school. That means he spent about 2,000 hours in school each year, which is double the amount of time we spend in school.

7. One of the most well-known quotes by William Shakespeare is.
   (A) 'to be not to be'
   (B) 'to bee not to be'
   (C) 'to be or not to be'
   (D) 'too be or not to be'
8. From the given options select the one which is CORRECT according to the passage.
   'Christian way of life' as mentioned in the passage would mean.
   (A) Validating the crusades or wars fought in the name of religion.
   (B) Holding the bible as the only source of valid knowledge.
   (C) Leading a moral life and respecting values that protect and promote life and society.
   (D) Watch films made only by Christian filmmakers only.
9. From the given options choose the one which is CORRECT according to the passage.
   (A) Shakespeare was known only as a great Nordic Lyricist.
   (B) Shakespeare's incredible writing style includes the use of iambic pentameter.
   (C) Shakespeare is a character of a great English drama.
   (D) Shakespeare never used the famous iambic pentameter.
10. From the options given below select the one which is CORRECT according to the passage. 'Petty schools', which Shakespeare himself attended, were?
    (A) Schools run by the English Government.
    (B) Formal schools run by the rich theatre guilds in England.
    (C) Schools that were held in someone's house and were taught by a very well-educated housewife.
    (D) Schools held in neighbourhood farms and taught by the wives of the English nobles.

11. Match List–I with List–II.

	List-I		List-II
i.	Hamlet is a	a.	Home of William Shakespeare.
ii.	Henley street, Stratford-upon-Avon is the	b.	Common English words that were invented by William Shakespeare.
iii.	Private usher	c.	Taught William Shakespeare in the grammar school.
iv.	1,700	d.	Play written by William Shakespeare.

Choose the CORRECT answer from the options given below:

(A) i– d, ii– a, iii–c, iv– b
(B) i– d, ii– c, iii– b, iv– a
(C) i– a, ii– b, iii–c, iv– d
(D) i– b, ii– d, iii– a, iv– c

12. From the options given below, select the one which is CORRECT according to the passage. We can assume while reading the passage that as a child William Shakespeare's life was not all fun and games because.

(A) He had to attend school for over 40 hours every week along with attending to household chores and learning to be polite.
(B) He had to attend the English parliament as a child member.
(C) He was Queen Elizabeth's personal assistant as a child.
(D) He was the head of Eton.

[Note: *Question has been modified to get the answer.* **]**

Read the passage carefully and answer questions from 13 to 18:

The young liftman in a city office, who threw a passenger out of his lift the other morning and was fined for the offence, was undoubtedly in the wrong. It was a question of 'Please'. The complainant entering the lift, said, 'Top'. The liftman demanded 'top-please' and this concession being refused he not only declined to comply with the instruction but hurled the passenger out of the lift. This, of course, was carrying a comment on manner too far. Discourtesy is not a legal offence, and it does not excuse assault and battery. If a burglar breaks into my house and I knock him down, the law will acquit me, and if I am physically assaulted, it will permit me to retaliate with reasonable violence. It does this because the burglar and my assailant have broken quite definite commands of the law, but no legal system could attempt to legislate against bad manners or could sanction the use of violence against something which it does not itself recognise as a legally punishable offence. And whatever our sympathy with the liftman, we must admit that the law is reasonable. It would never do if we were at liberty to box people's ears because we did not like their behaviour, or the tone of their voices, or the scowl on their faces. Our fists would never be idle, and the gutters of the city would run with blood all day. I may be as uncivil as I may please, and the law will protect me against violent retaliation. I may be haughty or boorish and there is no penalty to pay except the penalty of being written down an ill-mannered fellow.

13. From the given options select the one which is true and CORRECT according to the passage. The term 'discourtesy' means that we are:

(A) Lovely, pretty, and cute
(B) Strange and ridiculous
(C) Sad and unhappy
(D) Fail to be polite with others by not saying simple courteous words like 'please' and 'thank you'.

14. From the passage it may be concluded that often we invoke violent reaction from others, quiet like the young liftman in a city office who threw a passenger out of the lift, due to our own:

(A) Bad manners, impolite behaviour
(B) Patient and kind attitude
(C) Generosity and decency
(D) Daydreams

15. The young liftman in the passage by throwing the man out of the lift had committed a:

i. Heinous crime worth a capital punishment.

ii. Religious sin that only a holy pilgrimage can a tone.

iii. Grammatical error that cannot be corrected.

iv. An offence provoked by bad manners.

Choose the CORRECT answer from the options given below:

(A) i. only
(B) ii. only
(C) iii. only
(D) iv. only

16. The passage mentions 'This of course, was carrying a comment on manners too far':

    What do you think is the CORRECT explanation of this expression? (Choose the correct option)

    i. The comment could be heard a mile away from the city office.

    ii. Loudspeakers were used to carry the sound of the commit to far thing places.

    iii. Placing undue importance on social manners.

    iv. Manners are to become our staple food.

    Choose the CORRECT answer from the options given below:

    (A) i. only (B) ii. only
    (C) iii. only (D) iv. only

17. From the given select one of the options which is CORRECT according to the passage and explain the following:

    Burglary, unlike bad manners, is a legal offence because

    (A) Discourtesy is not a legal offence, but burglary is.
    (B) Bad manners are serious legal offence, but burglary is not a crime at all.
    (C) Democratic societies remit burglary as legal.
    (D) No sane and well-educated adult is ever rude.

18. Match List–I with List–II.

	List-I		List-II
i.	Man is thrown out of the lift because he	a.	did not say 'please' to the liftman.
ii.	Discourtesy	b.	is not a legal offence.
iii.	Law cannot punish violence	c.	against rude behaviour.
iv.	Uncivil, impolite, and rude behaviour	d.	can provoke violent reaction in people.

Choose the CORRECT answer from the options given below:

(A) i– d, ii– a, iii– b, iv– c
(B) i– a, ii– b, iii–c, iv– d
(C) i– c, ii– a, iii–d, iv– b
(D) i– b, ii– d, iii– c, iv– a

19. From the given options select the rightly spelt word.

    (A) Pariferal (B) Perripharal
    (C) Peripheral (D) Peryferal

20. From the given options select the rightly spelt word.

    (A) Disseminate (B) Dicceminate
    (C) Disaminate (D) Disiminate

21. From the given options select the rightly spelt word.

    (A) Opproximately
    (B) Approximately
    (C) Aproxemately
    (D) Aprroxemately

22. From the given options select the rightly spelt word.

    (A) Centemprary
    (B) Cantemporary
    (C) Contemporary
    (D) Kontemporary

23. From the given options select the one which can rightly substitute the given expression.

    The study of the human mind and behaviour.

    (A) Sociology (B) Philology
    (C) Physiology (D) Psychology

24. From the given options select the one which can rightly substitute the given expression. Handwriting which is difficult or impossible to read is.

    (A) Illegible (B) Illogical
    (C) Irrational (D) Edible

25. From the given options select the one which can rightly substitute the given expression.

    A book that contains information on various subject.

    (A) Dictionary (B) Novel
    (C) Thesaurus (D) Encyclopedia

26. From the given options select the one which can rightly substitute the given expression.

    A person interested in the study of coins and medals.

    (A) Numismatist
    (B) Numerologist
    (C) Medallist
    (D) Idealist

27. From the given options select the one which is similar in meaning to the given word. STRINGENT

    (A) Semblance (B) Semantics
    (C) Strict (D) Stringy

28. From the given options select the one which is similar in meaning to the given word. RESCUE

(A) Command (B) Help
(C) Restrict (D) Hinder

29. From the given options select the one which is similar in meaning to the given word.

CANDID

(A) Explore (B) Appeal
(C) Shine (D) Frank

30. From the given options select the one which is similar in meaning to the given word. HOMAGE

(A) Celebrate (B) Tribute
(C) Abide (D) Grateful

31. From the given options select the one that carries the same relation as:

Demolish : Construct

(A) Courageous : Cowardly
(B) Absurd : Ridiculous
(C) Submissive : Humble
(D) Blemish : Tarnish

[Note: *Question has been modified to get the answer.***]**

32. From the given options select the one that carries the same relation as:

Deficient : Surplus

(A) Wrath : Anger
(B) Extravagant : Frugal
(C) Valiant : Brave
(D) Unique : Rare

33. From the given options select the one that carries the same relation as:

Provoke : Incite

(A) Transient : Permanent
(B) Eradicate : Eliminate
(C) Advance : Deteriorate
(D) Abolish : Restore

34. From the given options select the one that carries the same relation as:

Commence : Initiate

(A) Proficient : Incompetent
(B) Candid : Sly
(C) Curious : Eager
(D) Delicious : Tasteless

35. From the given options select the one word which is opposite in meaning to the given word.

Alleviate

(A) Remove (B) Dissolve
(C) Intensify (D) Surprise

[Note: *Question has been modified to get the answer.***]**

36. From the given options select the one which is opposite in meaning to the given word.

Deception

(A) Falsehood (B) Scholarship
(C) Monstrous (D) Honesty

37. From the given options select the one which is opposite in meaning to the given word.
Apprentice

(A) Novice (B) Expert
(C) Hungry (D) Naïve

38. From the given options select the one which is opposite in meaning to the given word 'Translucent'

(A) Smart (B) Intelligent
(C) Compassionate (D) Opaque

39. From the given options select the one that rightly explains the given expression.

A man of straw

(A) a man of no substance
(B) a man who sells straws
(C) a worthy fellow
(D) a straw doll

40. From the given options select the one that rightly explains the given expression.

To leave someone in the lurch

(A) to argue with someone
(B) to desert someone in his difficulties
(C) to comfort someone
(D) to annoy someone

41. From the given options select the one that rightly explains the given expression

'at the eleventh hour'

(A) At the very last moment
(B) Every now and then
(C) Before the sun reaches the highest point in the sky
(D) Late in the evening after the sun has set

42. From the given options select the one that rightly explains the given expression.

To get into hot waters

(A) To get into trouble
(B) To be dishonest
(C) To suffer from stomach pain
(D) To be confused

43. Rearrange the given jumbled groups of words to make a meaningful sentence.

i. A temple you must

ii. Take off your shoes

iii. At the entrance

iv. Whenever you go to

Choose the CORRECT answer from the options given below:

(A) ii, i, iii, iv (B) iii, ii, i, iv
(C) i, iv, iii, ii (D) iv, i, ii, iii

44. Rearrange the given jumbled groups of words to make a meaningful sentence.

i. Some of the improvised fabric and garments

ii. Are displayed in the main pavilion

iii. Sales in the domestic market

iv. To facilitate export and to improve

Choose the CORRECT answer from the options given below:

(A) ii, iii, iv, i (B) i, iii, iv, ii
(C) iv, iii, i, ii (D) i, ii, iii, iv

45. Rearrange the given jumbled groups of words to make a meaningful sentence.

i. A lot of travel delay

ii. And lack of good management

iii. On the part of the railways

iv. Is caused due to the inefficiency

Choose the CORRECT answer from the options given below:

(A) i, iv, ii, iii (B) iii, i, ii, iv
(C) iv, i, iii, ii (D) iv, ii, iii, i

46. Rearrange the given jumbled groups of words to make a meaningful sentence.

i. A book he will lend

ii. You will never get it back

iii. If you lend him

iv. It to someone else and

Choose the CORRECT answer from the options given below:

(A) i, ii, iii, iv (B) iii, i, iv, ii
(C) i, iv, ii, iii (D) ii, i, iii, iv

47. From the given options, select the Figure of Speech (Poetic Device) used in the expression.

Betty Botter bought some bitter butter

(A) Alliteration (B) Simile
(C) Oxymoron (D) Pun

48. From the given options, select the Figure of Speech (Poetic Device) used in the expression.

Both wry with laboured ease of loss

(A) Personification (B) Oxymoron
(C) Simile (D) Pun

49. From the given options, select the Figure of Speech (Poetic Device) used in the expression. My alarm clock yells at one 'to get out of my bed'

(A) Pun (B) Simile
(C) Personification (D) Oxymoron

50. From the given options, select the Figure of Speech (Poetic Device) used in the expression.

The dust settled like a falling veil

(A) Simile (B) Metaphor
(C) Personification (D) Pun

ANSWERS – CUET 2022 ENGLISH PAPER

1	D	9	B	17	A	25	D	33	B	41	A	49	C
2	A	10	C	18	B	26	A	34	C	42	A	50	A
3	C	11	A	19	C	27	C	35	C	43	D		
4	D	12	A	20	A	28	B	36	D	44	C		
5	D	13	D	21	B	29	D	37	B	45	A		
6	A	14	A	22	C	30	B	38	D	46	B		
7	C	15	D	23	D	31	A	39	A	47	A		
8	C	16	D	24	A	32	B	40	B	48	B		

CUET UG - 2021 English Paper 23.09.2021 Shift 1 and 2

1. Choose the word opposite in meaning to the underlined word in the following sentence:
   The leader had a derisive attitude towards some of the members of his team.
   i. Respectful ii. Negative
   iii. Deprecatory iv. Critical
2. Choose the word that best fits into the blank space of the following sentence:
   Ambition is one of those __________ which are never satisfied.
   i. Ideas ii. Activities
   iii. Fancies iv. passions
3. Monika is not ______ for this kind of a job.
   i. cut up ii. cut in
   iii. cut out iv. cut through
4. Ramesh decided to set __________ sometime everyday for gardening.
   i. up ii. of
   iii. on iv. aside
5. Get me a cup of coffee, __________
   i. shall you? ii. will you?
   iii. won't you? iv. wouldn't you?
6. She took that person ___________ a thief
   i. To ii. As
   iii. For iv. After
7. As the Ratha Yatra festival approaches, the number of pilgrims in Puri _______.
   i. Increases
   ii. is increasing
   iii. will be increased
   iv. would have been increased
8. If you suffer from fever, the best remedy lies ________ complete rest.
   i. with ii. in
   iii. on iv. upon
9. Choose the word that best fits into the blank space of the following sentence: Education facilitates the ________ of specific skills.
   i. creation ii. procurement
   iii. acquisition iv. requirement
10. The book has passed ________ fifteen editions.
    i. By ii. On
    iii. From iv. Through
11. It was _______ cold ________ we couldn't go out.
    i. so, that ii. too, to
    iii. neither, nor iv. either, or
12. She never _______ with him.
    i. Agrees ii. Agreeing
    iii. was agreed iv. is agree
13. My uncle _________ tomorrow.
    i. will arrived ii. is arriving
    iii. arrive iv. has arrived
14. A person who breaks the law is
    i. Rogue ii. Criminal
    iii. Guilty iv. sinner
15. Which is the nearest meaning of the phrase, 'to build castles in the air'?
    i. Unimaginative
    ii. to be practical
    iii. to be very optimistic
    iv. day dream
16. Choose the correct option for the use of 'the'.
    i. The Canada
    ii. The Netherlands
    iii. The India
    iv. The South Africa
17. Synonym of Tangible is
    i. Concrete ii. Actual
    iii. Sensible iv. Abstract
18. Antonym of Outcast is
    i. Unwanted
    ii. Persona non grata
    iii. Favorite
    iv. Gypsy

19. I hurt my knee quite badly so _________.
   i. I did not have the right running shoes
   ii. I did not have the bandage
   iii. It was bleeding profusely
   iv. I had to go to hospital

20. Choose the correct spelling.
   i. Rith ii. Wreath
   iii. Reeth iv. Writh

21. We _________ in the London, but now we live in Delhi.
   i. Lived
   ii. used to live
   iii. were
   iv. happen to live

Answer Key

Q. No.	*Options*	*Q. No.*	*Options*
1.	(i)	12.	(i)
2.	(iii)	13.	(ii)
3.	(iii)	14.	(ii)
4.	(iv)	15.	(iv)
5.	(iv)	16.	(ii)
6.	(iii)	17.	(i)
7.	(ii)	18.	(iii)
8.	(ii)	19.	(iv)
9.	(iii)	20.	(ii)
10.	(iv)	21.	(ii)
11.	(i)		

Miscellaneous
CUET Exam Overview

Candidates must note that the CUET (erstwhile CUCET) will have **Section 1A, Section 1B**, General Test and domain-specific subjects.

Section 1A, which will be compulsory, will be conducted in **13 languages** and candidates will be given the option to choose the language of their choice. The options are English, Hindi, Assamese, Bengali, Gujarati, Kannada, Malayalam, Marathi, Odia, Punjabi, Tamil, Telugu and Urdu.

Section 1B will be optional and for students who want to opt for another language apart from the ones that are a part of Section 1A. Some of the languages on offer are French, Arabic, German, etc.

CUET Marking Scheme

It is important to know the latest CUET 2023 marking scheme for a candidate in order to make an intelligent strategy and get better marks. Lack of knowledge about the CUET 2023 marking scheme can lead to poor performance in the entrance exam. Therefore, candidates must avoid such errors and go through the Marking scheme provided below:

Correct answer	+1 mark
Incorrect answer	-0.25 marks
Non-attempted questions	No marks

The duration of Language tests and Subject tests is 45 minutes each.

NTA CUET Exam Day General Instructions

You are advised to carry the following with you to the examination centre:

- A clear admit card along with self-declaration.
- Transparent ballpoint pens.
- Carry additional photographs (same as uploaded) on the online application form. It will be required to be pasted on the attendance sheet in the examination room/hall.
- A seat indicating roll number will be allocated. You will be required to sit in the allotted seat only.
- You should also ensure that the question paper is available on the computer as per the opted subjects indicated in the admit card. If you find other question papers than opted, bring them to the notice of the invigilator.
- Do not furnish false information as it may lead to the cancellation of the NTA CUET result.
- There shall be no re-test under any circumstances for the students who fail to appear on the scheduled dates of the test.

- Under no circumstances will the choice of the cities for the centre and timings of the examinations provided in the admit card be changed.
- You are advised to report to the Examination centre before 2 hours of the commencement of the exam time. The NTA will not be responsible for any delay.
- You will be required to show the admit card on-demand whenever asked.
- You can download the admit card from the official website of NTA CUET , i.e., https://cuet.samarth.ac.in/
- If you do not possess a valid admit card and authorised Photo ID, you shall not be permitted to take the examination under any circumstances by the Centre Superintendent.
- All calculations/rough work are to be done only in the blank sheets. You are required to write their Roll Number and name on the rough sheets, as soon as the exam commences. On completion of the test, you must drop these rough sheets along with Admit card and Undertaking in the designated box, as instructed by the invigilator on duty.
- For PwD candidates, extra time is allowed to PwD candidates eligible for it.

List of must bring documents on the day of examination at the test centre:

- Photocopy of the NTA CUET Admit Card with self-declaration.
- One passport size photograph (same as uploaded on the online application form).
- Any original photo IDs (valid and non-expired).
- Identity Card/ PAN card/ Driving License/ Voter ID/ Passport/ Aadhaar Card (Witness photograph)/ E-Aadhaar with photograph/ Ration Card with photograph/ Class 12 Board / Admit Card with photograph/ Bank Passbook with Photograph.
- PwD certificate issued by the authorized medical officer, if you are claiming under the PwD category. or PwD certificate regarding physical limitation in an examination to write.